Acura Integra & Legend Automotive Repair Manual

by Larry Warren, Alan Ahlstrand and John H Haynes

Member of the Guild of Motoring Writers

Models covered:

Acura Integra models - 1990 through 1993
Acura Legend models - 1991 through 1995

ABCDE
FGHIJ
KLMNO
PQRST

Haynes Publishing Group
Sparkford Nr Yeovil
Somerset BA22 7JJ England

Haynes North America, Inc
861 Lawrence Drive
Newbury Park
California 91320 USA

About this manual

Its purpose

The purpose of this manual is to help you get the best value from your vehicle. It can do so in several ways. It can help you decide what work must be done, even if you choose to have it done by a dealer service department or a repair shop; it provides information and procedures for routine maintenance and servicing; and it offers diagnostic and repair procedures to follow when trouble occurs.

We hope you use the manual to tackle the work yourself. For many simpler jobs, doing it yourself may be quicker than arranging an appointment to get the vehicle into a shop and making the trips to leave it and pick it up. More importantly, a lot of money can be saved by avoiding the expense the shop must pass on to you to cover its labor and overhead costs. An added benefit is the sense of satisfaction and accomplishment that you feel after doing the job yourself.

Using the manual

The manual is divided into Chapters. Each Chapter is divided into numbered Sections, which are headed in bold type between horizontal lines. Each Section consists of consecutively numbered paragraphs.

At the beginning of each numbered Section you will be referred to any illustrations which apply to the procedures in that Section. The reference numbers used in illustration captions pinpoint the pertinent Section and the Step within that Section. That is, illustration 3.2 means the illustration refers to Section 3 and Step (or paragraph) 2 within that Section.

Procedures, once described in the text, are not normally repeated. When it's necessary to refer to another Chapter, the reference will be given as Chapter and Section number. Cross references given without use of the word "Chapter" apply to Sections and/or paragraphs in the same Chapter. For example, "see Section 8" means in the same Chapter.

References to the left or right side of the vehicle assume you are sitting in the driver's seat, facing forward.

Even though we have prepared this manual with extreme care, neither the publisher nor the author can accept responsibility for any errors in, or omissions from, the information given.

NOTE

A **Note** provides information necessary to properly complete a procedure or information which will make the procedure easier to understand.

CAUTION

A **Caution** provides a special procedure or special steps which must be taken while completing the procedure where the Caution is found. Not heeding a Caution can result in damage to the assembly being worked on.

WARNING

A **Warning** provides a special procedure or special steps which must be taken while completing the procedure where the Warning is found. Not heeding a Warning can result in personal injury.

Acknowledgements

Wiring diagrams originated exclusively for Haynes North America, Inc. by Valley Forge Technical Communications.

© **Haynes North America, Inc. 1999**

With permission from J.H. Haynes & Co. Ltd.

A book in the Haynes Automotive Repair Manual Series

Printed in the U.S.A.

ISBN 1 56392 335 1

Library of Congress Catalog Card Number 99-60417

Contents

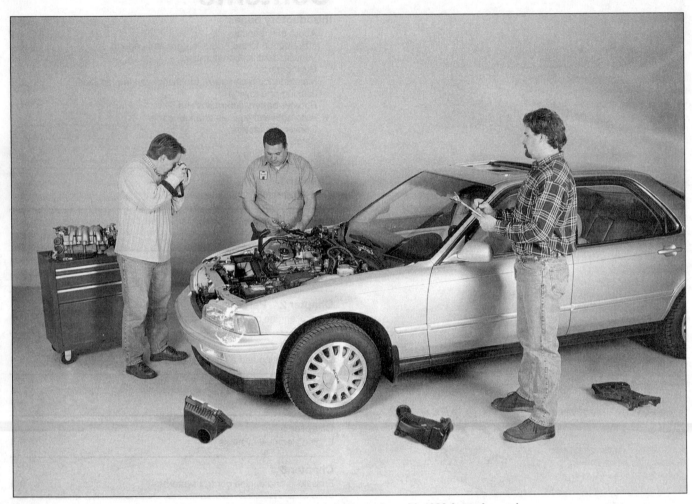

Haynes mechanic, author and photographer with 1993 Acura Legend

Introduction to the Acura Integra and Legend

Integra models are available in two-door coupe, three-door hatchback and four-door sedan body styles. Legend models are available as a two-door coupe or four-door sedan.

Integra models use a transversely mounted inline four cylinder dual overhead cam engine. The longitudinally mounted Legend V6 engine is a single overhead camshaft design. All models are equipped with electronic fuel injection.

On Integra models, the engine drives the front wheels through a four- or five-speed manual or a four-speed automatic transaxle by way of independent driveaxles. Legend models use a five-or six-speed manual or a four-speed automatic transmission. Power passes via an extension shaft from the transmission to the differential housing mounted on the right side of the engine. Independent driveaxles then take the power to the front wheels.

Independent suspension, featuring coil spring/shock absorber units, is used on all four wheels. The power-assisted rack-and-pinion steering unit is mounted behind the engine.

The brakes on all models are disc at all four wheels, with power assist standard. An Anti-lock Braking System (ABS) is available on most models.

Vehicle identification numbers

Modifications are a continuing and unpublicized process in vehicle manufacturing. Since spare parts manuals and lists are compiled on a numerical basis, the individual vehicle numbers are essential to correctly identify the component required.

Vehicle identification number (VIN)

This very important number is stamped on the firewall in the engine compartment and on a plate attached to the dashboard inside the windshield on the driver's side of the vehicle (see illustration). The VIN also appears on the Vehicle Certificate of Title and Registration. It contains information such as where and when the vehicle was manufactured, the model year and the body style (see illustration).

Model year

L = 1990	O = 1993
M = 1991	R = 1994
N = 1992	S = 1995

Engine number

The engine code number, which is commonly needed when ordering engine parts, can be found near the right (passenger's side) end of the engine, near the exhaust manifold on Integra models. On Legend mod-

The Vehicle Identification Number (VIN) can be found on the edge of the dashboard and is visible through the left side windshield of the vehicle

els, the number is stamped on the left (driver's side) front corner of the cylinder block, below the cylinder head. The engine code on all models is the first three to five digits of the number. The three engines covered by this manual are:

Integra
   B17A1 - 1.7L DOHC 16-valve VTEC
   B18A1 - 1.8L DOHC 16-valve
Legend
   C32A1 - 3.2L SOHC V6

Transmission/transaxle number

The transmission/transaxle number is commonly needed when ordering parts. On Integra models with manual transaxles it's located on the bellhousing, opposite the starter motor. On automatic transaxles, it's located on the right front of the transaxle case, above the dipstick. On Legend models, the transmission number is located on the right side of the bellhousing, near the firewall.

2HGEH236 * SH100001

1st, 2nd and 3rd Digits	4th, 5th and 6th Digits	7th Digit	8th Digit	9th Digit	10th Digit	11th Digit	12th to 17th Digits
Manufacturer, make and type of vehicle	Line, body and engine type	Body/ trans type	Vehicle grade	Check digit	Model year	Plant	Serial number

The Vehicle Identification Number (VIN) contains important information on the vehicle

Buying parts

Replacement parts are available from many sources, which generally fall into one of two categories - authorized dealer parts departments and independent retail auto parts stores. Our advice concerning these parts is as follows:

Retail auto parts stores: Good auto parts stores will stock frequently needed components which wear out relatively fast, such as clutch components, exhaust systems, brake parts, tune-up parts, etc. These stores often supply new or reconditioned parts on an exchange basis, which can save a considerable amount of money. Discount auto parts stores are often very good places to buy materials and parts needed for general vehicle maintenance such as oil, grease, filters, spark plugs, belts, touch-up paint, bulbs, etc. They also usually sell tools and general accessories, have convenient hours, charge lower prices and can often be found not far from home.

Authorized dealer parts department: This is the best source for parts which are unique to the vehicle and not generally available elsewhere (such as major engine parts, transmission parts, trim pieces, etc.).

Warranty information: If the vehicle is still covered under warranty, be sure that any replacement parts purchased - regardless of the source - do not invalidate the warranty!

To be sure of obtaining the correct parts, have engine and chassis numbers available and, if possible, take the old parts along for positive identification.

Maintenance techniques, tools and working facilities

Maintenance techniques

There are a number of techniques involved in maintenance and repair that will be referred to throughout this manual. Application of these techniques will enable the home mechanic to be more efficient, better organized and capable of performing the various tasks properly, which will ensure that the repair job is thorough and complete.

Fasteners

Fasteners are nuts, bolts, studs and screws used to hold two or more parts together. There are a few things to keep in mind when working with fasteners. Almost all of them use a locking device of some type, either a lockwasher, locknut, locking tab or thread adhesive. All threaded fasteners should be clean and straight, with undamaged threads and undamaged corners on the hex head where the wrench fits. Develop the habit of replacing all damaged nuts and bolts with new ones. Special locknuts with nylon or fiber inserts can only be used once. If they are removed, they lose their locking ability and must be replaced with new ones.

Rusted nuts and bolts should be treated with a penetrating fluid to ease removal and prevent breakage. Some mechanics use turpentine in a spout-type oil can, which works quite well. After applying the rust penetrant, let it work for a few minutes before trying to loosen the nut or bolt. Badly rusted fasteners may have to be chiseled or sawed off or removed with a special nut breaker, available at tool stores.

If a bolt or stud breaks off in an assembly, it can be drilled and removed with a special tool commonly available for this purpose. Most automotive machine shops can perform this task, as well as other repair procedures, such as the repair of threaded holes that have been stripped out.

Flat washers and lockwashers, when removed from an assembly, should always be replaced exactly as removed. Replace any damaged washers with new ones. Never use a lockwasher on any soft metal surface (such as aluminum), thin sheet metal or plastic.

Grade 1 or 2   Grade 5   Grade 8

Bolt strength marking (standard/SAE/USS; bottom - metric)

Grade	Identification
Hex Nut Grade 5	3 Dots
Hex Nut Grade 8	6 Dots

Standard hex nut strength markings

Grade	Identification
Hex Nut Property Class 9	Arabic 9
Hex Nut Property Class 10	Arabic 10

Metric hex nut strength markings

Class 10.9   Class 9.8   Class 8.8

Metric stud strength markings

00-1 HAYNES

Fastener sizes

For a number of reasons, automobile manufacturers are making wider and wider use of metric fasteners. Therefore, it is important to be able to tell the difference between standard (sometimes called U.S. or SAE) and metric hardware, since they cannot be interchanged.

All bolts, whether standard or metric, are sized according to diameter, thread pitch and length. For example, a standard 1/2 - 13 x 1 bolt is 1/2 inch in diameter, has 13 threads per inch and is 1 inch long. An M12 - 1.75 x 25 metric bolt is 12 mm in diameter, has a thread pitch of 1.75 mm (the distance between threads) and is 25 mm long. The two bolts are nearly identical, and easily confused, but they are not interchangeable.

In addition to the differences in diameter, thread pitch and length, metric and standard bolts can also be distinguished by examining the bolt heads. To begin with, the distance across the flats on a standard bolt head is measured in inches, while the same dimension on a metric bolt is sized in millimeters (the same is true for nuts). As a result, a standard wrench should not be used on a metric bolt and a metric wrench should not be used on a standard bolt. Also, most standard bolts have slashes radiating out from the center of the head to denote the grade or strength of the bolt, which is an indication of the amount of torque that can be applied to it. The greater the number of slashes, the greater the strength of the bolt. Grades 0 through 5 are commonly used on automobiles. Metric bolts have a property class (grade) number, rather than a slash, molded into their heads to indicate bolt strength. In this case, the higher the number, the stronger the bolt. Property class numbers 8.8, 9.8 and 10.9 are commonly used on automobiles.

Strength markings can also be used to distinguish standard hex nuts from metric hex nuts. Many standard nuts have dots stamped into one side, while metric nuts are marked with a number. The greater the number of dots, or the higher the number, the greater the strength of the nut.

Metric studs are also marked on their ends according to property class (grade). Larger studs are numbered (the same as metric bolts), while smaller studs carry a geometric code to denote grade.

It should be noted that many fasteners, especially Grades 0 through 2, have no distinguishing marks on them. When such is the case, the only way to determine whether it is standard or metric is to measure the thread pitch or compare it to a known fastener of the same size.

Standard fasteners are often referred to as SAE, as opposed to metric. However, it should be noted that SAE technically refers to a non-metric fine thread fastener only. Coarse thread non-metric fasteners are referred to as USS sizes.

Since fasteners of the same size (both standard and metric) may have different

Metric thread sizes

	Ft-lbs	Nm
M-6	6 to 9	9 to 12
M-8	14 to 21	19 to 28
M-10	28 to 40	38 to 54
M-12	50 to 71	68 to 96
M-14	80 to 140	109 to 154

Pipe thread sizes

	Ft-lbs	Nm
1/8	5 to 8	7 to 10
1/4	12 to 18	17 to 24
3/8	22 to 33	30 to 44
1/2	25 to 35	34 to 47

U.S. thread sizes

	Ft-lbs	Nm
1/4 - 20	6 to 9	9 to 12
5/16 - 18	12 to 18	17 to 24
5/16 - 24	14 to 20	19 to 27
3/8 - 16	22 to 32	30 to 43
3/8 - 24	27 to 38	37 to 51
7/16 - 14	40 to 55	55 to 74
7/16 - 20	40 to 60	55 to 81
1/2 - 13	55 to 80	75 to 108

Standard (SAE and USS) bolt dimensions/grade marks

G   Grade marks (bolt strength)
L   Length (in inches)
T   Thread pitch (number of threads per inch)
D   Nominal diameter (in inches)

Metric bolt dimensions/grade marks

P   Property class (bolt strength)
L   Length (in millimeters)
T   Thread pitch (distance between threads in millimeters)
D   Diameter

strength ratings, be sure to reinstall any bolts, studs or nuts removed from your vehicle in their original locations. Also, when replacing a fastener with a new one, make sure that the new one has a strength rating equal to or greater than the original.

Tightening sequences and procedures

Most threaded fasteners should be tightened to a specific torque value (torque is the twisting force applied to a threaded component such as a nut or bolt). Overtightening the fastener can weaken it and cause it to break, while undertightening can cause it to eventually come loose. Bolts, screws and studs, depending on the material they are made of and their thread diameters, have

specific torque values, many of which are noted in the Specifications at the beginning of each Chapter. Be sure to follow the torque recommendations closely. For fasteners not assigned a specific torque, a general torque value chart is presented here as a guide. These torque values are for dry (unlubricated) fasteners threaded into steel or cast iron (not aluminum). As was previously mentioned, the size and grade of a fastener determine the amount of torque that can safely be applied to it. The figures listed here are approximate for Grade 2 and Grade 3 fasteners. Higher grades can tolerate higher torque values.

Fasteners laid out in a pattern, such as cylinder head bolts, oil pan bolts, differential cover bolts, etc., must be loosened or tightened in sequence to avoid warping the com-

Micrometer set

Dial indicator set

ponent. This sequence will normally be shown in the appropriate Chapter. If a specific pattern is not given, the following procedures can be used to prevent warping.

Initially, the bolts or nuts should be assembled finger-tight only. Next, they should be tightened one full turn each, in a criss-cross or diagonal pattern. After each one has been tightened one full turn, return to the first one and tighten them all one-half turn, following the same pattern. Finally, tighten each of them one-quarter turn at a time until each fastener has been tightened to the proper torque. To loosen and remove the fasteners, the procedure would be reversed.

Component disassembly

Component disassembly should be done with care and purpose to help ensure that the parts go back together properly. Always keep track of the sequence in which parts are removed. Make note of special characteristics or marks on parts that can be installed more than one way, such as a grooved thrust washer on a shaft. It is a good idea to lay the disassembled parts out on a clean surface in the order that they were removed. It may also be helpful to make sketches or take instant photos of components before removal.

When removing fasteners from a component, keep track of their locations. Sometimes threading a bolt back in a part, or putting the washers and nut back on a stud, can prevent mix-ups later. If nuts and bolts cannot be returned to their original locations, they should be kept in a compartmented box or a series of small boxes. A cupcake or muffin tin is ideal for this purpose, since each cavity can hold the bolts and nuts from a particular area (i.e. oil pan bolts, valve cover bolts, engine mount bolts, etc.). A pan of this type is especially helpful when working on assemblies with very small parts, such as the carburetor, alternator, valve train or interior dash and trim pieces. The cavities can be marked with paint or tape to identify the contents.

Whenever wiring looms, harnesses or connectors are separated, it is a good idea to

identify the two halves with numbered pieces of masking tape so they can be easily reconnected.

Gasket sealing surfaces

Throughout any vehicle, gaskets are used to seal the mating surfaces between two parts and keep lubricants, fluids, vacuum or pressure contained in an assembly.

Many times these gaskets are coated with a liquid or paste-type gasket sealing compound before assembly. Age, heat and pressure can sometimes cause the two parts to stick together so tightly that they are very difficult to separate. Often, the assembly can be loosened by striking it with a soft-face hammer near the mating surfaces. A regular hammer can be used if a block of wood is placed between the hammer and the part. Do not hammer on cast parts or parts that could be easily damaged. With any particularly stubborn part, always recheck to make sure that every fastener has been removed.

Avoid using a screwdriver or bar to pry apart an assembly, as they can easily mar the gasket sealing surfaces of the parts, which must remain smooth. If prying is absolutely necessary, use an old broom handle, but keep in mind that extra clean up will be necessary if the wood splinters.

After the parts are separated, the old gasket must be carefully scraped off and the gasket surfaces cleaned. Stubborn gasket material can be soaked with rust penetrant or treated with a special chemical to soften it so it can be easily scraped off. A scraper can be fashioned from a piece of copper tubing by flattening and sharpening one end. Copper is recommended because it is usually softer than the surfaces to be scraped, which reduces the chance of gouging the part. Some gaskets can be removed with a wire brush, but regardless of the method used, the mating surfaces must be left clean and smooth. If for some reason the gasket surface is gouged, then a gasket sealer thick enough to fill scratches will have to be used during reassembly of the components. For most applications, a non-drying (or semi-drying) gasket sealer should be used.

Hose removal tips

Warning: *If the vehicle is equipped with air conditioning, do not disconnect any of the A/C hoses without first having the system depressurized by a dealer service department or a service station.*

Hose removal precautions closely parallel gasket removal precautions. Avoid scratching or gouging the surface that the hose mates against or the connection may leak. This is especially true for radiator hoses. Because of various chemical reactions, the rubber in hoses can bond itself to the metal spigot that the hose fits over. To remove a hose, first loosen the hose clamps that secure it to the spigot. Then, with slip-joint pliers, grab the hose at the clamp and rotate it around the spigot. Work it back and forth until it is completely free, then pull it off. Silicone or other lubricants will ease removal if they can be applied between the hose and the outside of the spigot. Apply the same lubricant to the inside of the hose and the outside of the spigot to simplify installation.

As a last resort (and if the hose is to be replaced with a new one anyway), the rubber can be slit with a knife and the hose peeled from the spigot. If this must be done, be careful that the metal connection is not damaged.

If a hose clamp is broken or damaged, do not reuse it. Wire-type clamps usually weaken with age, so it is a good idea to replace them with screw-type clamps whenever a hose is removed.

Tools

A selection of good tools is a basic requirement for anyone who plans to maintain and repair his or her own vehicle. For the owner who has few tools, the initial investment might seem high, but when compared to the spiraling costs of professional auto maintenance and repair, it is a wise one.

To help the owner decide which tools are needed to perform the tasks detailed in this manual, the following tool lists are offered: *Maintenance and minor repair, Repair/overhaul* and *Special.*

The newcomer to practical mechanics

Dial caliper

Hand-operated vacuum pump

Timing light

Compression gauge with spark plug hole adapter

Damper/steering wheel puller

General purpose puller

Hydraulic lifter removal tool

Valve spring compressor

Valve spring compressor

Ridge reamer

Piston ring groove cleaning tool

Ring removal/installation tool

Ring compressor

Cylinder hone

Brake hold-down spring tool

Brake cylinder hone

Clutch plate alignment tool

Tap and die set

should start off with the *maintenance and minor repair* tool kit, which is adequate for the simpler jobs performed on a vehicle. Then, as confidence and experience grow, the owner can tackle more difficult tasks, buying additional tools as they are needed. Eventually the basic kit will be expanded into the *repair and overhaul* tool set. Over a period of time, the experienced do-it-yourselfer will assemble a tool set complete enough for most repair and overhaul procedures and will add tools from the special category when it is felt that the expense is justified by the frequency of use.

Maintenance and minor repair tool kit

The tools in this list should be considered the minimum required for performance of routine maintenance, servicing and minor repair work. We recommend the purchase of combination wrenches (box-end and open-end combined in one wrench). While more expensive than open end wrenches, they offer the advantages of both types of wrench.

Combination wrench set (1/4-inch to 1 inch or 6 mm to 19 mm)
Adjustable wrench, 8 inch
Spark plug wrench with rubber insert
Spark plug gap adjusting tool
Feeler gauge set
Brake bleeder wrench

Standard screwdriver (5/16-inch x 6 inch)
Phillips screwdriver (No. 2 x 6 inch)
Combination pliers - 6 inch
Hacksaw and assortment of blades
Tire pressure gauge
Grease gun
Oil can
Fine emery cloth
Wire brush
Battery post and cable cleaning tool
Oil filter wrench
Funnel (medium size)
Safety goggles
Jackstands (2)
Drain pan

Note: *If basic tune-ups are going to be part of routine maintenance, it will be necessary to purchase a good quality stroboscopic timing light and combination tachometer/dwell meter. Although they are included in the list of special tools, it is mentioned here because they are absolutely necessary for tuning most vehicles properly.*

Repair and overhaul tool set

These tools are essential for anyone who plans to perform major repairs and are in addition to those in the maintenance and minor repair tool kit. Included is a comprehensive set of sockets which, though expensive, are invaluable because of their versatil-

ity, especially when various extensions and drives are available. We recommend the 1/2-inch drive over the 3/8-inch drive. Although the larger drive is bulky and more expensive, it has the capacity of accepting a very wide range of large sockets. Ideally, however, the mechanic should have a 3/8-inch drive set and a 1/2-inch drive set.

Socket set(s)
Reversible ratchet
Extension - 10 inch
Universal joint
Torque wrench (same size drive as sockets)
Ball peen hammer - 8 ounce
Soft-face hammer (plastic/rubber)
Standard screwdriver (1/4-inch x 6 inch)
Standard screwdriver (stubby - 5/16-inch)
Phillips screwdriver (No. 3 x 8 inch)
Phillips screwdriver (stubby - No. 2)
Pliers - vise grip
Pliers - lineman's
Pliers - needle nose
Pliers - snap-ring (internal and external)
Cold chisel - 1/2-inch
Scribe
Scraper (made from flattened copper tubing)
Centerpunch
Pin punches (1/16, 1/8, 3/16-inch)
Steel rule/straightedge - 12 inch

Allen wrench set (1/8 to 3/8-inch or
    4 mm to 10 mm)
A selection of files
Wire brush (large)
Jackstands (second set)
Jack (scissor or hydraulic type)

Note: Another tool which is often useful is an
electric drill with a chuck capacity of 3/8-inch
and a set of good quality drill bits.

Special tools

The tools in this list include those which
are not used regularly, are expensive to buy,
or which need to be used in accordance with
their manufacturer's instructions. Unless
these tools will be used frequently, it is not
very economical to purchase many of them.
A consideration would be to split the cost
and use between yourself and a friend or
friends. In addition, most of these tools can
be obtained from a tool rental shop on a temporary basis.

This list primarily contains only those
tools and instruments widely available to the
public, and not those special tools produced
by the vehicle manufacturer for distribution to
dealer service departments. Occasionally,
references to the manufacturer's special
tools are included in the text of this manual.
Generally, an alternative method of doing the
job without the special tool is offered. However, sometimes there is no alternative to
their use. Where this is the case, and the tool
cannot be purchased or borrowed, the work
should be turned over to the dealer service
department or an automotive repair shop.

Valve spring compressor
Piston ring groove cleaning tool
Piston ring compressor
Piston ring installation tool
Cylinder compression gauge
Cylinder ridge reamer
Cylinder surfacing hone
Cylinder bore gauge
Micrometers and/or dial calipers
Hydraulic lifter removal tool
Balljoint separator
Universal-type puller
Impact screwdriver
Dial indicator set
Stroboscopic timing light (inductive
    pick-up)
Hand operated vacuum/pressure pump
Tachometer/dwell meter
Universal electrical multimeter
Cable hoist
Brake spring removal and installation
    tools
Floor jack

Buying tools

For the do-it-yourselfer who is just starting to get involved in vehicle maintenance
and repair, there are a number of options
available when purchasing tools. If maintenance and minor repair is the extent of the
work to be done, the purchase of individual
tools is satisfactory. If, on the other hand,
extensive work is planned, it would be a good
idea to purchase a modest tool set from one

of the large retail chain stores. A set can usually be bought at a substantial savings over
the individual tool prices, and they often
come with a tool box. As additional tools are
needed, add-on sets, individual tools and a
larger tool box can be purchased to expand
the tool selection. Building a tool set gradually allows the cost of the tools to be spread
over a longer period of time and gives the
mechanic the freedom to choose only those
tools that will actually be used.

Tool stores will often be the only source
of some of the special tools that are needed,
but regardless of where tools are bought, try
to avoid cheap ones, especially when buying
screwdrivers and sockets, because they
won't last very long. The expense involved in
replacing cheap tools will eventually be
greater than the initial cost of quality tools.

Care and maintenance of tools

Good tools are expensive, so it makes
sense to treat them with respect. Keep them
clean and in usable condition and store them
properly when not in use. Always wipe off any
dirt, grease or metal chips before putting
them away. Never leave tools lying around in
the work area. Upon completion of a job,
always check closely under the hood for tools
that may have been left there so they won't
get lost during a test drive.

Some tools, such as screwdrivers, pliers, wrenches and sockets, can be hung on a
panel mounted on the garage or workshop
wall, while others should be kept in a tool box
or tray. Measuring instruments, gauges,
meters, etc. must be carefully stored where
they cannot be damaged by weather or
impact from other tools.

When tools are used with care and
stored properly, they will last a very long
time. Even with the best of care, though,
tools will wear out if used frequently. When a
tool is damaged or worn out, replace it. Subsequent jobs will be safer and more enjoyable
if you do.

How to repair damaged threads

Sometimes, the internal threads of a nut
or bolt hole can become stripped, usually
from overtightening. Stripping threads is an
all-too-common occurrence, especially when
working with aluminum parts, because aluminum is so soft that it easily strips out.

Usually, external or internal threads are
only partially stripped. After they've been
cleaned up with a tap or die, they'll still work.
Sometimes, however, threads are badly damaged. When this happens, you've got three
choices:

1) Drill and tap the hole to the next suitable
    oversize and install a larger diameter
    bolt, screw or stud.
2) Drill and tap the hole to accept a
    threaded plug, then drill and tap the plug
    to the original screw size. You can also
    buy a plug already threaded to the origi-
    nal size. Then you simply drill a hole to

the specified size, then run the threaded
plug into the hole with a bolt and jam
nut. Once the plug is fully seated,
remove the jam nut and bolt.
3) The third method uses a patented
    thread repair kit like Heli-Coil or Slimsert.
    These easy-to-use kits are designed to
    repair damaged threads in straight-
    through holes and blind holes. Both are
    available as kits which can handle a vari-
    ety of sizes and thread patterns. Drill the
    hole, then tap it with the special
    included tap. Install the Heli-Coil and the
    hole is back to its original diameter and
    thread pitch.

Regardless of which method you use,
be sure to proceed calmly and carefully. A little impatience or carelessness during one of
these relatively simple procedures can ruin
your whole day's work and cost you a bundle
if you wreck an expensive part.

Working facilities

Not to be overlooked when discussing
tools is the workshop. If anything more than
routine maintenance is to be carried out,
some sort of suitable work area is essential.

It is understood, and appreciated, that
many home mechanics do not have a good
workshop or garage available, and end up
removing an engine or doing major repairs
outside. It is recommended, however, that
the overhaul or repair be completed under
the cover of a roof.

A clean, flat workbench or table of com-
fortable working height is an absolute neces-
sity. The workbench should be equipped with
a vise that has a jaw opening of at least four
inches.

As mentioned previously, some clean,
dry storage space is also required for tools,
as well as the lubricants, fluids, cleaning solvents, etc. which soon become necessary.

Sometimes waste oil and fluids, drained
from the engine or cooling system during normal maintenance or repairs, present a disposal problem. To avoid pouring them on the
ground or into a sewage system, pour the
used fluids into large containers, seal them
with caps and take them to an authorized
disposal site or recycling center. Plastic jugs,
such as old antifreeze containers, are ideal
for this purpose.

Always keep a supply of old newspapers and clean rags available. Old towels are
excellent for mopping up spills. Many
mechanics use rolls of paper towels for most
work because they are readily available and
disposable. To help keep the area under the
vehicle clean, a large cardboard box can be
cut open and flattened to protect the garage
or shop floor.

Whenever working over a painted surface, such as when leaning over a fender to
service something under the hood, always
cover it with an old blanket or bedspread to
protect the finish. Vinyl covered pads, made
especially for this purpose, are available at
auto parts stores.

Jacking and towing

Jacking

Warning: *The jack supplied with the vehicle should only be used for changing a tire or placing jackstands under the frame. Never work under the vehicle or start the engine while this jack is being used as the only means of support.*

The vehicle should be on level ground. Place the shift lever in Park, if you have an automatic, or Reverse if you have a manual transmission or transaxle. Block the wheel diagonally opposite the wheel being changed. Set the parking brake.

Remove the spare tire and jack from stowage. Remove the wheel cover and trim ring (if so equipped) with the tapered end of the lug nut wrench by inserting and twisting the handle and then prying against the back of the wheel cover. **Caution:** *On some models the wheel cover can't be removed by prying; the wheel nuts must be removed first. Loosen, but do not remove, the lug nuts (one-half turn is sufficient).*

Place the scissors-type jack under the side of the vehicle and adjust the jack height until the slot in the jack head engages with the raised portion of the ridge on the vertical rocker panel flange nearest the wheel to be changed. There is a front and rear jacking point on each side of the vehicle (**see illustration**).

Turn the jack handle clockwise until the tire clears the ground. Remove the lug nuts and pull the wheel off. Replace it with the spare.

Install the lug nuts with the beveled edges facing in. Tighten them snugly. Don't

attempt to tighten them completely until the vehicle is lowered or it could slip off the jack. Turn the jack handle counterclockwise to lower the vehicle. Remove the jack and tighten the lug nuts in a criss-cross pattern.

Install the cover (and trim ring, if used) and be sure it's snapped into place all the way around.

Stow the tire, jack and wrench. Unblock the wheels.

Towing

As a general rule, the vehicle should be towed with the front (drive) wheels off the ground (the best method is to have the vehicle placed on a flat-bed tow truck). If they can't be raised, place them on a dolly. The ignition key must be in the OFF position, since the steering lock mechanism isn't strong enough to hold the front wheels straight while towing.

Vehicles equipped with an automatic transmission/transaxle can be towed from the front with all four wheels on the ground, provided that speeds don't exceed 35 mph and the distance is not over 50 miles. Before towing, check the transmission fluid level (see Chapter 1). If the level is below the HOT line on the dipstick, add fluid or use a towing dolly. Additionally, perform the following steps:

a) *Release the parking brake*
b) *Start the engine*
c) *Move the transmission/transaxle gear selector into D4, then to Neutral*
d) *Turn off the engine*
e) *Place the ignition key in the OFF (not the LOCK position).*

The jacking points are located near the front and rear wheel on each side of the vehicle

Caution: *Never tow a vehicle with an automatic transmission/transaxle from the rear with the front wheels on the ground.*

When towing a vehicle equipped with a manual transmission/transaxle or Continuously Variable Transaxle with all four wheels on the ground, be sure to place the shift lever in neutral and release the parking brake.

Equipment specifically designed for towing should be used. It should be attached to the main structural members of the vehicle, not the bumpers or brackets.

Safety is a major consideration when towing and all applicable state and local laws must be obeyed. A safety chain system must be used at all times. Remember that power steering and power brakes will not work with the engine off.

Booster battery (jump) starting

Observe these precautions when using a booster battery to start a vehicle:

a) *Before connecting the booster battery, make sure the ignition switch is in the Off position.*
b) *Turn off the lights, heater and other electrical loads.*
c) *Your eyes should be shielded. Safety goggles are a good idea.*
d) *Make sure the booster battery is the same voltage as the dead one in the vehicle.*
e) *The two vehicles MUST NOT TOUCH each other!*
f) *Make sure the transaxle is in Neutral (manual) or Park (automatic).*
g) *If the booster battery is not a maintenance-free type, remove the vent caps and lay a cloth over the vent holes.*

Connect the red jumper cable to the positive (+) terminals of each battery (**see illustration**).

Connect one end of the black jumper cable to the negative (-) terminal of the booster battery. The other end of this cable should be connected to a good ground on the vehicle to be started, such as a bolt or bracket on the body.

Start the engine using the booster battery, then, with the engine running at idle speed, disconnect the jumper cables in the reverse order of connection.

Make the booster battery cable connections in the numerical order shown (note that the negative cable of the booster battery is NOT attached to the negative terminal of the dead battery)

Automotive chemicals and lubricants

A number of automotive chemicals and lubricants are available for use during vehicle maintenance and repair. They include a wide variety of products ranging from cleaning solvents and degreasers to lubricants and protective sprays for rubber, plastic and vinyl.

Cleaners

Carburetor cleaner and choke cleaner is a strong solvent for gum, varnish and carbon. Most carburetor cleaners leave a dry-type lubricant film which will not harden or gum up. Because of this film it is not recommended for use on electrical components.

Brake system cleaner is used to remove grease and brake fluid from the brake system, where clean surfaces are absolutely necessary. It leaves no residue and often eliminates brake squeal caused by contaminants.

Electrical cleaner removes oxidation, corrosion and carbon deposits from electrical contacts, restoring full current flow. It can also be used to clean spark plugs, carburetor jets, voltage regulators and other parts where an oil-free surface is desired.

Demoisturants remove water and moisture from electrical components such as alternators, voltage regulators, electrical connectors and fuse blocks. They are non-conductive, non-corrosive and non-flammable.

Degreasers are heavy-duty solvents used to remove grease from the outside of the engine and from chassis components. They can be sprayed or brushed on and, depending on the type, are rinsed off either with water or solvent.

Lubricants

Motor oil is the lubricant formulated for use in engines. It normally contains a wide variety of additives to prevent corrosion and reduce foaming and wear. Motor oil comes in various weights (viscosity ratings) from 5 to 80. The recommended weight of the oil depends on the season, temperature and the demands on the engine. Light oil is used in cold climates and under light load conditions. Heavy oil is used in hot climates and where high loads are encountered. Multi-viscosity oils are designed to have characteristics of both light and heavy oils and are available in a number of weights from 5W-20 to 20W-50.

Gear oil is designed to be used in differentials, manual transmissions and other areas where high-temperature lubrication is required.

Chassis and wheel bearing grease is a heavy grease used where increased loads and friction are encountered, such as for wheel bearings, balljoints, tie-rod ends and universal joints.

High-temperature wheel bearing grease is designed to withstand the extreme temperatures encountered by wheel bearings in disc brake equipped vehicles. It usually contains molybdenum disulfide (moly), which is a dry-type lubricant.

White grease is a heavy grease for metal-to-metal applications where water is a problem. White grease stays soft under both low and high temperatures (usually from -100 to +190-degrees F), and will not wash off or dilute in the presence of water.

Assembly lube is a special extreme pressure lubricant, usually containing moly, used to lubricate high-load parts (such as main and rod bearings and cam lobes) for initial start-up of a new engine. The assembly lube lubricates the parts without being squeezed out or washed away until the engine oiling system begins to function.

Silicone lubricants are used to protect rubber, plastic, vinyl and nylon parts.

Graphite lubricants are used where oils cannot be used due to contamination problems, such as in locks. The dry graphite will lubricate metal parts while remaining uncontaminated by dirt, water, oil or acids. It is electrically conductive and will not foul electrical contacts in locks such as the ignition switch.

Moly penetrants loosen and lubricate frozen, rusted and corroded fasteners and prevent future rusting or freezing.

Heat-sink grease is a special electrically non-conductive grease that is used for mounting electronic ignition modules where it is essential that heat is transferred away from the module.

Sealants

RTV sealant is one of the most widely used gasket compounds. Made from silicone, RTV is air curing, it seals, bonds, waterproofs, fills surface irregularities, remains flexible, doesn't shrink, is relatively easy to remove, and is used as a supplementary sealer with almost all low and medium temperature gaskets.

Anaerobic sealant is much like RTV in that it can be used either to seal gaskets or to form gaskets by itself. It remains flexible, is solvent resistant and fills surface imperfections. The difference between an anaerobic sealant and an RTV-type sealant is in the curing. RTV cures when exposed to air, while an anaerobic sealant cures only in the absence of air. This means that an anaerobic sealant cures only after the assembly of parts, sealing them together.

Thread and pipe sealant is used for sealing hydraulic and pneumatic fittings and vacuum lines. It is usually made from a Teflon compound, and comes in a spray, a paint-on liquid and as a wrap-around tape.

Chemicals

Anti-seize compound prevents seizing, galling, cold welding, rust and corrosion in fasteners. High-temperature anti-seize, usually made with copper and graphite lubricants, is used for exhaust system and exhaust manifold bolts.

Anaerobic locking compounds are used to keep fasteners from vibrating or working loose and cure only after installation, in the absence of air. Medium strength locking compound is used for small nuts, bolts and screws that may be removed later. High-strength locking compound is for large nuts, bolts and studs which aren't removed on a regular basis.

Oil additives range from viscosity index improvers to chemical treatments that claim to reduce internal engine friction. It should be noted that most oil manufacturers caution against using additives with their oils.

Gas additives perform several functions, depending on their chemical makeup. They usually contain solvents that help dissolve gum and varnish that build up on carburetor, fuel injection and intake parts. They also serve to break down carbon deposits that form on the inside surfaces of the combustion chambers. Some additives contain upper cylinder lubricants for valves and piston rings, and others contain chemicals to remove condensation from the gas tank.

Miscellaneous

Brake fluid is specially formulated hydraulic fluid that can withstand the heat and pressure encountered in brake systems. Care must be taken so this fluid does not come in contact with painted surfaces or plastics. An opened container should always be resealed to prevent contamination by water or dirt.

Weatherstrip adhesive is used to bond weatherstripping around doors, windows and trunk lids. It is sometimes used to attach trim pieces.

Undercoating is a petroleum-based, tar-like substance that is designed to protect metal surfaces on the underside of the vehicle from corrosion. It also acts as a sound-deadening agent by insulating the bottom of the vehicle.

Waxes and polishes are used to help protect painted and plated surfaces from the weather. Different types of paint may require the use of different types of wax and polish. Some polishes utilize a chemical or abrasive cleaner to help remove the top layer of oxidized (dull) paint on older vehicles. In recent years many non-wax polishes that contain a wide variety of chemicals such as polymers and silicones have been introduced. These non-wax polishes are usually easier to apply and last longer than conventional waxes and polishes.

Conversion factors

Length (distance)
Inches (in)	X	25.4	= Millimetres (mm)	X	0.0394 = Inches (in)
Feet (ft)	X	0.305	= Metres (m)	X	3.281 = Feet (ft)
Miles	X	1.609	= Kilometres (km)	X	0.621 = Miles

Volume (capacity)
Cubic inches (cu in; in³)	X	16.387	= Cubic centimetres (cc; cm³)	X	0.061 = Cubic inches (cu in; in³)
Imperial pints (Imp pt)	X	0.568	= Litres (l)	X	1.76 = Imperial pints (Imp pt)
Imperial quarts (Imp qt)	X	1.137	= Litres (l)	X	0.88 = Imperial quarts (Imp qt)
Imperial quarts (Imp qt)	X	1.201	= US quarts (US qt)	X	0.833 = Imperial quarts (Imp qt)
US quarts (US qt)	X	0.946	= Litres (l)	X	1.057 = US quarts (US qt)
Imperial gallons (Imp gal)	X	4.546	= Litres (l)	X	0.22 = Imperial gallons (Imp gal)
Imperial gallons (Imp gal)	X	1.201	= US gallons (US gal)	X	0.833 = Imperial gallons (Imp gal)
US gallons (US gal)	X	3.785	= Litres (l)	X	0.264 = US gallons (US gal)

Mass (weight)
Ounces (oz)	X	28.35	= Grams (g)	X	0.035 = Ounces (oz)
Pounds (lb)	X	0.454	= Kilograms (kg)	X	2.205 = Pounds (lb)

Force
Ounces-force (ozf; oz)	X	0.278	= Newtons (N)	X	3.6 = Ounces-force (ozf; oz)
Pounds-force (lbf; lb)	X	4.448	= Newtons (N)	X	0.225 = Pounds-force (lbf; lb)
Newtons (N)	X	0.1	= Kilograms-force (kgf; kg)	X	9.81 = Newtons (N)

Pressure
Pounds-force per square inch (psi; lbf/in²; lb/in²)	X	0.070	= Kilograms-force per square centimetre (kgf/cm²; kg/cm²)	X	14.223 = Pounds-force per square inch (psi; lbf/in²; lb/in²)
Pounds-force per square inch (psi; lbf/in²; lb/in²)	X	0.068	= Atmospheres (atm)	X	14.696 = Pounds-force per square inch (psi; lbf/in²; lb/in²)
Pounds-force per square inch (psi; lbf/in²; lb/in²)	X	0.069	= Bars	X	14.5 = Pounds-force per square inch (psi; lbf/in²; lb/in²)
Pounds-force per square inch (psi; lbf/in²; lb/in²)	X	6.895	= Kilopascals (kPa)	X	0.145 = Pounds-force per square inch (psi; lbf/in²; lb/in²)
Kilopascals (kPa)	X	0.01	= Kilograms-force per square centimetre (kgf/cm²; kg/cm²)	X	98.1 = Kilopascals (kPa)

Torque (moment of force)
Pounds-force inches (lbf in; lb in)	X	1.152	= Kilograms-force centimetre (kgf cm; kg cm)	X	0.868 = Pounds-force inches (lbf in; lb in)
Pounds-force inches (lbf in; lb in)	X	0.113	= Newton metres (Nm)	X	8.85 = Pounds-force inches (lbf in; lb in)
Pounds-force inches (lbf in; lb in)	X	0.083	= Pounds-force feet (lbf ft; lb ft)	X	12 = Pounds-force inches (lbf in; lb in)
Pounds-force feet (lbf ft; lb ft)	X	0.138	= Kilograms-force metres (kgf m; kg m)	X	7.233 = Pounds-force feet (lbf ft; lb ft)
Pounds-force feet (lbf ft; lb ft)	X	1.356	= Newton metres (Nm)	X	0.738 = Pounds-force feet (lbf ft; lb ft)
Newton metres (Nm)	X	0.102	= Kilograms-force metres (kgf m; kg m)	X	9.804 = Newton metres (Nm)

Vacuum
Inches mercury (in. Hg)	X	3.377	= Kilopascals (kPa)	X	0.2961 = Inches mercury
Inches mercury (in. Hg)	X	25.4	= Millimeters mercury (mm Hg)	X	0.0394 = Inches mercury

Power
Horsepower (hp)	X	745.7	= Watts (W)	X	0.0013 = Horsepower (hp)

Velocity (speed)
Miles per hour (miles/hr; mph)	X	1.609	= Kilometres per hour (km/hr; kph)	X	0.621 = Miles per hour (miles/hr; mph)

Fuel consumption*
Miles per gallon, Imperial (mpg)	X	0.354	= Kilometres per litre (km/l)	X	2.825 = Miles per gallon, Imperial (mpg)
Miles per gallon, US (mpg)	X	0.425	= Kilometres per litre (km/l)	X	2.352 = Miles per gallon, US (mpg)

Temperature
Degrees Fahrenheit = (°C x 1.8) + 32   Degrees Celsius (Degrees Centigrade; °C) = (°F - 32) x 0.56

*It is common practice to convert from miles per gallon (mpg) to litres/100 kilometres (l/100km), where mpg (Imperial) x l/100 km = 282 and mpg (US) x l/100 km = 235

Safety first!

Regardless of how enthusiastic you may be about getting on with the job at hand, take the time to ensure that your safety is not jeopardized. A moment's lack of attention can result in an accident, as can failure to observe certain simple safety precautions. The possibility of an accident will always exist, and the following points should not be considered a comprehensive list of all dangers. Rather, they are intended to make you aware of the risks and to encourage a safety conscious approach to all work you carry out on your vehicle.

Essential DOs and DON'Ts

DON'T rely on a jack when working under the vehicle. Always use approved jackstands to support the weight of the vehicle and place them under the recommended lift or support points.

DON'T attempt to loosen extremely tight fasteners (i.e. wheel lug nuts) while the vehicle is on a jack - it may fall.

DON'T start the engine without first making sure that the transmission is in Neutral (or Park where applicable) and the parking brake is set.

DON'T remove the radiator cap from a hot cooling system - let it cool or cover it with a cloth and release the pressure gradually.

DON'T attempt to drain the engine oil until you are sure it has cooled to the point that it will not burn you.

DON'T touch any part of the engine or exhaust system until it has cooled sufficiently to avoid burns.

DON'T siphon toxic liquids such as gasoline, antifreeze and brake fluid by mouth, or allow them to remain on your skin.

DON'T inhale brake lining dust - it is potentially hazardous (see *Asbestos* below).

DON'T allow spilled oil or grease to remain on the floor - wipe it up before someone slips on it.

DON'T use loose fitting wrenches or other tools which may slip and cause injury.

DON'T push on wrenches when loosening or tightening nuts or bolts. Always try to pull the wrench toward you. If the situation calls for pushing the wrench away, push with an open hand to avoid scraped knuckles if the wrench should slip.

DON'T attempt to lift a heavy component alone - get someone to help you.

DON'T rush or take unsafe shortcuts to finish a job.

DON'T allow children or animals in or around the vehicle while you are working on it.

DO wear eye protection when using power tools such as a drill, sander, bench grinder, etc. and when working under a vehicle.

DO keep loose clothing and long hair well out of the way of moving parts.

DO make sure that any hoist used has a safe working load rating adequate for the job.

DO get someone to check on you periodically when working alone on a vehicle.

DO carry out work in a logical sequence and make sure that everything is correctly assembled and tightened.

DO keep chemicals and fluids tightly capped and out of the reach of children and pets.

DO remember that your vehicle's safety affects that of yourself and others. If in doubt on any point, get professional advice.

Asbestos

Certain friction, insulating, sealing, and other products - such as brake linings, brake bands, clutch linings, torque converters, gaskets, etc. - may contain asbestos. Extreme care must be taken to avoid inhalation of dust from such products, since it is hazardous to health. If in doubt, assume that they do contain asbestos.

Fire

Remember at all times that gasoline is highly flammable. Never smoke or have any kind of open flame around when working on a vehicle. But the risk does not end there. A spark caused by an electrical short circuit, by two metal surfaces contacting each other, or even by static electricity built up in your body under certain conditions, can ignite gasoline vapors, which in a confined space are highly explosive. Do not, under any circumstances, use gasoline for cleaning parts. Use an approved safety solvent.

Always disconnect the battery ground (-) cable at the battery before working on any part of the fuel system or electrical system. Never risk spilling fuel on a hot engine or exhaust component. It is strongly recommended that a fire extinguisher suitable for use on fuel and electrical fires be kept handy in the garage or workshop at all times. Never try to extinguish a fuel or electrical fire with water.

Fumes

Certain fumes are highly toxic and can quickly cause unconsciousness and even death if inhaled to any extent. Gasoline vapor falls into this category, as do the vapors from some cleaning solvents. Any draining or pouring of such volatile fluids should be done in a well ventilated area.

When using cleaning fluids and solvents, read the instructions on the container carefully. Never use materials from unmarked containers.

Never run the engine in an enclosed space, such as a garage. Exhaust fumes contain carbon monoxide, which is extremely poisonous. If you need to run the engine, always do so in the open air, or at least have the rear of the vehicle outside the work area.

If you are fortunate enough to have the use of an inspection pit, never drain or pour gasoline and never run the engine while the vehicle is over the pit. The fumes, being heavier than air, will concentrate in the pit with possibly lethal results.

The battery

Never create a spark or allow a bare light bulb near a battery. They normally give off a certain amount of hydrogen gas, which is highly explosive.

Always disconnect the battery ground (-) cable at the battery before working on the fuel or electrical systems.

If possible, loosen the filler caps or cover when charging the battery from an external source (this does not apply to sealed or maintenance-free batteries). Do not charge at an excessive rate or the battery may burst.

Take care when adding water to a non maintenance-free battery and when carrying a battery. The electrolyte, even when diluted, is very corrosive and should not be allowed to contact clothing or skin.

Always wear eye protection when cleaning the battery to prevent the caustic deposits from entering your eyes.

Household current

When using an electric power tool, inspection light, etc., which operates on household current, always make sure that the tool is correctly connected to its plug and that, where necessary, it is properly grounded. Do not use such items in damp conditions and, again, do not create a spark or apply excessive heat in the vicinity of fuel or fuel vapor.

Secondary ignition system voltage

A severe electric shock can result from touching certain parts of the ignition system (such as the spark plug wires) when the engine is running or being cranked, particularly if components are damp or the insulation is defective. In the case of an electronic ignition system, the secondary system voltage is much higher and could prove fatal.

Troubleshooting

Contents

This Section provides an easy reference guide to the more common problems which may occur during the operation of your vehicle. These problems and their possible causes are grouped under headings denoting various components or systems, such as Engine, Cooling system, etc. They also refer you to the Chapter and/or Section which deals with the problem.

Remember that successful troubleshooting is not a mysterious art practiced only by professional mechanics. It is simply the result of the right knowledge combined with an intelligent, systematic approach to the problem. Always work by a process of elimination, starting with the simplest solution and working through to the most complex - and never overlook the obvious. Anyone can run the gas tank dry or leave the lights on overnight, so don't assume that you are exempt from such oversights.

Finally, always establish a clear idea of why a problem has occurred and take steps to ensure that it doesn't happen again. If the electrical system fails because of a poor connection, check the other connections in the system to make sure that they don't fail as well. If a particular fuse continues to blow, find out why - don't just replace one fuse after another. Remember, failure of a small component can often be indicative of potential failure or incorrect functioning of a more important component or system.

Engine

1 Engine will not rotate when attempting to start

1 Battery terminal connections loose or corroded (Chapter 1).
2 Battery discharged or faulty (Chapter 1).
3 Automatic transmission/transaxle not completely engaged in Park (Chapter 7) or clutch not completely depressed (Chapter 8).
4 Broken, loose or disconnected wiring in the starting circuit (Chapters 5 and 12).
5 Starter motor pinion jammed in flywheel ring gear (Chapter 5).
6 Starter solenoid faulty (Chapter 5).
7 Starter motor faulty (Chapter 5).
8 Ignition switch faulty (Chapter 12).
9 Starter pinion or flywheel teeth worn or broken (Chapter 5).

2 Engine rotates but will not start

1 Fuel tank empty.
2 Battery discharged (engine rotates slowly) (Chapter 5).
3 Battery terminal connections loose or corroded (Chapter 1).
4 Leaking fuel injector(s), faulty fuel pump, pressure regulator, etc. (Chapter 4).
5 Fuel not reaching fuel rail (Chapter 4).

6 Ignition components damp or damaged (Chapter 5).
7 Worn, faulty or incorrectly gapped spark plugs (Chapter 1).
8 Broken, loose or disconnected wiring in the starting circuit (Chapter 5).
9 Loose distributor is changing ignition timing (Chapter 5).
10 Broken, loose or disconnected wires at the ignition coil or faulty coil (Chapter 5).

3 Engine hard to start when cold

1 Battery discharged or low (Chapter 1).
2 Malfunctioning fuel system (Chapter 4).
3 Injector(s) leaking (Chapter 4).
4 Distributor rotor carbon tracked (Chapter 5).

4 Engine hard to start when hot

1 Air filter clogged (Chapter 1).
2 Fuel not reaching the fuel injection system (Chapter 4).
3 Corroded battery connections, especially ground (Chapter 1).

5 Starter motor noisy or excessively rough in engagement

1 Pinion or flywheel gear teeth worn or broken (Chapter 5).
2 Starter motor mounting bolts loose or missing (Chapter 5).

6 Engine starts but stops immediately

1 Loose or faulty electrical connections at distributor, coil or alternator (Chapter 5).
2 Insufficient fuel reaching the fuel injector(s) (Chapters 1 and 4).
3 Vacuum leak at the gasket between the intake manifold and throttle body (Chapters 1 and 4).

7 Oil puddle under engine

1 Oil pan gasket and/or oil pan drain bolt washer leaking (Chapter 2).
2 Oil pressure sending unit leaking (Chapter 2).
3 Cylinder head covers leaking (Chapter 2).
4 Engine oil seals leaking (Chapter 2).

8 Engine lopes while idling or idles erratically

1 Vacuum leakage (Chapters 2 and 4).
2 Leaking EGR valve (Chapter 6).
3 Air filter clogged (Chapter 1).

4 Fuel pump not delivering sufficient fuel to the fuel injection system (Chapter 4).
5 Leaking head gasket (Chapter 2).
6 Timing belt and/or pulleys worn (Chapter 2).
7 Camshaft lobes worn (Chapter 2).

9 Engine misses at idle speed

1 Spark plugs worn or not gapped properly (Chapter 1).
2 Faulty spark plug wires (Chapter 1).
3 Vacuum leaks (Chapter 1).
4 Incorrect ignition timing (Chapter 1).
5 Uneven or low compression (Chapter 2).

10 Engine misses throughout driving speed range

1 Fuel filter clogged and/or impurities in the fuel system (Chapter 1).
2 Low fuel pressure (Chapter 4).
3 Faulty or incorrectly gapped spark plugs (Chapter 1).
4 Incorrect ignition timing (Chapter 5).
5 Cracked distributor cap, disconnected distributor wires or damaged distributor components (Chapters 1 and 5).
6 Leaking spark plug wires (Chapters 1 or 5).
7 Faulty emission system components (Chapter 6).
8 Low or uneven cylinder compression pressures (Chapter 2).
9 Weak or faulty ignition system (Chapter 5).
10 Vacuum leak in fuel injection system, intake manifold, air control valve or vacuum hoses (Chapter 4).

11 Engine stumbles on acceleration

1 Spark plugs fouled (Chapter 1).
2 Fuel injection system faulty (Chapter 4).
3 Fuel filter clogged (Chapters 1 and 4).
4 Incorrect ignition timing (Chapter 5).
5 Intake manifold air leak (Chapters 2 and 4).

12 Engine surges while holding accelerator steady

1 Intake air leak (Chapter 4).
2 Fuel pump faulty (Chapter 4).
3 Loose fuel injector wire harness connectors (Chapter 4).
4 Defective ECU or information sensor (Chapter 6).

13 Engine stalls

1 Idle speed incorrect (Chapter 1).
2 Fuel filter clogged and/or water and

impurities in the fuel system (Chapters 1 and 4).
3 Distributor components damp or damaged (Chapter 5).
4 Faulty emissions system components (Chapter 6).
5 Faulty or incorrectly gapped spark plugs (Chapter 1).
6 Faulty spark plug wires (Chapter 1).
7 Vacuum leak in the fuel injection system, intake manifold or vacuum hoses (Chapters 2 and 4).
8 Valve clearances incorrectly set (Chapter 1).

14 Engine lacks power

1 Incorrect ignition timing (Chapter 5).
2 Excessive play in distributor shaft (Chapter 5).
3 Worn rotor, distributor cap or wires (Chapters 1 and 5).
4 Faulty or incorrectly gapped spark plugs (Chapter 1).
5 Fuel injection system out of adjustment or excessively worn (Chapter 4).
6 Faulty coil (Chapter 5).
7 Brakes binding (Chapter 9).
8 Automatic transmission/transaxle fluid level incorrect (Chapter 1).
9 Clutch slipping (Chapter 8).
10 Fuel filter clogged and/or impurities in the fuel system (Chapters 1 and 4).
11 Emission control system not functioning properly (Chapter 6).
12 Catalytic converter plugged (Chapter 6).
13 Low or uneven cylinder compression pressures (Chapter 2).
14 Obstructed exhaust system (Chapter 4).

15 Engine backfires

1 Emission control system not functioning properly (Chapter 6).
2 Ignition timing incorrect (Chapter 5).
3 Faulty secondary ignition system (cracked spark plug insulator, faulty plug wires, distributor cap and/or rotor) (Chapters 1 and 5).
4 Fuel injection system malfunctioning (Chapter 4).
5 Vacuum leak at fuel injector(s), intake manifold, air control valve or vacuum hoses (Chapters 2 and 4).
6 Valve clearances incorrectly set and/or valves sticking (Chapter 1).

16 Pinging or knocking engine sounds during acceleration or uphill

1 Incorrect grade of fuel.
2 Ignition timing incorrect (Chapter 5).
3 Fuel injection system faulty (Chapter 4).

4 Improper or damaged spark plugs or wires (Chapter 1).
5 Worn or damaged distributor components (Chapter 5).
6 EGR valve not functioning (Chapters 1 and 6).
7 Vacuum leak (Chapters 2 and 4).

17 Engine runs with oil pressure light on

1 Low oil level (Chapter 1).
2 Short in wiring circuit (Chapter 12).
3 Faulty oil pressure sender (Chapter 2).
4 Worn engine bearings and/or oil pump (Chapter 2).

18 Engine diesels (continues to run) after switching off

1 Idle speed too high (Chapter 5).
2 Excessive engine operating temperature (Chapter 3).
3 Ignition timing in need of adjustment (Chapter 5).

Engine electrical system

19 Battery will not hold a charge

1 Alternator drivebelt defective or not adjusted properly (Chapter 1).
2 Battery electrolyte level low (Chapter 1).
3 Battery terminals loose or corroded (Chapter 1).
4 Alternator not charging properly (Chapter 5).
5 Loose, broken or faulty wiring in the charging circuit (Chapter 5).
6 Short in vehicle wiring (Chapter 12).
7 Internally defective battery (Chapters 1 and 5).

20 Alternator light fails to go out

1 Faulty alternator or charging circuit (Chapter 5).
2 Alternator drivebelt defective or out of adjustment (Chapter 1).
3 Alternator voltage regulator inoperative (Chapter 5).

21 Alternator light fails to come on when key is turned on

1 Warning light bulb defective (Chapter 12).
2 Fault in the printed circuit, dash wiring or bulb holder (Chapter 12).

Fuel system

22 Excessive fuel consumption

1 Dirty or clogged air filter element (Chapter 1).
2 Incorrectly set ignition timing (Chapter 5).
3 Emissions system not functioning properly (Chapter 6).
4 Fuel injection internal parts excessively worn or damaged (Chapter 4).
5 Low tire pressure or incorrect tire size (Chapter 1).

23 Fuel leakage and/or fuel odor

1 Leaking fuel feed or return line (Chapters 1 and 4).
2 Tank overfilled.
3 Evaporative canister filter clogged (Chapters 1 and 6).
4 Fuel injector internal parts excessively worn (Chapter 4).

Cooling system

24 Overheating

1 Insufficient coolant in system (Chapter 1).
2 Radiator core blocked or grille restricted (Chapter 3).
3 Thermostat faulty (Chapter 3).
4 Electric coolant fan blades broken or cracked (Chapter 3).
5 Radiator cap not maintaining proper pressure (Chapter 3).
6 Ignition timing incorrect (Chapter 5).

25 Overcooling

1 Faulty thermostat (Chapter 3).
2 Inaccurate temperature gauge sending unit (Chapter 3)

26 External coolant leakage

1 Deteriorated/damaged hoses; loose clamps (Chapters 1 and 3).
2 Water pump defective (Chapter 3).
3 Leakage from radiator core or coolant reservoir bottle (Chapter 3).
4 Engine drain or water jacket core plugs leaking (Chapter 2).

27 Internal coolant leakage

1 Leaking cylinder head gasket (Chapter 2).
2 Cracked cylinder bore or cylinder head (Chapter 2).

28 Coolant loss

1   Too much coolant in system (Chapter 1).
2   Coolant boiling away because of over-heating (Chapter 3).
3   Internal or external leakage (Chapter 3).
4   Faulty radiator cap (Chapter 3).

29 Poor coolant circulation

1   Inoperative water pump (Chapter 3).
2   Restriction in cooling system (Chapters 1 and 3).
3   Thermostat sticking (Chapter 3).

Clutch

30 Pedal travels to floor - no pressure or very little resistance

1   No fluid in reservoir (Legend models) (Chapter 1)
2   Faulty clutch master cylinder, release cylinder or hydraulic line (Legend models) (Chapter 8).
3   Broken clutch cable (Integra models) (Chapter 8).
4   Broken release bearing or fork (Chapter 8).

31 Unable to select gears

1   Faulty transmission/transaxle (Chapter 7).
2   Faulty clutch disc (Chapter 8).
3   Release lever and bearing not assembled properly (Chapter 8).
4   Faulty pressure plate (Chapter 8).
5   Pressure plate-to-flywheel bolts loose (Chapter 8).
6   Problem with the clutch hydraulic system (Legend models) (Chapter 8).
7   Clutch cable out of adjustment (Integra models) (Chapters 1 and 8).

32 Clutch slips (engine speed increases with no increase in vehicle speed)

1   Clutch plate worn (Chapter 8).
2   Clutch plate is oil soaked by leaking rear main seal (Chapter 8).
3   Clutch plate not seated. It may take 30 or 40 normal starts for a new one to seat.
4   Warped pressure plate or flywheel (Chapter 8).
5   Weak diaphragm spring (Chapter 8).
6   Clutch plate overheated. Allow to cool.

33 Grabbing (chattering) as clutch is engaged

1   Oil on clutch plate lining, burned or glazed facings (Chapter 8).
2   Worn or loose engine or transmission/transaxle mounts (Chapters 2 and 7).
3   Worn splines on clutch plate hub (Chapter 8).
4   Warped pressure plate or flywheel (Chapter 8).
5   Burned or smeared resin on flywheel or pressure plate (Chapter 8).

34 Transmission/transaxle rattling (clicking)

1   Release lever loose (Chapter 8).
2   Clutch plate damper spring failure (Chapter 8).
3   Low engine idle speed (Chapter 1).

35 Noise in clutch area

1   Fork shaft improperly installed (Chapter 8).
2   Faulty bearing (Chapter 8).

36 Clutch pedal stays on floor

1   Faulty clutch master or release cylinder (Legend models) (Chapter 8).
2   Broken clutch cable (Integra models) (Chapter 8).
3   Broken release bearing or fork (Chapter 8).
4   Damaged clutch cable (Integra models) (Chapters 1 and 8).

37 High pedal effort

1   Damaged or out of adjustment clutch cable (Integra models) (Chapters 1 and 8).
2   Pressure plate faulty (Chapter 8).

Manual transmission/transaxle

38 Knocking noise at low speeds

1   Worn driveaxle constant velocity (CV) joints (Chapter 8).
2   Worn driveaxle bore in differential case (Chapter 7A).*

39 Noise most pronounced when turning

Differential gear noise (Chapter 7A Integra models or 8 Legend models).*

40 Clunk on acceleration or deceleration

1   Loose engine or transmission/transaxle mounts (Chapters 2 and 7A).
2   Worn differential pinion shaft in case.*
3   Worn driveaxle bore in differential case (Chapter 7A Integra or 8 Legend).*
4   Worn or damaged driveaxle inboard CV joints (Chapter 8).

41 Clicking noise in turns

Worn or damaged outboard CV joint (Chapter 8).

42 Vibration

1   Rough wheel bearing (Chapters 1 and 10).
2   Damaged driveaxle (Chapter 8).
3   Out of round tires (Chapter 1).
4   Tire out of balance (Chapters 1 and 10).
5   Worn CV joint (Chapter 8).

43 Noisy in neutral with engine running

1   Damaged input gear bearing (Chapter 7A).*
2   Damaged clutch release bearing (Chapter 8).

44 Noisy in one particular gear

1   Damaged or worn constant mesh gears (Chapter 7A).*
2   Damaged or worn synchronizers (Chapter 7A).*
3   Bent reverse fork (Chapter 7A).*
4   Damaged fourth speed gear or output gear (Chapter 7A).*
5   Worn or damaged reverse idler gear or idler bushing (Chapter 7A).*

45 Noisy in all gears

1   Insufficient lubricant (Chapter 7A).
2   Damaged or worn bearings (Chapter 7A).*
3   Worn or damaged input gear shaft and/or output gear shaft (Chapter 7A).*

46 Slips out of gear

1   Worn or improperly adjusted linkage (Chapter 7A).
2   Transmission/transaxle loose on engine (Chapter 7A).
3   Shift linkage does not work freely, binds (Chapter 7A).

4   Input gear bearing retainer broken or loose (Chapter 7A).*
5   Dirt between clutch cover and engine block (Chapter 7A).
6   Worn shift fork (Chapter 7A).*

47   Leaks lubricant

1   Driveaxle oil seals worn (Chapters 7 Integra or 8 Legend).
2   Excessive amount of lubricant in transmission/transaxle (Chapters 1 and 7A).
3   Loose or broken input gear shaft bearing retainer (Chapter 7A).*
4   Input gear bearing retainer O-ring and/or lip seal damaged (Chapter 7A).*

48   Locked in gear

Lock pin or interlock pin missing (Chapter 7A).*

Although the corrective action necessary to remedy the symptoms described is beyond the scope of the home mechanic, the above information should be helpful in isolating the cause of the condition so that the owner can communicate clearly with a professional mechanic.

Automatic transmission/transaxle

Note: *Due to the complexity of the automatic transmission/transaxle, it is difficult for the home mechanic to properly diagnose and service this component. For problems other than the following, the vehicle should be taken to a dealer or transmission shop.*

49   Fluid leakage

1   Automatic transmission fluid is a deep red color. Fluid leaks should not be confused with engine oil, which can easily be blown onto the transmission/transaxle by air flow.
2   To pinpoint a leak, first remove all built-up dirt and grime from the transmission/transaxle housing with degreasing agents and/or steam cleaning. Then drive the vehicle at low speeds so air flow will not blow the leak far from its source. Raise the vehicle and determine where the leak is coming from. Common areas of leakage are:
a)   Pan (Chapters 1 and 7)
b)   Dipstick tube (Chapters 1 and 7)
c)   Transmission/transaxle oil lines (Chapter 7)
d)   Speed sensor (Chapter 7)

50   Transmission/transaxle fluid is brown or has a burned smell

Transmission/transaxle fluid burned (Chapter 1).

51   General shift mechanism problems

1   Chapter 7, Part B, deals with checking and adjusting the shift linkage on automatic transmission/transaxles. Common problems which may be attributed to poorly adjusted linkage are:
a)   Engine starting in gears other than Park or Neutral.
b)   Indicator on shifter pointing to a gear other than the one actually being used.
c)   Vehicle moves when in Park.
2   Refer to Chapter 7B for the shift linkage adjustment procedure.

52   Engine will start in gears other than Park or Neutral

Neutral start switch malfunctioning (Chapter 7B).

53   Transmission/transaxle will not downshift with accelerator pressed to the floor

Throttle valve cable out of adjustment (Integra only) (Chapter 7B).

54   Transmission/transaxle slips, shifts roughly, is noisy or has no drive in forward or reverse gears

There are many probable causes for the above problems, but the home mechanic should be concerned with only one possibility - fluid level. Before taking the vehicle to a repair shop, check the level and condition of the fluid as described in Chapter 1. Correct the fluid level as necessary or change the fluid and filter if needed. If the problem persists, have a professional diagnose the cause.

Driveaxles

55   Clicking noise in turns

Worn or damaged outboard CV joint (Chapter 8).

56   Shudder or vibration during acceleration

1   Excessive toe-in (Chapter 10).
2   Incorrect spring heights (Chapter 10).
3   Worn or damaged inboard or outboard CV joints (Chapter 8).
4   Sticking inboard CV joint assembly (Chapter 8).

57   Vibration at highway speeds

1   Out of balance front wheels and/or tires (Chapters 1 and 10).
2   Out of round front tires (Chapters 1 and 10).
3   Worn CV joint(s) (Chapter 8).

Brakes

Note: *Before assuming that a brake problem exists, make sure that:*
a)   *The tires are in good condition and properly inflated (Chapter 1).*
b)   *The front end alignment is correct (Chapter 10).*
c)   *The vehicle is not loaded with weight in an unequal manner.*

58   Vehicle pulls to one side during braking

1   Incorrect tire pressures (Chapter 1).
2   Front end out of line (have the front end aligned).
3   Front, or rear, tires not matched to one another.
4   Restricted brake lines or hoses (Chapter 9).
5   Malfunctioning drum brake or caliper assembly (Chapter 9).
6   Loose suspension parts (Chapter 10).
7   Loose calipers (Chapter 9).
8   Excessive wear of brake shoe or pad material or disc on one side.

59   Noise (high-pitched squeal when the brakes are applied)

Front disc brake pads worn out. The noise comes from the wear sensor rubbing against the disc (does not apply to all vehicles). Replace pads with new ones immediately (Chapter 9).

60   Brake roughness or chatter (pedal pulsates)

1   Excessive lateral runout (Chapter 9).
2   Uneven pad wear (Chapter 9).
3   Defective disc (Chapter 9).

61   Excessive brake pedal effort required to stop vehicle

1   Malfunctioning power brake booster (Chapter 9).

2   Partial system failure (Chapter 9).
3   Excessively worn pads (Chapter 9).
4   Piston in caliper stuck or sluggish (Chapter 9).
5   Brake pads contaminated with oil or grease (Chapter 9).
6   New pads installed and not yet seated. It will take awhile for the new material to seat against the disc.

62 Excessive brake pedal travel

1   Partial brake system failure (Chapter 9).
2   Insufficient fluid in master cylinder (Chapters 1 and 9).
3   Air trapped in system (Chapters 1 and 9).

63 Dragging brakes

1   Incorrect adjustment of brake light switch (Chapter 9).
2   Master cylinder pistons not returning correctly (Chapter 9).
3   Restricted brakes lines or hoses (Chapters 1 and 9).
4   Incorrect parking brake adjustment (Chapter 9).

64 Grabbing or uneven braking action

1   Malfunction of proportioning valve (Chapter 9).
2   Malfunction of power brake booster unit (Chapter 9).
3   Binding brake pedal mechanism (Chapter 9).

65 Brake pedal feels spongy when depressed

1   Air in hydraulic lines (Chapter 9).
2   Master cylinder mounting bolts loose (Chapter 9).
3   Master cylinder defective (Chapter 9).

66 Brake pedal travels to the floor with little resistance

1   Little or no fluid in the master cylinder reservoir caused by leaking caliper piston(s) (Chapter 9).
2   Loose, damaged or disconnected brake lines (Chapter 9).

67 Parking brake does not hold

Parking brake linkage improperly adjusted (Chapters 1 and 9).

Suspension and steering systems

Note: *Before attempting to diagnose the suspension and steering systems, perform the following preliminary checks:*
a)   *Tires for wrong pressure and uneven wear.*
b)   *Steering universal joints from the column to the steering gear for loose connectors or wear.*
c)   *Front and rear suspension and the steering gear assembly for loose or damaged parts.*
d)   *Out-of-round or out-of-balance tires, bent rims and loose and/or rough wheel bearings.*

68 Vehicle pulls to one side

1   Mismatched or uneven tires (Chapter 10).
2   Broken or sagging springs (Chapter 10).
3   Wheel alignment (Chapter 10).
4   Front brake dragging (Chapter 9).

69 Abnormal or excessive tire wear

1   Wheel alignment (Chapter 10).
2   Sagging or broken springs (Chapter 10).
3   Tire out of balance (Chapter 10).
4   Worn shock absorber (Chapter 10).
5   Overloaded vehicle.
6   Tires not rotated regularly (Chapter 10).

70 Wheel makes a thumping noise

1   Blister or bump on tire (Chapter 10).
2   Improper shock absorber action (Chapter 10).

71 Shimmy, shake or vibration

1   Tire or wheel out-of-balance or out-of-round (Chapter 10).
2   Loose or worn front hub or wheel bearings (Chapters 1, 8 and 10).
3   Worn tie-rod ends (Chapter 10).
4   Worn suspension components (Chapters 1 and 10).
5   Excessive wheel runout (Chapter 10).
6   Blister or bump on tire (Chapter 10).

72 Hard steering

1   Lack of lubrication at balljoints and tie-rod ends (Chapters 1 and 10).
2   Front wheel alignment (Chapter 10).
3   Low tire pressure(s) (Chapters 1 and 10).

73 Poor returnability of steering to center

1   Lack of lubrication at balljoints and tie-rod ends (Chapters 1 and 10).
2   Binding in balljoints (Chapter 10).
3   Binding in steering column (Chapter 10).
4   Lack of lubricant in steering gear assembly (Chapter 10).
5   Front wheel alignment (Chapter 10).

74 Abnormal noise at the front end

1   Lack of lubrication at balljoints and tie-rod ends (Chapters 1 and 10).
2   Damaged shock absorber mounting (Chapter 10).
3   Worn control arm bushings or tie-rod ends (Chapter 10).
4   Loose stabilizer bar (Chapter 10).
5   Loose wheel nuts (Chapters 1 and 10).
6   Loose suspension bolts (Chapter 10)

75 Wander or poor steering stability

1   Mismatched or uneven tires (Chapter 10).
2   Lack of lubrication at balljoints and tie-rod ends (Chapters 1 and 10).
3   Worn shock absorber assemblies (Chapter 10).
4   Loose stabilizer bar (Chapter 10).
5   Broken or sagging springs (Chapter 10).
6   Wheels out of alignment (Chapter 10).

76 Erratic steering when braking

1   Front hub bearings worn (Chapter 10).
2   Broken or sagging springs (Chapter 10).
3   Leaking caliper (Chapter 9).
4   Warped brake discs (Chapter 9).

77 Excessive pitching and/or rolling around corners or during braking

1   Loose stabilizer bar (Chapter 10).
2   Worn shock absorbers or mountings (Chapter 10).
3   Broken or sagging springs (Chapter 10).
4   Overloaded vehicle.

78 Suspension bottoms

1   Overloaded vehicle.
2   Worn shock absorbers (Chapter 10).
3   Incorrect, broken or sagging springs (Chapter 10).

79 Cupped tires

1   Front wheel or rear wheel alignment (Chapter 10).

2   Worn shock absorbers (Chapter 10).
3   Wheel bearings worn (Chapter 10).
4   Excessive tire or wheel runout (Chapter 10).
5   Worn balljoints (Chapter 10).

80 Excessive tire wear on outside edge

1   Inflation pressures incorrect (Chapter 1).
2   Excessive speed in turns.
3   Front end alignment incorrect (excessive toe-in). Have professionally aligned.
4   Suspension arm bent or twisted (Chapter 10).

81 Excessive tire wear on inside edge

1   Inflation pressures incorrect (Chapter 1).
2   Front end alignment incorrect (toe-out). Have professionally aligned.
3   Loose or damaged steering or suspension components (Chapter 10).

82 Tire tread worn in one place

1   Tires out of balance.
2   Damaged or buckled wheel. Inspect and replace if necessary.
3   Defective tire (Chapter 1).

83 Excessive play or looseness in steering system

1   Front hub bearing(s) worn (Chapter 10).
2   Tie-rod end loose (Chapter 10).
3   Steering gear loose or worn (Chapter 10).
4   Worn or loose steering intermediate shaft (Chapter 10).

84 Rattling or clicking noise in steering gear

1   Steering gear loose (Chapter 10).
2   Steering gear defective.

Chapter 1
Tune-up and routine maintenance

Contents

1

Specifications

Recommended lubricants and fluids

Note: *Listed here are manufacturer recommendations at the time the manual was written. Manufacturers occasionally upgrade their fluid and lubricant specifications, so check with your local auto parts store for the most current recommendations.*

Engine oil
Type.. API grade SJ or better multigrade and fuel efficient oil
Viscosity .... See accompanying chart

Recommended lubricants and fluids (continued)

Automatic transmission/transaxle fluid	DEXRON type automatic transmission fluid
Manual transmission/transaxle	
Lubricant type	API grade SJ or better engine oil
Viscosity	10W-30 or 10W-40 engine oil
Differential lubricant type (Legend only)	API GL4 or GL5 80W90 gear oil
Brake fluid type..	DOT 3 brake fluid
Power steering system fluid	Honda power steering fluid or equivalent (not ATF)
Fuel	
Integra (except GSR)..	Unleaded gasoline, 87 octane or higher
Integra GSR and Legend......................................	Unleaded gasoline, 91 octane or higher

Capacities*

Engine oil (including filter)	
Integra (except GSR model)	4.0 qts
Integra GSR model	4.2 qts
Legend	5.0 qts
Automatic transmission/transaxle (drain and refill)	
Integra	3.2 qts
Legend	3.5 qts
Manual transmission/transaxle	2.4 qts
Differential (Legend models) (drain and refill)	1.1 qts
Coolant	
Integra	5.0 qts
Legend	7.9 qts

All capacities approximate. Add as necessary to bring to the appropriate level.

Cylinder location and distributor rotor rotation diagram (Acura Integra)

Ignition system

Spark plug type and gap	
Integra	
1990 and 1991	
Conventional type..............................	NGK BCPR5E-11 or equivalent
Gap	0.039 to 0.043 inch
Platinum type.....................................	NGK BCPR5EVX-11 or equivalent
Gap	0.039 to 0.043 inch
1992 and 1993 non-VTEC engine	
Conventional type..............................	NGK ZFR5FE-11 or equivalent
Gap	0.039 to 0.043 inch
1992 and 1993 VTEC engine	
Platinum type.....................................	NGK PFR6G-13 or equivalent
Gap	0.039 to 0.043 inch
Legend	
1991 and 1992 engine	
Platinum type.....................................	NGK PFR6G-11 or equivalent
Gap	0.039 to 0.043 inch
1993 though 1995 engine	
Platinum type.....................................	NGK PZFR6G-11 or equivalent
Gap	0.039 to 0.043 inch
Spark plug wire resistance	Less than 25,000 ohms
Engine firing order	
Integra	1-3-4-2
Legend	1-4-2-5-5-3-6
Ignition timing	
Integra	
Non-VTEC engine	16 +/- 2-degrees @750 +/- 50 rpm
VTEC engine	16 +/- 2-degrees @ 800 +/- 50 rpm
Legend	
Manual	15 +/- 2-degrees @ 650 +/- 50 rpm
Automatic..	15 +/- 2-degrees @ 600 +/- 50 rpm

Front

12021-1-specs HAYNES

Acura Legend cylinder location diagram

Idle Speed

Integra	
With EACV/IAC valve disconnected (for adjusting)	
Non-VTEC engine	600 +/- 50 rpm
VTEC engine	800 +/- 50 rpm
With EACV valve/IAC connected	
Non-VTEC engine	750 +/- 50 rpm
VTEC engine	800 +/- 50 rpm

Legend
    Manual transaxle .... 650 +/- 50 rpm
    Automatic transaxle .... 600 +/- 50 rpm

Cooling system

Thermostat rating
    Starts to open.. 173-degrees F
    Fully open .... 194-degrees F

Accessory drivebelt deflection

Power steering pump
    Integra .... 1/2 to 5/8-inch
    Legend .... 7/16 to 1/2-inch
Alternator
    Integra .... 3/8 to 1/2-inch
    Legend .... 1/4 to 7/16-inch
Air conditioning compressor
    Integra .... 3/8 to 1/2-inch
    Legend .... 3/16 to 5/16-inch

Brakes

Disc brake pad lining thickness (minimum) 1/16-inch
Parking brake shoe lining thickness (minimum) 3/32-inch
Parking brake adjustment.. 6 to 10 clicks

Clutch pedal/release lever

Integra
    Pedal height .... 7 inches
    Pedal freeplay.. 19/32 to 25/32 inch
    Release arm freeplay... 5/32 to 13/64 inch
Legend
    Pedal height
        1991 through 1993... 7-27/32 inches
        1994 on .... 7-19/32 inches
    Pedal freeplay
        1991 and 1992 .... 3/64 to 9/32 inch
        1993 on .... 11/32 to 19/32 inch

Valve clearances (engine cold)

Integra
    1990 and 1991
        Intake .... 0.006 to 0.007-inch
        Exhaust .... 0.007 to 0.008-inch
    1992 and 1993
        Non-VTEC engine
            Intake.. 0.003 to 0.005-inch
            Exhaust... 0.006 to 0.008-inch
        VTEC engine
            Intake .... 0.006 to 0.007-inch
            Exhaust .... 0.007 to 0.008-inch
Legend .... Not adjustable

Torque specifications

                                                                             Ft-lbs (unless otherwise indicated)
ABS high-pressure hose banjo bolts....................................... 25
Automatic transmission/transaxle
    Drain plug 29
    Fill plug 33
Manual transmission/transaxle drain/fill plugs
    Drain 29
    Fill 33
Legend differential
    Drain plug 29
    Fill plug 33
Fuel filter
    Banjo bolt .... 132 in-lbs
    Banjo nut 16
Spark plugs.. 156 in-lbs
Wheel lug nuts 80

Acura Integra engine compartment layout

1	Fuse block	7	Power steering fluid reservoir	12	Radiator cap
2	ABS brake fluid reservoir	8	Windshield washer fluid reservoir	13	Radiator hose
3	Fuel filter	9	Engine coolant reservoir	14	Distributor cap
4	Brake master cylinder reservoir	10	Engine oil dipstick	15	Battery
5	Engine oil filler cap	11	Spark plug wires	16	Air filter housing
6	Spark plug				

Acura Legend engine compartment layout

1 Anti-lock Braking System (ABS) fluid reservoir	9 Battery
2 Automatic transmission fluid dipstick	10 Engine oil filler cap
3 Fuel filter	11 Engine oil dipstick
4 Brake master cylinder reservoir	12 Coil assemblies (spark plugs underneath)
5 Evaporative Emissions system canister	13 Radiator hose
6 Fuse block	14 Radiator cap
7 Engine coolant reservoir	15 Power steering fluid reservoir
8 Windshield washer fluid reservoir	16 Air filter housing

Acura Integra engine compartment underside components

1	Radiator drain	3	Driveaxle	5	Exhaust pipe	7	Outer driveaxle boot
2	Front brake caliper	4	Engine oil drain plug	6	Transaxle drain plug		

Acura Legend engine compartment underside components

1   Radiator drain
2   Outer driveaxle boot
3   Driveaxle
4   Engine oil drain plug
5   Engine oil filter
6   Exhaust pipe
7   Transmission drain plug
8   Disc brake
9   Differential drain plug
10 Differential check/filler plug

Acura Legend rear underside components

1 Exhaust pipe
2 Fuel tank
3 Parking brake cable
4 Rear disc brake caliper
5 Shock and spring assembly
6 Muffler
7 Brake hose

Acura Integra rear underside components

1 Exhaust pipe
2 Fuel tank
3 Parking brake cable
4 Rear disc brake caliper
5 Muffler
6 Brake hose
7 Shock and spring assembly

1

1 Maintenance schedule

The maintenance intervals in this manual are provided with the assumption that you, not the dealer, will be doing the work. These are the minimum maintenance intervals recommended by the factory for vehicles that are driven daily. If you wish to keep your vehicle in peak condition at all times, you may wish to perform some of these procedures even more often. Because frequent maintenance enhances the efficiency, performance and resale value of your car, we encourage you to do so. If you drive in dusty areas, tow a trailer, idle or drive at low speeds for extended periods or drive for short distances (less than four miles) in below freezing temperatures, shorter intervals are also recommended.

When your vehicle is new, it should be serviced by a factory authorized dealer service department to protect the factory warranty. In many cases, the initial maintenance check is done at no cost to the owner.

Every 250 miles or weekly, whichever comes first

Check the engine oil level (Section 4)
Check the engine coolant level (Section 4)
Check the windshield washer fluid level (Section 4)
Check the brake fluid level (Section 4)
Check the tires and tire pressures (Section 5)

Every 3000 miles or 3 months, whichever comes first

All items listed above plus:
Check the power steering fluid level (Section 6)
Check the automatic and transmission/transaxle fluid level (Section 7)
Change the engine oil and oil filter (Section 8)

Every 7500 miles or 6 months, whichever comes first

All items listed above plus:
Inspect and replace, if necessary, the windshield wiper blades (Section 9)
Check and service the battery (Section 10)
Check and adjust, if necessary, the engine drivebelts (Section 11)
Inspect and replace, if necessary, all underhood hoses (Section 12)
Check the cooling system (Section 13)
Rotate the tires (Section 14)
Check the front disc brake pads (Section 15)

Every 15,000 miles or 12 months, whichever comes first

All items listed above plus:
Inspect the brake system (Section 15)*
Check the clutch pedal height and freeplay (Section 16)
Inspect the seatbelts (Section 17)
Replace the air conditioning air filter (1992 and later Legend models) (Section 18)
Adjust the valve clearances (Section 19)

Replace the air filter (Section 20)*
Inspect the fuel system (Section 21)
Check the manual transmission/transaxle lubricant level (Section 22)*
Check the differential lubricant level (Legend models) (Section 22)
Inspect the suspension and steering components and driveaxle boots (Section 23)*
Inspect the exhaust system (Section 24)

Every 30,000 miles or 24 months, whichever comes first

All items listed above plus:
Replace the spark plugs (conventional [non -platinum] spark plugs) (Section 25)
Inspect and replace, if necessary, the spark plug wires, distributor cap and rotor (Section 26)
Check and replace, if necessary, the PCV valve (Section 27)
Replace the fuel filter (Section 28)
Service the cooling system (drain, flush and refill) (Section 29)
Replace the brake fluid (Section 30)
Change the automatic transmission/transaxle fluid (Section 31)
Change the manual transmission/transaxle lubricant (Section 32)
Change the differential lubricant (Legend models) (Section 32)
Check the Exhaust Gas Recirculation (EGR) system (Section 33)
Check and replace, if necessary, the engine idle speed (Section 34)
Check and replace, if necessary, the engine ignition timing (Section 35)
Replace the Anti-lock Brake System (ABS) high pressure hose (Section 36)
Reset the Maintenance Required Indicator (Legend models) (Section 37)

Every 60,000 miles or 24 months, whichever comes first

All items listed above plus:
Replace the spark plugs (platinum-tipped spark plugs) (Section 25)

Every 90,000 miles or 72 months, whichever comes first

Replace timing belt (Chapter 2A or 2B)

* This item is affected by "severe" operating conditions as described below. If your vehicle is operated under "severe" conditions, perform all maintenance indicated with a * at 7500 mile/6 month intervals. Severe conditions are indicated if you mainly operate your vehicle under one or more of the following conditions:
Operating in dusty areas
Towing a trailer
Idling for extended periods and/or low speed operation
Operating when outside temperatures remain below freezing and when most trips are less than four miles
** If operated under one or more of the following conditions, change the automatic transmission/transaxle fluid every 15,000 miles):
In heavy city traffic where the outside temperature regularly reaches 90-degrees F (32-degrees C) or higher
In hilly or mountainous terrain

2 Introduction

This chapter is designed to help the home mechanic maintain his/her car for peak performance, economy, safety and long life.

The following sections deal specifically with each item on the maintenance schedule. Visual checks, adjustments, component replacement and other helpful items are included. Refer to the accompanying photos of the engine compartment and the under-side of the vehicle for the location of various components.

Servicing your vehicle in accordance with the mileage/time maintenance schedule and the following Sections will provide it with a planned maintenance program that should result in a long and reliable service life. This is a comprehensive plan, so maintaining some items but not others at the specified service intervals will not produce the same results.

As you service your car, you will discover that many of the procedures can - and should - be grouped together because of the nature of the particular procedure you're performing or because of the close proximity of two otherwise unrelated components to one another. For example, if the vehicle is raised for chassis lubrication, you should inspect the exhaust, suspension, steering and fuel systems while you're under the vehicle. When you're rotating the tires, it makes good sense to check the brakes and wheel bearings since the wheels are already removed.

Finally, let's suppose you have to borrow or rent a torque wrench. Even if you only need to tighten the spark plugs, you might as well check the torque of as many critical fasteners as time allows.

The first step of this maintenance program is to prepare yourself before the actual work begins. Read through all sections pertinent to the procedures you're planning to do, then make a list of and gather together all the parts and tools you will need to do the job. If it looks as if you might run into problems during a particular segment of some procedure, seek advice from your local parts man or dealer service department.

3 Tune-up general information

The term tune-up is used in this manual to represent a combination of individual operations rather than one specific procedure.

If, from the time the vehicle is new, the routine maintenance schedule is followed closely and frequent checks are made of fluid levels and high wear items, as suggested throughout this manual, the engine will be kept in relatively good running condition and the need for additional work will be minimized.

More likely than not, however, there will be times when the engine is running poorly due to lack of regular maintenance. This is even more likely if a used vehicle, which has

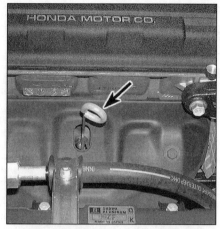

4.2a The Integra oil dipstick (arrow) extends through the exhaust manifold heat shield

4.2b The Legend engine oil dipstick (arrow) is located at left (drivers) front corner of the engine, near the battery

not received regular and frequent maintenance checks, is purchased. In such cases, an engine tune-up will be needed outside of the regular routine maintenance intervals.

The first step in any tune-up or engine diagnosis to help correct a poor running engine would be a cylinder compression check. A check of the engine compression (see Chapter 2 Part B) will give valuable information regarding the overall performance of many internal components and should be used as a basis for tune-up and repair procedures. If, for instance, a compression check indicates serious internal engine wear, a conventional tune-up will not help the running condition of the engine and would be a waste of time and money. Because of its importance, compression checking should be performed by someone with the proper compression testing gauge and the knowledge to use it properly.

The following series of operations are those most often needed to bring a generally poor running engine back into a proper state of tune.

Minor tune-up

Check all engine related fluids (Section 4)
Clean, inspect and test the battery (Section 10)
Check and adjust the drivebelts (Section 11)
Check all underhood hoses (Section 12)
Check the cooling system (Section 13)
Check the air filter (Section 20)
Replace the spark plugs (conventional non-platinum) (Section 25)
Inspect the distributor cap and rotor (Section 26)
Check and adjust the idle speed (Section 34)

Major tune-up

All items listed under minor tune-up, plus . . .
Replace the air filter (Section 20)
Check the fuel system (Section 21)

Replace the spark plugs (platinum) (Section 25)
Replace the distributor cap and rotor (Section 26)
Inspect the spark plug and coil wires (Section 26)
Replace the spark plug wires (Section 26)
Check the charging system (Chapter 5)

4 Fluid level checks (every 250 miles or weekly)

1   Fluids are an essential part of the lubrication, cooling, brake, clutch and other systems. Because these fluids gradually become depleted and/or contaminated during normal operation of the vehicle, they must be periodically replenished. See *Recommended lubricants and fluids* and *Capacities* at the beginning of this Chapter before adding fluid to any of the following components. **Note:** *The vehicle must be on level ground before fluid levels can be checked.*

Engine oil

Refer to illustrations 4.2a, 4.2b, 4.4, 4.6a and 4.6b

2   Engine oil level is checked with a dipstick located at the side of the engine **(see illustrations)**. The dipstick extends through a metal tube from which it protrudes down into the engine oil pan.

3   The oil level should be checked before the vehicle has been driven, or about 15 minutes after the engine has been shut off. If the oil is checked immediately after driving the vehicle, some of the oil will remain in the upper engine components, producing an inaccurate reading on the dipstick.

4   Pull the dipstick from the tube and wipe all the oil from the end with a clean rag or paper towel. Insert the clean dipstick all the way back into its metal tube and pull it out again. Observe the oil at the end of the dip-

4.4 The oil level should be between the two holes in the dipstick - if it isn't, add enough oil to bring the level to or near the upper hole (it takes one quart to raise the level from the lower hole to the upper hole)

4.6a The threaded oil filler cap is located on the rear corner of the valve cover on Integra models.

4.6b On Legend models the oil filler cap is on the left valve cover - to prevent dirt from contaminating the engine, always make sure the area around this opening is clean before unscrewing the cap

4.9 Make sure the coolant level is between the MAX and MIN lines - if it's below the MIN line, add a sufficient quantity of the specified mixture of antifreeze and water

stick. At its highest point, the level should be between the upper and lower holes **(see illustration)**.

5   It takes one quart of oil to raise the level from the lower hole to the upper hole on the dipstick. Do not allow the level to drop below the lower hole or oil starvation may cause engine damage. Conversely, overfilling the engine (adding oil above the upper hole) may cause oil fouled spark plugs, oil leaks or oil seal failures.

6   Remove the threaded cap from the valve cover to add oil **(see illustrations)**. Use a funnel to prevent spills. After adding the oil, install the filler cap hand tight. Start the engine and look carefully for any small leaks around the oil filter or drain plug. Stop the engine and check the oil level again after it has had sufficient time to drain from the upper block and cylinder head galleys.

7   Checking the oil level is an important preventive maintenance step. A continually dropping oil level indicates oil leakage through damaged seals, from loose connections, or past worn rings or valve guides. If the oil looks milky in color or has water droplets in it, a cylinder head gasket may be blown or the oil cooler could be leaking. The engine should be checked immediately. The condition of the oil should also be checked. Each time you check the oil level, slide your thumb and index finger up the dipstick before

wiping off the oil. If you see small dirt or metal particles clinging to the dipstick, the oil should be changed (see Section 8).

Engine coolant

Refer to illustration 4.9

Warning: *Do not allow antifreeze to come in contact with your skin or painted surfaces of the vehicle. Rinse off spills immediately with plenty of water. Antifreeze is highly toxic if ingested. Never leave antifreeze lying around in an open container or in puddles on the floor; children and pets are attracted by its sweet smell and may drink it. Check with local authorities about disposing of used antifreeze. Many communities have collection centers, which will see that antifreeze is disposed of safely.* **Note:** *Non-toxic antifreeze is now manufactured and available at auto parts stores, but even this should be disposed of properly.*

8   All vehicles covered by this manual are equipped with a pressurized coolant recovery system. A coolant reservoir located on the right side of the engine compartment is connected by a hose to the base of the radiator filler neck. If the coolant heats up excessively during engine operation, coolant can escape through the pressurized filler cap, then through the connecting hose into the reservoir. As the engine cools, the coolant is automatically drawn back into the cooling system

to maintain the correct level.

9   The coolant level in the reservoir should be checked regularly. It must be between the MAX and MIN lines on the tank. The level will vary with the temperature of the engine. When the engine is cold, the coolant level should be at or slightly above the MIN mark on the tank. Once the engine has warmed up, the level should be at or near the MAX mark. If it isn't, allow the fluid in the tank to cool, then remove the cap from the reservoir **(see illustration)** and add coolant to bring the level up to the MAX line. **Warning:** *Do not remove the radiator cap to check the coolant level when the engine is warm! Use only ethylene glycol type coolant and water in the mixture ratio recommended by your owner's manual. Do not use supplemental inhibitors or additives. If only a small amount of coolant is required to bring the system up to the proper level, water can be used. However, repeated additions of water will dilute the recommended antifreeze and water solution. In order to maintain the proper ratio of antifreeze and water, it is advisable to top up the coolant level with the correct mixture. Refer to your owner's manual for the recommended ratio.*

10   If the coolant level drops within a short time after replenishment, there may be a leak in the system. Inspect the radiator, hoses, engine coolant filler cap, drain plugs, air bleeder bolt and water pump. If no leak is evident, have the radiator cap pressure tested. **Warning:** *Never remove the radiator cap or the coolant recovery reservoir cap when the engine is running or has just been shut down, because the cooling system is hot. Escaping steam and scalding liquid could cause serious injury.*

11   If it is necessary to open the radiator cap, wait until the system has cooled completely, then wrap a thick cloth around the cap and turn it to the first stop. If any steam escapes, wait until the system has cooled further, then remove the cap.

12   When checking the coolant level, always note its condition. It should be relatively

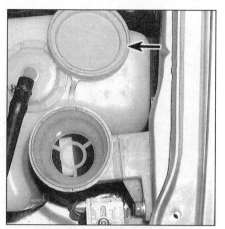

4.14 The windshield washer fluid reservoir is located at left front corner of the engine compartment - flip up the cap (arrow) to add fluid

4.16a The brake fluid should be kept between the MIN and MAX marks on the reservoir - turn and lift up the cap to add fluid

4.16b The ABS system brake fluid reservoir is located on the right rear corner of the engine compartment

clear. If it is brown or rust colored, the system should be drained, flushed and refilled. Even if the coolant appears to be normal, the corrosion inhibitors wear out with use, so it must be replaced at the specified intervals.

13   Do not allow antifreeze to come in contact with your skin or painted surfaces of the vehicle. Flush contacted areas immediately with plenty of water.

Windshield washer fluid

Refer to illustration 4.14

14   Fluid for the windshield washer system is stored in a plastic reservoir that is located at the left front corner of the engine compartment **(see illustration)**. In milder climates, plain water can be used to top up the reservoir, but the reservoir should be kept no more than 2/3 full to allow for expansion should the water freeze. In colder climates, the use of a specially designed windshield washer fluid, available at your dealer and any auto parts store, will help lower the freezing point of the fluid. Mix the solution with water in accordance with the manufacturer's directions on the container. Do not use regular antifreeze. It will damage the vehicle's paint.

Brake and clutch fluid

Refer to illustrations 4.16a and 4.16b

15   The brake master cylinder is mounted on the front of the power booster unit and the clutch master cylinder next to it on the firewall within the engine compartment. Models with an Anti-lock Brake System (ABS) also have a reservoir for the ABS modulator located on the right side of the engine compartment. ABS-equipped vehicles should be driven for a few minutes to equalize the fluid in the system before checking the fluid level in the reservoirs. If the level rises significantly above the MAX mark, have the system checked by a dealer because this could indicate a malfunction in the ABS system.

16   To check the fluid level of the brake or clutch master cylinder, simply look at the

MAX and MIN marks on the reservoir **(see illustration)**. The level should be between the two marks. If the vehicle is equipped with an Anti-lock Brake System (ABS), the fluid level in the ABS unit reservoir must also be checked. It's located on the right (passenger) side of the engine compartment **(see illustration)**.

17   If the level is low, wipe the top of the reservoir cover with a clean rag to prevent contamination of the brake system before lifting the cap.

18   Add only the specified brake fluid to the brake, clutch or ABS reservoir (refer to *Recommended lubricants and fluids* at the front of this chapter or to your owner's manual). Mixing different types of brake fluid can damage the system. Fill the brake master cylinder reservoir only to about 3/4-inch below the MAX line - this brings the fluid to the correct level when you put the cap back on. **Warning:** *Use caution when filling the reservoir - brake fluid can harm your eyes and damage painted surfaces. Do not use brake fluid that has been opened for more than one year or has been left open. Brake fluid absorbs moisture from the air. Moisture in the brake system can boil, causing a dangerous loss of braking.*

19   While the reservoir cap is removed, inspect the master cylinder reservoir for contamination. If deposits, dirt particles or water droplets are present, the system should be drained and refilled (see Chapters 8 and 9).

20   After filling the reservoir to the proper level, make sure the lid is properly seated to prevent fluid leakage and/or system pressure loss.

21   The brake fluid in the master cylinder will drop slightly as the brake pads at each wheel wear down during normal operation. If the master cylinder requires repeated replenishing to keep it at the proper level, this is an indication of leakage in the brake system, which should be corrected immediately. Check all brake lines and connections, along with the wheel cylinders and booster (see Section 15 for more information). A drop in

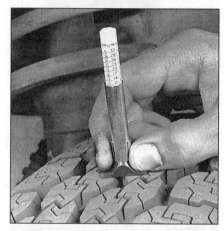

5.2 Use a tire tread depth gauge to monitor tire wear - they are available at auto parts stores and service stations and cost very little

the clutch reservoir level indicates a leak in the clutch hydraulic system (see Chapter 8).

22   If, upon checking the brake master cylinder fluid level, you discover an empty or nearly empty reservoir, the brake system should be bled (see Chapter 9).

---

5   Tire and tire pressure checks (every 250 miles or weekly)

Refer to illustrations 5.2, 5.3, 5.4a, 5.4b and 5.8

1   Periodic inspection of the tires may spare you from the inconvenience of being stranded with a flat tire. It can also provide you with vital information regarding possible problems in the steering and suspension systems before major damage occurs.

2   Normal tread wear can be monitored with a simple, inexpensive device known as a tread depth indicator **(see illustration)**. When the tread depth reaches the specified minimum, replace the tire(s).

UNDERINFLATION

CUPPING

Cupping may be caused by:
- Underinflation and/or mechanical irregularities such as out-of-balance condition of wheel and/or tire, and bent or damaged wheel.
- Loose or worn steering tie-rod or steering idler arm.
- Loose, damaged or worn front suspension parts.

OVERINFLATION

INCORRECT TOE-IN OR EXTREME CAMBER

FEATHERING DUE TO MISALIGNMENT

5.3 This chart will help you determine the condition of the tires, the probable cause(s) of abnormal wear and the corrective action necessary

5.4a If a tire loses air on a steady basis, check the valve core first to make sure it's snug (special inexpensive wrenches are commonly available at auto parts stores)

5.4b If the valve core is tight, raise the corner of the vehicle with the low tire and spray a soapy water solution onto the tread as the tire is turned slowly - leaks will cause small bubbles to appear

5.8 To extend the life of the tires, check the air pressure at least once a week with an accurate gauge (don't forget the spare)

3   Note any abnormal tread wear **(see illustration)**. Tread pattern irregularities such as cupping, flat spots and more wear on one side than the other are indications of front end alignment and/or balance problems. If any of these conditions are noted, take the vehicle to a tire shop or service station to correct the problem.

4   Look closely for cuts, punctures and embedded nails or tacks. Sometimes a tire will hold its air pressure for a short time or leak down very slowly even after a nail has embedded itself into the tread. If a slow leak persists, check the valve core to make sure it is tight **(see illustration)**. Examine the tread for an object that may have embedded itself into the tire or for a "plug" that may have begun to leak (radial tire punctures are repaired with a plug that is installed in a puncture). If a puncture is suspected, it can be easily verified by spraying a solution of soapy water onto the puncture area **(see illustration)**. The soapy solution will bubble if there is a leak. Unless the puncture is inordinately large, a tire shop or gas station can usually repair the punctured tire.

5   Carefully inspect the inner side of each tire for evidence of brake fluid leakage. If you see any, inspect the brakes immediately.

6   Correct tire air pressure adds miles to the lifespan of the tires, improves mileage and enhances overall ride quality. Tire pressure cannot be accurately estimated by looking at a tire, particularly if it is a radial. A tire pressure gauge is therefore essential. Keep an accurate gauge in the glovebox. The pres-

6.4a The power steering fluid reservoir (arrow) is translucent so the fluid level can be checked without removing the cap - keep the fluid between the two lines (Integra shown)

6.4b On Legend models, the power steering fluid reservoir (arrow) is located in the right front corner of the engine compartment

7.3a The automatic transaxle fluid dipstick (arrow) is located on the right (passenger) side of the engine compartment on Integra models

1

7.3b On Legend models, the automatic transmission dipstick (arrow) is located near the center of the firewall

7.5 The automatic transaxle fluid level should be in the cross-hatched area (between the arrows) on the dipstick (Legend shown)

sure gauges fitted to the nozzles of air hoses at gas stations are often inaccurate.

7   Always check tire pressure when the tires are cold. "Cold," in this case, means the vehicle has not been driven over a mile in the three hours preceding a tire pressure check. A pressure rise of four to eight pounds is not uncommon once the tires are warm.

8   Unscrew the valve cap protruding from the wheel or hubcap and push the gauge firmly onto the valve **(see illustration)**. Note the reading on the gauge and compare this figure to the recommended tire pressure shown on the tire placard on the left door jamb. Be sure to reinstall the valve cap to keep dirt and moisture out of the valve stem mechanism. Check all four tires and, if necessary, add enough air to bring them up to the recommended pressure levels.

9   Don't forget to keep the spare tire inflated to the specified pressure (consult your owner's manual). Note that the air pressure specified for the compact spare is significantly higher than the pressure of the regular tires.

6   Power steering fluid level check (every 3000 miles or 3 months)

Refer to illustrations 6.4a and 6.4b

1   The power steering system relies on fluid that may, over a period of time, require replenishing.

2   The fluid reservoir for the power steering pump is located on the inner fender panel near the left (Integra models) or right (Legend models) front of the engine compartment.

3   For the check, the front wheels should be pointed straight ahead and the engine should be off. The fluid should be cold when checking the level.

4   On all models, the reservoir is translucent plastic and the fluid level can be checked visually **(see illustrations)**.

5   If additional fluid is required, pour the

specified type directly into the reservoir, using a funnel to prevent spills.

6   If the reservoir requires frequent fluid additions, all power steering hoses, hose connections, the power steering pump and the steering gear should be carefully checked for leaks.

7   Automatic transmission/transaxle fluid level check (every 3000 miles or 3 months)

Refer to illustrations 7.3a, 7.3b and 7.5

1   The level of the automatic transmission/transaxle fluid should be carefully maintained. Low fluid level can lead to slipping or loss of drive, while overfilling can cause foaming, loss of fluid and transaxle damage.

2   The transmission/transaxle fluid level should only be checked on level ground within one minute of the engine being shut off.

3   Remove the dipstick. On Integra models it's located down low on the front of the transaxle (in the passenger's side of the

engine compartment) **(see illustration)**. On Legend models, the transmission dipstick is located at the rear of the engine **(see illustration)**. Check the level of the fluid on the dipstick and note its condition.

4   Wipe the fluid from the dipstick with a clean rag and reinsert it.

5   Pull the dipstick out again and note the fluid level. The level should be between the upper and lower marks on the dipstick **(see illustration)**. If the level is low, add the specified automatic transmission fluid through the dipstick opening with a funnel.

6   Add just enough of the specified fluid to fill the transmission/transaxle to the proper level. It takes about one pint to raise the level from the lower mark to the upper mark, so add the fluid a little at a time and keep checking the level until it is correct.

7   The condition of the fluid should also be checked along with the level. If the fluid at the end of the dipstick is black or a dark reddish brown color, or if it emits a burned smell, the fluid should be changed (see Section 31). If you are in doubt about the condition of the fluid, purchase some new fluid and compare the two for color and smell.

8.2 These tools are required when changing the engine oil and filter

1   *Drain pan* - It should be fairly shallow in depth, but wide to prevent spills
2   *Rubber gloves* - When removing the drain plug and filter, you will get oil on your hands (the gloves will prevent burns)
3   *Breaker bar* - Sometimes the oil drain plug is tight, and a long breaker bar is needed to loosen it
4   *Socket* - To be used with the breaker bar or a ratchet (must be the correct size to fit the drain plug)
5   *Filter wrench* - This is a metal band-type wrench, which requires clearance around the filter to be effective
6   *Filter wrench* - This type fits on the bottom of the filter and can be turned with a ratchet or breaker bar (different-size wrenches are available for different types of filters)

8   Engine oil and oil filter change (every 3000 miles or 3 months)

Refer to illustrations 8.2, 8.7, 8.12a, 8.12b and 8.14

1   Frequent oil changes are the best preventive maintenance the home mechanic can give the engine, because aging oil becomes diluted and contaminated, which leads to premature engine wear.
2   Make sure you have all the necessary tools before you begin this procedure **(see illustration)**. You should also have plenty of rags or newspapers handy for mopping up any spills.
3   Access to the underside of the vehicle is greatly improved if the vehicle can be lifted on a hoist, driven onto ramps or supported by jackstands. **Warning:** *Do not work under a vehicle which is supported only by a bumper, hydraulic or scissors-type jack.*
4   If this is your first oil change, get under the vehicle and familiarize yourself with the locations of the oil drain plug and the oil filter.

8.7 Use the proper size box-end wrench or socket to remove the oil drain plug without rounding off the corners

8.12b The Legend oil filter is located at the front of the engine

The engine and exhaust components will be warm during the actual work, so try to anticipate any potential problems before the engine and accessories are hot.
5   Park the vehicle on a level spot. Start the engine and allow it to reach its normal operating temperature. Warm oil and sludge will flow out more easily. Turn off the engine when it's warmed up. Remove the filler cap from the valve cover.
6   Raise the vehicle and support it securely on jackstands. **Warning:** *Never get beneath the vehicle when it is supported only by a jack. The jack provided with your vehicle is designed solely for raising the vehicle to remove and replace the wheels. Always use jackstands to support the vehicle when it becomes necessary to place your body underneath the vehicle.*
7   Being careful not to touch the hot exhaust components, place the drain pan under the drain plug in the bottom of the pan and remove the plug **(see illustration)**. You may want to wear gloves while unscrewing the plug the final few turns if the engine is hot.
8   Allow the old oil to drain into the pan. It may be necessary to move the pan farther under the engine as the oil flow slows to a trickle. Inspect the old oil for the presence of metal shavings and chips.

8.12a The oil filter is usually on very tight and will require a special wrench for removal - DO NOT use the wrench to tighten the new filter (Integra shown)

8.14 Lubricate the oil filter gasket with clean engine oil before installing the filter on the engine

9   After all the oil has drained, wipe off the drain plug with a clean rag. Even minute metal particles clinging to the plug would immediately contaminate the new oil.
10   Clean the area around the drain plug opening, reinstall the plug and tighten it securely, but do not strip the threads.
11   Move the drain pan into position under the oil filter.
12   Loosen the oil filter **(see illustrations)** by turning it counterclockwise with the filter wrench. Any standard filter wrench will work. Sometimes the oil filter is screwed on so tightly that it cannot be loosened. If this situation occurs, punch a metal bar or long screwdriver directly through the side of the canister and use it as a T-bar to turn the filter. Be prepared for oil to spurt out of the canister as it is punctured. Once the filter is loose, use your hands to unscrew it from the block. Just as the filter is detached from the block, immediately tilt the open end up to prevent the oil inside the filter from spilling out. **Warning:** *The exhaust system may still be hot, so be careful.*
13   With a clean rag, wipe off the mounting surface on the block. If a residue of old oil is allowed to remain, it will smoke when the block is heated up. Also make sure that none of the old gasket remains stuck to the mount-

9.6 Press in on the tab and push the blade assembly out of the hook at the end to remove it

9.7 Squeeze the blade element tabs, then pull the element out of the metal frame and remove it

9.8 The metal retainers must be inserted into the slots in the rubber before installation

ing surface. It can be removed with a scraper if necessary.

14 Compare the old filter with the new one to make sure they are the same type. Smear some clean engine oil on the rubber gasket of the new filter and screw it into place **(see illustration)**. Because overtightening the filter will damage the gasket, do not use a filter wrench to tighten the filter. Tighten it by hand until the gasket contacts the seating surface. Then seat the filter by giving it an additional 3/4-turn.

15 Remove all tools, rags, etc. from under the vehicle, being careful not to spill the oil in the drain pan, then lower the vehicle.

16 Add new oil to the engine through the oil filler cap in the valve cover. Use a funnel, if necessary, to prevent oil from spilling onto the top of the engine. Pour three quarts of fresh oil into the engine. Wait a few minutes to allow the oil to drain into the pan, then check the level on the oil dipstick (see Section 4 if necessary). If the oil level is at or near the upper hole on the dipstick, install the filler cap hand tight, start the engine and allow the new oil to circulate.

17 Allow the engine to run for about a minute. While the engine is running, look under the vehicle and check for leaks at the oil pan drain plug and around the oil filter. If either is leaking, stop the engine and tighten the plug or filter.

18 Wait a few minutes to allow the oil to trickle down into the pan, then recheck the level on the dipstick and, if necessary, add enough oil to bring the level to the upper hole.

19 During the first few trips after an oil change, make it a point to check frequently for leaks and proper oil level.

20 The old oil drained from the engine cannot be re-used in its present state and should be discarded. Check with your local refuse disposal company or environmental agency to see if they will accept the oil for recycling. Don't pour used oil into drains or onto the ground. After the oil has cooled, it can be drained into a suitable container (capped plastic jugs, topped bottles, milk cartons, etc.) for transport to one of these disposal sites.

9   Windshield wiper blade inspection and replacement (every 7500 miles or 6 months)

Refer to illustrations 9.6, 9.7 and 9.8

1 The windshield wiper and blade assembly should be inspected periodically for damage, loose components and cracked or worn blade elements.

2 Road film can build up on the wiper blades and affect their efficiency, so they should be washed regularly with a mild detergent solution.

3 The action of the wiping mechanism can loosen bolts, nuts and fasteners, so they should be checked and tightened, as necessary, at the same time the wiper blades are checked.

4 If the wiper blade elements are cracked, worn or warped, or no longer clean adequately, they should be replaced with new ones.

5 Lift the arm assembly away from the glass for clearance.

6 Press in on the lock tab and push the blade assembly down the wiper arm, out of the hook at the end **(see illustration)**.

7 Squeeze the blade element tabs tightly and pull the element out of the metal frame **(see illustration)**.

8 Remove the metal retainers from the element and install them in the new element **(see illustration)**.

9 Insert the element into the frame and push it until the element tabs lock.

10 Place the metal arm assembly in the hook on the wiper arm and press it into place until the lock tab snaps into place.

10 Battery check, maintenance and charging (every 7500 miles or 6 months)

Refer to illustrations 10.1, 10.6, 10.7a, 10.7b, 10.8a, 10.8b and 10.13

Warning: *Certain precautions must be followed when checking and servicing the battery. Hydrogen gas, which is highly flammable, is always present in the battery cells, so keep lighted tobacco and all other open*

10.1 Tools and materials required for battery maintenance

1 **Face shield/safety goggles** - *When removing corrosion with a brush, the acidic particles can easily fly up into your eyes*

2 **Baking soda** - *A solution of baking soda and water can be used to neutralize corrosion*

3 **Petroleum jelly** - *A layer of this on the battery posts will help prevent corrosion*

4 **Battery post/cable cleaner** - *This wire brush cleaning tool will remove all traces of corrosion from the battery posts and cable clamps*

5 **Treated felt washers** - *Placing one of these on each post, directly under the cable clamps, will help prevent corrosion*

6 **Puller** - *Sometimes the cable clamps are very difficult to pull off the posts, even after the nut/bolt has been completely loosened. This tool pulls the clamp straight up and off the post without damage*

7 **Battery post/cable cleaner** - *Here is another cleaning tool that is a slightly different version of Number 4 above, but it does the same thing*

8 **Rubber gloves** - *Another safety item to consider when servicing the battery; remember that's acid inside the battery!*

10.6 The indicator "eye" can tell you a lot about your battery condition at a glance

10.7a Battery terminal corrosion usually appears as light, fluffy powder

10.7b Removing the cable from a battery post with a wrench - sometimes special battery pliers are required for this procedure if corrosion has caused deterioration of the nut hex (always remove the ground cable first and hook it up last!)

10.8a When cleaning the cable clamps, all corrosion must be removed (the inside of the clamp is tapered to match the taper on the post, so don't remove too much material)

10.8b Regardless of the type of tool used on the battery posts, a clean, shiny surface should be the result

Maintenance

7   If corrosion, which looks like white, fluffy deposits **(see illustration)** is evident, particularly around the terminals, the battery should be removed for cleaning. Loosen the cable clamp bolts with a wrench, being careful to remove the ground cable first, and slide them off the terminals **(see illustration)**. Then disconnect the hold-down clamp bolt and nut, remove the clamp and lift the battery from the engine compartment.

8   Clean the cable clamps thoroughly with a battery brush or a terminal cleaner and a solution of warm water and baking soda **(see illustration)**. Wash the terminals and the top of the battery case with the same solution but make sure that the solution doesn't get into the battery. When cleaning the cables, terminals and battery top, wear safety goggles and rubber gloves to prevent any solution from coming in contact with your eyes or hands. Wear old clothes too - even diluted, sulfuric acid splashed onto clothes will burn holes in them. If the terminals have been extensively corroded, clean them up with a terminal cleaner **(see illustration)**. Thoroughly wash all cleaned areas with plain water.

9   Whenever the battery is removed for cleaning or charging, inspect the battery carrier before reinstalling the battery in the engine compartment. If the carrier is dirty or covered with corrosion, clean it in the same solution of warm water and baking soda. Inspect the metal brackets that support the carrier to make sure that they are not covered with corrosion. If they are, wash them off. If corrosion is extensive, sand the brackets down to bare metal and spray them with a zinc-based primer (available in spray cans at auto paint and body supply stores).

10   Reinstall the battery back into the engine compartment. Make sure that no parts or wires are laying on the carrier during installation of the battery. Information on

flames and sparks away from the battery. The electrolyte inside the battery is actually dilute sulfuric acid, which will cause injury if splashed on your skin or in your eyes. It will also ruin clothes and painted surfaces. When removing the battery cables, always detach the negative cable first and hook it up last!

Check

1   A routine preventive maintenance program for the battery in your vehicle is the only way to ensure quick and reliable starts. But before performing any battery maintenance, make sure that you have the proper equipment necessary to work safely around the battery **(see illustration)**.

2   There are also several precautions that should be taken whenever battery maintenance is performed. Before servicing the battery, always turn the engine and all accessories off and disconnect the cable from the negative terminal of the battery.

3   The battery produces hydrogen gas, which is both flammable and explosive. Never create a spark, smoke or light a match

around the battery. Always charge the battery in a ventilated area.

4   Electrolyte contains poisonous and corrosive sulfuric acid. Do not allow it to get in your eyes, on your skin on your clothes. Never ingest it. Wear protective safety glasses when working near the battery. Keep children away from the battery.

5   Note the external condition of the battery. If the positive terminal and cable clamp on your vehicle's battery is equipped with a rubber protector, make sure that it's not torn or damaged. It should completely cover the terminal. Look for any corroded or loose connections, cracks in the case or cover or loose hold-down clamps. Also check the entire length of each cable for cracks and frayed conductors.

6   Some models with sealed batteries have a battery condition indicator on top of the battery **(see illustration)**. Compare the color showing in the window to the condition color chart on the battery. You may catch a low-charge battery condition before it strands you on the roadside. If the color indicate a low state of charge, charge the battery and examine the charging system (see Chapter 5 and this Section).

10.13 Make sure the battery hold-down nuts are tight

11.3a Here are some of the more common problems associated with drivebelts (check the belts very carefully to prevent an untimely breakdown)

STREAKED SIDEWALL

FRAYING

CRACKS

SEPARATION

GLAZING

OIL SOAKED

TENSILE BREAK

ACCEPTABLE

Cracks Running Across "V" Portions of Belt

1/2"

Missing Two or More Adjacent Ribs 1/2" or longer

UNACCEPTABLE

Cracks Running Parallel to "V" Portions of Belt

11.3b Small cracks in the underside of a V-ribbed belt are acceptable - lengthwise cracks, or missing pieces that cause the belt to make noise, are cause for replacement

removing and installing the battery can be found in Chapter 5. Information on jump starting can be found at the front of this manual. For more detailed battery checking procedures, refer to the *Haynes Automotive Electrical Manual*.

11   Install a pair of specially-treated felt washers around the terminals (available at auto parts stores), then coat the terminals and the cable clamps with petroleum jelly or grease to prevent further corrosion. Install the cable clamps and tighten the nuts, being careful to install the negative cable last.

12   Install the hold-down clamp and nuts. Tighten the nuts only enough to hold the battery firmly in place. Overtightening these nuts can crack the battery case.

13   Make sure that the battery tray is in good condition and the hold-down clamp bolts are tight **(see illustration)**. If the battery is removed from the tray, make sure no parts remain in the bottom of the tray when the battery is reinstalled. When reinstalling the hold-down clamp bolts, do not overtighten them.

Charging

Warning: *When batteries are being charged, hydrogen gas, which is very explosive and flammable, is produced. Do not smoke or allow open flames near a charging or a recently charged battery. Wear eye protection when near the battery during charging. Also, make sure the charger is unplugged before connecting or disconnecting the battery from the charger.*

14   Slow-rate charging is the best way to restore a battery that's discharged to the point where it will not start the engine. It's also a good way to maintain the battery charge in a vehicle that's only driven a few miles between starts. Maintaining the battery charge is particularly important in the winter when the battery must work harder to start the engine and electrical accessories that drain the battery are in greater use.

15   It's best to use a one or two-amp battery charger (sometimes called a "trickle" charger). They are the safest and put the least strain on the battery. They are also the least expensive. For a faster charge, you can use a higher amperage charger, but don't use

one rated more than 1/10th the amp/hour rating of the battery. Rapid boost charges that claim to restore the power of the battery in one to two hours are hardest on the battery and can damage batteries not in good condition. This type of charging should only be used in emergency situations.

16   The average time necessary to charge a battery should be listed in the instructions that come with the charger. As a general rule, a trickle charger will charge a battery in 12 to 16 hours.

11   Drivebelt check, adjustment and replacement (every 7500 miles or 6 months)

Refer to illustrations 11.3a, 11.3b, 11.4, 11.6a, 11.6b, 11.6c and 11.6d

Check

1   The drivebelts are located at the front of the engine and play an important role in the overall operation of the vehicle and its components. Due to their function and material make-up, the belts are prone to failure after a period of time and should be inspected and adjusted periodically to prevent major engine damage.

2   The number of belts used on a particular vehicle depends on the accessories installed. Drivebelts are used to turn the alternator, power steering pump, water pump and air conditioning compressor. Depending on the pulley arrangement, more than one of these components may be driven by a single belt.

3   With the engine off, open the hood and locate the drivebelts at the front of the engine. Using your fingers (and a flashlight if necessary), move along the belts chuckling for cracks and separation of the belt plies. Also check for fraying and glazing, which

11.4 Measuring drivebelt deflection with a straightedge and ruler

11.6a On Legend models, loosen the lockbolt (A) and pivot bolt (below the alternator, not visible in this photo), then turn the adjusting screw (B) in-or-out to adjust the alternator drivebelt tension

11.6b On Integra models, loosen the pivot bolt (A) and locknut (B), then move the alternator in-or-out to adjust the drivebelt tension

11.6c On Integra models, power steering pump adjustment requires loosening the lower mounting bolt (A), the upper mounting bolt (B), then turning the adjusting bolt (C) to tighten or loosen the belt

11.6d On Legend models, loosen the mounting bolt and nut (A) and turn the adjusting bolt (B) to adjust the drivebelt tension

gives the belt a shiny appearance **(see illustrations)**. Both sides of the belt should be inspected, which means you will have to twist the belt to check the underside.

4   The tension of each belt is checked by pushing the belt at a distance halfway between the pulleys. Push firmly with your thumb and see how much the belt moves (deflects) **(see illustration)**. As a rule of thumb, if the distance from pulley center-to-pulley center is between 7 and 11 inches, the belt should deflect 1/4-inch. If the belt travels between pulleys spaced 12 to 16-inches apart, the belt should deflect 1/2-inch for a V-belt and 1/4-inch for a ribbed belt.

Adjustment

5   If it is necessary to adjust the belt tension, either to make the belt tighter or looser, it is done by moving the belt-driven accessory on the bracket.

6   The alternator drivebelt is adjusted by loosening the pivot and adjusting bolts and moving the alternator to tension the drivebelt. After adjustment, tighten the pivot and adjusting bolts **(see illustrations)**. The air conditioning compressor is rigidly mounted and uses

an adjustable idler pulley that is mounted between the components to tension the belt. On Integra models, the power steering pump is adjusted by loosening the mounting bolts and turning the adjusting bolt to tension the belt **(see illustration)**. On Legend models, the adjustment is made by loosening the mounting bolt and mounting nut, then turning the adjusting bolt **(see illustration)**.

7   After the bolts have been loosened, move the component away from the engine to tighten the belt or toward the engine to loosen the belt. Measure the belt tension in accordance with the above methods. Repeat this step until the drivebelt is adjusted.

Replacement

8   To replace a belt, follow the above procedures for drivebelt adjustment but slip the belt off the pulleys and remove it. Since belts tend to wear out more or less at the same time, it's a good idea to replace them all at the same time. Mark each belt and the corresponding pulley groove so the replacement belts can be installed properly.

9   Take the old belts with you when purchasing new ones in order to make a direct comparison for length, width and design.

10   Adjust the belts as described earlier in this Section.

---

12   Underhood hose check and replacement (every 7500 miles or 6 months)

Caution: *Replacement of air conditioning hoses must be left to a dealer service department or air conditioning shop that has the equipment to depressurize the system safely. Never remove air conditioning components or hoses until the system has been depressurized.*

General

1   High temperatures in the engine compartment can cause the deterioration of the rubber and plastic hoses used for engine, accessory and emission systems operation. Periodic inspection should be made for cracks, loose clamps, material hardening and leaks.

2   Information specific to the cooling system hoses can be found in Section 13.
3   Some, but not all, hoses are secured to the fittings with clamps. Where clamps are used, check to be sure they haven't lost their tension, allowing the hose to leak. If clamps aren't used, make sure the hose has not expanded and/or hardened where it slips over the fitting, allowing it to leak.

Vacuum hoses

4   It's quite common for vacuum hoses, especially those in the emissions system, to be color coded or identified by colored stripes molded into them. Various systems require hoses with different wall thicknesses, collapse resistance and temperature resistance. When replacing hoses, be sure the new ones are made of the same material.
5   Often the only effective way to check a hose is to remove it completely from the vehicle. If more than one hose is removed, be sure to label the hoses and fittings to ensure correct installation.
6   When checking vacuum hoses, be sure to include any plastic T-fittings in the check. Inspect the fittings for cracks and the hose where it fits over the fitting for distortion, which could cause leakage.
7   A small piece of vacuum hose (1/4-inch inside diameter) can be used as a stethoscope to detect vacuum leaks. Hold one end of the hose to your ear and probe around vacuum hoses and fittings, listening for the "hissing" sound characteristic of a vacuum leak. **Warning:** *When probing with the vacuum hose stethoscope, be very careful not to come into contact with moving engine components such as the drivebelts, cooling fan, etc.*

Fuel hose

Warning: *Gasoline is extremely flammable, so take extra precautions when you work on any part of the fuel system. Don't smoke or allow open flames or bare light bulbs near the work area, and don't work in a garage where a natural gas-type appliance (such as a water heater or clothes dryer) with a pilot light is present. Since gasoline is carcinogenic, wear latex gloves when there's a possibility of being exposed to fuel, and, if you spill any fuel on your skin, rinse it off immediately with soap and water. Mop up any spills immediately and do not store fuel-soaked rags where they could ignite. The fuel system is under constant pressure, so, if any fuel lines are to be disconnected, the fuel pressure in the system must be relieved first (see Chapter 4 for more information). When you perform any kind of work on the fuel system, wear safety glasses and have a Class B type fire extinguisher on hand.*
8   Check all rubber fuel lines for deterioration and chafing. Check especially for cracks in areas where the hose bends and just before fittings, such as where a hose attaches to the fuel filter.
9   When replacing hose, use only hose that

is specifically designed for your fuel injection system.

Metal lines

10   Sections of metal line are often used for fuel line between the fuel pump and fuel injection unit. Check carefully to be sure the line has not been bent or crimped and that cracks have not started in the line.
11   If a section of metal fuel line must be replaced, only seamless steel tubing should be used, since copper and aluminum tubing don't have the strength necessary to withstand normal engine vibration.
12   Check the metal brake lines where they enter the master cylinder and brake proportioning unit (if used) for cracks in the lines or loose fittings. Any sign of brake fluid leakage calls for an immediate thorough inspection of the brake system.

13   Cooling system check (every 7500 miles or 6 months)

Refer to illustration 13.4
1   Many major engine failures can be attributed to a faulty cooling system. If the vehicle is equipped with an automatic transaxle, the cooling system also cools the transaxle fluid and thus plays an important role in prolonging transaxle life.
2   The cooling system should be checked with the engine cold. Do this before the vehicle is driven for the day or after the engine has been shut off for at least three hours.
3   Remove the radiator cap by turning it to the left until it reaches a stop. If you hear a hissing sound (indicating there is still pressure in the system), wait until it stops. Now press down on the cap with the palm of your hand and continue turning to the left until the cap can be removed. Thoroughly clean the cap, inside and out, with clean water. Also clean the filler neck on the radiator. All traces of corrosion should be removed. The coolant inside the radiator should be relatively transparent. If it's rust colored, the system should be drained and refilled (see Section 29). If the coolant level isn't up to the top, add additional antifreeze/coolant mixture (see Sec-tion 4).
4   Carefully check the large upper and lower radiator hoses along with the smaller diameter heater hoses that run from the engine to the firewall. Inspect each hose along its entire length, replacing any hose that is cracked, swollen or shows signs of deterioration. Cracks may become more apparent if the hose is squeezed **(see illustration)**. Regardless of condition, it's a good idea to replace hoses with new ones every two years.
5   Make sure that all hose connections are tight. A leak in the cooling system will usually show up as white or rust colored deposits on the areas adjoining the leak. If wire-type clamps are used at the ends of the hoses, it may be a good idea to replace them with more secure screw-type clamps.

Check for a chafed area that could fail prematurely.

Check for a soft area indicating the hose has deteriorated inside.

Overtightening the clamp on a hardened hose will damage the hose and cause a leak.

Check each hose for swelling and oil-soaked ends. Cracks and breaks can be located by squeezing the hose.

13.4 Hoses, like drivebelts, have a habit of failing at the worst possible time - to prevent the inconvenience of a blown radiator hose or heater hose, inspect them carefully as shown here

6   Use compressed air or a soft brush to remove bugs, leaves, etc. from the front of the radiator or air conditioning condenser. Be careful not to damage the delicate cooling fins or cut yourself on them.
7   Every other inspection, or at the first indication of cooling system problems, have the cap and system pressure tested. If you don't have a pressure tester, most gas stations and repair shops will do this for a minimal charge.

14   Tire rotation (every 7500 miles or 6 months)

Refer to illustration 14.2
1   The tires should be rotated at the specified intervals and whenever uneven wear is noticed. Since the vehicle will be raised and

1

the tires removed anyway, check the brakes (see Section 15) at this time.

2   Radial tires must be rotated in a specific pattern **(see illustration)**. Most models are equipped with non-directional tires, but some models have directional tires, which have a different rotation pattern. When choosing replacement tires, examine the sidewalls. Directional tires have arrows on the sidewall that indicate the direction they must turn, and a set of these tires includes two left-side tires and two right-side tires. The left and right side tires must not be rotated to the other side.

3   Refer to the information in *Jacking and towing* at the front of this manual for the proper procedures to follow when raising the vehicle and changing a tire. If the brakes are to be checked, do not apply the parking brake as stated. Make sure the tires are blocked to prevent the vehicle from rolling.

4   Preferably, the entire vehicle should be raised at the same time. This can be done on a hoist or by jacking up each corner and then lowering the vehicle onto jackstands placed under the frame rails. Always use four jackstands and make sure the vehicle is firmly supported.

5   After rotation, check and adjust the tire pressures as necessary and be sure to check the lug nut tightness. Ideally, lug nuts should be torque to Specifications with a torque wrench, and rechecked after 25 miles of driving.

6   For further information on the wheels and tires, refer to Chapter 10.

---

15   Brake check (every 7500 miles or 6 months)

Warning: *The dust created by the brake system may contain asbestos, which is harmful to your health. Never blow it out with compressed air and don't inhale any of it. An approved filtering mask should be worn when working on the brakes. Do not, under any circumstances, use petroleum-based solvents to clean brake parts. Use brake system cleaner only! Try to use non-asbestos*

RADIAL TIRE ROTATION

1-AJ HAYNES

14.2 The recommended tire rotation pattern for these models

---

replacement parts whenever possible.
Note: *For detailed photographs of the brake system, refer to Chapter 9.*

1   In addition to the specified intervals, the brakes should be inspected every time the wheels are removed or whenever a defect is suspected.

2   Any of the following symptoms could indicate a potential brake system defect: The vehicle pulls to one side when the brake pedal is depressed; the brakes make squealing or dragging noises when applied; brake pedal travel is excessive; the pedal pulsates; brake fluid leaks, usually onto the inside of the tire or wheel.

3   Loosen the wheel lug nuts.

4   Raise the vehicle and place it securely on jackstands.

5   Remove the wheels (see *Jacking and towing* at the front of this book, or your owner's manual, if necessary).

Disc brakes

Refer to illustrations 15.6, 15.9 and 15.11

6   There are two pads (an outer and an inner) in each caliper. They can be inspected

15.6 Remove the lower bolt and swing the caliper up for access to the pads

by removing the lower caliper bolt and swinging the caliper up for access **(see illustration)**.

7   Check the pad thickness. If the lining material is less than the thickness listed in this Chapter's Specifications, replace the pads. **Note:** *Keep in mind that the lining material is riveted or bonded to a metal backing plate and the metal portion is not included in this measurement.*

8   If it is difficult to determine the exact thickness of the remaining pad material by the above method, or if you are at all concerned about the condition of the pads, remove the pads from the mounting bracket for further inspection (refer to Chapter 9).

9   Once the pads are removed, clean them with brake cleaner and re-measure them with a ruler or a vernier caliper **(see illustration)**.

10   Measure the disc thickness with a micrometer to make sure that it still has service life remaining. If any disc is thinner than the specified minimum thickness, replace it (refer to Chapter 9). Even if the disc has service life remaining, check its condition. Look for scoring, gouging and burned spots. If these conditions exist, remove the disc and have it resurfaced (see Chapter 9).

11   Check all brake lines and hoses for damage, wear, deformation, cracks, corro-

15.9 If a more precise measurement of pad thickness is necessary, remove the pads and measure the remaining friction material

15.11 Inspect the brake fitting and hose connection for leaks or damage

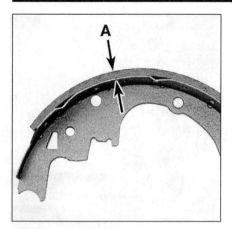

15.15 Measure the lining thickness of the parking brake shoe from the outer surface to the metal shoe, as shown here

15.16 Typical assembled view of a rear drum-type parking brake (left side shown)

Brake booster check

20   Sit in the driver's seat and perform the following sequence of tests.

21   With the brake fully depressed, start the engine - the pedal should move down a little when the engine starts.

22   With the engine running, depress the brake pedal several times - the travel distance should not change.

23   Depress the brake, stop the engine and hold the pedal in for about 30 seconds - the pedal should neither sink nor rise.

24   Restart the engine, run it for about a minute and turn it off. Then firmly depress the brake several times - the pedal travel should decrease with each application.

25   If your brakes do not operate as described, the brake booster has failed. Refer to Chapter 9 for the replacement procedure.

Parking brake

26   Slowly pull up on the parking brake and count the number of clicks you hear until the handle is up as far as it will go. The adjustment is correct if you hear the specified number of clicks (see this Chapter's Specifications). If you hear more or fewer clicks, it's time to adjust the parking brake (see Chapter 9).

27   An alternative method of checking the parking brake is to park the vehicle on a steep hill with the parking brake set and the transmission in Neutral (be sure to stay in the vehicle during this test). If the parking brake cannot prevent the vehicle from rolling, it is in need of adjustment (see Chapter 9).

sion, leakage, bends and twists, particularly in the vicinity of the rubber hoses at the calipers **(see illustration)**. Check the clamps for tightness and the connections for leakage. Make sure that all hoses and lines are clear of sharp edges, moving parts and the exhaust system. If any of the above conditions are noted, repair, reroute or replace the lines and/or fittings as necessary (see Chapter 9). Reinstall the pads and caliper, tightening the caliper mounting bolt to the torque listed in the Chapter 9 Specifications. Install the wheel and lug nuts and lower the vehicle. Tighten the lug nuts to the torque listed in this Chapter's Specifications.

Parking brake shoes (Legend models)

Refer to illustrations 15.15 and 15.16

12   Legend model rear disc brake assemblies incorporate a drum-type parking brake that should be inspected periodically.

13   Make sure the parking brake is off. Remove the rear brake discs.

14   With the discs removed, carefully clean the parking brake assembly with brake system cleaner. **Warning:** *Don't blow the dust out with compressed air and don't inhale any*

of it (it may contain asbestos, which is harmful to your health).

15   Note the thickness of the lining material on both front and rear parking brake shoes. If the material has worn away to within 1/16-inch of the metal backing, the shoes should be replaced **(see illustration)**. The shoes should also be replaced if they're cracked or glazed (shiny areas).

16   Make sure all the brake assembly springs are connected and in good condition **(see illustration)**.

17   Wipe the inside of the drum with a clean rag and denatured alcohol or brake cleaner. Again, be careful not to breathe the dangerous asbestos dust.

18   Check the inside of the drum for cracks, score marks, deep scratches and "hard spots" which will appear as small discolored areas. If imperfections cannot be removed with fine emery cloth, the drum must be taken to an automotive machine shop for resurfacing.

19   Repeat the procedure for the remaining wheel. If the inspection reveals that all parts are in good condition, reinstall the brake discs, install the wheels and lower the vehicle to the ground. Tighten the lug nuts to the torque listed in this Chapter's Specifications.

16 Clutch pedal height and freeplay check (every 15,000 miles or 12 months)

Pedal height

Refer to illustrations 16.1 and 16.2

1   The height of the clutch pedal is the distance the pedal sits off the floor **(see illustration)**. If the pedal height is not at the specified height, it must be adjusted.

2   To adjust the clutch pedal, loosen the

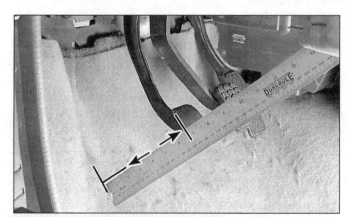

16.1 Pedal height is the distance between the pedal pad and the floor - measure the distance from the top of the pad to the floor with the pedal fully released

16.2 Back-out the stopper bolt or switch (A) for clearance, then loosen the locknut behind the pushrod clevis (B). Turn the pushrod to adjust the pedal height

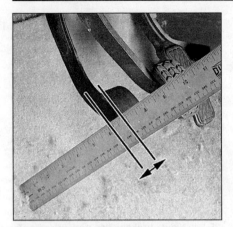

16.5 Pedal freeplay is the distance the pedal travels before resistance is felt

16.8 On Integra models, move the clutch release arm up-and-down and measure the freeplay - turn the knob (arrow) to adjust the freeplay

18.3 Remove the blower housing cover retaining screws (arrows)

18.4 After removing the bracket, slide the filter from the housing

locknut on the clutch switch or adjusting bolt and back the switch out until it no longer touches the pedal, then loosen the locknut on the clutch pushrod **(see illustration)**. Turn the pushrod to adjust the pedal height, then tighten the locknut.

3   Turn the switch or bolt clockwise until it just contacts the pedal arm, then turn it in an additional 1/4 to 1/2 turn. Tighten the locknut.

4   Check the operation of the starter/clutch interlock switch as described in Chapter 8, adjusting it if necessary.

Pedal freeplay

Refer to illustration 9.5

5   The freeplay is the pedal slack, or the distance the pedal can be depressed before it begins to have any effect on the clutch system **(see illustration)**. If the pedal freeplay is not within the specified range, it must be adjusted.

6   To adjust the pedal freeplay, loosen the locknut on the clutch pushrod. Then back off the pushrod to adjust the pedal freeplay to the specified range and retighten the locknut.

7   Check and, if necessary, adjust the starter/clutch interlock switch (see Chapter 8).

Clutch release arm freeplay (Integra models)

Refer to illustration 16.8

8   Move the clutch release arm up-and-down and measure the freeplay movement **(see illustration)**.

9   If the freeplay is not as specified at the beginning of this Chapter, adjust it by turning the knurled knob at the top of the bracket **(see illustration 16.8)**.

17 Seat belt check (every 15,000 miles or 12 months)

1   Check the seat belts, buckles, latch plates and guide loops for obvious damage and signs of wear.

2   See if the seat belt reminder light comes on when the key is turned to the Run or Start position. A chime should also sound. On passive restraint systems, the shoulder belt should move into position in the A-pillar.

3   The seat belts are designed to lock up during a sudden stop or impact, yet allow free movement during normal driving. Make sure the retractors return the belt against your chest while driving and rewind the belt fully when the buckle is unlatched.

4   If any of the above checks reveal problems with the seat belt system, replace parts as necessary.

18 Air conditioning filter replacement (1992 and later Legend models) (every 15,000 miles or 12 months)

Refer to illustrations 18.3 and 18.4

Warning : *The models covered by this manual are equipped with Supplemental Restraint Systems (SRS), more commonly known as airbags. Always disconnect the negative battery cable, then wait three minutes before working in the vicinity of the impact sensors, steering column or instrument panel to avoid the possibility of accidental deployment of the airbag, which could cause personal injury (see Chapter 12). Do not use any electrical test equipment on any of the airbag system wires or tamper with them in any way.*

1   These models are equipped with an air filtering element in the air conditioning system, located in the blower unit housing, under the right side of the instrument panel.

2   Refer to Chapter 11 for removal of the glove compartment assembly.

3   Remove the screws and the blower housing cover **(see illustration)**.

4   Remove the bracket and slide the filter assembly out of the housing **(see illustration)**.

5   Installation is the reverse of the removal procedure.

19 Valve clearance check and adjustment (Integra models) (every 15,000 miles or 12 months)

Check

1   Valve clearances generally do not need adjustment unless valvetrain components have been replaced, or a valve job has been performed.

2   The simplest check for proper valve adjustment is to listen carefully to the engine running with the hood open. If the valvetrain is noisy, adjustment is necessary.

Adjustment

Refer to illustrations 19.6, 19.7 and 19.8

3   The valve clearances must be checked and adjusted with the engine cold.

4   Place the number one piston (closest to the drivebelt end of the engine) at Top Dead Center (TDC) on the compression stroke. This is accomplished by rotating the crankshaft pulley clockwise until the timing pointer on the block lines up with the TDC mark on the front pulley. The distributor rotor should be pointing toward the number one spark plug wire terminal on the distributor cap. If it isn't, rotate the engine one complete turn and

19.6 Valve layout - non-VTEC engine shown, VTEC engine similar

19.7 Insert the feeler gauge between the rocker arm and the camshaft lobe

19.8 Make sure the adjusting screw doesn't move when the locknut is tightened - the locknuts are recessed and a special tool like this one (available at some auto parts stores) makes the job of tightening them securely much easier

20.2 On Integra models, the air cleaner housing cover is secured by four clips (arrows)

20.3 Move the cover out of the way and remove the filter (Legend shown)

realign the marks.

5   Remove the valve cover (see Chapter 2A).

6   With the engine in this position, the number one cylinder valves can be checked and adjusted **(see illustration)**.

7   Start with the exhaust valve clearance. Insert a feeler gauge of the correct thickness (see this Chapter's Specifications) between the camshaft lobe and the rocker arm **(see illustration)**. Withdraw it; you should feel a slight drag. If there's no drag or a heavy drag, loosen the adjuster nut and back off the adjuster screw. Carefully tighten the adjuster screw until you can feel a slight drag on the feeler gauge as you withdraw it.

8   Hold the adjuster screw with a screwdriver (to keep it from turning) and tighten the locknut **(see illustration)**. Recheck the clearance to make sure it hasn't changed. Repeat the procedure in this Step and the previous Step on the other exhaust valve, then on the two intake valves. **Note:** *A special tool is available at many auto parts that makes this step much easier. It is a combination screw-*

driver/nut driver setup which allows you to hold the adjuster screw steady while tightening the locknut.

9   Rotate the crankshaft pulley 180-degrees counterclockwise (the camshaft pulley will turn 90-degrees) until the number three cylinder is at TDC. With the number three cylinder at TDC, the UP mark on the camshaft sprockets should be at the exhaust side (nine o'clock position) and the distributor rotor should point at the number three spark plug wire terminal. Check and adjust the number three cylinder valves.

10   Rotate the crankshaft pulley 180-degrees counterclockwise until the number four cylinder is at TDC. With the number four cylinder at TDC, the UP mark on the camshaft sprockets should be pointed straight down. The distributor rotor should point at the number four spark plug wire terminal. Check and adjust the number four cylinder valves.

11   Rotate the crankshaft pulley 180-degrees counterclockwise to bring the number two cylinder to TDC. The UP mark on the camshaft sprockets should be on the intake side (three o'clock position). The distributor rotor should point at the number two spark

plug wire terminal. Check and adjust the number two cylinder valves.

12   Install the valve cover.

20   Air filter replacement (every 15,000 miles or 12 months)

Refer to illustrations 20.2 and 20.3

1   At the specified intervals, the air filter should be replaced with a new one.

2   On Integra models, detach the four clips at each corner of the housing and lift the cover up for access to the element **(see illustration)**. Later Integra models have a sub-filter mounted on top of the air cleaner housing. On these models first remove the four bolts, lift up the cover and replace the sub-filter. Reinstall the cover and perform the main filter replacement procedure. On Legend models detach the four clips, remove the resonance chamber bolt and lift the cover up.

3   Lift the air filter element out of the housing and wipe out the inside of the air cleaner housing with a clean rag **(see illustration)**.

4   While the air cleaner cover is off, be careful not to drop anything down into the air cleaner assembly.

1

21.6 Inspect the fuel filler hoses for cracks and make sure the clamps (arrows) are tight

21.7a Carefully inspect fuel line couplings (arrows) for damage (Integra models)

21.7b Legend model fuel line couplings (arrows)

5   Place the new filter in the air cleaner housing. Make sure it seats properly in the housing.

6   Install the air cleaner cover and secure the clips. On Legend models, tighten the resonance chamber bolt securely.

21   Fuel system check (every 15,000 miles or 12 months)

Refer to illustration 21.6, 21.7a, 21.7b and 21.9

Warning: *Gasoline is extremely flammable, so take extra precautions when you work on any part of the fuel system. Don't smoke or allow open flames or bare light bulbs near the work area, and don't work in a garage where a natural gas-type appliance (such as a water heater or clothes dryer) with a pilot light is present. Since gasoline is carcinogenic, wear latex gloves when there's a possibility of being exposed to fuel, and, if you spill any fuel on your skin, rinse it off immediately with soap and water. Mop up any spills immediately and do not store fuel-soaked rags where they could ignite. When you perform any kind of work on the fuel system, wear safety glasses and have a Class B type fire extinguisher on hand. The fuel system is under constant pressure, so, before any lines are disconnected, the fuel system pressure must be relieved (see Chapter 4).*

1   If you smell gasoline while driving or after the vehicle has been sitting in the sun, inspect the fuel system immediately.

2   Remove the fuel filler cap and inspect it for damage and corrosion. The gasket should have an unbroken sealing imprint. If the gasket is damaged or corroded, install a new cap.

3   Inspect the fuel feed and return lines for cracks. Make sure that the connections between the fuel lines and the fuel injection system and between the fuel lines and the in-line fuel filter are tight. **Warning:** *Your vehicle is fuel injected, so you must relieve the fuel*

system pressure before servicing fuel system components. The fuel system pressure-relief procedure is outlined in Chapter 4.

4   If the fuel injectors are visible, look for signs of fuel leakage (wet spots) around any of the injectors, they may need new O-rings (see Chapter 4).

5   Since some components of the fuel system - the fuel tank and part of the fuel feed and return lines, for example - are underneath the vehicle, they can be inspected more easily with the vehicle raised on a hoist. If that's not possible, raise the vehicle and support it on jackstands.

6   With the vehicle raised and safely supported, inspect the gas tank and filler neck for punctures, cracks and other damage. The connection between the filler neck and the tank is particularly critical. Sometimes a rubber filler neck will leak because of loose clamps or deteriorated rubber **(see illustration)**. Inspect all fuel tank mounting brackets and straps to be sure that the tank is securely attached to the vehicle. **Warning:** *Do not, under any circumstances, try to repair a fuel tank (except rubber components). A welding torch or any open flame can easily cause fuel vapors inside the tank to explode.*

7   Carefully check all rubber hoses and metal lines leading away from the fuel tank **(see illustrations)**. Check for loose connections, deteriorated hoses, crimped lines and other damage. Repair or replace damaged sections as necessary (see Chapter 4).

8   The evaporative emissions control system can also be a source of fuel odors. The function of the system is to store fuel vapors from the fuel tank in a charcoal canister until they can be routed to the intake manifold where they mix with incoming air before being burned in the combustion chambers.

9   The most common symptom of a faulty evaporative emissions system is a strong odor of fuel in the engine compartment. If a fuel odor has been detected, and you have already checked the areas described above, check the charcoal canister, located in the engine compartment, and the hoses connected to it **(see illustration)**.

21.9 Inspect the charcoal canister and hoses (arrows) for damage and cracks

22   Manual transmission/transaxle and differential lubricant level check (every 15,000 miles or 12 months)

Refer to illustrations 22.1, 22.2a and 22.2b

Transmission/transaxle lubricant level check

1   The manual transmission/transaxle does not have a dipstick. To check the fluid level, raise the vehicle and support it securely on jackstands. On Integra models, the check/fill plug is on the right side of the transaxle housing **(see illustration)**. On Legend models the check/fill plug is located on the right (passenger) side of the transmission rear housing, near the upper edge. Remove the plug. If the lubricant level is correct, it should be up to the lower edge of the hole.

2   If the transmission/transaxle needs more lubricant (if the level is not up to the hole), use a pump or a funnel to add more **(see illustrations)**. Stop filling the transmission/transaxle when the lubricant begins to run out the hole.

3   Install the plug and tighten it to the torque listed in this Chapter's Specifications. Drive the vehicle a short distance, then check for leaks.

22.1 The manual transaxle check/filler plug and drain plug (arrows) are located on the passenger side of the transaxle - use a box end wrench to remove the check/fill plug

22.2a Use two different size pieces of hose to make an adapter on the funnel . . .

Differential lubricant level check (Legend models only)

4   Raise the vehicle and support it securely on jackstands.
5   Locate the differential lubricant check/fill plug on the side of the differential (see the Legend undervehicle photo at the beginning of this Chapter). Remove the plug. If the lubricant level is correct, it should be up to the lower edge of the hole.
6   If the differential needs more lubricant (if the level is not up to the hole), use a pump or squeeze bottle to add more. Stop filling the differential when the lubricant begins to run out the hole.
7   Install the plug and tighten it to the torque listed in this Chapter's Specifications. Drive the vehicle a short distance, then check for leaks.

---

23 **Suspension, steering and driveaxle boot check (every 15,000 miles or 12 months)**

Note: *The steering linkage and suspension components should be checked periodically. Worn or damaged suspension and steering linkage components can result in excessive and abnormal tire wear, poor ride quality and vehicle handling and reduced fuel economy. For detailed illustrations of the steering and suspension components, refer to Chapter 10.*

Shock absorber check

Refer to illustration 23.6

1   Park the vehicle on level ground, turn the engine off and set the parking brake. Check the tire pressures (see Section 5).
2   Push down at one corner of the vehicle, then release it while noting the movement of the body. It should stop moving and come to rest in a level position within one or two bounces.
3   If the vehicle continues to move up-and-down or if it fails to return to its original position, a worn or weak shock absorber is probably the reason.

22.2b . . . so you can easily add lubricant to the transmission/transaxle from above

4   Repeat the above check at each of the three remaining corners of the vehicle.
5   Raise the vehicle and support it securely on jackstands.
6   Check the shock absorbers for evidence of fluid leakage **(see illustration)**. A light film of fluid is no cause for concern. Make sure that any fluid noted is from the shocks and not from some other source. If leakage is noted, replace the shocks as a set.
7   Check the shocks to be sure that they are securely mounted and undamaged. Check the upper mounts for damage and

23.6 Check the shock absorbers for leakage where the damper rod enters the shock body

wear. If damage or wear is noted, replace the shocks as a set (front or rear).
8   If the shocks must be replaced, refer to Chapter 10 for the procedure.

Steering and suspension check

Refer to illustrations 23.9a, 23.9b, 23.9c and 23.9d

9   Raise the vehicle and support it securely on jackstands. Visually inspect the steering and suspension components for damage and

23.9a Inspect the lower control arm for deteriorated bushings (A), the lower balljoints (B) and the tie-rod ends (C) for torn grease seals

23.9b Check the front lower control arm bushings (arrow)

23.9c Check the steering gear boots for cracks and leaking steering fluid

23.9d Check the stabilizer bar bushings for deterioration (arrow)

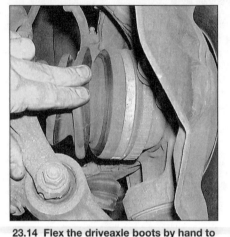

23.14 Flex the driveaxle boots by hand to check for tears, cracks and leaking grease

24.2a Check the exhaust pipe flange (arrow) connections

distortion. Look for damaged seals, boots and bushings and leaks of any kind **(see illustrations)**.

10   Clean the lower end of the steering knuckle. Have an assistant grasp the lower edge of the tire and move the wheel in-and-out while you look for movement at the steering knuckle-to-control arm balljoint. If there is any movement the suspension balljoint(s) must be replaced (be sure to check the upper balljoint as well).

11   Grasp each front tire at the front and rear edges, push in at the front, pull out at the rear and feel for play in the steering system components. If any freeplay is noted, check the tie-rod ends for looseness.

12   Similar checks can be performed on the rear suspension. Additional steering and suspension system information and illustrations can be found in Chapter 10.

Driveaxle boot check

Refer to illustration 23.14

13   The driveaxle boots are very important because they prevent dirt, water and foreign material from entering and damaging the constant velocity (CV) joints. Oil and grease can cause the boot material to deteriorate prematurely, so it's a good idea to wash the

boots with soap and water. Because it constantly pivots back and forth following the steering action of the front hub, the outer CV boot wears out sooner and should be inspected regularly.

14   Inspect the boots for tears and cracks as well as loose clamps **(see illustration)**. If there is any evidence of cracks or leaking lubricant, they must be replaced as described in Chapter 8.

24 Exhaust system check (every 6000 miles or 6 months)

Refer to illustrations 24.2a, 24.2b and 24.2c

1   With the engine cold (at least three hours after the vehicle has been driven), check the complete exhaust system from the engine to the end of the tailpipe. Ideally, the inspection should be done with the vehicle on a hoist to permit unrestricted access. If a hoist isn't available, raise the vehicle and support it securely on jackstands.

2   Check the exhaust pipes and connections for evidence of leaks, severe corrosion and damage. Make sure that all brackets and

hangers are in good condition and tight **(see illustrations)**.

3   At the same time, inspect the underside of the body for holes, corrosion, open seams, etc. which may allow exhaust gases to enter the passenger compartment. Seal all body

24.2b Inspect the exhaust pipe connections (arrow) for exhaust leaks - also check that the retaining nuts and bolts are securely tightened

24.2c Check the exhaust system hangers (arrows)

openings with silicone or body putty.
4   Rattles and other noises can often be traced to the exhaust system, especially the mounts and hangers. Try to move the pipes, muffler and catalytic converter. If the components can come in contact with the body or suspension parts, secure the exhaust system with new mounts.
5   Check the running condition of the engine by inspecting inside the end of the tailpipe. The exhaust deposits here are an indication of engine state-of-tune. If the pipe is black and sooty or coated with white deposits, the engine may need a tune-up, including a thorough fuel system inspection and adjustment.

25   Spark plug check and replacement (see the maintenance schedule for service interval)

Refer to illustrations 25.2, 25.5a, 25.5b, 25.6a, 25.6b, 25.9 and 25.10
Note: *Some engines are equipped with two different types of platinum spark plugs. If the original spark plugs are to be removed and reinstalled in the engine, the spark plugs must be marked and reinstalled in the original cylinder from which they were removed.*
1   The spark plugs are located on both sides of the engine on V6 models on top of the engine on four-cylinder models. Label each spark plug wire before proceeding any further.
2   In most cases, the tools necessary for spark plug replacement include a spark plug socket which fits onto a ratchet (spark plug sockets are padded inside to prevent damage to the porcelain insulators on the new plugs), various extensions and a gap gauge to check and adjust the gaps on the new plugs **(see illustration)**. A special plug wire removal tool is available for separating the wire boots from the spark plugs, but it isn't absolutely necessary. A torque wrench should be used to tighten the new plugs.

25.2 Tools required for changing spark plugs

1   *Spark plug socket - This will have special padding inside to protect the spark plug's porcelain insulator*
2   *Torque wrench - Although not mandatory, using this tool is the best way to ensure the plugs are tightened properly*
3   *Ratchet - Standard hand tool to fit the spark plug socket*
4   *Extension - Depending on model and accessories, you may need special extensions and universal joints to reach one or more of the plugs*
5   *Spark plug gap gauge - This gauge for checking the gap comes in a variety of styles. Make sure the gap for your engine is included*

3   The best approach when replacing the spark plugs is to purchase the new ones in advance, adjust them to the proper gap and replace the plugs one at a time. When buying the new spark plugs, be sure to obtain the correct plug type for your particular engine. This information can be found in the Specifications at the front of this Chapter and on the Emission Control Information label located under the hood. If these two sources list different plug types, assume that the emission control label is correct.
4   Allow the engine to cool completely before attempting to remove any of the plugs. While you are waiting for the engine to cool, check the new plugs for defects and adjust the gaps.
5   Check the gap by inserting the proper thickness gauge between the electrodes at the tip of the plug **(see illustration)**. The gap between the electrodes should be the same as the one specified on the *Emissions Control Information label* or in this Chapter's Specifications. The wire should slide between the electrodes with a slight amount of drag. If the gap is incorrect, use the adjuster on the gauge body to bend the curved side electrode slightly until the proper gap is obtained **(see illustration)**. If the side electrode is not exactly over the center electrode, bend it with the adjuster until it is. Check for cracks in the porcelain insulator (if any are found, the plug should not be used).
6   With the engine cool, remove the wire from one spark plug (Integra models). Pull

25.5a Spark plug manufacturers recommend using a wire-type gauge when checking the gap - if the wire does not slide between the electrodes with a slight drag, adjustment is required

25.5b To change the gap, bend the side electrode only, as indicated by the arrows, and be very careful not to crack or chip the porcelain insulator surrounding the center electrode

only on the boot at the end of the wire - do not pull on the wire. A plug wire removal tool should be used if available. Legend models are equipped with individual coil packs that must be removed first to access the spark plugs **(see illustrations)**.

25.6a On Legend models, remove the coil bolts (arrows) . . .

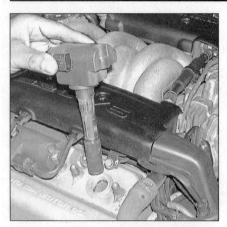

25.6b . . . and lift out the coils for access to the spark plugs

25.9 A light coat of anti-seize compound applied to the threads of the spark plugs will keep the threads in the cylinder head from being damaged the next time the plugs are removed

7   If compressed air is available, use it to blow any dirt or foreign material away from the spark plug hole. The idea here is to eliminate the possibility of debris falling into the cylinder as the spark plug is removed. **Warning:** *Wear eye protection when using compressed air.*

8   The spark plugs on these models are recessed so a spark plug socket incorporating a long extension will be necessary. Place the spark plug socket over the plug and remove it from the engine by turning it in a counterclockwise direction.

9   Compare the spark plug with the chart on the inside back cover of this manual to get an indication of the general running condition of the engine. Before installing the new plugs, it is a good idea to apply a thin coat of anti-seize compound to the threads **(see illustration)**.

10   Thread one of the new plugs into the hole until you can no longer turn it with your fingers, then tighten it with a torque wrench (if available) or the ratchet. It's a good idea to slip a length of rubber hose over the end of the plug to use as a tool to thread it into place **(see illustration)**. The hose will grip the plug well enough to turn it, but will start to slip if the plug begins to cross-thread in the hole - this will prevent damaged threads and the accompanying repair costs.

11   Before pushing the spark plug wire (or coil) onto the end of the plug, inspect it fol-

lowing the procedures outlined in the next Section.

12   Attach the plug wire or coil to the new spark plug, again using a twisting motion on the boot until it's seated on the spark plug. On Legend models install the coil bolts, tightening them securely.

13   Repeat the procedure for the remaining spark plugs, replacing them one at a time to prevent mixing up the spark plug wires.

---

26   Spark plug wire, distributor cap and rotor check and replacement (Integra models) (every 30,000 miles or 24 months)

Refer to illustrations 26.11a, 26.11b, 26.11c, 26.12a and 26.12b

1   The spark plug wires should be checked whenever new spark plugs are installed (see Section 25).

2   Begin this procedure by making a visual check of the spark plug wires while the engine is running. In a darkened garage (make sure there is ventilation) start the engine and observe each plug wire. Be careful not to come into contact with any moving engine parts. If there is a break in the wire,

you will see arcing or a small spark at the damaged area. If arcing is noticed, make a note to obtain new wires, then allow the engine to cool and check the distributor cap and rotor.

3   The spark plug wires should be inspected one at a time to prevent mixing up the order, which is essential for proper engine operation. Each original plug wire should be numbered to help identify its location. If the number is illegible, a piece of tape can be marked with the correct number and wrapped around the plug wire.

4   Disconnect the plug wire from the spark plug. A removal tool can be used for this purpose or you can grasp the rubber boot, twist the boot half a turn and pull the boot free. Do not pull on the wire itself.

5   Check inside the boot for corrosion, which will look like a white crusty powder.

6   Push the wire and boot back onto the end of the spark plug. It should fit tightly onto the end of the plug. If it doesn't, remove the wire and use pliers to carefully crimp the metal connector inside the wire boot until the fit is snug.

7   Using a clean rag, wipe the entire length of the wire to remove built-up dirt and grease. Once the wire is clean, check for burns, cracks and other damage. Do not bend the wire sharply, because the conductor inside might break.

8   Disconnect the wire from the distributor. Again, pull only on the rubber boot. Check for corrosion and a tight fit. Replace the wire in the distributor.

9   Inspect the remaining spark plug wires, making sure that each one is securely fastened at the distributor and spark plug when the check is complete.

10   If new spark plug wires are required, purchase a set for your specific engine model. Pre-cut wire sets with the boots already installed are available. Remove and replace the wires one at a time to avoid mix-ups in the firing order.

11   Detach the distributor cap by removing the cap retaining screws **(see illustration)**. Check the outside for cracks and damage, then look inside it for cracks, carbon tracks and worn, burned or loose contacts **(see illustrations)**.

12   Loosen the retaining screw and pull the

25.10 A length of rubber hose will save time and prevent damaged threads when installing the spark plugs

26.11a Use a screwdriver or nut driver to remove the distributor cap screws

26.11b Inspect the outside of the distributor cap for carbon tracks, broken or cracked towers and damage (if in doubt about its condition, install a new one)

26.11c Check the inside of the distributor cap for carbon tracks, charred or eroded terminals and a worn or eroded button (if in doubt about its condition, install a new one)

26.12a Loosen the retaining screw and remove the distributor rotor

26.12b The ignition rotor should be checked for wear and corrosion as indicated here (if in doubt about its condition, buy a new one)

27.2a On Integra models the PCV valve (arrow) is located in the intake manifold near the fuel rail

27.2b On Legend models, the PCV valve (arrow) is located in the left valve cover

wires from the old cap one at a time and attach them to the new cap in the exact same location. **Note:** *If an accidental mix-up occurs, refer to the firing order at the beginning of this Chapter. On most models, the location of the number one plug wire tower is marked on the distributor cap.*

---

27 Positive Crankcase Ventilation (PCV) valve and hose check and replacement (every 30,000 miles or 24 months)

Refer to illustrations 27.2a, 27.2b and 27.4

1   The Positive Crankcase Ventilation (PCV) system directs blow-by gases from the crankcase through the PCV valve and hose back into the intake manifold so they can be burned in the engine. The system consists of a hose leading from the valve cover to the intake manifold and a fresh air hose between the air cleaner assembly and the valve cover.

2   The PCV valve and hose is located in the intake manifold near the fuel rail on Integra models, and in the left (driver side) valve cover on Legend models **(see illustrations)**.

rotor off the distributor shaft **(see illustration)**. It may be necessary to use a small screwdriver to gently pry off the rotor and examine it for cracks and carbon tracks **(see illustration)**. Replace the cap and rotor if any damage or defects are noted.

13   It is common practice to install a new

cap and rotor whenever new spark plug wires are installed, but if you wish to continue using the old cap, check the resistance between the spark plug wires and the cap first. If the indicated resistance is more than the specified maximum value (see this Chapter's Specifications), replace the cap and/or wires.

14   When installing a new cap, remove the

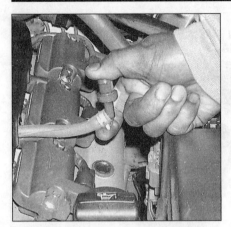

27.4 Pull the PCV valve out of the rubber grommet and put your finger over the opening

28.4a Integra fuel filter location and fuel line connection details (arrows)

28.4b Use a flare-nut wrench like the one shown here, if available, to disconnect the fuel line (Legend model shown) . . .

3   With the engine idling at normal operating temperature, pull the PCV valve (with hose attached) from the manifold or valve cover.
4   Place your finger over the valve opening **(see illustration)**. If there is no vacuum, check for a plugged hose, manifold port, or the valve itself. Replace any plugged or deteriorated hoses.
5   Turn off the engine and shake the PCV valve, listening for a rattle. If the valve doesn't rattle, replace it with a new one.
6   To replace the valve, pull it out of the end of the hose, noting its installed position and direction.
7   When purchasing a replacement PCV valve, make sure it's for your particular vehicle, model vehicle and engine size. Compare the old valve with the new one to make sure they are the same.
8   Push the valve into the end of the hose until it's seated.
9   Inspect all the rubber hoses grommets for damage and hardening. Replace them, if necessary.
10   Press the PCV valve and hose securely into position. For further information on the PCV system refer to Chapter 6.

28 Fuel filter replacement (every 30,000 miles or 24 months)

Refer to illustrations 28.4a, 28.4b, 28.4c and 28.4d
Warning: *Gasoline is extremely flammable, so take extra precautions when you work on any part of the fuel system. Don't smoke or allow open flames or bare light bulbs near the work area, and don't work in a garage where a natural gas-type appliance (such as a water heater or clothes dryer) with a pilot light is present. Since gasoline is carcinogenic, wear latex gloves when there's a possibility of being exposed to fuel, and, if you spill any fuel on your skin, rinse it off immediately with soap and water. Mop up any spills immediately and do not store fuel-soaked rags where*

28.4c . . . unscrew the banjo bolt (it isn't necessary to remove the small service port bolt in the center of the banjo bolt) . . .

they could ignite. The fuel system is under constant pressure, so, if any fuel lines are to be disconnected, the fuel pressure in the system must be relieved first (see Chapter 4 for more information). When you perform any kind of work on the fuel system, wear safety glasses and have a Class B type fire extinguisher on hand.
1   This job should be done with the engine cold (after sitting at least three hours).
2   The fuel filter is located on the firewall in the engine compartment.
3   Relieve the fuel system pressure as described in Chapter 4.
4   Place shop towels around and under the filter. Remove the banjo bolt(s), unscrew the threaded fitting (Legend models), remove the clamp bolt and lift the filter from the engine compartment **(see illustrations)**. **Note:** *If available, use a flare-nut wrench when disconnecting the fuel line fitting at the filter (Legend models).*
5   Installation is the reverse of removal. Use new sealing washers on either side of the banjo fitting and tighten the banjo bolt to the torque listed in this Chapter's Specifications. Tighten the threaded line fitting securely. Start the engine and check for leaks.

28.4d . . . then use a socket and extension to remove the filter clamp bolt

29 Cooling system servicing (draining, flushing and refilling) (every 30,000 miles or 24 months)

Refer to illustrations 29.5 and 29.6
Warning 1: *Wait until the engine is completely cool before beginning this procedure.*
Warning 2: *Do not allow antifreeze to come in contact with your skin or painted surfaces of the vehicle. Rinse off spills immediately with plenty of water. Antifreeze is highly toxic if ingested. Never leave antifreeze lying around in an open container or in puddles on the floor; children and pets are attracted by its sweet smell and may drink it. Check with local authorities about disposing of used antifreeze. Many communities have collection centers that will see that antifreeze is disposed of safely.*
Note: *Non-toxic antifreeze solutions are now widely available, but even these should be disposed of properly.*
1   Periodically, the cooling system should be drained, flushed and refilled to replenish the antifreeze mixture and prevent formation of rust and corrosion, which can impair the performance of the cooling system and

29.5 Remove the radiator cap with the engine cool to the touch

29.6 On most models you will have to remove a cover for access to the radiator drain fitting located at the bottom of the radiator (arrow)

29.13 With the thermostat removed, disconnect the upper radiator hose and flush the radiator and engine block with a garden hose

cause engine damage.

2   At the same time the cooling system is serviced, all hoses and the radiator cap should be inspected and replaced if defective (see Section 13).

3   Since antifreeze is a corrosive and poisonous solution, be careful not to spill any of the coolant mixture on the vehicle's paint or your skin. If this happens, rinse it off immediately with plenty of clean water. Consult local authorities about where to recycle or dispose of antifreeze before draining the cooling system. In many areas, reclamation centers have been set up to collect automobile oil and drained antifreeze/water mixtures, rather than allowing them to be added to the sewage system.

Draining

4   Apply the parking brake and block the wheels. If the vehicle has just been driven, wait several hours to allow the engine to cool down before beginning this procedure.

5   Once the engine is completely cool, remove the radiator cap and the coolant reservoir cap (see illustration).

6   Place a drain pan under the radiator. Drain the radiator by opening the drain plug at the bottom of the radiator (see illustra-

tion). If the drain plug is corroded and can't be turned easily, or if the radiator isn't equipped with a plug, disconnect the lower radiator hose to allow the coolant to drain. Be careful not to get antifreeze on your skin or in your eyes.

7   After the coolant stops flowing out of the radiator, remove the lower radiator hose and allow the remaining fluid in the upper half of the engine block to drain.

8   While the coolant is draining from the engine block, disconnect the hose from the coolant reservoir and remove the reservoir (see Chapter 3 if necessary). Flush the reservoir out with water until it's clean, and if necessary, wash the inside with soapy water and a brush to make reading the fluid level easier.

9   While the coolant is draining, check the condition of the radiator hoses, heater hoses and clamps (refer to Section 13 if necessary).

10   Replace any damaged clamps or hoses (refer to Chapter 3 for detailed replacement procedures).

Flushing

Refer to illustration 29.13

11   Once the system is been completely drained, remove the thermostat from the engine (see Chapter 3). Then reinstall the thermostat housing without the thermostat. This will allow the system to be flushed.

12   Reinstall the lower radiator hose and tighten the radiator drain plug. Turn your heating system controls to Hot, so that the heater core will be flushed at the same time as the rest of the cooling system.

13   Disconnect the upper radiator hose, then place a garden hose in the upper radiator inlet and flush the system until the water runs clear at the upper radiator hose (see illustration).

14   In severe cases of contamination or clogging of the radiator, remove the radiator (see Chapter 3) and have a radiator repair facility clean and repair it if necessary.

15   Many deposits can be removed by the chemical action of a cleaner available at auto parts stores. Follow the procedure outlined in the manufacturer's instructions. **Note:** *When the coolant is regularly drained and the system refilled with the correct antifreeze/water mixture, there should be no need to use chemical cleaners or descalers.*

Refilling

Refer to illustration 29.18

16   To refill the system, install the thermostat, reconnect any radiator hoses and install the reservoir and the overflow hose.

17   Place the heater temperature control in the maximum heat position.

18   Be sure to use the proper coolant mixture listed in this Chapter's Specifications. Loosen the air bleed bolt, located on the water outlet (where the upper radiator hose connects to the engine). Slowly fill the radiator with the recommended mixture of antifreeze and water to the base of the filler

29.18 The air bleed bolt (arrow) is located on the water outlet - use a wrench to open it during the filling process to bleed air from the system (Integra shown)

neck, make sure a steady, bubble-free stream flows out from the bleed bolt, then tighten the bleed bolt securely **(see illustration)**. Add coolant to the reservoir until it reaches the FULL COLD mark. Wait five minutes and recheck the coolant level in the radiator, adding if necessary.

19   Leave the radiator cap off and run the engine in a well-ventilated area until the thermostat opens (coolant will begin flowing through the radiator and the upper radiator hose will become hot).

20   Turn the engine off and let it cool. Add more coolant mixture to bring the level back up to the base of the filler neck.

21   Squeeze the upper radiator hose to expel air, then add more coolant mixture if necessary. Reinstall the radiator cap.

22   Start the engine, allow it to reach normal operating temperature and check for leaks.

30   Brake fluid change (every 30,000 miles or 24 months)

Warning: *Brake fluid can harm your eyes and damage painted surfaces, so use extreme caution when handling or pouring it. Do not use brake fluid that has been standing open or is more than one year old. Brake fluid absorbs moisture from the air. Excess moisture can cause a dangerous loss of braking effectiveness.*

1   At the specified intervals, the brake fluid should be drained and replaced. Since the brake fluid may drip or splash when pouring it, place plenty of rags around the master cylinder to protect any surrounding painted surfaces.

2   Before beginning work, purchase the specified brake fluid (see *Recommended lubricants and fluids* at the beginning of this Chapter).

3   Remove the cap from the master cylinder reservoir.

4   Using a hand suction pump or similar device, withdraw the fluid from the master cylinder reservoir.

31.7 Use a 3/8-inch ratchet to remove the automatic transmission/transaxle drain plug (Legend shown)

5   Add new fluid to the master cylinder until it rises to the base of the filler neck.

6   Bleed the brake system as described in Chapter 9 at all four brakes until new and uncontaminated fluid is expelled from the bleeder screw. Be sure to maintain the fluid level in the master cylinder as you perform the bleeding process. If you allow the master cylinder to run dry, air will enter the system.

7   Refill the master cylinder with fluid and check the operation of the brakes. The pedal should feel solid when depressed, with no sponginess. **Warning:** *Do not operate the vehicle if you are in doubt about the effectiveness of the brake system.*

31   Automatic transmission/transaxle fluid change (every 30,000 miles or 24 months)

Refer to illustration 31.7

Note: *Refer to Section 32 for the differential lubricant changing procedure (Legend models only).*

1   At the specified intervals, the automatic transmission/transaxle fluid should be drained and replaced.

2   Before beginning work, purchase the specified transmission fluid (see *Recommended lubricants and fluids* at the beginning of this Chapter).

3   Other tools necessary for this job include jackstands to support the vehicle in a raised position, a 3/8-inch drive ratchet and extension, a drain pan capable of holding at least eight pints, newspapers and clean rags.

4   The fluid should be drained immediately after the vehicle has been driven. Hot fluid is more effective than cold fluid at removing built-up sediment. **Warning:** *Fluid temperature can exceed 350-degrees F in a hot transmission/transaxle. Wear protective gloves.*

5   After the vehicle has been driven to warm up the fluid, raise it and place it on jackstands for access to the transmission/transaxle and differential drain plugs.

6   Move the necessary equipment under the vehicle, being careful not to touch any of the hot exhaust components.

7   Place the drain pan under the drain plug in the transmission/transaxle and remove the drain plug with the ratchet - it's located on the right (passenger's) side of the transaxle, near the bottom on Integra models and at the bottom edge of the transmission on Legend models **(see illustration)** . Be sure the drain pan is in position, as fluid will come out with some force. Once the fluid is drained, clean the drain plug, reinstall it and tighten it to the torque listed in this Chapter's Specifications.

8   Lower the vehicle.

9   With the engine off pull out the dipstick, then add new fluid to the transaxle through the dipstick hole (see *Recommended fluids and lubricants* for the recommended fluid type and capacity). Use a funnel to prevent spills. It is best to add a little fluid at a time, continually checking the level with the dip-

stick (see Section 7). Allow the fluid time to drain into the pan.

10   Start the engine and shift the selector into all positions from P through 2, then shift into P and apply the parking brake.

11   Turn off the engine and check the fluid level. Add fluid to bring the level into the cross-hatched area on the dipstick.

32   Manual transmission/transaxle and differential lubricant change (every 30,000 miles or 24 months)

Refer to illustration 32.4

1   At the specified time intervals, the manual transmission/transaxle lubricant (and, on Legend models, the differential lubricant) should be drained and replaced.

2   Before beginning work, purchase the specified lubricant (see *Recommended lubricants and fluids* and *Capacities* at the beginning of this Chapter). Other tools necessary for this job include jackstands to support the vehicle in a raised position, 3/8-inch drive ratchet, a drain pan capable of holding at least four quarts, newspapers and clean rags.

3   Drive the vehicle to warm up the transmission/transaxle (and on Legend models the differential) lubricant, then park the vehicle on a level surface. Raise the front of the vehicle and support it securely on jackstands.

Transmission/transaxle lubricant change

4   Remove the drain and check/filler plugs and allow the old lubricant to drain into a drain pan **(see illustration)**.

5   Reinstall the drain plug and tighten it to the torque listed in this Chapter's Specifications.

6   Add new lubricant until it begins to run out of the filler hole (see Section 22). Install the check/filler plug and tighten it to the torque listed in this Chapter's Specifications.

32.4 Remove the manual transmission/transaxle drain plug (right arrow) with a 3/8-inch ratchet; the left arrow points to the check/filler plug (Integra)

33.1 The EGR valve (arrow) is located on the intake manifold (Legend shown)

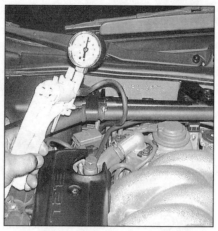

33.2 Apply vacuum directly to the EGR valve and observe that the valve holds vacuum and the engine stumbles or stalls

34.8 On Integra models, use a screwdriver to turn the adjusting screw (arrow) until the idle speed is correct with the EACV or IAC valve connector disconnected

Differential lubricant change (Legend models only)

7   Locate the differential lubricant check/fill plug and the drain plug on the side of the differential (see the Legend undervehicle photo at the beginning of this Chapter). Remove the plugs. Allow the old lubricant to drain into a drain pan.

8   Reinstall the drain plug and tighten it to the torque listed in this Chapter's Specifications.

9   Add new lubricant until it begins to run out of the filler hole (see Section 22).

10   Install the check/filler plug and tighten it to the torque listed in this Chapter's Specifications. Drive the vehicle a short distance, then check for leaks.

33   Exhaust Gas Recirculation (EGR) system check (every 60,000 miles or 48 months)

Refer to illustrations 33.1 and 33.2

1   On models so equipped, the EGR valve is located on the intake manifold **(see illustration)**. Most of the time when a problem develops in this emissions system, it's due to a stuck or defective EGR valve or a clogged EGR passage.

2   With the engine at normal operating temperature, disconnect the vacuum hose from the EGR valve and connect a hand-held vacuum pump to the valve. Start the engine and run it at idle, then apply vacuum to the EGR valve. **(see illustration)**. The idle speed should drop considerably or even stall as vacuum is applied. This indicates that the EGR system is operating properly.

3   If the engine speed does not change, this indicates a faulty EGR valve (if vacuum hoses are not damaged and EGR passages are not blocked). If in doubt about the condition of the EGR valve, replace it with a new one.

4   Refer to Chapter 6 for more information on the EGR system.

34   Idle speed check and adjustment (every 60,000 miles or 48 months)

1   Engine idle speed is the speed at which the engine operates when no accelerator pedal pressure is applied, as when stopped at a traffic light. This speed is critical to the performance of the engine itself, as well as many subsystems.

Check

2   Start the engine and allow it to warm up to normal operating temperature (the cooling fan should come on at least twice).

3   Stop the engine. Hook up a hand-held tachometer in accordance with the tool manufacturer's instructions.

4   Set the parking brake firmly and block the wheels to prevent the vehicle from rolling. On Canadian models it is imperative that the parking brake is applied so the headlights are off during the procedure. Place the transmission/transaxle in Neutral (manual transmission/transaxle) or Park (automatic transmission/transaxle).

5   Start the engine. Make sure all accessories are turned off.

6   Note the idle speed rpm on the tachometer and compare it to that listed on the VECI label or in this Chapter's Specifications. **Note:** *If the idle speed listed on the VECI label is different than that listed in this Chapter's Specifications, use the specification shown on the VECI label.*

Adjustment

Integra models

Refer to illustration 34.8

7   If the idle speed is too low or too high, disconnect the electrical connector from the Electronic Air Control Valve (EACV) or Idle Air Control (IAC) valve (see Chapter 4).

8   Turn the screw to obtain the specified idle speed **(see illustration)**.

34.13 With the carpet pulled back, the ECM's yellow LED light (arrow) is visible

9   Plug in the electrical connector to the IAC valve and remove the 7.5 amp HAZARD (1990 models), BACKUP (1991 and later U.S. models) or HAZARD/BACKUP (1991 and later Canadian models) fuse from the underhood fuse block for ten seconds. This will clear any trouble codes from the ECM's memory.

10   Turn on the engine and let it idle for one minute, then recheck the idle speed.

11   Turn off the engine and disconnect the tachometer.

Legend models

Refer to illustrations 34.13 and 34.14

12   If the idle speed is too low or too high, connect a jumper wire to the two terminals of the service check connector under the right side of the instrument panel **(see illustration 35.5b)**.

13   Peel back the carpeting on the right side floorboard for access to the ECM's yellow LED light **(see illustration)**.

14   If the light is off, the idle doesn't require adjustment. If the light is blinking, the engine

34.14 Location of the idle speed adjusting screw (Legend models)

idle speed adjusting screw should be turned clockwise 1/4-turn **(see illustration)**. If the light is on, but not blinking, the idle screw should be turned 1/4-turn counterclockwise.
15   After adjustment, the LED should go out within 30 seconds. If it doesn't, turn the screw an additional 1/4-turn in the same direction, repeating until the LED goes out.
16   Turn off the engine, remove the jumper wire from the service check connector and disconnect the tachometer.

35   Ignition timing check and adjustment (every 60,000 miles or 48 months)

Refer to illustrations 35.2, 35.4, 35.5a, 35.5b, 35.10 and 35.11
Note: *It is imperative that the procedures included on the tune-up or Vehicle Emissions Control Information (VECI) label be followed when adjusting the ignition timing. The label will include all information concerning preliminary steps to be performed before adjusting the timing, as well as the timing specifications. If now VECI label is found, refer to the Specifications chart at the beginning of this Chapter.*

Check

1   Start the engine and allow it to warm up to normal operating temperature (the cooling fan should come on at least twice).
2   With the ignition off, locate the VECI label under the hood and read through and perform all preliminary instructions concerning ignition timing. Several special tools will be needed for this procedure **(see illustration)**.
3   Stop the engine. Hook up a hand-held tachometer in accordance with the tool manufacturer's instructions.
4   Locate the pointer on the timing belt cover **(see illustration)**.
5   Locate the service check connector under the dash on the far right of the dash **(see illustrations)**. With the engine off con-

35.2 Tools needed to check and adjust the ignition timing

1   **Vacuum plugs** - *Vacuum hoses will, in most cases, have to be disconnected and plugged. Molded plugs in various shapes and sizes are available for this*
2   **Inductive pick-up timing light** - *Flashes a bright, concentrated beam of light when the number one spark plug fires. Connect the leads according to the instructions supplied with the light*
3   **Distributor wrench** - *On some models, the hold-down bolt for the distributor is difficult to reach and turn with conventional wrenches or sockets. A special wrench like this must be used*

nect a jumper wire between the green/white and brown terminals on Integra models and the white and black terminals on Legend models.
6   Start the engine and point the timing light at the timing pointer.
7   The red mark on the pulley will appear stationary and be aligned with the pointer if the timing is correct.

35.5b On Legend models, insert a jumper wire into the white and black terminals of the service check connector (arrow) located under the right side of the dash

35.4 Be sure when viewing the timing mark on the pulley that you are directly above the pointer (arrow), aiming the timing light down so as not to create an extreme angle (you'll get an accurate reading this way)

35.5a On Integra models, the service connector (arrow) is located under the dash, next to the blower motor - insert a jumper wire between the green/white and brown terminals

35.10 On Legend models, grasp the control box cover securely and pull it straight out to detach it

35.11 Drill out the rivets (arrows) and detach the adjuster cover

36.2a Integra model ABS bleeder screw (arrow) location - note that the battery has been removed for access

36.2b Legend model ABS bleeder screw location (arrow)

36.3 The high pressure ABS hoses are retained by a banjo fitting (arrow) at each end

37.2 Insert the ignition key into the slot in the dash to reset the Maintenance Required indicator

Adjustment

Integra

8   If an adjustment is required on, loosen the three adjusting bolts and rotate the distributor slightly until the timing is correct.
9   Tighten the adjusting bolts and recheck the timing. Proceed to Step 14.

Legend

10   Detach the control box cover **(see illustration)**.
11   Use a drill with a 3/16-inch drill bit to remove the retaining rivets, then detach the ignition timing adjuster cover **(see illustration)**.
12   Use a screwdriver to turn the adjusting screw until the timing is correct.
13   After adjustment, attach the cover with new rivets and install the control box cover.

All models

14   Turn off the engine and remove the timing light.
15   Remove the jumper wire from the service check connector.

36 Anti-lock Brake System (ABS) high pressure hose replacement (every 60,000 miles or 48 months)

Refer to illustrations 36.2a, 36.2b and 36.3
Warning: *Brake fluid can harm your eyes and damage painted surfaces, so use extreme caution when handling or pouring it. Do not use brake fluid that has been standing open or is more than one year old. Brake fluid absorbs moisture from the air. Excess moisture can cause a dangerous loss of braking effectiveness.*
1   Remove the brake fluid from the master cylinder and ABS modulator.
2   Remove the cap on the top of the power unit **(see illustrations)**. Connect a length of snug-fitting hose to the bleeder and direct the other end of the hose into a container. Loosen the bleeder a little to allow the pressurized brake fluid to escape, then once the fluid flow slows, loosen the bleeder a little more to drain out the residual brake fluid.
Warning: *The fluid in the power unit is under extremely high pressure. Open the bleeder slowly to prevent brake fluid from shooting*

out with force.
3   Disconnect the banjo fittings and remove the hose **(see illustration)**.
4   Install the new hose and tighten the banjo fittings to the torque listed in the Specifications Section at the beginning of this Chapter. Be sure to use new sealing washers on either side of the banjo fittings.
5   Refill the system with fluid and bleed any air from the system (see Chapter 9).

37 Maintenance Required Indicator resetting (Legend models)

Refer to illustration 37.2
1   The Maintenance Required Indicator will turn yellow as your vehicle nears 7500 miles since a service. If you exceed 7,500 miles since the last service, it will turn red.
2   After performing the required maintenance (see the maintenance schedule), reset the Maintenance Required Indicator by inserting the ignition key into the slot in the instrument cluster below the indicator **(see illustration)**.

1

Notes

Chapter 2 Part A
Integra engines

Contents

Specifications

General

Firing order	1-3-4-2
Cylinder numbers (front-to-rear)	1-2-3-4
Displacement (cubic inch displacement)	
1.7L (VTEC)	102 cid
1.8L	112 cid
Bore	3.19 inches
Stroke	
1.7L (VTEC)	3.20 inches
1.8L	3.50 inches

Cylinder location and distributor rotor rotation

FRONT OF VEHICLE

12021-2A-specs HAYNES

Camshaft

Endplay	
Standard	0.002 to 0.006 inch
Service limit	0.020 inch maximum
Lobe height	
1.7L (VTEC)	
Intake	
Primary	1.3026 inches
Mid	1.4343 inches
Secondary	1.3771 inches
Exhaust	
Primary	1.2907 inches
Mid	1.4063 inches
Secondary (1992)	1.3644 inches
Secondary (1993)	1.3658 inches
1.8L	
Intake	
1990 and 1991	1.3160 inches
1992 and 1993	1.3274 inches
Exhaust	1.3083 inches

Camshaft (continued)

Runout
    1990 through 1992
        Standard .... 0.0006 inch
        Service limit... 0.001 inch maximum
    1993
        Standard .... 0.001 inch
        Service limit... 0.002 inch maximum
Journal oil clearance
    Standard .... 0.002 to 0.004 inch
    Service limit .... 0.006 inch maximum

Oil pump

Rotor-to-cover clearance
    Standard .... 0.001 to 0.003 inch
    Service limit .... 0.006 inch maximum
Tooth tip clearance
    Standard .... 0.002 to 0.006 inch
    Service limit .... 0.008 inch maximum
Outer rotor-to-pump body clearance
    Standard .... 0.004 to 0.007 inch
    Service limit .... 0.008 inch maximum

Torque specifications   **Ft-lbs** (unless otherwise indicated)

Camshaft bearing holder bolts (1.7L VTEC)
    6 mm bolts .... 96 in-lbs
    8 mm bolts .... 192 in-lbs
Camshaft bearing cap bolts (1.8L) .... 84 in-lbs
Camshaft sprocket bolts
    1.7L (VTEC).. 37
    1.8L 27
Crankshaft pulley bolt
    1990 87
    1991 and later (used bolt and crankshaft)............................... 130
    1991 and later (new bolt or crankshaft)
        First step 145
        Second step.. Loosen completely
        Third step 130
Cylinder head bolts
    First step 22
    Second step... 61
Driveplate-to-crankshaft bolts... 54
Intake manifold bolts/nuts 17
Exhaust manifold-to-cylinder head nuts...................................... 23
Exhaust pipe-to-manifold nuts 40
Exhaust manifold upper cover bolts 17
Flywheel-to-crankshaft bolts 76
Oxygen sensor.. 33
Oil jet bolts... 144 in-lbs
Oil pressure switch .... 156 in-lbs
Oil pan baffle plate bolts.. 96 in-lbs
Oil pan drain plug 33
Oil pan-to-engine bolts .... 108 in-lbs
Oil pump pick-up tube to pump housing nuts............................... 96 in-lbs
Oil pump screen-to-main bearing cap.. 96 in-lbs
Oil pump housing-to-block bolts
    6 mm bolts .... 96 in-lbs
    8 mm bolts .... 204 in-lbs
Oil pump cover-to-housing... 48 in-lbs
Oil pump relief valve plug .... Not specified
Rear main oil seal housing bolts.. 96 in-lbs
Timing belt cover bolts
    1990 and 1991 .... 108 in-lbs
    1992 and 1993 .... 84 in-lbs
Timing belt tensioner bolt 40
Valve cover nuts .... 84 in-lbs
VTEC lock-up solenoid bolts .... 108 in-lbs
VTEC oil pressure inspection hole bolt.. 168 in-lbs
Water pump bolts .... 108 in-lbs

1 General information

This Part of Chapter 2 is devoted to in-vehicle repair procedures for 1.7 and 1.8 liter, fuel injected, four cylinder engines. All information concerning engine removal and installation and engine block and cylinder head overhaul can be found in Part C of this Chapter.

There are two different versions of engines covered in this Part of Chapter 2. All versions are Dual Overhead Camshaft (DOHC), with 4 valves per cylinder (16V).

All 1.7 liter engines use the VTEC (Variable Valve Timing and Lift Electronic Control) system. For more information on VTEC engines see Section 9 of this Chapter.

Engines covered include:	Engine designation:
1.7L DOHC VTEC	B17A1
1.8L DOHC	B18A1

The following repair procedures are based on the assumption that the engine is installed in the vehicle. If the engine has been removed from the vehicle and mounted on a stand, many of the steps outlined in this Part of Chapter 2 will not apply.

The Specifications included in this Part of Chapter 2 apply only to the procedures contained in this chapter. Chapter 2C contains the Specifications necessary for cylinder head and engine block rebuilding.

It is a compact and lightweight engine with an aluminum alloy block (with steel cylinder liners) and an aluminum alloy cylinder head. The crankshaft rides in the main webs of the engine block and uses renewable insert-type main bearings, with separate thrust bearings at the number four bearing position assigned the task of controlling crankshaft endplay.

The pistons have two compression rings and one oil control ring. The semi-floating piston pins are press fitted into the small end of the connecting rod. The connecting rod big ends are also equipped with renewable insert-type plain bearings.

The engine is liquid-cooled, utilizing a centrifugal impeller-type pump, driven by the timing belt, to circulate coolant around the cylinders and combustion chambers and through the intake manifold.

Lubrication is handled by a rotor-type oil pump mounted on the front of the engine under the timing belt cover. It is driven directly by the crankshaft. The oil is filtered continuously by a cartridge-type filter mounted on the firewall side of the engine.

2 Repair operations possible with the engine in the vehicle

Clean the engine compartment and the exterior of the engine with some type of degreaser before any work is done. It will make the job easier and help keep dirt out of the internal areas of the engine.

Depending on the components involved, it may be helpful to remove the hood to improve access to the engine as repairs are performed (refer to Chapter 11 if necessary). Cover the fenders to prevent damage to the paint. Special pads are available, but an old bedspread or blanket will also work.

If vacuum, exhaust, oil or coolant leaks develop, indicating a need for gasket or seal replacement, the repairs can generally be made with the engine in the vehicle. The intake and exhaust manifold gaskets, oil pan gasket, crankshaft oil seals and cylinder head gasket are all accessible with the engine in place.

Exterior engine components, such as the intake and exhaust manifolds, the oil pan, the water pump, the starter motor, the alternator, the distributor and the fuel system components can be removed for repair with the engine in place.

Since the cylinder head can be removed without pulling the engine, camshaft and valve component servicing can also be accomplished with the engine in the vehicle. Replacement of the timing belt and sprockets is also possible with the engine in the vehicle.

In extreme cases caused by a lack of necessary equipment, repair or replacement of piston rings, pistons, connecting rods and rod bearings is possible with the engine in the vehicle. However, this practice is not recommended because of the cleaning and preparation work that must be done to the components involved.

3 Top Dead Center (TDC) for number one piston - locating

Refer to illustrations 3.10 and 3.11
Note: *The following procedure is based on the assumption that the spark plug wires and distributor are correctly installed. If you are trying to locate TDC to install the distributor correctly, piston position must be determined by feeling for compression at the number one spark plug hole, then aligning the ignition timing marks as described in Step 11.*

1 Top Dead Center (TDC) is the highest point in the cylinder that each piston reaches as it travels up-and-down when the crankshaft turns. Each piston reaches TDC on the compression stroke and again on the exhaust stroke, but TDC generally refers to piston position on the compression stroke.
2 Positioning the piston(s) at TDC is an essential part of many procedures such as camshaft and timing belt/sprocket removal and distributor removal.
3 Before beginning this procedure, be sure to place the transaxle in Neutral and apply the parking brake or block the rear wheels.
4 Disable the ignition system by detaching the connectors at the distributor (see Chapter 5).

5 Disable the fuel system (see Chapter 4).
6 Remove the spark plugs (see Chapter 1).
7 In order to bring any piston to TDC, the crankshaft must be turned using one of the methods outlined below. When looking at the front (drive belt end) of the engine, normal crankshaft rotation is counterclockwise. Always rotate the engine counterclockwise; clockwise rotation may cause incorrect adjustment of the timing belt.

  a) *The preferred method is to turn the crankshaft with a socket and ratchet attached to the bolt threaded into the front of the crankshaft.*
  b) *A remote starter switch, which may save some time, can also be used. Follow the instructions included with the switch. Once the piston is close to TDC, use a socket and ratchet as described in the previous paragraph.*
  c) *If an assistant is available to turn the ignition switch to the Start position in short bursts, you can get the piston close to TDC without a remote starter switch. Make sure your assistant is out of the vehicle, away from the ignition switch, then use a socket and ratchet as described in Paragraph a) to complete the procedure.*

8 Note the position of the terminal for the number one spark plug wire on the distributor cap. If the terminal isn't marked, follow the plug wire from the number one cylinder spark plug to the cap.
9 Detach the cap from the distributor and set it aside (see Chapter 1 if necessary).
10 Mark the distributor cover directly under the rotor terminal **(see illustration)** for the number 1 cylinder.
11 Locate the timing marks on the crankshaft pulley. Turn the crankshaft (see Step 7 above) until the TDC mark (white mark) on the crankshaft pulley is aligned with

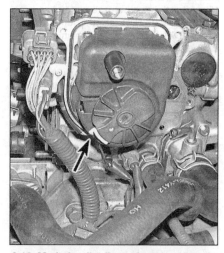

3.10 Mark the distributor housing directly beneath the number one spark plug wire terminal (double check the distributor cap to verify that the rotor points to the number 1 spark plug wire)

2A

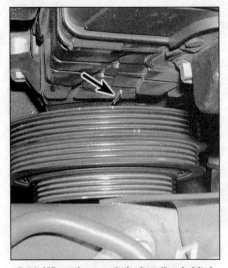

3.11 When the crankshaft pulley (white) mark aligns with the pointer on the timing belt cover and the distributor rotor is pointing to number 1 cylinder's terminal - the no. 1 cylinder is at TDC on the compression stroke

4.5 Valve cover bolt locations (VTEC engine shown, non-VTEC similar)

the pointer on the timing belt cover **(see illustration)**.

12   Look at the distributor rotor - it should be pointing directly at the mark you made on the distributor body (cover). If the rotor is 180-degrees off, the number one piston is at TDC on the exhaust stroke.

13   To get the piston to TDC on the compression stroke, turn the crankshaft one complete turn (360-degrees) counterclockwise. The rotor should now be pointing at the mark on the distributor.

14   When the rotor is pointing at the number one spark plug wire terminal in the distributor cap and the ignition timing marks are aligned, the number one piston is at TDC on the compression stroke.

15   After the number one piston has been positioned at TDC on the compression stroke, TDC for any of the remaining pistons can be located by turning the crankshaft and following the firing order. Mark the remaining spark plug wire terminal locations on the distributor body just like you did for the number one terminal, then number the marks to correspond with the cylinder numbers. As you turn the crankshaft, the rotor will also turn. When it's pointing directly at one of the marks on the distributor, the piston for that particular cylinder is at TDC on the compression stroke.

4   Valve cover - removal and installation

Removal

Refer to illustration 4.5

1   Detach the cable from the negative terminal of the battery. **Caution:** *If the radio in your vehicle is equipped with an anti-theft*

system, *make sure you have the correct activation code before disconnecting the battery.*

2   Remove the spark plug wires from the valve cover (see Chapter 1). Be sure to mark each wire for correct installation. **Note:** *On VTEC engines it will be necessary to remove the spark plug wire cover before removing the spark plug wires from the valve cover.*

3   Mark and detach any hoses or wires from the valve cover that will interfere with the removal of the valve cover.

4   Wipe off the valve cover thoroughly to prevent debris from falling onto the exposed cylinder head or camshaft/valve train assembly.

5   Remove the valve cover nuts and washers **(see illustration)**.

6   Carefully lift off the valve cover and gasket. If the valve cover is stuck to the cylinder head, tap it with a rubber mallet to break the seal. Do not pry between the cover and cylinder head or you'll damage the gasket mating surfaces.

Installation

7   Remove the old gasket and clean the mating surfaces of the cylinder head and the valve cover. Clean the surfaces with a rag soaked in lacquer thinner or acetone.

8   Inspect the sealing grommets or the O-rings that fit at the bottoms of the spark plug wells. Replace them if they're cracked or flattened, or if the rubber has hardened.

9   Apply beads of RTV sealant to the corners where the cylinder head mates with the front and rear camshaft caps. Wait five minutes or so and let the RTV "set-up" (slightly harden). **Note:** *Make sure the RTV sealant has slightly hardened before installing the valve cover. If the weather is damp and cold, the sealant will take some extra time to set.*

10   Install a new molded rubber gasket onto the valve cover by pushing it into the slot that circles the valve cover perimeter. Install the valve cover sealing grommets or O-rings, lubricate them with light coat of grease (this will ease the installation of the sealing grommets and hold the O-rings in place). Install the valve cover and tighten the nuts to the

torque listed in this Chapter's Specifications. Tighten the nuts in several stages in a criss-cross pattern. **Note:** *Make sure the rubber spark plug seals are in position before tightening the valve cover.*

11   The remainder of installation is the reverse of removal.

5   Intake manifold - removal and installation

Warning: *Gasoline is extremely flammable, so take extra precautions when you work on any part of the fuel system. Don't smoke or allow open flames or bare light bulbs near the work area, and don't work in a garage where a natural gas-type appliance (such as a water heater or clothes dryer) with a pilot light is present. If you spill any fuel on your skin, rinse it off immediately with soap and water. When you perform any kind of work on the fuel system, wear safety glasses and have a Class B type fire extinguisher on hand.*

Removal

Refer to illustrations 5.8 and 5.9

1   Detach the cable from the negative terminal of the battery. **Caution:** *If the radio in your vehicle is equipped with an anti-theft system, make sure you have the correct activation code before disconnecting the battery.*

2   Drain the cooling system (see Chapter 1).

3   Remove the intake air duct. If you're working on a VTEC model, remove the air cleaner housing as well (see Chapter 4).

4   Clearly label and detach any vacuum lines and electrical connectors which will interfere with removal of the manifold.

5   Detach the accelerator cable from the throttle lever (see Chapter 4).

6   Remove the coolant hoses from the throttle body.

7   Relieve the fuel system pressure and disconnect the fuel feed and return lines at the fuel rail (see Chapter 4).

8   Working under the engine compartment,

5.8 Working under the vehicle, remove the intake manifold brace (arrow)

5.9 Disconnect the coolant bypass hoses (arrows) (non-VTEC engine shown, VTEC similar)

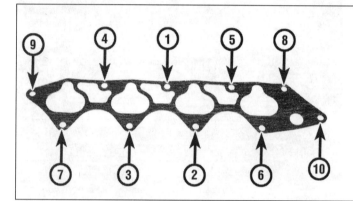

5.16 Intake manifold TIGHTENING sequence - tighten evenly in stages, from the center outward

gasket material from the cylinder head and manifold mating surfaces. Clean the surfaces with lacquer thinner or acetone.

16   Install the intake manifold with a new gasket and tighten the nuts finger-tight. Follow the recommended tightening sequence **(see illustration)**, tighten the nuts until the torque listed in this Chapter's Specifications is reached.

17   The remainder of the installation procedure is the reverse of removal. Refer to Chapter 1 and refill the cooling system.

6   Exhaust manifold - removal and installation

Removal

Refer to illustrations 6.2 and 6.3

1   Disconnect the battery cable from the negative battery terminal. **Caution:** *If the radio in your vehicle is equipped with an anti-theft system, make sure you have the correct activation code before disconnecting the battery.*

2   Raise the front of the vehicle and support it securely on jackstands. Unbolt the brace and detach the exhaust pipe from the exhaust manifold **(see illustration)**. Apply penetrating oil to the fastener threads if they are difficult to remove.

3   Remove the heat shield from the exhaust manifold **(see illustration)**. Be sure to soak the bolts and nuts with penetrating oil before attempting to remove them from the manifold.

4   Remove the exhaust manifold nuts in the reverse order of the tightening sequence and detach the exhaust manifold from the cylinder head **(see illustration 6.6)**.

Installation

Refer to illustration 6.6

5   Discard the old gasket and use a scraper to clean the gasket mating surfaces on the manifold and head, then clean the surfaces with a rag soaked in lacquer thinner or acetone.

remove the brace that supports the intake manifold **(see illustration)**.

9   Disconnect the coolant by-pass hose from the timing belt end of the intake manifold **(see illustration)**.

10   Remove the intake manifold bolts in the reverse order of the tightening sequence and remove the manifold from the engine **(see illustration 5.16)**.

Installation

Refer to illustration 5.16

11   Clean the manifold nuts with solvent

and dry them with compressed air, if available.

12   Check the mating surfaces of the manifold for flatness with a precision straightedge and feeler gauges.

13   Inspect the manifold for cracks and distortion. If the manifold is cracked or warped, replace it or see if it can be resurfaced at an automotive machine shop.

14   Check carefully for any stripped or broken intake manifold bolts/studs. Replace any defective bolts with new parts.

15   Using a scraper, remove all traces of old

6.2 Spray the flange nuts and bracket bolts (arrows) with penetrating lubricant, remove them and lower the exhaust pipe

6.3 Remove the bolts (arrows) and lift off the heat shield (fourth bolt not visible)

6.6 Exhaust manifold TIGHTENING sequence - tighten evenly in stages, from the center outward

7.9 Hold the crankshaft pulley and remove the bolt

7.14 If you intend to reuse the belt, make an arrow to indicate direction of rotation and match marks to align the sprockets with the belt

7.15a Center timing cover bolts (arrows)

6   Place the exhaust manifold in position on the cylinder head and install the nuts. Following the recommended tightening sequence **(see illustration)**, tighten the nuts to the torque listed in this Chapter's Specifications.

7   The remainder of installation is the reverse of removal.

8   Start the engine and check for exhaust leaks between the manifold and the cylinder head and between the manifold and the exhaust pipe.

---

7   Timing belt and sprockets - removal, inspection and installation

---

Removal

Refer to illustrations 7.9, 7.14, 7.15a, 7.15b and 7.16

1   Disconnect the cable from the negative terminal of the battery. **Caution:** *If the radio in your vehicle is equipped with an anti-theft system, make sure you have the correct activation code before disconnecting the battery.*

2   Remove the spark plugs and drivebelts (see Chapter 1).

3   Remove the valve cover (see Section 4).

4   Unbolt the power steering pump without disconnecting the hoses and set it aside (see Chapter 10).

5   Place blocks behind the rear wheels and set the parking brake.

6   Loosen the lug nuts on the front wheels and raise the front of the vehicle. Support the front of the vehicle securely on jackstands.

7   Remove the left front wheel and remove the splash shield from the left wheel well.

8   Position the number one piston at Top Dead Center (see Section 3). **Caution:** *Always rotate the crankshaft counterclockwise (viewed from the pulley end of the engine). Clockwise rotation may cause incorrect adjustment of the timing belt.*

9   Keep the crankshaft pulley from turning with a strap wrench or chain wrench. Loosen the pulley-to-crankshaft bolt with a socket and breaker bar **(see illustration)**.

10   Slip the pulley off the crankshaft.

11   Support the engine with a floor jack. Place a wood block between the jack pad and the oil pan to avoid damaging the pan.

12   Working in the engine compartment, remove the cruise control actuator (if equipped) and position it aside.

13   Remove the driver's side engine mount (see Section 17).

7.15b Lower timing cover bolts (arrows)

14   If you intend to reuse the timing belt, use white paint or chalk to make match marks to align the sprockets with the belt and an arrow to indicate the direction of rotation **(see illustration)**.

15   Remove the center and lower timing belt covers **(see illustrations)**. The upper cover is an integral part of the valve cover.

16   Loosen the timing belt tensioner pulley bolt **(see illustration)**. Push on the tensioner to release the tension on the belt, then

7.16 Timing belt tensioner pulley (arrow) (belt removed for clarity)

7.19 Carefully inspect the timing belt for wear or damage

2A

7.21 Be sure the word UP is at the twelve o'clock position and the two timing marks (arrows) align with each other and the rear cover mark

EXHAUST CAM   INTAKE CAM

7.22 Align the line on the crankshaft sprocket with the pointer on the oil pump (arrows)

retighten the bolt. Slip the belt off.

17 If you're replacing the camshafts or camshaft oil seals, slip a large screwdriver through the camshaft sprocket to keep it from rotating and remove the bolt, then pull off the sprocket.

Inspection

Refer to illustration 7.19

18 Rotate the belt tensioner pulley by hand and move it from side-to-side, checking for play and rough rotation **(see illustration 7.16)**. Replace it if roughness or play is detected.

19 Check the timing belt for wear (especially on the thrust side of the teeth), cracks, splits, fraying and oil contamination **(see illustration)**. Replace the belt if any of these conditions are noted. **Note:** *Unless the engine has very low mileage, it's common practice to replace the timing belt with a new one every time it's removed. Don't reinstall the original belt unless it's in like-new condition. Never reinstall a belt in questionable condition.*

Installation

Refer to illustrations 7.21 and 7.22

20 If you removed the camshaft sprockets, reinstall them aligning them with the camshaft keys. Tighten the camshaft sprocket bolts to the torque listed in this Chapter's specifications.

21 Before installing the timing belt, make

sure the dots or "UP" marks on the camshaft sprockets are at the top and the two index marks are in line with each other and the rear cover mark **(see illustration)**.

22 Make sure the timing marks on the crankshaft sprocket and the pointer on the oil pump are aligned **(see illustration)**. If the crankshaft was disturbed, temporarily reinstall the crankshaft pulley bolt and turn the crankshaft until the marks are aligned.

23 Install the timing belt, making sure there is no slack, first on the crankshaft sprocket, then in order on the tensioner pulley, water pump pulley, exhaust camshaft sprocket and intake camshaft sprocket. Loosen the belt tensioner bolt, let the tensioner move to take up the slack and tighten the bolt.

24 Carefully turn the crankshaft through six revolutions and recheck the timing marks and camshaft sprocket index marks for proper alignment **(see illustrations 7.21 and 7.22)**. If the crankshaft binds or seems to hit something, do not force it, as the valves may be hitting the pistons. If this happens, valve timing is incorrect. Remove the belt and repeat the installation procedure and verify that the installation is correct.

25 Install the outer belt guide onto the crankshaft (if removed) **(see illustration 8.3a)**. Reinstall the remaining parts in the reverse order of removal.

26 Refer to Chapter 1 and adjust the drivebelts.

27 Run the engine and check for proper operation.

8 Crankshaft front oil seal - replacement

Refer to illustrations 8.3a, 8.3b, 8.3c and 8.4

1 Remove the drivebelts (see Chapter 1).

2 Remove the crankshaft pulley and the timing belt (see Section 7).

3 Remove the outer belt guide and crankshaft sprocket from the crankshaft. If

8.3a Remove the outer belt guide - note that the curved edge faces away from the timing belt

8.3b Remove the crankshaft sprocket

8.3c After removing the sprocket, slide off the inner belt guide (if equipped) – note that the curved edge faces away from the timing belt

8.4 Carefully pry the oil seal out with a removal tool or a screwdriver - don't nick or scratch the crankshaft or the seal bore or the new seal will leak

the inner belt guide is a separate piece from the sprocket, remove it **(see illustrations)**.

4   Carefully pry the seal out of the oil pump housing with a seal removal tool or a screwdriver **(see illustration)**. Don't scratch the seal bore or damage the crankshaft in the process (if the crankshaft is damaged, the new seal will end up leaking).

5   Clean the bore in the oil pump housing and coat the outer edge of the new seal with engine oil or multi-purpose grease. Using a socket with an outside diameter slightly smaller than the outside diameter of the seal, carefully drive the seal into place with a hammer. If a socket is not available, a short section of a large diameter pipe will work. Check the seal after installation to be sure the spring did not pop out.

6   Install the inner belt guide (if equipped), crankshaft sprocket and outer belt guide. Install the timing belt and the timing belt covers (see Section 7).

7   Lubricate the sleeve of the crankshaft pulley with engine oil or multi-purpose grease, then install the crankshaft pulley. The remainder of installation is the reverse of removal.

8   Run the engine and check for leaks.

9   VTEC system - description and component checks

Description

1   The VTEC system (Variable Valve Timing and Lift Electronic Control) is used on engines across the entire Honda line of cars.

2   The differences between the base engines and their VTEC counterparts is strictly in the components and operation of the valve train. The engine short block, oiling and cooling systems are identical, as are all attached components. Models equipped with VTEC engines can be distinguished by the letters "VTEC" molded into the top of the valve cover.

3   The intake camshaft has three lobes for each intake valve. The Powertrain Control Module (PCM) has the ability to decide which

set of lobes will be used for a given set of engine operating conditions. The PCM turns the system ON or OFF, depending on sensor input.

4   The following are used to determine VTEC operation:

a) *Engine speed (rpm)*
b) *Vehicle speed (mph)*
c) *Throttle position*
d) *Engine load measured by Manifold Absolute Pressure (MAP) sensor*
e) *Coolant temperature*

5   At low speeds, the secondary intake valve operates on its own camshaft lobe, which has very low lift and duration (compared to the primary valve). The opening is intended to be just enough to keep atomized fuel from building up, "puddling", at the valve head. This limited valve operation is designed to provide good low end torque and responsiveness, by inducing swirl in the combustion chamber from the primary intake valve, which operates with a normal profile.

6   When performance is needed, the primary and secondary rocker arms are locked together through the use of an electrically controlled hydraulic system. Hydraulically operated synchronizing pistons lock all three rocker arms together. When activated, both intake valves open to the higher lift and duration of the middle rocker arm, which has its own camshaft lobe. **Note:** *The secondary rocker arm no longer contacts its own camshaft lobe until the system is disengaged.*

Component checks

VTEC lock-up control solenoid valve

Refer to illustrations 9.9, 9.14, 9.18, 19.19 and 9.20

7   The lock-up VTEC solenoid valve, which includes an oil pressure switch, is mounted to the cylinder head next to the distributor.

8   A problem in the VTEC solenoid valve and pressure switch circuit will set a diagnostic trouble code, and light the CHECK engine light on the dash. Refer to Chapter 6 for

9.9 Location of the VTEC oil pressure switch connector (A) and the lock-up control solenoid valve connector (B)

accessing trouble codes.

9   Disconnect the round electrical connector from the pressure switch **(see illustration)**.

10   Connect an ohmmeter between the terminals of the switch. There should be continuity. If there is no continuity, replace the switch.

11   Connect a voltmeter between body ground and the blue-black wire's terminal in the harness side of the connector. With the ignition key ON (engine not running), there should be approximately 12 volts. If not, look for a break or bad connection in the blue-black wire between the connector and its terminal at the PCM (terminal D6).

12   Once you've got the correct voltage at the blue-black wire's terminal in the connector, connect the voltmeter between both of the terminals in the harness side of the connector (blue-black and black wires). With the key ON, there should still be approximately 12 volts. If not, check the black wire (which supplies the ground for this circuit) for a break or bad connection between the connector and body ground.

13   With the ignition key OFF, disconnect the single-pin connector from the VTEC

9.14 Connect an oil pressure gauge to the VTEC solenoid port

9.18 VTEC solenoid valve mounting bolts (arrows)

9.19 Whenever problems are suspected in the VTEC system, check the filter and O-ring (arrow) located between solenoid valve and the cylinder head

2A

9.20 Push on the solenoid plunger and check for free movement

9.22 Press the mid rocker arm with a finger; it should move independently of the others

Clean and reinstall with a new O-ring. If the filter was clogged, change the engine oil and filter to keep it from clogging again **(see illustration)**.

20   Unbolt the solenoid from the solenoid valve assembly, separate the solenoid and push the plunger to check for free movement **(see illustration)**. Use a new O-ring when reinstalling the solenoid.

Rocker arms and oil control orifices

Refer to illustrations 9.22, 9.23 and 9.24

21   Remove the valve cover (see Section 4) and place the no. 1 cylinder at TDC (see Section 3).

22   Press on the mid rocker arm with a finger **(see illustration)**. It should move separately from the primary and secondary rocker arms. If it doesn't, remove and disassemble the rocker arms for inspection (see Section 10).

23   Once the rocker arm assemblies have been removed and disassembled separate the rocker arms and synchronizing pistons **(see illustration)**.

24   Inspect all other parts (rocker arms and synchronizing pistons) for wear, galling, scor-

solenoid **(see illustration 9.9)**. Connect an ohmmeter between the terminal pin in the solenoid (not in the harness) and body ground. If the ohmmeter doesn't indicate 14-to-30 ohms, replace the solenoid as described below.

14   Remove the 10 mm bolt from the oil pressure test port on the cylinder head. Attach a mechanical oil pressure gauge, using an adapter with 10.0 x 1 mm threads **(see illustration)**.

15   Warm the engine to normal operating temperature (until the electric cooling fan comes on).

16   Briefly run the engine at 1000 rpm, 3000 rpm and 5000 rpm, noting the oil pressure reading at each engine speed. **Caution:**

Don't run the engine for more than one minute at no-load.

17   The oil pressure should be less than 7 psi. If it isn't, inspect the VTEC solenoid.

18   Connect a length of wire between the battery positive terminal and the VTEC solenoid terminal **(see illustration 9.9)**. Briefly run the engine at 5,000 rpm (no more than one minute) and check the oil pressure reading. It should now be 57 psi or more. If not, remove the solenoid valve **(see illustration)** and inspect the VTEC solenoid valve filter.

19   Check the filter/O-ring for clogging.

A B C

D E

9.23 VTEC rocker arms and synchronizing assembly

a)   Primary rocker arm
b)   Mid rocker arm
c)   Secondary rocker arm
d)   Short piston
e)   Long piston

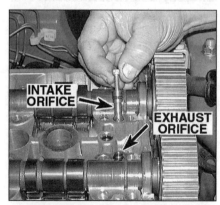

INTAKE ORIFICE

EXHAUST ORIFICE

9.24 To remove an oil control orifice for cleaning, thread a machine screw into the top and pull upward - don't get the intake and exhaust orifices mixed up

9.28 Check the lost motion assemblies for free movement

10.1 To check camshaft endplay, set a dial indicator like this, with the gauge plunger touching the nose of the camshaft

10.11 Measure the camshaft lobe heights with a micrometer

10.13a Lay a strip of Plastigage along each camshaft journal

ing or signs of overheating (bluish in color). Replace any parts necessary. Remove the oil control orifice from the intake and exhaust sides of the cylinder head **(see illustration)**, clean and reinstall them.

25   Reassembly is the reverse of removal. **Note:** *Reassemble and hold together (rubber bands work well) each cylinder's components before trying to assemble on the rocker shaft (see Section 10).*

Lost motion assemblies

Refer to illustration 9.28

26   The four lost motion assemblies sit in pockets in the cylinder head.

27   Remove the individual lost motion assemblies from the head (see Section 10).

28   Test each lost motion assembly by pushing the plunger with your finger **(see illustration)**. A light pressure should move the plunger slightly, and firmer pressure will move it further. If the assembly doesn't move smoothly, replace it.

10   Camshafts and rocker arms - removal, inspection and installation

Endplay and runout check

Refer to illustration 10.1

1   To check camshaft endplay:

a)   *Install the camshaft and secure it with the caps.*

b)   *Mount a dial indicator on the head **(see illustration)**.*

c)   *Using a large screwdriver as a lever at the opposite end, move the camshaft forward-and-backward and note the dial indicator reading.*

d)   *Compare the reading with the endplay listed in this Chapter's Specifications.*

e)   *If the indicated reading is higher, either the camshaft or the head is worn. Replace parts as necessary.*

2   To check camshaft runout:

a)   *Support the camshaft with a pair of V-blocks and set up a dial indicator with the plunger resting against the center bearing journal on the camshaft.*

b)   *Rotate the camshaft and note the indicated runout.*

c)   *Compare the results to the camshaft runout listed in this Chapter's Specifications.*

d)   *If the indicated runout exceeds the specified runout, replace the camshaft.*

1.8L engine

Removal

3   Remove the distributor (see Chapter 5).

4   Remove the valve cover (see Section 4). Loosen the valve adjusting screws all the way (see Chapter 1).

5   Position the number one piston at Top Dead Center (see Section 3).

6   Remove the timing belt and camshaft sprockets (see Section 7).

7   Check the camshaft bearing caps for arrow marks pointing to the timing belt end of the engine. If you can't see them, make your own marks with a sharp scribe. Also number the bearing caps (1 through 6, starting at the timing belt end of the engine) and label them with an I for intake or E for exhaust. **Caution:** *Reinstalling the camshaft holders in the wrong positions (or turned around backwards) may cause the camshaft to seize.*

8   Loosen the camshaft bearing cap bolts 1/4-turn at a time, starting from the center and working outward, until the valve spring pressure is relieved.

9   Lift the camshafts from the cylinder head, then lift out the rocker arms. Label the rocker arms so they can be returned to their original locations.

Inspection

Refer to illustrations 10.11, 10.13a and 10.13b

10   Thoroughly clean the parts and inspect them for wear and damage. Check the rocker arm faces that contact the camshaft, the rocker arm tips and the rocker arm pivots. Replace any parts that are damaged or excessively worn.

11   Check the cam lobes for wear:

a)   *Check the toe and ramp areas of each*

cam lobe for score marks or uneven wear. Also check for flaking and pitting.

b)   *If there's wear on the toe or the ramp, replace the camshaft, but first try to find the cause of the wear. Look for abrasive substances in the oil and inspect the oil pump and oil passages for blockage. Lobe wear is usually caused by inadequate lubrication or dirty oil.*

c)   *Using a micrometer, measure the cam lobe height **(see illustration)**.*

12   Check the camshaft bearing journals and caps for signs of scoring and wear. If they are worn, replace the cylinder head with a new or rebuilt unit.

13   Check the oil clearance of each camshaft journal with Plastigage as follows.

a)   *Clean the bearing caps and camshaft journals with lacquer thinner or acetone and a clean cloth.*

b)   *Carefully lay the camshafts in place in the head. Don't use any lubricant. **Note:** Do not turn the camshaft during this procedure.*

c)   *Lay a strip of Plastigage on each journal **(see illustration)**.*

d)   *Install the camshaft bearing caps and tighten the bolts in stages to the torque listed in this Chapter's Specifications, working from the center bolts outward.*

10.13b Measure the width of the flattened Plastigage

10.25 Wrap a rubber band around each rocker arm set so the parts don't get mixed up

10.27a The intake rocker shaft (A) is secured by a threaded plug - the exhaust rocker shaft (B) is accessible after removing the VTEC control valve

2A

e) Loosen the cam bearing cap bolts and lift the caps off.
f) Compare the width of the crushed Plastigage at its widest point to the scale on the Plastigage envelope (see illustration).
g) If the clearance is greater than that listed in this Chapter's Specifications, replace the worn parts as necessary.
h) Scrape off the Plastigage with your fingernail or the edge of a credit card - don't nick or scratch the journals or bearing caps.

Installation

14   Lubricate all components with assembly lube or engine oil and reinstall the rocker arms. When installing the rocker arms, be sure to return them to their original locations.
15   Coat the cam lobes and journals with camshaft installation lubricant. Lay the camshafts in their bearings, making sure the intake and exhaust camshafts are installed in the correct side of the head. Apply anaerobic-type sealant to the cylinder head contact surfaces of bearing caps 1 and 6 and install the bearing caps. Tighten the caps evenly in stages, working from the center outward, to the torque listed in this Chapter's Specifications.
16   The remainder of installation is the reverse of removal. Adjust the valve clearance, if necessary (see Chapter 1).
17   Run the engine and check for oil leaks and proper operation.

1.7L (VTEC) engine

Removal

Refer to illustrations 10.25, 10.27a, 10.27b and 10.28

18   Remove the valve cover (see Section 4).
19   Remove the timing belt and sprockets (see Section 7).
20   Remove the distributor (see Chapter 5).
21   Loosen the valve adjustment locknuts and back off the screws all the way.
22   Check the camshaft bearing caps for arrow marks pointing to the timing belt end of the engine. If you can't see them, make your own marks with a sharp scribe or marker. Also number the bearing caps (1 through 5,

10.27b Thread a bolt into each rocker shaft and use it to pull the shaft out

starting at the timing belt end of the engine) and label the end caps with an I for intake or E for exhaust. **Caution:** *Reinstalling the camshaft holders in the wrong positions (or turned around backwards) may cause the camshaft to seize.*
23   Loosen the camshaft holder plate and bearing cap bolts 1/4-turn at a time, starting from the center and working outward, until the spring pressure is relieved (see illustration 10.37). Lift off the holder plates and bearing caps. There's a dowel with an O-ring in the underside of the no. 3 (center) bearing cap. Locate these so they won't be lost.
24   Lift the camshafts from the cylinder head.
25   Wrap each set of rocker arms with a rubber band before you remove them so the sets can be kept together (see illustration).
26   Remove the oil control orifice from each rocker shaft and the VTEC lock-up control valve (see Section 9).
27   Remove the intake rocker shaft sealing plug from the distributor end of the engine. Thread a 12 mm bolt into the end of each rocker shaft and use it to pull the rocker shafts from the head (see illustrations).
28   Remove the lost motion assemblies from the head (see illustration). Inspect them as described in Section 9.

10.28 Remove the lost motion assemblies (arrow) from their bores in the cylinder head

Inspection

29   Check the rocker arm faces that contact the camshaft and the rocker arm tips. Check the surfaces of the shafts that the rocker arms ride on, as well as the bearing surfaces inside the rocker arms, for scoring and excessive wear. Also, make sure the oil holes in the shafts are not plugged. Disassemble each set of rocker arms and check the rocker arms and synchronizing pistons as described in Section 9. Replace any parts that are damaged or excessively worn. **Note:** *Be sure to keep the components from each set together. Reassemble the sets after inspection if you're going to reinstall them, then secure each set together with a rubber band.*
30   Inspect the camshaft and rocker arms as described in Steps 11 through 13 above.

Installation

Refer to illustrations 10.35 and 10.37

31   Install the lost motion assemblies (**see illustration 10.28**).
32   Lubricate all components with assembly lube or engine oil. Loosen the valve adjusting screws all the way. Lay the assembled rocker arms in their original locations, then install the shafts. There's a bore in each rocker shaft that accepts the oil control orifice. If the

10.35 Install new oil seals on the timing belt end of the engine

10.37 Camshaft holder TIGHTENING sequence

bores don't line up after the rocker shafts are installed, insert a 12 mm bolt into the end of the rocker shaft and use it as a handle to move the rocker shaft around until they do line up.

33 Replace the O-ring on each oil control orifice, then install the orifices in the cylinder head (see Section 9). Be sure to install the intake and exhaust orifices in the correct locations. Also make sure the orifices fit into their bores in the rocker shafts. They should prevent the rocker shafts from turning when correctly installed. Replace the O-ring on the intake rocker shaft sealing plug and install it onto the cylinder head **(see illustration 10.27a)**.

34 Coat the cam lobes and journals with camshaft installation lubricant. Lay the camshafts in their bearings, making sure the intake and exhaust camshafts are installed in the correct side of the head.

35 Make sure the oil seal contact surfaces of the cylinder head are clean and dry and install new oil seals **(see illustration)**. The oil seal springs face toward the cylinder head.

36 Apply anaerobic-type sealant to the cylinder head contact surfaces of bearing caps 1 and 5 (intake and exhaust) and install the bearing caps.

37 Install the holders on the bearing caps. Tighten the caps evenly in stages, in the correct sequence, to the torque listed in this Chapter's Specifications **(see illustration)**.

38 The remainder of installation is the reverse of removal. Adjust the valve clearance (see Chapter 1).

39 Run the engine and check for oil leaks and proper operation.

---

11 Valve springs, retainers and seals - replacement

Refer to illustrations 11.6 and 11.8

1 Replacing broken valve springs and defective valve stem seals requires removing the head from the engine on VTEC models. On these engines, remove the camshafts and cylinder head (Sections 10 and 12), then refer

11.6 This valve spring compressor allows in-vehicle replacement of valve stem seals on non-VTEC engines

to Part C of this Chapter to remove the valve springs, retainers and seals.

2 On non-VTEC models, the valve springs, retainers and seals can be replaced without removing the cylinder head, but a special type of valve spring compressor is required.

3 Place no. 1 cylinder at TDC compression and remove the valve cover (see Sections 3 and 4).

4 Remove the distributor (see Chapter 5).

5 Remove the camshafts and rocker arms (Section 10).

6 Install a valve spring compressor of the type shown in the accompanying illustration **(see illustration)**. The compressor lever fulcrum on this type of compressor is bolted to the engine in place of the camshafts.

7 Connect an air hose to the spark plug hole of no. 1 cylinder. With the cylinder at TDC, pump air into the cylinder to keep the valve from falling in when the spring is removed.

8 Compress the valve spring and remove the keepers **(see illustration)**. Slowly release the spring tension and remove the spring.

9 Remove the valve stem seal and install a new one (see Part C of this Chapter for details).

10 Repeat the procedure of the remaining valve on no. 1 cylinder, then for the remaining valves on the engine.

11 Install all removed components.

11.8 Compress the valve spring, remove the keepers and slowly release the spring

---

12 Cylinder head - removal and installation

Caution: *Allow the engine to cool completely before beginning this procedure.*

Removal

Refer to illustration 12.2

1 Position the number one piston at Top Dead Center (see Section 3).

2 Disconnect the negative cable from the battery and disconnect the ground cable from the engine **(see illustration)**. **Caution:** *If the radio in your vehicle is equipped with an anti-theft system, refer to the information at the front of this manual before detaching the battery cable.*

3 Drain the cooling system and remove the spark plugs (see Chapter 1).

4 Remove the air cleaner duct. If you're working on a VTEC model, remove the air cleaner housing as well (see Chapter 4).

5 Remove the drivebelts (see Chapter 1). Unbolt the power steering pump and set it aside with out disconnecting any hoses, then remove the power steering pump bracket (see Chapter 10).

6 Disconnect the throttle cable and relieve the fuel system pressure (see Chapter 4).

7 If you're working on an automatic transaxle model, disconnect the transaxle throttle cable.

12.2 Cylinder head removal points, Integra (non-VTEC shown)

1 *Air intake duct*
2 *Power steering pump*
3 *Fuel feed line*
4 *Fuel return line*
5 *PCV hose*
6 *Brake booster vacuum hose*
7 *Engine ground cable*
8 *Coolant hoses*
9 *Distributor*
10 *Cruise control actuator*
11 *Driver's side engine mount*

8   Disconnect the following hoses and lines (see Chapters 4 and 6):

  a) *Fuel feed and return hoses*
  b) *Evaporative emission control hose*
  c) *Breather hose*
  d) *PCV hose*
  e) *Brake booster vacuum hose*

9   Disconnect the coolant bypass hose, heater hose and upper radiator hose (see Chapter 3).
10 Disconnect the following electrical connectors:

  a) *Fuel injectors*
  b) *Engine coolant temperature sensor and switch*
  c) *Temperature gauge sender*
  d) *Distributor*
  e) *Crankshaft fluctuation sensor*
  f) *Ignition coil*
  g) *Throttle position sensor*
  h) *Manifold absolute pressure (MAP) sensor*
  i) *Evap purge control solenoid*
  j) *VTEC solenoid (1.7L engines)*
  k) *VTEC pressure switch (1.7L engines)*
  l) *Idle air control (IAC) valve*
  m) *Intake air temperature sensor (IAT) (1.7L engines)*
  n) *EACV (1.8L engines)*
  o) *oxygen sensor (1.8L engines)*
  p) *Throttle angle (TA) sensor (1.8L engines)*
  q) *EGR valve lift sensor connector (1.8L engines with automatic transaxle)*

11 Remove the cruise control actuator, if equipped.
12 Remove the left front wheel and remove the splash shield from the left wheel well.
13 Support the engine with a floor jack. Place a wood block between the jack pad and the oil pan to avoid damaging the pan. Remove the driver's side engine mount (see Section 17).
14 Remove the intake manifold brace and

exhaust manifold flange bolts. **Note:** *You may wish to detach the intake manifold (see Section 5) and/or exhaust manifold (see Section 6), rather than removing it with the cylinder head, to make the cylinder head easier to handle.*
15 Remove the valve cover (see Section 4).
16 Remove the distributor (see Chapter 5), including the cap and wires.
17 Remove the timing belt (see Section 7), camshafts and the rocker arm assembly (see Section 10).
18 Loosen the head bolts in 1/4-turn increments until they can be removed by hand. Work in a pattern that's the reverse of the tightening sequence **(see illustration 12.26)** to avoid warping the head. Note where each bolt goes so it can be returned to the same location on installation.
19 Lift the head off the engine. If resistance is felt, don't pry between the head and block gasket mating surfaces or damage to the mating surfaces will result. Instead, pry between the power steering pump bracket and the engine block. Set the head on blocks of wood to prevent damage to the gasket sealing surfaces.
20 Cylinder head disassembly and inspection procedures are covered in detail in Chapter 2, Part C. It's a good idea to have the head checked for warpage, even if you're just replacing the gasket.

Installation

Refer to illustrations 12.25 and 12.26
21 The mating surfaces of the cylinder head and block must be perfectly clean when the head is installed.
22 Use a gasket scraper to remove all traces of carbon and old gasket material, then clean the mating surfaces with lacquer thinner or acetone. If there's oil on the mating surfaces when the head is installed, the gasket may not seal correctly and leaks may develop. When working on the block, stuff the cylinders with clean shop rags to keep out debris. Use a vacuum cleaner to remove material that falls into the cylinders. Since the head and block are made of aluminum, aggressive scraping can cause damage. Be extra careful not to nick or gouge the mating surfaces with the scraper.
23 Check the block and head mating surfaces for nicks, deep scratches and other damage. If damage is slight, it can be removed with a file; if it's excessive, machining may be the only alternative.
24 Use a tap of the correct size to chase the threads in the head bolt holes. Mount each head bolt in a vise and run a die down the threads to remove corrosion and restore the threads. Dirt, corrosion, sealant and damaged threads will affect torque readings.
25 Place a new gasket on the block. Check

12.25 Cylinder head dowel locations (arrows)

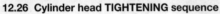

12.26 Cylinder head TIGHTENING sequence

13.5 Oil pan bolt locations

14.4 Remove the oil pick-up tube (A) and the oil pump mounting bolts (arrows)

to see if there are any markings (such as "TOP") on the gasket that say how it is to be installed. Those identification marks must face UP. Make sure the dowels are in the correct locations **(see illustration)**, and install the cylinder head oil orifice with a new O-ring. Set the cylinder head in position.

26 Lubricate the threads and the seats of the cylinder head bolts with clean engine oil, then install them. Tighten the cylinder head bolts following the recommended sequence **(see illustration)**, in stages, to the torque listed in this Chapter's Specifications.

27 Install the rocker arms and camshafts (see section 10). Attach the camshaft sprockets to the camshafts and install the timing belt (see Section 7).

28 Reinstall the remaining parts in the reverse order of removal.

29 Be sure to refill the cooling system and check all fluid levels.

30 Rotate the crankshaft counterclockwise slowly by hand through two complete revolutions. **Caution:** *If you feel any resistance while turning the engine over, stop and recheck the camshaft timing. The valves may be hitting the pistons.*

31 Start the engine and check the ignition timing (see Chapter 1).

32 Run the engine until normal operating temperature is reached. Check for leaks and proper operation.

---

13 Oil pan - removal and installation

Removal

Refer to illustration 13.5

1 Warm up the engine, then drain the oil and replace the oil filter (see Chapter 1).

2 Detach the cable from the negative terminal of the battery. **Caution:** *If the radio in your vehicle is equipped with an anti-theft system, make sure you have the correct activation code before disconnecting the battery.*

3 Raise the vehicle and support it securely on jackstands. Remove the splash shield from under the engine.

4 Remove the front exhaust pipe (see Chapter 5) and the center support brace from

below the oil pan.

5 Remove the bolts securing the oil pan to the engine block **(see illustration)**.

6 Tap on the pan with a soft-face hammer to break the gasket seal, then detach the oil pan from the engine. Don't pry between the block and oil pan mating surfaces.

7 Using a gasket scraper, remove all traces of old gasket and/or sealant from the engine block and oil pan. Remove the seals from each end of the engine block or oil pan. Clean the mating surfaces with lacquer thinner or acetone. Make sure the threaded bolt holes in the block are clean.

Installation

8 Clean the oil pan with solvent and dry it thoroughly. Check the gasket flanges for distortion, particularly around the bolt holes. If necessary, place the pan on a wood block and use a hammer to flatten and restore the gasket surfaces.

9 Apply a 1/8-inch wide bead of RTV sealant to the oil pan gasket surfaces. Make sure the sealant is applied to the inside edge of the bolt holes.

10 Carefully place the oil pan in position.

11 Install the bolts and tighten them in small increments to the torque listed in this Chapter's Specifications. Start with the bolts closest to the center of the pan and work out in a spiral pattern. Don't overtighten them or leakage may occur.

12 Add oil (see Chapter 1), run the engine and check for oil leaks.

---

14 Oil pump - removal, inspection and installation

Removal

Refer to illustrations 14.4 and 14.5

1 Remove the timing belt and the crankshaft sprocket (see Section 7).

2 Remove the oil pan (see Section 13).

3 Remove the oil pick-up tube and screen from the pump housing.

4 Remove the bolts from the oil pump housing and separate the assembly from the engine **(see illustration)**.

5 Remove the screws and disassemble the oil pump **(see illustration)**. You may need to use an impact screwdriver to loosen the pump cover screws without stripping the heads.

Inspection

Refer to illustrations 14.6a, 14.6b and 14.6c

6 Check the oil pump rotor-to-cover clearance, tooth tip clearance and outer rotor-to-pump body clearance **(see illustrations)**. Compare your measurements to the figures listed in this Chapter's Specifications. Replace the pump if any of the measurements are outside of the specified limits.

7 Remove the pressure relief valve plug and extract the spring and pressure relief valve plunger from the pump housing. Check the spring for distortion and the relief valve plunger for scoring. Replace parts as necessary.

14.5 Remove the oil pump cover screws (arrows)

14.6a Use a feeler gauge and straight-edge to check the clearance between the rotors and the cover

2A

8   Install the pump rotors. Pack the spaces between the rotors with petroleum jelly (this will prime the pump).
9   Apply thread-locking compound to the pump cover screws, install the cover and tighten the screws to the torque listed in this Chapter's Specifications. Install the oil pressure relief valve and spring assembly. Use a new sealing washer on the plug and tighten the plug securely.

Installation

10   Apply a thin coat of RTV sealant to the pump housing-to-block sealing surface and a new O-ring in the pump housing. Install the pump housing to the engine block and tighten the bolts to the torque listed in this Chapter's Specifications.
11   Install the oil pick-up tube and screen, using a new gasket. Tighten the bolts to the torque listed in this Chapter's Specifications.
12   Install the oil pan (see Section 13).
13   The remainder of installation is the reverse of removal. Add the specified type and quantity of oil and coolant (see Chapter 1), run the engine and check for leaks.

15   Flywheel/driveplate - removal and installation

Removal

Refer to illustration 15.3
1   Raise the vehicle and support it securely on jackstands, then refer to Chapter 7 and remove the transaxle.
2   Remove the pressure plate and clutch disc (see Chapter 8) (manual transaxle equipped vehicles). Now is a good time to check/replace the clutch components and pilot bearing.
3   Remove the bolts that secure the flywheel/driveplate to the crankshaft **(see illustration)**. If the crankshaft turns, install a flywheel holder tool (available at most auto parts stores) around the ring gear teeth (manual transaxle models), or insert a long punch through one of the holes in the driveplate and allow it to rest against a projection on the

14.6b Use a feeler gauge to check the tooth-tip clearance between the inner and outer rotors

14.6c Use a feeler gauge to check the outer rotor-to-pump body clearance

engine block (automatic transaxle models).
4   Remove the flywheel/driveplate from the crankshaft. Since the flywheel is fairly heavy, be sure to support it while removing the last bolt.
5   Clean the flywheel to remove grease and oil. Inspect the surface for cracks, rivet grooves, burned areas and score marks. Light scoring can be removed with emery cloth. Check for cracked and broken ring gear teeth. Lay the flywheel on a flat surface and use a straightedge to check for warpage.
6   Clean and inspect the mating surfaces of the flywheel/driveplate and the crankshaft. If the rear main oil seal is leaking, replace it before reinstalling the flywheel/driveplate (see Section 16).

Installation

7   Position the flywheel/driveplate against the crankshaft. **Note:** *Some engines have an alignment dowel or staggered bolt holes to ensure correct installation and automatic transaxle equipped vehicles may use a large washer instead of single retaining washers for each bolt.* Before installing the bolts, apply thread-locking compound to the threads.
8   Prevent the flywheel/driveplate from turning by using one of the methods described in Step 3. Using a crossing pattern, tighten the bolts to the torque listed in this Chapter's Specifications.

15.3 Remove the flywheel/driveplate bolts (arrows) from the crankshaft

9   The remainder of installation is the reverse of the removal procedure.

16   Rear main oil seal - replacement

Refer to illustrations 16.2 and 16.3
1   The transaxle must be removed from the vehicle for this procedure and the flywheel/driveplate must be separated from the engine (see Section 15 and Chapter 7).
2   The seal can be replaced without removing the oil pan or removing the seal retainer. However, the lip of the seal is quite

16.2 Carefully pry the rear cover seal out -
don't damage the surface of the
crankshaft or the seal will leak

16.3 Drive the new seal in squarely

17.9a Passenger side engine
mount (arrow)

17.9b Front engine mount (arrow)

17.9c Driver's side engine mount (A) and
the cruise control actuator (B)

17.9d Rear engine mount (arrow)

stiff and it's possible to cock the seal in the retainer bore or damage it during installation. If you want to take the chance, use a screwdriver and a rag to carefully pry the seal out of the housing **(see illustration)**.

3   Apply multi-purpose grease to the crankshaft seal journal and the lip of the new seal and carefully drive the seal into place **(see illustration)**. Install the seal with the spring side in. Use a socket, section of pipe or seal driver. The lip is stiff so carefully work it onto the seal journal of the crankshaft with a smooth object like the end of a socket extension. Don't rush it or you may damage the seal.

4   The rear main oil seal replacement described in Chapter 2C is recommended but requires removal of the oil pan and the seal retainer. If you use this method, you can also measure the clearance between the seal and the bottom of the seal bore, which should be 0.020 to 0.030 inch. The seal should not bottom out. This clearance can't be easily measured with the cover in place on the block.

5   The remaining steps are the reverse of removal.

6   Run the engine and check for oil leaks.

17   Engine mounts - check and replacement

1   Engine mounts seldom require attention, but broken or deteriorated mounts should be replaced immediately or the added strain placed on the driveline components may cause damage or wear.

Check

2   During the check, the engine must be raised slightly to remove the weight from the mounts.

3   Raise the vehicle and support it securely on jackstands, then position a jack under the engine oil pan. Place a large wood block between the jack head and the oil pan, then carefully raise the engine just enough to take the weight off the mounts. **Warning:** *DO NOT place any part of your body under the engine when it's supported only by a jack!*

4   Check the mount insulators to see if the rubber is cracked, hardened or separated from the metal plates. Sometimes the rubber will split right down the center.

5   Check for relative movement between the mount plates and the engine or frame (use a large screwdriver or pry bar to attempt to move the mounts). If movement is noted, lower the engine and tighten the mount fasteners.

6   Rubber preservative should be applied to the insulators to slow deterioration.

Replacement

Refer to illustrations 17.9a, 17.9b, 17.9c and 17.9d

7   Disconnect the cable from the negative terminal of the battery. **Caution:** *If the radio in your vehicle is equipped with an anti-theft system, make sure you have the correct activation code before disconnecting the battery.* Raise the vehicle and support it securely on jackstands (if not already done). Support the engine as described in Step 3.

8   Remove the fasteners, raise the engine with the jack and detach the mount from the frame bracket and engine.

9   Install the new mount, making sure it is correctly positioned in its bracket **(see illustrations)**. Install the fasteners and tighten them securely.

Chapter 2 Part B
Legend engine

Contents

Specifications

General

Cylinder numbers	
Right side	1-2-3
Left side	4-5-6
Firing order	1-4-2-5-3-6

Camshaft and rocker arms

Camshaft bearing oil clearance	
Standard	0.0020 to 0.0035 inch
Service limit	0.004 inch
Camshaft lobe height	
1991 through 1995 (except GS models)	
Intake	1.5750 inches
Exhaust	1.4868 inches
1994 and later (GS models)	
Intake	1.5885
Exhaust	1.4935

Front

12021-2b-specs HAYNES

Acura legend cylinder locations

Camshaft and rocker arms

Camshaft endplay	
Standard	0.002 to 0.006 inch
Service limit	0.006 inch
Camshaft runout (total indicator reading)	
Standard	0.001 inch
Limit	0.002 inch
Rocker arm-to-shaft oil clearance	
Standard	0.0007 to 0.0021 inch
Service limit	0.003 inch

Oil pump clearances

Outer rotor-to-body	
Standard	0.004 to 0.007 inch
Limit	0.008 inch
Outer rotor-to-inner rotor	
Standard	0.002 to 0.006 inch
Limit	0.008 inch
Housing-to-rotor clearance	
Standard	0.001 to 0.003 inch
Limit	0.005 inch

Torque specifications

	Ft-lbs
Camshaft and rocker shaft holder bolts	
6mm	108 in-lbs
8mm	16
Camshaft sprocket bolts	23
Crankshaft pulley bolt	174
Cylinder head bolts	56
Driveplate bolts	54
Exhaust manifold nuts	22
Exhaust heat shield bolts	16
Flywheel bolts	76
Intake manifold bolts/nuts	16
Oil pan baffle plate bolts	108 in-lbs
Oil pan bolts/nuts	16
Oil pan drain plug	33
Oil pick-up screen mounting bolts	108 in-lbs
Oil pump cover screws	60 in-lbs
Oil pump mounting bolts	
6mm bolts	108 in-lbs*
8mm bolts	16*
Rear main oil seal retainer bolts	108 in-lbs*
Timing belt tensioner bolt	31
Timing belt rear cover bolts	108 in-lbs
Valve cover nuts/bolts	84 in-lbs

Replace with new ones whenever the bolts are removed.

1   General information

This Part of Chapter 2 is devoted to in-vehicle repair procedures for the V6 engine. All information concerning engine removal and installation and engine block and cylinder head overhaul can be found in Part C of this Chapter.

The following repair procedures are based on the assumption that the engine is installed in the vehicle. If the engine has been removed from the vehicle and mounted on a stand, many of the steps outlined in this Part of Chapter 2 will not apply.

The Specifications included in this Part of Chapter 2 apply only to the procedures contained in this Part. Part C of Chapter 2 contains the Specifications necessary for cylinder head and engine block rebuilding.

2   Repair operations possible with the engine in the vehicle

Many major repair operations can be accomplished without removing the engine from the vehicle.

Clean the engine compartment and the exterior of the engine with some type of degreaser before any work is done. It will make the job easier and help keep dirt out of the internal areas of the engine.

Depending on the components involved, it may be helpful to remove the hood to improve access to the engine as repairs are performed (refer to Chapter 11 if necessary). Cover the fenders to prevent damage to the paint. Special pads are available, but an old bedspread or blanket will also work.

If vacuum, exhaust, oil or coolant leaks develop, indicating a need for gasket or seal replacement, the repairs can generally be made with the engine in the vehicle. The intake and exhaust manifold gaskets, oil pan gasket, crankshaft oil seals and cylinder head gaskets are all accessible with the engine in place.

Exterior engine components, such as the intake and exhaust manifolds, the oil pan, the oil pump, the water pump (see Chapter 3), the starter motor, the alternator, the distributor (see Chapter 5) and the fuel system components (see Chapter 4) can be removed for repair with the engine in place.

Since the cylinder heads can be removed without pulling the engine, valve component servicing can also be accomplished with the engine in the vehicle. Replacement of the camshafts, timing belt and sprockets is also possible with the engine in the vehicle.

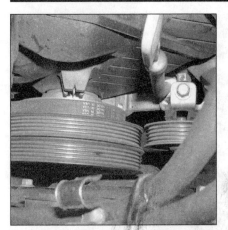

3.6 Align the TDC mark with the notch in the pointer

4.5a Disconnect the connector (arrow) and move this harness . . .

4.5b . . . and this one at the rear of the valve cover

In extreme cases caused by a lack of necessary equipment, repair or replacement of piston rings, pistons, connecting rods and rod bearings is possible with the engine in the vehicle. However, this practice is not recommended because of the cleaning and preparation work that must be done to the components involved.

3 Top Dead Center (TDC) for number one piston - locating

Refer to illustration 3.6
Note: *Although this engine does not have a distributor, timing marks on the crankshaft damper and a stationary pointer on the engine front cover will help you to locate Top Dead Center (TDC) for cylinders 1 and 5.*
1   Top Dead Center (TDC) is the highest point in the cylinder that each piston reaches as it travels upward when the crankshaft turns. Each piston reaches TDC on the compression stroke and on the exhaust stroke, but TDC generally refers to piston position on the compression stroke.
2   Positioning one or more pistons at TDC is an essential part of many procedures such as camshaft removal and timing belt replacement.
3   To place any piston at TDC, turn the crankshaft using one of the methods described below. When you look at the front of the engine, crankshaft rotation is clockwise. **Warning:** *Before using any of the following methods to turn the crankshaft, be sure the transmission is in neutral (manual) or park (automatic). Also deactivate the ignition system to prevent accidental starting.*

a) *The best way to turn the crankshaft is to use a socket and breaker bar on the crankshaft damper bolt on the front of the crankshaft.*
b) *You also can use a remote starter switch. Follow the instructions included with the switch. Operate the remote switch in short intervals until the piston is close to TDC. Then use a socket and breaker bar for the final rotation to TDC.*

c) *If an assistant is available to operate the ignition switch in short intervals, you can rotate the crankshaft until the piston is close to TDC. Then use a socket and breaker bar for the final rotation to TDC.*
4   Remove the spark plug from number 1 cylinder and install a compression gauge in its place.
5   Rotate the crankshaft by one of the methods described in Step 3, until a compression reading is indicated on the gauge. The piston should be approaching TDC.
6   Continue turning the crankshaft with a socket and breaker bar until the TDC mark aligns with the notch in the front cover pointer **(see illustration)**. At this point number one cylinder is at TDC on the compression stroke. If the marks aligned but there was no compression, the piston was on the exhaust stroke. Continue rotating the engine until compression is indicated.
7   If you go past TDC, rotate the engine backwards (counterclockwise) until the timing marks indicate that the piston is before TDC. Then rotate the crankshaft clockwise until the marks align. Final rotation should always be clockwise.
8   After the number one piston is at TDC on the compression stroke, TDC for any of the remaining cylinders can be located by turning the crankshaft and following the firing order (refer to the Specifications). Divide the crankshaft pulley into three equal sections with chalk marks at three points, each indicat-

ing 120 degrees of crankshaft rotation. For example, rotating the engine 120-degrees past TDC for number one piston will place the engine at TDC for cylinder number 4.

4 Valve covers - removal and installation

Removal
1   Disconnect the cable from the negative terminal of the battery. **Caution:** *The radio in your vehicle is equipped with an anti-theft system. Make sure you have the correct activation code before disconnecting the battery.*
2   Remove the fuel rail covers **(see illustration 5.4)**.

Left side
Refer to illustrations 4.5a, 4.5b and 4.6
3   Remove the EGR pipe.
4   Remove the ignition coils from the spark plugs (see Chapter 1) and lay them out of the way. Mark them clearly with pieces of masking tape to prevent confusion during installation.
5   Detach the wiring harnesses and hoses that rest on the valve cover **(see illustrations)**. These include the following:

a) *CRANK/CYL sensor connector*
b) *Throttle Position Sensor (TPS) connector*
c) *Knock sensor connector*
6   Remove the valve cover bolts and nuts

4.6 Left valve cover retaining bolts (arrows)

and detach the valve cover **(see illustration).**
Caution: *If the cover is stuck to the head, bump one end with a block of wood and a hammer to jar it loose. If that doesn't work, try to slip a flexible putty knife between the head and cover to break the gasket seal. Don't pry at the cover-to-head joint or damage to the sealing surfaces may occur (leading to oil leaks in the future).*

Right side
Refer to illustrations 4.8a, 4.8b, 4.8c, 4.8d and 4.8e

7　Refer to Chapter 5 for removal of the ignition coils.

8　Disconnect the air inlet pipe and any electrical connectors necessary to move wiring harnesses out of the way **(see illustrations)**. Move the air conditioning hose if necessary to provide clearance for valve cover removal. **Warning:** *The air conditioning system is under high pressure. Don't disconnect any air conditioning hoses or fittings until the system has been discharged by a dealer service department or air conditioning shop (see Chapter 3).*

9　Remove the valve cover bolts and nuts and remove the valve cover.

Installation

10　The mating surfaces of each cylinder head and valve cover must be perfectly clean when the covers are installed. Use a gasket scraper to remove all traces of sealant and old gasket material, then clean the mating surfaces with lacquer thinner or acetone. If there's sealant or oil on the mating surfaces when the cover is installed, oil leaks may develop.

11　If necessary, clean the mounting bolt and nut threads with a die to remove any corrosion and restore damaged threads. Make sure the threaded holes in the head are clean - run a tap into them to remove corrosion and restore damaged threads.

12　The gaskets should be mated to the covers before the covers are installed. Apply a bead of RTV sealant to the front and rear camshaft towers where the corners of the gasket contact them, then position the gas-

4.8a　Right valve cover details

1　*Vacuum pipe and wiring harness*
2　*Ground wire (secured by valve cover bolt)*
3　*Air conditioning line*
4　*Wiring harness*
5　*Breather hose*

4.8b　Vacuum pipe assembly bolts (arrows)

4.8c　You'll need to move this wiring harness (arrow)

ket firmly inside the groove around the cover.
13　Install the round seal on top of each spark plug well.
14　Carefully position the cover on the head and install the bolts.
15　Tighten the bolts and nuts in three or four steps to the torque listed in this Chapter's Specifications.
17　The remaining installation steps are the reverse of removal.
18　Start the engine and check carefully for oil leaks as the engine warms up.

5　Intake manifold - removal and installation

Removal
Refer to illustrations 5.4, 5.6a, 5.6b, 5.6c, 5.6d, 5.6e, 5.7, 5.10a, 5.10b and 5.12

1　Relieve the fuel pressure (see Chapter 4) and then disconnect the negative cable from the battery. **Caution:** *The radio in your vehicle is equipped with an anti-theft system. Make sure you have the correct activation*

4.8d　Disconnect the breather hose (right arrow) and ground wire (left arrow)

4.8e　Right valve cover bolts

5.4　Fuel rail cover bolts (arrows)

5.6a Intake manifold disconnection points

1   *EGR valve (pipe and vacuum hose)*
2   *Fast idle thermo valve*
3   *Engine coolant temperature sensor*
4   *Idle air control valve*
5   *Air boost valve*
6   *Intake air temperature sensor*
7   *Throttle cables*
8   *Throttle body*

5.6b The oil pressure connector (left arrow) and ground wire (right arrow) are inside the front wiring harness cover

5.6c Disconnect the hose (upper arrow) and IAT electrical connector (lower arrow)

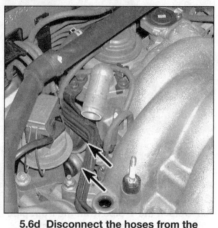

5.6d Disconnect the hoses from the intake air bypass diaphragm (arrows)

5.6e Disconnect the hoses from the fast idle thermo valve (arrow)

code before disconnecting the battery.
2   Drain the coolant into a clean container (see Chapter 1).
3   Remove the intake air duct (see Chapter 4).
4   Remove the fuel rail covers **(see illustration)**.
5   Remove the ignition coils and spark plugs (see Chapter 1).
6   Clearly label, then detach all wires, hoses and brackets attached to the intake manifold **(see illustrations)**. Once the vacuum hoses are disconnected, remove the vacuum pipe assembly.
7   Remove the air inlet pipe from the right side of the engine **(see illustration)**.
8   Disconnect the accelerator cable from the throttle body (see Chapter 4).
9   Detach the air suction pipe from the back of the intake manifold.

10   Remove the mounting nuts/bolts **(see illustration)**, then detach the manifold from the engine. If it's stuck, don't pry between the gasket mating surfaces or damage may result **(see illustration)**.
11   Carefully use a scraper to remove all traces of old gasket material and sealant from the manifold and cylinder heads, then clean the mating surfaces with lacquer thinner or acetone.

5.7 Remove the secondary air inlet pipe

5.10a Remove the intake manifold mounting bolts/nuts (arrows)

5.10b Carefully pry the manifold loose, using external tabs such as this

5.12 Air bypass valve mounting bolts/nuts (arrows)

6.5a The right front exhaust pipe or warm-up catalyst is secured to the manifold with nuts (upper nut hidden)

6.5b The left front exhaust pipe or warm-up catalyst is secured to the manifold with nuts (upper nut hidden)

6.6 Detach the Y-pipe from the front pipe or warm-up catalyst on each side

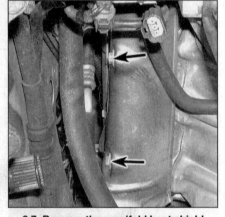

6.7 Remove the manifold heat shield bolts (arrows)

12   If necessary, remove the bolts/nuts and separate the manifold and bypass valve body **(see illustration)**. Clean the valve body and reassemble with new gaskets and tighten securely.

Installation

13   Install new gaskets, then position the manifold on the engine. Make sure the gaskets haven't shifted and install the nuts/bolts.
14   Tighten the nuts/bolts, in three equal steps, to the torque listed in this Chapter's Specifications. Work from the center out towards the ends to avoid warping the manifold.
15   Install the remaining parts in the reverse order of removal.
16   Refill the cooling system. Run the engine and check for fuel, vacuum and coolant leaks.

6   Exhaust manifolds - removal and installation

Refer to illustrations 6.5a, 6.5b, 6.6, 6.7 and 6.8
Warning: *The engine must be completely cool before starting this procedure.*

1   Disconnect the cable from the negative terminal of the battery. **Caution:** *The radio in your vehicle is equipped with an anti-theft system. Make sure you have the correct activation code before disconnecting the battery.*
2   Spray penetrating oil on the exhaust manifold fasteners and allow it to soak in.
3   Block the rear wheels to prevent the vehicle from rolling. Set the parking brake.
4   Raise the front of the vehicle and support it securely on jackstands. Remove the lower splash guard.
5   Remove the nuts that secure each manifold to the front exhaust pipe or warmup catalytic converter on 1994 and later GS models **(see illustrations)**.

6   Remove the nuts that secure the rear end of each front exhaust pipe or warmup catalyst to the exhaust Y-pipe **(see illustrations)**.
7   Remove the heat shield from each manifold **(see illustration)**. Remove the Pulsed Air Injection (PAIR) pipe, if removing the left exhaust manifold.
8   Remove the self-locking nuts retaining the manifold to the cylinder head and slip it off the mounting studs **(see illustration)**.
9   Carefully inspect the manifold and fasteners for cracks and damage. If the manifold is cracked, replace it with a new one.
10   Use a scraper to remove any traces of old gasket material and carbon deposits from

6.8 Exhaust manifold bolts/nuts (viewed from below; upper nuts hidden)

7.4a Remove the wiring harness cover from the right front of the engine . . .

7.4b . . . and from the left front

7.9 Mark the direction of rotation on the timing belt

7.10a Right camshaft timing marks (arrows) - the pointer on the cover is colored yellow, while the TDC mark on the sprocket is red

7.10b Left camshaft timing marks (arrows) - the cover mark is yellow and the sprocket mark is blue

7.11 Hold the crankshaft pulley with a chain wrench and remove the pulley bolt

the manifold and cylinder head mating surfaces. If the gasket was leaking, have the manifold checked for warpage at an automotive machine shop and resurfaced if necessary.
11   Position a new gasket over the cylinder head studs.
12   Install the manifold and thread the mounting nuts into place.
13   Working from the center out, tighten the nuts to the torque listed in this Chapter's Specifications in three equal steps.
14   Reinstall the remaining parts in the reverse order of removal. Use anti-seize compound on all bolts and nuts.
15   Run the engine and check for exhaust leaks.

7   Timing belt and sprockets - removal, inspection and installation

Removal

Refer to illustrations 7.4a, 7.4b, 7.9, 7.10a, 7.10b, 7.11, 7.12a, 7.12b, 7.12c, 7.13 and 7.14

1   Disconnect the cable from the negative terminal of the battery. **Caution:** *The radio in your vehicle is equipped with an anti-theft*

system. *Make sure you have the correct activation code before disconnecting the battery.*
2   If you're working on a 1993 or later model, support the engine safely and remove the center mount, bracket and damper (see Section 17).
3   If the vehicle is equipped with a Traction Control System (TCS), detach the TCS control electrical connectors and remove the intake air duct (see Chapter 4).
4   Remove the wiring harness covers from the front of the engine **(see illustrations)** and detach the harness. Disconnect the oil pressure switch connector and engine ground cable from the front of the engine.
5   If you're working on a 1991 or 1992 model, remove the breather pipe and vacuum pipe bracket from the right front of the engine.
6   Remove the drivebelts (see Chapter 1) and the air conditioning idler pulley.
7   Remove the upper timing belt covers **(see illustration 7.4a and 7.4b).**
8   Remove the spark plugs to make it easier to turn the crankshaft (see Chapter 1). Position the number one piston at TDC (see Section 3).
9   If you intend to re-use the belt, mark the belt to indicate the direction of rotation **(see illustration).**

7.12a Remove the timing belt lower cover

10   Make sure the timing marks are properly aligned **(see illustrations).**
11   Remove the crankshaft pulley **(see illustration).** To keep the crankshaft from turning, hold the pulley with a chain wrench while you loosen the crank pulley bolt. **Note:** *When the crankshaft pulley bolt is loosened, the position of the timing marks on the crankshaft pulley and the camshafts may be disturbed. Check and align them again. Temporarily reinstall the crankshaft pulley bolt to turn the crankshaft.*
12   Remove the lower timing belt cover **(see**

2B

7.12b Crankshaft sprocket timing marks

7.12c Loosen the timing belt tensioner bolt (arrow)

7.13 Prevent the camshaft from turning with this special tool or by inserting a screwdriver through a hole in the sprocket while you loosen the bolts, then pull the sprocket off

7.14 Carefully work the crankshaft sprocket off without damaging anything

7.21 Install the outer timing belt guide as shown

tion: *If you feel any resistance, back up and recheck the belt timing. Do not force the crankshaft to turn or engine damage will occur!*

23   Install the lower timing belt cover.

24   Slip the drivebelt pulley onto the crankshaft, aligning the pulley keyway with the crankshaft key. Install the bolt and tighten it to the torque listed in this Chapter's Specifications. Use the method described in Step 11 to keep the crankshaft from turning.

25   Loosen the tensioner bolt again, allow the tensioner to settle against the belt, and retighten the bolt.

26   Recheck the timing marks. **Caution:** *If the timing marks are not aligned exactly as shown, repeat the timing belt installation procedure. DO NOT start the engine until you're absolutely certain that the timing belt is installed correctly. Serious and costly engine damage could occur if the belt is installed wrong.* **Note:** *Both upper timing belt covers have inspection holes (remove the rubber plugs) that allows checking the camshaft sprocket timing marks even when the covers are in place.*

27   Reinstall the remaining parts in the reverse order of removal.

8   Crankshaft front oil seal - replacement

Refer to illustrations 8.2 and 8.4

1   Remove the timing belt and crankshaft sprocket (see Section 7).

2   Carefully pry the seal out of the engine with a screwdriver or seal removal tool **(see illustration)**. If you use a screwdriver, don't scratch the housing bore or damage the crankshaft (if the crankshaft is damaged, the new seal will end up leaking).

3   Clean the oil seal bore and coat the outer edge of the new seal with a small amount of engine oil to ease installation. Apply multi-purpose grease to the seal lip.

4   Using a socket with an outside diameter

illustration). Slip the timing belt guide off the crankshaft sprocket, noting how it's installed. Also note the alignment of the crankshaft sprocket timing marks **(see illustration).** Loosen the timing belt tensioner bolt, move the tensioner (use a flat screwdriver against the tensioner bracket, **not** the belt) to relieve tension on the belt and retighten the bolt. Remove the timing belt **(see illustration).**

13   The camshaft sprockets can be removed at this point, if they are damaged or to replace the oil seals **(see illustration).** Remove the keys from the shafts so they don't fall out and get lost.

14   If it's worn or damaged, or if you're replacing the crankshaft front oil seal, the crankshaft sprocket can now be removed. If it won't come off by hand, carefully pry it off **(see illustration).** Also remove the inner timing belt guide, noting how it's installed.

Inspection

15   Refer to Chapter 2, Part A for the timing belt inspection procedure.

16   If the engine has high mileage, now is the best time to remove and inspect the water pump (see Chapter 3).

Installation

Refer to illustration 7.21

17   Remove all dirt and oil from the timing

belt area.

18   If any of the timing belt sprockets were removed, install them now with their keys and tighten the bolts to the torque listed in this Chapter's Specifications.

19   If removed, install the inner timing belt guide over the crankshaft sprocket with the chamfered edge facing away from the belt. Also install the crankshaft sprocket.

20   Recheck the position of the timing marks **(see illustrations 7.10a, 7.10b and 7.12b).** Install the timing belt, starting at the crankshaft sprocket and tensioner pulley, then left camshaft sprocket, water pump, and right camshaft sprocket. For ease of installation, temporarily advance the right camshaft sprocket about one-half tooth. If you're re-using the original belt, the arrow you made in Step 9 should point in the direction of normal rotation.

21   Install the outer timing belt guide over the crankshaft sprocket with the chamfered edge facing away from the belt **(see illustration).**

22   Loosen the tensioner adjustment bolt, allow the tensioner to move into position and retighten the bolt.

22   Turn the crankshaft slowly six revolutions clockwise using a socket and breaker bar on the crankshaft pulley bolt to seat the belt, then return to TDC. Recheck the alignment of cam and crank timing marks. **Cau-**

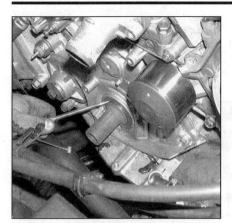

8.2 Carefully pry out the oil seal

8.4 Lubricate the seal lip and tap the new crankshaft seal into place with a large socket or piece of pipe and a hammer

9.5a Remove the mounting bolts from the left timing belt rear cover (arrows) . . .

9.5b . . . and take it off the engine - use a new gasket on installation

9.5c Remove the mounting bolts from the right timing belt rear cover (arrows) . . .

9.5d . . . and take it off the engine - use a new O-ring on installation

2B

slightly smaller than the outside diameter of the seal, carefully drive the new seal into place with a hammer **(see illustration)**. Make sure it's installed squarely and driven in to the same depth as the original. If a socket isn't available, a short section of large-diameter pipe will also work. Check the seal after installation to make sure the garter spring didn't pop out of place.
5   Reinstall the crankshaft sprocket and timing belt (see Section 7).
6   Run the engine and check for oil leaks at the front seal.

9   Rocker arm assemblies - removal, inspection and installation

Note: *While the camshaft bearing caps are off, inspect them, as well as the camshaft bearing journals, as described in Section 10.*

Removal

Refer to illustrations 9.5a, 9.5b, 9.5c, 9.5d, 9.7a and 9.7b

1   Remove the timing belt upper covers (see Section 7).
2   Position the number one piston at Top Dead Center (see Section 3).

9.7a Leave the bolts in the rocker assembly to hold it together while you lift it off the engine

3   Loosen the timing belt tensioner bolt, push the tensioner back then tighten the bolt to relieve tension on the belt (see Section 7).
4   Remove the camshaft sprocket bolts **(see illustration 7.13)**.
5   Remove the camshaft sprockets from the camshafts, then remove the timing belt rear covers from the cylinder heads **(see illustrations)**.
6   Loosen the camshaft and rocker shaft

9.7b Install new O-rings on the spark plug wells (arrows)

holder bolts 1/4-turn at a time, in the reverse of the tightening sequence, until the spring pressure is relieved **(see illustration 9.15)**. Loosen all of the bolts completely, but don't remove them; you'll need them in place to hold the rocker assembly together while you lift it off the head.
7   Lift the rocker arms and shaft assembly from the cylinder head **(see illustration)**. Locate the O-rings around the spark plug wells - they may have stuck to the undersides of the camshaft holders **(see illustration)**.

9.8a The rocker arms are stamped with location letters A or B

9.8b Make sure the rocker arms are returned to their proper positions

9.9 Inspect the rocker arm and lash adjuster contact surfaces (A) - be sure to reinstall the wave washers (B) in their correct locations

9.10 Install a new O-ring (arrow) whenever a lash adjuster is removed

Inspection

Refer to illustrations 9.8a, 9.8b, 9.9 and 9.10

8   If you wish to disassemble and inspect the rocker arm assembly, (a good idea as long as you have them off), remove the retaining bolts and slip the rocker arms, springs and bearing caps off the shafts. Mark the relationship of the shafts to the bearing caps and keep the parts in order. They must be reassembled in the same positions they were removed from. There are two different types of intake rocker shaft, two types of intake rocker arms and two types of exhaust rocker arms **(see illustrations)**.

9   Thoroughly clean the parts and inspect them for wear and damage. Check the rocker arm faces that contact the camshaft and the tips of the hydraulic lash adjusters **(see illustration)**. Check the surfaces of the shafts that the rocker arms ride on, as well as the bearing surfaces inside the rocker arms, for scoring and excessive wear. Replace any parts that are damaged or excessively worn. Also, make sure the oil holes in the shafts are not plugged.

10   If the lash adjusters show signs of wear, pull them out of the rocker arms **(see illustration)**. Once a lash adjuster has been removed, replace the O-ring.

Installation

Refer to illustration 9.15

11   Place each lash adjuster with its open end upward in a container of clean 10W-30 engine oil. Insert a thin, stiff wire into the open end of the lash adjuster, then pump the check ball up and down until bubbles stop emerging from the lash adjuster.

12   Install the lash adjusters in their rocker arms (if they were removed).

13   Lubricate all components with assembly lube or engine oil and reassemble the shafts. When installing the rocker arms, shafts and springs, note the markings and the difference between the left and right side parts.

14   Coat the cam lobes and journals with camshaft installation lubricant. Apply anaerobic-type sealant to the cylinder head contact surfaces of camshaft holders 1 and 7 and install the rocker arm assembly.

15   Tighten the camshaft bearing cap bolts a little at a time, in the proper sequence **(see illustration)** to the torque listed in this Chapter's Specifications.

16   The remainder of installation is the reverse of removal.

17   Run the engine and check for oil leaks and proper operation.

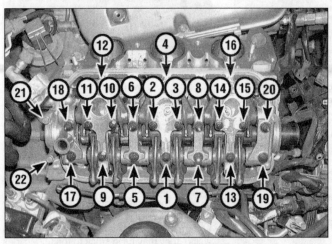

9.15 Rocker assembly TIGHTENING sequence

10.1 Set up a dial indicator against the end of the camshaft and pry the camshaft back-and-forth to measure endplay

10.4 Pull the end plug off the rear of the cylinder head and the oil seal off the front of the camshaft

10 Camshafts - removal, inspection and installation

Endplay and runout check

Refer to illustration 10.1

1   To check camshaft endplay:

a) *Perform this check while the camshaft is still secured by the rocker assembly.*

b) *Mount a dial indicator on the head* **(see illustration).**

c) *Using a large screwdriver as a lever at the opposite end, move the camshaft forward-and-backward and note the dial indicator reading.*

d) *Compare the reading with the endplay listed in this Chapter's Specifications.*

e) *If the indicated reading is higher, either the camshaft or the head is worn. Replace parts as necessary.*

2   To check camshaft runout:

a) *Support the camshaft with a pair of V-blocks and set up a dial indicator with the plunger resting against the center bearing journal on the camshaft.*

b) *Rotate the camshaft and note the indicated runout.*

c) *Compare the results to the camshaft runout listed in this Chapter's Specifications.*

d) *If the indicated runout exceeds the specified runout, replace the camshaft.*

Removal

Refer to illustration 10.4

3   Remove the valve covers, timing belt, sprockets and inner covers, and the rocker assemblies (see Sections 4, 7 and 9).

4   Remove the rear camshaft sealing plug **(see illustration)**. Note the position of the sprocket locating dowel pin for reassembly and lift out the camshaft.

5   Remove the oil seal by slipping it off the end of the camshaft.

Inspection

6   Refer to Chapter 2, Part A and check the

10.13 Seat the seal in its bore with a hammer and socket

camshaft lobes and bearing journals. Be sure to use the Specifications in this Part of Chapter 2 for the V6 engine.

Installation

Refer to illustration 10.13

7   Apply camshaft installation lube to the contact surfaces of all moving parts.

8   Install the camshaft front seal with its spring side inward and the rear camshaft sealing plug **(see illustration 10.4).**

9   Apply camshaft installation lube to the camshaft lobes, bearing journals and thrust faces.

10   Reinstall the rocker assembly (which includes the camshaft holders) in the reverse order of removal.

11   Install the other camshaft in the same manner (if removed).

12   Install the valve cover(s).

13   Make sure the camshaft front seal is seated by tapping against it with a socket or piece of pipe the same diameter as the seal **(see illustration)**.

14   The remainder of installation is the reverse of the removal steps.

11 Valve springs, retainers and seals - replacement

Refer to illustrations 11.5, 11.8, 11.9 and 11.17

Note: *Broken valve springs and defective valve stem seals can be replaced without removing the cylinder heads. Two special tools and a compressed air source are normally required to perform this operation, so read through this Section carefully and rent or buy the tools before beginning the job.*

1   Refer to Section 4 and remove the valve cover.

2   Remove the spark plug from the cylinder that has the defective component. If all of the valve stem seals are being replaced, all of the spark plugs should be removed.

3   Turn the crankshaft until the piston in the affected cylinder is at top dead center on the compression stroke (refer to Section 3 for

11.5 This is what the air hose adapter that threads into the spark plug hole looks like - they're commonly available from auto parts stores

instructions). If you're replacing all of the valve stem seals, begin with cylinder number one and work on the valves for one cylinder at a time. Move from cylinder-to-cylinder following the firing order sequence (see this Chapter's Specifications).

4   Remove the rocker arm assembly (see Section 9).

5   Thread an adapter into the spark plug hole and connect an air hose from a compressed air source to it **(see illustration)**. Most auto parts stores can supply the air hose adapter. **Note:** *Many cylinder compression gauges utilize a screw-in fitting that may work with your air hose quick-disconnect fitting.*

6   Apply compressed air to the cylinder. **Warning:** *The piston may be forced down by compressed air, causing the crankshaft to turn suddenly. If the wrench used when positioning the number one piston at TDC is still attached to the bolt in the crankshaft nose, it could cause damage or injury when the crankshaft moves.*

7   The valves should be held in place by the air pressure. Lightly tap on the top of each retainer with a socket and hammer (this will loosen the valve keepers and retainers so they can be easily removed).

8   Stuff shop rags into the cylinder head holes around the valves to prevent parts and tools from falling into the engine, then use a valve spring compressor to compress the

11.8 Compress the valve spring using a valve spring compressor . . .

2B

11.9 . . . then remove the keepers with a small magnet

11.17 Apply a small dab of grease to each keeper as shown here before installation - it'll hold them in place on the valve stem as the spring is released

12.13 Carefully pry the head loose, using an external projection

spring **(see illustration)**.

9   Remove the keepers with small needle-nose pliers or a magnet **(see illustration)**.

10   Remove the spring retainer and the valve spring, then remove the valve guide seal. **Note:** *If air pressure fails to hold the valve in the closed position during this operation, the valve face or seat is probably damaged. If so, the cylinder head will have to be removed for additional repair operations.*

11   Wrap a rubber band or tape around the top of the valve stem so the valve won't fall into the combustion chamber, then release the air pressure.

12   Inspect the valve stem for damage. Rotate the valve in the guide and check the end for eccentric movement, which would indicate that the valve is bent.

13   Move the valve up-and-down in the guide and make sure it doesn't bind. If the valve stem binds, either the valve is bent or the guide is damaged. In either case, the head will have to be removed for repair.

14   Reapply air pressure to the cylinder to retain the valve in the closed position, then remove the tape or rubber band from the valve stem.

15   Lubricate the valve stem with clean engine oil and install a new guide seal. **Note:** *The springs on the valve stem seals are color coded; white for the intake valves and black for the exhaust valves.*

16   Install the valve spring in position over the valve. Place the end of the spring with the closely wound coils toward the cylinder head.

17   Install the valve spring retainer. Compress the valve spring and carefully position the keepers in the groove. Apply a small dab of grease to the inside of each keeper to hold it in place **(see illustration)**.

18   Remove the pressure from the spring tool and make sure the keepers are seated.

19   Disconnect the air hose and remove the adapter from the spark plug hole.

20   Refer to Section 9 and install the rocker arm assembly.

21   Refer to Section 4 and install the valve cover.

22   Install the spark plug(s) and hook up the

ignition coil packs.

23   Start and run the engine, then check for oil leaks and unusual sounds coming from the valve cover area.

12 Cylinder heads - removal and installation

Caution: *Allow the engine to cool completely before beginning this procedure.*

Removal

Refer to illustration 12.13

1   Relieve the fuel pressure (see Chapter 4).

2   Disconnect the cable from the negative terminal of the battery. **Caution:** *The radio in your vehicle is equipped with an anti-theft system. Make sure you have the correct activation code before disconnecting the battery.*

3   If you're removing the left cylinder head, remove the battery (see Chapter 5). Also remove the bolts and reposition the engine compartment fuse box.

4   Disconnect the engine ground cables from the cylinder head and engine block.

5   Drain the cooling system, including both block drains (see Chapter 1).

6   Disconnect the brake booster vacuum hose (see Chapter 9).

7   Remove the intake manifold (see Section 5).

8   Remove the exhaust manifolds (see Section 6).

9   Detach the timing belt, camshaft sprockets and inner timing belt cover (see Sections 7 and 9).

10   Disconnect the EGR tube from the back of both cylinder heads.

11   Remove the camshaft from the head you intend to remove (see Section 10).

12   Using a socket, loosen the cylinder head bolts in 1/4-turn increments until they can be removed by hand. Loosen them in a sequence opposite that of the tightening sequence **(see illustration 12.24)**.

13   Lift the cylinder head off the engine

block. If the head is stuck, pry against an external casting protrusion **(see illustration)**. **Caution:** *Don't pry between the head and block. The gasket surfaces may be damaged and leaks could result.*

14   Locate the dowels (two per head). They may stay in the block or come off with the head. Remove the two oil control orifices by threading a 6mm bolt into them and pulling.

15   Check the cylinder heads for warpage as shown in Chapter 2C.

Installation

Refer to illustrations 12.21 and 12.24

16   The mating surfaces of the cylinder heads and block must be perfectly clean when the heads are installed.

17   Use a gasket scraper to remove all traces of carbon and old gasket material. Be careful not to gouge the delicate aluminum. Clean the mating surfaces with lacquer thinner or acetone. If there's oil on the mating surfaces when the head is installed, the gasket may not seal correctly and leaks could develop. When working on the block, stuff the cylinders with clean shop rags to keep out debris. Use a vacuum cleaner to remove material that falls into the cylinders.

18   Check the block and head mating surfaces for nicks, deep scratches and other damage. If damage is slight, it can be removed with a file; if it's excessive, machining may be the only alternative.

19   Use a tap of the correct size to chase the threads in the head bolt holes, then clean the holes with compressed air - make sure that nothing remains in the holes. **Warning:** *Wear eye protection when using compressed air!*

20   Mount each bolt in a vise and run a die down the threads to remove corrosion and restore the threads. Dirt, corrosion, sealant and damaged threads will affect torque readings.

21   Clean the oil-control orifices thoroughly and reinstall them with new O-rings. Position the new gaskets over the oil-control jets and locating dowels in the block **(see illustration)**.

22   Carefully set the head on the block with-

12.21 There's an R mark on the right head gasket; be sure the dowels and oil control orifices are located correctly

A   Dowel locations
B   Oil control orifice locations

12.24 Cylinder head bolt TIGHTENING sequence

out disturbing the gasket.

23   Before installing the head bolts, apply a small amount of clean engine oil to the threads.

24   Install the bolts and special washers and tighten them finger tight. Following the recommended sequence **(see illustration)**, tighten the bolts to the torque listed in this Chapter's Specifications in three steps.

25   Repeat the entire procedure to install the other cylinder head, if necessary.

26   The remaining installation steps are the reverse of removal.

27   Refill the cooling system, change the oil and filter (see Chapter 1), run the engine and check for leaks.

13   Oil pan and oil pick-up - removal and installation

Removal

Refer to illustrations 13.13, 13.14, 13.15 and 13.16

1   Disconnect the cables from the negative terminal of the battery. **Caution:** *The radio in your vehicle is equipped with an anti-theft system. Make sure you have the correct activation code before disconnecting the battery.*

2   Block the rear wheels and set the parking brake. Raise the front of the vehicle and support it securely on jackstands.

3   Remove the splash shield from beneath the engine. Remove the stiffener brace from beneath the steering gear (see Chapter 10).

4   Drain the engine oil and remove the oil filter (see Chapter 1).

5   Remove the damper fork from the bottom of each suspension strut and separate the lower arm balljoints (see Chapter 10).

6   Separate the inner ends of the driveaxles from the differential (see Chapter 8). **Caution:** *Support the driveaxles so they don't hang by their own weight.*

13.13 Use a soft-face hammer to break the oil pan loose

7   Drain the cooling system and differential (see Chapter 1).

8   Remove the vehicle speed sensor (VSS) (see Chapter 6).

9   Remove the stiffener brace located between the front and rear engine crossmembers (just to the right of the differential).

10   Remove the differential and intermediate shaft (see Chapter 8).

11   Unbolt the air conditioning compressor from the engine and move it out of the way without disconnecting any hoses (see Chapter 3). Support the compressor so it doesn't hang by the hoses.

12   Detach the lower bellhousing cover, if equipped.

13   Loosen the bolts/nuts in the reverse of the tightening sequence **(see illustration 13.22)** and lower the oil pan. The bolts adjacent to the driveaxle can be removed with a 1/4-inch drive socket, extension and ratchet. If the pan is stuck, break it loose with a soft-face hammer **(see illustration)**. Don't damage the mating surfaces of the pan and block or oil leaks could develop.

14   Locate the pickup and pump fitting O-

13.14 Be sure the oil pickup and pump O-rings (arrows) are in place before installing the oil pan

13.15 Oil pan baffle plate locations (arrows)

rings **(see illustration)**. They may have stayed on the engine or come off with the oil pan.

15   Unbolt the baffle from the inside of the oil pan **(see illustration)**.

13.16 Oil pickup screen bolt locations (arrows)

13.22 Oil pan bolt TIGHTENING sequence

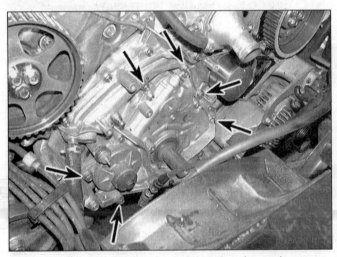

14.3 Oil pump housing bolt locations (arrows)

14.4 Locate the O-rings (A) and remove the screws from the pump cover (B)

16   Unbolt the oil pickup from inside the pan (see illustration).

Installation

Refer to illustration 13.22

17   Use a scraper to remove all traces of old sealant from the block and oil pan. Be careful not to gouge the delicate aluminum block. Clean the mating surfaces with lacquer thinner or acetone.

18   Make sure the threaded bolt holes in the block are clean.

19   Check the oil pan flange for distortion, particularly around the bolt holes. If necessary, place the pan on a block of wood and use a hammer to flatten and restore the gasket surface.

20   Inspect the oil pump pick-up screen assembly for damage and a blocked strainer. If the pick-up and/or baffle was removed, install it now. Use new O-rings on the pick-up and pan. Tighten the fasteners to the torque listed in this Chapter's Specifications.

21   Apply a bead of RTV sealant to the mating flange of the oil pan. Be sure to route the bead of sealant around the inside edge of the

bolt holes. **Note:** *Install the oil pan within 15 minutes of applying the sealant.*

22   Carefully position the oil pan on the engine block and install the bolts/nuts. Tighten them to the torque listed in this Chapter's Specifications in three steps, following the specified sequence (see illustration).

23   The remainder of installation is the reverse of removal. Be sure to add oil and install a new oil filter. **Note:** *Wait 30 minutes (to allow the sealant to cure) before adding oil.*

24   Run the engine and check for oil pressure and leaks.

14   Oil pump - removal and installation

Removal

Refer to illustrations 14.3, 14.4 and 14.5

1   Remove the timing belt and crankshaft sprocket (see Section 7).

2   Remove the oil pan and oil pickup (see Section 13).

3   Remove the bolts and detach the oil pump housing from the engine (see illustration). You may have to pry carefully between the main bearing cap and the pump housing with a screwdriver.

4   Use a large Phillips screwdriver to remove the screws holding the pump cover to the rear of the housing (see illustration). **Note:** *It may be necessary to remove the screws with an impact screwdriver.*

5   Lift the cover off and inspect the pump rotors (see illustration). If any wear or damage is evident, replace the pump. Check the rotor clearances with feeler gauges and compare to this Chapter's Specifications.

6   Use a scraper to remove any traces of old sealant from the pump body and engine block, being careful not to damage the delicate aluminum.

Installation

7   Replace the old crankshaft oil seal (see Section 8). Apply multi-purpose grease to the seal lip.

8   Pack the pump cavity with petroleum jelly and install the cover. Apply a non-hard-

14.5 Inspect the condition of the rotors and the inside of the cover - with feeler gauges, measure the clearances at A (outer rotor to housing) and B (inner rotor to outer rotor), lay a straightedge across the face of the pump housing and measure the housing-to-rotor axial clearance and compare to Specifications

15.2 Remove the bolts (arrows) with a 12-point socket

ening thread locking compound to the threads and tighten the screws securely following a criss-cross pattern.

9   Use acetone or lacquer thinner and a clean rag to remove all traces of oil from the gasket surfaces.

10   Apply a bead of sealant to the oil pump flange and the 8-mm x 1.25 x 45-mm bolt. Avoid using an excessive amount of sealant, especially around oil passages and bolt holes. Parts must be assembled within five minutes of sealant application, otherwise the material must be removed and reapplied. Wherever O-rings are employed, use new ones.

11   Engage the flat surfaces on the oil pump drive rotor with the matching flats on the crankshaft and slide the pump into place.

12   Install the pump mounting bolts in their original locations and tighten them to the torque listed in this Chapter's Specifications in a criss-cross pattern.

13   Reinstall the remaining parts in the reverse order of removal.

14   Wait 30 minutes (to allow the sealant to cure), then add oil, start the engine and check for oil leaks and pressure.

15   Recheck the engine oil level.

15 Flywheel/driveplate - removal and installation

Refer to illustration 15.2

1   Remove the transmission (see Chapter 7). If the front pump seal/O-ring on an automatic is leaking, now would be a very good time to replace it.

2   Remove the bolts that secure the flywheel/driveplate to the crankshaft (see illustration). Hold the crankshaft from turning with a large screwdriver wedged into the ring gear.

3   Remove the spacer washer and flywheel/driveplate from the crankshaft. Since it's fairly heavy, be sure to support it while removing the last bolt. **Warning:** *The ring gear teeth can be sharp, so wear gloves or handle the driveplate with rags.*

16.2 Carefully pry the rear main seal out - don't damage the surface of the crankshaft or the new seal will leak

4   Clean the flywheel/driveplate and inspect the surface for cracks. Check for worn, cracked or broken ring gear teeth. Use a straightedge to check for warpage.

5   Clean and inspect the mating surfaces of the flywheel/driveplate and the crankshaft. If the crankshaft oil seal is leaking, replace it before reinstalling the flywheel/driveplate.

6   Position the flywheel/driveplate against the crankshaft. Note that offset bolt holes ensure correct installation. Be sure to install the spacer washer with the driveplate.

7   Hold the crankshaft from turning as described above. Working in several stages, tighten the bolts in a criss-cross pattern to the torque listed in this Chapter's Specifications.

8   The remainder of installation is the reverse of the removal procedure.

16 Crankshaft rear oil seal - replacement

Refer to illustrations 16.2 and 16.3

1   The transmission must be removed from the vehicle for this procedure and the driveplate must be separated from the engine. Refer to Chapter 7 and Section 15

16.3 Drive the new seal in squarely

as necessary.

2   The seal can be replaced without removing the oil pan or removing the seal retainer. However, the lip of the seal is quite stiff and it's possible to cock the seal in the retainer bore or damage it during installation. If you want to take the chance, pry out the old seal with a screwdriver (see illustration).

3   Apply multi-purpose grease to the crankshaft seal journal and the lip of the new seal and carefully drive the new seal into place (see illustration). Install the seal with the spring side in. Use a seal driver or if one isn't available, a socket or section of pipe with an outside diameter slightly smaller than that of the seal. The lip is stiff so carefully work it onto the seal journal of the crankshaft. Don't rush it or you may damage the seal.

4   The crankshaft seal replacement method described in Chapter 2C is recommended but requires removal of the oil pan and the seal retainer. If you use this method, you can also measure the clearance between the seal and the bottom of the seal bore, which should be 0.008 to 0.020 inch. The seal should not bottom out. This clearance can't be easily measured with the cover in place on the block.

5   The remaining steps are the reverse of removal.

17.9a Center bracket mounting bolts (inner arrows) and center beam mounting bolts (outer arrows) (rear view)

17.9b The center bracket is mounted in front of the engine (arrow)

17.9c Passenger side engine mount through-bolt

17.9d Driver's side engine mount nut (left arrow) and through-bolt (right arrow)

17.9e Driver's side mid-mount nut and bolts

17 Engine mounts - check and replacement

1   Engine mounts seldom require attention, but broken or deteriorated mounts should be replaced immediately or the added strain placed on the driveline components may cause damage or wear.

Check

2   During the check, the engine must be raised slightly to remove the weight from the mounts. A floor jack (with a block of wood placed on the jack head) can be used, or an engine hoist can be attached to the engine lifting brackets from above. **Warning:** *DO NOT place any part of your body under the engine when it's supported only by a hoist!*

3   You may also need to jack up the vehicle to get at the engine mounts from below. If this is necessary, jack it up and support it securely on jackstands.

4   Check the mount insulators to see if the rubber is cracked, hardened or separated from the metal plates. Sometimes the rubber will split right down the center.

5   Check for relative movement between the mount plates and the engine or frame (use a large screwdriver or prybar to attempt to move the mounts). If movement is noted, lower the engine and tighten the mount fasteners.

6   Rubber preservative should be applied to the insulators to slow deterioration.

Replacement

Refer to illustrations 17.9a, 17.9b, 17.9c, 17.9d, 17.9e and 17.9f

7   Disconnect the cable from the negative terminal of the battery. **Caution:** *If the radio in your vehicle is equipped with an anti-theft system, make sure you have the correct activation code before disconnecting the battery. Raise the vehicle and support it securely on jackstands (if not already done). Support the engine as described in Step 3.*

8   Remove the fasteners, raise the engine with the jack and detach the mount from the frame bracket and engine.

17.9f Passenger side mid-mount nut and bolts

9   Install the new mount, making sure it is correctly positioned in its bracket **(see illustrations)**. Install the fasteners and tighten them securely.

Chapter 2 Part C
General engine overhaul procedures

Contents

2C

Specifications

Integra

General

Cylinder compression pressure	
Standard	184 psi
Minimum	135 psi
Maximum variation between cylinders	28 psi
Oil pressure (hot)	
At idle	10 psi
At 3000 rpm	50 psi

Engine block

Cylinder bore	
Standard	3.1890 to 3.1898 inches
Service limit	3.1917 inches
Cylinder taper limit	0.002 inch
Cylinder out-of-round limit	0.002 inch
Cylinder overbore limit	0.010 inch
Block deck warpage	
B17A, B17A1	
Standard	0.002 inch
Service limit	0.003 inch
B18A, B18A1	
Standard	0.003 inch
Service limit	0.004 inch

Integra (continued)

Pistons and rings

Piston diameter	
Standard	3.1882 to 3.1886 inches
Service limit	3.1878 inches
Diameter measurement point (from bottom)	19/32 inch
Piston to cylinder wall clearance	
Standard	0.0004 to 0.0014 inch
Service limit	0.002 inch maximum
Ring groove clearance	
Compression rings	
Standard	0.002 to 0.003 inch
Service limit	0.005 inch
Ring end gap	
B17A	
Top compression ring	
Standard	0.008 to 0.014 inch
Service limit	0.024 inch
Second compression ring	
Standard	0.016 to 0.022 inch
Service limit	0.028 inch
Oil control ring (Teikoku)	
Standard	0.008 to 0.018 inch
Service limit	0.032 inch
Oil control ring (Riken)	
Standard	0.008 to 0.020 inch
Service limit	0.032 inch
B17A1	
Top compression ring (Teikoku)	
Standard	0.008 to 0.012 inch
Service limit	0.024 inch maximum
Top compression ring (Riken)	
Standard	0.008 to 0.014 inch
Service limit	0.024 inch maximum
Second compression ring	
Standard	0.016 to 0.022 inch
Service limit	0.028 inch maximum
Oil control ring (Teikoku)	
Standard	0.008 to 0.018 inch
Service limit	0.028 inch maximum
Oil control ring (Riken)	
Standard	0.008 to 0.020 inch
Service limit	0.028 inch maximum
B18A	
Top compression ring	
Standard	0.008 to 0.014 inch
Service limit	0.024 inch
Second compression ring	
Standard	0.016 to 0.022 inch
Service limit	0.028 inch
Oil control ring	
Standard	0.008 to 0.028 inch
Service limit	0.032 inch
B18A1	
Top compression ring	
Standard	0.008 to 0.014 inch
Service limit	0.024 inch
Second compression ring	
Standard	0.016 to 0.022 inch
Service limit	0.028 inch
Oil control ring	
Standard	0.008 to 0.028 inch
Service limit	0.032 inch

Crankshaft and connecting rods

Endplay	
Standard	0.004 to 0.014 inch
Service limit	0.018 inch maximum

Main bearing journals
  Diameter
    Journals 1, 2, 4 and 5 .... 2.1644 to 2.1654 inches
    Journal 3 .... 2.1642 to 2.1651
  Taper and out-of-round
    Standard .... 0.0002 inch
    Service limit .... 0.0004 inch maximum
  Runout
    Standard .... 0.001 inch
    Service limit .... 0.002 inch
Main bearing oil clearance
  Journals no. 1, 2, 4 and 5
    Standard .... 0.0009 to 0.0017 inch
    Service limit .... 0.002 inch
  Journal no. 3
    Standard .... 0.0012 to 0.0019 inch
    Service limit .... 0.002 inch
Connecting rod journal
  Diameter .... 1.7707 to 1.7717 inches
  Taper and out-of-round (B18A, B18A1)
    Standard .... 0.0002 inch
    Service limit .... 0.0004 inch
  Taper and out-of-round limit (B17A, B17A1) .... 0.0002 inch
  Runout
    Standard .... 0.001 inch
    Service limit .... 0.002 inch
Connecting rod bearing oil clearance (B18A, B18A1)
  Standard .... 0.0008 to 0.0015 inch
  Service limit .... 0.002 inch
Connecting rod bearing oil clearance (B17A, B17A1)
  Standard .... 0.0013 to 0.0020 inch
  Service limit .... 0.0024 inch
Connecting rod side clearance (endplay)
  Standard .... 0.006 to 0.012 inch
  Service limit .... 0.016 inch maximum

Cylinder head and valves

Head warpage limits .... 0.002 inch
Cylinder head height
  B17A, B17A1 .... 5.589 to 5.593 inches
  B18A, B18A1 .... 5.195 to 5.199 inches
Valve seat angle 45-degrees
Valve face angle 45-degrees
Valve margin width (B18, B18A)
  Intake
    Standard .... 0.053 to 0.065 inch
    Service limit .... 0.045 inch
  Exhaust
    Standard .... 0.065 to 0.077 inch
    Service limit .... 0.057 inch
Valve margin width (B17, B17A)
  Intake
    Standard .... 0.041 to 0.053 inch
    Service limit .... 0.033 inch
  Exhaust
    Standard .... 0.065 to 0.077 inch
    Service limit .... 0.057 inch
Valve stem diameter
  Intake
    Standard .... 0.2591 to 0.2594 inch
    Service limit .... 0.2579 inch
  Exhaust
    Standard .... 0.2579 to 0.2583 inch
    Service limit .... 0.2567 inch
Valve guide inside diameter
  Standard .... 0.260 to 0.261 inch
  Service limit .... 0.262 inch

2C

Integra (continued)

Cylinder head and valves (continued)

Valve stem-to-guide clearance
  Intake
    Standard .... 0.001 to 0.002 inch
    Service limit.. 0.003 inch
  Exhaust
    Standard .... 0.002 to 0.003 inch
    Service limit.. 0.004 inch
Valve stem installed height
  B17A, B17A1
    Intake
      Standard .... 1.4750 to 1.4935 inch
      Service limit .... 1.5033 inch
    Exhaust
      Standard .... 1.4632 to 1.4817 inch
      Service limit .... 1.7120 inch
  B18A, B18A1
    Intake
      Standard .... 1.6049 to 1.6234 inch
      Service limit .... 1.6333 inch
    Exhaust
      Standard .... 1.6837 to 1.7022 inch
      Service limit .... 1.7120 inch
Valve spring free length
  B18A, B18A1
    Intake
      Standard .... 1.7354 inch
      Service limit .... 1.7016 inch
    Exhaust
      Standard .... 1.8657 inch
      Service limit .... 1.8307 inch
  B17A, B17A1 (intake)
    Inner spring .... 1.445 inch
    Outer spring
      Nihon Hatsujo .... 1.611 inch
      Chuo Hatsujo .... 1.610 inch
  B17A, B17A1 (exhaust)
    Nihon Hatsujo .... 1.652 inch
    Chuo Hatsujo .... 1.651 inch

Torque specifications*   **Ft-lbs** (unless otherwise indicated)

Main bearing cap bolts
  First step 22
  Second step 56
Connecting rod bearing cap nuts 30

Refer to Part A or Part B for additional torque specifications.

Legend

General

Cylinder compression pressure
  B18B1
    Standard
      1991 through 1993 .... 192 psi
      1994 on .... 199 psi
    Minimum .... 142 psi
    Maximum variation between cylinders .... 28 psi
Oil pressure (hot)
  At idle .... 10 psi
  At 3000 rpm... 50 psi

Engine block

Cylinder bore
  Standard... 3.543 to 3.544 inches
  Service limit .... 3.546 inches
Cylinder taper limit... 0.002 inch maximum
Cylinder out-of-round limit .... Not specified

Cylinder overbore limit.. 0.020 inch
Block deck warpage
    Standard... 0.003 inch
    Service limit... 0.004 inch

Pistons and rings

Piston diameter
    A or no letter piston
        Standard .... 3.5425 to 3.5429 inches
        Service limit.. 3.5421 inches
    B piston
        Standard .... 3.5421 to 3.5425 inches
        Service limit.. 3.54217 inches
Diameter measurement point (from bottom) .... 0.67 inch
Piston to cylinder wall clearance
    Standard... 0.001 to 0.002 inch
    Service limit... 0.003 inch
Ring groove clearance
    Top compression ring
        Standard .... 0.0014 to 0.0024 inch
        Service limit.. 0.005 inch
    Second compression ring
        Standard .... 0.0012 to 0.0021 inch
        Service limit.. 0.005 inch
Ring end gap
    Top compression ring
        Standard .... 0.010 to 0.016 inch
        Service limit.. 0.027 inch
    Second compression ring
        Standard .... 0.016 to 0.022 inch
        Service limit.. 0.033 inch
    Oil control ring (1991 and 1992)
        Standard .... 0.008 to 0.028 inch
        Service limit.. 0.032 inch
    Oil control ring (1993 on)
        Riken brand (standard) .... 0.008 to 0.028 inch
        Teikoku brand (standard) .... 0.008 to 0.020 inch
            Service limit (all)...................................... 0.031 inch

Crankshaft and connecting rods

Endplay
    Standard... 0.004 to 0.011 inch
    Service limit... 0.018 inch
Main bearing journals
    Diameter... 2.6762 to 2.6772 inches
    Taper and out-of-round
        Standard .... 0.0002 inch
        Service limit.. 0.0004 inch
    Runout (1991 and 1992)
        Standard .... 0.0004 inch
        Service limit.. 0.0006 inch
    Runout (1993-on)
        Standard .... 0.0008 inch
        Service limit.. 0.0012 inch
Main bearing oil clearance
    Standard... 0.0008 to 0.0017 inch
    Service limit... 0.002 inch
Connecting rod journal
    1991 and 1992
        Diameter... 2.1250 to 2.0866 inch
    Taper and out-of-round
        Standard .... 0.0002 inch
        Service limit.. 0.0004 inch
    Runout
        Standard .... 0.0004 inch
        Service limit.. 0.0006 inch maximum
Connecting rod bearing oil clearance
    Standard... 0.0009 to 0.0018 inch
    Service limit... 0.002 inch maximum
Connecting rod side clearance (endplay) .... 0.006 to 0.012 inch

Legend (continued)

Cylinder head and valves

Head warpage limit..	0.002 inch
Cylinder head height...	3.935 to 3.939 inches
Valve seat angle...	45-degrees
Valve face angle...	45-degrees
Valve margin width	
Intake	
Standard	0.033 to 0.045 inch
Service limit..	0.026 inch
Exhaust	
Standard	0.053 to 0.065 inch
Service limit..	0.045 inch
Valve stem diameter	
Intake	
Standard	0.2157 to 0.2161inch
Service limit..	0.2146 inch
Exhaust	
Standard	0.2146 to 0.2159 inch
Service limit..	0.2134 inch
Valve guide inside diameter	
Standard	0.2169 to 0.2177 inch
Service limit..	0.2185 inch
Valve stem-to-guide clearance	
Intake	
Standard	0.001 to 0.002 inch
Service limit..	0.003 inch maximum
Exhaust	
Standard	0.002 to 0.003 inch
Service limit..	0.004 inch maximum
Valve stem installed height	
Intake	
Standard	1.8478 to 1.8671 inches
Service limit..	1.875 inches maximum
Exhaust	
Standard	1.8852 to 1.9045 inches
Service limit..	1.9124 inches maximum
Valve spring free length	
All except 1995 sedan L and LS models	
Intake	1.935 inches
Exhaust	1.975 inches
1995 sedan L and LS models	
Intake	1.975 inches
Exhaust	1.983 inches

Torque specifications*

Ft-lbs (unless otherwise indicated)

Main bearing cap bolts	
9 mm vertical bolts..	29
11 mm vertical bolts..	57
Horizontal bolts..	36
Connecting rod bearing cap nuts...	33

* Refer to Part A or Part B for additional torque specifications.

1   General information

Included in this portion of Chapter 2 are the general overhaul procedures for the cylinder head and internal engine components.

The information ranges from advice concerning preparation for an overhaul and the purchase of replacement parts to detailed, step-by-step procedures covering removal and installation of internal engine components and the inspection of parts.

The following Sections have been written based on the assumption that the engine has been removed from the vehicle. For infor-

mation concerning in-vehicle engine repair, as well as removal and installation of the external components necessary for the overhaul, see Chapter 2A or 2B.

The Specifications included in this Part are only those necessary for the inspection and overhaul procedures which follow. Refer to Chapter 2, Part A or Part B for additional Specifications.

It's not always easy to determine when, or if, an engine should be completely overhauled, as a number of factors must be considered.

High mileage is not necessarily an indication that an overhaul is needed, while low

mileage doesn't preclude the need for an overhaul. Frequency of servicing is probably the most important consideration. An engine that's had regular and frequent oil and filter changes, as well as other required maintenance, will most likely give many thousands of miles of reliable service. Conversely, a neglected engine may require an overhaul very early in its life.

Excessive oil consumption is an indication that piston rings, valve seals and/or valve guides are in need of attention. Make sure that oil leaks aren't responsible before deciding that the rings and/or guides are bad. Perform a cylinder compression check to deter-

2.2a This is the Integra oil pressure sending unit

2.2b This is the Legend oil pressure sending unit

mine the extent of the work required (see Section 3). Also check the vacuum readings under various conditions (see Section 4).

Loss of power, rough running, knocking or metallic engine noises, excessive valve train noise and high fuel consumption rates may also point to the need for an overhaul, especially if they're all present at the same time. If a complete tune-up doesn't remedy the situation, major mechanical work is the only solution.

An engine overhaul involves restoring the internal parts to the specifications of a new engine. During an overhaul, the piston rings are replaced and the cylinder walls are reconditioned (re-bored and/or honed). If a re-bore is done by an automotive machine shop, new oversize pistons will also be installed. The main bearings, connecting rod bearings and camshaft bearings are generally replaced with new ones and, if necessary, the crankshaft may be reground to restore the journals. Generally, the valves are serviced as well, since they're usually in less-than-perfect condition at this point. While the engine is being overhauled, other components, such as the distributor, starter and alternator, can be rebuilt as well. The end result should be a like new engine that will give many trouble free miles. **Note:** *Critical cooling system components such as the hoses, drivebelts, thermostat and water pump should be replaced with new parts when an engine is overhauled. The radiator should be checked carefully to ensure that it isn't clogged or leaking (see Chapter 3). If you purchase a rebuilt engine or short block, some rebuilders will not warranty their engines unless the radiator has been professionally flushed. Also, be sure to check the oil pump carefully, as described in Chapter 2A or 2B.*

Before beginning the engine overhaul, read through the entire procedure to familiarize yourself with the scope and requirements of the job. Overhauling an engine isn't difficult, but it is time-consuming. Plan on the vehicle being tied up for a minimum of two weeks, especially if parts must be taken to an automotive machine shop for repair or recon-

ditioning. Check on availability of parts and make sure that any necessary special tools and equipment are obtained in advance. Most work can be done with typical hand tools, although a number of precision measuring tools are required for inspecting parts to determine if they must be replaced. Often an automotive machine shop will handle the inspection of parts and offer advice concerning reconditioning and replacement. **Note:** *Always wait until the engine has been completely disassembled and all components, especially the engine block, have been inspected before deciding what service and repair operations must be performed by an automotive machine shop.* Since the block's condition will be the major factor to consider when determining whether to overhaul the original engine or buy a rebuilt one, never purchase parts or have machine work done on other components until the block has been thoroughly inspected. As a general rule, time is the primary cost of an overhaul, so it doesn't pay to install worn or substandard parts.

As a final note, to ensure maximum life and minimum trouble from a rebuilt engine, everything must be assembled with care in a spotlessly-clean environment.

2   Oil pressure check

Refer to illustrations 2.2a and 2.2b

1   Low engine oil pressure can be a sign of an engine in need of rebuilding. A "low oil pressure" indicator (often called an "idiot light") is not a test of the oiling system. Such indicators only come on when the oil pressure is dangerously low. Even a factory oil pressure gauge in the instrument panel is only a relative indication, although much better for driver information than a warning light. A better test is with a mechanical (not electric) oil pressure gauge. When used in conjunction with an accurate tachometer, an engine's oil pressure performance can be compared to factory Specifications for that year and model.

2   Find the oil pressure sending unit **(see illustrations)**.
3   Remove the oil pressure sending unit and install a fitting which will allow you to directly connect your hand-held, mechanical oil pressure gauge. Use Teflon tape or sealant on the threads of the adapter and the fitting on the end of your gauge's hose.
4   Connect an accurate tachometer to the engine, according to the tachometer manufacturer's instructions.
5   Check the oil pressure with the engine running (full operating temperature) at the specified engine speed, and compare it to this Chapter's Specifications. If it's extremely low, the bearings and/or oil pump are probably worn out.

3   Cylinder compression check

Refer to illustration 3.7

1   A compression check will tell you what mechanical condition the upper end (pistons, rings, valves, head gaskets) of the engine is in. Specifically, it can tell you if the compression is down due to leakage caused by worn piston rings, defective valves and seats or a blown head gasket. **Note:** *The engine must be at normal operating temperature and the battery must be fully charged for this check.*
2   Begin by cleaning the area around the spark plugs before you remove them. Compressed air should be used, if available, otherwise a small brush or even a bicycle tire pump will work. The idea is to prevent dirt from getting into the cylinders as the compression check is being done.
3   Remove all of the spark plugs from the engine (see Chapter 1).
4   Block the throttle wide open.
5   Disable the fuel system by removing the PGM-FI (main) relay (see Chapter 4).
6   Disable the ignition system by detaching the primary connectors at the distributor (Integra) or by removing fuse no. 25 (30A) from the under-dash fuse box (Legend) (see Chapter 5).
7   Install the compression gauge in the

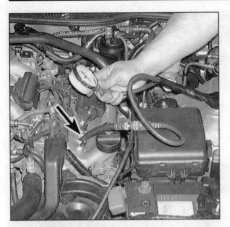

3.7 To use a compression gauge, you must have a gauge with a hose long enough to reach down the spark plug tubes (arrow) - be sure to open the throttle as far as possible during the compression check

4.6 Vacuum gauge readings

number one spark plug hole **(see illustration)**.

8   Crank the engine over at least seven compression strokes and watch the gauge. The compression should build up quickly in a healthy engine. Low compression on the first stroke, followed by gradually increasing pressure on successive strokes, indicates worn piston rings. A low compression reading on the first stroke, which doesn't build up during successive strokes, indicates leaking valves or a blown head gasket (a cracked head could also be the cause). Deposits on the undersides of the valve heads can also cause low compression. Record the highest gauge reading obtained.

9   Repeat the procedure for the remaining cylinders and compare the results to this Chapter's Specifications.

10   If the readings are below normal, add some engine oil (about three squirts from a plunger-type oil can) to each cylinder, through the spark plug hole, and repeat the test.

11   If the compression increases significantly after the oil is added, the piston rings are definitely worn. If the compression doesn't increase significantly, the leakage is occurring at the valves or head gasket. Leakage past the valves may be caused by burned valve seats and/or faces or warped, cracked or bent valves.

12   If two adjacent cylinders have equally low compression, there's a strong possibility the head gasket between them is blown. The appearance of coolant in the combustion chambers or the crankcase would verify this condition.

13   If one cylinder is about 20-percent lower than the others, and the engine has a slightly rough idle, a worn exhaust lobe on the camshaft could be the cause.

14   If the compression is unusually high, the combustion chambers are probably coated with carbon deposits. If that's the case, the cylinder head(s) should be removed and

decarbonized.

15   If compression is way down or varies greatly between cylinders, it would be a good idea to have a leak-down test performed by an automotive repair shop. This test will pinpoint exactly where the leakage is occurring and how severe it is.

4   Vacuum gauge diagnostic checks

Refer to illustration 4.6

A vacuum gauge provides valuable information about what is going on in the engine at a low-cost. You can check for worn rings or cylinder walls, leaking head or intake manifold gaskets, incorrect carburetor adjustments, restricted exhaust, stuck or burned valves, weak valve springs, improper ignition or valve timing and ignition problems.

Unfortunately, vacuum gauge readings are easy to misinterpret, so they should be used in conjunction with other tests to confirm the diagnosis.

Both the absolute readings and the rate of needle movement are important for accurate interpretation. Most gauges measure vacuum in inches of mercury (in-Hg). The following references to vacuum assume the

diagnosis is being performed at sea level. As elevation increases (or atmospheric pressure decreases), the reading will decrease. For every 1,000 foot increase in elevation above approximately 2000 feet, the gauge readings will decrease about one inch of mercury.

Connect the vacuum gauge directly to intake manifold vacuum, not to ported (throttle body) vacuum. Be sure no hoses are left disconnected during the test or false readings will result.

Before you begin the test, allow the engine to warm up completely. Block the wheels and set the parking brake. With the transmission in Park, start the engine and allow it to run at normal idle speed. **Warning:** *Keep your hands and the vacuum gauge clear of the fans.*

Read the vacuum gauge; an average, healthy engine should normally produce about 17 to 22 inches of vacuum with a fairly steady needle **(see illustration)**. Refer to the following vacuum gauge readings and what they indicate about the engine's condition:

1   A low steady reading usually indicates a leaking gasket between the intake manifold and cylinder head(s) or throttle body, a leaky vacuum hose, late ignition timing or incorrect camshaft timing. Check ignition timing with a timing light and eliminate all other possible causes, utilizing the tests provided in this

Chapter before you remove the timing chain cover to check the timing marks.

2   If the reading is three to eight inches below normal and it fluctuates at that low reading, suspect an intake manifold gasket leak at an intake port or a faulty fuel injector.

3   If the needle has regular drops of about two-to-four inches at a steady rate, the valves are probably leaking. Perform a compression check or leak-down test to confirm this.

4   An irregular drop or down-flick of the needle can be caused by a sticking valve or an ignition misfire. Perform a compression check or leak-down test and read the spark plugs.

5   A rapid vibration of about four in.-Hg vibration at idle combined with exhaust smoke indicates worn valve guides. Perform a leak-down test to confirm this. If the rapid vibration occurs with an increase in engine speed, check for a leaking intake manifold gasket or head gasket, weak valve springs, burned valves or ignition misfire.

6   A slight fluctuation, say one inch up and down, may mean ignition problems. Check all the usual tune-up items and, if necessary, run the engine on an ignition analyzer.

7   If there is a large fluctuation, perform a compression or leak-down test to look for a weak or dead cylinder or a blown head gasket.

8   If the needle moves slowly through a wide range, check for a clogged PCV system, incorrect idle fuel mixture, carburetor/throttle body or intake manifold gasket leaks.

9   Check for a slow return after revving the engine by quickly snapping the throttle open until the engine reaches about 2,500 rpm and let it shut. Normally the reading should drop to near zero, rise above normal idle reading (about 5 in.-Hg over) and then return to the previous idle reading. If the vacuum returns slowly and doesn't peak when the throttle is snapped shut, the rings may be worn. If there is a long delay, look for a restricted exhaust system (often the muffler or catalytic converter). An easy way to check this is to temporarily disconnect the exhaust ahead of the suspected part and redo the test.

5   Engine removal - methods and precautions

If you've decided the engine must be removed for overhaul or major repair work, several preliminary steps should be taken.

Locating a suitable place to work is extremely important. Adequate work space, along with storage space for the vehicle, will be needed. If a shop or garage isn't available, at the very least a flat, level, clean work surface made of concrete or asphalt is required.

Cleaning the engine compartment and engine before beginning the removal procedure will help keep tools clean and organized.

An engine hoist or A-frame will also be necessary. Make sure the equipment is rated in excess of the combined weight of the engine/transmission and its accessories.

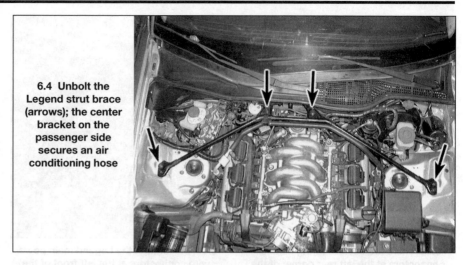

6.4 Unbolt the Legend strut brace (arrows); the center bracket on the passenger side secures an air conditioning hose

Safety is of primary importance, considering the potential hazards involved in lifting the engine out of the vehicle.

If the engine is being removed by a novice, a helper should be available. Advice and aid from someone more experienced would also be helpful. There are many instances when one person cannot simultaneously perform all of the operations required when lifting the engine out of the vehicle.

Plan the operation ahead of time. Arrange for or obtain all of the tools and equipment you'll need prior to beginning the job. Some of the equipment necessary to perform engine removal and installation safely and with relative ease are (in addition to an engine hoist) a heavy duty floor jack, complete sets of wrenches and sockets as described in the front of this manual, wooden blocks and plenty of rags and cleaning solvent for mopping up spilled oil, coolant and gasoline. If the hoist must be rented, be sure to arrange for it in advance and perform all of the operations possible without it beforehand. This will save you money and time.

Plan for the vehicle to be out of use for quite a while. A machine shop will be required to perform some of the work which the do-it-yourselfer can't accomplish without special equipment. These shops often have a busy schedule, so it would be a good idea to consult them before removing the engine in order to accurately estimate the amount of time required to rebuild or repair components that may need work.

Always be extremely careful when removing and installing the engine. Serious injury can result from careless actions. Plan ahead, take your time and a job of this nature, although major, can be accomplished successfully.

6   Engine - removal and installation

Refer to illustrations 6.4, 6.6a, 6.6b, 6.6c, 6.6d, 6.26a and 6.26b

Warning: Gasoline is extremely flammable, so take extra precautions when you work on

any part of the fuel system. Don't smoke or allow open flames or bare light bulbs near the work area, and don't work in a garage where a natural gas-type appliance (such as a water heater or clothes dryer) with a pilot light is present. If you spill any fuel on your skin, rinse it off immediately with soap and water. When you perform any kind of work on the fuel system, wear safety glasses and have a Class B type fire extinguisher on hand. Also, the air conditioning system is under high pressure - have a dealer service department or service station discharge the system before disconnecting any of the hoses or fittings.

Note 1: Read through the following steps carefully and familiarize yourself with the procedure before beginning work. Also at this point it may be helpful to use a penetrating fluid or spray on nuts and bolts that may be difficult to remove, such as exhaust manifolds, engine mounts, etc.

Note 2: The engine and transmission are removed together, as a single unit.

Removal

1   Refer to Chapter 4 and relieve the fuel system pressure.

2   Disconnect the negative battery cable. **Caution:** If the radio in your vehicle is equipped with an anti-theft system, make sure you have the correct activation code before disconnecting the battery. Disconnect the positive cable, then disconnect the other ends of the cables and remove them. Remove the battery and battery tray from the engine compartment (see Chapter 5). If you're working on an Integra, disconnect the transmission ground cable that passes under the battery tray.

3   Cover the fenders and cowl. Remove the hood support bolts and prop the hood open as wide as possible (see Chapter 11). Special pads are available to protect the fenders, but an old bedspread or blanket will also work.

4   If you're working on a Legend, remove the strut brace that passes across the engine compartment **(see illustration)**.

5   Remove the air cleaner assembly (see Chapter 4), and the air intake duct.

2C

6.6a There are several wiring harness connectors at the left rear corner of the engine compartment (Legend shown; Integra similar)

6.6b Disconnect the Legend main power wire connectors at the left front of the engine compartment and remove the fuse/relay box (arrows)

6.6c The Legend igniter connectors are at the left side of the engine compartment (arrows)

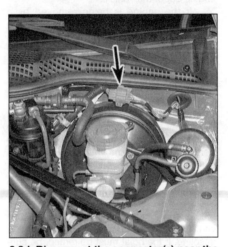

6.6d Disconnect the connector(s) near the brake booster (Legend shown)

6   Label the vacuum lines, emissions system hoses, electrical connectors, ground straps and fuel lines to ensure correct reinstallation, then detach them **(see illustrations)**. Pieces of masking tape with numbers or letters written on them work well. If there's any possibility of confusion, make a sketch of the engine compartment and clearly label the lines, hoses and wires.

7   If you're working on a Legend, unbolt the control box from the firewall after disconnecting its electrical connectors. Leave the vacuum hoses connected to the control box. Also detach the bypass solenoids and vacuum tank from the right front corner of the engine compartment and set them out of the way. Again, leave the vacuum hoses connected.

8   If you're working on an Integra, detach the starter cable and the engine wiring harness cable from the underhood fuse/relay box. If you're working on a Legend, remove the underhood fuse/relay box from the engine compartment (see Chapter 12).

9   Drain the cooling system (see Chapter 1). Label and detach all coolant hoses from the engine.

10   Remove the coolant reservoir, cooling fan, shroud and radiator (see Chapter 3).

11   Remove the drivebelt(s) and idler, if equipped (see Chapter 1).

12   Disconnect the fuel lines running from the engine to the chassis (see Chapter 4). Plug or cap all open fittings and lines.

13   Disconnect the accelerator linkage from the engine (see Chapter 4). Disconnect the cruise control cable and remove the cruise control actuator (if equipped). If you're working on a Legend with traction control, remove the TCS control valve from the throttle body (see Chapter 9).

14   Unbolt the power steering pump and set it aside (see Chapter 10). Leave the lines/hoses attached and make sure the pump is kept in an upright position in the engine compartment. Disconnect the power

steering speed sensor (see Chapter 10). If you're working on a Legend, unbolt the power steering fluid reservoir and set it out of the way.

15   Unbolt the air conditioning compressor (see Chapter 3) and set it aside. Do not disconnect the hoses.

16   Unbolt the alternator and mounting strap and set it aside. If you're working on an Integra, remove the distributor (see Chapter 5).

17   Raise the vehicle and support it securely on jackstands.

18   Drain the engine oil and remove the filter (see Chapter 1).

19   Remove the exhaust system from the vehicle (see Chapter 4).

20   Remove the splash shields from the underside of the engine compartment (see Chapter 11). If you're working on a Legend, remove the lower plate from under the rear beam of the subframe, then tighten the steering gear bolts to the torque listed in the Chapter 10 Specifications.

Automatic transmission equipped models

21   Remove the throttle control cable and shift control cable from the transmission. Also, disconnect the electrical connectors and shift cable from the transmission (see Chapter 7B).

22   Remove the transmission cooler lines. Cover the ends of the lines with plastic bags to keep out dirt.

23   If you're working on an Integra, remove the engine stiffeners and the torque converter cover.

Manual transmission/transaxle equipped models

24   Disconnect the shift linkage and disconnect the clutch cable (Integra) or remove the slave cylinder (Legend) (see Chapters 7A and 8). Leave the clutch hose attached to the slave cylinder on Legend models.

All models

25   Support the transmission/transaxle with a jack (preferably a transmission jack). If you're not using a transmission jack, position a wood block on the jack head to prevent damage to the transmission/transaxle.

26   Attach an engine sling or a length of chain to the lifting brackets on the engine **(see illustrations)**. If you're working on a Legend, also remove the EGR passage bolt from the rear of the engine and install an engine hanger in its place.

27   Roll the hoist into position and connect the sling to it. Take up the slack in the sling or chain, but don't lift the engine. **Warning:** *DO NOT place any part of your body under the engine when it's supported only by a hoist or other lifting device.*

28   Remove the driveaxles (see Chapter 8).

29   Remove the engine mount-to-chassis bolts (see Chapter 2A or 2B).

30   Recheck to be sure nothing is still connecting the engine to the vehicle. Disconnect anything still remaining.

31   Raise the engine slightly to disengage the mounts. Also, slightly raise the jack sup-

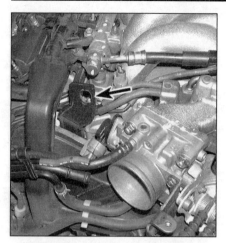

6.26a Attach the hoist chain to the hangers (arrow) mounted to the engine; this is the Legend front hanger . . .

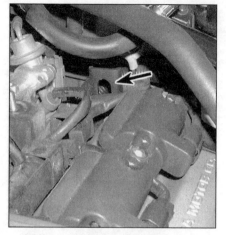

6.26b . . . and this is the Legend rear hanger; DO NOT forget to remove the EGR passage bolt and install another hanger on Legends

porting the transmission. Slowly raise the engine/ transmission assembly out of the engine compartment. Check carefully to make sure nothing is hanging up as the hoist is raised.

32 Lower the engine/transmission assembly to the ground and support it with wood blocks. Separate the transmission from the engine at this time (see Chapter 7).

33 Remove the clutch and flywheel or driveplate and mount the engine on an engine stand.

Installation

34 Check the engine and transmission mounts. If they're worn or damaged, replace them.

35 If you're working on a manual transmission equipped vehicle, install the clutch and pressure plate (see Chapter 8). Now is a good time to install a new clutch. Apply a dab of high-temperature grease to the input shaft.

36 Attach the transmission to the engine. **Caution:** *DO NOT use the bolts to force the transmission and engine together. If you're working on an automatic transmission equipped vehicle, take great care when installing the torque converter, following the procedure outlined in Chapter 7B.* Line up the holes in the engine mounts with the frame and install the bolts, tightening them securely.

37 Attach a chain hoist to the engine/transmission assembly and lower the assembly into the engine compartment.

38 The remainder of installation is the reverse of the removal steps. Tighten the engine mounting bolts in the correct sequence to prevent vibration and strain on the mounts as described in the following steps.

Integra

39 Tighten the bolts and nuts in order:
a) *Rear transaxle mount insulator*
b) *Rear transaxle mount bracket to frame*

c) *Rear transaxle mount bracket to insulator (snug only at this time)*
d) *Front transaxle mount insulator to engine*
e) *Front transaxle mount insulator to bracket (snug only at this time)*
f) *Side transaxle mount insulator to bracket*
g) *Side transaxle mount insulator bracket to transaxle*
h) *Side transaxle mount insulator through-bolt (snug only at this time)*
i) *Side engine mount insulator through-bolt (snug only at this time)*
j) *Side engine mount insulator to engine*
k) *Side transaxle mount insulator through-bolt (to specified torque)*
l) *Side engine mount insulator through-bolt (to specified torque)*
m) *Rear transaxle mount bracket to insulator (to specified torque)*
n) *Front transaxle mount insulator to bracket (to specified torque)*

Legend

40 Tighten the nuts and bolts in order:
a) *Mid mount bolts (both side of vehicle)*
b) *Mid mount nut (both sides of vehicle)*
c) *Left mount bracket bolts*
d) *Center bracket bolts (outer two of four bolts)*
e) *Right engine mount bracket to right bracket*
f) *Center bracket bolts (inner two of four bolts)*
g) *Center bracket insulator center bracket nut*
h *Left mount through-bolt*
h) *Center bracket damper*
i) *Rear transmission mount vertical bolt (finger-tight at this time)*
j *Transmission beam bolts (automatic) or bracket bolts (manual)*
k) *Transmission bracket bolts (automatic)*
l) *Rear transmission mount vertical bolt (to specified torque)*

41 Add coolant, oil, power steering and transmission fluid as needed (see Chapter 1).

42 Run the engine and check for leaks and proper operation of all accessories, then install the hood supports and test drive the vehicle.

43 If the air conditioning system was discharged, have it evacuated, recharged and leak tested by the shop that discharged it.

---

7 Engine rebuilding alternatives

The home mechanic is faced with a number of options when performing an engine overhaul. The decision to replace the engine block, piston/connecting rod assemblies and crankshaft depends on a number of factors, with the number one consideration being the condition of the block. Other considerations are cost, access to machine shop facilities, parts availability, time required to complete the project and the extent of prior mechanical experience.

Some of the rebuilding alternatives include:
Note: *The costs of alternatives described in this Section can vary, depending upon quality of parts, machine work required and the necessary tools and equipment to correctly do the work. Many automotive parts stores carry complete (long and short block) assemblies in addition to individual repair parts. Consult the local parts store on price and availability to make the final repair/replace decision.*

Individual parts - If the inspection procedures reveal the engine block and most engine components are in reusable condition, purchasing individual parts may be the most economical alternative. The block, crankshaft and piston/connecting rod assemblies should all be inspected carefully. Even if the block shows little wear, the cylinder bores should be surface honed.

Short block - A short block consists of an engine block with a crankshaft and piston/connecting rod assemblies already installed. All new bearings are incorporated and all clearances will be correct. The existing camshaft, valve train components, cylinder head(s) and external parts can be bolted to the short block with little or no machine shop work necessary.

Long block - A long block consists of a short block plus an oil pump, oil pan, cylinder head(s), valve cover, camshaft(s) and valve train components, timing sprockets and belt. All components are installed with new bearings, seals and gaskets incorporated throughout. The installation of manifolds and external parts is all that's necessary.

Give careful thought to which alternative is best for you and discuss the situation with local automotive machine shops, auto parts dealers and experienced rebuilders before ordering or purchasing replacement parts.

2C

9.2 A small plastic bag, with an appropriate label, can be used to store the valve train components so they can be kept together and reinstalled in the original position

9.3 Use a valve spring compressor to compress the springs, then remove the keepers from the valve stem with a magnet or small needle-nose pliers

9.4 If the valve won't pull through the guide, deburr the edge of the stem end and the area around the top of the keeper groove with a file or whetstone

8   Engine overhaul - disassembly sequence

1   It's much easier to disassemble and work on the engine if it's mounted on a portable engine stand. A stand can often be rented quite cheaply from an equipment rental yard. Before it's mounted on a stand, the flywheel/driveplate should be removed from the engine.

2   If a stand isn't available, it's possible to disassemble the engine with it blocked up on the floor. Be extra careful not to tip or drop the engine when working without a stand.

3   If you're going to obtain a rebuilt engine, all external components must come off first, to be transferred to the replacement engine, just as they will if you're doing a complete engine overhaul yourself. These include:

Alternator and brackets
Power steering pump and brackets
Emissions control components
Distributor (Integra only), coils (Legend), spark plug wires (Integra) and spark plugs
Thermostat and housing cover
Water pump
Fuel injection components
Intake/exhaust manifolds
Oil filter
Engine mounts
Clutch and flywheel or driveplate

Note: *When removing the external components from the engine, pay close attention to details that may be helpful or important during installation. Note the installed position of gaskets, seals, spacers, pins, brackets, washers, bolts, wiring and other small items.*

4   If you're obtaining a short block, which consists of the engine block, crankshaft, pistons and connecting rods all assembled, then the cylinder head(s), oil pan and oil pump will have to be removed as well. See *Engine*

rebuilding alternatives for additional information regarding the different possibilities to be considered.

5   If you're planning a complete overhaul, the engine must be disassembled and the internal components removed in the following general order :

Intake and exhaust manifolds
Valve cover(s)
Timing belt covers
Timing belt and sprockets
Rocker arm assembly(ies) and camshaft(s)
Cylinder head(s)
Water pump
Oil pan and pick-up tube
Oil pump
Oil jets (Integra models so equipped)
Piston/connecting rod assemblies
Rear main oil seal retainer
Crankshaft and main bearings

6   Before beginning the disassembly and overhaul procedures, make sure the following items are available. Also, refer to *Engine overhaul - reassembly sequence* for a list of tools and materials needed for engine reassembly.

Common hand tools
Small cardboard boxes or plastic bags for storing parts
Gasket scraper
Ridge reamer
Vibration damper puller
Micrometers
Telescoping gauges
Dial indicator set
Valve spring compressor
Cylinder surfacing hone
Piston ring groove cleaning tool
Electric drill motor
Tap and die set
Wire brushes
Oil gallery brushes
Cleaning solvent

9   Cylinder head - disassembly

Refer to illustrations 9.2, 9.3 and 9.4

Note 1: *New and rebuilt cylinder heads are commonly available for most engines at dealer parts departments and auto parts stores. Due to the fact that some specialized tools are necessary for the disassembly and inspection procedures, and replacement parts aren't always readily available, it may be more practical and economical for the home mechanic to purchase replacement head(s) rather than taking the time to disassemble, inspect and recondition the original(s).*

Note 2: *On Integra VTEC engines, remove the oil control orifice from the block immediately after cylinder head removal. Clean it and store it in a plastic bag for reassembly.*

1   Cylinder head disassembly involves removal of the intake and exhaust valves and related components. It's assumed that the rocker arms or rocker arm assemblies and camshaft(s) have already been removed (see Part A or Part B of this Chapter).

2   Before the valves are removed, arrange to label and store them, along with their related components, so they can be kept separate and reinstalled in their original locations **(see illustration)**.

3   Compress the springs on the first valve with a spring compressor and remove the keepers **(see illustration)**. Carefully release the valve spring compressor and remove the retainer, the spring and the spring seat (if used).

4   Pull the valve out of the head, then remove the oil seal from the guide. If the valve binds in the guide (won't pull through), push it back into the head and deburr the area around the stem and the keeper groove with a fine file or whetstone **(see illustration)**.

5   Repeat the procedure for the remaining valves. Remember to keep all the parts for

10.13 Check the cylinder head gasket surface for warpage by trying to slip a feeler gauge under the straightedge (see this Chapter's Specifications for the maximum warpage allowed and use a feeler gauge of that thickness)

10.15 A dial indicator can be used to determine the valve stem-to-guide clearance (move the valve stem as indicated by the arrows)

10.16 Check for valve wear at the points shown here

each valve together so they can be reinstalled in the same locations.

6   Once the valves and related components have been removed and stored in an organized manner, the head should be thoroughly cleaned and inspected. If a complete engine overhaul is being done, finish the engine disassembly procedures before beginning the cylinder head cleaning and inspection process.

10   Cylinder head - cleaning and inspection

Refer to illustrations 10.13, 10.15, 10.16, 10.17, 10.18 and 10.19

1   Thorough cleaning of the cylinder head and related valve train components, followed by a detailed inspection, will enable you to decide how much valve service work must be done during the engine overhaul. **Note:** *If the engine was severely overheated, the cylinder head(s) is probably warped.*

Cleaning

2   Scrape all traces of old gasket material and sealant off the head gasket, intake manifold and exhaust manifold mating surfaces. Be very careful not to gouge the cylinder head. Special gasket removal solvents that soften gaskets and make removal much easier are available at auto parts stores.

3   Remove all built-up scale from the coolant passages.

4   Run a stiff wire brush through the various holes to remove deposits that may have formed in them.

5   Run an appropriate size tap into each of the threaded holes to remove corrosion and thread sealant that may be present. If compressed air is available, use it to clear the holes of debris produced by this operation.

Warning: *Wear eye protection when using compressed air!*

6   Clean the exhaust and intake manifold stud threads with a wire brush.

7   Clean the cylinder head with solvent and dry it thoroughly. Compressed air will speed the drying process and ensure that all holes and recessed areas are clean. **Note:** *Decarbonizing chemicals are available and may prove very useful when cleaning cylinder heads and valve train components. They're very caustic and should be used with caution. Wear rubber gloves and goggles and be sure to follow the instructions on the container.*

8   Clean the rocker arms and bearing caps with solvent and dry them thoroughly (don't mix them up during the cleaning process). Compressed air will speed the drying process and can be used to clean out the oil passages. **Note:** *On VTEC engines, keep the three intake rockers for each cylinder bundled together with rubber bands.*

9   Clean all the valve springs, spring seats, keepers and retainers with solvent and dry them thoroughly. Do the components from one valve at a time to avoid mixing up the parts.

10   Scrape off any heavy deposits that may have formed on the valves, then use a motorized wire brush to remove deposits from the valve heads and stems. Again, make sure the valves don't get mixed up.

11   Remove, clean and store in order the lost motion assemblies (Integra VTEC models). **Note:** *The oil control orifices should be cleaned and put away at this time (if not already done). They're located in the top of the head ion Integra VTEC models and in the top of the block on non-VTEC Integra and all Legends.*

Inspection

Note: *Be sure to perform all of the following inspection procedures before concluding machine shop work is required. Make a list of the items that need attention. The inspection*

procedure for the rocker arms and camshafts, as well as the V6 lash adjusters, can be found in Part A or Part B of this Chapter.

Cylinder head

12   Inspect the head very carefully for cracks, evidence of coolant leakage and other damage. If cracks are found, check with an automotive machine shop concerning repair. If repair isn't possible, a new cylinder head should be obtained.

13   Using a straightedge and feeler gauge, check the head gasket mating surface for warpage **(see illustration)**. If the warpage exceeds the limit in this Chapter's Specifications, it can be resurfaced at an automotive machine shop.

14   Examine the valve seats in each of the combustion chambers. If they're pitted, cracked or burned, the head will require valve service that's beyond the scope of the home mechanic.

15   Check the valve stem-to-guide clearance by measuring the lateral movement of the valve stem with a dial indicator attached securely to the head **(see illustration)**. The valve must be in the guide and approximately 1/16-inch off the seat. The total valve stem movement indicated by the gauge needle must be divided by two to obtain the actual clearance. After this is done, if there's still some doubt regarding the condition of the valve guides, they should be checked by an automotive machine shop (the cost should be minimal).

Valves

16   Carefully inspect each valve face for uneven wear, deformation, cracks, pits and burned areas. Check the valve stem for scuffing and galling and the neck for cracks. Rotate the valve and check for any obvious indication that it's bent. Look for pits and excessive wear on the end of the stem **(see illustration)**. The presence of any of these conditions indicates the need for valve service by an automotive machine shop.

17   Check the margin width on each valve

2C

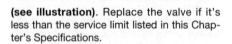

10.17 There must be a margin on each valve (if no margin exists, the valve cannot be reused)

10.18 Measure the free length of each valve spring with a dial or vernier caliper

10.19 Check each valve spring for squareness

(see illustration). Replace the valve if it's less than the service limit listed in this Chapter's Specifications.

Valve components

18   Check each valve spring for wear (on the ends) and pits. Measure the free length and compare it to this Chapter's Specifications **(see illustration)**. Any springs that are shorter than specified have sagged and shouldn't be reused. The tension of all springs should be checked with a special fixture before deciding they're suitable for use in a rebuilt engine (take the springs to an automotive machine shop for this check).
19   Stand each spring on a flat surface and check it for squareness **(see illustration)**. If any of the springs are distorted or sagged, replace all of them with new parts.
20   Check the spring retainers and keepers for obvious wear and cracks.
21   Any questionable parts should be replaced with new ones, as extensive damage will occur if they fail during engine operation.
22   If the inspection process indicates the valve components are in generally poor condition and worn beyond the limits specified, which is usually the case in an engine that's being overhauled, reassemble the valves in the cylinder head and refer to Section 11 for valve servicing recommendations.

11   Valves - servicing

1   Because of the complex nature of the job and the special tools and equipment needed, servicing of the valves, the valve seats and the valve guides, commonly known as a valve job, should be done by a professional.
2   The home mechanic can remove and disassemble the head, do the initial cleaning and inspection, then reassemble and deliver it to a dealer service department or an automotive machine shop for the actual service work. Doing the inspection will enable you to

see what condition the head and valvetrain components are in and will ensure that you know what work and new parts are required when dealing with an automotive machine shop.
3   The dealer service department, or automotive machine shop, will remove the valves and springs, recondition or replace the valves and valve seats, recondition the valve guides, check and replace the valve springs, rotators, spring retainers and keepers (as necessary), replace the valve seals with new ones, reassemble the valve components and make sure the installed height is correct. The cylinder head gasket surface will also be resurfaced if it's warped.
4   After the valve job has been performed by a professional, the head will be in like new condition. When the head is returned, be sure to clean it again before installation on the engine to remove any metal particles and abrasive grit that may still be present from the valve service or head resurfacing operations. Use compressed air, if available, to blow out all the oil holes and passages.

12.3 Drop the spring seats over the valve guides

12   Cylinder head - reassembly

Refer to illustrations 12.3, 12.4a, 12.4b, 12.6a, 12.6b and 12.8

1   Regardless of whether or not the head was sent to an automotive repair shop for valve servicing, make sure it's clean before beginning reassembly.
2   If the head was sent out for valve servicing, the valves and related components will already be in place. Begin the reassembly procedure with Step 8.
3   Slip the spring seats over the valve guides **(see illustration)**.
4   Install new seals on each of the valve guides. Using a hammer and a deep socket or seal installation tool, gently tap each seal into place until it's completely seated on the guide **(see illustration)**. Don't twist or cock the seals during installation or they won't seal properly on the valve stems. **Note:** *The valve stem seals are color coded - DO NOT mix them up! Exhaust valve seals have black springs and intake valve seals have white*

12.4a Gently tap the valve seals into place with a seal installation tool or a deep socket and hammer

12.4b The intake valve stem seals are color coded white and the exhaust seals are color coded black (arrows)

12.6a Install the spring (closely wound coils toward the head) and retainer over the valve stem

12.6b Apply a small dab of grease to each keeper as shown here before installation - it'll hold them in place on the valve stem as the spring is released

springs **(see illustration)**.

5   Beginning at one end of the head, lubricate and install the first valve. Apply molybase grease or clean engine oil to the valve stem.

6   Position the valve springs (and shims, if used) over the valves **(see illustration)**. Place the end of the valve spring with the closely wound coils toward the cylinder head Compress the springs with a valve spring compressor and carefully install the keepers in the groove, then slowly release the compressor and make sure the keepers seat properly. Apply a small dab of grease to each keeper to hold it in place if necessary **(see illustration)**.

7   Repeat the procedure for the remaining valves. Be sure to return the components to their original locations - don't mix them up!

8   Check the installed valve stem height (dimension L) with a vernier or dial caliper **(see illustration)**. If the head was sent out for service work, the installed height should be correct (but don't automatically assume it is). The measurement is taken from the spring seat to the top of the valve stem. If the height

is greater than listed in this Chapter's Specifications, shims can be added under the springs to correct it. **Caution:** *Do not shim the springs to the point where the installed height is less than specified.*

9   Apply camshaft assembly lube or molybase grease to the rocker arm faces, the camshaft and the rocker shafts, then install the camshaft, rocker arms and shafts (refer to Chapter 2A or 2B).

13 Pistons and connecting rods - removal

Refer to illustrations 13.1, 13.4, 13.5a, 13.5b and 13.7
Note: *Prior to removing the piston/connecting rod assemblies, remove the cylinder head(s), the oil pan, oil pump pick-up tube and pump and baffle plate (see Chapter 2A or 2B).*

1   Use your fingernail to feel if a ridge has formed at the upper limit of ring travel (about 1/4-inch down from the top of each cylinder).

If carbon deposits or cylinder wear have produced ridges, they must be completely removed with a special tool **(see illustration)**. Follow the manufacturer's instructions provided with the tool.

2   Failure to remove the ridges before attempting to remove the piston/connecting rod assemblies may result in piston breakage.

3   After the cylinder ridges (if any) have been removed, turn the engine upside-down so the crankshaft is facing up.

4   Before the connecting rods are removed, check the side clearance (endplay) with feeler gauges. Slide them between the first connecting rod and the crankshaft throw until the play is removed **(see illustration)**. The endplay is equal to the thickness of the feeler gauge(s). If the endplay exceeds the service limit, new connecting rods will be required. If new rods (or a new crankshaft) are installed, the endplay may fall under the specified minimum (if it does, the rods will have to be machined to restore it - consult an automotive machine shop for advice if neces-

2C

12.8 Be sure to check the valve stem installed height (the distance from the spring seat to the top of the valve stem)

13.1 A ridge reamer is required to remove the ridge from the top of each cylinder - do this before removing the pistons!

13.4 Check the connecting rod side clearance (endplay) with a feeler gauge

13.5a DO NOT confuse the stamped numbers on the parting surface, such as this 3 (arrow) with cylinder numbers - the numbers indicate big-end bore size

13.5b Mark the cylinder number on each connecting rod and cap with a center punch before removing them

13.7 To prevent damage to the crankshaft journals and cylinder walls, slip sections of rubber or plastic hose over the rod bolts before removing the pistons

sary). Repeat the procedure for the remaining connecting rods.

5   The existing numbers on the connecting rods indicate the rod bore size, not the position in the engine **(see illustration)**. Use a small center punch to make the appropriate number of indentations on each rod and cap (1, 2, 3, etc., depending on the engine type and cylinder they're associated with) **(see illustration)**.

6   Loosen each of the connecting rod cap nuts 1/2-turn at a time until they can be removed by hand. Remove the number one connecting rod cap and bearing insert. Don't drop the bearing insert out of the cap.

7   Slip a short length of plastic or rubber hose over each connecting rod cap bolt to protect the crankshaft journal and cylinder wall as the piston is removed **(see illustration)**.

8   Remove the bearing insert and push the connecting rod/piston assembly out through the top of the engine. Use a wooden hammer handle to push on the upper bearing surface

in the connecting rod. If resistance is felt, double-check to make sure that all of the ridge was removed from the cylinder.

9   Repeat the procedure for the remaining cylinders.

10   After removal, reassemble the connecting rod caps and bearing inserts in their respective connecting rods and install the cap nuts finger tight. Leaving the old bearing inserts in place until reassembly will help prevent the connecting rod bearing surfaces from being accidentally nicked or gouged.

11   Don't separate the pistons from the connecting rods (see Section 18 for additional information).

14   Crankshaft - removal

Refer to illustrations 14.1 and 14.3
Note: *The crankshaft can be removed only after the engine has been removed from the vehicle. It's assumed that the flywheel or driveplate, timing belt, oil pan, oil pick-up tube and oil pump, baffle plate and piston/connecting rod assemblies have already been removed. The rear main oil seal retainer must be unbolted and separated from the block before proceeding with crankshaft removal.*

1   Before the crankshaft is removed, check the endplay. Mount a dial indicator with the plunger in line with the crankshaft, touching the end **(see illustration)**. **Note:** *The main caps should be in place and torqued to Specifications.*

2   Push the crankshaft all the way to the rear and zero the dial indicator. Next, pry the crankshaft to the front as far as possible and check the reading on the dial indicator. The distance that it moves is the endplay. If it's greater than specified, check the crankshaft thrust surfaces for wear. If no wear is evident, new thrust washers should correct the endplay.

3   If a dial indicator isn't available, feeler gauges can be used. Gently pry or push the

crankshaft all the way to the front of the engine. Slip feeler gauges between the crankshaft and the back face of the front thrust bearing to determine the clearance **(see illustration)**. The thrust bearing is journal number four.

4   Check the main bearing caps to see if they're marked to indicate their locations. They should be numbered consecutively from the front of the engine to the rear. If they aren't, mark them with number-stamping dies or a center punch. Main bearing caps generally have a cast-in arrow, which points to the front of the engine. Loosen the main bearing cap bolts 1/4-turn at a time each, working around the engine until they can be removed by hand. **Note:** *On Legend V6 engines, there are side main cap bolts in addition to the conventional vertical bolts. Make sure all bolts are removed before trying to remove the caps.*

5   Gently tap the remaining caps with a soft-face hammer and separate them from the engine block. If necessary, use the bolts as levers to remove the caps. Try not to drop the bearing inserts if they come out with the caps.

14.1 Place a dial indicator against the end of the crankshaft and pry the crankshaft back-and-forth to check endplay

14.3 The endplay can also be checked with a feeler gauge at the thrust bearing journal

15.2 Some Integra models are equipped with oil jets (arrows)

15.5a A hammer and a large punch can be used to knock the core plugs sideways in their bores

15.5b Pull the core plugs from the block with pliers

6   Carefully lift the crankshaft out of the engine. It may be a good idea to have an assistant available, since the crankshaft is quite heavy. With the bearing inserts in place in the engine block, return the caps to their respective locations on the engine block and tighten the bolts finger tight.

15   Engine block - cleaning

Refer to illustrations 15.2, 15.5a, 15.5b, 15.9 and 15.11

1   Remove the main bearing caps and separate the bearing inserts from the caps and the engine block. Tag the bearings, indicating which cylinder they were removed from and whether they were in the cap or the block, then set them aside.

2   If you're working on an Integra with a VTEC engine, unbolt the oil jets from the block and remove them **(see illustration)**. The spout holes in the oil jets are 0.050-inch in diameter and you should be able to fit a 0.040-inch drill into them. Insert the shank end of the drill bit into the oil inlet and push against the check ball. It should move freely and return with spring pressure. If the spring seems weak, test it by blowing compressed air into the oil inlet. It should take at least 28 psi to push the check ball off its seat against the spring pressure. If the oil jet fails any of these tests, replace it.

3   Using a gasket scraper, remove all traces of gasket material from the engine block. Be very careful not to nick or gouge the gasket sealing surfaces.

4   Remove all of the covers and threaded oil gallery plugs from the block. The plugs are usually very tight - they may have to be drilled out and the holes retapped. Use new plugs when the engine is reassembled.

5   Remove the core plugs from the engine block. To do this, knock one side of each plug into the block with a hammer and a punch, then grasp them with large pliers and pull them out **(see illustrations)**.

6   If the engine is extremely dirty, it should be taken to an automotive machine shop to be cleaned.

7   After the block is returned, clean all oil holes and oil galleries one more time. Brushes specifically designed for this purpose are available at most auto parts stores. Flush the passages with warm water until the water runs clear, dry the block thoroughly and wipe all machined surfaces with a light, rust preventive oil. If you have access to compressed air, use it to speed the drying process and blow out all the oil holes and galleries. **Warning:** *Wear eye protection when using compressed air!*

8   If the block isn't extremely dirty or sludged up, you can do an adequate cleaning job with hot soapy water and a stiff brush. Take plenty of time and do a thorough job. Regardless of the cleaning method used, be sure to clean all oil holes and galleries very thoroughly, dry the block completely and coat all machined surfaces with light oil.

9   The threaded holes in the block must be clean to ensure accurate torque readings during reassembly. Run the proper size tap into each of the holes to remove rust, corro-

sion, thread sealant or sludge and restore damaged threads **(see illustration)**. If possible, use compressed air to clear the holes of debris produced by this operation. Now is a good time to clean the threads on the head bolts and the main bearing cap bolts as well.

10   Reinstall the main bearing caps and tighten the bolts finger tight.

11   After coating the sealing surfaces of the new core plugs with Permatex no. 1 sealant (or equivalent), install them in the engine block **(see illustration)**. Make sure they're driven in straight and seated properly or leakage could result. Special tools are available for this purpose, but a large socket, with an outside diameter that will just slip into the core plug, a 1/2-inch drive extension and a hammer will work just as well.

12   Apply non-hardening sealant (such as Permatex no. 2 or Teflon pipe sealant) to the new oil gallery plugs and thread them into the holes in the block. Make sure they're tightened securely.

13   If the engine isn't going to be reassembled right away, cover it with a large plastic trash bag to keep it clean.

15.9 All bolt holes in the block - particularly the main bearing cap and head bolt holes - should be cleaned and restored with a tap (be sure to remove debris from the holes after this is done)

15.11 A large socket on an extension can be used to drive the new core plugs into the bores

2C

16.4a Measure the diameter of each cylinder at a right angle to the engine centerline (A), and parallel to engine centerline (B) - out-of-round is the distance between A and B; taper is the difference between A and B at the top of the cylinder and A and B at the bottom of the cylinder

16.4b The ability to "feel" when the telescoping gauge is at the correct point will be developed over time, so work slowly and repeat the check until you're satisfied the bore measurement is accurate

16.4c The gauge is then measured with a micrometer to determine the bore size

16   Engine block - inspection

Refer to illustrations 16.4a, 16.4b, 16.4c, 16.10a and 16.10b

1   Before the block is inspected, it should be cleaned as described in Section 15.
2   Visually check the block for cracks, rust and corrosion. Look for stripped threads in the threaded holes. It's also a good idea to have the block checked for hidden cracks by an automotive machine shop that has the special equipment to do this type of work. If defects are found, have the block repaired, if possible, or replaced.
3   Check the cylinder bores for scuffing and scoring.
4   Check the cylinders for taper and out-of-round conditions as follows **(see illustrations)**.
5   Measure the diameter of each cylinder at the top (just under the ridge area), center and bottom of the cylinder bore, parallel to the crankshaft axis.

6   Next measure each cylinder's diameter at the same three locations perpendicular to the crankshaft axis.
7   The taper of the cylinder is the difference between the bore diameter at the top of the cylinder and the diameter at the bottom. The out-of-round specification of the cylinder bore is the difference between the parallel and perpendicular readings. Compare your results to those listed in this Chapter's Specifications.
8   Repeat the procedure for the remaining cylinders.
9   If the cylinder walls are badly scuffed or scored, or if they're out-of-round or tapered beyond the limits given in this Chapter's Specifications, have the engine block rebored and honed at an automotive machine shop. If a rebore is done, oversize pistons and rings will be required.
10   Using a precision straightedge and feeler gauge, check the block deck (the surface that mates with the cylinder head) for distortions **(see illustrations)**.
11   If the cylinders are in reasonably good

condition and not worn to the outside of the limits, and if the piston-to-cylinder clearances can be maintained properly, then they don't have to be rebored. Honing is all that's necessary (see Section 17).

17   Cylinder honing

Refer to illustrations 17.3a and 17.3b

1   Prior to engine reassembly, the cylinder bores must be honed so the new piston rings will seat correctly and provide the best possible combustion chamber seal. **Note:** *If you don't have the tools or don't want to tackle the honing operation, most automotive machine shops will do it for a reasonable fee.*
2   Before honing the cylinders, install the main bearing caps and tighten the bolts to the specified torque.
3   Two types of cylinder hones are commonly available - the flex hone or "bottle-brush" type and the more traditional surfacing hone with spring-loaded stones. Both will do the job, but for the less experienced mechanic the "bottle brush" hone will probably be easier to use. You'll also need some honing oil (kerosene will work if honing oil

16.10a Check the block deck with a precision straightedge and feeler gauges

16.10b Lay the straightedge across the block, diagonally and from end-to-end when making the check

17.3a A spring-loaded, stone-edged hone is the most common type of cylinder hone, but a bottle-brush hone is easier to use

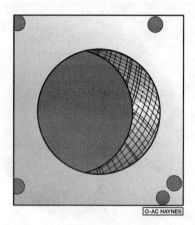

17.3b The cylinder hone should leave a smooth, crosshatch pattern with the lines intersecting at approximately a 60-degree angle

18.4a The piston ring grooves can be cleaned with a special tool, as shown here . . .

2C

18.4b . . . or a section of a broken ring

isn't available), rags and an electric drill motor. Proceed as follows:

a) *Mount the hone in the drill motor, compress the stones and slip it into the first cylinder* **(see illustration)**. *Be sure to wear safety goggles or a face shield!*

b) *Lubricate the cylinder with plenty of honing oil, turn on the drill and move the hone up-and-down in the cylinder at a pace that will produce a fine crosshatch pattern on the cylinder walls. Ideally, the crosshatch lines should intersect at approximately a 60-degree angle* **(see illustration)**. *Be sure to use plenty of lubricant and don't take off any more material than is absolutely necessary to produce the desired finish.* **Note:** *Piston ring manufacturers may specify a smaller crosshatch angle than the traditional 60-degrees - read and follow any instructions included with the new rings.*

c) *Don't withdraw the hone from the cylinder while it's running. Instead, shut off the drill and continue moving the hone up-and-down in the cylinder until it comes to a complete stop, then compress the stones and withdraw the hone. If you're using a "bottle brush" type hone, stop the drill motor, then turn the chuck in the normal direction of rotation while withdrawing the hone from the cylinder.*

d) *Wipe the oil out of the cylinder and repeat the procedure for the remaining cylinders.*

4   After the honing job is complete, chamfer the top edges of the cylinder bores with a small file so the rings won't catch when the pistons are installed. Be very careful not to nick the cylinder walls with the end of the file.

5   The entire engine block must be washed again very thoroughly with warm, soapy water to remove all traces of the abrasive grit produced during the honing operation. **Note:** *The bores can be considered clean when a lint-free white cloth - dampened with clean engine oil - used to wipe them out doesn't*

pick-up any more honing residue, which will show up as gray areas on the cloth. Be sure to run a brush through all oil holes and galleries and flush them with running water.

6   After rinsing, dry the block and apply a coat of light rust preventive oil to all machined surfaces. Wrap the block in a plastic trash bag to keep it clean and set it aside until reassembly.

18 Pistons and connecting rods - inspection

Refer to illustrations 18.4a, 18,4b, 18.10 and 18.11

1   Before the inspection process can be carried out, the piston/connecting rod assemblies must be cleaned and the original piston rings removed from the pistons. **Note:** *Always use new piston rings when the engine is reassembled.*

2   Using a piston ring expander tool, carefully remove the rings from the pistons. Be careful not to nick or gouge the pistons in the process.

3   Scrape all traces of carbon from the top of the piston. A hand held wire brush or a piece of fine emery cloth can be used once the majority of the deposits have been scraped away. Do not, under any circumstances, use a wire brush mounted in a drill motor to remove deposits from the pistons. The piston material is soft and may be eroded away by the wire brush.

4   Use a piston ring groove cleaning tool to remove carbon deposits from the ring grooves. If a tool isn't available, a piece broken off the old ring will do the job. Be very careful to remove only the carbon deposits - don't remove any metal and do not nick or scratch the sides of the ring grooves **(see illustrations)**.

5   Once the deposits have been removed, clean the piston/rod assemblies with solvent

and dry them with compressed air (if available). **Warning:** *Wear eye protection.* Make sure the oil return holes in the back sides of the ring grooves are clear.

6   If the pistons and cylinder walls aren't damaged or worn excessively, and if the engine block isn't rebored, new pistons won't be necessary. Normal piston wear appears as even vertical wear on the piston thrust surfaces and slight looseness of the top ring in its groove. New piston rings, however, should always be used when an engine is rebuilt.

7   Carefully inspect each piston for cracks around the skirt, at the pin bosses and at the ring lands.

8   Look for scoring and scuffing on the thrust faces of the skirt, holes in the piston crown and burned areas at the edge of the crown. If the skirt is scored or scuffed, the engine may have been suffering from overheating and/or abnormal combustion, which caused excessively high operating temperatures. The cooling and lubrication systems should be checked thoroughly. A hole in the piston crown is an indication that abnormal combustion (pre-ignition) was occurring. Burned areas at the edge of the piston crown

18.10 Check the ring side clearance with a feeler gauge at several points around the groove

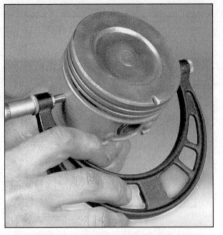

18.11 Measure the piston diameter at a 90-degree angle to the piston pin, at the specified distance from the bottom of the skirt

19.1 The oil holes should be chamfered so sharp edges don't gouge or scratch the new bearings

are usually evidence of spark knock (detonation). If any of the above problems exist, the causes must be corrected or the damage will occur again. The causes may include intake air leaks, incorrect fuel/air mixture, low octane fuel, ignition timing and EGR system malfunctions.

9   Corrosion of the piston, in the form of small pits, indicates coolant is leaking into the combustion chamber and/or the crankcase. Again, the cause must be corrected or the problem may persist in the rebuilt engine.

10   Measure the piston ring side clearance by laying a new piston ring in each ring groove and slipping a feeler gauge in beside it **(see illustration)**. Check the clearance at three or four locations around each groove. Be sure to use the correct ring for each groove - they are different. If the side clearance is greater than specified in this Chapter's Specifications, new pistons will have to be used.

11   Check the piston-to-bore clearance by measuring the bore (see Section 16) and the piston diameter. Make sure the pistons and bores are correctly matched. Measure the

piston across the skirt, at a 90-degree angle to the piston pin, at the height from the bottom of the skirt listed in this Chapter's Specifications **(see illustration)**.

12   Subtract the piston diameter from the bore diameter to obtain the clearance. If it's greater than listed in this Chapter's Specifications, the block will have to be rebored and new pistons and rings installed.

13   Check the piston-to-rod clearance by twisting the piston and rod in opposite directions. Any noticeable play indicates excessive wear, which must be corrected. The piston/connecting rod assemblies should be taken to an automotive machine shop to have the pistons and rods re-sized and new pins installed.

14   If the pistons must be removed from the connecting rods for any reason, they should be taken to an automotive machine shop. While they are there have the connecting rods checked for bend and twist, since automotive machine shops have special equipment for this purpose. **Note:** *Unless new pistons and/or connecting rods must be installed, do*

not disassemble the pistons and connecting rods.

15   Check the connecting rods for cracks and other damage. Temporarily remove the rod caps, lift out the old bearing inserts, wipe the rod and cap bearing surfaces clean and inspect them for nicks, gouges and scratches. After checking the rods, replace the old bearings, slip the caps into place and tighten the nuts finger tight. **Note:** *If the engine is being rebuilt because of a connecting rod knock, be sure to install new rods.*

19 Crankshaft - inspection

Refer to illustrations 19.1, 19.2, 19.5 and 19.7

1   Remove all burrs from the crankshaft oil holes with a stone, file or scraper **(see illustration)**.

2   Clean the crankshaft with solvent and dry it with compressed air (if available). **Warning:** *Wear eye protection when using compressed air.* Be sure to clean the oil holes with a stiff brush **(see illustration)** and flush them with solvent.

3   Check the main and connecting rod bearing journals for uneven wear, scoring, pits and cracks.

4   Check the rest of the crankshaft for cracks and other damage. It should be magnafluxed to reveal hidden cracks - an automotive machine shop will handle the procedure.

5   Using a micrometer, measure the diameter of the main and connecting rod journals and compare the results to this Chapter's Specifications **(see illustration)**. By measuring the diameter at a number of points around each journal's circumference, you'll be able to determine whether or not the journal is out-of-round. Take the measurement at each end of the journal, near the crank throws, to determine if the journal is tapered.

6   If the crankshaft journals are damaged, tapered, out-of-round or worn beyond the limits given in the Specifications, the

19.2 Use a wire or stiff plastic bristle brush to clean the oil passages in the crankshaft

19.5 Measure the diameter of each crankshaft journal at several points to detect taper and out-of-round conditions

19.7 If the seals have worn grooves in the crankshaft journals, or if the seal contact surfaces are nicked or scratched, the new seals will leak

20.1 Typical bearing failures

crankshaft will have to be replaced; the manufacturer states that it can't be reground.

7   Check the oil seal journals at each end of the crankshaft for wear and damage. If the seal has worn a groove in the journal, or if it's nicked or scratched **(see illustration)**, the new seal may leak when the engine is reassembled. In some cases, an automotive machine shop may be able to repair the journal by pressing on a thin sleeve. If repair isn't feasible, a new or different crankshaft should be installed.

8   Place the crankshaft in V-blocks or a lathe and set up a dial indicator contacting each of the main bearing journals in turn. Rotate the crankshaft through two complete revolutions at each position and compare the reading on the dial indicator to the runout limit listed in this Chapter's Specifications. Replace the crankshaft if it's beyond the limit.

9   Refer to Section 20 and examine the main and rod bearing inserts.

20 Main and connecting rod bearings - inspection and selection

Inspection

Refer to illustration 20.1

1   Even though the main and connecting rod bearings should be replaced with new ones during the engine overhaul, the old bearings should be retained for close examination, as they may reveal valuable information about the condition of the engine **(see illustration)**.

2   Bearing failure occurs because of lack of lubrication, the presence of dirt or other foreign particles, overloading the engine and corrosion. Regardless of the cause of bearing failure, it must be corrected before the engine is reassembled to prevent it from happening again.

3   When examining the bearings, remove them from the engine block, the main bearing caps, the connecting rods and the rod caps and lay them out on a clean surface in the same general position as their location in the engine. This will enable you to match any bearing problems with the corresponding crankshaft journal.

4   Dirt and other foreign particles get into the engine in a variety of ways. It may be left in the engine during assembly, or it may pass through filters or the PCV system. It may get into the oil, and from there into the bearings. Metal chips from machining operations and normal engine wear are often present. Abrasives are sometimes left in engine components after reconditioning, especially when parts are not thoroughly cleaned using the proper cleaning methods. Whatever the source, these foreign objects often end up embedded in the soft bearing material and are easily recognized. Large particles will not embed in the bearing and will score or gouge the bearing and journal. The best prevention for this cause of bearing failure is to clean all parts thoroughly and keep everything spotlessly clean during engine assembly. Frequent and regular engine oil and filter changes are also recommended.

5   Lack of lubrication (or lubrication breakdown) has a number of interrelated causes. Excessive heat (which thins the oil), overloading (which squeezes the oil from the bearing face) and oil leakage or throw off (from excessive bearing clearances, worn oil pump or high engine speeds) all contribute to lubrication breakdown. Blocked oil passages, which usually are the result of misaligned oil holes in a bearing shell, will also oil starve a bearing and destroy it. When lack of lubrication is the cause of bearing failure, the bearing material is wiped or extruded from the steel backing of the bearing. Temperatures may increase to the point where the steel backing turns blue from overheating.

6   Driving habits can have a definite effect on bearing life. Full throttle, low speed operation (lugging the engine) puts very high loads on bearings, which tends to squeeze out the oil film. These loads cause the bearings to flex, which produces fine cracks in the bearing face (fatigue failure). Eventually the bearing material will loosen in pieces and tear away from the steel backing. Short-trip driving leads to corrosion of bearings because insufficient engine heat is produced to drive off the condensed water and corrosive gases. These products collect in the engine oil, forming acid and sludge. As the oil is carried to the engine bearings, the acid attacks and corrodes the bearing material.

7   Incorrect bearing installation during engine assembly will lead to bearing failure as well. Tight-fitting bearings leave insufficient bearing oil clearance and will result in oil starvation. Dirt or foreign particles trapped behind a bearing insert result in high spots on the bearing which lead to failure.

2C

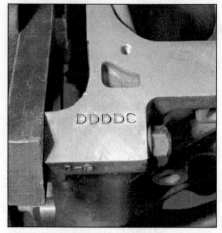

20.10 The crankcase journal designations are stamped onto the engine block

20.11a The crankshaft journal designations are stamped onto the crankshaft; this is an Integra crankshaft . . .

20.11b . . . and this is a Legend crankshaft

	A	B	C	D
1 or I	Red	Pink	Yellow	Green
2 or II	Pink	Yellow	Green	Brown
3 or III	Yellow	Green	Brown	Black
4 or IIII	Green	Brown	Black	Blue

20.12a Main bearing selection chart for four-cylinder engines

	A or I	B or II	C or III	D or IIII
1 or I	Pink	Pink Yellow	Yellow	Yellow Green
2 or II	Pink Yellow	Yellow	Yellow Green	Green
3 or III	Yellow	Yellow Green	Green	Green Brown
4 or IIII	Yellow Green	Green	Green Brown	Brown
5 or IIIII	Green	Green Brown	Brown	Brown Black
6 or IIIIII	Green Brown	Brown	Brown Black	Black

20.12b Main bearing selection chart for V6 engines; where two colors are listed together, use one bearing half of each color

20.14 Connecting rod journal designation

Selection

Refer to illustrations 20.10, 20.11a, 20.11b, 20.12a, 20.12b, 20.14, 20.15a, 20.15b, 20.16a and 20.16b

8   If the original bearings are worn or damaged, or if the oil clearances are incorrect (see Section 23 or 25), the following procedures should be used to select the correct new bearings for engine reassembly. Regardless of how the bearing sizes are determined, use the oil clearance, measured with Plastigage, as a guide to ensure the bearings are the right size. **Note:** *If the thickest bearings (smallest inside diameter) won't bring bearing clearance within the specified range, replace the crankshaft.*

Main bearings

9   If you need to use a STANDARD-size main bearing, install one that has the same color code as the original bearing.
10   If the color code on the original main bearing has been obscured, locate the codes stamped into the block for the corresponding cap location **(see illustration)**.
11   Locate the main journal grade numbers on the crankshaft as well **(see illustrations)**.
12   Use the accompanying chart to determine the correct bearings for each journal **(see illustrations)**.

Connecting rod bearings

13   If you need to use a STANDARD-size rod bearing, install one that has the same color code as the original.
14   If the color code has been obscured, locate the number stamped on each connecting rod cap **(see illustration)**. This code indicates the connecting rod big-end-bearing bore size, **not** the cylinder number it came from.
15   Locate the letters stamped on the

20.15a Crankshaft journal designations for four-cylinder connecting rods

	1	2	3	4
A or I	Red	Pink	Yellow	Green
B or II	Pink	Yellow	Green	Brown
C or III	Yellow	Green	Brown	Black
D or IIII	Green	Brown	Black	Blue

20.16a Connecting rod bearing selection chart for four-cylinder engines

20.15b Crankshaft journal designations for V6 connecting rods

	1 or I	2 or II	3 or III	4 or IIII
A or I	Pink	Pink Yellow	Yellow	Yellow Green
B or II	Pink Yellow	Yellow	Yellow Green	Green
C or III	Yellow	Yellow Green	Green	Green Brown
D or IIII	Yellow Green	Green	Green Brown	Brown
E or IIIII	Green	Green Brown	Brown	Brown Black
F or IIIIII	Green Brown	Brown	Brown Black	Black

20.16b Connecting rod bearing selection chart for V6 engines; where two colors are listed together, use one bearing half of each color

2C

crankshaft (**see illustrations**). These denote the size of their respective connecting rod journals.
16   Use the accompanying chart (**see illustrations**) to determine the correct bearings for each journal.

All bearings

17   Remember, the oil clearance is the final judge when selecting new bearing sizes. If you have any questions or are unsure which bearings to use, get help from your dealer parts or service department.

21   Engine overhaul - reassembly sequence

1   Before beginning engine reassembly, make sure you have all the necessary new parts, gaskets and seals as well as the following items on hand:

Common hand tools
Torque wrench (1/2-inch drive)
Piston ring installation tool
Piston ring compressor
Short lengths of rubber or plastic hose to fit over connecting rod bolts
Plastigage
Feeler gauges
Fine-tooth file
New engine oil
Engine assembly lube or moly-base grease

Gasket sealant
Thread locking compound

2   To save time and avoid problems, engine reassembly must be done in the following general order:

Crankshaft and main bearings
Rear main oil seal and retainer
Piston/connecting rod assemblies
Oil pan baffle and oil pump pick-up
Oil pan
Oil pump
Cylinder head(s)
Camshaft(s) and rocker arm assembly(ies)
Water pump
Timing belt and sprockets
Intake and exhaust manifolds
Timing belt covers
Valve cover(s)
Flywheel/driveplate

22   Piston rings - installation

Refer to illustrations 22.3, 22.4, 22.9a, 22.9b and 22.12

1   Before installing the new piston rings, the ring end gaps must be checked. It's assumed the piston ring side clearance has been checked and verified correct (see Section 18).
2   Lay out the piston/connecting rod assemblies and the new ring sets so the ring sets will be matched with the same piston and cylinder during the end gap measurement and engine assembly.
3   Insert the top (number one) ring into the first cylinder and square it up with the cylinder walls by pushing it in with the top of the piston (**see illustration**). The ring should be near the bottom of the cylinder, at the lower limit of ring travel.

22.3 When checking piston ring end gap, the ring must be square in the cylinder bore (this is done by pushing the ring down with the top of a piston as shown)

22.4　With the ring square in the cylinder, measure the end gap with a feeler gauge

22.9a　Installing the spacer/expander in the oil control ring groove

22.9b　DO NOT use a piston ring installation tool when installing the oil ring side rails

4　To measure the end gap, slip feeler gauges between the ends of the ring until a gauge equal to the gap width is found **(see illustration)**. The feeler gauge should slide between the ring ends with a slight amount of drag. Compare the measurement to this Chapter's Specifications. If the gap is larger or smaller than specified, double-check to make sure you have the correct rings before proceeding.

5　If the gap is too small, it must be enlarged or the ring ends may come in contact with each other during engine operation, which can cause serious engine damage. The end gap can be increased by filing the ring ends very carefully with a fine file. Mount the file in a vise equipped with soft jaws, slip the ring over the file with the ends contacting the file teeth and slowly move the ring to remove material from the ends. When performing this operation, file only from the outside in.

6　Excess end gap isn't critical unless it's greater than 0.040-inch. Again, double-check to make sure you have the correct rings for the engine.

7　Repeat the procedure for each ring that will be installed in the first cylinder and for each ring in the remaining cylinders. Remember to keep rings, pistons and cylinders matched up.

8　Once the ring end gaps have been checked/corrected, the rings can be installed

on the pistons.

9　The oil control ring (lowest one on the piston) is usually installed first. It's composed of three separate components. Slip the spacer/expander into the groove **(see illustration)**. If an anti-rotation tang is used, make sure it's inserted into the drilled hole in the ring groove. Next, install the lower side rail. Don't use a piston ring installation tool on the oil ring side rails, as they may be damaged. Instead, place one end of the side rail into the groove between the spacer/expander and the ring land, hold it firmly in place and slide a finger around the piston while pushing the rail into the groove **(see illustration)**. Next, install the upper side rail in the same manner.

10　After the three oil ring components have been installed, check to make sure both the upper and lower side rails can be turned smoothly in the ring groove.

11　The number two (middle) ring is installed next. It's usually stamped with a mark, which must face up, toward the top of the piston. **Note:** *Always follow the instructions printed on the ring package or box - different manufacturers may require different approaches. Don't mix up the top and middle rings, as they have different cross-sections.*

12　Use a piston ring installation tool and make sure the identification mark is facing the top of the piston, then slip the ring into the middle groove on the piston **(see illustration)**. Don't expand the ring any more than necessary to slide it over the piston.

13　Install the number one (top) ring in the same manner. Make sure the mark is facing up. Be careful not to confuse the number one and number two rings.

14　Repeat the procedure for the remaining pistons and rings.

23　Crankshaft - installation and main bearing oil clearance check

Refer to illustrations 23.6, 23.11, 23.13 and 23.15

1　It's assumed at this point that the engine block and crankshaft have been cleaned, inspected and repaired or reconditioned.

2　Position the engine with the bottom

facing up.

3　Remove the main bearing caps (if not already done) and make sure the original bearings are not in place in the block or caps.

4　If they're still in place, remove the original bearing inserts from the block and the main bearing caps. Wipe the bearing surfaces of the block and caps with a clean, lint-free cloth. They must be kept spotlessly clean.

Main bearing oil clearance check

Note: *Don't touch the faces of the new bearing inserts with your fingers. Oil and acids from your skin can etch the bearings.*

5　Clean the back sides of the new main bearing inserts and lay one in each main bearing saddle in the block. If one of the bearing inserts from each set has a large groove in it, make sure the grooved insert is installed in the block. Lay the other bearing from each set in the corresponding main bearing cap. Make sure the tab on the bearing insert fits into the recess in the block or cap.

6　The flanged thrust bearings must be installed in the number four cap and saddle (counting from the front of the engine) **(see illustration)**.

22.12　Installing the compression rings with a ring expander - the mark on the ring must face up

23.6　Location of the four-cylinder number four thrust bearings (arrows); the V6 thrust bearings are on the rear journal - the grooved sides on all models face OUT

23.11 Lay the Plastigage strips on the main bearing journals, parallel to the crankshaft centerline

7   Clean the faces of the bearings in the block and the crankshaft main bearing journals with a clean, lint-free cloth.

8   Check or clean the oil holes in the crankshaft, as any dirt here can go only one way - straight through the new bearings.

9   Once you're certain the crankshaft is clean, carefully lay it in position in the main bearings.

10   Before the crankshaft can be permanently installed, the main bearing oil clearance must be checked.

11   Cut several pieces of the appropriate size Plastigage (they should be slightly shorter than the width of the main bearings) and place one piece on each crankshaft main bearing journal, parallel with the journal axis **(see illustration)**.

12   Clean the faces of the bearings in the main bearing caps and install the assembly. Don't disturb the Plastigage.

23.15 Compare the width of the crushed Plastigage to the scale on the envelope to determine the main bearing oil clearance (always take the measurement at the widest point of the Plastigage); be sure to use the correct scale - standard and metric ones are included

23.13 Main bearing cap bolt TIGHTENING sequence - four-cylinder engine

13   Starting with the center bolts and working out toward the ends, tighten the main bearing cap bolts, in three steps, to the torque figure listed in this Chapter's Specifications **(see illustration)**. Don't rotate the crankshaft at any time during this operation. **Note:** *If you're working on a V6 engine, tighten the 9 x 1.25 mm cap bolts first, the 11 x 1.5 mm cap bolts second, and the 10 x 1.25 mm side bolts last.*

14   Remove the bolts and carefully lift off the main bearing caps. Keep them in order. Don't disturb the Plastigage or rotate the crankshaft. If any of the main bearing caps are difficult to remove, tap them gently from side-to-side with a soft-face hammer to loosen them.

15   Compare the width of the crushed Plastigage on each journal to the scale printed on the Plastigage envelope to obtain the main bearing oil clearance **(see illustration)**. Check the Specifications at the beginning of this Chapter to make sure it's correct.

16   If the clearance is not as specified, the bearing inserts may be the wrong size (which means different ones will be required). Before deciding different inserts are needed, make sure no dirt or oil was between the bearing inserts and the caps or block when the clearance was measured. If the Plastigage was wider at one end than the other, the journal may be tapered (see Section 19).

17   Carefully scrape all traces of the Plastigage material off the main bearing journals and/or the bearing faces. Use your fingernail or the edge of a credit card - don't nick or scratch the bearing faces.

Final crankshaft installation

18   Carefully lift the crankshaft out of the engine.

19   Clean the bearing faces in the block, then apply a thin, uniform layer of moly-base grease or engine assembly lube to each of the bearing surfaces. Be sure to coat the thrust faces as well as the journal face of the thrust bearing.

20   Make sure the crankshaft journals are clean, then lay the crankshaft back in place in the block.

21   Clean the faces of the bearings in the caps, then apply lubricant to them.

22   Install the main bearing caps.

23   Install the bolts.

24   Tighten all main bearing cap bolts to the torque listed in this Chapter's Specifications, starting with the center main and working out toward the ends **(see illustration 23.13**. If you're working on a V6 engine, be sure to tighten the bolts in the order described in Step 13.

25   Rotate the crankshaft a number of times by hand to check for any obvious binding.

26   The final step is to check the crankshaft endplay with feeler gauges or a dial indicator as described in Section 14. The endplay should be correct if the crankshaft thrust faces aren't worn or damaged and new bearings have been installed.

27   Refer to Section 24 and install the new rear main oil seal.

24   Rear main oil seal - installation

Refer to illustrations 24.1, 24.2a and 24.2b
Note: *The crankshaft must be installed and the main bearing caps bolted in place before the new seal and retainer assembly can be bolted to the block.*

1   Remove the old seal from the retainer with a hammer and punch by driving it out from the back side **(see illustration)**. Be sure to note how far it's recessed into the retainer

24.1 Support the retainer on wood blocks and drive out the old seal with a punch and hammer

2C

24.2a Drive the new seal into the retainer with a wood block or a section of pipe, if you have one large enough - make sure you don't cock the seal in the retainer bore

24.2b Be sure to check the clearance between the seal and retainer using a feeler gauge

25.5 Position the ring gaps as shown before installing the piston/connecting rod assemblies into the engine

bore before removing it; the new seal will have to be recessed an equal amount. Be very careful not to scratch or otherwise damage the bore in the retainer or oil leaks could develop.

2   Make sure the retainer is clean, then apply a thin coat of engine oil to the outer edge of the new seal. The seal must be pressed squarely into the retainer bore, so hammering it into place isn't recommended. If you don't have access to a press, sandwich the retainer and seal between two smooth pieces of wood and press the seal into place with the jaws of a large vise. If you don't have a vise big enough, lay the retainer on a workbench and drive the seal into place with a wood block and hammer **(see illustration)**. The piece of wood must be thick enough to distribute the force evenly around the entire circumference of the seal. Work slowly and make sure the seal enters the bore squarely. **Note:** *Using a feeler gauge, confirm that the clearance between the seal and the retainer is equal all the way around* **(see illustration)**. **It should be 0.020 to 0.030-inch (four-cylinder) or 0.008 to 0.030-inch (V6).**

3   Place a thin coat of RTV sealant to the

entire edge of the retainer.

4   Lubricate the seal lips with multi-purpose grease or engine oil before you slip the seal/retainer over the crankshaft and bolt it to the block. Be sure to use a new gasket. **Note:** *Apply a film of RTV sealant to both sides of the gasket before installation.*

5   Tighten the retainer bolts, a little at a time, to the torque listed in the Chapter 2, Part A or Part B Specifications. Trim the gasket flush with the oil pan gasket surface, being careful not to scratch it.

25 Pistons and connecting rods - installation and rod bearing oil clearance check

Refer to illustrations 25.5, 25.9, 25.11, 25.13 and 25.17

1   Before installing the piston/connecting rod assemblies, the cylinder walls must be perfectly clean, the top edge of each cylinder must be chamfered, and the crankshaft must be in place.

2   Remove the cap from the end of the number one connecting rod (check the marks

made during removal). Remove the original bearing inserts and wipe the bearing surfaces of the connecting rod and cap with a clean, lint-free cloth. They must be kept spotlessly clean.

Connecting rod bearing oil clearance check

Note: *Don't touch the faces of the new bearing inserts with your fingers. Oil and acids from your skin can etch the bearings.*

3   Clean the back side of the new upper bearing insert, then lay it in place in the connecting rod. Make sure the tab on the bearing fits into the recess in the rod. Don't hammer the bearing insert into place and be very careful not to nick or gouge the bearing face. Don't lubricate the bearing at this time.

4   Clean the back side of the other bearing insert and install it in the rod cap. Again, make sure the tab on the bearing fits into the recess in the cap, and don't apply any lubricant. It's critically important that the mating surfaces of the bearing and connecting rod are perfectly clean and oil free when they're assembled.

5   Position the piston ring gaps at intervals around the piston **(see illustration)**. **Caution:** *DON'T position any ring gap at piston thrust surfaces (90-degrees to piston pin).*

6   Slip a section of plastic or rubber hose over each connecting rod cap bolt.

7   Lubricate the piston and rings with clean engine oil and attach a piston ring compressor to the piston. Leave the skirt protruding about 1/4-inch to guide the piston into the cylinder. The rings must be compressed until they're flush with the piston.

8   Rotate the crankshaft until the number one connecting rod journal is at BDC (bottom dead center) and apply a coat of engine oil to the cylinder walls.

9   With the mark or notch on top of the piston facing the front of the engine **(see illustration)**, gently insert the piston/connecting rod assembly into the number one cylinder

25.9 The pliers-and-band type ring compressor is the easiest to use; the arrow on the piston points toward the front of the engine

25.11 Drive the piston gently into the cylinder bore with the end of a wooden or plastic hammer handle

25.13 Lay the Plastigage strips on each rod bearing journal, parallel to the crankshaft centerline

2C

bore and rest the bottom edge of the ring compressor on the engine block.

10   Tap the top edge of the ring compressor to make sure it's contacting the block around its entire circumference.

11   Gently tap on the top of the piston with the end of a wooden or plastic hammer handle **(see illustration)** while guiding the end of the connecting rod into place on the crankshaft journal. The piston rings may try to pop out of the ring compressor just before entering the cylinder bore, so keep some pressure on the ring compressor. Work slowly, and if any resistance is felt as the piston enters the cylinder, stop immediately. Find out what's hanging up and fix it before proceeding. Do not, for any reason, force the piston into the cylinder - you might break a ring and/or the piston.

12   Once the piston/connecting rod assembly is installed, the connecting rod bearing oil clearance must be checked before the rod cap is permanently bolted in place.

13   Cut a piece of the appropriate size Plastigage slightly shorter than the width of the connecting rod bearing and lay it in place on the number one connecting rod journal, parallel with the journal axis **(see illustration)**.

14   Clean the connecting rod cap bearing face, remove the protective hoses from the connecting rod bolts and install the rod cap. Make sure the mating mark on the cap is on the same side as the mark on the connecting rod.

15   Install the nuts and tighten them to the torque listed in this Chapter's Specifications. Work up to it in two steps. **Note:** *Use a thin-wall socket to avoid erroneous torque readings that can result if the socket is wedged between the rod cap and nut. If the socket tends to wedge itself between the nut and the cap, lift up on it slightly until it no longer contacts the cap. Do not rotate the crankshaft at any time during this operation.*

16   Remove the nuts and detach the rod cap, being very careful not to disturb the Plastigage.

17   Compare the width of the crushed Plas-

tigage to the scale printed on the Plastigage envelope to obtain the oil clearance **(see illustration)**. Compare it to this Chapter's Specifications to make sure the clearance is correct.

18   If the clearance is not as specified, the bearing inserts may be the wrong size (which means different ones will be required). Before deciding different inserts are needed, make sure no dirt or oil was between the bearing inserts and the connecting rod or cap when the clearance was measured. Also, recheck the journal diameter. If the Plastigage was wider at one end than the other, the journal may be tapered.

Final connecting rod installation

19   Carefully scrape all traces of the Plastigage material off the rod journal and/or bearing face. Be very careful not to scratch the bearing - use your fingernail or the edge of a credit card.

20   Make sure the bearing faces are perfectly clean, then apply a uniform layer of clean moly-base grease or engine assembly lube to both of them. You'll have to push the piston into the cylinder to expose the face of

the bearing insert in the connecting rod - be sure to slip the protective hoses over the rod bolts first.

21   Slide the connecting rod back into place on the journal, remove the protective hoses from the rod cap bolts, install the rod cap and tighten the nuts to the torque listed in this Chapter's Specifications. Again, work up to the torque in two steps. **Note:** *Again, make sure the mating mark on the cap is on the same side as the mark on the connecting rod.*

22   Repeat the entire procedure for the remaining pistons/connecting rods.

23   The important points to remember are:

a) *Keep the back sides of the bearing inserts and the insides of the connecting rods and caps perfectly clean when assembling them.*

b) *Make sure you have the correct piston/rod assembly for each cylinder.*

c) *The arrow or mark on the piston must face the front (timing belt end) of the engine.*

d) *Lubricate the cylinder walls with clean oil.*

e) *Lubricate the bearing faces when installing the rod caps after the oil clearance has been checked.*

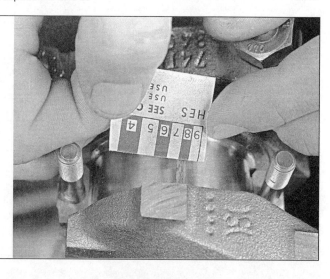

25.17 Measuring the width of the crushed Plastigage to determine the rod bearing oil clearance (be sure to use the correct scale - standard and metric ones are included)

24   After all the piston/connecting rod assemblies have been properly installed, rotate the crankshaft a number of times by hand to check for any obvious binding.

25   As a final step, the connecting rod endplay must be checked. Refer to Section 13 for this procedure.

26   Compare the measured endplay to this Chapter's Specifications to make sure it's correct. If it was correct before disassembly and the original crankshaft and rods were reinstalled, it should still be right. If new rods or a new crankshaft were installed, the endplay may be inadequate. If so, the rods will have to be removed and taken to an automotive machine shop for re-sizing.

26   Initial start-up and break-in after overhaul

Warning: *Have a fire extinguisher handy when starting the engine for the first time.*

1   Once the engine has been installed in the vehicle, double-check the engine oil and coolant levels.

2   With the spark plugs out of the engine and the ignition system and fuel system disabled (see Section 3), crank the engine until oil pressure registers on the gauge or the light goes out.

3   Install the spark plugs, hook up the plug wires and restore the ignition system functions.

4   Start the engine. It may take a few moments for the fuel system to build up pressure, but the engine should start without a great deal of effort. **Note:** *If backfiring occurs through the throttle body, recheck the valve timing and ignition timing.*

5   After the engine starts, it should be allowed to warm up to normal operating temperature at idle speed, then allowed to idle for about 15 minutes. This is especially important after main or connecting rod bearings have been replaced. While the engine is warming up, make a thorough check for fuel,

oil and coolant leaks.

6   Shut the engine off and recheck the engine oil and coolant levels.

7   Drive the vehicle to an area with minimum traffic, accelerate quickly, from 30 to 50 mph, then allow the vehicle to slow to 20 or 30 mph with the throttle closed. Repeat the procedure 10 or 12 times. This will load the piston rings and cause them to seat properly against the cylinder walls. Check again for oil and coolant leaks.

8   Drive the vehicle easily for the first 500 miles (no sustained high speeds or towing) and keep a constant check on the oil level. It isn't unusual for an engine to use oil during the break-in period.

9   At approximately 500 to 600 miles, change the oil **and** filter.

10   For the next few hundred miles, drive the vehicle normally. Don't pamper or abuse it.

11   After 2000 miles, change the oil and filter again and consider the engine broken in.

Chapter 3
Cooling, heating and air conditioning systems

Contents

3

Specifications

General

Coolant capacity..	See Chapter 1
Drivebelt tension..	See Chapter 1
Radiator pressure cap rating	14 to 18 psi
Thermostat rating	195 degrees F
Refrigerant type	
Integra	R-12
Legend	
1992 and earlier	R-12
1993 and later	R-134a
Refrigerant capacity	
Integra	32.0 to 34.0 ounces
Legend	24.5 to 26.5 ounces

Torque specifications

	Ft-lbs (unless otherwise indicated)
Alternator adjustment bracket-to-water pump bolt............................	33
Thermostat housing cover bolts	108 in-lbs
Upper radiator hose fitting-to-block bolts	96 in-lbs
Water pump-to-block bolts	
Integra	108 in-lbs
Legend	
8 mm bolts	16
6 mm bolts	108 in-lbs

1.1a Typical cooling, heater and air conditioning systems underhood component locations (Acura Integra)

1	Upper radiator hose	4	Cooling fan	7	Coolant reservoir
2	Lower radiator hose	5	Air conditioning refrigerant hose	8	Heater hose
3	Radiator cap	6	Air conditioning compressor		

1   General information

Engine cooling system

Refer to illustrations 1.1a and 1.1b

All vehicles covered by this manual employ a pressurized engine cooling system with thermostatically controlled coolant circulation **(see illustrations)**. An impeller-type water pump mounted on the engine block pumps coolant through the engine. The coolant flows around each cylinder and toward the rear of the engine. Cast-in coolant passages direct coolant around the intake and exhaust ports, near the spark plug areas and in close proximity to the exhaust valve guides.

A wax pellet type thermostat controls engine coolant temperature. During warm up, the closed thermostat prevents coolant from circulating through the radiator. As the engine nears normal operating temperature, the thermostat opens and allows hot coolant to travel through the radiator, where it's cooled before returning to the engine.

The cooling system is sealed by a pressure type radiator cap, which raises the boiling point of the coolant and increases the

cooling efficiency of the radiator. If the system pressure exceeds the cap pressure relief value, the excess pressure in the system forces the spring-loaded valve inside the cap off its seat and allows the coolant to escape through the overflow tube into a coolant reservoir. When the system cools the excess coolant is automatically drawn from the reservoir back into the radiator.

The coolant reservoir serves as both the point at which fresh coolant is added to the cooling system to maintain the proper fluid level and as a holding tank for overheated coolant.

This type of cooling system is known as a closed design because coolant that escapes past the pressure cap is saved and reused.

Heating system

The heating system consists of a blower fan and heater core located in the heater box, the hoses connecting the heater core to the engine cooling system and the heater/air conditioning control head on the dashboard. Hot engine coolant is circulated through the heater core. When the heater mode is activated, a flap door opens to expose the heater box to the passenger compartment. A fan

switch on the control head activates the blower motor, which forces air through the core, heating the air.

Air conditioning system

The air conditioning system consists of a condenser mounted in front of the radiator, an evaporator mounted adjacent to the heater core, a compressor mounted on the engine, a receiver-drier which contains a high pressure relief valve and the plumbing connecting all of the above components.

A blower fan forces the warmer air of the passenger compartment through the evaporator core (sort of a radiator-in-reverse), transferring the heat from the air to the refrigerant. The liquid refrigerant boils off into low-pressure vapor, taking the heat with it when it leaves the evaporator.

2   Antifreeze - general information

Warning: *Do not allow antifreeze to come in contact with your skin or painted surfaces of the vehicle. Rinse off spills immediately with plenty of water. Antifreeze is highly toxic if ingested. Never leave antifreeze lying around*

1.1b Typical cooling, heater and air conditioning systems underhood component locations (Acura Legend)

1	Cooling fans	4	Air conditioning compressor	7	Low-pressure service fitting
2	Radiator cap	5	Coolant reservoir	8	Heater hose
3	Upper radiator hose	6	Air conditioning refrigerant hose		

in an open container or in puddles on the floor; children and pets are attracted by its sweet smell and may drink it. Check with local authorities about disposing of used antifreeze. Many communities have collection centers that will see that antifreeze is disposed of safely.

The cooling system should be filled with a water/ethylene glycol based antifreeze solution, which will prevent freezing down to at least -20-degrees F, or lower if local climate requires it. It also provides protection against corrosion and increases the coolant boiling point.

The cooling system should be drained, flushed and refilled at the specified intervals (see Chapter 1). Old or contaminated antifreeze solutions are likely to cause damage and encourage the formation of rust and scale in the system. Use distilled water with the antifreeze.

Before adding antifreeze, check all hose connections, because antifreeze tends to leak through very minute openings. Engines don't normally consume coolant, so if the level goes down, find the cause and correct it.

The exact mixture of antifreeze-to-water, which you should use, depends on the relative weather conditions. The mixture should contain at least 50-percent antifreeze, but should never contain more than 70-percent antifreeze. Consult the mixture ratio chart on the antifreeze container before adding coolant. Hydrometers are available at most auto parts stores to test the coolant. Use antifreeze that meets the vehicle manufacturer's specifications.

3   Thermostat - check and replacement

Warning: *Do not remove the radiator cap, drain the coolant or replace the thermostat until the engine has cooled completely. Read the warning at the beginning of Section 2.*

Check

Refer to illustration 3.5

1   Before assuming the thermostat is to blame for a cooling system problem, check the coolant level, drivebelt tension (see Chapter 1) and temperature gauge operation.

2   If the engine seems to be taking a long time to warm up (based on heater output or temperature gauge operation), the thermostat is probably stuck open. Replace the thermostat with a new one.

3   If the engine runs hot, use your hand to check the temperature of the upper radiator hose. If the hose isn't hot, but the engine is, the thermostat is probably stuck closed, preventing the coolant inside the engine from escaping to the radiator. Replace the thermostat. **Caution:** *Don't drive the vehicle without a thermostat. The computer may stay in open loop and emissions and fuel economy will suffer.*

4   If the upper radiator hose is hot, it means that the coolant is flowing and the thermostat is open. Consult the Troubleshooting section at the front of this manual for cooling system diagnosis.

5   To accurately test the thermostat, remove it from the engine and suspend the

3.5 Testing the thermostat opening temperature

(closed) thermostat on a length of string in a container of cold water, with a cooking thermometer beside it **(see illustration)**. Ensure that neither touches the sides or bottom of the container.

6   Heat the water and check the temperature at which the thermostat fully opens. Compare this value with the value listed in this Chapter's Specifications. Remove the container from the heat, allow it to cool and confirm the thermostat closes fully.

7   If the thermostat does not fully open at

3.16 Install a new rubber seal onto the thermostat

3.17 Install the new thermostat in the housing with the spring towards the engine and the jiggle pin (arrow) at the top

3.13a Thermostat housing cover bolt locations (arrows) - Integra

the specified temperature and close as described, replace the thermostat.

Replacement

Refer to illustrations 3.13a, 3.13b, 3.16 and 3.17

8   Disconnect the cable from the negative battery terminal. **Caution:** *If the radio in your vehicle is equipped with an anti-theft system, make sure you have the correct activation code before disconnecting the battery.*

9   Drain the cooling system (see Chapter 1). If the coolant is relatively new or in good condition (see Chapter 1), save it and reuse it.

10   Follow the upper radiator hose to the engine to locate the thermostat housing cover.

11   Loosen the hose clamp, then detach the hose from the fitting. If it's stuck, grasp it near the end with a pair of adjustable pliers and twist it to break the seal, then pull it off. If the hose is old or deteriorated, cut it off and install a new one.

12   If the outer surface of the large fitting that mates with the hose is deteriorated (corroded, pitted, etc.) it may be damaged further by hose removal. If it is, the thermostat housing cover will have to be replaced.

13   Disconnect the engine coolant temperature (ECT) sensor, remove the thermostat housing cover bolts and detach the housing cover **(see illustrations)**. If the cover is stuck, tap it with a soft-face hammer to jar it loose. Be prepared for some coolant to spill as the gasket seal is broken.

14   Note how it's installed - with the jiggle pin up - then remove the thermostat.

15   Remove all traces of old gasket material and/or sealant from the housing and cover.

16   Install a new rubber gasket onto the thermostat **(see illustration)**.

17   Install the new thermostat in the housing without using sealant. Make sure the jiggle pin, if equipped, is at the top and the spring end is directed into the engine **(see illustration)**.

18   Install the housing cover and bolts. Tighten the bolts to the torque listed in this

3.13b Thermostat housing cover bolt locations (arrows) - Legend

Chapter's Specifications.

19   Reattach the hose and tighten the hose clamp securely. Install all components that were removed for access.

20   Refill the cooling system. **Caution:** *When refilling the cooling system, be sure to bleed the air from the system or engine damage could result,* see Chapter 1 - Cooling system servicing.

21   Start the engine and allow it to reach normal operating temperature, then check for leaks and proper thermostat operation (as described in Steps 2 through 4).

---

4   Engine cooling fan and circuit - description, check and fan motor replacement

Warning 1: *Be very careful when working around the cooling fans, the fans can operate with the engine stopped. Keep hair, loose clothing, tools, test equipment leads, etc. away from the fan blades at all times.*

Warning 2: *To avoid possible injury or damage, DO NOT operate the engine with a damaged fan. Do not attempt to repair fan blades - replace a damaged fan with a new one.*

Description

Note: *Refer to the wiring diagrams at the end of Chapter 12 for diagrams of the cooling fan circuits.*

Integra models

1   On models without air conditioning, the circuit consists simply of the ignition switch, fuse box, fan motor, fan switch and related wiring. When the fan switch closes (at approximately 194 degrees F) it completes the circuit to ground and the motor runs. When the coolant cools sufficiently, the switch opens and the motor stops.

2   On models with air conditioning, the radiator fan circuit consists of the ignition switch, fuse box, fan motor, fan relay, fan switch and related wiring. Operation is similar to models without air conditioning, except

4.6 Radiator cooling and condenser fan motor electrical connector locations (arrows) - Legend models

4.7a Integra cooling fan relay location (arrow)

4.7b Integra condenser cooling fan relay location (arrow)

4.7c Legend model radiator fan relay locations

A   *Radiator fan main relay*
B   *Condenser fan relay*
C   *Radiator fan relay*

that when the switch closes it completes the relay control circuit to ground, the relay completes the motor power circuit to ground and the motor runs. The condenser fan circuit is complex. It consists of the ignition switch, fuse box, fan control module, condenser fan relay, condenser fan motor, engine oil temperature switch and the ECM. The condenser fan motor is powered by the condenser fan relay. The relay control circuit is controlled by the fan control module, air conditioning control switch and the ECM. When the air conditioning is switched On and certain criteria are

met, the ECM completes the relay control circuit to ground and the condenser fan motor is energized.

3   The condenser fan motor will also run with the engine stopped. If the engine oil temperature is above approximately 226 degrees F, the engine oil temperature switch (threaded into the engine block at the rear, firewall-side, of the engine) closes, signaling the fan control module to turn on the condenser fan motor.

The timer circuitry inside the fan control module allows the condenser fan motor to run for approximately 15 minutes.

Legend models

4   The radiator and condenser fan circuits consist of the ignition switch, fuse box, fan relays (three total), fan motors (radiator and condenser), fan control sensor, engine oil temperature switch, fan control unit, fan control module and the ECM. The fan control unit controls the operation of the fan relays depending on information provided by the fan control sensor, ECM and air conditioning system. The fan control sensor is a variable resistor whose resistance values decrease as coolant temperature increases. The fan control unit operates both fans at low speed or high speed, depending on coolant temperature and air conditioning demand.

5   When the engine is stopped and the engine oil temperature is above 198 degrees F the engine oil temperature switch closes, signaling the fan control module to energize the condenser fan relay. The timer circuitry inside the fan control module allows the condenser fan motor to run at low speed for approximately 15 minutes. The oil temperature switch is located at the rear of the right valve cover.

Check

Refer to illustrations 4.6, 4.7a, 4.7b, 4.7c, 4.7d, 4.7e, 4.7f and 4.9
Note: *The following procedures apply only to the radiator fans, relays and temperature switches. The fan control unit, fan control module and the ECM and cannot be tested without the proper equipment. If the following checks fail to locate the problem, have the fan control module and/or fan control unit diagnosed by a dealership service department or other qualified repair facility.*

6   To test a fan motor, disconnect the electrical connector at the motor **(see illustration)** and use jumper wires to connect the fan directly to the battery. If the fan doesn't work, replace the motor.

7   If the motor tests OK, refer to Chapter 12 and check the fuses and relays **(see illustrations)**. Check the fan switch (see

1	2	3	4
5	6	7	8

4.7d On Integra models, the radiator fan control module (arrow) is attached to the right side of the heater unit

1   *Condenser fan relay positive*
2   *Battery voltage with ignition switch On*
3   *Not used*
4   *Ground*
5   *Engine oil temperature switch*
6   *Battery power at all times*
7   *Ignition switch (timer reset signal)*
8   *Condenser fan relay ground*

3

4.7e On Legend models, the fan control unit is located under the right side of the instrument panel

1   Radiator fan control
    sensor ground
2   Radiator fan relay and
    radiator fan main relay
    control ground
3   Air conditioning
    pressure switch -
    terminal A
4   Ground
5   Not used

6   Air conditioning
    pressure switch - terminal B
7   Radiator fan control
    sensor positive
8   Not used
9   Radiator fan control
    module
10 Not used
11 ECM
12 Ignition switch

4.7f On Legend models, the radiator fan control module (arrow) is located behind the right kick panel

1   Ground
2   Fan control unit
3   Condenser fan relay
    positive
4   Battery power with
    ignition switch On

5   Condenser fan relay
    ground
6   Battery power with
    ignition switch Off
7   Not used
8   Engine oil temperature
    sensor

below) and the wiring and connectors connecting the components. Disconnect the electrical connector from the appropriate fan control module and check the circuits for the proper input **(see illustrations)**.

8   To test the radiator fan switch on an Integra, drain the cooling system (see Chapter 1) and remove the switch from the cylinder head (the switch is located on the rear, firewall-side, of the cylinder head). Suspend the switch in a container of water with only the sensor portion of the switch submerged and place a cooking thermometer beside it. Connect an ohmmeter to the switch terminals and check for continuity as the water is heated. The switch should not have continuity below 189 degrees F. The radiator fan switch should indicate continuity when the water reaches 196 to 203 degrees F. If the switch fails to indicate continuity above this temperature, replace it. **Caution:** *When refilling the cooling system, be sure to bleed the air from the system or engine damage could result,* see Chapter 1 - Cooling system servicing.

9   To test the radiator fan sensor on a Legend, drain the cooling system (see Chapter 1) and remove the switch from the radiator **(see illustration)**. Suspend the switch in a container of water with only the sensor portion of the switch submerged and place a cooking thermometer beside it. Connect an ohmmeter to the switch terminals and check the resistance as the water is heated. The switch should indicate approximately 1000 to 1250 ohms at 183 degrees F and 870 to 1025

4.9 On Legend models, the fan control sensor (arrow) is located at the bottom of the radiator

ohms at 194 degrees F. If the switch fails to indicate the specified resistance, replace it. **Caution:** *When refilling the cooling system, be sure to bleed the air from the system or engine damage could result,* see Chapter 1 - Cooling system servicing.

Fan motor replacement

Refer to illustrations 4.16, 4.17, 4.18, 4.19 and 4.20

10   Disconnect the battery cable from the negative battery terminal. **Caution:** *If the radio in your vehicle is equipped with an anti-theft system, make sure you have the correct*

4.16 The lower fan shroud bolts are accessible from below

activation code before disconnecting the battery.

11   Set the parking brake and block the rear wheels to prevent the vehicle from rolling. Raise the front of the vehicle and support it securely with jackstands. Remove the lower splash pan, if equipped, from under the radiator.

12   Drain the cooling system and detach the upper radiator hose from the radiator.

13   Disconnect the electrical connector from the cooling fan.

14   On Integra models, remove the air conditioning line bracket and position the lines back toward the engine as far as possible.

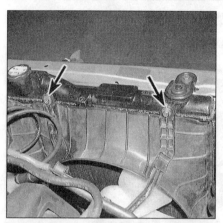

4.17 Each upper fan shroud has two retaining bolts (arrows)

4.18 on Integra models, remove the air conditioning line bracket bolts, push the bracket and lines aside, then carefully lift the fan out of the engine compartment

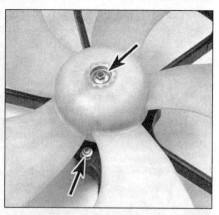

4.19 To remove the fan, unscrew the nut in the center (upper arrow), then pull the fan blade from the motor shaft (the lower arrow points to one of the motor mounting screws)

4.20 To detach the fan motor from the shroud, remove these screws (arrows)

5.4 If the vehicle is equipped with an automatic transmission/transaxle, disconnect the cooler lines protruding from the radiator (only one line shown, other line similar)

5.6a Loosen the hose clamp and detach the upper radiator hose (arrow) . . .

5.6b . . . then loosen the hose clamp and detach the lower radiator hose (arrow)

15   On Legend models, detach the under-hood relay box and position it aside.

16   Remove the fan shroud lower mounting bolts **(see illustration)**.

17   Remove the fan shroud upper mounting bolts **(see illustration)**.

18   Carefully lift the fan out of the engine compartment **(see illustration)**.

19   To detach the fan from the motor, remove the motor shaft nut **(see illustration)**.

20   To detach the fan motor from the shroud, remove the mounting screws **(see illustration)**.

21   Installation is the reverse of removal. **Caution:** *When refilling the cooling system, be sure to bleed the air from the system or engine damage could result,* see Chapter 1 - Cooling system servicing.

---

5   Radiator and coolant reservoir - removal and installation

---

Warning: *Wait until the engine is completely cool before beginning these procedures. Read the warning at the beginning of Section 2.*

Radiator

Removal

Refer to illustrations 5.4, 5.6a, 5.6b and 5.8

1   Disconnect the cable from the negative battery terminal. **Caution:** *If the radio in your vehicle is equipped with an anti-theft system, make sure you have the correct activation code before disconnecting the battery.*

2   Set the parking brake and block the rear wheels. Raise the front of the vehicle and support it securely on jackstands. Remove the splash pan beneath the radiator.

3   Drain the cooling system (see Chapter 1). If the coolant is relatively new or in good condition, save it and reuse it.

4   If the vehicle is equipped with an automatic transmission/transaxle, disconnect the cooler lines from the radiator **(see illustration)**. Use a drip pan to catch spilled fluid and plug the lines and fittings.

5   Disconnect the electrical connectors for the cooling fan motors.

6   Loosen the hose clamps, then detach the radiator hoses from the fittings **(see illus-**

trations). If they're stuck, grasp each hose near the end with a pair of slip joint pliers and twist it to break the seal, then pull it off - be careful not to damage the radiator fittings! If the hoses are old or deteriorated, cut them off and install new ones.

7   Remove the engine cooling fans (see Section 4).

5.8 Remove these bolts (arrows) and brackets that attach the radiator to the radiator support

6.1 Oil cooler location (arrow)

8   Unbolt and remove the small brackets that attach the upper end of the radiator to the radiator support **(see illustration)**.
9   Carefully lift out the radiator. Don't spill coolant on the vehicle or scratch the paint.
10   Inspect the radiator for leaks and damage. If it needs repair, have a radiator shop or dealer service department perform the work as special techniques are required.
11   Bugs and dirt can be removed from the radiator by spraying with a garden hose from the back side.
12   Check the radiator mounts for deterioration and replace if necessary.

Installation

13   Installation is the reverse of the removal procedure. Guide the radiator into the mounts until they seat properly.
14   After installation, fill the cooling system with the proper mixture of antifreeze and water. **Caution:** *When refilling the cooling system, be sure to bleed the air from the system or engine damage could result,* see Chapter 1 - Cooling system servicing.
15   Start the engine and check for leaks. Allow the engine to reach normal operating temperature, indicated by the upper radiator hose becoming hot. Recheck the coolant level and add more if required.
16   If you're working on an automatic transaxle equipped vehicle, check and add fluid as needed.

Coolant reservoir

17   The coolant reservoir is mounted adjacent to the radiator in the right front corner of the engine compartment.
18   Trace the overflow hose from the radiator neck to the top of coolant reservoir. Remove the cap with the hose still attached. Lift the reservoir straight up out of the bracket.
19   Pour the coolant into a container.
20   Wash out and inspect the reservoir for cracks and chafing. Examine the reservoir closely. If it's damaged, replace it.
21   Installation is the reverse of removal.

7.3a The weep holes (arrows) are located on the firewall side of the water pump on Integra models

6   Oil cooler - removal and installation

Warning: *Allow the engine to cool completely before beginning this procedure.*

Removal

Refer to illustration 6.1

1   The oil cooler used on some Integra models is mounted between the oil filter and engine block **(see illustration)**.
2   Remove the oil filter and drain the coolant (see Chapter 1).
3   Detach the two coolant lines from the oil cooler. Be prepared for coolant to escape from the open fittings. Cap or plug the open fittings.
4   Remove the large nut (actually part of the hollow retaining bolt) in the center of the oil cooler and separate the oil cooler from the engine.

Installation

5   Installation is the reverse of removal. Be sure to use a new O-ring between the block

7.3b Legend water pump weep hole location (arrow)

and oil cooler (lubricate the O-ring with clean engine oil before installation). Tighten the coolant hoses securely at the fittings.
6   Install a new oil filter and change the engine oil (see Chapter 1).
7   Refill the cooling system. **Caution:** *When refilling the cooling system, be sure to bleed the air from the system or engine damage could result,* see Chapter 1 - Cooling system servicing.
8   Start the engine and check for oil and coolant leaks.
9   Recheck the coolant and oil levels.

7   Water pump - check

Refer to illustrations 7.3a and 7.3b

1   A failure in the water pump can cause serious engine damage due to overheating.
2   There are two ways to check the operation of the water pump while it's installed on the engine. If the pump is defective, it should be replaced with a new or rebuilt unit.
3   Water pumps are equipped with weep (or vent) holes **(see illustrations)**. If a failure occurs in the pump seal, coolant will leak

8.6a Integra water pump bolt locations (arrows)

8.6b Legend water pump bolt locations (arrows) (not all bolts visible)

8.11 Apply a thin layer of RTV sealant to the O-ring groove of the new pump, then carefully set a new O-ring in the groove

9.1a Location of the Integra model coolant temperature sending unit (arrow)

9.1b Legend model coolant temperature sending unit location (arrow)

from the hole. With the timing belt cover removed, you'll need a flashlight and small mirror to find the hole on the water pump from underneath to check for leaks.

4   If the water pump shaft bearings fail there may be a howling sound at the pump while it's running. Shaft wear can be felt with the timing belt removed if the water pump pulley is rocked up and down (with the engine off). Don't mistake drivebelt slippage, which causes a squealing sound, for water pump bearing failure.

8   Water pump - replacement

Refer to illustrations 8.6a, 8.6b and 8.11
Warning: *Wait until the engine is completely cool before beginning this procedure. Read the warning at the beginning of Section 2.*
1   Disconnect the cable from the negative battery terminal. **Caution:** *If the radio in your vehicle is equipped with an anti-theft system, make sure you have the correct activation code before disconnecting the battery.*
2   Drain the cooling system (see Chapter 1). If the coolant is relatively new or in good condition, save it and reuse it.
3   Remove the drivebelts (see Chapter 1).

4   Remove the timing belt (see Chapter 2, Part A). On Integra models, remove the pulleys from the camshafts and the timing belt rear cover from the engine.
5   Remove any accessory brackets from the water pump. On Legend models, remove the thermostat housing-to-water pump bolts and detach the coolant hoses from the water pump.
6   Remove the bolts and detach the water pump from the engine **(see illustration)**. Note the location of the longer bolts on Legend models.
7   Clean the bolt threads and the threaded holes in the engine to remove corrosion and sealant.
8   Compare the new pump to the old one to make sure they're identical.
9   Remove all traces of old gasket sealant and O-ring from the engine.
10   Clean the engine and new water pump mating surfaces with lacquer thinner or acetone.
11   Apply a thin layer of RTV sealant to the O-ring groove of the new pump, then carefully set a new O-ring in the groove **(see illustration)**.
12   Carefully attach the pump to the engine and thread the bolts into the holes finger tight.

13   Install the remaining bolts (if they also hold an accessory bracket in place, be sure to reposition the bracket at this time). Tighten them to the torque listed in this Chapter's Specifications in 1/4-turn increments. Don't overtighten them or the pump may be distorted.
14   Reinstall all parts removed for access to the pump.
15   Refill the cooling system and check the drivebelt tension (see Chapter 1). **Caution:** *When refilling the cooling system, be sure to bleed the air from the system or engine damage could result,* see Chapter 1 - Cooling system servicing.
16   Run the engine and check for leaks.

9   Coolant temperature gauge sending unit - check and replacement

Warning: *Wait until the engine is completely cool before beginning this procedure.*
Refer to illustrations 9.1a and 9.1b
1   The coolant temperature indicator system consists of a temperature gauge mounted in the instrument panel and a coolant temperature sending unit mounted

3

10.3 Blower motor connector (arrow) - Integra models

10.5 Blower motor resistor terminals - with the connector disconnected, there should be approximately 2.5 ohms between terminals 2 and 4

| 1 | 2 | 3 |
| 4 | 5 | 6 |

SWITCH POSITION	CONTINUITY BETWEEN
LOW	3, 5 AND 6
MEDIUM 1	2, 5 AND 6
MEDIUM 2	1, 5 AND 6
HIGH	4, 5 AND 6

10.6 Blower switch terminal guide and continuity table (Integra)

on the engine **(see illustrations)**.

2   If an overheating indication occurs even when the engine is cold, check the wiring between the dash and the sending unit for a short circuit to ground.

3   If the gauge is inoperative, test the circuit by briefly grounding the wire to the sending unit while the ignition is on (engine not running for safety). If the gauge begins to deflects full scale, replace the sending unit. Don't let the gauge fully deflect full scale as this could damage it. **Warning:** *This vehicle is equipped with electric cooling fans. Stay clear of the fan blades, which can come on even when the engine is not running.* If the sending unit is suspect, remove it and check the resistance across the terminals with the unit cold and hot (suspend the probe in hot water). With the unit cool (133 degrees F), the resistance should be 142 ohms and from 49 to 32 ohms when it is hot (186 to 212 degrees F).

4   If the gauge doesn't respond in the test outlined in Step 3, check for an open circuit in the gauge wiring.

5   If the sending unit must be replaced, simply unscrew it from the engine and quickly install the replacement. Use sealant on the threads. Make sure the engine is cool before removing the defective sending unit. There will be some coolant loss as the unit is removed, so be prepared to catch it. Check the level after the replacement part has been installed.

10   Blower motor and circuit - check

Warning: *The models covered by this manual are equipped with a Supplemental Restraint system (SRS), more commonly known as airbags. Always disable the airbag system before working in the vicinity of the impact sensors, steering column or instrument panel to avoid the possibility of accidental deployment of the airbag, which could cause personal injury (see Chapter 12). Do not use electrical test equipment on any of the airbag system wiring or tamper with them in any way.*

Integra

Refer to illustrations 10.3, 10.5 and 10.6

1   After disabling the airbags (see Chapter 12), reconnect the battery cables. Check the fuse and all connections in the circuit for looseness and corrosion. Make sure the battery is fully charged. Remove the under-dash panels for access to the circuit connectors.

2   Place the transaxle in Park (automatic) or neutral (manual) and apply the parking brake. Turn the ignition switch On (engine not running) and place the blower speed switch in the Hi position.

3   If the blower motor does not operate at any speed, disconnect the electrical connector at the blower motor and check for battery voltage between the connector blue/white wire terminal and ground **(see illustration)**. If no battery voltage is present, check the circuit from the ignition switch to the blower motor.

4   If battery voltage was present at the blower motor connector, reconnect the connector to the blower motor and insert a jumper wire into the backside of the blower motor connector blue/black wire and connect the other end of the jumper wire to a good chassis ground. If the blower motor now runs the fault lies with the blower switch, the blower resistors or related wiring (see Steps 5, 6 and 7). If there is battery voltage present

at the connector and the motor didn't run when grounded, replace the blower motor (see Section 11).

5   If the blower motor runs, but one or more speeds are inoperative, remove the blower resistor from the heater case mounting location (above the blower motor) and visually check for damage. Using an ohmmeter, check the resistance between terminals 2 and 4 **(see illustration)**. The resistance should be approximately 2.5 ohms. If the resistance is not as specified, replace the blower resistor assembly.

6   If the blower resistor tests good, remove the control panel (see Section 12) and check the continuity of the blower switch **(see illustration)**. If the continuity is not as specified, replace the switch.

7   If the switch tests good, check the wiring from the resistor connector to the switch connector for continuity. Check for continuity to chassis ground at the black wire terminal of the switch connector. If any of the circuits are open, repair the wiring.

Legend

Refer to illustrations 10.9, 10.10 and 10.13

8   After disabling the airbags (see Chapter 12), reconnect the battery cables. Check the fuse and all connections in the circuit for looseness and corrosion. Make sure the bat-

10.9 Blower motor connector location (arrow) and terminal details

10.10 Blower motor relay (A), high speed relay (B) and terminal details for the blower motor relay harness connector

10.13 To check the blower motor relay, connect an ohmmeter to terminals (A) and (B); connect battery power to terminal (C) and ground terminal (D); the relay should click and continuity should be indicated on the meter

tery is fully charged. Remove the under-dash panels for access to the circuit connectors.

9   If the blower motor does not operate, disconnect the blower motor electrical connector **(see illustration)**. Using a voltmeter or test light, turn the ignition key On and check for battery voltage at the blue/red wire terminal of the harness connector. If voltage is present, reconnect the connector and using a jumper wire, connect the blue/black terminal to a good chassis ground. The blower motor should run at full speed, if it doesn't, the motor is faulty and should be replaced.

10   If battery voltage is not present at the blue/red terminal of the blower motor connector, disconnect the electrical connector from the blower motor relay **(see illustration)**.

11   Using a voltmeter or test light, check for battery voltage at the blue/white wire terminal of the blower relay harness connector with the ignition key Off. Turn the ignition key On

and check for battery voltage at the blue/yellow wire terminal. If battery voltage is not present at the connector check the circuits from the fuse box or ignition switch to the connector.

12   Using an ohmmeter or self-powered continuity tester, check for continuity between the black wire terminal of the relay connector and chassis ground. If there is no continuity, check an open circuit in the wire or a bad ground connection.

13   If the blower relay power and ground circuits are good, detach the relay from the housing and check the relay terminals for continuity when connected to battery power and ground **(see illustration)**. If the relay is faulty, replace it.

14   The high speed relay can be checked in the same manner as the blower speed relay. Check for battery voltage on the black/yellow terminal of the high speed relay connector. Using a jumper wire, connect the orange/white terminal to a good chassis ground (without disconnecting the connector). If all the above tests are good, the blower motor should run at high speed. If it doesn't, remove the relay and test it as described in Step 13.

15   The blower speeds are controlled by power transistor unit mounted on the heater/evaporator assembly and cannot be checked using conventional methods. If there is a problem with the blower motor speed control, have the power transistor and control assembly checked by a dealer service department or other qualified repair facility.

11   Blower motor - removal and installation

Warning: *The models covered by this manual are equipped with a Supplemental Restraint System (SRS), more commonly known as airbags. Always disable the airbag system before working in the vicinity of the SRS unit, steering column or instrument panel to avoid*

the possibility of accidental deployment of the airbag, which could cause personal injury (see Chapter 12).

1   Disconnect the cable from the negative battery terminal. Disable the airbag (see Chapter 12). **Caution:** *If the radio in your vehicle is equipped with an anti-theft system, make sure you have the correct activation code before disconnecting the battery.*

2   The blower unit is located under the dash, behind the glovebox. remove the necessary under-dash panels to access the blower motor.

Integra

Refer to illustration 11.4

3   Disconnect the electrical connector from the blower motor.

4   Remove the three retaining screws and remove the blower motor **(see illustration)**.

5   If you're replacing the blower motor itself, separate the blower motor from the fan wheel and place the fan on the new blower motor.

6   Installation is the reverse of removal. Check for proper operation.

11.4 Blower motor mounting screws (arrows) - Integra models

3

11.11 Remove the screws (arrows) and separate the blower motor cover from the blower unit

12.4 On Integra models, remove the mounting screws retaining the heater/air conditioner control assembly to the dash panel (arrows)

Legend

Refer to illustration 11.11

Note: *On Legend models, the complete blower unit must be removed from the vehicle to access the blower motor.*

7   Remove the glovebox, instrument panel side cover and glovebox frame (see Chapter 11).

8   Disconnect the wiring harness electrical connectors from the blower unit. Remove the four bolts retaining the blower unit to the dash frame.

9   Detach the assembly and pull it out from under the instrument panel.

10   Remove the blower relay bracket and blower relays from the unit.

11   Remove the remainder of the screws and separate the lower cover from the housing **(see illustration)**. Remove the blower motor from the unit.

12   Installation is the reverse of removal.

12   Heater and air conditioning control assembly - removal, installation and cable adjustment

Warning: *The models covered by this manual are equipped with a Supplemental Restraint System (SRS), more commonly known as airbags. Always disable the airbag system before working in the vicinity of the SRS unit, steering column or instrument panel to avoid the possibility of accidental deployment of the airbag, which could cause personal injury* (see Chapter 12).

1   Disconnect the cable from the negative battery terminal. **Caution:** *If the radio in your vehicle is equipped with an anti-theft system, make sure you have the correct activation code before disconnecting the battery.*

Integra

Refer to illustration 12.4

2   Remove the instrument cluster bezel, knee bolster and passenger side lower cover (see Chapter 11). Remove the radio (see

12.8 Detach the air mix control cable from the clamp (arrow)

Chapter 12). Remove the center console (see Chapter 11).

3   Disconnect the air mix control cable from the heater unit **(see illustration12.8)**. disconnect the mode control and recircula-tion control cables (if equipped) from the heater unit. Disconnect the heater valve cable from the heater valve **(see illustration12.16)**.

4   Remove the heater/air conditioner con-trol assembly mounting screws **(see illustra-tion)**.

5   Pull the assembly out and disconnect electrical connectors. Do not attempt to remove the cables from the control unit, they are permanently attached.

6   Installation is the reverse of removal. Adjust the control cables.

7   Run the engine and check for proper functioning of the heater and air conditioning system.

Adjustment

Refer to illustration 12.8

Air mix control cable

8   Disconnect the cable from the control arm clamp **(see illustration)**.

9   Set the temperature control lever to COOL. Rotate the air mix control arm to the

12.15 Disconnect the cable from the clamp and rotate the heater valve arm forward

front of the vehicle and connect the cable to the arm.

10   Slide the cable housing back from the end to take up any slack without allowing the control lever to move and connect the cable housing to the clamp.

Mode control cable

11   Disconnect the cable from the control arm clamp. Move the mode control lever to the DEFROST position.

12   Rotate the control shaft toward the front of the vehicle, then connect the cable end to the arm.

13   Slide the cable housing back from the end to take up any slack without allowing the control lever to move and connect the cable housing to the clamp.

Heater valve cable

Refer to illustration 12.15

14   Disconnect the cable from the cable clamp in the engine compartment.

15   Set the temperature control lever to COOL. Rotate the heater control valve arm toward the front of the vehicle and connect the cable to the arm **(see illustration)**.

16   Slide the cable housing back from the

12.18 To remove the heater and air conditioning control assembly, remove the screws (A) and press down on the clips (B) (unit removed for clarity)

13.3 Detach the control cable (arrow) from the heater valve lever arm using a small screwdriver to lift the cable end off the pin

13.4a Loosen the two heater hose clamps and disconnect the heater hoses (arrows) from the heater core inlet and outlet pipes at the firewall

13.4b Remove the nut (arrow) retaining the heater unit to the firewall

13.12 Detach the cable (arrow) from the heater valve arm (Legend models)

end to take up any slack without allowing the control lever to move and connect the cable housing to the clamp.

Legend

Refer to illustration 12.18

17   Remove the radio (see Chapter 12). **Caution:** *If the radio in your vehicle is equipped with an anti-theft system, make sure you have the correct activation code before disconnecting the battery.*

18   Remove the two retaining screws through the radio opening **(see illustration)**. Using a small screwdriver, push down on the two clips along the upper edge and pull the trim panel and control assembly out of the dash. Disconnect the electrical connectors from the control assembly.

19   Installation is reverse of removal.

13   Heater core - replacement

Warning 1: *The models covered by this manual are equipped with a Supplemental Restraint System (SRS), more commonly known as airbags. Always disable the airbag system before working in the vicinity of the SRS unit, steering column or instrument panel to avoid the possibility of accidental deployment of the airbag, which could cause personal injury (see Chapter 12).*

Warning 2: *The air conditioning system is under high pressure. Do not loosen any hose fittings or remove any components until after the system has been discharged. Air conditioning refrigerant should be properly discharged into an EPA-approved recovery/recycling unit at a dealer service department or an automotive air conditioning repair facility. Always wear eye protection when disconnecting air conditioning system fittings.*

1   If the vehicle is equipped with air conditioning, have the system discharged by a

dealer service department or automotive air conditioning repair facility. Disconnect the cable from the negative battery terminal. Disable the airbags, if equipped (see Chapter 12). **Caution:** *If the radio in your vehicle is equipped with an anti-theft system, make sure you have the correct activation code before disconnecting the battery.*

2   Drain the cooling system (see Chapter 1).

Integra

Refer to illustrations 13.3, 13.4a and 13.4b

3   Disconnect the heater valve cable **(see illustration)**.

4   Working in the engine compartment, disconnect the heater hoses where they enter the firewall **(see illustration)**. Place a drain pan underneath the hoses to catch any coolant that runs out when the hoses are disconnected. Remove the heater unit mounting nut located above the heater hose inlet and outlet tubes **(see illustration)**. **Caution:** *Be careful not to damage or bend the fuel lines or brake pipes when removing the nut.*

5   Remove the heater/air conditioner control assembly (see Section 12).

6   Remove the instrument cluster bezel, the knee bolster, the center console and the instrument panel (see Chapter 11).

7   Remove the evaporator unit (see Section 19).

8   Remove the steering column bracket.

9   Remove the wire harness clip from the heater unit, the two nuts retaining the heater unit to the bulkhead and remove the heater unit from the vehicle.

10   Remove the screws from the heater core cover and the heater pipe clamp. Lift the heater core from the housing.

11   Installation is the reverse of removal. Be sure to check the operation of the air control flaps. If any parts bind, correct the problem before installation.

Legend

Refer to illustrations 13.12, 13.13, 13.14, 13.15, 13.19a, 13.19b and 13.20

12   Disconnect the heater valve cable **(see illustration)**.

3

13.13 Loosen the two heater hose clamps and disconnect the heater hoses (arrows) from the heater core pipes at the firewall (Legend models)

13   Working in the engine compartment, disconnect the heater hoses **(see illustration)** where they enter the firewall. Place a drain pan underneath the hoses to catch any

13.19a Heater unit left side retaining nuts (arrows)

13.14 Remove the bolt (arrow) and detach the air conditioning lines

coolant that runs out when the hoses are disconnected.

14   Disconnect the air conditioning lines from the evaporator sealing plate on the firewall **(see illustration)**. Be sure to cap the lines to avoid contaminating the system.

15   Remove the two nuts and detach the evaporator sealing plate **(see illustration)**.

16   Remove the heater/air conditioner control assembly (see Section 12).

17   Remove the instrument cluster bezel, the console and the instrument panel (see Chapter 11).

18   Remove the steering column bracket.

19   Remove the air ducts and disconnect the wiring harness. Remove the nuts and bolts retaining the heater unit to the bulkhead and remove the heater unit from the vehicle **(see illustrations)**.

20   Remove the inlet and outlet pipe bracket bolts and lift the heater core from the housing **(see illustration)**.

21   Installation is the reverse of removal. Be sure to check the operation of the air control flaps. If any parts bind, correct the problem before installation.

13.15 Remove the evaporator sealing plate nuts (arrows)

All models

22   Refill the cooling system (see Chapter 1). **Caution:** *When refilling the cooling system, be sure to bleed the air from the system or engine damage could result,* see Chapter 1 - Cooling system servicing.

23   Reconnect the battery and run the engine. Check for coolant leaks and proper heater system operation. If equipped with air conditioning, have the system charged by a dealer service department or automotive air conditioning repair facility.

14   Air conditioning and heating system - check and maintenance

Air conditioning system

Refer to illustration 14.1

Warning: *The air conditioning system is under high pressure. Do not loosen any hose fittings or remove any components until after the system has been discharged. Air conditioning refrigerant should be properly dis-*

13.19b Heater unit right side retaining nuts and bolts (arrows)

13.20 Heater core inlet and outlet pipe bracket clamp screws (arrows)

14.1 Air conditioner condensation drain tube (arrow)

14.9 Insert a thermometer in the center vent while operating the air conditioning system - the output air should be 35 - 45 degrees F less than the ambient temperature, depending on humidity (but not lower than 40-degrees F

charged into an EPA-approved recovery/recycling unit at a dealer service department or an automotive air conditioning repair facility. Always wear eye protection when disconnecting air conditioning system fittings.

Caution 1: *There are two types of refrigerants used on the models covered by this manual. 1992 and earlier Legend and all Integra models use R-12 refrigerant while 1993 and later Legend models use environmentally-friendly R-134a. The two refrigerants (and their appropriate refrigerants oils) are not compatible and must never be mixed or components will be damaged.*

Caution 2: *When replacing entire components, additional refrigerant oil should be added equal to the amount that is removed with the component being replaced. Be sure to read the can before adding any oil to the system, to make sure it is compatible with either the R-12 or R-134a system.*

1   The following maintenance checks should be performed on a regular basis to ensure that the air conditioning continues to operate at peak efficiency.

  a) *Inspect the condition of the compressor drivebelt. If it is worn or deteriorated, replace it (see Chapter 1).*
  b) *Check the drivebelt tension and, if necessary, adjust it (see Chapter 1).*
  c) *Inspect the system hoses. Look for cracks, bubbles, hardening and deterioration. Inspect the hoses and all fittings for oil bubbles or seepage. If there is any evidence of wear, damage or leakage, replace the hose(s).*
  d) *Inspect the condenser fins for leaves, bugs and any other foreign material that may have embedded itself in the fins. Use a "fin comb" or compressed air to remove debris from the condenser.*
  e) *Make sure the system has the correct refrigerant charge.*
  f) *If you hear water sloshing around in the dash area or have water dripping on the carpet, check the evaporator housing drain tube* **(see illustration)** *and insert a piece of wire into the opening to check for blockage.*

2   It's a good idea to operate the system for about ten minutes at least once a month. This is particularly important during the winter months because long term non-use can cause hardening, and subsequent failure, of the seals. Note that using the Defrost function operates the compressor.

3   If the air conditioning system is not working properly, first make sure the compressor clutch is operating (see Section 15).

4   Because of the complexity of the air conditioning system and the special equipment necessary to service it, in-depth troubleshooting and repairs are not included in this manual. However, simple checks and component replacement procedures are provided in this Chapter. For more complete information on the air conditioning system, refer to the *Haynes Automotive Heating and Air Conditioning Manual*. However, simple component replacement procedures are provided in this Chapter.

5   The most common cause of poor cooling is simply a low system refrigerant charge. If a noticeable drop in system cooling ability occurs, one of the following quick checks will help you determine whether the refrigerant level is low. Should the system lose its cooling ability, the following procedure will help you pinpoint the cause.

Check

Refer to illustration 14.9

6   Warm the engine up to normal operating temperature.

7   Place the air conditioning temperature selector at the coldest setting and put the blower at the highest setting. Open the doors (to make sure the air conditioning system doesn't cycle off as soon as it cools the passenger compartment).

8   After the system reaches operating temperature, feel the two pipes connected to the evaporator at the firewall.

9   The pipe (thinner tubing) leading from the condenser outlet to the evaporator should be cold, and the evaporator outlet line (the thicker tubing that leads back to the compressor) should be slightly colder (3 to 10 degrees F). If the evaporator outlet is considerably warmer than the inlet, the system needs a charge. Insert a thermometer in the center air distribution duct **(see illustration)** while operating the air conditioning system - the temperature of the output air should be 35 to 40 degrees F below the ambient air temperature (down to approximately 40 degrees F). If the ambient (outside) air temperature is very high, say 110 degrees F, the duct air temperature may be as high as 60 degrees F, but generally the air conditioning is 35 to 40 degrees F cooler than the ambient air.

10   If the air isn't as cold as it used to be, the system probably needs a charge. Further inspection or testing of the system is beyond the scope of the home mechanic and should be left to a professional.

Adding refrigerant

Refer to illustrations 14.12 and 14.15

Caution: *Make sure any refrigerant, refrigerant oil or replacement component your purchase is designated as compatible with environmentally-friendly R-134a systems.*

11   Integra models and 1992 and later Legend models use R-12 refrigerant. Because of federal restrictions on the sale of R-12 refrigerant, it isn't practical for refrigerant to be added by the home mechanic. When the system needs recharging, take the vehicle to a dealer service department or professional air conditioning shop for evacuation, leak testing and recharging. On 1993 and later Legend models using R-134a refrigerant, make sure any refrigerant, oil or replacement component is designated for environmentally-friendly R-134a systems.

12   Buy an R-134a automotive charging kit at an auto parts store **(see illustration)**. A charging kit includes a 12-ounce can of refrigerant, a tap valve and a short section of hose that can be attached between the tap

3

14.12 A basic charging kit for 134A systems is available at most auto parts stores - it must say 134a (not R-12) and so should the 12-ounce can of refrigerant

14.15 Add refrigerant only to the low-side - the procedure is easier if you wrap the can with a warm, wet towel to prevent icing

14.26 Air mix control motor connector (arrow) and terminal details

valve and the system low side service valve. Because one can of refrigerant may not be sufficient to bring the system charge up to the proper level, it's a good idea to buy an additional can. **Warning:** *Never add more than two cans of refrigerant to the system.*

13   Hook up the charging kit by following the manufacturer's instructions. **Warning:** *DO NOT hook the charging kit hose to the system high side!* The fittings on the charging kit are designed to fit **only** on the low side of the system.

14   Back off the valve handle on the charging kit and screw the kit onto the refrigerant can, making sure first that the O-ring or rubber seal inside the threaded portion of the kit is in place. **Warning:** *Wear protective eyewear when dealing with pressurized refrigerant cans.*

15   Remove the dust cap from the low-side charging and attach the quick-connect fitting on the kit hose **(see illustration)**.

16   Warm up the engine and turn on the air conditioning. Keep the charging kit hose away from the fan and other moving parts. **Note:** *The charging process requires the compressor to be running. If the clutch cycles off, you can put the air conditioning switch on High and leave the car doors open to keep the clutch on and compressor working.* **Note:** *The compressor can be kept on during the charging by removing the connector from the low-pressure switch (combination high-limit and low-limit switch on some models) and bridging it with a jumper wire during the procedure.*

17   Turn the valve handle on the kit until the stem pierces the can, then back the handle out to release the refrigerant. You should be able to hear the rush of gas. Add refrigerant to the low side of the system, keeping the can upright at all times, but shaking it occasionally. Allow stabilization time between each addition.

18   If you have an accurate thermometer, you can place it in the center air conditioning duct inside the vehicle and keep track of the output air temperature **(see illustration 14.9)**.

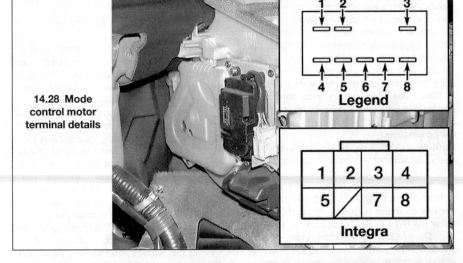

14.28 Mode control motor terminal details

Legend

Integra

A charged system that is working properly should cool down to approximately 40-degrees F. If the ambient (outside) air temperature is very high, say 110 degrees F, the duct air temperature may be as high as 60 degrees F, but generally the air conditioning is 30-40 degrees F cooler than the ambient air.

19   When the can is empty, turn the valve handle to the closed position and release the connection from the low-side port. Replace the dust cap.

20   Remove the charging kit from the can and store the kit for future use with the piercing valve in the UP position, to prevent inadvertently piercing the can on the next use.

Heating systems

21   If the carpet under the heater core is damp, or if antifreeze vapor or steam is coming through the vents, the heater core is leaking. Remove it (see Section 13) and install a new unit.

22   If the air coming out of the heater vents isn't hot, the problem could stem from any of the following causes:

a)   *The thermostat is stuck open, prevent-*

ing the engine coolant from warming up enough to carry heat to the heater core. Replace the thermostat (see Section 3).

b)   *There is a blockage in the system, preventing the flow of coolant through the heater core. Feel both heater hoses at the firewall. They should be hot. If one of them is cold, there is an obstruction in one of the hoses or in the heater core, or the heater control valve is shut. Detach the hoses and back flush the heater core with a water hose. If the heater core is clear but circulation is impeded, remove the two hoses and flush them out with a water hose.*

c)   *If flushing fails to remove the blockage from the heater core, the core must be replaced (see Section 13).*

Air mix control motor check (Legend only)

Refer to illustration 14.26

26   Remove the electrical connector from the air mix control motor. Attach a jumper wire with battery voltage to the number 1 ter-

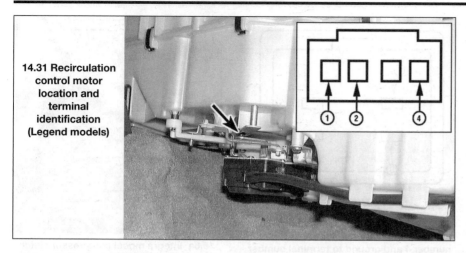

14.31 Recirculation control motor location and terminal identification (Legend models)

14.32 Recirculation motor terminal details (Integra models)

minal on the motor, and apply ground to terminal 2 **(see illustration)**. The motor should run and stop at Cool. If it doesn't operate, reverse the two jumper wires and the motor should operate the other direction and stop at Hot. If it doesn't operate in either direction, replace the motor.

27   If you suspect the problem may be in the operation of the door, disconnect the control motor's rod from the linkage and perform the jumper wire tests above. If the motor now operates, repair or replace the air mix door or linkage.

Mode control motor check

Refer to illustration 14.28

28   On Legend models, connect a jumper wire with battery power to terminal 3 and ground to terminal 2 **(see illustration)**. On Integra models, connect a jumper wire with battery power to terminal 5 and ground to terminal 1. Use another jumper wire to connect the number 1 terminal to the number 4 through number 8 terminals in order. The mode control motor should start and run smoothly as each connection is made. If does not, replace the mode motor with a new one.

Recirculation control motor check

Refer to illustrations 14.31 and 14.32

31   On Legend models, disconnect the electrical connector at the recirculation control motor **(see illustration)**. Connect a jumper wire with battery power to terminal 1, then ground terminals 2 and 4. The motor should run smoothly. The motor should stop at either Fresh or Recirculate when the ground jumpers are removed.

32   On Integra models, the recirculation control motor is located on the side of the blower unit. Disconnect the electrical connector at the recirculation control motor and connect a jumper wire with battery power to terminal 3 and ground terminal 2 **(see illustration)**. Use another jumper wire to connect the number 2 terminal to the number 1 and number 4 terminals in order. The motor should run 1/2-turn to the Fresh or Recirculate positions when the 1 and 4 terminals are grounded.

33   If the motor does not operates described, disconnect it from the door linkage and test again. If it works now, check the door and linkage for binding.

Eliminating air-conditioning odors

34   Unpleasant odors that often develop in air-conditioning systems are caused by the growth of a fungus, usually on the surface of the evaporator core. The warm, humid environment there is a perfect breeding ground for mildew to develop.

35   The evaporator core on most vehicles is difficult to access, and factory dealerships have a lengthy, expensive process for eliminating the fungus by opening up the evaporator case and using a powerful disinfectant and rinse on the core until the fungus is gone. You can service your own system at home, but it takes something much stronger than basic household germ-killers or deodorizers.

36   Aerosol disinfectants for automotive air-conditioning systems are available in most auto parts stores, but remember when shopping for them that the most effective treatments are also the most expensive. The basic procedure for using these sprays is to start by running the system in the RECIRC mode for ten minutes with the blower on its highest speed. Use the highest heat mode to dry out the system and keep the compressor from engaging by disconnecting the wiring connector at the compressor (see Section 17).

37   The disinfectant can usually comes with a long spray hose. Remove the blower motor (see Section 10), point the nozzle inside the hole and to the left towards the evaporator core, and spray according to the manufacturer's recommendations. Try to cover the whole surface of the evaporator core, by aiming the spray up, down and sideways. Follow the manufacturer's recommendations for the length of spray and waiting time between applications.

38   Once the evaporator has been cleaned, the best way to prevent the mildew from coming back again is to make sure your evaporator housing drain tube is clear **(see illustration 14.1)**.

15   Air conditioning compressor clutch circuit - check

Refer to illustrations 15.3a, 15.3b, 15.5, 15.6a and 15.6b

1   Proper operation of the compressor clutch is essential to the function of the air conditioning system. If your system doesn't seem to get cold, first check the clutch operation.

2   With the engine warmed up, set the air conditioning temperature selector on the coldest setting and the fan on high. Open the doors (to make sure the air conditioning system doesn't cycle off as soon as it cools the passenger compartment down).

3   Have an assistant push the A/C button while you observe the front of the compressor. The clutch will make an audible click and the center of the clutch should rotate. If it doesn't, shut the engine off and disconnect the air conditioning system pressure switch **(see illustrations)**. On Integra models, insert a jumper wire between the two terminals of the connector. On legend models, insert a jumper wire between the light blue and blue/red wire terminals of the connector. Try the air conditioning again as in Steps 1 and 2. If it works now, the system pressure is too

15.3a Integra air conditioning pressure switch location (arrow)

15.3b Legend air conditioning pressure switch location (arrow)

12021 3-15.5 HAYNES

15.5 Compressor clutch relay terminals - with battery power connected to terminal number 4 and ground to terminal number 2, there should be continuity between terminals number 1 and number 3

15.6a Integra model compressor clutch connector (arrow)

15.6b Legend compressor clutch connector location (arrow)

16.4 In the engine compartment, remove the bolts (arrows) and disconnect both refrigerant line fittings (Integra model shown)

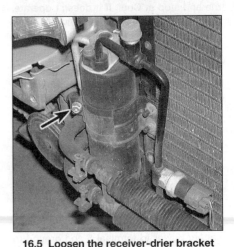

16.5 Loosen the receiver-drier bracket pinch bolt (arrow) (Legend model shown)

high or too low. Have your system tested by a dealer service department or air conditioning shop.

4   If the clutch still didn't operate, check the appropriate fuses. Inspect the fuse in the interior fuse panel under the driver's side of the dash and in the large relay/fuse box at the engine side of the firewall.

5   Remove the compressor clutch relay from the underhood relay/fuse box and test the relay **(see illustration)** (see Chapter 12 for additional information on testing relays). With the relay out and the ignition Off, check for battery power at the relay connector in the relay box that correspond to the number 1 terminal of the compressor clutch relay. There should be battery power. With the key On, there should be battery power at terminal number 4.

6   Connect the terminals in the fuse box that correspond to the relay terminals 1 and 3 with a jumper wire. Turn the ignition On and listen for the clutch to click. If the clutch doesn't respond, disconnect the clutch connector at the compressor and check for battery voltage at the compressor clutch connector **(see illustrations)**. If power is avail-

able and the clutch doesn't operate when connected, the compressor clutch is defective.

7   If the compressor clutch, relay and related circuits are good and the system is fully charged with refrigerant and the compressor does not operate under normal conditions, have the PCM and related circuits checked by a dealer service department or other properly equipped repair facility.

16   Air conditioning receiver-drier - removal and installation

Refer to illustrations 16.4 and 16.5

1   Have the air conditioning system refrigerant discharged by dealership service department or air conditioning repair facility (see the **Warnings** and **Cautions** in Section 14).

2   Disconnect the battery. **Caution:** *If the radio in your vehicle is equipped with an anti-theft system make sure you have the correct*

activation code before disconnecting the battery.

3   On Legend models, remove the front bumper for access to the receiver-drier.

4   Disconnect the refrigerant lines from the receiver-drier and cap the open fittings to prevent dirt and moisture entry **(see illustration)**.

5   Loosen the receiver-drier bracket pinch bolt and remove the receiver-drier from the vehicle **(see illustration)**.

6   Installation is the reverse of removal, using new O-rings where the lines connect to the receiver-drier.

7   Have the system evacuated, charged and leak tested by an air conditioning technician. If the receiver-drier was replaced, add 1/3 fluid ounce of refrigerant oil.

17   Air conditioning compressor - removal and installation

Refer to illustrations 17.7 and 17.9
Note : *The receiver-drier should be replaced whenever the compressor is replaced.*

1   Have the air conditioning system refrig-

17.7 Disconnect the refrigerant lines (arrows) and plug the open fittings to prevent entry of dirt and moisture

17.9 Remove the compressor mounting bolts (arrows) and lower the compressor out from under the vehicle

erant discharged by dealership service department or air conditioning repair facility (see the **Warnings** and **Cautions** in Section 14).

2   Disconnect the cable from the negative battery terminal. **Caution:** *If the radio in your vehicle is equipped with an anti-theft system, make sure you have the correct activation code before disconnecting the battery.*

3   Set the parking brake, block the rear wheels and raise the front of the vehicle, supporting it securely on jackstands.

4   Remove the drivebelt (see Chapter 1).

5   On Integra models, remove the power steering pump without disconnecting the hoses at position it aside (see Chapter 10). Remove the condenser fan and shroud (see Section4).

6   Remove the cruise control actuator (if equipped).

7   Disconnect the refrigerant lines from the compressor **(see illustration)**. Plug the open fittings to prevent entry of dirt and moisture.

8   Disconnect the compressor clutch wiring harness.

9   Unbolt the compressor **(see illustration)** from the mounting bracket and remove it from the vehicle.

10   The clutch may have to be transferred from the old compressor to the new unit.

11   Calculate and add the proper amount of refrigerant oil for the new compressor:

a) *Drain the refrigerant oil from the old compressor through the suction fitting and measure it in fluid ounces.*

b) *Subtract this volume from 2-2/3 fluid ounces (Integra) or 4-2/3 fluid ounces (Legend).*

c) *The difference between these two figures is equal to the amount you should drain from the new compressor.*

12   Installation is otherwise the reverse of removal.

13   Have the system evacuated, recharged and leak tested by a dealership service department or automotive air conditioning repair facility.

18   Air conditioning condenser - removal and installation

Refer to illustrations 18.4 and 18.5

1   Have the refrigerant discharged by a dealership service department or air condi-

tioning repair facility (see the **Warnings** and **Cautions** in Section 14).

2   Disconnect the cable from the negative battery terminal. **Caution:** *If the radio in your vehicle is equipped with an anti-theft system, make sure you have the correct activation code before disconnecting the battery.* On Legend models, remove the battery and the battery tray.

3   Remove the air intake duct. On Integra models, remove the coolant reservoir. On Legend models, remove the condenser fan and shroud.

4   Disconnect the condenser hose and discharge line from the condenser **(see illustration)**.

5   Remove the condenser brackets **(see illustration)**.

6   Lift the condenser from the vehicle. Be careful not to damage the condenser fins or the radiator when removing or installing the condenser.

7   Installation is the reverse of removal. **Note:** *Always replace all O-rings with new ones and lightly lubricate them with refrigerant oil before assembly.*

8   Have the system evacuated, charged and leak tested by a dealership service department or air conditioning repair facility. If a new condenser was installed, add 1/3 fluid ounce (Integra) or 1-fluid ounce (Legend) of refrigerant oil.

3

19   Air conditioning evaporator and expansion valve - removal and installation

Warning: *The models covered by this manual are equipped with a Supplemental Restraint System (SRS), more commonly known as airbags. Always disable the airbag system before working in the vicinity of the SRS unit, steering column or instrument panel to avoid the possibility of accidental deployment of the airbag, which could cause personal injury (see Chapter 12).*

1   Have the air conditioning system discharged by a dealer service department or

18.4 Disconnect the condenser line and discharge line attaching bolt (arrow) from the condenser

18.5 Remove the condenser retaining bracket bolts (arrows) and lift off the brackets

19.3 Disconnect the suction line (A) and the receiver line (B) from the evaporator at the firewall

19.8 Typical evaporator core and expansion valve installation

A   Expansion valve
B   Capillary tube (taped to suction line)
C   Pipe connections
D   Evaporator core

automotive air conditioning repair facility (see the **Warnings** and **Cautions** in Section 14).

2   Disconnect the cable from the negative battery terminal. Disable the airbag, if equipped (see Chapter 12). **Caution:** *If the radio in your vehicle is equipped with an anti-theft system, make sure you have the correct activation code before disconnecting the battery.*

Integra

Refer to illustrations 19.3 and 19.8

3   Disconnect the receiver line and suction line from the evaporator at the firewall **(see illustration)**. Plug both lines to prevent the entry of contaminants and moisture into air conditioning system.

4   Remove lower instrument panel covers from both sides. Remove the glovebox and the glovebox frame. Remove the center console (see Chapter 11).

5   Disconnect the connector from the air conditioning thermostat and remove the wiring harness clips from the evaporator housing.

6   Remove the evaporator unit retaining strap screws and detach the straps from the dash panel. Remove the evaporator unit mounting bolts/nuts. Pull the evaporator unit out far enough to disconnect the drain hose and remove the unit from the vehicle.

7   Remove the screws and clips retaining the evaporator case halves together, remove the air conditioning thermostat and separated the housing.

8   Remove the evaporator core from the housing and remove the expansion valve, if necessary **(see illustration)**.

9   Installation is the reverse of removal. Make sure the expansion valve is taped to the suction line as originally installed and install the thermostat sensor in the original location.

10   Have the system evacuated, charged

and leak tested by a dealer service department or automotive air conditioning repair facility. If a new evaporator was installed, add 1-fluid ounce of refrigerant oil.

Legend

Refer to illustrations 19.12a and 19.12b

11   Refer to Section 13 and remove the heater/evaporator unit.

12   Remove the screws and clips and separate the evaporator core cover from the heater/evaporator housing **(see illustrations)**.

13   Remove the evaporator core from the housing and remove the expansion valve, if necessary.

14   Installation is the reverse of removal. Make sure the expansion valve is taped to the suction line as originally installed.

15   Have the system evacuated, charged and leak tested by a dealer service department or automotive air conditioning repair facility. If a new evaporator was installed, add 2 fluid ounces of refrigerant oil.

19.12a Remove the screws and detach the clips from the front . . .

19.12b . . . and back side of the evaporator housing

Chapter 4
Fuel and exhaust systems

Contents

4

Specifications

Fuel pressure

Integra
  With vacuum hose attached
    1990 .... 26 to 32 psi
    1991 .... 28 to 35 psi
    1992 and 1993
      B18A1, B18B1 .... 32 to 39 psi
      B17A1, B17B1 .... 39 to 46 psi
  With vacuum hose disconnected
    1990 .... 35 to 41 psi
    1991 .... 37 to 41 psi
    1992 and 1993
      B18A1, B18B1 .... 41 to 48 psi
      B17A1, B17B1 .... 48 to 56 psi
Legend
  With vacuum hose attached
    1991 and 1992 .... 31 to 37 psi
    1993 .... 29 to 35 psi
    1994
      GS model .... 36 to 43 psi
      L, LS model .... 30 to 37 psi
  With vacuum hose disconnected
    1991 and 1992 .... 38 to 46 psi
    1993 .... 35 to 41 psi
    1994
      GS model .... 44 to 51 psi
      L, LS model .... 38 to 46 psi

Resistance values

Fuel injector resistor resistance (Legend only) .... 5 to 7 ohms
Fuel injector resistance
  Integra
    1990 and 1991 .... 1.5 to 2.5 ohms
    1992 on .... 10 to 13 ohms
  Legend .... 1.5 to 2.5 ohms
Fuel level sender resistance
  Full position .... 2 to 5 ohms
  Half position
    1990 and 1991 Integra .... 25 to 39 ohms
    All others .... 25.5 to 39.5 ohms
  Empty position .... 105 to 110 ohms

Torque specifications

Ft-lbs (unless otherwise indicated)

Fuel injection service bolt (6 mm bolt)
  Integra
    1990 .... 108 inch-lbs
    1991 on .... 132 inch-lbs
  Legend .... 108 inch-lbs
12 mm banjo bolt (all models)
  Integra 25
  Legend 20
Throttle body mounting nuts/bolts 16
Fuel rail mounting nuts
  Integra .... 132 in-lbs
  Legend .... 108 inch-lbs

1.1a Typical fuel injection system components (Integra)

1	*Air cleaner duct*	*3*	*Fuel rail and injectors*	*5*	*Fuel pressure regulator*
2	*Throttle body*	*4*	*Fuel filter*		

1   General information

Refer to illustrations 1.1a and 1.1b

The fuel system consists of a fuel tank, an electric fuel pump (located in the fuel tank), a PGM-FI (main) relay, the fuel rail(s) and fuel injectors, an air cleaner assembly and a throttle body unit. All models are equipped with a Sequential Electronic Fuel Injection (SEFI) system **(see illustrations)**.

Programmed Fuel Injection (PGM-FI) system

Programmed Fuel Injection uses timed impulses to inject the fuel directly into the intake port of each cylinder according to its firing order. The injectors are controlled by the Powertrain Control Module (PCM). The PCM monitors various engine parameters and delivers the exact amount of fuel required into the intake ports. The throttle

body serves only to control the amount of air passing into the system. Because each cylinder is equipped with its own injector, much better control of the fuel/air mixture ratio is possible.

Fuel pump and lines

Fuel is circulated from the fuel tank to the fuel injection system, and back to the fuel tank, through a pair of metal lines running along the underside of the vehicle. An electric

1.1b Typical fuel injection system components (Legend)

1	Throttle body	3	Fuel rails and injectors	5	Air cleaner housing
2	Fuel filter	4	Fuel pressure regulator		

fuel pump and fuel level sending unit is located inside the fuel tank. A vapor return system routes all vapors back to the fuel tank through a separate return line.

The PGM-FI main relay (fuel pump relay) is equipped with a primary and secondary voltage circuit. With the ignition switch ON, the primary circuit supplies current to the PCM, the fuel injectors and the secondary circuit. The secondary circuit supplies current to the fuel pump. The secondary circuit is energized for two seconds with the ignition switch ON and the engine not running, and constantly with the engine running.

Exhaust system

The exhaust system includes an exhaust manifold, (two on Legend models), an oxygen sensor (two on Legend models), a three-way (reduction) catalytic converter, a muffler and a tail pipe. Legend models use warmup catalytic converters, one bolted to each exhaust manifold.

The catalytic converter(s) is an emission control device added to the exhaust system to reduce pollutants. Refer to Chapter 6 for more information regarding the catalytic converter.

2 Fuel pressure relief procedure

Refer to illustrations 2.1, 2.4a and 2.4b
Warning: *Gasoline is extremely flammable, so take extra precautions when you work on any part of the fuel system. Don't smoke or allow open flames or bare light bulbs near the work area, and don't work in a garage where a natural gas-type appliance (such as a water heater or a clothes dryer) with a pilot light is present. Since gasoline is carcinogenic, wear latex gloves when there's a possibility of being exposed to fuel, and, if you spill any fuel on your skin, rinse it off immediately with soap and water. Mop up any spills immediately and do not store fuel-soaked rags where they could ignite. The fuel system is under constant pressure, so, if any fuel lines are to be disconnected, the fuel pressure in the system must be relieved first. When you perform any kind of work on the fuel system, wear safety glasses and have a Class B type fire extinguisher on hand.*

1   Remove the rear seat and locate the fuel pump electrical connector **(see illustration)**. On Legend models it will be necessary to remove a cover plate for access to the connector; see Section 5 for more information.

2.1 Disconnect the fuel pump electrical connector (Integra shown)

Unplug the connector and start the engine, allowing it to run until it stalls.
2   Detach the cable from the negative battery terminal. Unscrew the fuel filler cap to relieve pressure built up in the fuel tank. **Caution:** *If the stereo in your vehicle is equipped with an anti-theft system, make sure you have the correct activation code before disconnecting the battery. On all models, write down the preset radio stations.*

4

2.4a Be sure to use a back-up wrench to prevent the fitting from turning - before the bolt is loosened, cover the wrenches with a shop rag to catch the escaping fuel; this is the Integra fuel filter . . .

3   To relieve any residual pressure in the lines you'll need to open the fuel line at the fuel filter. This is done by loosening the service bolt that's threaded into the banjo bolt, as described in the following Steps.

4   You'll need two wrenches for this procedure - one to loosen the service bolt and one to hold the banjo bolt **(see illustrations)**.

5   Place a shop rag around the fuel line fitting on top of the fuel filter.

6   While holding the banjo bolt or fuel line fitting, *slowly* loosen the service bolt or banjo bolt one complete turn - fuel will begin to flow from the fitting. Allow the pressure to be relieved completely, then remove the bolt.

7   After all work to the fuel system has been performed, install the service bolt with a new sealing washer and tighten it to the torque listed in this Chapter's Specifications.

3   Fuel pump/fuel pressure - check

Warning: *Gasoline is extremely flammable, so take extra precautions when you work on*

2.4b . . . and this is the Legend fuel filter

*any part of the fuel system. See the **Warning** in Section 2.*

Note: *In order to perform the fuel pressure test, you will need to obtain a fuel pressure gauge capable of measuring high fuel pressure and an adapter set for the fuel injection system being tested.*

General checks

1   Check that there is adequate fuel in the fuel tank.

2   Make sure the fuel pump operates. Have an assistant turn the ignition switch to ON - you should hear a brief whirring noise (approximately two seconds) as the pump comes on and pressurizes the system. **Note:** *The fuel pump is easily heard through the fuel tank filler neck.* If there is no response from the fuel pump (makes no sound) proceed to Step 9 and check the fuel pump electrical circuit.

Fuel pump output and pressure check

Refer to illustrations 3.3, 3.6a, 3.6b and 3.6c

3   Relieve the fuel pressure (see Section 2), then connect a fuel pressure gauge to the

3.3 This aftermarket fuel pressure testing kit contains all the necessary fittings and adapters, along with a fuel pressure gauge, to test most automotive fuel systems

test port on the fuel filter **(see illustration)**. The gauge is connected in place of the service bolt (see Section 2).

4   Turn the ignition switch ON (engine not running) with the air conditioning off. The fuel pump should run for about two seconds - pressure should register on the gauge and should hold steady.

5   Start the engine and let it idle at normal operating temperature. Compare the pressure reading with the value listed in this Chapter's Specifications. Now, disconnect the vacuum hose from the fuel pressure regulator **(see illustrations 3.6a and 3.6b)** - the pressure should increase immediately to the value listed in this Chapter's Specifications. If the pressure readings are correct, the system is operating properly.

6   If the pressure did not increase when the hose was disconnected, apply 12 to 14 inches of vacuum to the pressure regulator, using a hand-held vacuum pump **(see illustrations)**. If the pressure drops, repair the vacuum source to the regulator. If the pres-

3.6a Detach the vacuum hose from the fuel pressure regulator (arrow); this is the Integra . . .

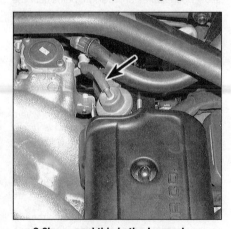

3.6b . . . and this is the Legend . . .

3.6c . . . connect a vacuum pump to the regulator and apply vacuum - fuel pressure should decrease as vacuum increases

3.10a The Integra fuel injection main relay is on the left side of the cowl (arrow) - the inset shows terminal identification for testing (see text)

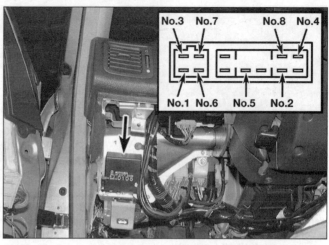

3.10b The Legend fuel injection main relay is also on the left side of the cowl (arrow) - the inset shows terminal identification for testing (see text)

sure does not drop, replace the regulator.

7   If the fuel pressure is not within specifications, check the following:

a) *If the pressure is higher than specified, check for vacuum to the fuel pressure regulator. Vacuum must fluctuate with the increase or decrease in the engine rpm. If vacuum is present, check for a pinched or clogged fuel return hose or pipe. If the return line is OK, replace the regulator.*

b) *If the pressure is lower than specified, change the fuel filter to rule out the possibility of a clogged filter (see Chapter 1). If the pressure is still low, start the engine (if possible) and slowly pinch the return hose shut. If the pressure rises to or above the "vacuum hose disconnected" fuel pressure listed in this Chapter's Specifications, replace the regulator (see Section 14).* **Warning:** *Don't allow the fuel pressure to exceed 60 psi.*

c) *If the pressure is still low with the fuel return line restricted, an injector (or injectors) may be leaking (see Section 15) or the in-tank fuel pump may be faulty.*

8   After the testing is done, relieve the fuel pressure (see Section 2) and remove the fuel pressure gauge.

Fuel pump electrical circuit check

Refer to illustrations 3.10a and 3.10b

Note: *Refer to Chapter 12 for additional wiring schematics that detail the fuel pump relay and circuit.*

9   If the pump does not turn on (makes no sound) with the ignition switch in the ON position, check the fuel injection (PGM-FI) main relay fuse (see Chapter 12). If the fuse is blown, replace the fuse and see if the pump works. If the pump now works, check for a short in the circuit between the fuel pump relay and the fuel pump.

10   If the pump still does not work, check

the fuel pump relay circuit. First check the relay, as follows **(see illustrations)**:

a) *Remove the relay and connect a fused jumper wire between terminal 4 of the relay and the positive battery terminal. Connect terminal 8 to the negative battery terminal. With these connections made, check for continuity between terminals 5 and 7. If there is no continuity, replace the relay.*

b) *Connect a fused jumper wire between terminal 5 (Integra) or 6 (Legend) of the relay and the positive battery terminal. Connect terminal 2 to the negative battery terminal. With these connections made, check for continuity between terminals 1 and 3. If there is no continuity, replace the relay.*

c) *Connect a fused jumper wire between terminal 3 of the relay and the positive battery terminal. Connect terminal 8 to the negative battery terminal. With these connections made, check for continuity between terminals 5 and 7. If there is no continuity, replace the relay.*

11   If the fuel pump still does not work and the relay tested OK, check for voltage at the relay connector. There should be battery voltage at Terminal 1 of the harness connector and ground. When the ignition key is cycled on and off, there should be battery voltage at terminal 5 (Integra) or terminals 5 and 6 (Legend). With the ignition key in the Start position (be sure the vehicle is not in gear!), there should be battery voltage between the Number 4 terminal and ground. If there is not voltage in any of these tests, check the fuses and wiring. **Note 1:** *On some vehicles, if oil pressure drops below the specified pressure level, the oil pressure switch will act as a fuel pressure cut-off device. Be sure to check the oil pressure switch and circuit in the event of a difficult problem diagnosing the fuel pump circuit (refer to the wiring diagrams at the end of Chapter 12).* **Note 2:** *The theft deterrent system (if equipped) is equipped with a fuel enable cir-*

cuit. If this system is malfunctioning it will not allow the PCM to signal the fuel pump relay or the engine to crank over. Be sure to check the theft deterrent system and circuit in the event of a difficult problem diagnosing the fuel pump circuit.

12   If everything checks out in Steps 10 and 11, check for power to the fuel pump at the fuel tank. Remove the rear seat and check for battery voltage at the electrical connector near the tank. If voltage is present at the fuel pump connector, replace the fuel pump. If there is not voltage and you passed the Steps 10 and 11 checks, there is a problem in the wiring to the fuel pump. When checking voltage, keep in mind that voltage will only be present for about two seconds after the key is cycled to "ON." An assistant will be necessary during this check to cycle the key while you make the check.

4   Fuel lines and fittings - repair and replacement

Warning: *Gasoline is extremely flammable, so take extra precautions when you work on any part of the fuel system. Don't smoke or allow open flames or bare light bulbs near the work area, and don't work in a garage where a natural gas-type appliance (such as a water heater or a clothes dryer) with a pilot light is present. Since gasoline is carcinogenic, wear latex gloves when there's a possibility of being exposed to fuel, and, if you spill any fuel on your skin, rinse it off immediately with soap and water. Mop up any spills immediately and do not store fuel-soaked rags where they could ignite. The fuel system is under constant pressure, so, if any fuel lines are to be disconnected, the fuel pressure in the system must be relieved first (see Chapter 4 for more information). When you perform any kind of work on the fuel system, wear safety glasses and have a Class B type fire extinguisher on hand.*

4

5.4 The Legend has a cover that must be removed for access to the fuel pump and sending unit - remove the screws and take it off (arrows)

5.5 Detach the fuel line (A), return line (B) and the nuts that retain the fuel pump to the fuel tank (C) (Legend)

5.6 Lift the pump from the access hole; angle it to avoid damaging the screen attached to the bottom (Legend shown)

1   Always relieve the fuel pressure before servicing fuel lines or fittings (see Section 2).
2   The fuel feed, return and vapor lines extend from the fuel tank to the engine compartment. The lines are secured to the underbody with clip and screw assemblies. These lines must be occasionally inspected for leaks, kinks and dents.
3   If evidence of dirt is found in the system or fuel filter during disassembly, the line should be disconnected and blown out. Check the fuel strainer on the fuel gauge sending unit (see Section 5) for damage and deterioration.

Steel tubing

4   If replacement of a fuel line or emission line is called for, use welded steel tubing meeting the manufacturer's specifications or its equivalent.
5   Don't use copper or aluminum tubing to replace steel tubing. These materials cannot withstand normal vehicle vibration.
6   Because fuel lines used on fuel-injected vehicles are under high pressure, they require special consideration.
7   Some fuel lines have threaded fittings with O-rings. Any time the fittings are loosened to service or replace components:

  a) Use a backup wrench while loosening and tightening the fittings.
  b) Check all O-rings for cuts, cracks and deterioration. Replace any that appear hardened, worn or damaged.
  c) If the lines are replaced, always use original equipment parts, or parts that meet the original equipment standards specified in this Section.

Flexible hose

Warning: *Use only original equipment replacement hoses or their equivalent. Others may fail from the high pressures of this system.*

8   Don't route fuel hose within four inches of any part of the exhaust system or within ten inches of the catalytic converter. Metal lines and rubber hoses must never be allowed to chafe against the frame. A mini-

mum of 1/4-inch clearance must be maintained around a line or hose to prevent contact with the frame.

Removal and installation

9   Relieve the fuel pressure (see Section 2).
10   Remove all fasteners attaching the lines to the vehicle body.
11   Detach the clamp(s) that attach the fuel hoses to the metal lines, then pull the hoses off the fitting. Twisting the hoses back and forth will allow them to separate more easily.
12   Installation is the reverse of removal. Be sure to use new O-rings at the threaded fittings (if equipped) and new sealing washer(s) at the fuel filter.

Repair

13   In the event of any fuel line damage (metal or flexible lines) it is necessary to replace the damaged lines with factory replacement parts or their equivalents. Repairs are not recommended because of the high pressures in the system.

---

5   Fuel pump - removal and installation

Refer to illustrations 5.4, 5.5, 5.6, 5.7, 5.8 and 5.11

Warning: *Gasoline is extremely flammable, so take extra precautions when you work on any part of the fuel system. Don't smoke or allow open flames or bare light bulbs near the work area, and don't work in a garage where a natural gas-type appliance (such as a water heater or a clothes dryer) with a pilot light is present. Since gasoline is carcinogenic, wear latex gloves when there's a possibility of being exposed to fuel, and, if you spill any fuel on your skin, rinse it off immediately with soap and water. Mop up any spills immediately and do not store fuel-soaked rags where they could ignite. The fuel system is under constant pressure, so, if any fuel lines are to be disconnected, the fuel pressure in the system must be relieved first (see Section 2 for more information). When you perform any kind of work on the fuel system, wear safety*

glasses and have a Class B type fire extinguisher on hand.

1   Relieve the fuel system pressure (see Section 2).
2   Detach the cable from the negative battery terminal. **Caution:** *If the stereo in your vehicle is equipped with an anti-theft system, make sure you have the correct activation code before disconnecting the battery.*
3   If you're working on an Integra, remove the fuel tank (see Section 7) and proceed to Step 6. If you're working on a Legend, remove the rear seat (see Chapter 11).
4   On Legend models, remove the screws that retain the fuel pump access cover **(see illustration)**.
5   Unplug the electrical connector from the fuel pump and detach the fuel lines **(see illustration)**.
6   Remove the fuel pump assembly retaining nuts and remove the fuel pump from the tank **(see illustration)**.
7   Remove the electrical connector protective cover **(see illustration)**.
8   Remove the electrical connector from the fuel pump **(see illustration)**.
9   Squeeze the hose clamps with a pair of pliers - remove the upper clamp from the hose and slide the lower clamp half-way up the hose, off the fuel pump inlet.
10   Separate the pump from the fuel pump bracket.

5.7 Remove the protective cover from the main electrical connector

5.8 Lift the tab on the main electrical connector and disconnect it from the fuel pump

5.11 Pry off the retaining clip with a small screwdriver and detach the filter (sock) from the pump

6.2 Integras have an access cover for the sending unit - remove the screws (arrows)

6.4 Disconnect the electrical connector (arrow); if there's a locking ring, use a brass punch to remove it; a steel punch may cause sparks

6.5 If the sending unit is secured by nuts, remove them (arrows)

6.6 Lift the fuel level sending unit through the access hole (Legend shown)

11 Remove the sock filter from the end of the pump (see illustration).

12 Installation is the reverse of removal. Be sure to use a new gasket on the cover plate flange.

6 Fuel level sending unit - check and replacement

Refer to illustrations 6.2, 6.4, 6.5, 6.6 and 6.7
Warning: *Gasoline is extremely flammable, so take extra precautions when you work on any part of the fuel system. Don't smoke or allow open flames or bare light bulbs near the work area, and don't work in a garage where a natural gas-type appliance (such as a water heater or a clothes dryer) with a pilot light is present. Since gasoline is carcinogenic, wear latex gloves when there's a possibility of being exposed to fuel, and, if you spill any fuel on your skin, rinse it off immediately with soap and water. Mop up any spills immediately and do not store fuel-soaked rags where they could ignite. The fuel system is under constant pressure, so, if any fuel lines are to be disconnected, the fuel pressure in the sys-*

tem must be relieved first (see Section 2 for more information). When you perform any kind of work on the fuel system, wear safety glasses and have a Class B type fire extinguisher on hand.

1 Remove the rear seat (see Chapter 11).

2 Remove the access cover (see illustration 5.4 or the accompanying illustration).

3 Disconnect the electrical connector from the sender.

4 If the sending unit is held in place by a locking ring, use a brass punch and tap the locking ring counterclockwise (see illustration) until the tabs line up with the recess in the housing. **Warning:** *A steel punch shouldn't be used, since a spark could cause an explosion.*

5 If the sending unit is held in place by nuts, remove them (see illustration).

6 Lift the fuel level sending unit from the tank (see illustration). Be careful not to damage the float arm.

7 Connect the probes of an ohmmeter to the electrical connector terminals and check the resistance (see illustration).

8 First, check the resistance of the sending unit with the float in the bottom (fuel tank empty) position. The resistance of the sending unit should be within the range listed in this Chapter's Specifications.

9 Now check the resistance of the unit

6.7 Measure the resistance of the fuel level sending unit with the float raised (full tank), halfway down and near the bottom (empty)

with the float in the half-tank position and compare the reading to the value listed in this Chapter's Specifications.

10 Finally, lift the float to the full tank position and measure the resistance.

11 If the readings are incorrect or there is very little change in resistance as the float travels from full to empty, replace the sending unit.

12 Installation is the reverse of removal. Be sure to use a new gasket under the sealing flange.

4

7.7a Remove the small cover; this is the Integra (arrow) . . .

7.7b . . . and this is the Legend (arrow)

7.8a Remove the clamp that retains the rubber fuel line to the inlet pipe (arrow)

7.8b Follow the fuel and EVAP lines (arrow) to the tank and disconnect them

7.10 Support the fuel tank and remove the nuts from the strap bolts (arrows)

7 Fuel tank - removal and installation

Refer to illustrations 7.7a, 7.7b, 7.8a, 7.8b and 7.10

Warning: *Gasoline is extremely flammable, so take extra precautions when you work on any part of the fuel system. Don't smoke or allow open flames or bare light bulbs near the work area, and don't work in a garage where a natural gas-type appliance (such as a water heater or a clothes dryer) with a pilot light is present. Since gasoline is carcinogenic, wear latex gloves when there's a possibility of being exposed to fuel, and, if you spill any fuel on your skin, rinse it off immediately with soap and water. Mop up any spills immediately and do not store fuel-soaked rags where they could ignite. The fuel system is under constant pressure, so, if any fuel lines are to be disconnected, the fuel pressure in the system must be relieved first (see Section 2 for more information). When you perform any kind of work on the fuel system, wear safety glasses and have a Class B type fire extinguisher on hand.*

Note: *The following procedure is much easier to perform if the fuel tank is empty.*

1   Remove the fuel tank filler cap to relieve

fuel tank pressure.

2   Relieve the fuel system pressure (see Section 2).

3   Detach the cable from the negative terminal of the battery. **Caution:** *If the stereo in your vehicle is equipped with an anti-theft system, make sure you have the correct activation code before disconnecting the battery.*

4   Remove the tank drain plug and drain the fuel into an approved gasoline container. If it doesn't have a drain plug, siphon the fuel into an approved gasoline container, using a siphoning kit (available at most auto parts stores).

5   Remove the rear seat (see Chapter 11) and disconnect the fuel pump (Legend only) and fuel gauge electrical connectors (see Section 4 and 5).

6   Raise the rear of the vehicle and place it securely on jackstands.

7   Remove the splash panels that protect the fuel tank and the fuel lines **(see illustrations)**.

8   Working under the vehicle, disconnect any additional fuel lines, line brackets and electrical connectors **(see illustrations)**.

9   Support the fuel tank with a floor jack. Position a wood block between the jack head and the fuel tank to protect the tank.

10   Disconnect both fuel tank retaining straps and pivot them down until they are

hanging out of the way **(see illustration)**.

11   Remove the tank from the vehicle.

12   Installation is the reverse of removal.

8 Fuel tank cleaning and repair - general information

1   All repairs to the fuel tank or filler neck should be carried out by a professional who has experience in this critical and potentially dangerous work. Even after cleaning and flushing of the fuel system, explosive fumes can remain and ignite during repair of the tank.

2   If the fuel tank is removed from the vehicle, it should not be placed in an area where sparks or open flames could ignite the fumes coming out of the tank. Be especially careful inside garages where a natural gas-type appliance is located, because the pilot light could cause an explosion.

9 Air cleaner housing - removal and installation

Refer to illustrations 9.1a, 9.1b, 9.2a and 9.2b

1   Undo the clips and lift off the air cleaner cover **(see illustrations)**.

2   Remove the mounting bolts and remove the air cleaner housing **(see illustrations)**.

3   If you're working on a Legend, remove the air intake duct and resonator.

4   Installation is the reverse of removal.

10 Accelerator cable - removal, installation and adjustment

Refer to illustrations 10.2, 10.3a, 10.3b, 10.4 and 10.5

Replacement

1   Detach the cable from the negative terminal of the battery. **Caution:** *If the stereo in your vehicle is equipped with an anti-theft system, make sure you have the correct acti-*

9.1a Remove the cover clips (this is an Integra) . . .

9.1b . . . and this is a Legend

9.2a Integra air cleaner housing bolts (arrows)

9.2b Legend air cleaner housing bolts (arrows)

10.2 On Legends, remove the throttle cable cover bolts (arrows)

10.3a Measure side-to-side cable deflection (left arrows); adjusting nut and locknut (right arrows)

4

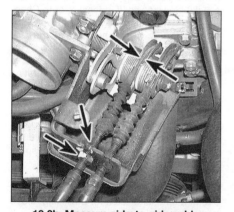

10.3b Measure side-to-side cable deflection (upper arrows); adjusting nut and locknut locations (lower arrows)

10.4 Disconnect the throttle cable end from the bellcrank at the throttle body

10.5 Working under the dash on the driver's side, pull the accelerator cable end (arrow) out and then lift the cable out of the recess in the pedal

vation code before disconnecting the battery.

2   If you're working on a Legend, remove the throttle cable cover (see illustration).

3   Loosen the locknut and remove the accelerator cable from its bracket (see illustrations).

4   Rotate the throttle shaft bellcrank until the cable is out of its guide groove in the bellcrank and detach the cable from the bellcrank (see illustration).

5   Working underneath the dash, detach the cable from the accelerator pedal (see illustration).

6   Pull the grommet from the firewall and pull the cable through the firewall from the engine compartment side.

7   Installation is the reverse of removal. Use the locknut and adjusting nut to get the throttle cable deflection as close as possible to the correct final setting, then adjust the cable as described below.

Adjustment

8   Start the engine and warm it up until the cooling fan comes on, then turn it off.

9   Check cable deflection (side-to-side slack) in the cable between the bellcrank and the cable bracket (see illustration 10.3a or 10.3b). Deflection should be 3/8 to 1/2-inch. If deflection is not within specifications,

12.7 Use a stethoscope or screwdriver to determine if the injectors are working properly - they should make a steady clicking sound that rises and falls with engine speed changes

12.8 Install the "noid" light into each injector harness electrical connector and confirm that it blinks when the engine is cranking or running

12.9 To check the Legend injector resistor, measure the resistance between the power terminal (A) and each of the injector terminals (B through H)

loosen the locknut and turn the adjusting nut until the deflection is as specified, then tighten the locknut.

10   After you have adjusted the throttle cable, have an assistant help you verify that the throttle valve opens all the way when you depress the accelerator pedal to the floor and that it returns to the idle position when you release the accelerator. Verify the cable operates smoothly. It must not bind or stick.

11   If the vehicle is equipped with an automatic transaxle, adjust the transaxle Throttle Valve (TV) cable (see Chapter 7B).

11   Fuel injection system - general information

The Programmed Fuel Injection (PGM-FI) system **(see illustrations 1.1a and 1.1b)** consists of three sub-systems: air intake, electronic control and fuel delivery. The system uses a Powertrain Control Module (PCM), along with the sensors (coolant temperature sensor, Throttle Position Sensor (TPS), Manifold Absolute Pressure (MAP) sensor etc.) to determine the proper air/fuel ratio under all operating conditions.

The fuel injection system and the emissions control system are closely linked in function and design. For additional information, refer to Chapter 6.

Air intake system

The air intake system consists of the air cleaner, the air intake ducts, the throttle body, the idle control system and the intake manifold. A resonator in the air intake tube provides silencing as air is drawn into the system.

The throttle body is a single barrel design, side-draft on all models. The lower portion of the throttle body is heated by engine coolant to prevent icing in cold weather. The idle adjusting screw is located on top of the throttle body. A throttle position sensor is attached to the throttle shaft to monitor changes in the throttle opening.

Electronic control system

The electronic control system and the Powertrain Control Module (PCM) are explained in detail in Chapter 6.

Fuel delivery system

The fuel delivery system consists of these components: The fuel pump, the pressure regulator, the fuel injectors, the fuel pulsation damper (some models) and the main relay.

The fuel pump is an in-tank type. Fuel is drawn through a filter into the pump, flows through the fuel delivery line, passes through another filter and is delivered to the injectors.

The pressure regulator maintains a constant fuel pressure to the injectors. Excess fuel is routed back to the fuel tank through the return line.

The injectors are solenoid-actuated, constant stroke, pintle types consisting of a solenoid, plunger, needle valve and housing. When current is applied to the solenoid coil, the needle valve raises and pressurized fuel fills the injector housing and squirts out the nozzle. The injection quantity is determined by the length of time the valve is open (the length of time during which current is supplied to the solenoid coils).

Injector open time is determined by the Powertrain Control Module (PCM). It contains a basic open time for various combinations of engine speed and air flow. This information is combined with inputs from the engine sensors to arrive at a final open time for a given set of conditions.

The main relay is installed in the left or right side of the cowl depending on model. It contains two relays: One relay supplies power to the Powertrain Control Module (PCM), fuel injectors and to the other relay. The other relay supplies power to the fuel pump.

12   Fuel injection system - check

Refer to illustrations 12.7, 12.8, 12.9 and 12.10

Warning: *Gasoline is extremely flammable,*

so take extra precautions when you work on any part of the fuel system. See the **Warning** *in Section 2.*

1   Check all electrical connectors - especially ground connections - for the system. Loose connectors and poor grounds can cause at least half of all engine control system problems.

2   Verify that the battery is fully charged because the powertrain control module (PCM) and sensors cannot operate properly without adequate supply voltage.

3   Refer to Chapter 1 and check the air filter element. A dirty or partially blocked filter will reduce performance and economy.

4   Check fuel pump operation (Section 3). If the fuel pump fuse is blown, replace it and see if it blows again. If it does, refer to Chapter 12 and the wiring diagrams and look for a grounded wire in the harness to the fuel pump.

5   Inspect the vacuum hoses connected to the intake manifold for damage, deterioration and leakage.

6   Remove the air intake duct from the throttle body and check for dirt, carbon, varnish, or other residue in the throttle body, particularly around the throttle plate. If it's dirty, clean it with carburetor cleaner and a toothbrush.

7   With the engine running, place an automotive stethoscope against each injector, one at a time, and listen for a clicking sound that indicates operation **(see illustration)**. If you don't have a stethoscope, you can place the tip of a long screwdriver against the injector and listen through the handle.

8   If an injector does not seem to be operating electrically (not clicking), purchase a special injector test light (sometimes called a "noid" light) and install it into the injector wiring harness connector **(see illustration)**. Start the engine and see if the noid light flashes. If it does, the injector is receiving proper voltage. If it doesn't flash, further diagnosis is necessary. If you're working on a Legend, test the injector resistor as described below. If you're working on an Integra, you might want to have the injector

12.10 Disconnect the fuel injector electrical connectors and measure the resistance of each injector

13.3a Disconnect the MAP sensor and charcoal canister hoses from the Integra throttle body (arrows)

13.3b Disconnect the electrical connector, vacuum hoses and coolant hoses from the Legend throttle body (arrows)

circuit checked by a dealership service department or other qualified repair shop.

9   If you're working on a Legend, locate the injector resistor in the corner of the engine compartment **(see illustration)**. Disconnect its electrical connector. Connect an ohmmeter between the power wire's terminal in the connector (the injector side, not the harness side). Connect the other ohmmeter lead to each of the injector terminals in turn. Resistance should be 5 to 7 ohms; if not, replace the resistor.

10   With the engine off and the fuel injector electrical connectors disconnected, measure the resistance of each injector with an ohmmeter **(see illustration)**. Check the specifications at the beginning of this chapter for the correct resistance.

11   Refer to Chapter 6 for other system checks.

13.6a On Integras, remove the nuts (arrows) and separate the throttle body from the air intake plenum

13.6b The Legend throttle body is secured either by four nuts or two nuts and two bolts (arrows)

13   Throttle body - removal and installation

Refer to illustrations 13.3a, 13.3b, 13.6a and 13.6b

Warning: *Wait until the engine is completely cool before beginning this procedure.*

1   Detach the cable from the negative battery terminal. **Caution:** *If the stereo in your vehicle is equipped with an anti-theft system, make sure you have the correct activation code before disconnecting the battery.*

2   Remove the air duct that connects the air cleaner assembly to the throttle body. If you're working on a Legend with traction control, remove the TCS assembly (see Chapter 10).

3   Unplug the electrical connector from the throttle body (Legend). Also label and detach all vacuum hoses from the throttle body **(see illustrations)**.

4   Detach the accelerator cable (see Section 10) and, if equipped, the automatic transaxle Throttle Valve (TV) cable (see Chapter 7B).

5   Detach the coolant hoses from the

throttle body. Plug the lines to prevent coolant loss.

6   Unscrew the four mounting nuts and/or bolts **(see illustrations)**. Remove the throttle body and gasket. Remove all traces of old gasket material from the throttle body and air intake plenum.

7   Installation is the reverse of removal. Be sure to use a new gasket. Tighten the mounting bolts or nuts to the torque listed in this Chapter's Specifications. Adjust the accelerator cable (see Section 10) and, if equipped, the Throttle Valve (TV) cable (see Chapter 7B). Check the coolant level and add some, if necessary (see Chapter 1).

14   Fuel pressure regulator - replacement

Refer to illustrations 14.3a and 14.3b

Warning: *Gasoline is extremely flammable, so take extra precautions when you work on any part of the fuel system. Don't smoke or allow open flames or bare light bulbs near the work area, and don't work in a garage where*

a natural gas-type appliance (such as a water heater or a clothes dryer) with a pilot light is present. Since gasoline is carcinogenic, wear latex gloves when there's a possibility of being exposed to fuel, and, if you spill any fuel on your skin, rinse it off immediately with soap and water. Mop up any spills immediately and do not store fuel-soaked rags where they could ignite. The fuel system is under constant pressure, so, if any fuel lines are to be disconnected, the fuel pressure in the system must be relieved first (see Section 2 for more information). When you perform any kind of work on the fuel system, wear safety glasses and have a Class B type fire extinguisher on hand.

Note: *Pressure regulator diagnosis is covered in Section 3.*

1   Relieve the system fuel pressure (see Section 2).

2   Detach the cable from the negative battery terminal. **Caution:** *If the stereo in your vehicle is equipped with an anti-theft system, make sure you have the correct activation code before disconnecting the battery.*

3   Detach the vacuum hose and fuel hose from the pressure regulator, then unscrew

4

14.3a The Integra fuel pressure regulator (arrow) is near the brake master cylinder

14.3b The Legend fuel pressure regulator is at the left rear corner of the engine (arrow)

15.3a Use a small screwdriver or sharp pick to remove the bail from the fuel injector electrical connector

15.3b If you're working on a Legend, remove the engine harness holder nuts (arrows)

15.7a Remove the fuel rail mounting nuts (arrows); this is an Integra . . .

the mounting bolts **(see illustrations)**.

4   Remove the pressure regulator.

5   Installation is the reverse of removal. Be sure to use a new O-ring. Lubricate the O-ring with a light coat of clean engine oil before installation.

6   Check for fuel leaks after installing the pressure regulator.

15   Fuel injectors - removal and installation

Warning: *Gasoline is extremely flammable, so take extra precautions when you work on any part of the fuel system. Don't smoke or allow open flames or bare light bulbs near the work area, and don't work in a garage where a natural gas-type appliance (such as a water heater or a clothes dryer) with a pilot light is present. Since gasoline is carcinogenic, wear latex gloves when there's a possibility of being exposed to fuel, and, if you spill any fuel on your skin, rinse it off immediately with soap and water. Mop up any spills immedi-*

ately and do not store fuel-soaked rags where they could ignite. The fuel system is under constant pressure, so, if any fuel lines are to be disconnected, the fuel pressure in the system must be relieved first (see Section 2 for more information). When you perform any kind of work on the fuel system, wear safety glasses and have a Class B type fire extinguisher on hand.

Removal

Refer to illustrations 15.3a, 15.3b, 15.7a, 15.7b, 15.8a and 15.8b

1   Relieve the fuel pressure (see Section 2).

2   Detach the cable from the negative battery terminal. **Caution:** *If the stereo in your vehicle is equipped with an anti-theft system, make sure you have the correct activation code before disconnecting the battery.*

3   Unplug the injector connectors **(see illustration)**. If you're working on a Legend, remove the engine harness holder nuts **(see illustration)**.

4   Detach the vacuum hose and fuel return hose from the fuel pressure regulator (see Section 14).

5   Detach any ground cables from the fuel rail.

6   Detach the fuel feed line from the fuel rail.

7   Remove the mounting nuts **(see illustrations)** and detach the fuel rail from the injectors.

8   Remove the injector(s) from the bores in the intake manifold and remove and discard the O-ring, cushion ring and seal ring **(see illustrations)**. **Note:** *Whether you're replacing an injector or a leaking O-ring, it's a good idea to remove all the injectors from the intake manifold and replace all the O-rings, seal rings and cushion rings.*

Installation

Refer to illustrations 15.10a and 15.10b

Caution: *To protect the injector seals, install all of the injectors in the fuel rail, then install the injector and fuel rail assembly in the intake manifold.*

9   Coat the new cushion rings with clean engine oil and slide them onto the injectors.

10   Coat the new O-rings with clean engine oil and install them on the injector(s), then

15.7b ... and this is a Legend

15.8a Carefully remove the injector O-rings

15.8b Remove the seal ring and cushion ring from the injector

insert each injector into its corresponding bore in the fuel rail **(see illustrations)**.

11   Coat the new seal rings with clean engine oil and press them into the injector bore(s) in the intake manifold.

12   Install the injector and fuel rail assembly on the intake manifold. Tighten the fuel rail mounting nuts to the torque listed in this Chapter's Specifications.

13   The remainder of installation is the reverse of removal.

14   After the injector/fuel rail assembly installation is complete, turn the ignition switch to ON, but don't operate the starter (this activates the fuel pump for about two seconds, which builds up fuel pressure in the fuel lines and the fuel rail). Repeat this about two or three times, then check the fuel lines, rail and injectors for fuel leakage.

16   Exhaust system servicing - general information

Refer to illustrations 16.4a, 16.4b, 16.4c and 16.4d
Warning: *Inspection and repair of exhaust system components should be done only*

after enough time has elapsed after driving the vehicle to allow the system components to cool completely. Also, when working under the vehicle, make sure it is securely supported on jackstands.

1   The exhaust system consists of the exhaust manifold(s), a pair of warm-up catalytic converters on Legend models, a catalytic converter on all models, the muffler, the tailpipe and all connecting pipes, brackets, hangers and clamps. The exhaust system is attached to the body with mounting brackets and rubber hangers. If any of the parts are improperly installed, excessive noise and vibration will be transmitted to the body.

2   Conduct regular inspections of the exhaust system to keep it safe and quiet. Look for any damaged or bent parts, open seams, holes, loose connections, excessive corrosion or other defects which could allow exhaust fumes to enter the vehicle. Deteriorated exhaust system components should not be repaired; they should be replaced with new parts.

3   If the exhaust system components are extremely corroded or rusted together, welding equipment will probably be required to remove them. The convenient way to accomplish this is to have a muffler repair shop

remove the corroded sections with a cutting torch. If, however, you want to save money by doing it yourself (and you don't have a welding outfit with a cutting torch), simply cut off the old components with a hacksaw. If you have compressed air, special pneumatic cutting chisels can also be used. If you do

4

15.10a Install the injectors in the fuel rail, then install the assembly in the intake manifold ...

15.10b ... making sure the alignment marks on the injector and fuel rail are lined up (arrows)

16.4a Be sure to apply penetrating lubricant to the exhaust system fasteners before attempting to remove them

16.4b Unscrew the exhaust system fasteners with a pair of wrenches

16.4c Be sure to reinstall all catalytic converter heat shields

16.4d Check for any broken or missing rubber hangers (arrows)

decide to tackle the job at home, be sure to wear safety goggles to protect your eyes from metal chips and work gloves to protect your hands.

4   Here are some simple guidelines to follow when repairing the exhaust system:

a) *Work from the back to the front when removing exhaust system components* **(see illustrations)**.

b) *Apply penetrating oil to the exhaust system component fasteners to make them easier to remove.*

c) *Use new gaskets, hangers and clamps when installing exhaust systems components.*

d) *Apply anti-seize compound to the threads of all exhaust system fasteners during reassembly.*

e) *Be sure to allow sufficient clearance between newly installed parts and all points on the underbody to avoid overheating the floor pan and possibly damaging the interior carpet and insulation. Pay particularly close attention to the catalytic converter(s) and heat shield.*

Chapter 5
Engine electrical systems

Contents

Specifications

5

Ignition system
Coil
Integra
Primary resistance .... 0.6 to 0.8 ohms
Secondary resistance
1990 through 1992 .... 9.76 to 14.64 K-ohms
1993 .... 12.8 to 19.2 K-ohms
Legend
Primary resistance .... 0.9 to 1.1 ohms
Secondary resistance .... Not specified
Ignition timing .... See Chapter 1

Charging system
Alternator brush length (minimum)
Integra
1990 through 1992 .... 1/16 inch
1993 .... 1/4 inch
Legend .... 1/16 inch

1 General information

Refer to illustrations 1.1a and 1.1b

The engine electrical systems include all ignition, charging and starting components **(see illustrations)**. Because of their engine-related functions, these components are considered separately from chassis electrical devices like the lights, instruments, etc.

Be very careful when working on the engine electrical components. They are easily damaged if checked, connected or handled improperly. The alternator is driven by an engine drivebelt which could cause serious injury if your hands, hair or clothes become entangled in it with the engine running. Both the starter and alternator are connected directly to the battery and could arc or even cause a fire if mishandled, overloaded or shorted out.

Never leave the ignition switch on for long periods of time with the engine off. Don't disconnect the battery cables while the engine is running. Correct polarity must be maintained when connecting battery cables from another source, such as another vehi-

1.1a Engine electrical system components (Integra)

1   Powertrain Control Module (PCM) (in passenger compartment)
2   Spark plug wires
3   TDC/CKP/CYP sensor (inside distributor cap)
4   Ignition coil (inside distributor (cap)

5   Ignition control module (inside distributor cap)
6   Spark plugs
7   Starter motor (not visible in photo)
8   Alternator

1.1b Engine electrical system components (Legend)

1   Powertrain Control Module (PCM) (in passenger compartment)
2   Ignition coils (spark plugs underneath)
3   CKP/CYP sensor
4   Ignition control module
5   Starter motor
6   Alternator

3.2 To test the open circuit voltage of the battery, simply touch the black probe of the voltmeter to the negative terminal and the red probe to the positive terminal of the battery - a fully charged battery should read approximately 12.5 volts (but may vary a little depending on the ambient temperature)

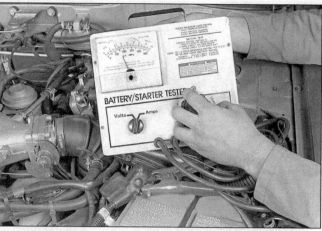

3.3 This load tester has an ammeter so the battery load can be precisely dialed in - less expensive testers have a load switch and a voltmeter only

cle, during jump starting. Always disconnect the negative cable first and hook it up last or the battery may be shorted by the tool being used to loosen the cable clamps.

Additional safety related information on the engine electrical systems can be found in *Safety first* near the front of this manual. It should be referred to before beginning any operation included in this Chapter.

2   Battery - emergency jump starting

Refer to the *Booster battery (jump) start-ing* procedure at the front of this manual.

3   Battery - check and replacement

Check

Refer to illustrations 3.2 and 3.3

1   Disconnect the negative battery cable, then the positive cable from the battery. **Caution 1:** *Always disconnect the negative cable first and hook it up last or the battery may be shorted by the tool being used to loosen the cable clamps.* **Caution 2:** *The radio in your vehicle is equipped with an anti-theft system, make sure you have the correct activation code before disconnecting the battery.*
2   Check the battery state of charge. Visually inspect the indicator eye on the top of the battery; if the indicator eye is black in color, charge the battery as described in Chapter 1. Next perform an open voltage circuit test using a digital voltmeter **(see illustration)**. **Note:** *The battery's surface charge must be removed before accurate voltage measurements can be made. Turn the high beam headlights on for ten seconds, then turn them off and let the vehicle stand for two minutes. With the engine and all accessories off, touch the negative probe of the voltmeter to the negative terminal of the battery and the posi-*

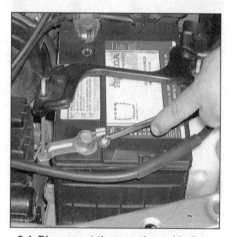

3.4 Disconnect the negative cable first, then the positive cable

tive probe to the positive terminal of the battery. The battery voltage should be approximately 12.5 volts or slightly more. If the battery has less than the specified voltage, charge the battery before proceeding to the next test. Do not proceed with the battery load test unless the battery charge is correct.
3   Perform a battery load test. An accurate check of the battery condition can only be performed with a load tester (available at most auto parts stores). This test evaluates the ability of the battery to operate the starter and other accessories during periods of heavy amperage draw (load). Install a special battery load testing tool onto the terminals **(see illustration)**. Load test the battery according to the manufacturer's instructions furnished with the tool. This tool utilizes a carbon pile to increase the load demand (amperage draw) on the battery. Maintain the load on the battery for 15 seconds or less and confirm that the battery voltage does not drop below 9.6 volts. If the battery condition is weak or defective, the tool will indicate this condition immediately. **Note:** *Cold tempera-tures will cause the minimum voltage read-*

3.5 Remove the hold-down strap (arrow) to detach the battery

ings to drop slightly. Follow the chart given in the manufacturer's instructions to compen-sate for cold climates. Minimum load voltage for freezing temperatures (32 degrees F) should be approximately 9.1 volts.

Replacement

Refer to illustrations 3.4, 3.5 and 3.8

4   Disconnect both cables from the battery terminals **(see illustration)**. **Caution 1:** *Always disconnect the negative cable first and hook it up last or the battery may be shorted by the tool being used to loosen the cable clamps.* **Caution 2:** *If the radio in your vehicle is equipped with an anti-theft system, make sure you have the correct activation code before disconnecting the battery.*
5   Remove the battery hold-down clamp **(see illustration)**.
6   Lift out the battery. Be careful - it's heavy. **Note:** *Battery straps and handles are available at most auto parts stores for a rea-sonable price. They make it easier to remove and carry the battery.*
7   While the battery is out, remove and inspect the carrier (tray) for corrosion.

5

3.8 Unbolt the battery tray (arrows) (Legend shown)

4.2a The lower end of the positive cable connects to the starter motor (arrow) (Legend shown)

4.2b Positive cables connect to the underhood fuse/relay box on some models (arrow)

4.2c The lower end of the negative cable is attached to the engine block (arrow) . . .

4.2d . . . and sub-frame (arrow)

4.4 Note the positions of the cable clamps (arrows)

8   If corrosion exists on the battery tray, detach the bolts and remove the tray from the engine compartment **(see illustration)**. Clean the deposits from the metal to prevent the battery tray from further corrosion.

9   If you are replacing the battery, make sure you get one that's identical, with the same dimensions, amperage rating, cold cranking rating, etc.

10   Installation is the reverse of removal.

4   Battery cables - check and replacement

Refer to illustrations 4.2a, 4.2b, 4.2c, 4.2d and 4.4

1   Periodically inspect the entire length of each battery cable for damage, cracked or burned insulation and corrosion. Poor battery cable connections can cause starting problems and decreased engine performance.

2   Check the cable-to-terminal connections at the ends of the cables for cracks, loose wire strands and corrosion **(see illustrations)**. The presence of white, fluffy deposits under the insulation at the cable terminal connection is a sign that the cable is corroded and should be replaced. Check the terminals for distortion, missing mounting bolts and corrosion.

3   When removing the cables, always disconnect the negative cable first and hook it up last or the battery may be shorted by the tool used to loosen the cable clamps. Even if only the positive cable is being replaced, be sure to disconnect the negative cable from the battery first (see Chapter 1 for further information regarding battery cable removal). **Caution:** *If the radio in your vehicle is equipped with an anti-theft system, make sure you have the correct activation code before disconnecting the battery.*

4   Disconnect the old cables from the battery, then trace each of them to their opposite ends and detach them from the starter solenoid and ground terminals. Disconnect the cables from the fuse/relay box under the hood (and from the ABS fuse/relay box, if equipped). Note the routing of each cable to ensure correct installation and detach it from any retaining clips **(see illustration)**.

5   If you are replacing any of the cables, take the old cable(s) with you to the parts store. It is vitally important that you replace the cables with identical parts. Cables have characteristics that make them easy to iden-

tify: positive cables are usually red and larger in cross-section; ground cables are usually black and smaller in cross-section.

6   Clean the threads of the solenoid or ground connection with a wire brush to remove rust and corrosion. Apply a light coat of battery terminal corrosion inhibitor, or petroleum jelly, to the threads to prevent future corrosion.

7   Attach the cable to the solenoid or ground connection and tighten the mounting nut/bolt securely.

8   Before connecting a new cable to the battery, make sure that it reaches the battery post without having to be stretched.

9   Connect the positive cable first, followed by the negative cable.

5   Ignition system - general information

Warning: *The transistorized electronic ignition systems used on the models covered by this manual generate considerably higher voltage than conventional systems. Be extra careful when servicing these ignition systems.*

    The Programmed Ignition (PGM-IG) sys-

6.2 Here's a calibrated ignition tester in use on an Integra

6.3 With the key ON, probe the positive terminal in the ignition coil connector to make sure voltage is getting to the coil

6.6 Here's a calibrated ignition tester in use on a Legend

tem provides complete control of the ignition timing by determining the optimum timing using a micro computer in response to engine speed, coolant temperature, throttle position and vacuum in the intake manifold. These parameters are relayed to the PCM by the TDC/CKP/CYP Sensor (Integra), CKP/CYP Sensor (Legend), Throttle Position Sensor (TPS), Engine Coolant Temperature (ECT) Sensor and Manifold Absolute Pressure (MAP) Sensor. Ignition timing is altered during warm-up, idling and warm running conditions by the PGM-IG system. This electronic ignition system also consists of the ignition switch, battery, coil and distributor (Integra only), individual coils (Legend only) spark plug wires and spark plugs **(see illustration 1.1a or 1.1b)**.

The distributor on Integra models is driven by the intake camshaft. The distributor is advanced and retarded by the Powertrain Control Module (PCM). Integra models employ a crankshaft position sensor which is located inside the distributor; these distributors must be replaced as a single unit if they become defective. Refer to a dealer parts department or auto parts store for any questions concerning the availability of the distributor parts and assemblies. Testing the sensors is covered in Chapter 6.

6   Ignition system - check

Warning: *Because of the high voltage generated by the ignition system, extreme care should be taken whenever an operation is performed involving ignition components. This not only includes the ignition control module, coil, distributor and spark plug wires, but related components such as plug connectors, tachometer and other test equipment also.*

1   If a malfunction occurs in the ignition system, do not immediately assume that the distributor (Integra) or ignition coils (Legend) are causing the problem. First, check the following items:

a) *Make sure the battery cable clamps,*

where they connect to the battery, are clean and tight.
b) Test the condition of the battery (see Section 3). If it does not pass all the tests, replace it with a new battery.
c) Check the distributor (Integra only) wiring and connections.
d) Check the ignition system fuses (see Chapter 12). If they're burned, determine the cause and repair the circuit.

Integra

Refer to illustrations 6.2 and 6.3

2   Check the ignition spark at the plug. If the engine turns over but won't start, disconnect the spark plug wire from any spark plug and attach it to a calibrated tester (available at most auto parts stores) **(see illustration)**. Connect the clip on the tester to a bolt or metal bracket on the engine. Crank the engine and watch the end of the tester or spark plug wire to see if a bright blue, well-defined sparks occur.

a) *If sparks occur, sufficient voltage is reaching the plug to fire it (repeat the check at the remaining plug wires to verify that the distributor cap and rotor are OK). However, the plugs themselves may be fouled, so remove and check them as described in Chapter 1.*
b) *If no sparks or intermittent sparks occur, remove the distributor cap (and cover if equipped) and check the cap and rotor as described in Chapter 1. If moisture is present, dry out the cap and rotor, then reinstall the cap and repeat the spark test.*
c) *These models are equipped with an integral coil assembly mounted within the distributor. Check the condition of the spring and carbon button inside the distributor cap for burn marks or damage. Replace the cap if necessary.*

3   If no sparks occur, check the primary wire connections at the coil to make sure they're clean and tight. Check for voltage to the coil on the primary circuit from the ignition switch **(see illustration)**.

4   If voltage is present, check the ignition coil (see Section 7).
5   If the ignition coil is good, check the Ignition Control Module (ICM) for proper operation (see Section 8).

Legend

Refer to illustrations 6.6, 6.9 and 6.10

6   If the engine turns over but won't start, disconnect the ignition coil from any spark plug (see Section 7) and attach it to a calibrated tester (available at most auto parts stores). Connect the clip on the tester to a bolt or metal bracket on the engine **(see illustration)**.
7   Crank the engine and watch the end of the tester to see if bright blue, well-defined sparks occur.
8   If sparks occur, sufficient voltage is reaching the plug to fire it (repeat the check at the remaining coils to verify that they're functioning). However, the plugs themselves may be fouled, so remove and check them as described in Chapter 1.
9   If no sparks or intermittent sparks occur, check for battery voltage to the ignition coil **(see illustration)** with the ignition key ON (engine not running). Attach a 12-volt test light to a good ground. Disconnect the coil

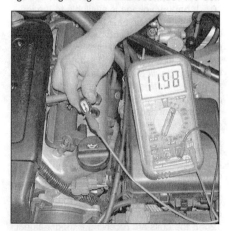

6.9 On Legends, check voltage at each ignition coil's positive terminal . . .

5

6.10 . . . and use an LED test light to check for a trigger signal at each of the ignition coils' negative terminals

7.4 Disconnect the coil electrical connectors and check the resistance between the primary terminals

7.5 Check the resistance between the coil primary and secondary terminals

7.10 Remove the screws (arrows) and pull the coil out of the distributor

7.12 Measure the resistance between each coil's primary terminals

7.16 Remove the mounting bolts (arrows) and work the coil free of the spark plug

electrical connectors and check for power to the positive (+) terminals. Battery voltage should be available with the ignition key ON (engine not running). If there is no battery voltage, check the no. 25 (30 amp) fuse in the under-dash fuse and relay box (see Chapter 12 for additional information on the fuses and the wiring diagrams). **Note:** *Inspect the connectors for dirt, corrosion and damage.*

10   If battery voltage is available to the ignition coils, attach an LED test light to the battery positive terminal and each coil's negative terminal (connectors still unplugged), one at a time **(see illustration)** and crank the engine. **Warning:** *It will be necessary to disconnect all of the ignition coil wiring connectors to prevent the engine from starting.* This test checks for the trigger signal (ground) from the computer.

11   The test light should flash as the engine is cranked over. If the test light does not flash, check the crankshaft position and cylinder position sensors (see Chapter 6). If the sensors check out OK, have the PCM checked by a dealer service department or other qualified automotive repair facility.

12   If the coils are receiving a trigger signal, check the individual ignition coils (see Section 7).

7   Ignition coil - check and replacement

Integra

Check

Refer to illustrations 7.4 and 7.5

1   Make sure the ignition switch is turned OFF for the following checks.

2   Remove the distributor cap, rotor and the leak cover (if equipped).

3   Disconnect the primary electrical connectors from the ignition coil.

4   Using an ohmmeter, touch the probes to the primary terminals of the coil, measure the primary resistance and compare your reading to the value listed in this Chapter's Specifications **(see illustration)**.

5   Touch the probes to the secondary winding terminal and the positive primary terminal **(see illustration)**, measure the secondary resistance and compare your reading to the resistance value listed in this Chapter's Specifications.

6   The figures in the specifications will vary somewhat with the temperature of the coil. The specified resistance values are for a coil

temperature of about 70-degrees F.

7   If the coil fails either check, replace it with a new part.

Replacement

Refer to illustration 7.10

8   Detach the cable from the negative terminal of the battery. **Caution:** *If the radio in your vehicle is equipped with an anti-theft system, make sure you have the correct activation code before disconnecting the battery.*

9   Remove the distributor cap (see Chapter 1) and cover (if equipped). Remove the screws and detach the wires from the primary terminals.

10   Remove the two screws and slide the coil out **(see illustration)**.

11   Installation is the reverse of removal.

Legend

Check

Refer to illustration 7.12

12   Disconnect the electrical connectors from each coil assembly. Connect an ohmmeter across the coil primary terminals **(see illustration)**. The resistance should be as listed in this Chapter's Specifications. If not, replace the coil.

8.1 Check for battery voltage between the black/yellow wire and body ground

8.3 Check for battery voltage on the white/blue wire

8.9 Remove the screw(s) (arrow) and pull the ICM unit straight out from the distributor body

Replacement

Refer to illustration 7.16

13   Disconnect the cable from the negative terminal of the battery. **Caution:** *If the radio in your vehicle is equipped with an anti-theft system, make sure you have the correct activation code before disconnecting the battery.*

14   Disconnect the ignition coil electrical connector from each individual coil. If necessary, mark each electrical connector with tape to prevent mix-ups during reassembly.

15   If you're planning to remove the no. 6 ignition coil, unbolt the air conditioning hose and position it out of the way. DO NOT disconnect the hose.

16   Remove the bolts securing the ignition coil **(see illustration)**, then pull the coil from the cylinder head.

17   Installation is the reverse of the removal procedure with the following additions:

  a) *Prior to installing the coil into the cylinder head, coat the interior of the assembly with silicone dielectric compound.*

  b) *Connect each coil electrical connector to its correct coil and make sure they are tight and secure.*

8   Igniter/Ignition Control Module (ICM) - check and replacement

Note: *Integra models are equipped with an igniter, Legend models are equipped with an Ignition Control Module (ICM).*

Integra

Check

Refer to illustrations 8.1 and 8.3

1   Check for battery voltage to the igniter. Remove the distributor cap and the rotor and detach the black/yellow wire from the igniter **(see illustration)**. Check for battery voltage directly at the electrical connector with the ignition key ON (engine not running).

2   If there is no voltage to the igniter, check the circuit from the igniter to the battery (see Chapter 12). First check the ignition switch

fuses in the underhood fuse/relay box, as follows:

  a) *1990 and 1991: no. 30 (70 amps) and no. 32 (50 amps)*

  b) *1992 and 1993: no. 30 (80 amps) and no. 32 (50 amps)*

Follow the circuit carefully and make sure the ignition switch delivers battery voltage to the igniter with the key ON. Also check the yellow/green wire between the igniter and Powertrain Control Module (PCM), and the blue wire that connects to the tachometer or tachometer service connector. If there isn't continuity between the ends of each wire, there is a break in the wire. If there is continuity between either end of the wire and body ground, there is a short in the wire. Refer to the wiring diagrams at the end of Chapter 12 for additional information.

3   Check for battery voltage from the ignition coil to the igniter. With the ignition key turned ON (engine not running), check for voltage between the white/blue wire and body ground **(see illustration)**. There should be battery voltage.

4   Check the circuit from the ignition coil to the igniter. If there is no voltage, check the circuit between the corresponding wire and the ignition coil. Also check for an open circuit inside the ignition coil by checking for continuity between the primary terminals of the ignition coil (see Section 7).

5   If the ignition coil and circuits are good and there is still no spark, replace the igniter.

Replacement

Refer to illustration 8.9

6   Disconnect the negative battery cable from the battery terminal. **Caution:** *If the radio in your vehicle is equipped with an anti-theft system, make sure you have the correct activation code before disconnecting the battery.*

7   Remove the distributor cap and cover from the distributor (see Chapter 1).

8   Remove all the electrical connectors from the igniter unit.

9   Remove the retaining screw(s) from the igniter and pull the igniter unit straight out

(see illustration).

10   Installation is the reverse of removal.

Legend

Check

Refer to illustration 8.12

11   The Legend ICM is tested by process of elimination; if all the wiring connections and voltage inputs are correct, the ICM is assumed to be defective. Since there are many causes of ignition failure and electrical parts can't be returned once purchased, it's a good idea to have the system tested by a dealer or other qualified shop before replacing the ICM. A problem in the ignition output signal circuit, of which the ICM is a part, is indicated by a Code 15 (see Chapter 6).

12   Locate the ICM and disconnect its eight-pin electrical connector **(see illustration)**. Check for continuity between each of the black wires in the harness and body ground with an ohmmeter. If there's no continuity (or high resistance), follow the harness back to the ground connection at the right valve cover, checking as you go for a break or poor connection.

13   Disconnect the six-pin electrical con-

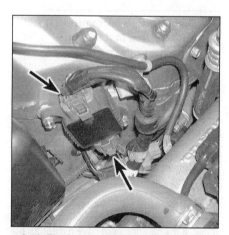

8.12 The Legend ICM has an eight-pin connector (upper arrow) and a six-pin connector (lower arrow)

5

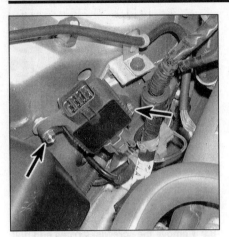

8.17 Disconnect both connectors and remove the mounting bolts (arrows) to remove the ICM

9.5a Mark the relationship of the rotor to the distributor body, and the distributor body to the cylinder head (arrows) . . .

9.5b . . . and remove the mounting nuts or bolts (arrows)

nector from the ICM. Follow the wires back to the PCM (see Chapter 6) and check for breaks or poor connections.

14   Reconnect the six-pin connector to the ICM.

15   Connect the negative lead of a voltmeter to body ground. Turn the ignition key to ON (engine not running). Connect the voltmeter positive lead to each of the remaining terminals in the harness side of the eight-pin connector (all wire colors except black). In each case, there should be battery voltage.

16   If there's no voltage, check the no. 25 fuse (30 amps) in the under-dash fuse/relay box (see Chapter 12). If the fuse is good, check or a break or poor connection in one of the wires. An ignition coil may also be defective (see Section 7).

Replacement

Refer to illustration 8.17

17   Disconnect the electrical connectors from the top and bottom of the ICM. Remove its mounting bolts and take it out **(see illustration)**.

18   Installation is the reverse of removal.

9   Distributor (Integra models) - removal and installation

Removal

Refer to illustrations 9.5a and 9.5b

1   Detach the cable from the negative battery terminal. **Caution:** *If the radio in your vehicle is equipped with an anti-theft system, make sure you have the correct activation code before disconnecting the battery.*

2   Detach any clamps and electrical connectors on the distributor.

3   Look for a raised number or letter on the distributor cap. This marks the location for the number one cylinder spark plug wire terminal. If the cap does not have a mark for the number one terminal, locate the number one spark plug and trace the wire back to the terminal on the cap.

4   Remove the distributor cap (see Chapter 1) and turn the engine over until the number one piston is at Top Dead Center and the rotor is pointing toward the number one spark plug terminal (see the locating TDC procedure in Chapter 2A or 2B).

5   Make a mark on the edge of the distributor base directly below the rotor tip and in line with it (if the rotor on your engine has more than one tip, use the center one for reference). Also, mark the distributor base and the cylinder head to ensure the distributor is installed correctly **(see illustrations).**

6   Remove the distributor hold-down bolt(s) and pull out the distributor. **Caution:** *Do not turn the crankshaft while the distributor is out of the engine, or the alignment marks will be useless.*

Installation

Note: *If the crankshaft has been moved while the distributor is out, the number one piston must be repositioned at TDC. This can be done by feeling for compression pressure at the number one plug hole as the crankshaft is turned. Once compression is felt, align the ignition timing zero mark with the pointer.*

7   Install a new O-ring on the distributor housing.

8   Insert the distributor into the cylinder head in exactly the same relationship to the head that it was when removed. **Note:** *The lugs on the end of the distributor and the corresponding grooves in the camshaft end are offset to eliminate the possibility of installing the distributor 180-degrees out of phase.*

9   Recheck the alignment marks between the distributor base and the cylinder head to verify the distributor is in the same position it was in before removal. Also check the rotor to see if it's aligned with the mark you made on the distributor.

10   Loosely install the hold-down bolt(s).

11   The remainder of installation is the reverse of removal. Check the ignition timing (see Chapter 1) and tighten the distributor hold-down bolt(s) securely.

10   Charging system - general information and precautions

The charging system includes the alternator, an internal voltage regulator, a charge indicator light, the battery, fuses and the wiring between all the components. The charging system supplies electrical power for the ignition system, the lights, the radio, etc. The alternator is driven by a drivebelt at the timing belt end of the engine.

The alternator control system within the ECU changes the voltage generated at the alternator in accordance with driving conditions. Depending upon electric load, vehicle speed, engine coolant temperature, accessories (air conditioning system, radio, cruise control etc.) and the intake air temperature, the system will adjust the amount of voltage generated, creating less load on the engine.

The purpose of the voltage regulator is to limit the alternator's voltage to a preset value. This prevents power surges, circuit overloads, etc., during peak voltage output.

The charging system doesn't ordinarily require periodic maintenance. However, the drivebelt, battery and wires and connections should be inspected at the intervals outlined in Chapter 1.

The dashboard warning light should come on when the ignition key is turned to On, but it should go off immediately after the engine is started. If it remains on, there is a malfunction in the charging system (see Section 11). Some vehicles are also equipped with a voltmeter. If the voltmeter indicates abnormally high or low voltage, check the charging system (see Section 11).

Be very careful when making electrical circuit connections to a vehicle equipped with an alternator and note the following:

a)   *When reconnecting wires to the alternator from the battery, be sure to note the polarity.*

b)   *Before using arc welding equipment to repair any part of the vehicle, disconnect the wires from the alternator and the battery terminals.*

11.3 Connect a voltmeter between the battery terminals to measure battery voltage

12.3a On Integras, loosen the adjustment nut at the top of the alternator . . .

12.3b . . . and the pivot bolt located at the bottom of the alternator

c) Never start the engine with a battery charger connected.

d) Always disconnect both battery cables before using a battery charger.

e) The alternator is turned by an engine drivebelt which could cause serious injury it your hands, hair or clothes become entangled in it with the engine running.

f) Because the alternator is connected directly to the battery, it could arc or cause a fire if overloaded or shorted out.

g) Wrap a plastic bag over the alternator and secure it with rubber bands before steam cleaning the engine.

11 Charging system - check

Refer to illustration 11.3

1 If a malfunction occurs in the charging circuit, do not immediately assume that the alternator is causing the problem. First, check the following items:

a) Make sure the battery cable clamps, where they connect to the battery, are clean and tight.

b) Test the condition of the battery (see Section 3). If it does not pass all the tests, replace it with a new battery.

c) Check the external alternator wiring and connections.

d) Check the drivebelt condition and tension (see Chapter 1).

e) Check the alternator mounting bolts for tightness.

f) Run the engine and check the alternator for abnormal noise.

g) Check the charging system fuses in the engine compartment and under-dash fuse boxes (see Chapter 12). If they're burned, determine the cause and repair the circuit.

h) Check the charge light on the dash. It should illuminate when the ignition key is turned ON (engine not running). If it does not, disconnect the multiple-wire connector from the back of the alternator. Check for battery voltage on the black-

yellow wire's terminal. If battery voltage is not available, check the black/yellow wire for a break or poor connection. If battery voltage is available, ground the white/blue wire's terminal. If the charge light now illuminates, replace the voltage regulator. If it does not, check the charge light fuse (see Chapter 12) and the charge light bulb. If either one is blown, replace it.

2 With the ignition key off, check the battery voltage with no accessories (blower fan, radio, cigarette lighter, cooling fan, etc.) operating. It should be approximately 12.5 volts. It may be slightly higher if the engine had been operating within the last hour.

3 Check the charging voltage with the engine running. Start the engine, raise the engine rpm to 1500 and check the battery voltage again. It should now be approximately 13.8 to 14.8 volts **(see illustration)**.

4 Load the battery and observe the charging voltage. Turn on the high beam headlights, the A/C blower on HIGH, the windshield wipers and the radio. The voltage should drop and then come back up as each accessory is selected. If the charging system is working properly the voltage should stay above 13.5 volts. If the voltage drops below 13 volts, the charging system is weak or defective.

5 Lower the engine rpm back to idle and observe the charging voltage. The charging voltage should not drop below 13 volts with the decrease in engine rpm. Apply the brakes and observe the charging voltage at idle. It should remain above 13 volts. **Note:** *Some smaller amperage alternators may drop below 13 volts but, if they are in good condition, they will regulate the charging voltage to normal.*

6 Turn off all the electrical loads (high beam headlights, the A/C blower on HIGH, the windshield wipers and the radio), run the engine at 1600 rpm and watch the charging voltage rise. It should not rise above 15 volts. **Note:** *Cold temperatures will cause the voltage readings to increase slightly while hot temperatures will lower the charging system voltage readings.*

7 If the charging voltages are low and the drivebelts and battery are all in good condition, the alternator is defective. In this situation, replace the alternator and voltage regulator as a single unit.

12 Alternator - removal and installation

1 Detach the cable from the negative terminal of the battery. **Caution:** *If the radio in your vehicle is equipped with an anti-theft system, make sure you have the correct activation code before disconnecting the battery.*

Integra

Refer to illustrations 12.3a, 12.3b and 12.5

2 Mark and detach the electrical connectors and any ground straps from the alternator.

3 Loosen the alternator adjusting bolt and pivot bolt, then detach the drivebelt **(see illustrations)**.

4 To remove the alternator from the engine compartment, it will be necessary to remove the left driveaxle (see Chapter 8).

5 Remove the adjusting and pivot bolts and lower the alternator from the engine **(see illustration)**.

12.5 After the driveaxle has been removed, lower the alternator from the engine compartment (Integra)

12.8 On Legend models, remove the lockbolt (arrow) and adjuster at the top of the alternator . . .

12.9 . . . and the pivot bolt at the bottom of the alternator (arrow)

13.2 Remove the three nuts (arrows) and detach the rear cover from the alternator

13.3 Once the rear cover is removed, remove the two screws (arrows) that retain the brush holder

13.5 Measure the exposed length of the brushes and compare your measurements to the specified minimum length to determine if they should be replaced

13.7 Remove the voltage regulator screws (arrows) and remove the regulator from the alternator assembly

Legend

Refer to illustrations 12.8 and 12.9

7   Remove the battery and battery tray (see Section 3).

8   Remove the lockbolt and adjusting rod, then remove the drivebelt **(see illustration)**.

9   Remove the lower mounting bolt **(see illustration)**.

10   Twist the alternator counterclockwise (viewed from the front of the engine) until it clears the bracket, then lower it clear of the engine and disconnect the electrical connectors. Remove the alternator from the engine compartment.

All models

11   If you are replacing the alternator, take the old one with you when purchasing a replacement unit. Make sure the new/rebuilt unit looks identical to the old alternator. Look at the terminals - they should be the same in number, size and location as the terminals on the old alternator. Finally, look at the identification numbers - they will be stamped into the housing or printed on a tag attached to the housing. Make sure the numbers are the same on both alternators.

12   Many new/rebuilt alternators DO NOT have a pulley installed, so you may have to switch the pulley from the old unit to the new/rebuilt one. When buying an alternator, find out the shop's policy regarding pulleys; some shops will perform this service free of charge.

13   Installation is the reverse of removal.

14   After the alternator is installed, adjust the drivebelt tension (see Chapter 1).

15   Check the charging voltage to verify proper operation of the alternator (see Section 11).

13   Voltage regulator and alternator brushes - replacement

Refer to illustrations 13.2, 13.3, 13.5 and 13.7
Note: *It's practical to replace the brushes and regulator on these models, but don't attempt to completely overhaul the alternator. If replacing the brushes and regulator does not solve the alternator problem, take the alternator to a dealer service department or other*

repair shop and have it rebuilt or exchange it for a rebuilt unit.

1   Remove the alternator (see Section 12) and place it on a clean workbench.

2   Remove the three rear cover nuts, the nut and terminal insulator and the rear cover **(see Illustration)**.

3   Remove the two brush holder retaining screws **(see illustration)**.

4   Remove the brush holder from the rear end frame.

5   Measure the exposed length of the brush **(see illustration)** and compare it to the minimum length in this Chapter's Specifications. If the length of the brush is less than specified, replace the brush.

6   Make sure that each brush moves smoothly in the brush holder.

7   .To remove the voltage regulator, remove the brushes as described above, then remove the mounting screws and take the regulator off **(see illustration)**.

8   Installation is the reverse of removal. Install the brush holder by depressing the brush with a small screwdriver to clear the shaft.

15.2 This is the Legend starter cut relay (arrow, it's mounted behind the left kick panel

15.4 Starter bench test setup

14 Starting system - general information and precautions

The sole function of the starting system is to turn over the engine quickly enough to allow it to start.

The starting system consists of the battery, the starter motor, the starter solenoid and the wires connecting them. The solenoid is mounted directly on the starter motor.

The solenoid/starter motor assembly is installed at the rear of the engine, next to the transaxle bellhousing.

When the ignition key is turned to the Start position, the starter solenoid is actuated through the starter control circuit. The starter solenoid then connects the battery to the starter. The battery supplies the electrical energy to the starter motor, which does the actual work of cranking the engine.

The starter motor on models equipped with manual transaxles can only be operated when the clutch pedal is depressed; the starter on models equipped with automatic transaxles can only be operated when the selector lever is in Park or Neutral.

Always observe the following precautions when working on the starting system:

a) *Excessive cranking of the starter motor can overheat it and cause serious damage. Never operate the starter motor for more than 15 seconds at a time without pausing to allow it to cool for at least two minutes.*

b) *The starter is connected directly to the battery and could arc or cause a fire if mishandled, overloaded or shorted out.*

c) *Always detach the cable from the negative terminal of the battery before working on the starting system.*

15 Starter motor and circuit - in-vehicle check

Refer to illustrations 15.2 and 15.4

1 If a malfunction occurs in the starting circuit, do not immediately assume that the starter is causing the problem. First, check the following items:

a) *Make sure the battery cable clamps, where they connect to the battery, are clean and tight.*

b) *Check the condition of the battery cables (see Section 4). Replace any defective battery cables with new parts.*

c) *Test the condition of the battery (see Section 3). If it does not pass all the tests, replace it with a new battery.*

d) *Check the starter solenoid wiring and connections. Refer to Chapter 12 wiring diagrams.*

e) *Check the starter mounting bolts for tightness.*

f) *Check the starting system fuses in the engine compartment fuse box (see Chapter 12). If they're burned, determine the cause and repair the circuit. Also, check the ignition switch circuit for correct operation (see Chapter 12).*

g) *Check the operation of the gear position switch (automatic transaxle) or clutch start circuit (manual transaxle) systems. Make sure the shift lever is in PARK or NEUTRAL (automatic transaxle) or the clutch pedal is pressed (manual transaxle). Refer to Chapter 7 for the gear position switch check and adjustment procedure. Refer to Chapter 12 wiring diagrams for the necessary circuit checks for the clutch activation system. These systems must operate correctly to provide battery voltage to the starter solenoid.*

2 If the starter does not actuate when the ignition switch is cranked, check for battery voltage to the solenoid. First determine if the solenoid is receiving the correct voltage signal from the ignition switch. Install a voltmeter to the starter solenoid terminal and while an assistant cranks the engine, observe the voltage. It should be approximately 12.6

volts. If voltage is not available, refer to the wiring diagrams in Chapter 12 and check all the fuses and relays in series with the starting system. On Legends, locate the fuse/relay panel in the driver's side dash area and check fuse number 14 (7.5 amps). Also, check the starter cut relay (Legend) or starter relay (Integra models with manual transaxle) for correct operation. On Legends, it's located on the fuse/relay box behind the left kick panel **(see illustration)**. On Integras it's located on the right side of the heater unit. Refer to Chapter 12 for the relay checking procedure. If voltage is available but there is no movement from the starter motor, remove the starter from the engine compartment (see Section 16) and bench test the starter (see Step 4).

3 If the starter turns over slowly, check the starter cranking voltage and the current draw from the battery. This test must be performed with the starter on the engine. Crank the engine over (for 10 seconds or less) and observe the battery voltage. It should not drop below 8.0 volts on Integras or 8.5 volts on Legends. Also, observe the current draw using an ammeter. It should not exceed 350 amps. If the starter motor exceeds these values, replace it with a new unit. There are several conditions that may affect the starter cranking potential. The battery must be in good condition and the cold-cranking rating must not be under-rated for the particular application. Be sure to check the battery specifications carefully. The battery terminals and cables must be clean and not corroded. Also, in cases of extreme cold temperatures, make sure the battery and/or engine block is warmed before performing the tests.

4 If the starter is receiving voltage but does not activate, remove and check the starter/solenoid assembly on the bench. Most likely the solenoid is defective. In some rare cases, the engine may be seized so be sure to try to rotate the crankshaft pulley (see

5

16.3a On Integras, disconnect the electrical connectors at the starter (arrow) and remove the upper mounting bolt . . .

16.3b . . . then remove the lower mounting bolt (arrow) and remove the starter

16.6a On Legends, disconnect the electrical connectors at the starter (arrow) and remove the lower mounting bolt (arrow) . . .

16.6b . . . then remove the upper mounting bolt (arrow) and remove the starter

17.4 Remove the screws and separate the solenoid from the starter

Legend

Refer to illustrations 16.6a and 16.6b

6   Clearly label, then disconnect the wires from the terminals on the starter motor solenoid **(see illustrations)**.

7   Unbolt the bracket from the starter motor.

8   Remove the left driveaxle (see Chapter 8).

9   Remove the forward section of the exhaust system (see Chapter 4).

10   Remove the starter mounting bolts **(see illustrations 16.6a and 16.6b)** and carefully maneuver the starter out from under the vehicle.

11   Installation is the reverse of removal.

---

17 Starter solenoid - replacement

Refer to illustration 17.4

Note: *Integra models are equipped with Nippondenso starters, which have non-replaceable solenoids. If an Integra solenoid is defective, the entire starter should be replaced. This procedure applies to the starters used on Legends.*

1   Detach the cable from the negative terminal of the battery. **Caution:** *If the radio in your vehicle is equipped with an anti-theft system, make sure you have the correct activation code before disconnecting the battery.*

2   Remove the starter motor (see Section 16).

3   Disconnect the large wire from the solenoid to the starter motor terminal.

4   Remove the screws and separate the solenoid from the starter motor **(see illustration)**.

5   Installation is the reverse of removal. Be sure to apply a slight amount of grease to the solenoid plunger and lever before installation.

Chapter 2A or 2B) before proceeding. With the starter/solenoid assembly mounted in a vise on the bench, install one jumper cable from the negative terminal (-) to the body of the starter **(see illustration)**. Install the other jumper cable from the positive terminal (+) on the battery to the B+ terminal on the starter. Install a starter switch and apply battery voltage to the solenoid S terminal (for 10 seconds or less) and see if the solenoid plunger, shift lever and overrunning clutch activate and rotate the pinion drive. If the pinion drive extends but does not rotate, the solenoid is operating but the starter motor is defective. If there is no movement but the solenoid clicks, the solenoid and/or the starter motor is defective. If the solenoid plunger extends and rotates the pinion drive, the starter/solenoid assembly is working properly.

16 Starter motor - removal and installation

1   Detach the cable from the negative terminal of the battery. **Caution:** *If the radio in your vehicle is equipped with an anti-theft system, make sure you have the correct activation code before disconnecting the battery.*

Integra

Refer to illustrations 16.3a and 16.3b

2   Remove the air cleaner intake air duct (see Chapter 4).

3   Clearly label, then disconnect the wires from the terminals on the starter motor solenoid **(see illustrations)**.

4   Remove the mounting bolts and detach the starter.

5   Installation is the reverse of removal.

Chapter 6
Emissions and engine control systems

Contents

Specifications

General

Integra
CKP sensor resistance	350 to 700 ohms
CYP sensor resistance	350 to 700 ohms
TDC sensor resistance	350 to 700 ohms

Legend
CKP sensor resistance	650 to 900 ohms
CYP sensor resistance	650 to 900 ohms
Intake air temperature sensor resistance	1,000 to 4,000 ohms at room temperature

1 General information

Refer to illustrations 1.1a, 1.1b and 1.6

To prevent pollution of the atmosphere from incompletely burned and evaporating gases, and to maintain good driveability and fuel economy, a number of emission and engine control systems are incorporated **(see illustrations)**. They include the:

Self diagnosis system
Electronic engine controls (PGM-FI)
Exhaust Gas Recirculation (EGR) system
Evaporative Emissions Control (EVAP) system
Positive Crankcase Ventilation (PCV) system
Catalytic converter

The Sections in this Chapter include general descriptions, checking procedures within the scope of the home mechanic and component replacement procedures (when possible) for each of the systems listed above.

Before assuming that an emissions control system is malfunctioning, check the fuel and ignition systems carefully. The diagnosis of some emission control devices requires specialized tools, equipment and training. If checking and servicing become too difficult or if a procedure is beyond your ability, consult a dealer service department or other repair shop. Remember, the most frequent cause of emissions problems is simply a loose or broken wire or vacuum hose, so always check the hose and wiring connections first.

This doesn't mean, however, that emissions control systems are particularly difficult to maintain and repair. You can quickly and easily perform many checks and do most of the regular maintenance at home with common tune-up and hand tools. **Note:** *Because of a Federally mandated extended warranty which covers the emissions control system components, check with your dealer about warranty coverage before working on any emissions-related systems. Once the warranty has expired, you may wish to perform some of the component checks and/or replacement procedures in this Chapter to save money.*

Pay close attention to any special precautions outlined in this Chapter. It should be noted that the illustrations of the various systems may not exactly match the system installed on your vehicle because of changes made by the manufacturer during production or from year-to-year.

A Vehicle Emissions Control Information (VECI) label is attached to the underside of the hood **(see illustration)**. This label contains important emissions specifications and adjustment information. Part of this label, the Vacuum Hose Routing Diagram, provides a vacuum hose schematic with emissions components identified. When servicing the engine or emissions systems, the VECI label and the vacuum hose routing diagram in your particular vehicle should always be checked for up-to-date information.

1.1a Typical emission and engine control components (Integra)

1	Fuel pressure regulator cut-off solenoid	5	Charcoal canister (below air duct)
2	Purge cut-off solenoid	6	Throttle Position Sensor (TPS) (on throttle body)
3	Manifold Absolute Pressure (MAP) sensor	7	Oxygen sensor (in exhaust manifold)
4	Air boost valve	8	TDC/CKP/CYP sensor (inside distributor)

1.1b Typical emission and engine control components (Legend)

1	Charcoal canister	5	Oxygen sensors (in exhaust manifolds)
2	CKP/CYP sensor	6	Ignition control module
3	EGR vacuum control valve	7	EVAP purge solenoid
4	Throttle Position Sensor (TPS)		

2   On-Board Diagnostic (OBD) system and trouble codes

Diagnostic tool information

Refer to illustrations 2.1 and 2.2

1   A digital multimeter is necessary for checking fuel injection and emission related components **(see illustration)**. A digital volt-ohmmeter is preferred over the older style analog multimeter for several reasons. The analog multimeter cannot display the volts-ohms or amps measurement in hundredths and thousandths increments. When working with electronic circuits which are often very low voltage, this accurate reading is most important. Another good reason for the digital multimeter is the high impedance circuit. The digital multimeter is equipped with a high resistance internal circuitry (10 million ohms). Because a voltmeter is hooked up in parallel with the circuit when testing, it is vital that none of the voltage being measured should be allowed to travel the parallel path set up by the meter itself. This dilemma does not show itself when measuring larger amounts of voltage (9 to 12 volt circuits) but if you are measuring a low voltage circuit such as the oxygen sensor signal voltage, a fraction of a volt may be a significant amount when diagnosing a problem.

2   Hand-held scanners are the most powerful and versatile tools for analyzing engine management systems used on later model vehicles **(see illustration)**. Each brand scan tool must be examined carefully to match the year, make and model of the vehicle you are working on. Often, interchangeable cartridges are available to access the particular manufacturer (Ford, GM, Chrysler, etc.). Some manufacturers will specify by continent (Asia, Europe, USA, etc.).

OBD system general description

3   These models use the first-generation On-Board Diagnostic (OBD) system. This system incorporates a series of diagnostic monitors that detect and identify emissions systems faults and store the information in the computer memory.

4   Stored fault information is displayed in the form of numeric trouble codes. The trouble code is flashed by an LED on top of the PCM (1990 and 1991 Integras) or by the Check Engine light (all others).

5   The PCM is the "brain" of the engine management system. It receives data from a number of sensors and other electronic components (switches, relays, etc.). Based on the information it receives, the PCM generates output signals to control various relays, solenoids and other actuators. The PCM is specifically calibrated to optimize the emissions, fuel economy and driveability of the vehicle.

6   Because of a Federally mandated extended warranty which covers the engine

1.6 The Vehicle Emission Control Information and vacuum hose routing diagram decals are located under the hood

management system components and because any owner-induced damage to the PCM, the sensors and/or the control devices may void the warranty, it isn't a good idea to attempt diagnosis or replacement of the PCM at home while the vehicle is under warranty. Take the vehicle to a dealer service department if the PCM or a system component malfunctions.

Information sensors

7   **Oxygen sensor or heated oxygen sensor (O2S or HO2S) -** The oxygen sensor generates a voltage signal that varies with the difference between the oxygen content of the exhaust and the oxygen in the surrounding air. The oxygen sensors in 1992 and later Integras and all Legends use internal heaters to stabilize their output.

8   **Crankshaft Position/Cylinder Position (CKP/CYP) sensor -** This sensor, used on Legend, models, provides information on crankshaft position, the position of the no. 1 cylinder and the engine speed to the PCM. The PCM uses this information to time fuel injection and ignition.

9   **Top Dead Center/Crankshaft Position/Cylinder Position (TDC/CKP/CYP) sensor -** This sensor, used on Integras, produces a signal which the PCM uses to identify number 1 cylinder and to time the sequential fuel injection and ignition.

10   **Engine Coolant Temperature (ECT) sensor -** The ECT monitors engine coolant temperature and sends the PCM a voltage signal that affects PCM control of the fuel mixture, ignition timing, and EGR operation.

11   **Intake Air Temperature (IAT) sensor -** The IAT provides the PCM with intake air temperature information. The PCM uses this information to control fuel flow, ignition timing, and EGR system operation (if equipped).

12   **Throttle Position Sensor (TPS) -** The Throttle Position Sensor (TPS) is located on the end of the throttle shaft on the throttle body. By monitoring the output voltage from the TPS, the ECM can determine fuel delivery based on throttle valve angle (driver

2.1 Digital multimeters can be used for testing all types of circuits; because of their high impedance, they are much more accurate than analog meters for measuring low-voltage computer circuits

2.2 Scanners like the Actron Scantool and the AutoXray XP240 are powerful diagnostic aids, programmed with comprehensive diagnostic information

demand). A broken or loose TPS can cause intermittent bursts of fuel from the injectors and an unstable idle because the ECM thinks the throttle is moving.

13   **Manifold Absolute Pressure (MAP) sensor -** The Manifold Absolute Pressure (MAP) sensor monitors the intake manifold pressure changes resulting from changes in engine load and speed and converts the information into a voltage output. The PCM uses the MAP sensor to control fuel delivery and ignition timing. The PCM will receive information as a voltage signal that will vary from 1.0 to 1.5 volts at closed throttle (high vacuum) and 4.0 to 4.5 volts at wide open throttle (low vacuum). The MAP sensor is located on the throttle body.

14   **Barometric pressure (BARO) sensor -** This sensor signals the atmospheric pressure to the PCM. It's built into the PCM.

15   **Vehicle Speed Sensor (VSS) -** The VSS provides information to the PCM to indicate vehicle speed.

6

16   Power Steering Pressure (PSP) switch - The PSP switch is used to increase transaxle hydraulic line pressure during low-speed vehicle maneuvers.

17   Knock sensor - The knock sensor detects the sound of spark knock and gives this information to the PCM, which in turn retards ignition timing to eliminate the spark knock condition.

Output actuators

18   PGM-FI main (fuel pump) relay - This relay is activated by the PCM with the ignition switch in the Start or Run position. When the ignition switch is turned on, the relay is activated to supply initial line pressure to the system. The PGM-FI main relay is in the power distribution box in the engine compartment. For more information on fuel pump check and replacement, refer to Chapter 4.

19   Fuel injectors - The PCM opens the fuel injectors individually in firing order sequence. The PCM also controls the time the injector is open, called the "pulse width." The pulse width of the injector (measured in milliseconds) determines the amount of fuel delivered. For more information on the fuel delivery system and the fuel injectors, including injector replacement, refer to Chapter 4.

20   Igniter/Ignition Control Module (ICM) - Integra models use an ignition module which is incorporated in the distributor. The ICM on Legend models triggers the ignition coils and determines proper spark advance based on inputs from the PCM. Refer to Chapter 5 for more information on the Igniter and Ignition Control Module.

21   Idle Air Control (IAC) valve - The IAC valve (called the Electronic Air Control Valve or EACV on some models) controls the amount of air to bypass the throttle plate when the throttle valve is closed or at idle position. This allows the PCM to maintain correct idle speed while the engine is cold and during increased loads on the engine caused by the air conditioning compressor, alternator, power steering pump or automatic

2.22a The service check connector, under the passenger side glove box behind the kick panel, can be used to read trouble codes with the CHECK engine light

transaxle (shifting into gear). The IAC valve opening and the resulting airflow is controlled by the PCM.

Obtaining trouble codes

Refer to illustrations 2.22a, 2.22b and 2.22c

22   The service check connector is located under the dashboard, on the passenger side **(see illustrations)**. The codes can be read by jumping this connector and reading the CHECK engine light on the instrument panel (all except 1990 and 1991 Integra) or the LED on top of the PCM (1990 and 1991 Integra).

23   To view self-diagnosis information from the ECM memory, install a jumper wire into the service check connector **(see illustration 2.22b or 2.22c)** located in the far right corner under the dash, then turn the ignition switch to the ON position. The codes are stored in the memory of the PCM and when accessed, they blink a sequence on the CHECK light on the instrument panel (or the LED on the PCM) to relay a number or code that represents a system or component failure.

24   The light will blink a longer blink to rep-

2.22b Bridge the connector with a short jumper wire; this is the Integra connector . . .

2.22c . . . and this is the Legend connector

resent the first digit of a two digit number and then will blink short for the second digit (for example, 1 long blink then 6 short blinks for the code 16). **Note:** *If the system has more than one problem, the codes will be displayed in sequence, then a there will be pause, then the codes will repeat.*

Integra trouble codes

Trouble code	Circuit or system	Corrective action
Code 0	Faulty ECM	Check the ECM electrical connector. If no loose connectors are found, have the ECM diagnosed by a dealer service department or other qualified repair shop.
Code 1	Oxygen content	Check the oxygen sensor, heater and the oxygen sensor circuit (see Section 11).
Codes 3 and 5	Manifold Absolute Pressure	Check the MAP sensor and circuit (see Section 5).
Code 4	Crankshaft Position sensor (CKP)	Check the Crankshaft Position sensor and circuit (see Section 8).
Code 6	Coolant temperature	Check the coolant temperature sensor (ECT) and circuit (see Section 7).
Code 7	Throttle Position Sensor (TPS)	Check the Throttle Position Sensor (TPS) and circuit (see Section 4).

Trouble code	Circuit or system	Corrective action
Code 8	TDC Position	Check the TDC sensor and the circuit (see Section 8).
Code 9	No. 1 cylinder position (CYP)	Check the CYP sensor and the circuit (see Section 8).
Code 10	Intake Air Temperature (IAT) sensor	Check the IAT sensor and the circuit (see Section 6).
Code 12	Exhaust Gas Recirculation	Check the hoses, the EGR valve lift sensor and the System EGR valve (see Section 19).
Code 13	Barometric Pressure	Have the vehicle checked at a dealer service department or other qualified repair shop.
Code 14	Idle Air Control (IAC) valve	Check the IAC valve and system (see Chapter 4).
Code 15	Ignition output signal	Check the ignition system (see Chapter 5).
Code 16	Fuel injector	Check the fuel injection system and the fuel injectors (see Chapter 4).
Code 17	Vehicle Speed Sensor (VSS)	Check the VSS (see Section 13).
Code 21	Variable Valve Timing and Valve Lift Solenoid	See Chapter 2A VTEC Solenoid checks.
Code 22	Variable Valve Timing and control pressure switch	See Chapter 2A VTEC Pressure switch checks.
Code 23	Knock sensor	Check the knock sensor and circuit (see Section 12).
Code 41	Oxygen sensor heater	Check the heater for the proper voltage signal (see Section 11).
Code 43	Fuel supply system	Check the fuel pressure, fuel pressure regulator (see Chapter 4). Check the oxygen sensor (see Section 11). Also, check for vacuum leaks.

Legend trouble codes

Trouble code	Circuit or system	Corrective action
Code 0	Faulty ECM	Check the ECM electrical connector. If no loose connectors are found, have the ECM diagnosed by a dealer service department or other qualified repair shop.
Code 1	Left HO2S	Check the oxygen sensor, heater and the oxygen sensor circuit (see Section 11).
Code 2	Right HO2S	Check the oxygen sensor, heater and the oxygen sensor circuit (see Section 11).
Codes 3 and 5	Manifold Absolute Pressure (MAP)	Check the MAP sensor and circuit (see Section 5).
Code 4	Crankshaft Position sensor (CKP)	Check the Crankshaft Position sensor and circuit (see Section 8).
Code 6	Coolant temperature	Check the coolant temperature sensor (ECT) and circuit (see Section 7).
Code 7	Throttle Position Sensor (TPS)	Check the Throttle Position Sensor (TPS) and circuit (see Section 4).
Code 9	No. 1 cylinder position (CYP)	Check the CYP sensor and the circuit (see Section 4).
Code 10	Intake Air Temperature (IAT) sensor	Check the IAT sensor and the circuit (see Section 6).
Code 12	Exhaust Gas Recirculation	Check the hoses, the EGR valve lift sensor and the System EGR valve (see Section 19).
Code 13	Barometric Pressure	Have the vehicle checked at a dealer service department or other qualified repair shop.

6

Legend trouble codes (continued)

Trouble code	Circuit or system	Corrective action
Code 14	Idle Air Control (IAC) valve	Check the IAC valve and system (see Chapter 14).
Code 15	Ignition output signal	Check the ignition system (see Chapter 5).
Code 16	Fuel injector	Check the fuel injection system and the fuel injectors (see Chapter 4).
Code 17	Vehicle Speed Sensor (VSS)	Check the VSS (see Section 13).
Code 18	Ignition timing adjuster	Check the ignition timing adjuster and circuit (see Section 9).
Code 23	Left knock sensor	Check the knock sensor and circuit (see Section 12).
Code 35	Traction control system	Check the traction control system (see Chapter 9)
Code 36	Traction control system	Check the traction control system (see Chapter 9)
Code 41	Left oxygen sensor heater	Check the heater for the proper voltage signal (see Section 11).
Code 42	Right oxygen sensor heater	Check the heater for the proper voltage signal (see Section 11).
Code 43	Left fuel supply system	Check the fuel pressure, fuel pressure regulator (see Chapter 4). Check the oxygen sensors (see Section 11). Also, check for vacuum leaks.
Code 44	Right fuel supply system	Check the fuel pressure, fuel pressure regulator (see Chapter 4). Check the oxygen sensors (see Section 11). Also, check for vacuum leaks (see Section 4).
Code 45	Left fuel metering	Check the MAP sensor (see Section 5). Also check the fuel injectors and check for a blocked fuel rail (see Chapter 4).
Code 46	Right fuel metering	Check the MAP sensor (see Section 5). Also check the fuel injectors and check for a blocked fuel rail (see Chapter 4).
Code 53	Right knock sensor	Check the knock sensor and circuit (see Section 12).
Code 54	Crankshaft position 2 (CKP sensor)	Check the sensor and circuit (see Section 8).
Code 59	Cylinder position 2 (CYL or CYP sensor)	Check the sensor and circuit (see Section 8).

Clearing codes

25   When the PCM sets a trouble code, the CHECK engine light will come on and a trouble code will be stored in the memory. The trouble code will stay in the PCM memory until the voltage to the PCM is interrupted.

26   To clear the memory on Integra models, remove the BACK-UP fuse from the engine compartment fuse/relay box for at least ten seconds. Also, be sure to remove the jumper wire.

27   To clear the memory on Legend models, remove the no. 15 (ACGS) fuse from the under-dash fuse relay box for at least ten seconds. Also, be sure to remove the jumper wire.

3   Powertrain Control Module (PCM) - removal and installation

Refer to illustrations 3.4 and 3.5

Warning: *Legend models covered by this manual are equipped with a Supplemental Restraint System (SRS), more commonly known as an airbag(s). Always disable the airbag system before working in the vicinity of the SRS unit, steering column or instrument panel to avoid the possibility of accidental deployment of the airbag, which could cause personal injury (see Chapter 12).*

1   The Powertrain Control Module (PCM) is located inside the passenger compartment under the dashboard behind the kick plate (right side).

2   Disable the airbag system (see Chapter 12). **Caution:** *If the stereo in your vehicle is equipped with an anti-theft system, make sure you have the correct activation code before disconnecting the battery.*

3   Remove the carpet from the lower panel assembly and the floor area (see Chapter 11) under the right end of the dash. Place the carpet sufficiently out of the way.

4   Remove the kick plate to expose the PCM **(see illustration). Caution:** *Avoid any static electricity damage to the computer by grounding yourself to the body before touching the PCM and using a special anti-static*

3.4 Remove the mounting nuts to detach the PCM from the kick panel; lift off the panel . . .

3.5 . . . and disconnect the connectors to remove the PCM

4.1a Integra Throttle Position Sensor (TPS)

pad to store the PCM on once it is removed.

5   Unplug the electrical connectors from the PCM **(see illustration). Caution:** *The ignition switch must be turned OFF when pulling out or plugging in the electrical connectors to prevent damage to the PCM.*

6   Remove the retaining nuts from the PCM bracket.

7   Carefully remove the PCM.

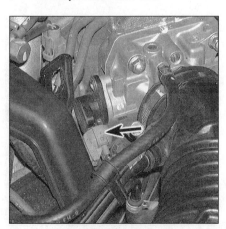

4.1b Legend Throttle Position Sensor (TPS)

4   Throttle Position Sensor (TPS) - check and replacement

Check

Refer to illustrations 4.1a and 4.1b

1   Make sure the ignition key is OFF, then disconnect the three-pin electrical connector from the Throttle Position Sensor **(see illustrations).**

2   Using a digital voltmeter, check the reference voltage from the ECM. Turn the ignition key to ON and connect the positive probe to the yellow/white wire and the negative probe to the green/white wire. It should read approximately 5.0 volts.

3   If there is no voltage, repeat the test, but this time connect the voltmeter negative probe to body ground. If it now reads 5.0 volts, follow the green/white wire from the Throttle Position Sensor back to the PCM, checking for breaks or poor connections.

4   If there's still no voltage, follow the yellow/white wire back to the PCM and check for breaks or poor connections.

5   Next, check the TPS signal voltage. With the engine Off, throttle fully closed and TPS electrical connector connected, connect the

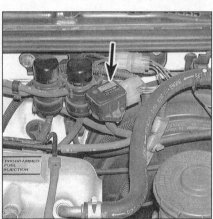

5.3a Integra MAP sensor

probes of the voltmeter onto the red/blue wire (positive probe) and ground (negative probe) **(see illustrations).** Gradually open the throttle valve and observe the TPS sensor voltage. With the throttle valve fully closed, the voltage should read approximately 0.5 volts. Slowly move the throttle valve and observe a distinct change in the voltage values as the sensor travels from idle to full throttle. The voltage should increase smoothly to approximately 4.8 volts. If the readings are incorrect, follow the red/blue wire back to the PCM and check for breaks or poor connections. If the wire is good, replace the TPS.

6   A problem in any of the TPS circuits will set a code (see Section 2). Once a trouble code is set, the ECM will use an artificial default value for throttle angle and some vehicle performance will return.

Replacement

7   The Throttle Position Sensor is riveted to the throttle body and is not available as a separate component. If the TPS fails, replace the throttle body (see Chapter 4).

5   Manifold Absolute Pressure (MAP) sensor - check and replacement

Check

1   Check the electrical connector at the sensor for a snug fit. Check the terminals in the connector and the wires leading to it from the PCM for looseness and breaks. Repair as required. Also check the vacuum hose to the sensor for cracks. The following tests are based on the assumption that the wires are good.

Code 3 indicated

Refer to illustrations 5.3a and 5.3b

2   Code 3 indicates an electrical problem in the MAP sensor.

3   Disconnect the electrical connector from the MAP sensor **(see illustrations).**

6

5.3b Legend MAP sensor

5.10 Connect a vacuum gauge to the MAP sensor hose and apply vacuum

6.1a Intake Air Temperature (IAT) sensor (Integra)

4   With the ignition key ON (engine not running), connect a voltmeter positive probe to the yellow/red wire (Integra) or yellow/white wire (Legend) and the negative probe to the green/white wire (in the harness side of the connector, not the MAP sensor side). There should be approximately 5 volts.

5   Move the positive probe to the white wire (Integra) or red wire (Legend). Again, there should be approximately 5 volts.

6   If there's no voltage and the wires are good in Step 4 or 5, the PCM may be at fault. Have it tested by a dealer service department or other qualified repair shop.

7   If the voltmeter does indicate 5 volts, turn the ignition key to OFF and connect the electrical connector to the MAP sensor.

8   Backprobe the connector and connect the voltmeter positive terminal to the white wire (Integra) or red wire (Legend). Connect the negative terminal to the green/white wire, then switch the ignition key to ON. There should now be approximately 3 volts. If not, replace the MAP sensor. If there are three volts, the PCM may be at fault. Have it tested by a dealer service department or other qualified repair shop.

Code 5 indicated

Refer to illustration 5.10

9   Code 5 indicates a vacuum problem in the MAP sensor.

10   Disconnect the MAP sensor hose (no. 21) from the throttle body. Connect a vacuum pump to the hose and apply vacuum **(see illustration)**. If it leaks, proceed to the next Step. If it doesn't leak, check the vacuum port to make sure it isn't plugged.

11   Connect the vacuum pump directly to the MAP sensor and apply vacuum. If it leaks, replace the MAP sensor. If the sensor doesn't leak, check the hose for a leak.

12   Connect the vacuum pump into the MAP sensor vacuum hose using a T-fitting.

13   Start the engine and let it idle. If the vacuum pump's gauge doesn't show vacuum, look for blockage in the throttle body vacuum port.

14   Shut the engine off, then turn the key back to ON but don't restart the engine.

15   With the MAP sensor vacuum line and electrical connector connected, backprobe the MAP sensor connector with a voltmeter. Connect the positive prove to the white wire (Integra) or red wire (Legend). Connect the negative probe to the green/white wire. There should be three volts. If not, replace the MAP sensor.

16   Start the engine and let it idle. There should now be one volt. If not, replace the MAP sensor.

Replacement

17   Disconnect the electrical connector and vacuum hose from the MAP sensor **(see illustration 5.3a or 5.3b)**. Remove the mounting screws and the MAP sensor.

18   Installation is the reverse of removal.

---

6   Intake Air Temperature (IAT) sensor - check and replacement

---

Check

Refer to illustrations 6.1a and 6.1b

1   With the ignition switch ON, disconnect the electrical connector from the IAT sensor, which is located on the intake manifold **(see illustrations)**. Using an ohmmeter, measure

the resistance between the two terminals on the sensor when the engine is cold, then again when the engine is hot. As the sensor temperature INCREASES, the resistance values will DECREASE; when the sensor temperature DECREASES, the resistance values will INCREASE. If the sensor does not perform as described, replace it.

2   Follow the yellow/red and green/white wires back to the PCM, checking for breaks or poor connections as you go. Repair as necessary. The following steps are based on the assumption that the wires are good.

3   With the ignition key ON (engine not running), check for 5 volts between the two wires in the IAT sensor connector (the wiring harness side). If there's no voltage and the wires are good, have the vehicle checked at a dealer service department or other qualified repair shop, as the PCM may be malfunctioning.

Replacement

Refer to illustration 6.5

4   Disconnect the electrical connector from the IAT sensor.

5   Remove the screws that retain the sensor to the intake manifold and remove the IAT sensor **(see illustration)**.

6   Installation is the reverse of removal.

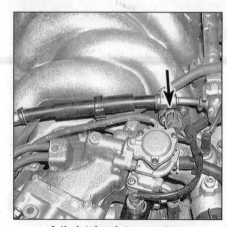

6.1b Intake air temperature sensor (Legend)

6.5 Remove the screws to detach the IAT sensor (Legend shown)

7.3a Engine Coolant Temperature (ECT) sensor (Integra)

7.3b Engine Coolant Temperature (ECT) sensor (Legend)

8.2 The Integra Crankshaft Position/Top Dead Center/Cylinder Position (CKP/TDC/CYP) sensor is mounted in the distributor; its connector (arrow) is accessible from outside

7 Engine Coolant Temperature (ECT) sensor - check and replacement

Check

Refer to illustrations 7.3a and 7.3b

1   The Engine Coolant Temperature (ECT) sensor is a thermistor (a resistor which varies its resistance in accordance with temperature changes). The change in the resistance values will directly affect the voltage signal from the ECT to the PCM. As the sensor temperature DECREASES, the resistance values will INCREASE. As the sensor temperature INCREASES, the resistance values will DECREASE. A trouble code for this sensor indicates a failure in the sensor circuit, so in most cases the appropriate solution to the problem will be either repair of a wire or replacement of the sensor.

2   Warm the engine to normal operating temperature and shut it off.

3   Disconnect the electrical connector from the ECT sensor, which is located on the intake manifold on Legends and near the distributor on Integras **(see illustrations)**. Using an ohmmeter, measure the resistance between the two terminals on the sensor. There should be 200 to 400 ohms. If the resistance isn't as specified, replace the sensor.

4   With the ignition key ON (engine not running), check for 5 volts between the two wires in the ECT sensor connector (the wiring harness side). If there's no voltage, follow the red/white and green/white wires back to the PCM, checking for breaks or poor connections as you go. Repair as necessary.

5   If the wires are good, have the vehicle checked at a dealer service department or other qualified repair shop, as the PCM may be malfunctioning.

Replacement

Warning: *Wait until the engine has cooled completely before beginning this procedure.*

6   Before installing the new sensor, wrap the threads with Teflon sealing tape to prevent leakage and thread corrosion.

7   To remove the sensor, depress the locking tab, unplug the electrical connector, then carefully unscrew the sensor. Coolant will leak out when the sensor is removed, so install the new sensor as quickly as possible. **Caution:** *Handle the coolant sensor with care. Damage to this sensor will affect the operation of the entire fuel injection system.*

8   Installation is the reverse of removal. Check the coolant level and add some, if necessary, to bring to the appropriate level (see Chapter 1).

8 Crankshaft Position (CKP) sensor - check and replacement

Integra

Check

Refer to illustration 8.2

1   On Integras, the TDC/CKP/CYP is a three-part sensor consisting of the CKP (Crankshaft Position) sensor, which determines the timing for the fuel injection and ignition on each cylinder and detects engine RPM; the TDC (Top Dead Center) sensor, which determines the ignition timing at startup (engine cranking); and the CYP (Cylinder Position) sensor, which determines the position of the no. 1 cylinder for sequential fuel injection to each cylinder. All three sensors are built into the distributor. Diagnostics for all three sensors are performed by checking for the diagnostic codes (see Section 2) and then checking for the proper resistance at the electrical connector.

2   Disconnect the connector at the distributor **(see illustration)**. Check the terminals for bending or corrosion. Follow the wires to the connector at the right shock tower, then to the PCM, checking for breaks or poor connections as you go. The following tests are based on the assumption that the wires are good.

3   To check the CKP sensor, disconnect the electrical connector at the distributor and probe terminals C and D (1990-91) or B and F (1992-93) of the sensor with an ohmmeter **(see illustration 8.2)**. Compare your reading

to the resistance listed in this Chapter's Specifications.

4   Check for continuity to body ground on terminals C and D (1990-91) or B and F (1992-93). Continuity should NOT exist. If the test results are incorrect, replace the distributor unit (see Chapter 5).

5   If the test results are all correct, have the system diagnosed by a dealer service department or other qualified repair shop.

6   To check the TDC sensor, disconnect the ignition harness connector at the distributor and probe terminals A and B (1990-91) or C and G (1992-93) with an ohmmeter **(see illustration 8.2)**. Compare the reading to the resistance listed in this Chapter's Specifications.

7   Check for continuity to ground on terminals A and B (1990-91) or C and G (1992-93). Continuity should NOT exist. If the test results are incorrect, replace the distributor unit (see Chapter 5). If the test results are correct, have the system diagnosed by a dealer service department.

8   To check the CYP sensor, disconnect the ignition harness connector at the distributor and probe terminals F and G (1990-91) or D and H (1992-93) with an ohmmeter **(see illustration 8.2)**. Compare the reading to the resistance listed in this Chapter's Specifications.

9   Check for continuity to ground on terminals F and G (1990-91) or D and H (1992-93). Continuity should NOT exist. If the test results are incorrect, replace the distributor unit (see Chapter 5).

10   If the test results are all correct, have the system diagnosed by a dealer service department or other qualified repair shop.

Legend

Refer to illustration 8.12

11   On Legends, the sensor is a two-part sensor consisting of the CKP, which times ignition and fuel injection and detects engine rpm; and the CYP, which indicates the position of no. 1 cylinder. The sensor unit mounted on the left cylinder head, inside the rear plate of the left camshaft. Diagnostics for

6

8.12 The Legend Crankshaft Position/Cylinder Position (CKP/CYP) sensor is mounted behind the left camshaft sprocket (arrow)

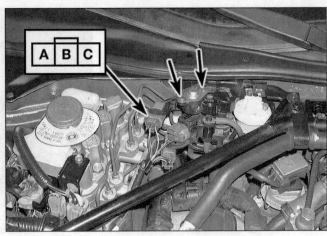

9.2 Ignition timing adjuster connector (left arrow) and cover screws (right arrows)

both sensors are performed by checking for the diagnostic codes (see Section 2) and then checking for the proper resistance at the electrical connector.

12   Follow the wiring harness from the sensor to the eight-pin connector and disconnect it **(see illustration)**. Check the terminals for bending or corrosion. Follow the wires to the connector at the right shock tower, then to the PCM, checking for breaks or poor connections as you go. The following tests are based on the assumption that the wires are good.

13   To check the CKP sensor, disconnect the eight-pin electrical connector at the distributor and probe terminals A and B, then terminals C and D with an ohmmeter **(see illustration 8.12)**. Compare to the resistance listed in this Chapter's Specifications.

14   Check for continuity to body ground on terminals A through D. Continuity should NOT exist. If the test results are incorrect, replace the sensor unit.

15   If the test results are all correct, have the system diagnosed by a dealer service department or other qualified repair shop.

16   To check the CYP sensor, disconnect the electrical connector at the sensor and probe terminals E and F, then terminals G

10.3a Power steering pressure switch connector (Integra)

and H with an ohmmeter **(see illustration 8.12)**. Compare the reading to the resistance listed in this Chapter's Specifications.

17   Check for continuity to body ground on terminals F through G. Continuity should NOT exist. If the test results are incorrect, replace the sensor unit.

18   If the test results are all correct, have the system diagnosed by a dealer service department or other qualified repair shop.

Replacement

19   Remove the timing belt and the left camshaft sprocket (see Chapter 2B).

20   Disconnect the sensor electrical connector. Remove the mounting screws and take the sensor off.

21   Installation is the reverse of removal.

---

9   Ignition timing adjuster (Legend models) - check and replacement

Refer to illustration 9.2

Check

1   The ignition timing adjuster allows the ignition timing at idle to be set at 15-degrees BTDC.

2   Locate the adjuster connector, next to the control box on the firewall, and disconnect it **(see illustration)**.

3   Connect an ohmmeter between terminals A and C in the adjuster side of the connector (not the harness side). It should indicate 3.5 to 6.5 K-ohms. If it doesn't, replace the unit.

4   Measure resistance between terminals A and B, then between terminals B and C. The total of the two measurements should be 3.5 to 6.5 K-ohms. If it doesn't, replace the unit.

5   Turn the ignition key to ON but don't start the engine. Connect a voltmeter between the yellow/white and green/white wire terminals in the harness side of the connector. There should be approximately 5 volts. If not, follow the wires back to the

PCM, checking for breaks or poor connections as you go.

6   Plug in the connector to the unit again. With the key ON, backprobe the connector and check voltage between the blue/yellow and green/white wire terminals. There should now be 0.5 to 4.5 volts. If not, check the blue/yellow wire back to the PCM for breaks or poor connections.

7   If the wire is good and the voltage reading is wrong, the PCM may be at fault. Have the system tested by a dealer service department or other qualified repair shop.

Replacement

8   Remove the control box cover from the firewall. Disconnect the electrical connector from the adjuster, drill out the rivets and remove it.

9   Installation is the reverse of removal.

---

10   Power Steering Pressure (PSP) switch - check and replacement

1   The power steering pressure (PSP) switch sends a signal to the PCM that the PCM uses to maintain engine idle speed during parking maneuvers. The OBD system can detect switch problems and set trouble codes to indicate specific faults.

Check

Refer to illustrations 10.3a and 10.3b

2   Check the operation of the PSP switch if the engine stalls or lopes during parking or if the engine runs continuously at high rpm.

3   Backprobe the power steering switch connector with a voltmeter and turn the ignition key to ON (but don't start the engine) **(see illustrations)**. There should be at least one volt.

4   Start the engine, let it idle and turn the steering wheel slowly from side to side. The voltmeter should indicate 10 volts or more as the steering wheel turns.

10.3b Power steering pressure switch and connector (Legend)

10.9 Integra Power Steering Pressure (PSP) switch (arrow)

11.7a Legend oxygen sensor connector (arrow) (left side shown, right side connector is located near the front of the right valve cover)

5   If the switch passes both tests, it is OK. If not, disconnect the electrical connector with the voltmeter still connected. If the meter now indicates 10 volts, replace the switch. If the meter does not indicate 10 volts, follow the switch wires back to the PCM, checking for breaks or poor connections as you go.
6   If the wires are good, the PCM may be at fault. Have the system tested by a dealer service department or other qualified repair shop.

Replacement

Refer to illustration 10.9

7   If necessary for access, raise the vehicle and support it securely on jackstands.
8   Disconnect the cable from the negative terminal of the battery. **Caution:** *If the radio in your vehicle is equipped with an anti-theft system, make sure you have the correct activation code before disconnecting the battery.*
9   Disconnect the electrical connector from the switch and unscrew the switch from its fitting **(see accompanying illustration and illustration 10.3b)**.
10   Install and connect the new switch. Lower the vehicle to the ground if it was raised.
11   Refer to Chapter 10 and bleed air from the power steering system. Add fluid as required (see Chapter 1).

11   Oxygen sensor (O2S) - check and replacement

General description

1   The oxygen sensor, which is located in the exhaust manifold, monitors the oxygen content of the exhaust gas stream (legend models have an oxygen sensor in each exhaust manifold). The oxygen content in the exhaust reacts with the oxygen sensor to produce a voltage output which varies from 0.1-volt (high oxygen, lean mixture) to 0.9-volts (low oxygen, rich mixture). The PCM constantly monitors this variable voltage output to determine the ratio of oxygen to fuel in the mixture. The PCM alters the air/fuel mix-

ture ratio by controlling the pulse width (open time) of the fuel injectors. A mixture ratio of 14.7 parts air to 1 part fuel is the ideal mixture ratio for minimizing exhaust emissions, thus allowing the catalytic converter to operate at maximum efficiency. It is this ratio of 14.7 to 1 which the PCM and the oxygen sensor attempt to maintain at all times.
2   The oxygen sensor produces no voltage when it is below its normal operating temperature of about 600-degrees F. During this initial period before warm-up, the PCM operates in OPEN LOOP mode.
3   If the engine reaches normal operating temperature and/or has been running for two or more minutes, and if the oxygen sensor is producing a steady signal voltage below 0.45-volts at 1,500 rpm or greater, the PCM will set a Code. The PCM will also set a code if it detects any problem with the heater circuit.
4   When there is a problem with the oxygen sensor or its circuit, the PCM operates in the open loop mode - that is, it controls fuel delivery in accordance with a programmed default value instead of feedback information from the oxygen sensor.
5   The proper operation of the oxygen sensor depends on four conditions:

a) **Electrical** - *The low voltages generated by the sensor depend upon good, clean connections which should be checked whenever a malfunction of the sensor is suspected or indicated.*
b) **Outside air supply** - *The sensor is designed to allow air circulation to the internal portion of the sensor. Whenever the sensor is removed and installed or replaced, make sure the air passages are not restricted.*
c) **Proper operating temperature** - *The ECM will not react to the sensor signal until the sensor reaches approximately 600-degrees F. This factor must be taken into consideration when evaluating the performance of the sensor.*
d) **Unleaded fuel** - *The use of unleaded fuel is essential for proper operation of the sensor. Make sure the fuel you are using is of this type.*

6   In addition to observing the above conditions, special care must be taken whenever the sensor is serviced.

a) *The oxygen sensor has a permanently attached pigtail and electrical connector which should not be removed from the sensor. Damage or removal of the pigtail or electrical connector can adversely affect operation of the sensor.*
b) *Grease, dirt and other contaminants should be kept away from the electrical connector and the louvered end of the sensor.*
c) *Do not use cleaning solvents of any kind on the oxygen sensor.*
d) *Do not drop or roughly handle the sensor.*
e) *The silicone boot must be installed in the correct position to prevent the boot from being melted and to allow the sensor to operate properly.*

Check

Refer to illustrations 11.7a and 11.7b

7   Locate the oxygen sensor electrical connector **(see illustrations)** and insert a long pin into the terminal for the oxygen sensor connector signal voltage wire, which is the white wire on Integra O2 sensor connec-

11.7b Integra oxygen sensor connector (arrow)

6

11.15 A special socket that allows clearance for the wiring harness is required for oxygen sensor removal

12.1a The Integra knock sensor is threaded into a coolant passage (arrow) (intake manifold removed for clarity)

12.1b Legend knock sensor (right arrow); the left arrow points to the other knock sensor, which isn't visible in this photo

tors and left-side Legend oxygen sensor connectors; on Legend right-side O2 sensor connectors it's the terminal with the red/blue wire. Connect the positive probe of a digital voltmeter to the pin and the negative probe to ground.

8   Monitor the voltage signal (millivolts) as the engine goes from cold to warm.

9   The oxygen sensor will produce a steady voltage signal at first (open loop) of approximately 0.1 to 0.2 volts with the engine cold. After a period of approximately two minutes, the engine will reach operating temperature and the oxygen sensor will start to fluctuate between 0.1 to 0.9 volts (closed loop). If the oxygen sensor fails to reach the closed loop mode or there is a very long period of time until it does switch into closed loop mode (lazy oxygen sensor), replace the oxygen sensor with a new part.

10   Also inspect the oxygen sensor heater. **Note:** *1990 and 1991 Integras do not have heated O2 sensors.* Disconnect the oxygen sensor electrical connector and connect an ohmmeter between the heater terminals: On 1992 and 1993 Integras, probe the terminals for the orange/black wire and the yellow/black wire; on Legends, probe the terminals for the green/blue wire and the black/yellow wire (left side) or the green/red wire and the black/yellow wire (right side). It should measure 10 to 40 ohms on Integras, 10 to 20 ohms on Legends.

11   Check for proper supply voltage to the heater on the harness side of the oxygen sensor electrical connector. On Integras, measure the voltage between the terminals for the yellow/black wire and the orange/black wire. On Legends, measure the voltage between the terminals for the green/blue wire and the black/yellow wire (left side) or the terminals for the green/red wire and the black/yellow wire. There should be battery voltage with the ignition key ON (engine not running). If there is no voltage, check the circuit between the main relay, the PCM and the sensor.

12   If the oxygen sensor fails the tests described in Steps 9 or 10, replace it with a new part.

Replacement

Refer to illustration 11.15

Note: *Because it is installed in the exhaust manifold or pipe, which contracts when cool, the oxygen sensor may be very difficult to loosen when the engine is cold. Rather than risk damage to the sensor (assuming you are planning to reuse it in another manifold or pipe), start and run the engine for a minute or two, then shut it off. Be careful not to burn yourself during the following procedure.*

13   Disconnect the cable from the negative terminal of the battery. **Caution:** *If the stereo in your vehicle is equipped with an anti-theft system, make sure you have the correct activation code before disconnecting the battery.*

14   Disconnect the electrical connector from the sensor **(see illustrations 11.7a and 11.7b).** If you're working on an Integra, raise the vehicle and place it securely on jackstands.

15   Carefully unscrew the sensor from the exhaust manifold **(see illustration).**

16   Anti-seize compound must be used on the threads of the sensor to facilitate future removal. The threads of new sensors will already be coated with this compound, but if an old sensor is removed and reinstalled, recoat the threads.

17   Install the sensor and tighten it securely.

18   Reconnect the electrical connector of the pigtail lead to the main engine wiring harness.

19   Take the vehicle on a test drive and check to see that no trouble codes set.

12 Knock sensor(s) - check and replacement

Refer to illustrations 12.1a, 12.1b and 12.3

1   Knock sensors detect abnormal vibration in the engine. The knock control system is designed to reduce spark knock during periods of heavy detonation. This allows the engine to use maximum spark advance to improve driveability. Knock sensors produce AC output voltage which increases with the severity of the knock. The signal is fed into

the PCM and the timing is retarded to reduce the detonation.

2   Knock sensors are used on the following models:

a) Integra with the 1.7L VTEC engine
b) Legend (all)

On Integra models the sensor is threaded into the cylinder block, below the intake manifold **(see illustration).** Legend models use two knock sensors, both mounted in the engine block in the valley between the cylinder banks **(see illustration).**

Check

3   Disconnect the electrical connector **(see illustration 12.1a and the accompanying illustration).**

4   On Integra models, connect the positive probe of a digital voltmeter to the terminal on the sensor and connect the negative probe to a good ground. **Note:** *You may have to raise the front of the vehicle and support it securely on jackstands for access to the sensor.*

5   On Legend models, connect the positive probe of the voltmeter to one of the outer terminals of the electrical connector in the side of the harness that leads to the sensors (it is routed under the upper intake manifold). Connect the negative probe to a good ground.

12.3 Knock sensor electrical connector location (arrow) - Legend

13.2 To test the Integra VSS, remove the instrument cluster and check for continuity on terminals A and B and you rotate the speedometer

13.5 The Vehicle Speed Sensor (VSS) is mounted on the transaxle (arrow); Legend

Note: *Each outer terminal in this electrical connector is for a knock sensor; the terminal connected to the red/blue wire is for the left (driver's side) knock sensor, and the terminal connected to the white wire is for the right knock sensor). You'll have to perform this check on each terminal to check both sensors.*
6   With the voltmeter set to the lowest AC voltage scale, tap sharply on the intake manifold (or, if you're working from underneath on an Integra, tap on the cylinder block) and watch the meter - a small AC voltage signal should be generated if the sensor is functioning. If no voltage fluctuations can be detected, the sensor is probably bad and should be replaced with a new part. **Note:** *On Legend models you'll have to check the continuity of the harness between the electrical connector and the sensor to verify that an open circuit condition does not exist.*

Replacement

Warning: *Wait until the engine is completely cool before beginning this procedure.*
Note: *New sensors are pre-coated with thread sealant. Don't use any additional sealant or the operation of the sensor may be affected.*

Integra

7   The knock sensor is threaded into the engine block coolant passage **(see illustration 12.1a)**. When it is removed, coolant will drain from the block, so be prepared for leakage. Place a drain pan under the sensor, disconnect the electrical connector and unscrew the sensor. Install the new sensor as quickly as possible to minimize coolant loss. Tighten the sensor to 23 ft-lbs.

Legend

8   Remove the intake manifold (see Chapter 2B).
9   Unplug the electrical connector, unscrew the sensor **(see illustration 12.1b)** and install the new sensor as quickly as possible to minimize coolant loss. Tighten the sensor to 23 ft-lbs.
10   Install the intake manifold (see Chapter 2B).

All models

11   Check the coolant and add some, if necessary, to bring to the appropriate level (see Chapter 1).

13   Vehicle Speed Sensor (VSS) - check and replacement

Integra

Refer to illustration 13.2
1   The Vehicle Speed Sensor is incorporated into the speedometer. The sensor is a reed-switch type sensor. As the speedometer rotates, the switch opens and closes producing a pulsating signal to the PCM.
2   To check the VSS, remove the instrument cluster (see Chapter 12). Connect an ohmmeter to terminals A and B on the back of the speedometer **(see illustration)**. Insert a dull pencil onto the speedometer cable hole and rotate the speedometer (counterclockwise). The meter should indicate continuity four times per revolution.
3   If the VSS doesn't respond as described replace the speedometer assembly.

Legend

Refer to illustration 13.5
4   The Vehicle Speed Sensor (VSS) is located on the transaxle. This sensor is a permanent magnetic variable reluctance sensor that produces a pulsing voltage whenever vehicle speed is over 3 mph. These pulses are translated by the PCM and provided for other systems for fuel and transaxle shift control.
5   To check the vehicle speed sensor, unplug the electrical connector in the wiring harness at the sensor **(see illustration)**. Using a voltmeter, check for voltage at the black/yellow wire terminal. The circuit should have battery voltage available. If there is no voltage available, check for an open circuit between the VSS and the fuse box. Using an ohmmeter, check the black wire of the connector for continuity to body ground. If there's no continuity, check the black wire for breaks or poor connections.
6   Raise the front of the vehicle and place it securely on jackstands. Block the rear wheels and place the transaxle in Neutral. Connect the electrical connector to the VSS, turn the ignition to On and backprobe the VSS connector yellow/red wire with a voltmeter posi-

tive lead. Connect the negative lead of the meter to body ground. While holding one wheel steady, rotate the other wheel by hand. The voltmeter should pulse between zero and 5 volts. If it doesn't, replace the sensor.
7   To replace the VSS, disconnect the electrical connector from the VSS.
8   Remove the retaining bolt and lift the VSS from the transaxle.
9   Installation is the reverse of removal.

14   Idle Air Control (IAC) valve - check and replacement

Note: *This valve is sometimes referred to as the Electric Air Control Valve (EACV).*
1   When the engine is idling, the air/fuel ratio is controlled by the idle air control (IAC) system. The IAC valve is activated by the PCM depending upon the running conditions of the engine (air conditioning system, power steering, cold and warm running etc.). This valve regulates the amount of airflow past the throttle plate and into the intake manifold. The PCM receives information from the sensors (vehicle speed, coolant temperature, air conditioning, power steering mode etc.) and adjusts the idle according to the demands of the engine and driver. Finally, to prevent rough running after the engine starts, the IAC valve is opened during cranking and immediately after starting to provide additional air into the intake manifold.

Check

Refer to illustrations 14.3a and 14.3b
2   Apply the parking brake, block the wheels and place the transaxle in Neutral (manual) or Park (automatic). Connect a tachometer, according to the manufacturer's instructions, to the engine. Start the engine and hold the accelerator steady at 3,000 rpm until the coolant fan comes on. Return the engine to idle and disconnect the electrical connector from the IAC valve. **Warning:** *Keep hands, loose clothing, etc. away from any moving engine parts while working on a*

6

14.3a   Idle Air Control (IAC) valve connector (Integra)

14.3b   Idle Air Control (IAC) valve connector (Legend)

14.7a   Integra IAC valve mounting bolts (arrows)

running engine or personal injury may result. There should be a noticeable reduction in idle speed with the IAC valve disconnected. If there isn't, the IAC valve is probably defective. If there was a drop in idle with the IAC valve disconnected and an intermittent idle problem still persists, check the wiring harness from the IAC valve to the ECM for poor connections or damaged wires.

3   Disconnect the electrical connector from the IAC valve, turn the ignition key ON (engine not running) and measure the voltage between the positive terminal of the wiring harness connector (yellow/black wire) and body ground **(see illustrations)**. There should be battery voltage. If no voltage is present, check for an open circuit in the yellow/black wire from the IAC valve to the PGM-FI main relay. In any case, leave the IAC valve connector disconnected for the next steps.

4   Momentarily connect the IAC valve directly to battery voltage with a pair of jumper wires (positive to the terminal that corresponds to the black/yellow wire, negative to the other terminal). The valve should click each time voltage is applied. If not, replace it.

5   If the IAC valve performs correctly in

Step 4 or 5, have the PCM and the electrical circuit for the IAC valve diagnosed by a dealer service department or other qualified repair shop.

Replacement

Refer to illustrations 14.7a and 14.7b

6   Disconnect the electrical connector from the IAC valve.

7   Remove the mounting fasteners from the valve and lift it from the air intake plenum **(see illustrations)**. On Integra models, disconnect the hoses from the bottom of the valve.

8   Installation is the reverse of removal. Be sure to install a new O-ring.

---

15   Fast Idle Thermo (FIT) valve - check and replacement

Note: *On some models this valve is referred to as the Fast Idle Valve (FIV).*

1   The Fast Idle Thermo (FIT) valve, used on some models, allows extra air into the intake manifold when the engine is cold, causing the idle speed to increase.

Check

Refer to illustrations 15.3a and 15.3b

2   Start this procedure with the engine cold. On Integra models, disconnect the intake duct from the throttle body (see Chapter 4). On Legend models, disconnect the rubber air hose from the large pipe at the front of the right (passenger's side) cylinder head.

3   Start the engine and let it idle. On Integras, reach inside the throttle body and place a finger over the port that connects to the FIT valve **(see illustration)**. On Legends, place your finger over the end of the pipe **(see illustration)**. You should feel suction.

4   Warm the engine to normal operating temperature and check for suction again. There should not be any. If there is, the valve hasn't closed. This might be caused by a low coolant level or air bubbles in the coolant passages. Make sure the engine coolant is full and free of air bubbles. If the coolant level is not correct, add coolant, bleed the cooling system (see Chapter 1) and repeat the check.

5   If the test results weren't correct, replace the FIT valve.

14.7b   Legend IAC valve mounting bolts (arrows)

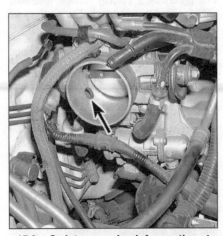

15.3a   On Integras, check for suction at this port inside the throttle body (with the engine cold)

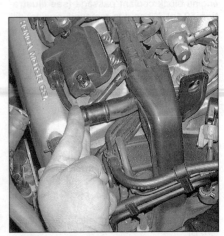

15.3b   On Legends, check for suction at this pipe (with the engine cold)

15.6a The Integra FIT valve is mounted to the underside of the throttle body

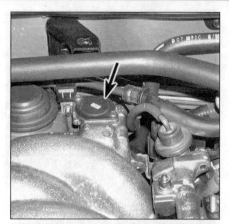

15.6b The Legend FIT valve is at the rear of the intake manifold (arrow) . . .

15.6c . . . remove its mounting bolts (two bolts hidden) to detach it

Replacement

Refer to illustrations 15.6a, 15.6b and 15.6c
Warning: *Wait until the engine is completely cool before beginning this procedure.*
6   Disconnect the hoses from the valve and unscrew the mounting bolts **(see illustrations)**. Be prepared for coolant leakage. Take off the valve and its O-rings. **Note:** *It may be easier to detach the hoses from the valve after the valve has been unbolted and partially removed.*
7   Install the valve using new O-rings, connect the hoses and tighten the mounting bolts to 84 inch-lbs.
8   Check the coolant and add some, if necessary, to bring it to the appropriate level (see Chapter 1).

16 Air boost valve - check and replacement

1   This valve, called the starting air valve on some models, admits additional air to the intake manifold while the starter is cranking the engine.

Check

2   Connect a vacuum pump to the valve and apply vacuum with the engine off. If the valve holds vacuum, replace it.
3   Disconnect the vacuum pump from the valve, reconnect the air boost valve hose and start the engine.
4   Reconnect the vacuum pump/gauge to the valve. With the engine idling, there should not be any vacuum indicated on the gauge. If there is, replace the valve.

Replacement

Refer to illustration 16.5
5   Disconnect the hose and remove the mounting bolts **(see illustration)**. Take the valve off and make sure the mounting surface is clean.
6   Installation is the reverse of removal.

17 Intake Air Bypass (IAB) system - check and component replacement

1   Legend models are equipped with an Intake Air Bypass (IAB) system. The IAB sys-

tem allows the intake manifold to divert the path of intake air flowing into the combustion chamber. Two air intake paths are provided in the intake manifold to allow the option of the intake volume most favorable for the particular engine speed. Optimum performance is achieved by switching the valves from either the closed position (for high torque at low RPM) or the open position (for maximum horsepower at high RPM).

Check

Refer to illustration 17.2
2   Locate the high and low control solenoids in the engine compartment **(see illustration)**. Follow their vacuum hoses to the two control diaphragms, at the back of the engine near the intake manifold.
3   With the engine off, disconnect the vacuum hose from the IAB low diaphragm and connect a vacuum pump to it. If the diaphragm rod doesn't move when vacuum is applied, replace the diaphragm.
4   With the engine idling, check for vacuum at the disconnected end of the hose. There should be vacuum at idle, and no vacuum when engine speed is raised to 3400 rpm.

6

16.5 Remove the mounting bolts (arrows; one hidden) and remove the air boost valve (Legend shown)

17.2 Legend Intake Air Bypass (IAB) solenoids; low (left arrow) and high (right arrow)

5   Repeat Steps 2 and 3 on the high diaphragm, There should be no vacuum when engine speed is raised to 4300 rpm.

6   If there isn't any vacuum at idle, follow the vacuum hose from the diaphragm to the control valve under the intake manifold, and then to the vacuum tank. Disconnect the hose that leads from the tank to the intake manifold and check for vacuum. If there isn't any, look for a blocked or cracked vacuum hose.

7   Disconnect the electrical connector from the IAB solenoids **(see illustration 17.2)**. To test the low solenoid, connect a voltmeter positive probe to the solenoid no. 1 black/yellow wire and the negative probe to the red/blue wire (in the harness side of the connector). To test the high solenoid, connect a voltmeter positive probe to the solenoid no. 2 black/yellow wire and the negative probe to the yellow wire (in the harness side of the connector). With the ignition key ON, there should be battery voltage. If not, check the wiring harness for breaks or poor connections.

8   If there's battery voltage at the wiring harness terminals and the vacuum lines are good, but test results weren't correct in Step 3, replace the solenoid.

Replacement

9   To replace a diaphragm, remove its mounting screws.

10   To replace a solenoid, loosen its mounting clamp and remove it from the intake manifold **(see illustration 17.2)**.

11   To replace the IAB valve body, refer to the intake manifold procedures in Chapter 4.

12   Installation is the reverse of removal.

18   Positive Crankcase Ventilation (PCV) system - check and component replacement

1   The Positive Crankcase Ventilation (PCV) system reduces hydrocarbon emissions by scavenging crankcase vapors. It does this by circulating fresh air from the air cleaner through the crankcase, where it mixes with blow-by gases and is then rerouted through a PCV valve to the intake manifold.

2   The main components of the PCV system are the PCV valve, a blow-by filter and the vacuum hoses connecting these two components with the engine.

3   To maintain idle quality, the PCV valve restricts the flow when the intake manifold vacuum is high. If abnormal operating conditions (such as piston ring problems) arise, the system is designed to allow excessive amounts of blow-by gases to flow back through the crankcase vent tube into the air cleaner to be consumed by normal combustion.

4   Checking and replacement of the PCV valve is covered in Chapter 1.

19.12 Connect a vacuum gauge to the EGR valve hose

19   Exhaust Gas Recirculation (EGR) system - check and component replacement

General description

1   The EGR system reduces oxides of nitrogen by recirculating exhaust gas through the EGR valve and intake manifold into the combustion chambers. It is used on some automatic transmission models. If you aren't sure whether your vehicle has an EGR system, refer to the VECI label under the hood (see Section 1).

2   The EGR system consists of the EGR valve, the CVC valve (early Integra only), the EGR control solenoid valve, the Powertrain Control Module (PCM) and various sensors. The PCM memory is programmed to produce the ideal EGR valve lift for each operating condition. An EGR valve lift sensor detects the amount of EGR valve lift and sends this information to the PCM. The PCM then compares it with the ideal EGR valve lift, which is determined by data received from the other sensors. If there's any difference between the two, the PCM triggers the EGR control solenoid valve to reduce the amount of vacuum applied to the EGR valve.

Check
Integra

3   Start the engine and warm it to its normal operating temperature (wait for the electric cooling fan to come on).

4   Detach the vacuum hose from the EGR valve and attach a vacuum gauge to the hose.

5   There should be NO vacuum. If there is no vacuum, proceed to Step 7.

6   If vacuum exists, disconnect the electrical connector from the EGR solenoid and check for vacuum at the EGR vacuum hose. If vacuum does not exist, have the PCM diagnosed by a dealer service department. If vacuum is present, check all the vacuum lines to make sure they are routed properly.

19.15 The engine should run roughly or stall when vacuum is applied to the EGR valve

7   If there originally was no vacuum, install a hand held vacuum pump to the EGR valve and apply 8 in-Hg of vacuum to the valve and observe that the engine stalls. Also, does the EGR valve hold vacuum? If not, replace the EGR valve.

8   Check for battery voltage to the EGR control solenoid valve. Disconnect the four-pin connector from the control box on the firewall and check for battery voltage at the black/yellow (+) terminal on the main harness. There should be battery voltage.

9   Reconnect the vacuum gauge to the EGR vacuum hose, start the engine and allow it to idle. Connect the battery positive cable with a jumper wire to the B+ wire's terminal on the four-pin connector (the control box side, not the harness side). While observing the vacuum gauge, ground the red wire terminal with another jumper wire. Vacuum should increase within one second. If there is no vacuum, replace the EGR control solenoid.

10   Further checking of the EGR control system requires special tools and equipment. Take the vehicle to a dealer service department or other qualified repair shop for checking.

Legend

Refer to illustrations 19.12, 19.15 and 19.16

11   Start the engine and warm it to its normal operating temperature (wait for the electric cooling fan to come on).

12   Detach the vacuum hose from the EGR valve and attach a vacuum gauge to the hose **(see illustration)**.

13   There should be NO vacuum. If there is no vacuum, proceed to Step 15.

14   If vacuum exists, disconnect the EGR solenoid electrical connector from the side of the control box and check for vacuum at the EGR vacuum hose. If vacuum does not exist, have the PCM diagnosed by a dealer service department. If vacuum is present, check all the vacuum lines to make sure they are routed properly.

15   If there originally was no vacuum, install a hand-held vacuum pump to the EGR valve,

19.16 Legend EGR control solenoid (upper arrow) and its electrical connector (lower arrow)

19.20 Remove the EGR valve mounting nuts (one nut hidden)

apply vacuum to the valve and see if the engine runs roughly or stalls **(see illustration)**. Also, does the EGR valve hold vacuum? If not, replace the EGR valve.

16   Check for battery voltage to the EGR control solenoid valve. Disconnect the four-pin solenoid connector and check for battery voltage at the black/yellow (+) terminal on the main harness **(see illustration)**. There should be battery voltage.

17   Reconnect the vacuum gauge to the EGR vacuum hose, start the engine and allow it to idle. Connect the battery positive cable with a jumper wire to the A terminal on the four-pin connector (the solenoid side, not the harness side) **(see illustration 19.16)**. While observing the vacuum gauge, ground the B terminal with another jumper wire. Vacuum should increase within one second. If there is no vacuum, replace the EGR control solenoid.

18   Further checking of the EGR control system requires special tools and equipment. Take the vehicle to a dealer service department or other qualified repair shop for checking.

Component replacement

EGR valve

Refer to illustration 19.20

19   Unplug the electrical connector for the EGR valve lift sensor.

20   Remove the two nuts that secure the EGR valve to the intake manifold and detach the EGR valve **(see illustration)**.

21   Clean the mating surfaces of the EGR valve and adapter.

22   Install the EGR valve, using a new gasket. Tighten the nuts securely.

23   Connect the electrical connector.

EGR control solenoid

24   Locate the EGR control solenoid **(see illustration 19.16)**. Remove the mounting screws and lift the solenoid off.

25   Installation is the reverse of removal.

EGR vacuum control valve

Refer to illustration 19.26

26   The vacuum control valve is used on early models. To remove it, disconnect the vacuum hoses and detach it from the firewall **(see illustration)**.

27   Installation is the reverse of removal.

20   Evaporative emissions control (EVAP) system

General description

1   The fuel evaporative emissions control system absorbs fuel vapors and, during engine operation, releases them into the engine intake where they mix with the incoming air-fuel mixture.

2   Every evaporative system employs a canister filled with activated charcoal to absorb fuel vapors. The means by which these vapors are controlled, however, varies considerably from one system to another. The following descriptions of a typical system for the models covered by this manual should provide you enough information to under-

stand the system on your vehicle. **Note:** *The following descriptions are not intended as a specific description of the evaporative system on your particular vehicle. Rather, they are intended as a general description of a typical system used on fuel-injected vehicles. Although the following components are most likely all used on your particular system, there may also be other devices, not included here, which are unique to your system. Check with the VECI label and the Vacuum Hose Routing Diagram under the hood.*

3   The fuel filler cap is fitted with a two-way valve as a safety device. The valve vents fuel vapors to the atmosphere if the evaporative control system fails.

4   Another fuel cut-off valve (two-way valve), mounted on the fuel tank, regulates fuel vapor flow from the fuel tank to the charcoal canister, based on the pressure or vacuum caused by temperature changes.

5   After passing through the two-way valve, fuel vapor is carried by vent hoses to the charcoal canister in the engine compartment. The activated charcoal in the canister absorbs and stores these vapors.

6   When the engine is running and warmed to a pre-set temperature, a purge cut-off

6

19.26 Legend EGR vacuum control valve

20.10a Disconnect the canister purge hose - here's an Integra hose . . .

20.10b . . . and here's the Legend hose (arrow)

20.13 Canister purge control solenoid (Legend)

solenoid valve near the canister closes, allowing a purge control diaphragm valve in the charcoal canister to be opened by intake manifold vacuum. Fuel vapors from the canister are then drawn through the purge control diaphragm valve by intake manifold vacuum.

Check

Note: *Complete checking of the evaporative emissions control system is beyond the scope of the average home mechanic. Fortunately, the evaporative control system, like all emission control systems, is protected by a Federally mandated extended warranty (5 years or 50,000 miles at the time this manual was written). The EVAP system probably won't fail during the service life of the vehicle; however, if it does, the hoses or charcoal canister are usually to blame.*

7   Always check the hoses first. A disconnected, damaged or missing hose is the most likely cause of a malfunctioning EVAP system. Refer to the Vacuum Hose Routing Diagram (attached to the underside of the hood) to determine whether the hoses are correctly routed and attached. Repair any damaged hoses or replace any missing hoses as necessary.

Purge control solenoid

Refer to illustrations 20.10a, 20.10b and 20.13

8   The purge control solenoid allows intake manifold vacuum to purge vapors from the canister when the engine is warm, and cuts off vacuum to the canister when the engine is cold.

9   Make sure the engine temperature is below 158-degrees F.

10   Locate the purge hose on top of the canister **(see illustrations)**. Follow the vacuum hose from the purge control valve on the intake manifold to the canister to make sure you've got the right hose.

11   Once you've found the hose, disconnect it from the canister and connect a vacuum

gauge to the disconnected end of the hose. Start the engine and allow it to idle. There should be NO vacuum present.

12   Let the engine idle until it warms up. There should now be vacuum at the end of the hose.

13   If the vacuum test results weren't correct, locate the purge control solenoid and disconnect its electrical connector **(see illustration)**. Disconnect its vacuum hoses and connect a piece of rubber hose to one of the fittings on the solenoid.

14   Connect the battery directly to the solenoid with jumper wires. Try to blow into the piece of hose (through the solenoid). The solenoid should open (allowing air to flow) and close (blocking the flow of air) as the jumper wires are connected and disconnected. (Some models will open when voltage is applied and close when it's removed; others will do the opposite. The important thing is that the solenoid open and close consistently as battery power is connected and disconnected.)

15   If the solenoid test results aren't correct, replace the solenoid.

21   Catalytic converter

Note: *Because of a Federally mandated extended warranty which covers emissions-related components such as the catalytic converter, check with a dealer service department before replacing the converter at your own expense.*

General description

1   The catalytic converter is an emission control device added to the exhaust system to reduce pollutants from the exhaust gas stream. There are two types of converters. The conventional oxidation catalyst reduces the levels of hydrocarbon (HC) and carbon

monoxide (CO). The three-way catalyst lowers the levels of oxides of nitrogen (NOx) as well as hydrocarbons (HC) and carbon monoxide (CO).

Check

2   The test equipment for a catalytic converter is expensive and highly sophisticated. If you suspect that the converter on your vehicle is malfunctioning, take it to a dealer or authorized emissions inspection facility for diagnosis and repair.

3   Whenever the vehicle is raised for servicing of underbody components, check the converter for leaks, corrosion, dents and other damage. Check the welds/flange bolts that attach the front and rear ends of the converter to the exhaust system. If damage is discovered, the converter should be replaced.

4   Although catalytic converters don't break too often, they can become plugged. The easiest way to check for a restricted converter is to use a vacuum gauge to diagnose the effect of a blocked exhaust on intake vacuum.

a) *Open the throttle until the engine speed is about 2000 rpm.*

b) *Release the throttle quickly.*

c) *If there is no restriction, the gauge will quickly drop to not more than 2 in-Hg or more above its normal reading.*

d) *If the gauge does not show 5 in-Hg or more above its normal reading, or seems to momentarily hover around its highest reading for a moment before it returns, the exhaust system, or the converter, is plugged (or an exhaust pipe is bent or dented, or the core inside the muffler has shifted).*

Component replacement

5   Refer to the exhaust system removal and installation section in Chapter 4.

Chapter 7 Part A
Manual transmission/transaxle

Contents

Specifications

Torque specifications

Ft-lbs (unless otherwise indicated)

Integra

Lower rear engine-to-transaxle bolt	
Self-locking bolt	87
Non-self-locking bolts	47
Non-self-locking bolt with washer	61
Upper transaxle-to-engine bolts	42
Short bolt	47
Starter bolt	33
Front transaxle mount	
Mount bolt and nuts	47
Engine bracket-to-mount through bolt	43
Side transaxle mount	
Mount bolt and nuts	54
Engine bracket-to-mount through bolt	43
Engine stiffeners	
Short bolts	17
Long bolts	42
Splash shield bolts	84 in-lbs
Clutch cover bolts	108 in-lbs

Legend

Upper transmission-to-engine bolts	55
Lower rear transmission-to-engine bolt	47
Transmission bracket bolt	29
Engine stiffener bolts	16
Clutch cover bolts	108 in-lbs
Steering gear cover plate	29
Exhaust pipe bracket	29
Splash shield bolts	84 in-lbs
Shift rod bolt	16

7A

1.1 An underside view of the manual transaxle and its related components (Integra model)

1 *Transaxle*	2 *Shift rod*	3 *Shift extension*	4 *Driveaxle*

1   General information

Refer to illustration 1.1

Integra models covered by this manual are equipped with a five-speed manual or a four-speed automatic transaxle **(see illustration)**. Legend models are equipped with either a five - or six-speed manual or a four-speed automatic transmission.

All information on the manual transmission/transaxle is included in this Part of Chapter 7. Service procedures for the four-speed automatic transmission/transaxle can be found in Chapter 7, Part B. You'll also find certain procedures common to both manual and automatic transaxles (Integra models) - such as oil seal replacement - in Part B of this Chapter.

Depending on the expense involved in

having a transmission/transaxle overhauled, it might be a better idea to consider replacing it with either a new or rebuilt unit. Your local dealer or transaxle shop should be able to supply information concerning cost, availability and exchange policy. Regardless of how you decide to remedy a transmission/transaxle problem, you can still save a lot of money by removing and installing the unit yourself.

2   Transmission/transaxle mount - check and replacement

Refer to illustrations 2.2 and 2.4

1   Raise the front of the vehicle and place it securely on jackstands.
2   Insert a large screwdriver or prybar between the mount and the transmission/transaxle and try to lever the transmission/transaxle up or down **(see illustration)**.
3   The transmission/transaxle should not move more than about 1/2 to 3/4-inch away from the mount. If it does, replace the mount.
4   To replace the mount, support the transmission/transaxle with a jack and remove the through-bolt. Remove the nuts and bolts and remove the mount **(see illustration)**. It may be necessary to raise the transmission/transaxle slightly to provide enough

2.2 To check a transmission/transaxle mount, lever the transaxle up and down and check for movement at the point shown

2.4 To remove the mount, support the transaxle with a jack, remove the through-bolt (A) and the mount-to-transaxle bolts/nut (B) (Integra model)

3.1 Remove this shift lever boot and the dust seal underneath

3.3 To disconnect the extension rod from its bracket on the transaxle, remove this bolt (arrow)

3.4 To disconnect the shift rod from the transaxle, push the dust boot forward, remove the clip and drive out the spring pin (arrow) - discard the old pin and install a new one when reassembling the linkage

clearance to remove the mount. **Warning:** *Do not place any part of your body under the transmission/transaxle when it's supported only by a jack.*

5   Installation is the reverse of removal.

3   Shift lever and linkage - removal and installation

Refer to illustrations 3.1, 3.3, 3.4 and 3.5

1   Unscrew the shift lever knob. Remove the center console (see Chapter 11). Remove the rubber shift lever boot and the dust seal underneath **(see illustration)**.

2   Raise the vehicle and place it securely on jackstands.

3   To disconnect the extension rod from the transaxle, remove the bolt that attaches it to the extension bracket **(see illustration)**.

4   To disconnect the shift rod from the transaxle, push the dust boot forward **(see illustration)**, remove the clip and drive out the spring pin with a pin punch. Discard the spring pin - do not re-use it.

5   To disconnect the rear end of the shift rod from the shift lever, remove the nut and bolt **(see illustration)**.

6   Remove the two nuts and washers that retain the change ball holder to the underside of the extension rod **(see illustration 3.5)** and remove the change ball holder, lower shift lever dust seal, shift lever ball seat, shift lever and extension rod.

7   Inspect the bushing at the front end of the extension rod and replace it if it's cracked, torn or worn.

8   Replace the O-rings in the base of the shift lever.

9   Installation is the reverse of removal. Lubricate the new O-rings and the bushings with silicone grease. Use a new spring pin to attach the shift rod to the transaxle. Tighten all fasteners to the torque values listed in this Chapter's Specifications.

10   Check the operation of the shift lever.

3.5 To disconnect the shift rod from the shift lever, remove the nut and bolt (1); to disconnect the extension rod from the shift lever, remove the nuts above (2) and the two bolts (3) retaining the extension mounting bracket and cushion

4   Back-up light switch - check and replacement

Check

Refer to illustration 4.4

1   Before testing the back-up light switch, check the No. 1 10-amp fuse (Integra) or No. 13 7.5-amp fuse (Legend) in the under-dash fuse/relay box.

2   Put the shift lever in Reverse and turn the ignition switch to the On position. The back-up lights should go on. Turn off the ignition switch.

3   If the back-up lights don't go on, check the back-up light bulbs in the tail light assembly.

4   If the fuse and bulbs are both okay, locate the back-up light switch on top of the

4.4 The back-up light switch (arrow) is located on the side of the transaxle housing (Integra shown, Legend similar)

transmission/transaxle **(see illustration)**, trace the leads back to the electrical connector, unplug the connector and hook up an ohmmeter or continuity tester across the two terminals.

5   With the shift lever in Reverse, there should be continuity; with the shifter in any other gear, there should be no continuity.

6   If the switch fails this test, replace it (see below).

7   If the switch is OK, but the back-up lights aren't coming on, check for a poor ground in the circuit; if the grounds are good, look for opens in the circuits.

Replacement

8   Unplug the back-up light switch electrical connector.

9   Unscrew the back-up light switch.

10   Discard the old washer.

11   Using a new washer, install the new switch.

12   Plug in the connector.

7A

5.12 Remove the stiffener bolts (arrows)

5.15 Remove the bolts (arrows) and detach the center beam

5   Manual transmission/transaxle - removal and installation

Integra

Removal

Refer to illustrations 5.12, 5.15, 5.17, 5.18, 5.19, and 5.21

1   Disconnect the negative cable from the battery. **Caution:** *If the radio in your vehicle is equipped with an anti-theft system, make sure you have the correct activation code before disconnecting the battery.*

2   Remove the battery and the battery tray (see Chapter 5).

3   Remove the resonator, intake air duct and air cleaner (see Chapter 4).

4   Disconnect the starter motor cables and remove the upper starter motor mounting bolt (see Chapter 5).

5   Disconnect the transaxle ground cable, unplug the back-up light switch connector (see Section 4) and detach the wiring harness

clamp from the transaxle. Unplug the vehicle speed sensor electrical connector. without disconnecting the hoses, remove the power steering speed sensor.

6   Loosen the front wheel lug nuts, raise the vehicle and support it securely on jackstands. Remove the front wheels.

7   Drain the transaxle lubricant (see Chapter 1). Remove the splash shield, if equipped.

8   Remove the elbow-shaped exhaust pipe section under the transaxle (see Chapter 4).

9   Disconnect the shift and extension rods from the transaxle (see Section 3).

10   Loosen the clutch cable adjuster nut, then detach the clutch cable from the arm.

11   Remove the driveaxles (see Chapter 8). Tie plastic bags over the inner CV joints to keep them clean. Remove the intermediate shaft.

12   Remove the engine stiffener (if equipped) **(see illustration)**.

13   Remove the clutch access cover bolts and remove the cover.

14   Remove the distributor (see Chapter 5).

Attach a engine support fixture or engine hoist to the cylinder head to support the engine, then lift the engine slightly to take the load off the engine and transaxle mounts.

15   Remove the splash guard (if equipped). On models so equipped, remove the center beam **(see illustration)**

16   Place a floor jack under the transaxle, place a block of wood between the jack head and the transmission/transaxle and raise it just enough to take the weight off the mounts.

17   Remove the transaxle mounting bracket bolts and nuts **(see illustration)**.

18   Remove the upper transaxle-to-engine mounting bolts **(see illustration)**.

19   Remove the clutch cable bracket **(see illustration)**.

20   Remove the rear lower transaxle-to-engine bolt immediately above the right driveaxle.

21   Remove the lower transaxle-to-engine bolt and transaxle mounting bracket bolts **(see illustration)**.

5.17 Remove the front transaxle bolts (arrows)

5.18 Remove the upper transaxle-to-engine mounting bolts (arrows)

5.19 Remove the clutch cable bracket bolts (arrows)

5.21 Remove the three rear transaxle mounting bracket bolts (arrows)

22 Make a final check that all wires and hoses have been disconnected from the transaxle, then carefully pull the transaxle and jack away from the engine.

23 Once the input shaft is clear, lower the transaxle and remove it from under the vehicle.

24 With the transaxle removed, the clutch components are now accessible and can be inspected. In most cases, new clutch components should be routinely installed when the transaxle is removed (see Chapter 8).

Installation

25 If removed, install the clutch components (see Chapter 8).

26 Make sure the two dowel pins are installed. With the transaxle secured to the jack with a chain, raise it into position behind the engine, then carefully slide it forward, engaging the two dowel pins on the transaxle with the corresponding holes in the block and the input shaft with the clutch plate hub splines. Do not use excessive force to install the transaxle - if the input shaft does not slide into place, readjust the angle of the transaxle so it is level and/or turn the input shaft so the splines engage properly with the clutch plate hub.

27 Install the transaxle housing-to-engine bolts and the transaxle rear mounting bracket bolts and tighten them to the torque listed in this Chapter's Specifications.

28 Install the three upper transaxle-to-engine bolts and the lower starter motor mounting bolt and tighten them to the torque listed in this Chapter's Specifications.

29 Raise the transaxle slightly, then install the right transaxle mounting bracket and the bracket bolt and nuts. First, tighten the bolt and nuts that attach the mount to the body, then tighten the longer through bolt that attaches the engine bracket to the mount. Tighten the bolts and nuts to the torque listed in this Chapter's Specifications.

30 Install the front stopper bracket and tighten the bolts to the torque listed in this Chapter's Specifications.

31 Install the splash shield and tighten the bolts to the torque listed in this Chapter's Specifications.

32 Remove the engine support fixture or hoist.

33 Install the clutch cover and, on models so equipped, install the engine stiffeners. Tighten the clutch cover and engine stiffener bolts to the torque listed in this Chapter's Specifications.

34 The remainder of installation is the reverse of removal wit the following additions:

a) Refill the transaxle with the specified amount of lubricant (see Chapter 1).

b) Road test the vehicle for proper operation and check for leaks.

Legend

Removal

35 Disconnect the negative cable from the battery. **Caution:** If the radio in your vehicle is equipped with an anti-theft system, make sure you have the correct activation code before disconnecting the battery.

36 Remove the control box located in the engine compartment for access. Disconnect the electrical connectors for the reverse lockout solenoid (if equipped), back-up light switch and neutral position sensor.

37 Remove the strut bar. Remove the clutch hose bracket from the engine rear hanger.

38 Remove the three upper transmission mounting bolts, then raise the vehicle and support it securely on jackstands. Drain the transaxle lubricant (see Chapter 1).

39 Remove the exhaust pipe section and catalytic converter mounted under the transmission (see Chapter 4). Remove the heat shield and the heat shield bracket.

40 Shift the transmission into second gear and remove the differential extension shaft cover and sealing bolt. Using a special puller tool, remove the extension shaft from the differential (see Chapter 8).

41 Disconnect the shift and extension rods from the transmission (see Section 3).

42 Disconnect the clutch fluid hose-to-clutch fluid pressure line junction, the clutch fluid pressure line, the release cylinder and the release cylinder pushrod (see Chapter 8). **Caution:** Be careful not to bend or kink the clutch fluid pressure line, and don't depress the clutch pedal while the clutch release cylinder is removed.

43 Remove the cover plate under the steering gear for access, then reinstall the bolts so they won't be mislaid.

44 Remove the exhaust system brackets, followed by the transmission mount/bracket.

45 Remove the clutch access cover bolts and remove the cover. Pull the clutch release fork out and detach it from the pivot and release arm. Allow the release fork to hang from the clutch housing.

46 Place a floor jack under the transmission, place a block of wood between the jack head and the transmission and raise it just enough to take the weight off the mounts.

47 Remove the transmission mounts and the engine stiffener plate.

48 Remove the remaining transmission retaining bolt and its shim, followed by the clutch housing cover.

49 Make a final check that all wires and hoses have been disconnected from the transmission, then carefully pull the transmission and jack away from the engine. Once the input shaft is clear, lower the transmission and remove it from under the vehicle.

50 With the transmission removed, the clutch components are now accessible and can be inspected. In most cases, new clutch components should be routinely installed when the transmission is removed (see Chapter 8).

Installation

51 If removed, install the clutch components (see Chapter 8).

52 Place the clutch release fork in position in the clutch housing. Install a new retaining

7A

ring on the differential extension shaft and place it in position in the transmission. Make sure the two dowel pins are installed in the clutch housing.

53   With the transmission secured to the jack with a chain, raise it into position behind the engine, then carefully slide it forward, engaging the two dowel pins on the transmission with the corresponding holes in the block and the input shaft with the clutch plate hub splines. Do not use excessive force to install the transmission - if the input shaft does not slide into place, readjust the angle of the transmission so it is level and/or turn the input shaft so the splines engage properly with the clutch plate hub.

54   Install the transmission housing-to-engine bolts, the clutch cover and the transmission mount and bracket bolts and tighten them to the torque listed in this Chapter's Specifications.

55   The remainder of installation is the reverse of removal with the following additions:

a)   *Install the differential extension shaft (see Chapter 8).*
b)   *Bleed the clutch hydraulic system (see Chapter 8).*

c)   *Refill the transmission with the specified amount of lubricant (see Chapter 1).*
d)   *Road test the vehicle for proper operation and check for leaks.*

---

6   Manual transmission/transaxle overhaul - general information

---

1   Overhauling a manual transmission/transaxle is a difficult job for the do-it-yourselfer. It involves the disassembly and reassembly of many small parts. Numerous clearances must be precisely measured and, if necessary, changed with select fit spacers and snap-rings. As a result, if transmission/transaxle problems arise, it can be removed and installed by a competent do-it-yourselfer, but overhaul should be left to a transmission/transaxle repair shop. Rebuilt transmission/transaxles may be available - check with your dealer parts department and auto parts stores. At any rate, the time and money involved in an overhaul is almost sure to exceed the cost of a rebuilt unit.

2   Nevertheless, it's not impossible for an inexperienced mechanic to rebuild a trans-

mission/transaxle if the special tools are available and the job is done in a deliberate step-by-step manner so nothing is overlooked.

3   The tools necessary for an overhaul include internal and external snap-ring pliers, a bearing puller, a slide hammer, a set of pin punches, a dial indicator and possibly a hydraulic press. In addition, a large, sturdy workbench and a vise or transmission/transaxle stand will be required.

4   During disassembly of the transmission/transaxle, make careful notes of how each piece comes off, where it fits in relation to other pieces and what holds it in place. Noting how the parts are installed when you remove them will make it much easier to get the transmission/transaxle back together.

5   Before taking the transmission/transaxle apart for repair, it will help if you have some idea what area of the transmission/transaxle is malfunctioning. Certain problems can be closely tied to specific areas in the transmission/transaxle, which can make component examination and replacement easier. Refer to the *Troubleshooting* section at the front of this manual for information regarding possible sources of trouble.

Chapter 7 Part B
Automatic transmission/transaxle

Contents

Specifications

General

Shift lock solenoid clearance..	3/32 ± 1/64-inch
Accelerator kickdown travel	7/16 to 11/16-inch
Lock-up control solenoid resistance	12 to 25 ohms
Shift control solenoid resistance	12 to 25 ohms
Linear solenoid resistance (Legend)	4 to 6 ohms

Torque specifications
Ft-lbs (unless otherwise indicated)

Integra

Engine-to-transaxle bolts	47
Rear engine mount bracket bolts	43
Front engine mount bracket bolts	47
Front engine mount through-bolt	43
Transaxle mount bracket-to-transaxle bolts	43
Transaxle mount-to-bracket bolt/nut	43
Transaxle mount through-bolt	40
Torque converter cover	108 in-lbs
Driveplate-to-torque converter bolts	108 in-lbs
Engine stiffeners	
Bolts-to-transaxle..	42
Bolts-to-engine	17
Shift lock solenoid self-locking nuts.................................	84 in-lbs
Lock-up control solenoid valve assembly bolts	108 in-lbs

Legend

Transmission-to-engine bolts..	47
Lower engine-to-transmission bolt (with shim)...................	54
Engine stiffeners	
Bolt-to-transmission..	54
Bolts-to-engine	16
Rear engine mount	
Bracket-to-transaxle bolts	28
Mount-to-crossmember nuts	35
Rear transmission mount bolts (all)	28
Torque converter cover	108 in-lbs
Driveplate-to-torque converter bolts	20
Lower reinforcement plate bolts..	28
Steering gear mounting bolts	43
Shift lock solenoid self-locking nuts..................................	84 in-lbs
Lock-up control solenoid valve assembly bolts	108 in-lbs

7B

1   General information

Refer to illustrations 1.1a and 1.1b

Integra models covered by this manual are equipped with a five-speed manual or a four-speed automatic transaxle. Legend models use a five-speed or six-speed manual or a four-speed automatic transmission.

All information on automatic transmission/transaxles is included in this Part of Chapter 7. Information for the manual transmission/transaxle can be found in Part A of this Chapter.

Due to the complexity of the automatic transmission/transaxles covered in this manual and to the specialized equipment necessary to perform most service operations, this Chapter contains only those procedures related to general diagnosis, routine maintenance, adjustment and removal and installation.

If the transaxle requires major repair work, this should be left to a dealer service department or an automotive or transmission repair shop. You can, however, remove and install the transmission/transaxle yourself and the expense, even if a transmission shop does the repair work (but be sure a proper diagnosis has been made before removing the transaxle).

2   Diagnosis - general

Note: *Automatic transmission/transaxle malfunctions may be caused by five general conditions: poor engine performance, improper adjustments, hydraulic malfunctions, mechanical malfunctions or malfunctions in the computer or its signal network. Diagnosis of these problems should always begin with a check of the easily repaired items: fluid level and condition (see Chapter 1), shift control cable adjustment and throttle control cable adjustment. Next, perform a road test to determine if the problem has been corrected or if more diagnosis is necessary. If the problem persists after the preliminary tests and corrections are completed, additional diagnosis should be done by a dealer service department or transmission repair shop. Refer to the Troubleshooting section at the front of this manual for information on symptoms of transaxle problems.*

Preliminary checks

1   Drive the vehicle to warm the transaxle to normal operating temperature.
2   Check the fluid level as described in Chapter 1:

a) *If the fluid level is unusually low, add enough fluid to bring the level within the designated area of the dipstick, then check for external leaks (see below).*

b) *If the fluid level is abnormally high, drain off the excess, then check the drained fluid for contamination by coolant. The presence of engine coolant in the automatic transmission fluid indicates that a failure has occurred in the internal radiator walls that separate the coolant from the transmission fluid (see Chapter 3).*

c) *If the fluid is foaming, drain it and refill the transaxle, then check for coolant in the fluid, or a high fluid level.*

3   Check the engine idle speed. **Note:** *If the engine is malfunctioning, do not proceed with the preliminary checks until it has been repaired and runs normally.*
4   Check the throttle control cable for freedom of movement. Adjust it if necessary (see Chapter 4).
5   Inspect the shift cable linkage (see Section 3). Make sure that it's properly adjusted and that the linkage operates smoothly.

Fluid leak diagnosis

6   Most fluid leaks are easy to locate visually. Repair usually consists of replacing a seal or gasket. If a leak is difficult to find, the following procedure may help.
7   Identify the fluid. Make sure it's transmission fluid and not engine oil or brake fluid (automatic transmission fluid is a deep red color).
8   Try to pinpoint the source of the leak. Drive the vehicle several miles, then park it over a large sheet of cardboard. After a minute or two, you should be able to locate the leak by determining the source of the fluid dripping onto the cardboard.
9   Make a careful visual inspection of the suspected component and the area immediately around it. Pay particular attention to gasket mating surfaces. A mirror is often helpful for finding leaks in areas that are hard to see.
10   If the leak still cannot be found, clean the suspected area thoroughly with a degreaser or solvent, then dry it.
11   Drive the vehicle for several miles at normal operating temperature and varying speeds. After driving the vehicle, visually inspect the suspected component again.
12   Once the leak has been located, the cause must be determined before it can be properly repaired. If a gasket is replaced but the sealing flange is bent, the new gasket will not stop the leak. The bent flange must be straightened.
13   Before attempting to repair a leak, check to make sure that the following conditions are corrected or they may cause another leak. **Note:** *Some of the following conditions cannot be fixed without highly specialized tools and expertise. Such problems must be referred to a transmission shop or a dealer service department.*

Gasket leaks

14   Check the right side cover periodically. Make sure the bolts are tight, no bolts are missing, the gasket is in good condition and the cover is not damaged.

1.1a   Underside view of the automatic transaxle and related components - Integra models

1	Transaxle	3	Driveaxle
2	Shift cable	4	Transaxle cooler lines

1.1b Underside view of the automatic transmission and related components - Legend model

1   *Transmission*   2   *Transaxle cooler lines*   3   *Driveaxle*

3.1 Make sure the shift lever lines up with the Neutral position on the shift indicator panel

3.5 Make sure the hole in the adjuster is perfectly aligned with the hole in the shift cable

17   Make sure the dipstick tube seal is in good condition and the tube is properly seated. Periodically check the area around the speedometer gear or sensor for leakage. If transmission fluid is evident, check the O-ring for damage.

Case leaks

18   If the case itself appears to be leaking, the casting is porous and will have to be repaired or replaced.
19   Make sure the oil cooler hose fittings are tight and in good condition.

Fluid comes out vent pipe or fill tube

20   If this condition occurs, the transmission/transaxle is overfilled, there is coolant in the fluid, the case is porous, the dipstick is incorrect, the vent is plugged or the drain-back holes are plugged.

3   Shift cable - check, adjustment and replacement

Warning: *Legend models are equipped with a Supplemental Restraint System (SRS), more commonly known as airbags. Always disable the airbag system before working in the vicinity of the SRS unit, steering column or instrument panel to avoid the possibility of accidental deployment of the airbag, which could cause personal injury (see Chapter 12).*
Caution: *If the radio in your vehicle is equipped with an anti-theft system, make sure you have the correct activation code before disconnecting the battery.*

Check

Refer to illustration 3.1

1   Verify that the shift lever is aligned with the Neutral position on the shift indicator panel when the transmission/transaxle is in Neutral **(see illustration)**.
2   Start the engine and check the shift lever in all gears. If any gear doesn't work properly, adjust the shift cable.

Adjustment

Refer to illustration 3.5

3   Remove the center console, if not already done (see Chapter 11).
4   Place the shift lever in the Neutral (Integra) or Reverse (Legend) position, then remove the retaining clip from the cable adjuster **(see illustrations 3.9a and 3.9b)**.
5   There are two holes in the end of the shift cable. They're positioned 90-degrees apart to allow cable adjustments in 1/4-turn increments. Verify that the hole in the adjuster is perfectly aligned with the hole in the shift cable **(see illustration)**.
6   If the two holes aren't perfectly aligned, loosen the locknut on the shift cable and adjust it as required, then retighten the locknut.
7   Install the retaining clip on the adjuster. If the clip feels as if it's binding as you reinstall it, the cable is still out of adjustment and must be readjusted.

15   If the leak is from the right side cover area, the bolts may be too tight, the sealing surface of the transmission/transaxle housing may be damaged, the gasket may be damaged or the transmission/transaxle casting may be cracked or porous. If sealant instead of gasket material has been used to form a seal between the cover and the transmission/transaxle housing, it may be the wrong sealant.

Seal leaks

16   If a transmission/transaxle seal is leaking, the fluid level or pressure may be too high, the vent may be plugged, the seal bore may be damaged, the seal itself may be damaged or improperly installed, the surface of the shaft protruding through the seal may be damaged or a loose bearing may be causing excessive shaft movement.

7B

3.9a Detach the shift cable retaining clip (arrow) (Integra)

3.9b Detach the shift cable retaining clip (arrow) (Legend)

3.10 Remove the shift cable bracket bolts (arrows) (Integra shown, Legend similar)

3.12a Integra shift cable cover bolts (arrows)

3.12b Legend shift cable cover bolts (arrows)

3.13a Integra shift cable-to-transaxle lever connection (arrow)

Replacement

Refer to illustrations 3.9a, 3.9b, 3.10, 3.12a, 3.12b, 3.13a and 3.13b

8   Remove the center console (see Chapter 11). On Legend models, remove the exhaust pipe, catalytic converter and heat shields.

9   Place the shift lever in the Neutral (Integra) or Reverse (Legend) position, then

3.13b Legend shift cable-to-lever connection (arrow)

remove the retaining clip from the cable adjuster **(see illustrations)**.

10   Unbolt the shift cable bracket **(see illustration)**.

11   Detach the shift cable holder from the floorpan and detach the cable from the brace.

12   Remove the shift cable cover **(see illustrations)**.

13   Remove the control lever from the control shaft, then remove the shift cable **(see illustrations)**. Be careful not to bend the cable when removing or installing it.

14   Installation is the reverse of removal. Be sure to adjust the shift cable when you're through.

---

4   Gear position switch - check, adjustment and replacement

Warning: *Legend models are equipped with a Supplemental Restraint System (SRS), more commonly known as airbags. Always disable the airbag system before working in the vicinity of the SRS unit, steering column or instrument panel to avoid the possibility of accidental deployment of the airbag, which could cause personal injury (see Chapter 12).*
Caution: *If the radio in your vehicle is*

equipped with an anti-theft system, make sure you have the correct activation code before disconnecting the battery.

Check

Refer to illustrations 4.3a, 4.3b, 4.3c and 4.3d

1   Remove the console (see Chapter 11).

2   Disconnect the 12-pin (Integra) or 14-pin (Legend) electrical connector from the gear position switch.

3   Check for continuity between the indicated terminals in each switch position in accordance with the accompanying tables **(see illustrations)**. Move the shift lever back and forth at each switch position without touching the push-button and check for continuity within the range of shift lever freeplay (about 5/64-inch).

4   If there's no continuity within the range of shift lever freeplay at each shift lever position, adjust the switch.

Adjustment

5   Move the shift lever to the Park position and loosen the switch mounting nuts **(see illustration 4.11)**.

6   Slide the switch toward the Drive position until there's continuity between terminals 6 and 7 (Integra) or 9 and 12 (Legend) within

4.3a Gear position switch terminal guide - Integra

SWITCH POSITION	CONTINUITY BETWEEN
Low	1,7 and 8
D3	1,7 and 9
D4	1,7 and 10
Neutral	7 and 5; 11 and 12
Reverse	7 and 4; 2 and 3
Park	7 and 6; 11 and 12

4.3b Gear position switch continuity table - Integra

4.3c Gear position switch terminal guide - Legend

SWITCH POSITION	CONTINUITY BETWEEN
1	9 and 4
2	9,3 and 5
D3	9,2 and 5
D4	9,1 and 5
Neutral	9 and 7; 6 and 14
Reverse	9 and 8; 10 and 11
Park	9 and 12; 6 and 14

4.3d Gear position switch continuity table - Legend

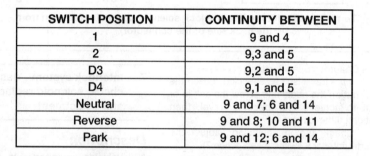

the range of shift lever freeplay (about 5/64-inch).

7   Recheck continuity as described above in Step 3. Make sure the engine starts when the shift lever is in the Park and Neutral positions.

8   If there's still no continuity at each shift lever position, inspect the shift lever detent and bracket for damage. If they're undamaged, replace the gear position switch.

Replacement

Refer to illustration 4.11

9   Remove the console (see Chapter 11).

10   Disconnect the electrical connector.

11   Remove the two gear position switch mounting nuts and washers **(see illustration)**.

12   Position the switch slider at the Neutral position.

13   Move the shift lever to the Neutral position, then install the new switch.

14   Attach the new switch with the two nuts and washers.

15   Test the new switch as described above in Step 3. Make sure the engine starts when the shift lever is in the Park or Neutral positions.

16   Reconnect the electrical connector. Clamp the harness.

17   Install the console (see Chapter 11).

4.11 Remove the nuts (arrows) and detach the gear position switch (note the position in which the switch slider must be when installing the new switch)

5   Kickdown switch (Legend models) - check, adjustment and replacement

Check

Refer to illustration 5.2

1   Disconnect the connector and check the kickdown switch for continuity. There should be continuity with the switch applied and

5.2 Loosen the locknut (A) and turn the adjusting screw (B) to adjust the kickdown travel (C)

none with it off. If there isn't, replace the switch with a new one. If the switch is operating properly, check and adjust the accelerator pedal kickdown travel to make sure it is operating the switch properly.

2   To measure the kickdown travel, press on the accelerator until the adjusting bolt contacts the switch, then measure the distance the pedal travels before it contacts the stopper on the floor **(see illustration)**. Compare this measurement with the one listed in

7B

7.6 Terminal guide for the key interlock solenoid connector (as seen from the back side of the connector)

7.12 Terminal guide for the shift lock solenoid connector (as seen from the back side of the connector)

this Chapter's Specifications.

3   If the travel isn't as specified, loosen the locknut on the pedal and screw the bolt in or out to achieve the specified travel, then retighten the locknut.

4   Check and, if necessary, adjust the starter/interlock switch (see Section 7).

Replacement

5   Remove the two retaining bolts, disconnect the electrical connector and lift the switch off.

6   Installation is the reverse of removal.

6   Vacuum modulator (Integra models) - check and replacement

Check

1   With the engine off, disconnect the pressure hose located at the vacuum modulator base and the vacuum hose between the modulator and the intake manifold. Inspect the hoses for damage or clogging. Replace the hoses with new ones if there is any doubt about their condition.

2   Disconnect the vacuum hose from the intake manifold. Connect a vacuum pump and apply vacuum to make sure the modulator holds vacuum. If it doesn't, replace the modulator with a new one.

3   As a final check, remove the modulator (see below) and apply vacuum while watching the movement of the actuating valve through the oil passage opening. If the valve binds or is sluggish, replace the vacuum modulator assembly.

Replacement

4   Detach the hoses, remove the three retaining bolts and remove the modulator.

5   Installation is the reverse of removal, taking care to install new O-rings between the modulator and the intake manifold.

7   Interlock system - description, check, solenoid replacement and adjustment

Description

1   Vehicles equipped with an automatic transmission/transaxle have an interlock system to prevent unintentional shifting. The interlock system consists of two subsystems: a shift lock system and a key interlock system.

Key interlock system

2   The key interlock system prevents the ignition key from being removed from the ignition switch unless the shift lever is in the Park position. If you insert the key when the shift lever is in any position other than Park, a solenoid is activated, making it impossible for you to remove the key until the shift lever is moved to the Park position.

Shift lock system

3   The shift lock system prevents the shift lever from moving from the Park position into the Reverse or Drive positions unless the brake pedal is depressed. Nor can the shift lever be shifted when the brake pedal and the accelerator pedal are depressed at the same time. In the event of a system malfunction, you can release the shift lever by inserting a key into the release slot near the shift lever.

Check

4   The following checks are simple tests of the key interlock solenoid and the shift lock solenoid you can do at home. Further testing of the interlock system should be left to a dealer service department.

Key interlock solenoid

Refer to illustration 7.6

5   Remove the lower instrument panel cover and knee bolster (see Chapter 11).

6   Disconnect the connector from the main wire harness **(see illustration)**.

7   On Integra models, check for continuity between the following terminals in each switch position:

a) *With the key pushed in, there should be continuity between terminals A, B and C.*

b) *With the key released, there should be continuity between terminals B and C.*

8   On Legend models, check for continuity between the following terminals in each switch position:

a) *With the key pushed in, there should be continuity between terminals A and C and continuity between terminals B and C*

b) *With the key released, there should be continuity between terminals A and B.*

9   Verify that the key can't be removed when battery power and ground are connected to the A and C terminals.

10   If the key can't be removed, the key interlock solenoid is okay; if the key can be removed, the steering lock assembly needs to be replaced (the key interlock solenoid isn't available separately).

Shift lock solenoid

Refer to illustration 7.12

11   Remove the console (see Chapter 11).

12   Disconnect the connector for the shift lock solenoid **(see illustration)**.

13   Using a pair of jumper wires, momentarily touch a positive battery lead to the (A) terminal of the connector and a negative lead to the (B) terminal and note whether the solenoid clicks on or not. **Caution:** *Make sure you don't connect the battery voltage leads to the wrong connector terminals. Reversing the polarity can damage or destroy the diode inside the solenoid.*

a) *If the solenoid doesn't operate, replace it.*

b) *If the solenoid does operate, but you have been having problems with the shift lock system, it may be necessary to adjust the solenoid at its Off and On positions (see below).*

14   While the solenoid is on, it's a good idea

7.17 Shift lock solenoid assembly (arrow)

2118-7B-7.18 HAYNES

7.19 With the solenoid energized, check the clearance between the shift lock lever and the lock pin groove

8.1a The lock-up control solenoid valve assembly (A and B) and connector (C) - Integra

8.1b The lock-up control solenoid valve assembly (A and B) and connector (C) - Legend

8.4a Disconnect the electrical connector from the shift control solenoid assembly (arrow) - Integra

to check the clearance between the shift lock lever and the lock pin groove (see below).
15 With the solenoid turned off, note whether or not the lock pin is blocked by the shift lock lever. If it isn't, adjust the position of the shift lock solenoid until it is (see below).

Solenoid replacement and adjustment

Refer to illustrations 7.17 and 7.19

Note: *The following procedure pertains only to the shift lock solenoid. For information on how to replace the key interlock solenoid, refer to the "Ignition switch/key lock cylinder replacement" Section in Chapter 12. The key interlock solenoid isn't available separately.*

16 Remove the shift lock collar and the solenoid pin.
17 Remove the self-locking nuts and the shift lock solenoid **(see illustration)**. Discard the old nuts.
18 Installation is the reverse of removal. Don't tighten the new nuts until you have adjusted the solenoid as follows.
19 To adjust the shift lock solenoid, energize the solenoid and check the clearance between the shift lock lever and the lock pin groove **(see illustration)** and compare your measurement to the clearance listed in this Chapter's Specifications. Position the solenoid so that the clearance is correct, then tighten the new self-locking nuts to the torque listed in this Chapter's specifications.

Note: *Be sure to use new self-locking nuts.*
20 With the solenoid turned off, note whether or not the lock pin is blocked by the shift lock lever. If it isn't, readjust the position of the shift lock solenoid until it is.

8 Lock-up control solenoid and shift control solenoid - check and replacement

Check

Lock-up control solenoid valves

Refer to illustrations 8.1a and 8.1b
1 Disconnect the electrical connector from the lock-up control solenoid valve assembly **(see illustrations)**.

2 Measure the resistance between each of the connector terminals (solenoid side) and ground and compare your measurements to the resistance listed in this Chapter's Specifications. If the resistance is out of specification for either terminal, replace the solenoid assembly.
3 Connect each of the connector terminals to the battery positive terminal with a jumper cable. You should hear a clicking sound as each solenoid valve is energized. If you don't, replace the solenoid assembly.

Shift control solenoid valves

Refer to illustrations 8.4a and 8.4b
4 Disconnect the connector from the shift control solenoid valve assembly **(see illustrations)**.

7B

8.4b On Legend models, the shift control solenoid valve assembly is located inside the transmission - disconnect the harness connector for testing

A Shift control solenoid valve A
B Shift control solenoid valve B
C Linear solenoid valve (-)
D Linear solenoid valve (+)

9.4 Insert the tip of a large screwdriver or prybar behind the oil seal and very carefully pry it out

9.6 Using a large socket or a section of pipe, drive the new seal squarely into the bore

5   Measure the resistance between each of the connector terminals (solenoid side) and ground and compare your measurements to the resistance listed in this Chapter's Specifications. On Legend models, also measure the resistance between the two terminals of the linear solenoid. If the resistance is out of specification for either terminal, replace the solenoid assembly.

6   Connect each of the connector terminals of the shift control solenoid, in turn, to the battery positive terminal with a jumper wire. You should hear a clicking sound as each solenoid valve is energized. If you don't, replace the solenoid assembly.

7   To check the linear solenoid on a Legend model, connect the two connector terminals to the battery power and ground with a jumper wires **(see illustration 8.4b)**. **Caution:** *Be sure you observe the correct polarity when connecting the jumper wires.* You should hear a clicking sound as the linear solenoid valve is energized. If you don't, replace the solenoid assembly.

Replacement

Integra

Note: *You cannot replace only one solenoid valve; both the lock-up and shift control solenoid valve assembly must be replaced as a single unit.*

8   Remove the mounting bolts and remove the lock-up control solenoid or shift control solenoid valve assembly.

9   Clean the mounting surface and oil passages; make sure all dirt and dust is removed.

10   Install a new base gasket and install the new solenoid valve assembly. Tighten the solenoid valve bolts to the torque listed in this Chapter's Specifications.

11   Check the electrical connector for dirt, corrosion and oil; clean it thoroughly if necessary. Reconnect it.

12   Check the solenoid valves as described above and make sure the new unit is functioning properly.

Legend

13   Replace the lock-up solenoid valve assembly in the same manner as the Integra model.

14   Replacement of the shift control solenoid valve assembly and linear solenoid requires partial disassembly of the transmission. Have the solenoids replaced by a dealer service department or qualified transmission repair facility.

---

9   Driveaxle oil seals (Integra models) - replacement

Refer to illustrations 9.4 and 9.6

1   Oil leaks frequently occur due to wear of the driveaxle oil seals. Replacement of these seals is relatively easy, since the repair can usually be performed without removing the transaxle from the vehicle.

2   Driveaxle oil seals are located at the sides of the transaxle, where the driveaxles are attached. If leakage at the seal is suspected, raise the vehicle and support it securely on jackstands. If the seal is leaking, lubricant will be found on the sides of the transaxle, below the seals.

3   Refer to Chapter 8 and remove the driveaxles.

4   Use a screwdriver or prybar to carefully pry the oil seal out of the transaxle bore **(see illustration)**.

5   If the oil seal cannot be removed with a screwdriver or prybar, a special oil seal removal tool (available at auto parts stores) will be required.

6   Using a large section of pipe or a large deep socket (as large as the outside diameter of the seal) as a drift, install the new oil seal **(see illustration)**. Drive it into the bore squarely and make sure it's completely seated. Coat the seal lip with transmission lubricant.

7   Install the driveaxle(s). Be careful not to damage the lip of the new seal.

---

10   Automatic transmission/transaxle - removal and installation

---

Integra

Removal

Refer to illustrations 10.20 and 10.26

1   Disconnect the negative cable from the battery. **Caution:** *If the radio in your vehicle is equipped with an anti-theft system, make sure you have the correct activation code before disconnecting the battery.*

2   Remove the intake air duct and air cleaner housing (see Chapter 4).

3   Remove the battery and the battery tray. Remove the starter motor cables and cable bracket from the starter. Remove the starter (see Chapter 5).

4   Disconnect the battery ground cable from the transaxle.

5   Disconnect the electrical connectors from the lock-up control solenoid valve assembly and the shift control solenoid valve assembly (see Section 7). Disconnect the vacuum hose from the modulator.

6   Disconnect the electrical connector from the vehicle speed sensor. Disconnect the speedometer cable. Without disconnecting the hoses, remove the power steering speed sensor from the transaxle and set it aside.

7   Remove the three upper transaxle-to-engine mounting bolts.

8   Raise the vehicle and support it securely on jackstands.

9   Drain the transmission fluid (see Chapter 1). Be sure to use a new sealing washer when you reinstall the drain plug.

10   Disconnect the transaxle fluid cooler hoses from the cooler lines. Turn the hoses up to prevent fluid from flowing out, then plug the lines to prevent contamination.

11   Remove center beam and the exhaust pipe section from underneath the engine (Chapter 4).

12   Disconnect the lower arms from the steering knuckles (see Chapter 10). Remove the damper fork bolts from the lower arms.

13   Separate the driveaxles from the transaxle and intermediate shaft (see Chapter 8). Cover the inner CV joints with plastic bags to keep them clean.

14   Remove the intermediate shaft.

15   Remove the engine splash shield and the right-side wheel well splash shield.

16   Remove the right damper fork and the right radius rod (see Chapter 10). Pivot the right driveaxle out and away from the transaxle and position it aside.

17   Remove the engine stiffener(s).

18   Remove the torque converter access cover and the shift cable cover.

19   Disconnect the shift cable from the control lever, remove the bracket bolts and position the shift cable aside.

20   Mark the relationship of the torque converter to the driveplate so that they can be reinstalled in the same relationship to one

10.20 Before removing the driveplate-to-torque converter bolts, mark the edge of the driveplate and torque converter or flywheel to ensure they're reattached in the same relationship when the transaxle is reinstalled

10.26 Remove the transaxle-to-engine mounting bolts (arrows)

10.37 Remove the three upper transmission mounting bolts (arrows)

10.40 Disconnect the transmission cooler lines (arrows)

another **(see illustration)**.

21   Remove the torque converter-to-driveplate bolts one at a time by rotating the crankshaft pulley for access to each bolt.

22   Attach a support fixture or engine hoist to the engine and raise the engine slightly.

23   Place a transmission jack or a floor jack under the transaxle. Raise the transaxle assembly just enough to take the load off the transaxle mount.

24   Remove the through-bolt from the front engine mount and remove the mount from the transaxle.

25   Remove the transaxle mount through-bolt and remove the mount and the mount bracket from the transaxle.

26   Remove the lower transaxle-to-engine bolt **(see illustration)**, the lower engine-to-transaxle bolts and the rear engine mount bolts.

27   Move the transaxle back to disengage it from the engine block dowel pins and make sure the torque converter is detached from the driveplate. Secure the torque converter to the transaxle so it will not fall out during removal.

28   Lower the transaxle from the vehicle. **Note:** *It may be necessary to slowly lower the hoist supporting the engine while the jack supporting the transaxle is being lowered. This will provide more clearance between the transaxle and the body.*

Installation

29   The manufacturer recommends flushing the transaxle cooler and the cooler hoses and lines with solvent whenever the transaxle is removed from the vehicle; use an approved flushing solvent. Flush the lines and fluid cooler thoroughly and make sure no solvent remains in the lines or cooler after flushing.

30   Prior to installation, make sure that the torque converter hub is securely engaged in the pump. With the transaxle secured to the jack, raise it into position. Be sure to keep it level so the torque converter does not slide out.

31   Turn the torque converter to line it up with the driveplate. The marks you made on the torque converter and the driveplate must line up. Make sure the two dowel pins are still installed, then move the transaxle forward carefully until the dowel pins and the torque converter are engaged.

32   Install the lower transaxle-to-engine bolt and the lower engine-to-transaxle bolts. Tighten them to the torque listed in this Chapter's Specifications. **Caution:** *Don't use the bolts to force the transaxle and engine together. If the transaxle doesn't slide easily up against the engine, find out why before you tighten the bolts.*

33   Install the front engine mount and the transaxle mount bracket and mount. Tighten the bolts to the torque listed in this Chapter's Specifications. Remove the transaxle jack and the engine support or hoist.

34   The remainder of installation is the reverse of removal with the following additions:

a) *Refill the transaxle with fluid to the specified level (see Chapter 1). Note that the transaxle may require more fluid than in a normal fluid and filter change, since the torque converter may be empty (the converter is not drained during a fluid change).*

b) *Start the engine, set the parking brake and shift the transaxle through all gears three times. Make sure the shift cable is working properly (see Section 4).*

c) *Check and, if necessary, adjust the ignition timing (see Chapter 1).*

d) *Allow the engine to reach its proper operating temperature with the transaxle in Park or Neutral, then turn it off and check the fluid level.*

e) *Road test the vehicle and check for fluid leaks.*

Legend

Removal

Refer to illustrations 10.37, 10.40, 10.43, 10.47a, 10.47b and 10.50

35   Disconnect the negative cable from the battery. **Caution:** *If the radio in your vehicle is equipped with an anti-theft system, make*

sure you have the correct activation code before disconnecting the battery.

36   Remove the air duct and the strut bar. Without disconnecting the vacuum hoses, remove the control box and position it aside.

37   Remove the three upper transmission mounting bolts **(see illustration)**. Remove the bolts retaining the transmission dipstick tube.

38   Raise the vehicle and support it securely on jackstands. Drain the transmission lubricant (see Chapter 1).

39   Remove the catalytic converter and the exhaust pipe section mounted under the transmission (see Chapter 4). Remove the heat shields.

40   Disconnect transmission cooler lines **(see illustration)**. Remove the bolt retaining the transmission dipstick tube to the transmission and detach the tube from the transmission.

41   Detach the transmission electrical harness retainer from the shift cable cover and remove the cover. Remove the shift cable holder from the base and remove the control lever from the control shaft. Position the shift cable assembly aside.

42   Disconnect the electrical connectors from the transmission control solenoids and speed sensors. Position the wiring harness aside.

7B

10.43 Remove the lower reinforcement plate bolts (arrows) (not all bolts shown)

10.47a Remove the engine stiffener (arrow) . . .

10.47b . . . and the torque converter cover bolts (arrows)

43   Remove the lower reinforcement plate **(see illustration)**. Reinstall the steering gear mounting bolts to secure the steering gear in position.

44   Shift the transmission into Park and remove the differential extension shaft cover and sealing bolt. Using the special puller tool, disconnect the extension shaft from the differential (see Chapter 8).

45   Remove the exhaust system brackets, the rear transmission mount and the transmission mount bracket. Remove the shift cable bracket.

46   Place a floor jack under the transmission, place a block of wood between the jack head and the transmission and raise it just enough to take the weight off the rear engine mounts and remove the mounts.

47   Remove the engine stiffener and the torque converter covers **(see illustrations)**.

48   Mark the relationship of the torque converter to the driveplate so that they can be reinstalled in the same relationship to one another.

49   Remove the torque converter-to-driveplate bolts one at a time by rotating the crankshaft pulley for access to each bolt.

50   Remove the remaining transmission mounting bolts **(see illustration)**. Remove the engine-to-transmission lower mounting bolt. **Note:** *A shim is used between the engine and transmission at this location. Remove the shim and place it with the bolt.*

51   Make a final check that all wires and hoses have been disconnected from the transmission, then carefully pull the transmission and jack away from the engine.

52   Once the dowel pin is clear, lower the transmission and remove it from under the vehicle.

Installation

53   The manufacturer recommends flushing the transmission cooler and the cooler hoses and lines with solvent whenever the transmission is removed from the vehicle; use an approved flushing solvent. Flush the lines and fluid cooler thoroughly and make sure no solvent remains in the lines or cooler after flushing.

54   Lubricate the differential extension shaft splines with high-temperature grease. Install the secondary spring into the differential side of the extension shaft.

55   Prior to installation, install a new O-ring (if the torque converter was removed from the transmission) and make sure that the torque converter hub is securely engaged in the pump. With the transmission secured to the jack, raise it into position. Be sure to keep it level so the torque converter does not slide out.

56   Turn the torque converter to align the bolt holes with the driveplate. The marks you made on the torque converter and the driveplate must align.

57   Make sure the two dowel pins are still installed, then move the transmission forward carefully until the dowel pins and the torque converter are engaged.

58   Install the lower transmission mounting bolts and the lower bolt with the shim. Tighten them to the torque listed in this Chapter's Specifications. **Caution:** *Don't use the bolts to force the transmission and engine together. If the transmission doesn't slide easily up against the engine, find out why before you tighten the bolts.*

59   Install the torque converter bolts and the torque converter covers. Tighten the bolts to the torque listed in this Chapter's Specifications.

60   Install the engine stiffener installing all the bolts snugly. Tighten the transmission mounting bolt first, followed by the stiffener-to-engine bolts. Tighten the bolts to the torque listed in this Chapter's Specifications.

61   Install the rear engine mounts. Tighten the mount bracket-to-transaxle bolts first followed by the mount to crossmember nuts. Tighten the bolts to the torque listed in this Chapter's Specifications. Remove the transmission jack.

62   Install the rear transmission mount, mount bracket and exhaust pipe bracket. Install all the bolts snugly. Tighten the four mount bracket-to-body bolts first, followed by the mount-to-transaxle bolts and lastly, the mount-to-bracket bolts. Tighten the bolts to the torque listed in this Chapter's Specifications.

63   Install the shift cable guide at the rear of the transmission.

64   Install the differential extension shaft in the transmission (see Chapter 8).

65   Remove the steering gear mounting bolts and install the lower reinforcement plate. Tighten the reinforcement plate bolts and the two steering gear bolts to the torque listed in this Chapter's Specifications.

66   The remainder of installation is the reverse of removal with the following additions:

a) *Refill the transmission with fluid to the specified level (see Chapter 1). Note that the transmission may require more fluid than in a normal fluid and filter change, since the torque converter may be empty (the converter is not drained during a fluid change).*

b) *Start the engine, set the parking brake and shift the transmission through all gears three times. Make sure the shift cable is working properly (see Section 4).*

c) *Check and, if necessary, adjust the ignition timing (see Chapter 1).*

d) *Allow the engine to reach its proper operating temperature with the transmission in Park or Neutral, then turn it off and check the fluid level.*

e) *Road test the vehicle and check for fluid leaks.*

10.50 Remove the transmission-to-engine bolts (arrow indicates one)

Chapter 8
Clutch, driveaxles and differential

Contents

Specifications

Driveaxle length

Integra
1990 through 1991 .... 19 to 19-3/16 inches
1992 through 1993 .... 19-1/8 to 19-5/16 inches
Dynamic damper - distance from inner CV boot 1-inch
Legend
1991 through 1992
Left .... 22-15/16 to 23-1/8 inches
Right .... 19-17/32 to 19-3/4 inches
1993 through 1995
Left .... 23-3/32 to 23-9/32 inches
Right .... 19-11/16 to 19-29/32 inches

Torque specifications

	Ft-lbs
Integra	
Clutch pressure plate bolts	19
Driveaxle/hub nut	134
Intermediate shaft bearing support bolts	28
Clutch release fork bolt	21
Legend	
Clutch pressure plate bolts	19
Driveaxle/hub nut	242
Intermediate shaft bearing support bolts	16

8

1 General information

The information in this Chapter deals with the components from the rear of the engine to the front wheels, except for the transmission/transaxle, which is dealt with in the previous Chapter. For the purposes of this Chapter, these components are grouped into two categories - clutch and driveaxles. Separate Sections within this Chapter offer general descriptions and checking procedures for components in each of the two groups.

Since nearly all the procedures covered in this Chapter involve working under the vehicle, make sure it's securely supported on sturdy jackstands or on a hoist where the vehicle can be easily raised and lowered.

2 Clutch - description and check

1   All vehicles with a five speed manual transmission/transaxle use a single dry-plate, diaphragm-spring type clutch. The clutch disc has a splined hub that allows it to slide along the splines of the transaxle input shaft. The clutch and pressure plate is held in contact by spring pressure exerted by the diaphragm in the pressure plate. On Legend models with a six-speed transmission, the flywheel is a two-piece "Dual Mass" design incorporating torsion springs. The clutch disc with this flywheel requires no torsion springs in its hub since the flywheel torsion springs perform this function.

2   On Integra models a cable is used to operate the clutch release system. The mechanical release system includes the clutch pedal, a clutch cable that actuates the clutch release lever and the release bearing. Legend models use hydraulic pressure to actuate the clutch release system. The hydraulic release system consists of the clutch pedal, a master cylinder and fluid reservoir, the hydraulic line, a release (or slave) cylinder which actuates the clutch release lever and the clutch release (or throwout) bearing.

3   When pressure is applied to the clutch pedal to release the clutch, the mechanical or hydraulic pressure is exerted against the outer end of the clutch release lever. As the lever pivots the shaft fingers push against the release bearing. The bearing pushes against the fingers of the diaphragm spring of the pressure plate assembly, which in turn releases the clutch plate.

4   Terminology can be a problem when discussing the clutch components because common names are in some cases different from those used by the manufacturer. For example, the driven plate is also called the clutch plate or disc, the clutch release bearing is sometimes called a throwout bearing, the release cylinder is sometimes called the operating or slave cylinder.

5   Other than to replace components with obvious damage, some preliminary checks should be performed to diagnose clutch problems. These checks assume that the transmission/transaxle is in good working condition.

a) *On Legend models, the first check should be of the fluid level in the clutch master cylinder (see Chapter 1). If the fluid level is low, add fluid as necessary and inspect the hydraulic system for leaks. If the master cylinder reservoir has run dry, bleed the system as described in Section 5 and retest the clutch operation. On Integra models, check the clutch pedal height and freeplay adjustment. If the pedal height and freeplay adjustment is out of specifications, adjust it before proceeding with the remaining clutch system checks.*

b) *To check "clutch spin-down time," run the engine at normal idle speed with the transmission/transaxle in Neutral (clutch pedal up - engaged). Disengage the clutch (pedal down), wait several seconds and shift the transmission/transaxle into Reverse. No grinding noise should be heard. A grinding noise would most likely indicate a problem in the pressure plate or the clutch disc.*

c) *To check for complete clutch release, run the engine (with the parking brake applied to prevent movement) and hold the clutch pedal approximately 1/2-inch from the floor. Shift the transmission/transaxle between 1st gear and Reverse several times. If the shift is rough, component failure is indicated. On Legend models, check the release cylinder pushrod travel. With the clutch pedal depressed completely, the release cylinder pushrod should extend substantially. If it doesn't, check the fluid level in the clutch master cylinder.*

d) *Visually inspect the pivot bushing at the top of the clutch pedal to make sure there is no binding or excessive play.*

e) *Crawl under the vehicle and make sure the clutch release lever is solidly mounted on its pivot.*

3.2 Loosen the adjuster wheel (arrow) to provide enough slack for removal of the cable

3 Clutch cable (Integra models) - removal and installation

Refer to illustrations 3.2, 3.3 and 3.4

1   Raise the vehicle and support it securely on jackstands.

2   Loosen the cable adjusting wheel until there's no tension on the cable **(see illustration)**.

3   Disconnect the cable from the release lever, pull it up and out of the slot **(see illustration)**. Pry out the clutch cable grommet from the firewall and detach any cable retaining clips.

4   Working under the dash with a flashlight, disengage the cable from the top of the clutch pedal and the cable retaining bracket **(see illustration)**. Push the cable into the engine compartment and remove the cable from the vehicle.

5   Installation is the reverse of removal, taking care there are no kinks in the cable that will cause it to bind.

6   After installation, adjust the clutch pedal freeplay (see Chapter 1).

3.3 Disconnect the cable from the release lever arm by pulling up on the lever, then pass the cable through the slot (arrow) in the arm

3.4 Detach the cable (A) from the top of the clutch pedal and the clutch cable bracket (B)

4.3a The remote reservoir for the clutch master cylinder is located in the left (driver's side) rear corner of the engine compartment, and the master cylinder is right below it; to get at the master cylinder, remove the bolt(s) (arrows) and lift the reservoir out of the way

4.3b Pinch off the fluid feed hose between the reservoir and the clutch master cylinder with a pair of locking pliers to prevent the fluid from running out of the end of the hose when you disconnect it from the clutch master cylinder

4   Clutch master cylinder (Legend models) - removal and installation

Removal

Refer to illustrations 4.3a, 4.3b and 4.5

1   Disconnect the cable from the negative terminal of the battery. **Caution:** *If the radio in your vehicle is equipped with an anti-theft system, make sure you have the correct activation code before disconnecting the battery.*
2   Working under the dashboard, remove the cotter pin from the master cylinder pushrod clevis. Pull out the clevis pin to disconnect the pushrod from the pedal.
3   Detach the clutch master cylinder reservoir **(see illustration)**. Clamp a pair of locking pliers onto the clutch fluid feed hoses, a couple of inches downstream of the reservoir **(see illustration)**. The pliers should be just tight enough to prevent fluid flow when the hose is disconnected.
4   Disconnect the hydraulic lines at the cylinder. Loosen the fluid feed hose clamp and detach the hose from the cylinder. Use a flare-nut wrench to loosen the line fitting. Have rags handy as some fluid will be lost as the line is removed. Cap or plug the ends of the line and hose to prevent fluid leakage and the entry of contaminants. **Caution:** *Don't allow brake fluid to come into contact with the paint as it will damage the finish.*
5   Working under the dash, unscrew the two clutch master cylinder retaining nuts and remove the cylinder **(see illustration)**.

Installation

6   Place the master cylinder in position and install the mounting bolts finger tight.
7   Connect the hydraulic line to the master cylinder. Move the cylinder slightly as necessary to thread the fitting into the cylinder (don't tighten the fitting yet). Attach the fluid feed hose to the cylinder and tighten the hose clamp.

8   Tighten the mounting bolts securely, then tighten the hydraulic line fitting securely.
9   Connect the pushrod to the clutch pedal. Use a new cotter pin to secure the clevis pin.
10   Remove the locking pliers from the feed hose. Fill the clutch master cylinder reservoir with brake fluid conforming to DOT 3 or DOT 4 specifications, bleed the clutch system as outlined in Section 6 and reconnect the cable to the negative terminal of the battery.

5   Clutch release cylinder (Legend models) - removal and installation

Removal

Refer to illustrations 5.3 and 5.4

1   Disconnect the cable from the negative terminal of the battery. **Caution:** *If the radio in your vehicle is equipped with an anti-theft system, make sure you have the correct activation code before disconnecting the battery.*
2   Raise the vehicle and support it securely on jackstands.
3   Remove the cover and disconnect the fluid hose at the release cylinder. Use a flare nut wrench so you don't strip the corners off

4.5 To disconnect the clutch master cylinder from the clutch pedal, remove the cotter pin and clevis pin that attach to the top of the pedal - to detach the master cylinder from the firewall, remove the two mounting nuts (arrows)

the fitting **(see illustration)**. Have a small can and rags handy, some fluid will be spilled as the line is removed.
4   Remove the two release cylinder mounting bolts **(see illustration)**.
5   Remove the release cylinder.

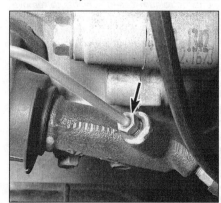

5.3 Using a flare-nut wrench, loosen the clutch fluid line fitting (arrow) at the release cylinder

5.4 Remove the two mounting bolts (arrows) from the clutch release cylinder

8

6.4 The setup for bleeding the clutch hydraulic system is simple - a length of hose between the bleeder screw and a small container with about two inches of brake fluid in it - make sure the hose is submerged in the fluid

7.5 Mark the relationship of the pressure plate to the flywheel (just in case you're going to re-use the old pressure plate)

7.6 Remove the pressure plate bolts (arrows) gradually and evenly in a criss-cross pattern

Installation

6   Install the release cylinder on the clutch housing, but don't completely tighten the bolts yet. Make sure the pushrod is seated in the release fork pocket.

7   Connect the hydraulic line to the release cylinder, then tighten the release cylinder mounting bolts securely. Using a flare-nut wrench, tighten the hydraulic fitting securely.

8   Fill the clutch master cylinder with brake fluid conforming to DOT 3 or DOT 4 specifications.

9   Bleed the system as described in Section 6.

10   Lower the vehicle and reconnect the cable to the negative terminal of the battery.

6   Clutch hydraulic system (Legend models) - bleeding

Refer to illustration 6.4

1   Bleed the hydraulic system whenever any part of the system has been removed or the fluid level has fallen so low that air has been drawn into the master cylinder. The bleeding procedure is very similar to bleeding a brake system.

2   Fill the master cylinder with new brake fluid conforming to DOT 3 or DOT 4 specifications. **Caution:** *Do not re-use any of the fluid coming from the system during the bleeding operation or use fluid which has been inside an open container for an extended period of time.*

3   Raise the vehicle and place it securely on jackstands to gain access to the release cylinder, which is located on the front of the transmission.

4   Remove the dust cap that fits over the bleeder valve and push a length of plastic hose over the valve **(see illustration)**. Place the other end of the hose into a clear container with about two inches of brake fluid. The hose end must be in the fluid at the bottom of the container.

5   Have an assistant depress the clutch pedal and hold it. Open the bleeder screw on the release cylinder, allowing fluid to flow through the hose. Close the bleeder screw when the flow of fluid (and bubbles) ceases. Once closed, have your assistant release the pedal.

6   Continue this process until all air is evacuated from the system, indicated by a solid stream of fluid being ejected from the bleeder valve each time with no air bubbles in the hose or container. Keep a close watch on the fluid level inside the clutch master cylinder reservoir - if the level drops too far, air will get into the system and you'll have to start all over again.

7   Install the dust cap onto the bleeder screw and lower the vehicle. Check carefully for proper operation before placing the vehicle into normal service.

7   Clutch components - removal, inspection and installation

Warning: *Dust produced by clutch wear and deposited on clutch components may contain asbestos, which is hazardous to your health. DO NOT blow it out with compressed air and DO NOT inhale it. DO NOT use gasoline or petroleum-based solvents to remove the dust. Brake system cleaner should be used to flush the dust into a drain pan. After the clutch components are wiped clean with a rag, dispose of the contaminated rags and cleaner in a covered, marked container.*

Removal

Refer to illustrations 7.5 and 7.6

1   Access to the clutch components is normally accomplished by removing the transmission/transaxle, leaving the engine in the vehicle. If the engine is being removed for major overhaul, check the clutch for wear and replace worn components as necessary. However, the relatively low cost of the clutch components compared to the time and trouble spent gaining access to them warrants their replacement anytime the engine or

transmission/transaxle is removed, unless they are new or in near-perfect condition. The following procedures are based on the assumption the engine will stay in place.

2   Remove the transmission/transaxle from the vehicle (see Chapter 7A). Support the engine while the transmission/transaxle is out. Preferably, an engine hoist should be used to support it from above. However, if a jack is used underneath the engine, make sure a piece of wood is positioned between the jack and oil pan to spread the load. **Caution:** *The pick-up for the oil pump is very close to the bottom of the oil pan. If the pan is bent or distorted in any way, engine oil starvation could occur.*

3   The clutch fork and release bearing on Integra models can remain attached to the transaxle housing for the time being.

4   To support the clutch disc during removal, install a clutch alignment tool through the clutch disc hub.

5   Carefully inspect the flywheel and pressure plate for indexing marks. The marks are usually an X, an O or a white letter. If they cannot be found, scribe or paint marks yourself so the pressure plate and the flywheel will be in the same alignment during installation **(see illustration)**.

6   Turning each bolt a little at a time, loosen the pressure plate-to-flywheel bolts **(see illustration)**. Work in a criss-cross pattern until all spring pressure is relieved. Then hold the pressure plate securely and completely remove the bolts, followed by the pressure plate and clutch disc.

Inspection

Refer to illustrations 7.9, 7.11a and 7.11b

7   Ordinarily, when a problem occurs in the clutch, it can be attributed to wear of the clutch driven plate assembly (clutch disc). However, all components should be inspected at this time.

8   Inspect the flywheel for cracks, heat checking, grooves and other obvious defects. If the imperfections are slight, a machine shop can machine the surface flat and smooth, which is highly recommended

regardless of the surface appearance. Refer to Chapter 2A or 2B for the flywheel removal and installation procedure.

9   Inspect the lining on the clutch disc. There should be at least 1/32-inch of lining above the rivet heads. Check for loose rivets, distortion, cracks, broken springs and other obvious damage (see illustration). As mentioned above, ordinarily the clutch disc is routinely replaced, so if in doubt about the condition, replace it with a new one.

10   The release bearing should also be replaced along with the clutch disc (see Section 9). This is also a good time to check the condition of the pilot bearing (see Section 8).

11   Check the machined surfaces and the diaphragm spring fingers of the pressure plate (see illustrations). If the surface is grooved or otherwise damaged, replace the pressure plate. Also check for obvious damage, distortion, cracking, etc. Light glazing can be removed with emery cloth or sandpaper. If a new pressure plate is required, new and factory-rebuilt units are available.

Installation

Refer to illustration 7.14

12   Before installation, clean the flywheel and pressure plate machined surfaces with brake cleaner, lacquer thinner or acetone. It's important that no oil or grease is on these surfaces or the lining of the clutch disc. Handle the parts only with clean hands.

13   On Legend models, install the clutch

7.9 Typical clutch disc

1 **Lining** - this will wear down in use
2 **Springs or dampers** - check for cracking and deformation
3 **Splined hub** - the splines must not be worn and should slide smoothly on the transaxle input shaft splines
4 **Rivets** - these secure the lining and will damage the flywheel or pressure plate if allowed to contact the surfaces

release bearing onto the pressure plate (see Section 9).

14   Position the clutch disc and pressure plate against the flywheel with the clutch held in place with an alignment tool (see illustration). Make sure the disc is installed properly (most replacement clutch discs will be marked "flywheel side" or something similar - if not marked, install the clutch disc with the damper springs toward the transmission/transaxle).

15   Center the clutch disc by ensuring the alignment tool extends through the splined hub and into the pilot bearing in the end of the crankshaft. Wiggle the tool up, down or side-to-side as needed to center the disc.

Tighten the pressure plate-to-flywheel bolts a little at a time, working in a criss-cross pattern to prevent distorting the cover. After all of the bolts are snug, tighten them to the torque listed in this Chapter's Specifications. Remove the alignment tool.

16   Using high-temperature grease, lubricate the inner groove of the release bearing (see Section 9). Also place grease on the release lever contact areas and the transmission/transaxle input shaft bearing retainer.

17   On Integra models, install the clutch release bearing (see Section 9).

18   Install the transmission/transaxle and all components removed previously.

NORMAL FINGER WEAR   EXCESSIVE FINGER WEAR   BROKEN OR BENT FINGERS

7.11a Replace the pressure plate if excessive wear or damage is noted

7.11b Inspect the pressure plate friction surface for score marks, cracks and signs of overheating

7.14 Center the clutch disc in the pressure plate with a clutch alignment tool

8

8 Pilot bearing - inspection and replacement

Refer to illustrations 8.5 and 8.6

1   The clutch pilot bearing is a needle roller or ball bearing type bearing which is pressed into the flywheel. It's greased at the factory and doesn't required additional lubrication. Its primary purpose is to support the front of the transmission/transaxle input shaft. The pilot bearing components should be inspected whenever the clutch components are removed from the engine. Because of its inaccessibility, replace it with a new one if you have any doubt about its condition. **Note:** *If the engine has been removed from the vehicle, disregard the following Steps, which don't apply.*

2   Remove the transmission/transaxle (see Chapter 7A).

3   Remove the clutch components (see Section 7).

4   Using a flashlight, inspect the bearing for excessive wear, scoring, dryness, roughness and any other obvious damage. If any of these conditions are noted, replace the bearing.

5   Removal can be accomplished with a special puller **(see illustration)**, which is available at most auto parts stores. Remove the bearing and clean the recess in the flywheel. **Note:** *If the special puller is not available, remove the flywheel (see Chapter 2A or 2B), then use a drift punch to drive the pilot bearing out from the backside of the flywheel.*

6   To install a new bearing, lightly lubricate the outside surface with grease, then drive it into the recess with a seal installer or a socket **(see illustration)**. The bearing seal must face out.

7   Install the clutch components, transmission/transaxle and other components removed previously. Tighten all fasteners to the recommended torque.

9 Clutch release bearing and lever - removal, inspection and installation

Warning: *Dust produced by clutch wear and deposited on clutch components may contain asbestos, which is hazardous to your health. DO NOT blow it out with compressed air and DO NOT inhale it. DO NOT use gasoline or petroleum-based solvents to remove the dust. Brake system cleaner should be used to flush the dust into a drain pan. After the clutch components are wiped clean with a rag, dispose of the contaminated rags and cleaner in a labeled, covered container.*

Removal

Integra

Refer to illustration 9.3

1   Disconnect the clutch cable from the release arm (see Section 3).

8.5 A small slide-hammer puller is handy for removing an old pilot bearing

2   Remove the transaxle (see Chapter 7A).

3   Remove the bolt which secures the release fork and bearing to the release lever shaft **(see illustration)**. Slide the release lever shaft out of the release fork.

4   Remove the fork and bearing from the input shaft, disengage the release fork spring from the bearing and remove the bearing from the release fork.

Legend

5   Unbolt the clutch release cylinder (see Section 5), but don't disconnect the fluid line between the master cylinder and the release cylinder. Suspend the release cylinder out of the way with a piece of wire.

8.6 Tap the bearing into place with a bearing installer or a socket that is slightly smaller than the outside diameter of the bearing

6   Pull out on the release fork to disengage it from the release bearing and the fork pivot located inside the bellhousing. Remove the transmission (see Chapter 7A) and the pressure plate (see Section 7).

7   Disengage the release bearing from the pressure plate.

Inspection

Refer to illustration 9.8

8   Hold the bearing by the outer race and rotate the inner race while applying pressure. If the bearing doesn't turn smoothly or if it's

9.3 Clutch fork, release bearing and related components (Integra models)

1   *Pressure plate retaining bolt(s)*
2   *Pressure plate*
3   *Clutch disc*
4   *Release bearing*
5   *Release fork retaining bolt*
6   *Release lever and shaft*
7   *Release fork spring*
8   *Release fork*

HAYNES 12021-09.03.I

9.8 To check the bearing, hold it by the outer race and rotate the inner race while applying pressure; if the bearing doesn't turn smoothly or if it's noisy, replace the bearing

9.10 Apply a light coat of high-temperature grease to the bearing surface of the retainer (before installing the transmission/transaxle, apply the same grease to the input shaft splines to help the shaft slide through the clutch hub)

9.17 Release bearing installation details (Legend models)

noisy, replace the bearing with a new one **(see illustration)**. Wipe the bearing with a clean rag and inspect it for damage, wear and cracks. It's common practice to replace the bearing with a new one whenever a clutch job is performed, to decrease the possibility of a bearing failure in the future.

9   Don't immerse the bearing in solvent - it's sealed for life and to do so would ruin it. Also check the release lever/fork assembly for cracks and bends.

Installation

Integra

Refer to illustration 9.10

10   Fill the inner groove of the release bearing with high temperature grease. Also apply a light coat of the same grease to the transaxle input shaft splines and the front bearing retainer **(see illustration)**.

11   Attach the release fork spring to the bearing, then align the release fork with the locating slots in the bearing.

12   Lubricate the release lever shaft with high temperature grease.

13   Slide the release bearing and fork assembly onto the transaxle input shaft front bearing retainer while passing the end of the release lever shaft through the opening in the transaxle housing. Push the release lever shaft into the release fork until it's firmly seated and the holes align **(see illustration 9.3)**. Install the bolt and tighten it to the torque listed in this Chapter's Specifications.

14   Apply a light coat of high temperature grease to the face of the release bearing where it contacts the pressure plate diaphragm fingers.

15   The remainder of installation is the reverse of the removal procedure.

Legend

Refer to illustration 9.17

16   Fill the inner groove of the release bearing with high temperature grease. Also apply a light coat of the same grease to the

transaxle input shaft splines and the front bearing retainer **(see illustration 9.10)**.

17   Attach the release bearing to the center of the pressure plate **(see illustration)**, then install the pressure plate onto the flywheel (see Section 7).

18   The remainder of installation is the reverse of the removal procedure.

10   Starter/clutch interlock switch - check, replacement and adjustment

Check

Refer to illustration 10.1

1   The starter/clutch interlock switch is located near the upper end of the clutch pedal **(see illustration)**. It has two wires - one coming from the starter relay and one going to ground. When the ignition switch key is turned to the Start position and the clutch pedal is depressed, the starter relay's path to ground is closed by the starter/clutch interlock switch and the starter motor is activated.

2   Verify that the engine will not start when the clutch pedal is released. Next verify that the engine will start when the clutch pedal is depressed all the way to the floor.

3   If the clutch start circuit does not perform as described, adjust the clutch interlock switch (see Step 9).

4   Verify that there is continuity between the clutch start switch terminals when the switch is On (pedal depressed).

5   Verify that there is no continuity between the clutch start switch terminals when the switch is Off (pedal released).

6   If the switch fails either of the tests, replace the switch.

Replacement

7   Unplug the electrical connector, loosen

the adjustment nut and unscrew the switch from its mounting bracket.

8   Installation is the reverse of removal. Adjust the switch as described in Step 9.

Adjustment

9   Loosen the switch locknut. Depress the clutch pedal to the floor, then release the clutch pedal 0.59 to 0.79 in. (approximately 3/4 of an inch). Turn the switch in or out, as necessary, to provide continuity through the switch when the clutch pedal is held in this position. Turn the switch inward an additional 1/4 to 1/2 turn and tighten the locknut.

10.1 On Integra models, the interlock switch (arrow) is located on a bracket near the top of the clutch pedal - Legend models have two switches on the clutch pedal; the interlock switch is the one located on the right side of the pedal arm and it faces in the opposite direction of the one shown here

8

11.1 If the driveaxle nut is "staked", use a center punch to unstake it

11.2 Loosen the driveaxle/hub nut with a long breaker bar

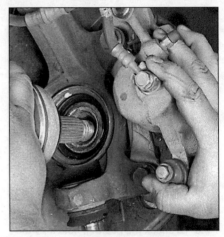

11.6 Swing the hub/knuckle out (away from the vehicle) and pull the driveaxle from the hub

11.7a Use a large screwdriver or a prybar to pop the inner end of the driveaxle from the transaxle, or . . .

11.7b . . . if you're removing the left driveaxle, insert the prybar between the intermediate shaft bearing and the driveaxle to pop it loose

11 Driveaxle - removal and installation

Removal

Refer to illustrations 11.1, 11.2, 11.6, 11.7a and 11.7b

1   Remove the wheel cover or hub cap. If the driveaxle/hub nut is staked, unstake it with a punch or chisel **(see illustration)**; if it's secured by locking tabs, bend the tabs out.

2   Break the hub nut loose with a socket and large breaker bar **(see illustration)**.

3   Loosen the wheel lug nuts, raise the vehicle and support it securely on jackstands. Remove the wheel. Drain the transmission/transaxle lubricant (see Chapter 1).

4   Disconnect the damper fork from the shock absorber assembly and the lower control arm (see Chapter 10).

5   Separate the lower control arm from the steering knuckle (see Chapter 10).

6   Swing the knuckle/hub assembly out (away from the vehicle) until the end of the driveaxle is free of the hub **(see illustration)**. Support the outer end of the driveaxle with a piece of wire to avoid unnecessary strain on the inner CV joint.

7   Carefully pry the inner end of the driveaxle from the transmission/transaxle or the intermediate shaft - using a large screwdriver or prybar positioned between transmission/transaxle or bearing support and the CV joint housing **(see illustrations)**. Support the CV joints and carefully remove the driveaxle from the vehicle. To prevent damage to the intermediate shaft seal or the differential seal, hold the inner CV joint horizontal until the driveaxle is clear of the intermediate shaft or transmission/transaxle.

Installation

Refer to illustrations 11.8a, 11.8b, 11.8c and 11.9

8   Pry the old spring clip from the inner end of the driveaxle and install a new one **(see illustrations)**. When installing the left driveaxle on Legend models, it will be necessary to pry the old spring clip from the outer end of the intermediate shaft and install a new one **(see illustration)**. Lubricate the

11.8a Pry the old spring clip from the inner end of the driveaxle with a small screwdriver or awl

11.8b To install the new spring clip, start one end in the groove and work the clip over the shaft end, into the groove

11.8c When installing the left driveaxle on Legend models, it will be necessary to remove and replace the spring clip on the intermediate shaft

11.9 When installing the driveaxle, make sure the spring clip pops into place in its groove - if it's seated properly, you shouldn't be able to pull it out by hand

SPRING CLIP

SPRING CLIP GROOVE

H.9773

differential or intermediate shaft seal with multi-purpose grease and raise the driveaxle into position while supporting the CV joints.

9   Insert the inner CV joint into the differential side gear or the intermediate shaft and make sure the spring clip locks in its groove **(see illustration)**.

10   Apply a light coat of multi-purpose grease to the outer CV joint splines, pull out on the strut/steering knuckle assembly and install the outer CV joint splines into the hub.

11   Insert the stud of the lower control arm balljoint into the steering knuckle and tighten the nut (see the torque specifications in Chapter 10). Be sure to use a new cotter pin. Install the damper fork (see Chapter 10).

12   Install the hub nut (and, if applicable, a new locking tab washer). Lock the disc so it can't turn, then tighten the hub nut securely. Don't try to tighten it to the actual torque specification until you've lowered the vehicle to the ground.

13   Grasp the inner CV joint housing (not the driveaxle) and pull out to make sure the driveaxle has seated securely in the transmission/transaxle.

14   Install the wheel and lug nuts, then lower the vehicle.

15   Tighten the lug nuts to the torque listed in the Chapter 1 Specifications. Tighten the hub nut to the torque listed in this Chapter's Specifications. Using a hammer and punch, stake the nut to the groove in the driveaxle. If the hub nut uses a locking tab, be sure to bend the tabs up against the nut. Install the wheel cover (if applicable).

16   Refill the differential or transaxle with the recommended type and amount of lubricant (see Chapter 1).

12 Intermediate shaft - removal and installation

Removal

Refer to illustrations 12.4a and 12.4b

1   Loosen the left (driver's side) front wheel lug nuts, raise the front of the vehicle and support it securely on jackstands. Remove the wheel.

2   Drain the transaxle lubricant on Integra models or the differential lubricant on Legend models (see Chapter 1).

3   Remove the left driveaxle (see Section 11).

4   Remove the three bearing support-to-engine block bolts **(see illustrations)** and slide the intermediate shaft out of the transaxle or differential on Legend models. Be careful not to damage the oil seal when pulling the shaft out.

5   Check the support bearing for smooth operation by turning the shaft while holding the bearing. If you feel any roughness, take the bearing support to a dealer service department or other repair shop to have a new bearing installed. To do the job at home, you'd need specialized tools.

8

12.4a Intermediate shaft bearing support bolts (arrows) (Integra models)

12.4b Intermediate shaft bearing support bolts (arrows) (Legend models)

Installation

6   Lubricate the lips of the differential or transaxle seal with multi-purpose grease. Carefully guide the intermediate shaft into the differential or transaxle side gear then install the mounting bolts through the bearing support. Tighten the bolts to the torque listed in this Chapter's Specifications.

7   Install a new spring clip on the inner CV joint on Integra models or the intermediate shaft on Legend models **(see illustrations 11.8a, 11.8b and 11.8c)**, then seat the driveaxle into the intermediate shaft splines.

8   The remainder of the installation is the reverse of removal. Refill the transaxle or differential with the proper type and amount of lubricant (see Chapter 1).

13   Driveaxle boot - replacement

Note 1: *If the CV joints are worn, indicating the need for an overhaul (usually due to torn boots), explore all options before beginning the job. Complete rebuilt driveaxles are available on an exchange basis, which eliminates much time and work. If you decide to rebuild a CV joint, check on the cost and availability of parts before disassembling the driveaxle.*

Note 2: *Some auto parts stores carry "split" type replacement boots, which can be installed without removing the driveaxle from the vehicle. This is a convenient alternative; however, the driveaxle should be removed and the CV joint disassembled and cleaned to ensure the joint is free from contaminants such as moisture and dirt which will accelerate CV joint wear.*

1   Remove the driveaxle from the vehicle (see Section 11).

2   Mount the driveaxle in a vise. The jaws of the vise should be lined with wood or rags to prevent damage to the driveaxle.

Inner CV joint and boot

Disassembly

Refer to illustrations 13.3a, 13.3b, 13.4, 13.5 and 13.6

3   If you have any doubts about the condition of the outer boot this would be a good time to replace it as well. Cut off both boot clamps and slide the boot towards the center of the driveaxle **(see illustrations)**.

4   Scribe or paint alignment marks on the outer race and the tri-pot bearing assembly **(see illustration)** so they can be returned to their original position, then slide the outer race off the tri-pot bearing assembly.

5   Remove the snap-ring from the end of the axleshaft, then mark the relationship of the tri-pot bearing assembly to the axleshaft **(see illustration)**.

6   Secure the bearing rollers with tape, then remove the tri-pot bearing assembly from the axleshaft with a brass drift and a hammer **(see illustration)**. Remove the tape, but don't let the rollers fall off and get mixed up.

13.3a Cut off the boot clamps and discard them - don't try to re-use old clamps

13.3b Slide the boot down the driveaxle, out of the way

13.4 Mark the relationship of the tri-pot assembly to the outer housing

7   Remove the stop-ring, slide the old boot off the driveaxle and discard it.

Inspection

8   Clean the old grease from the outer race and the tri-pot bearing assembly. Carefully disassemble each section of the tri-pot assembly, one at a time so as not to mix up the parts, and clean the needle bearings with solvent.

9   Inspect the rollers, tri-pot, bearings and outer race for scoring, pitting or other signs of abnormal wear, which will warrant the replacement of the inner CV joint.

Reassembly

Refer to illustrations 13.10a, 13.10b, 13.12, 13.13a, 13.13b, 13.14, 13.15, 13.16, 13.17a and 13.17b

10   Wrap the splines of the axleshaft with tape to avoid damaging the new boot, then slide the boot onto the axleshaft **(see illustration)**. Remove the tape and slide the inner stop-ring into place **(see illustration)**.

11   Align the match marks you made before disassembly and tap the tri-pot assembly onto the axleshaft with a hammer and brass drift.

13.5 Remove the snap-ring from the end of the axleshaft, then mark the relationship of the tri-pot bearing assembly to the axleshaft

13.6 Secure the bearing rollers with tape and drive the tri-pot off the shaft with a hammer and brass drift, then remove the stop-ring

13.10a Wrap the splined area of the axleshaft with tape to prevent damage to the boot when installing it

13.10b Install the stop-ring on the axleshaft, making sure it seats in its groove

13.12 Install the tri-pot assembly on the axleshaft, making sure the punch marks are lined up, then install the snap-ring

13.13a Use plenty of CV joint grease to hold the needle bearings in place when you install the roller assemblies on the tri-pot, and make sure you put each roller in its original position

13.13b If the bearing roller has a flange, the flange must be positioned facing the driveaxle

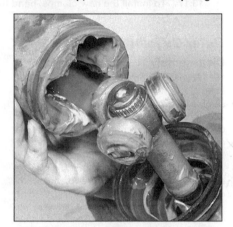

13.14 Pack the outer race with grease and slide it over the tri-pot assembly - make sure the match marks on the outer race and tri-pot line up

12   Install the outer snap-ring (see illustration).

13   Apply a coat of CV joint grease to the inner bearing surfaces to hold the needle bearings in place when reassembling the tri-pot assembly (see illustration). Make sure each roller is installed on the same post as before. Note: If the rollers are equipped with a flange, make sure the flange is positioned closest to the driveaxle (see illustration).

14   Pack the outer race with half of the grease furnished with the new boot and place the remainder in the boot. Install the outer race (see illustration). Make sure the marks you made on the tri-pot assembly and the outer race are aligned.

15   Seat the boot in the grooves in the outer race and the axleshaft, then adjust the driveaxle to the proper length (see illustration).

16   With the driveaxle set to the proper length, equalize the pressure in the boot by inserting a blunt screwdriver between the boot and the outer housing (see illustration). Don't damage the boot with the tool.

17   Install and tighten the new boot clamps (see illustrations).

18   Install the driveaxle assembly (see Section 11).

13.15 Before tightening the boot clamps, adjust the driveaxle length to the dimension listed in this Chapter's Specifications

13.16 Equalize the pressure inside the boot by inserting a small, dull screwdriver between the boot and the outer housing

8

13.17a To install the new clamps, bend the tang down . . .   **13.17b . . . and flatten the tabs to hold it in place**

Outer CV joint and boot

Disassembly

19   Following Steps 3 through 7, remove the inner CV joint from the driveaxle and disassemble it.

20   If the driveaxle is equipped with a dynamic damper, scribe or paint a location mark on the axleshaft along the outer edge of the damper (the side facing the outer CV joint), cut the retaining clamp and slide the damper off. **Note:** *If you're planning to replace the axleshaft and outer CV joint assembly, the specified distance between the inner CV joint boot and the dynamic damper is listed in this Chapter's Specifications.*

21   Cut the boot clamps from the outer CV joint. Slide the boot off the shaft. **Note:** *The outer CV joint can't be disassembled or removed from the shaft.*

Inspection

Refer to illustration 13.23

22   Thoroughly wash the inner and outer CV joints in clean solvent and blow them dry with compressed air, if available. **Warning:** *Wear eye protection when using compressed air.* **Note:** *Because the outer joint can't be*

disassembled, it is difficult to wash away all the old grease and to rid the bearing of solvent once it's clean. But it is imperative that the job be done thoroughly, so take your time and do it right.

23   Bend the outer CV joint housing at an angle to the axleshaft to expose the bearings, inner race and cage **(see illustration)**. Inspect the bearing surfaces for signs of wear. If the bearings are damaged or worn, replace the driveaxle.

Reassembly

24   Slide the new outer boot onto the axleshaft. It's a good idea to wrap tape around the splines of the shaft to prevent damage to the boot **(see illustration 13.10a)**. When the boot is in position, add the specified amount of grease (included in the boot replacement kit) to the outer joint and the boot (pack the joint with as much grease as it will hold and put the rest into the boot). Slide the boot on the rest of the way and install the new clamps **(see illustrations 13.17a and 13.17b)**.

25   Slide the dynamic damper, if equipped, onto the shaft. Make sure its outer edge is aligned with the previously applied mark. **Note:** *If you're using a new axleshaft and*

outer CV joint assembly, the specified distance between the inner CV joint boot and the dynamic damper is listed in this Chapter's Specifications. Install a new retaining clamp.

26   Clean and reassemble the inner CV joint by following Steps 8 through 17, then install the driveaxle as outlined in Section 11.

---

14   Differential oil seals (Legend models) - removal and installation

Refer to illustrations 14.4a, 14.4b and 14.6

1   Oil leaks frequently occur due to wear of the differential oil seals. Replacement of these seals is relatively easy, since the repair can usually be performed without removing the differential from the vehicle.

2   Oil seals are located at the sides of the differential, where the driveaxles are attached and on the pinion shaft. If leakage at the seal is suspected, raise the vehicle and support it securely on jackstands. If the seal is leaking, lubricant will be found on the sides or rear of the differential, below the seals. Replacement of the left side or pinion oil seals will require removal of the differential (see Section 15).

3   Refer to Section 11 and remove the driveaxles.

4   Use a screwdriver or prybar to carefully pry the oil seal out of the differential bore **(see illustrations)**.

5   If the oil seal cannot be removed with a screwdriver or prybar, a special oil seal removal tool (available at auto parts stores) will be required.

6   Using a large section of pipe or a large deep socket (as large as the outside diameter of the seal) as a drift, install the new oil seal **(see illustration)**. Drive it into the bore squarely and make sure it's completely seated. Coat the seal lip with transmission lubricant.

7   Install the driveaxle(s). Be careful not to damage the lip of the new seal.

13.23 After the old grease has been rinsed away and the solvent has been blown out with compressed air, rotate the outer joint assembly through its full range of motion and inspect the bearing surfaces for wear and damage - If any of the ball bearings, the race or the cage look damaged, replace the driveaxle and outer joint assembly

14.4a Insert the tip of a large screwdriver or prybar behind the driveaxle oil seal and very carefully pry it out

14.4b A special oil seal removal tool is necessary for replacing the pinion seal

14.6 Using a large socket or a section of pipe, drive the new seal squarely into the bore

15.6 Remove the bolt (arrow) and lift the speed sensor out of the differential

15.7 Disconnect the differential oil cooler lines (arrows)

15   Differential (Legend models) - removal and installation

Refer to illustrations 15.6, 15.7, 15.8a, 15,8b, 15.9, 15.10a, 15.10b, 15.10c and 15.11

1   Raise the vehicle and support it securely on jackstands.

2   Drain the engine coolant (see Chapter 1).
3   Drain the differential lubricant (see Chapter 1).
4   Remove the driveaxles and intermediate shaft (see Section 11 and Section 12).
5   Remove the steering gear cover plate (see Chapter 10).
6   Detach the vehicle speed sensor, leav-

ing the hoses connected (see illustration).
7   Disconnect the differential oil cooler lines (see illustration).
8   Remove the differential extension shaft cover and sealing plug (see illustrations).
9   Place the transmission in first gear (manual) or Park (automatic). Use a special puller tool to disconnect the extension shaft

8

15.8a Use a large screwdriver to pry out the differential extension shaft cover

15.8b Remove the sealing plug (arrow) with a ratchet and an extension

from the differential. Screw the tool into the threads in the end of the extension shaft, then pry the tool and shaft out far enough to release set ring in the end of the shaft so the differential can be separated from the transmission **(see illustration)**. If a factory tool isn't available, a long 8 mm bolt over a large washer can be threaded into the end of the extension shaft and used to pull the shaft out.

10   Remove the mounting bolts and shim, detach the differential and lower it from the vehicle **(see illustrations)**.

11   Installation is the reverse of removal, taking care on the following points. Before installing the set ring in the end of the extension shaft, lubricate the splines with high temperature grease. Prior to installing the sealing bolt, pack the area around the end of the extension shaft with this grease as well. If the special tool for installing the extension shaft isn't available, an 8 mm bolt, socket and a long extension can be used. Thread the bolt into the end of the shaft, install the

15.9 Screw the tool into the end of the extension shaft, then pry the tool and extension shaft back far enough to detach the set ring in the end of the shaft, allowing the differential to be removed from the transmission

socket and the extension onto the bolt. Tap on the end of the extension until the extension shaft set ring seats in the secondary gear. Finally, when installing the differential, be sure to reinstall the upper and lower differential mounting bolts loosely, place the shim

in the same position it was removed **(see illustration)**, then install and tighten the shim mounting bolt. Tighten the remaining bolts the torque listed in this Chapter's Specifications.

15.10a Remove the bolts (arrows) and detach the brace to provide access to the differential bolts

15.10b Differential upper bolt locations (arrows)

15.10c Remove the bolt and shim (A), noting the direction in which the shim is mounted, then remove the remaining two lower differential mounting bolts (B)

15.11 Insert the differential shim into position through the access hole (arrow) between the lower support brace and the steering gear, then install the shim retaining bolt

Chapter 9 Brakes

Contents

Specifications

General

Brake pedal height (with carpet removed) and freeplay
  Integra
    Pedal height
      Manual transaxle .... 6-1/8 inches
      Automatic transaxle .... 6-5/16 inches
    Freeplay .... 1/16 to 3/16 inch
  Legend
    Pedal height .... 8-13/32 inches
    Freeplay .... 1/16 to 3/16 inch
Parking brake lever travel
  Integra .... 6 to 10 clicks
  Legend .... 6 to 8 clicks
Power brake booster pushrod-to-master cylinder piston clearance
(with a vacuum of 20 in-Hg applied to booster)
  Integra .... 0.0 to 0.016 inch
  Legend .... 0.0 to 0.010 inch

Disc brakes

Brake pad minimum thickness .... See Chapter 1
Disc minimum thickness .... Refer to minimum thickness cast into disc
Thickness variation (parallelism) .... No more than 0.0006 inch
Runout limit .... 0.004 inch

Torque specifications

Ft-lbs (unless otherwise indicated)

General

Brake hose-to-caliper banjo bolt (front or rear) 25
Master cylinder mounting nuts .... 132 in-lbs
Strut brace mounting nuts 16
Brake booster mounting nuts .... 108 in-lbs
Wheel sensor mounting bolts .... 88 in-lbs

9

Torque specifications

Ft-lbs (unless otherwise indicated)

Front disc brake

Caliper mounting bolts
    Integra models 24
    Legend models 36
Caliper mounting bracket bolts
    Integra 56
    Legend 80

Rear disc brake

Caliper mounting bolts 17
Caliper mounting bracket bolts 28

---

1   General information

Refer to illustrations 1.1a and 1.1b

General

All vehicles covered by this manual are equipped with hydraulically operated, power-assisted brake systems. The brake systems are on all four wheels are disc type **(see illustrations)**.

All brakes are self-adjusting because disc brakes automatically compensate for pad wear.

The hydraulic system is a split design, meaning there are two separate circuits that control the brakes. If one circuit fails, the other circuit will remain functional and a warning indicator will light up on the dashboard when a substantial amount of brake fluid is lost, showing that a failure has occurred.

Master cylinder

The master cylinder is attached to the power brake booster, which is mounted on the left (driver's) side of the firewall. To locate the master cylinder, look for the large fluid reservoir on top. The fluid reservoir is a removable plastic cup, secured to the master cylinder by a clamp.

The master cylinder is designed for the "split system" mentioned earlier and has separate piston assemblies for each circuit.

Proportioning valve

The proportioning valve assembly is located on the firewall. On vehicles equipped with the Anti-lock Brake System (ABS), it's an integral part of the modulator/solenoid unit, which is located on the right (passenger's) side of the engine compartment.

The proportioning valve regulates the hydraulic pressure to the rear brakes during heavy braking to eliminate rear wheel lock-up. Under normal braking conditions, it allows full pressure to the rear brake system until a predetermined pedal pressure is reached. Above that point, the pressure to the rear brakes is limited.

The proportioning valve is not service-able - if a problem develops with the valve, it must be replaced as an assembly.

Power brake booster

The power brake booster, which uses engine manifold vacuum and atmospheric pressure to provide assistance to the hydraulically operated brakes, is mounted on the firewall in the engine compartment.

Parking brake

A parking brake lever inside the vehicle operates a rod attached to a pair of rear cables, each of which is connected to its respective rear brake. When the parking brake lever is pulled up on Integra models, the rear cables pull on levers that are attached to screw-type actuators in the caliper housings, which apply force to the caliper pistons, clamping the brake pads against the brake disc. When the parking brake cable is pulled up on Legend models, each rear cable pulls on a lever attached to the brake shoe assembly, causing the shoes to expand inside drum-type parking brake in the rear disc.

1.1a Typical front disc brake component layout

1   *Caliper*   2   *Brake hose*   3   *Disc*

1.1b Typical rear disc brake component layout

1 Brake hose	2 Caliper	3 Disc

Precautions

There are some general cautions and warnings involving the brake system on these vehicles:

a) *Use only brake fluid conforming to DOT 3 specifications.*

b) *The brake pads and linings may contain asbestos fibers, which are hazardous to your health if inhaled. Whenever you work on brake system components, clean all parts with brake system cleaner. Do not allow the fine dust to become airborne, and wear a filter/mask over your nose and mouth when cleaning or servicing brakes.*

c) *Safety should be paramount whenever any servicing of the brake components is performed. Do not use parts or fasteners, which are not in perfect condition, and be sure that all clearances and torque specifications are adhered to. If you are at all unsure about a certain procedure, seek professional advice. Upon completion of any brake system work, test the brakes carefully in a controlled area before putting the vehicle into normal service.*

d) *If a problem is suspected in the brake system, don't drive the vehicle until it's fixed.*

2.2a The ABS control unit (arrow) is located under a panel next to the right rear seat on two-door Integra models and in the trunk on four-door Integra models; on Legend models it's mounted behind the right rear seat back

2   Anti-lock Brake System (ABS) - general information and trouble codes

Refer to illustrations 2.2a, 2.2b, 2.2c, 2.5a and 2.5b

General information

1   In a conventional braking system, if you press the brake pedal too hard, the wheels can "lock up" (stop turning) and the vehicle can go into a skid. If the wheels lock up, you can lose control of the vehicle. The Anti-lock Brake System (ABS) prevents the wheels from locking up by modulating (pulsing on and off) the pressure of the brake fluid at each caliper.

2   The Anti-lock Brake System has two basic subsystems: One is an electrical system and the other is hydraulic. The electrical half has four "gear pulsers," four wheel sensors, a computer and an electrical circuit connecting all the components **(see illustrations)**. The hydraulic part of the system consists of a controller, solenoid/modulator, the disc brake calipers and the hydraulic fluid lines between the solenoid/modulator and the calipers **(see illustration)**.

3   In principle, the system is pretty simple: Each wheel has a wheel sensor monitoring a gear pulser (a ring with evenly-spaced raised ridges cast into its circumference). The wheel sensor "counts" the ridges of the gear pulser as they pass by, converts this information into an electrical output and transmits it back to the computer. The computer constantly "samples" the voltage inputs from all four wheel sensors and compares them to each other. As long as the gear pulsers at all four wheels are rotating at the same speed, the Anti-lock Brake System is inactive. But when a wheel locks up, the voltage signal from that wheel sensor deviates from the signals coming from the other wheels. So the computer "knows" the wheel is locking up. It sends an

2.2b The wheel speed sensors and toothed rings (arrows) are mounted in close proximity to one another

2.2c The hydraulic control/solenoid unit is mounted in the right rear corner of the engine compartment

9

TROUBLE CODE		MALFUNCTIONING COMPONENT/ SYSTEM	WHEELS-AFFECTED				OTHER COMPONENTS POSSIBLY INVOLVED
MAIN CODE	SUB-CODE		FRONT RIGHT	FRONT LEFT	REAR RIGHT	REAR LEFT	
1	–	Hydraulic controlled components	–	–	–	–	ABS main relay fuse **Motor relay (ON)** Pressure switch (OFF) Accumulator **Modulator**
2	–	Parking brake switch-related problem	–	–	–	–	Brake fluid level switch [BRAKE] light
3	1	Pulser(s)	O				
	2			O			
	4				O	O	
4	1	Speed sensor	O				
	2			O			
	4				O		
	8					O	
5	–	Speed sensor(s) **Rear wheel lock**			O	O	
	4				O		Modulator **Rear brake drag**
	8					O	
6	–	Fail-safe relay (Open, short)		O	O		
	1			O			
	4				O		
7	1	Solenoid related problem (Open)	O				ABS B1 fuse
	2			O			Front fail-safe relay
	4				O	O	Rear fail-safe relay

2118-9-2.5 HAYNES

2.5a Integra ABS trouble codes

electrical signal to the solenoid/modulator assembly, which releases the brake fluid pressure to the brake caliper at that wheel. As soon as the wheel unlocks and resumes turning at the same rate of speed as the other wheels, its wheel sensor voltage output once again matches the output of the other wheels and the computer deactivates the signal to the solenoid/modulator.

4   In reality, the Anti-lock Brake System is far more complex than it sounds, so we don't recommend that you attempt to service it. If the Anti-lock Brake System on your vehicle develops problems, take it to a dealer service department or other qualified shop.

ABS trouble codes

5   Normally, the ABS indicator light should come on when the engine is started, then go off immediately. Under certain conditions, however, the indicator light may remain on. If this occurs, the ABS computer has stored a diagnostic trouble code because it has detected a problem in the ABS system **(see illustrations)**. You can have the ABS indicator display the diagnostic trouble code as follows:

Integra

6   Remove the ABS control unit and detach the cover for access to the LED light.

7   On four-door models the ABS control unit is located under a cover in the right front corner of the trunk. On two-door models the control unit can be found under a trim panel in the right rear corner of the passenger compartment **(see illustration 2.2a)**.

8   Turn the ignition switch to On, but don't start the engine. After you turn on the ignition, the LED light on the ABS computer will begin displaying any stored diagnostic trouble code(s) by blinking on and off. The sequence begins with a 10-second pause, followed by a series of blinks representing the code, followed by a one-second pause, followed by another series of blinks representing the sub-code (if any), followed by a five-second pause, then the next blinks, another five second pause, the next main code/sub-code combination, etc. The ABS computer can indicate as many as three codes.

Legend

9   Unplug the service check connector from the connector cover located underneath

TROUBLE CODE		MALFUNCTIONING COMPONENT/ SYSTEM	WHEELS-AFFECTED				OTHER COMPONENTS POSSIBLY INVOLVED
MAIN CODE	SUB-CODE		FRONT RIGHT	FRONT LEFT	REAR RIGHT	REAR LEFT	
1	—	Pump motor over-run	—	—	—	—	**Motor fuse, motor relay** Pressure switch
	2	Pump motor circuit problem	—	—	—	—	Motor relay, Unit fuse
	3	High pressure leakage	—	—	—	—	Solenoid
	4	Pressure switch	—	—	—	—	
	8	Accumulator gas leakage	—	—	—	—	
2	1	Parking brake switch-related problem	—	—		—	Brake fluid level switch BRAKE light
3	1	Pulser(s)	○				
	2			○			
	4				○	○	
4	1	Speed sensor	○				
	2			○			
	4				○		
	8					○	
5	—	Speed sensor(s)			○	○	Modulator
	4				○		
	8					○	
6	—	Fail-safe relay (Open, short)	—	—	—	—	Front or rear fail-safe relay
	1		—	—	—	—	Front fail-safe relay
	4		—	—	—	—	Rear fail-safe relay
7	1	Solenoid related problem (Open)	○				ALB 3 or ABS B3 fuse
	2			○			ALB 1 or ABS B1 fuse Front fail-safe relay
	4				○	○	Rear fail-safe relay

2118-9-2.5 HAYNES

2.5b Legend ABS trouble codes

9

the glove box (see Chapter 6).
10 Bridge the two terminals of the service check connector with a jumper wire.
11 Turn the ignition switch to On, but don't start the engine. One second after you turn on the ignition, the ABS computer will begin displaying any stored diagnostic trouble code(s) by blinking the dash-mounted ABS indicator light on and off. The sequence begins with a two-second pause, followed by a series of blinks representing the main code, followed by a one-second pause, followed by another series of blinks representing the sub-code (if

any), followed by a five-second pause, then the next main code/sub-code blinks, another five second pause, the next main code/sub-code combination, etc. The ABS computer can indicate up to three codes.

All models

12 If you miscount, turn the ignition switch to Off, then back to On, to recycle the ABS computer. Record the number of main code and sub-code blinks. Most ABS repairs must be performed by a dealer service department or other qualified automotive repair facility.

Erasing diagnostic codes

13 Diagnostic codes must be cleared from the computer memory after the repairs have been performed.
14 Clear the diagnostic codes by removing the jumper wire from the electrical connector, then remove the 15 amp ABS B2 fuse or ALB B2 fuse (located in the engine compartment fuse block) for at least three seconds. Reinstall the fuse and plug in the service check connector.

3.5 Using a large C-clamp, push the piston back into the caliper - note that one end of the clamp is on the back side of the caliper and the other end (screw end) is pressing on the outer brake pad

3.6a Before removing anything, spray the caliper and brake pads with brake system cleaner to remove the dust produced by brake pad wear - DO NOT blow the dust off with compressed air!

3   Disc brake pads - replacement

Warning: *Disc brake pads must be replaced on both front or both rear wheels at the same time - never replace the pads on only one wheel. Also, the dust created by the brake system may contain asbestos, which is harmful to your health. Never blow it out with compressed air and don't inhale any of it. An approved filtering mask should be worn when working on the brakes. Do not, under any circumstances, use petroleum-based solvents to clean brake parts. Use brake system cleaner only!*

1   Remove the cap from the brake fluid reservoir.
2   Loosen the wheel lug nuts, raise the front or rear of the vehicle and support it securely on jackstands.
3   Remove the wheels. Work on one brake assembly at a time, using the assembled brake for reference if necessary.
4   Inspect the brake disc carefully as out-

lined in Section 5. If machining is necessary, follow the information in that Section to remove the disc, at which time the calipers and pads can be removed as well.

Front pads

Refer to illustrations 3.5 and 3.6a through 3.6m
5   Push the piston back into the bore to provide room for the new brake pads. A C-clamp can be used to accomplish this **(see illustration)**. As the piston is depressed to the bottom of the caliper bore, the fluid in the master cylinder will rise. Make sure it doesn't overflow. If necessary, siphon off some of the fluid.
6   Follow the accompanying illustrations, beginning with **3.6a**, for the actual pad replacement procedure. Be sure to stay in order and read the caption under each illustration. When you have completed the Steps described in the accompanying photos, proceed to Step 14.

3.6b On Integra models, remove the caliper lower mounting bolt (lower arrow; upper arrow points to the banjo fitting for the brake hose, which should not be disconnected unless you are removing the caliper from the vehicle for replacement)

3.6c Swing the caliper up and secure the caliper in this position with a piece of wire (Integra models; on Legend models remove both mounting bolts, detach the caliper and support it with a piece of wire)

3.6d Remove the outer brake pad and shim

- Chapter 9 Brakes

3.6e Remove the inner brake pad and shim(s)

3.6f Remove and inspect the upper and lower pad retainer clips

3.6g The pad retainer clips should fit snugly in the caliper mounting bracket; if they don't, replace them. Apply a thin film of high-temperature grease to the retainer

3.6h Apply anti-squeal compound to the back of the inner pads

3.6i Install the new inner pad and shim(s); make sure the "ears" on the upper and lower ends of the pad are fully engaged with their respective grooves and the pad retainer clips

3.6j Install the new outer pad and shim (if the new pad has no shim, take the old shim off the old pad and install it on the new outer pad)

3.6k Before installing the caliper, remove the caliper pin dust boots and inspect them for tears and cracks; if they're damaged, replace them

3.6l Clean off the caliper pin and coat it with high-temperature grease

3.6m Install the caliper (if the piston hits the inner pad, depress the piston further into the caliper bore with your C-clamp) and mounting bolt(s), tightening the bolt(s) to the torque listed in this Chapter's Specifications

9

3.7a Remove the brake hose retaining bolt (arrow) and detach the brake hose from the bracket

3.7b Remove the two caliper mounting bolts (arrows) . . .

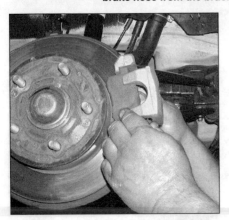

3.7c . . . and lift the caliper from its mounting bracket; hang the caliper out of the way with a piece of wire - don't let it hang by the brake hose

3.7d Remove the inner pad and shim

3.7e Remove the outer pad and shim

Rear pads

Refer to illustrations 3.7a through 3.7g, 3.8, 3.12a and 3.12b

7   Clean the brake assembly **(see illustration 3.6a)**. Follow the accompanying illustrations, beginning with **3.7a**, for the actual pad replacement procedure. Be sure to stay in order and read the caption under each illustration. When you have completed the Steps described in the accompanying photos, proceed to Step 8.

8   Apply a thin coat of disc brake anti-squeal compound, in accordance with the manufacturer's recommendations, on the backing plates of the new pads **(see illustration)**.

9   Install the shims onto their respective pads.

10   Install the pad retainers in the caliper mounting bracket. Lubricate the retainers with a thin film of high-temperature grease.

11   Install the new pads and shims to the caliper mounting bracket.

12   Retract the piston by engaging the tips of a pair of needle-nose pliers with two of the grooves in the face of the piston and turning

3.7f Remove the brake pad retainers from the caliper mount

3.7g Remove the pad spring from the caliper

3.8 Before installing the brake pads, apply a coat of disc brake anti-squeal compound to the backing plates of the pads - follow the manufacturer's instructions on the label

3.12a To provide clearance for the new brake pads, back the piston into the caliper bore by rotating it with a pair of needle-nose pliers

3.12b Make sure the piston is positioned so that one of the notches in the piston face will engage with the tab on the pad backing plate

it clockwise until it bottoms out **(see illustration)**. Now, rotate the piston out until one of its grooves is aligned with the tab on the inner brake pad when you install the caliper **(see illustration)**. You may have to adjust the piston position by turning it back and forth until the tab fits. If the piston dust boot becomes distorted when the piston is turned, turn the piston in the opposite direction to restore the shape of the boot, but make sure the cut-out still lines up.

13   Install the caliper and tighten the mounting bolts to the torque listed in this Chapter's Specifications. Connect the brake hose to the bracket on the knuckle. Proceed to the next step.

Front or rear pads

14   Install the wheel and lug nuts, lower the vehicle and tighten the lug nuts to the torque listed in the Chapter 1 Specifications.
15   Apply and release the brake pedal several times to bring the pads into contact with the brake discs.
16   Check the brake fluid level and add fluid, if necessary (see Chapter 1). Check the operation of the brakes in an isolated area before driving the vehicle in traffic.

4.2a Remove the brake hose banjo bolt (A), then unscrew the caliper mounting bolts (B)

4   Brake caliper - removal and installation

Warning: *Dust created by the brake system may contain asbestos, which is harmful to your health. Never blow it out with compressed air and don't inhale any of it. An approved filtering mask should be worn when working on the brakes. Do not, under any circumstances, use petroleum-based solvents to clean brake parts. Use brake system cleaner only!*
Note: *Always replace the calipers in pairs - never replace just one of them.*

Front brake caliper
Removal
Refer to illustrations 4.2a and 4.2b
1   Loosen - but don't remove - the lug nuts on the front wheels. Raise the front of the vehicle and place it securely on jackstands. Remove the front wheels.
2   Disconnect the brake line from the caliper and plug it to keep contaminants out of the brake system and to prevent losing any more brake fluid than is necessary **(see illustrations)**.
3   Remove the caliper mounting bolts.

4.2b Using a short piece of rubber hose of the appropriate diameter, plug the brake line banjo fitting like this

4   Detach the caliper from its mounting bracket.

Installation
5   Install the caliper by reversing the removal procedure. Remember to replace the sealing washer on either side of the brake line fitting with new ones. Tighten the caliper mounting bolts and the brake hose banjo bolt to the torque listed in this Chapter's Specifications.
6   Bleed the brake system (see Section 8).
7   Install the wheels and lug nuts and lower the vehicle. Tighten the lug nuts to the torque listed in the Chapter 1 Specifications.

Rear brake caliper
Removal
Refer to illustrations 4.9, 4.12a and 4.12b
8   Loosen - but don't remove - the lug nuts on the rear wheels. Raise the rear of the vehicle and place it securely on jackstands. Remove the rear wheels.
9   If you're working on an Integra model, release the parking brake handle and remove the clip from the parking brake cable **(see illustration)** located on the back side of the caliper.
10   Remove the lock pin and clevis pin and

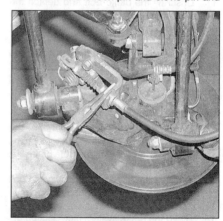

4.9 Remove the clip and separate the parking brake cable from the bracket (Integra models)

 9

4.12a Rear caliper mounting details (Integra)

A   *Brake hose banjo bolt*
B   *Caliper mounting bolts*

4.12b Rear caliper mounting details (Legend)

A   *Brake hose banjo bolt*
B   *Caliper mounting bolts*

5.3 The brake pads on this vehicle were obviously neglected, as they wore down to the rivets; the rivets then cut deep grooves into the disc, and now the disc must be replaced

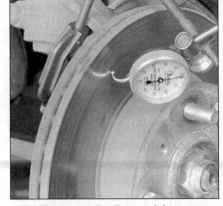

5.4a Make sure the disc retaining screws or lug nuts are tight, then rotate the disc and check the runout with a dial indicator - if the reading exceeds the maximum allowable runout limit, the disc will have to be machined or replaced

5.4b Using a swirling motion, remove the glaze from the disc with emery cloth or sandpaper

separate the parking brake cable from the lever on the caliper (Integra models).

11   Unscrew the banjo bolt and detach the brake line from the caliper. Plug the fitting to prevent fluid loss and contamination **(see illustration 4.2b)**

12   Remove the caliper mounting bolts **(see illustrations)**.

13   Detach the caliper from its mounting bracket.

Installation

14   Install the caliper by reversing the removal procedure. Remember to replace the sealing washer on either side of the brake line fitting with new ones. Tighten the caliper mounting bolts and the brake hose banjo bolt to the torque listed in this Chapter's Specifications.

15   Bleed the brake system (see Section 8).

16   Install the wheels and lug nuts. Lower the vehicle and tighten the lug nuts to the torque listed in the Chapter 1 Specifications.

5   Brake disc - inspection, removal and installation

Inspection

Refer to illustrations 5.3, 5.4a, 5.4b, 5.5a, 5.5b and 5.5c

1   Loosen the wheel lug nuts, raise the vehicle and support it securely on jackstands. Remove the wheel and install the lug nuts with 3 mm thick washers under them to hold the disc in place (if the two disc retaining screws are still in place, this will be unnecessary). If you're checking the rear disc, release the parking brake.

2   Remove the brake caliper (see Section 4). It's not necessary to disconnect the brake hose. After removing the caliper bolts, suspend the caliper out of the way with a piece of wire.

3   Visually inspect the disc surface for scoring or damage **(see illustration)**. Light

scratches and shallow grooves are normal after use and may not always be detrimental to brake operation, but deep scoring (over 0.015 inch) requires refinishing by an automotive machine shop. Be sure to check both sides of the disc.

4   If you've noted pulsation during braking, suspect disc runout. To check disc runout, place a dial indicator at a point about 1/2-inch from the outer edge of the disc **(see illustration)**. Set the indicator to zero and turn the disc. The indicator reading should not exceed the specified allowable runout limit. If it does, have the disc refinished by an automotive machine shop. **Note:** *Professionals recommend that the discs be resurfaced regardless of the dial indicator reading, as this will impart a smooth finish and ensure a perfectly flat surface, eliminating any brake pedal pulsation or other undesirable symptoms related to questionable discs. At the very least, if you elect not to have the discs resurfaced, remove the glazing from the surface with emery cloth or sandpaper using a swirling motion* **(see illustration)**.

5.5a The minimum allowable thickness is stamped into the disc (Integra)

5.5b Legend model minimum allowable thickness marking

5.5c A micrometer is used to measure disc thickness

5.6a Before you can remove the front disc, you'll have to remove these caliper mounting bracket-to-steering knuckle bolts (arrows) and the bracket

5.6b To remove the rear disc, remove the caliper mounting bracket bolts (arrows)

5   It is absolutely critical that the disc not be machined to a thickness less than the minimum allowable thickness. The minimum wear (or discard) thickness is stamped on the disc **(see illustrations)**. The disc thickness can be checked with a micrometer **(see illustration)**.

Removal

Refer to illustrations 5.6a, 5.6b, 5.7a and 5.7b
6   Remove the caliper mounting bracket bolts **(see illustrations)**, and remove the mounting bracket.
7   Remove the lug nuts which were put on to hold the disc in place, or the two disc retaining screws, if present **(see illustration)** and remove the disc from the hub. If the disc is stuck to the hub and won't come off, thread two bolts into the holes provided **(see illustration)** and tighten them. Alternate between the bolts, turning them a couple of turns at a time, until the disc is free.

Installation

8   Place the disc in position over the threaded studs. Install the disc retaining

screws and tighten them securely.
9   Install the caliper mounting bracket, brake pads and caliper over the disc. Tighten the mounting bracket bolts and caliper bolts to the torque listed in this Chapter's Specifications.
10   Install the wheel, then lower the vehicle

to the ground. Depress the brake pedal a few times to bring the brake pads into contact with the disc. Bleeding of the system will not be necessary unless the fluid hose was disconnected from the caliper. Check the operation of the brakes carefully before placing the vehicle into normal service.

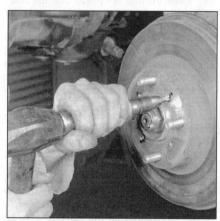

5.7a If the disc retaining screws are stuck, use an impact screwdriver to loosen them

5.7b If the disc is stuck, thread two bolts into the disc and tighten them to force the disc off the hub

9

6.4 Use a flare-nut wrench to unscrew the threaded fittings (1) at the master cylinder (a regular wrench can round off the corners); unplug the electrical connector (2); to detach the master cylinder from the brake booster, remove the two nuts (3) behind the reservoir)

6.8 The best way to bleed air from the master cylinder before installing it on the vehicle is with a pair of bleed tubes that directs brake fluid into the reservoir during bleeding

6   Master cylinder - removal and installation

Note: *If the master cylinder is defective, it must be replaced with a new one - the manufacturer does not recommend rebuilding it.*

Removal

Refer to illustration 6.4

1   The master cylinder is located in the engine compartment, mounted to the power brake booster.

2   Remove as much fluid as you can from the reservoir with a syringe, such as an old poultry baster. **Warning:** *If a baster is used, never again use it for the preparation of food.*

3   Place rags under the fluid fittings and prepare caps or plastic bags to cover the ends of the lines once they are disconnected. **Caution:** *Brake fluid will damage paint. Cover all painted surfaces and be careful not to spill fluid during this procedure.*

4   Loosen the fittings at the ends of the brake lines where they enter the master cylinder **(see illustration)**. To prevent rounding off the corners on these nuts, the use of a flare-nut wrench, which wraps around the nut, is preferred. Pull the brake lines slightly away from the master cylinder and plug the ends to prevent contamination.

5   Remove the strut brace from the engine compartment (if equipped).

6   Disconnect the electrical connector at the brake fluid level switch on the master cylinder, then remove the nuts attaching the master cylinder to the power booster **(see illustration 6.4)**. Pull the master cylinder off the studs and out of the engine compartment. Again, be careful not to spill the fluid as this is done.

Installation

Refer to illustration 6.8

7   Bench bleed the new master cylinder before installing it. Because it will be necessary to apply pressure to the master cylinder piston and, at the same time, control flow from the brake line outlets, it is recommended that the master cylinder be mounted in a vise, with the jaws of the vise clamping on the mounting flange.

8   Attach a pair of master cylinder bleeder tubes to the outlet ports of the master cylinder **(see illustration)**.

9   Fill the reservoir with brake fluid of the recommended type (see Chapter 1).

10   Slowly push the pistons into the master cylinder (a large Phillips screwdriver can be used for this) - air will be expelled from the pressure chambers and into the reservoir. Because the tubes are submerged in fluid, air can't be drawn back into the master cylinder when you release the pistons.

11   Repeat the procedure until no more air bubbles are present.

12   Remove the bleed tubes, one at a time, and install plugs in the open ports to prevent fluid leakage and air from entering. Install the reservoir cover.

13   Install the master cylinder over the studs on the power brake booster and tighten the attaching nuts only finger tight at this time.

14   Thread the brake line fittings into the master cylinder. Since the master cylinder is still a bit loose, it can be moved slightly in order for the fittings to thread in easily. Do not strip the threads as the fittings are tightened.

15   Fully tighten the mounting nuts, then the brake line fittings.

16   Install the strut brace and tighten the nuts to the torque listed in this Chapter's Specifications.

17   Fill the master cylinder reservoir with fluid, then bleed the master cylinder and the brake system as described in Section 8. To bleed the cylinder on the vehicle, have an assistant depress the brake pedal slowly and hold the pedal to the floor. Loosen the fitting nut to allow air and fluid to escape. Repeat this procedure on both fittings until the fluid is clear of air bubbles. **Caution:** *Have plenty of rags on hand to catch the fluid - brake fluid will ruin painted surfaces.*

18   Test the operation of the brake system carefully before placing the vehicle into normal service. **Warning:** *Do not operate the vehicle if you are in doubt about the effectiveness of the brake system.*

7   Brake hoses and lines - inspection and replacement

Refer to illustrations 7.4a, 7.4b and 7.5

1   About every six months the flexible hoses which connect the steel brake lines with the rear brakes and front calipers should be inspected for cracks, chafing of the outer cover, leaks, blisters, and other damage.

2   Replacement steel and flexible brake lines are commonly available from dealer parts departments and auto parts stores. Do not, under any circumstances, use anything other than genuine steel brake lines or approved flexible brake hoses as replacement items.

3   When installing the brake line, leave at least 3/4-inch clearance between the line and any moving or vibrating parts.

4   To disconnect a hose and line, use a flare-nut wrench **(see illustration)**. Then remove the clip and slide the hose out of the bracket **(see illustration)**.

5   Always install new washers on banjo fitting brake lines **(see illustration)**.

6   When disconnecting two hoses, use normal wrenches on the hose fittings. When connecting two hoses, make sure they are not twisted or strained.

7   Steel brake lines are usually retained along their span with clips. Always remove these clips completely before removing a rigid brake line. Always reinstall these clips, or new ones if the old ones are damaged,

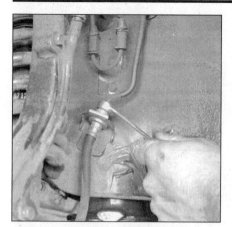

7.4a Use a flare-nut wrench to loosen the brake line-to-hose fitting . . .

7.4b . . . then remove the clip and slide the hose out of the bracket

7.5 Always install new sealing washers on either side of the brake line banjo fitting

when replacing a brake line, as they provide support and keep the lines from vibrating, which can eventually break them.

8   When replacing brake lines, be sure to use the correct parts. NEVER use copper tubing! Purchase steel brake lines from a dealer or auto parts store.

9   When installing a steel line, make sure it's securely supported in the brackets and has plenty of clearance between moving or hot components.

10   After installation, check the fluid level in the master cylinder and add fluid as necessary. Bleed the brake system as described in Section 8 and test the brakes carefully before driving the vehicle in traffic. **Warning:** *Do not operate the vehicle if you are in doubt about the effectiveness of the brake system.*

8   Brake hydraulic system - bleeding

Refer to illustration 8.8

Warning: *Wear eye protection when bleeding the brake system. If the fluid comes in contact with your eyes, immediately rinse them with water and seek medical attention.*

1   Bleeding the hydraulic system is necessary to remove any air that manages to find its way into the system when it's been opened during removal and installation of a hose, line, caliper or master cylinder. It will probably be necessary to bleed the system at all four brakes if air has entered the system due to low fluid level, or if the brake lines have been disconnected at the master cylinder.

2   If a brake line was disconnected only at a wheel, then only that caliper or wheel cylinder must be bled.

3   If a brake line is disconnected at a fitting located between the master cylinder and any of the brakes, that part of the system served by the disconnected line must be bled.

4   Remove any residual vacuum from the power brake booster by applying the brake several times with the engine off.

5   Remove the master cylinder reservoir

cover and fill the reservoir with brake fluid. Reinstall the cover. **Note:** *Check the fluid level often during the bleeding operation and add fluid as necessary to prevent the fluid level from falling low enough to allow air bubbles into the master cylinder.*

6   Have an assistant on hand, as well as a supply of new brake fluid, a clear container partially filled with clean brake fluid, a length of clear tubing to fit over the bleed screw and a wrench to open and close the bleed screw.

7   Beginning at the right rear wheel, loosen the bleed screw slightly, then tighten it to a point where it is snug but can still be loosened quickly and easily.

8   Place one end of the tubing over the bleed screw and submerge the other end in brake fluid in the container **(see illustration)**.

9   Have the assistant depress the brake pedal slowly, then hold the pedal firmly depressed.

10   While the pedal is held depressed, open the bleed screw just enough to allow a flow of fluid to leave the screw. Watch for air bubbles to exit the submerged end of the tube. When

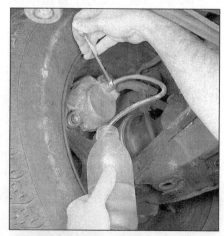

8.8 When bleeding the brakes, a hose is connected to the bleed screw at the caliper and then submerged in brake fluid - air will be seen as bubbles in the tube and container (all air must be expelled before moving to the next wheel)

the fluid flow slows after a couple of seconds, close the screw and have your assistant release the pedal.

11   Repeat Steps 9 and 10 until no more air is seen leaving the tube, then tighten the bleed screw and proceed to the left front wheel, the left rear wheel and the right front wheel, in that order, and perform the same procedure. Be sure to check the fluid in the master cylinder reservoir frequently.

12   Never use old brake fluid. It contains moisture which can boil during (or after) heavy braking, rendering the brakes inoperative.

13   Refill the master cylinder with fluid at the end of the operation.

14   Check the operation of the brakes. The pedal should feel solid when depressed, with no sponginess. If necessary, repeat the entire process. **Warning:** *Do not operate the vehicle if you are in doubt about the effectiveness of the brake system.*

9   Power brake booster - check, removal and installation

Operating check

1   Depress the brake pedal several times with the engine off and make sure there is no change in the pedal reserve distance.

2   Depress the pedal and start the engine. If the pedal goes down slightly, operation is normal.

Airtightness check

3   Start the engine and turn it off after one or two minutes. Depress the brake pedal several times slowly. If the pedal goes down farther the first time but gradually rises after the second or third depression, the booster is airtight.

4   Depress the brake pedal while the engine is running, then stop the engine with the pedal depressed. If there is no change in the pedal reserve travel after holding the pedal for 30 seconds, the booster is airtight.

9

Removal

Refer to illustration 9.10

5   Power brake booster units should not be disassembled. They require special tools not normally found in most automotive repair stations or shops. They are fairly complex and because of their critical relationship to brake performance it is best to replace a defective booster unit with a new or rebuilt one.

6   To remove the booster, first remove the brake master cylinder as described in Section 6.

7   Disconnect the hose leading from the engine to the booster. Be careful not to damage the hose when removing it from the booster fitting.

8   Locate the pushrod clevis pin connecting the booster to the brake pedal.

9   Remove the cotter pin with pliers and pull out the clevis pin.

10   Remove the four nuts and washers **(see illustration)** holding the brake booster to the firewall. You may need a light to see them, because they're up under the dash area.

11   Slide the booster straight out from the firewall until the studs clear the holes and pull the booster from the engine compartment.

Installation

Refer to illustrations 9.13a 9.13b, 9.13c, 9.13d, 9.14a and 9.14b

12   Installation procedures are basically the reverse of those for removal. Tighten the booster mounting nuts to the torque listed in this Chapter's Specifications. Also, be sure to use a new cotter pin on the clevis pin.

13   If a new power brake booster unit is being installed, check the pushrod clearance **(see illustration)** as follows:

   a) *Using a hand-held vacuum pump, apply a vacuum of 20 in-Hg to the booster. Measure the distance that the pushrod protrudes from the master cylinder mounting surface on the front of the power brake booster, including the gasket (if used). Write down this measurement* **(see illustration)**. *This is "dimension A."*

9.10 To remove the power brake booster, remove the cotter pin and clevis pin that connect the booster pushrod to the brake pedal, then remove the four mounting nuts (arrows)

   b) *Measure the distance from the mounting flange to the end of the master cylinder* **(see illustration)**. *Write down this measurement. This is "dimension B."*

   c) *Measure the distance from the end of the master cylinder to the bottom of the pocket in the piston* **(see illustration)**. *Write down this measurement. This is "dimension C."*

   d) *Subtract measurement B from measurement C, then subtract measurement A from the difference between B and C. This the pushrod clearance.*

   e) *Compare your calculated pushrod clearance to the pushrod clearance listed in this Chapter's Specifications. If necessary, adjust the pushrod length to achieve the correct clearance (see the next Step).*

14   If the clearance is more or less than specified:

    Integra models - loosen the star locknut and turn the adjuster on the booster pushrod until the clearance is as listed in this Chapter's Specifications **(see illustration)**. After adjustment, tighten the

9.13a There should be no (or very little) clearance between the booster pushrod and the master cylinder piston, but no interference either – if there is interference between the two, the brakes may drag; if there is clearance, there will be excessive brake pedal travel

9.13b Measure the distance that the pushrod protrudes from the brake booster at the master cylinder mounting surface (including the gasket, if equipped)

9.13c Measure the distance from the mounting flange to the end of the master cylinder

9.13d Measure the distance from the piston pocket to the end of the master cylinder

PUSHROD

ADJUSTER

STAR LOCKNUT

PUSHROD LOCKNUT

9.14a To adjust the length of the booster pushrod on an Integra, loosen the star locknut and turn the adjuster in or out, as necessary, to achieve the desired setting

9.14b To adjust the length of the booster pushrod on a Legend, hold the serrated portion of the rod with a pair of pliers and turn the adjusting screw in or out, as necessary, to achieve the desired setting

10.3a Parking brake details (Legend) - left side shown

1 *Return spring*
2 *Return spring*
3 *Parking brake shoe*
4 *Rod spring*
5 *Hold-down clip and pin*
6 *Return spring*
7 *Adjuster assembly*
8 *Parking brake shoe*
9 *Hold-down clip and pin*
10 *Connecting rod*

10.3b Before removing anything, clean the brake assembly with brake cleaner and allow it to dry - position a drain pan under the brake assembly to catch the residue - DO NOT USE COMPRESSED AIR TO BLOW BRAKE DUST OFF THE PARTS!

locknut. Recheck the clearance. Repeat this step as often as necessary until the clearance is correct.

Legend models - turn the adjusting screw on the end of the pushrod until the clearance is as listed in this Chapter's Specifications **(see illustration)**.

15   After the final installation of the master cylinder and brake hoses and lines, bleed the brakes as described in Section 8.

10 Parking brake shoes (Legend models) - replacement

Refer to illustrations 10.3a through 10.3n

1   Release the parking brake. Loosen the rear wheel lug nuts. Raise the vehicle and place it securely on jackstands. Remove the wheels.

2   Remove the brake calipers (see Section 4), the brake discs (see Section 5) and

the rear hubs (see Chapter 10).

3   Clean the parking brake assembly with brake system cleaner before beginning work. Follow **illustrations 10.3a through 10.3n** for the inspection and replacement of the parking brake shoes. Be sure to stay in order and read the caption under each illustration.

10.3c Remove the hold-down clip from each shoe

10.3d Lift the brake shoe assembly off the backing plate

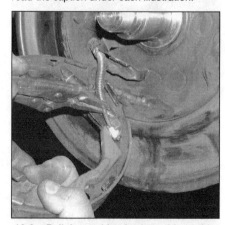

10.3e Pull the parking brake cable spring back and unhook the cable from the lever

9

10.3f Detach the return springs and separate the shoes

10.3g Pry open the parking brake lever retaining clip and separate the lever from the shoe; be careful not to lose the wave washer that is under the clip

10.3h Put the new shoe on the lever, place the wave washer over the pin, then install the retaining clip; crimp the ends of the clip together with a pair of needle-nose pliers

10.3i Clean the adjuster bolt and clevis, then lubricate the threads and ends with high-temperature grease

10.3j Install the connecting rod and rod spring

10.3k Install the adjuster and lower return spring to the bottom of the shoe assembly

4 Clean the brake disc/parking brake drum and check for score marks, deep grooves, hard spots (which will appear as small, discolored areas) and cracks. If the disc/drum is worn, scored or out-of-round, it can be resurfaced by an automotive machine shop. If it's worn excessively, however, it will have to be replaced.

5 Repeat this procedure for the other rear brake assembly.

6 Install the brake discs (see Section 5), brake calipers (see Section 4) and the rear hubs (see Chapter 10).

7 Install the rear wheels and lug nuts, lower the vehicle and tighten the lug nuts to the torque listed in the Chapter 1 Specifications.

8 Refer to Section 11 for adjustment of the parking brake shoes.

10.3l Compress the parking brake cable spring, hold it in position and connect the cable end to the parking brake lever

10.3m Place the shoes in position and connect the upper return springs

10.3n Install the shoe hold-down clips

11.3 On Integra models, make sure the rear brake caliper lever contacts the pin (arrow)

11.4 Location of the parking brake cable adjusting nut (arrow) - console removed for clarity

11   Parking brake - adjustment

Refer to illustrations 11.3, 11.4 and 11.6

1   Remove the rear console cover.

2   Block the front wheels, raise the rear of the vehicle and support it securely on jackstands. Apply the parking brake lever one click.

3   On Integra models, check that the rear caliper lever and pin are in contact **(see illustration)**.

4   Turn the adjusting nut on the equalizer clockwise while rotating the rear wheels **(see illustration)**. Stop turning the nut when the brakes just start to drag on the rear wheels.

5   Release the parking brake lever and check to see that the brakes don't drag when the rear wheels are turned. When properly adjusted, the travel on the parking brake lever should be as listed in this Chapter's Specifications.

6   On Legend models needing major adjustment, remove the plug, insert a flat-bladed screwdriver into the hub and turn the adjuster star wheel until the specified parking brake lever travel is achieved **(see illustration)**. Release the parking brake and check to be sure the brakes don't drag as the wheels are turned.

7   Lower the vehicle and reinstall the console cover.

12   Parking brake cable(s) - replacement

Refer to illustration 12.6

1   Block the front wheels and loosen the rear wheel lug nuts. Raise the rear of the vehicle and support it securely on jackstands.

2   On Legend models, remove the caliper(s) and brake disc(s) (see Sections 4 and 5).

3   Following the procedure in the previous Section, loosen the cable adjusting nut. Unhook the cable from the equalizer. Remove the cable clamps from the cable housing.

4   On Legend models, remove the parking brake shoes (see Section 10) and disconnect the cable end from the lever on the trailing shoe. Depress the tangs on the cable housing retainer and pass the cable through the backing plate using needle-nose pliers or a 12 mm off-set wrench (this compresses all the tangs simultaneously). **Note:** *If you do not have this wrench, you can also use a small screw-type hose clamp. Tighten the clamp around the tangs, start the cable through the hole and remove the hose clamp.*

5   On Integra models, remove the clip and clevis to disconnect the cable end from the actuator lever on the caliper, then remove the spring clip to free the cable housing from the support bracket.

6   Unbolt the cable housing clamps from the underbody, noting how the cable is routed, then remove the cable from the vehicle. It may be necessary to remove the exhaust pipe heat shield bolts at the rear to allow cable removal.

7   If both cables are to be removed, repeat the above steps to remove the remaining cable.

8   Installation is the reverse of the removal procedure. After the cable(s) are installed, be sure to adjust them according to the procedure described in Section 11.

11.6 On Legend models, remove the plug, insert a flat-bladed screwdriver and turn the star wheel to adjust the parking brake shoes

12.6 When removing a cable, unscrew the clamp bolts (arrows) and lift off the clamps

9

13.3 Location of the brake light switch (arrow)

13.5 Brake light switch terminal guide

13 Brake light switch - check, replacement and adjustment

Check

Refer to illustrations 13.3 and 13.5

1   To check the brake light switch, push on the brake pedal and verify that the brake lights come on as soon as the pedal is moved off its stop.

2   If they don't, check the brake light fuse (see Chapter 12 or check your owner's manual for fuse locations). Also check the brake light bulbs in both tail light assemblies (don't forget to check the high-mount brake light).

3   Locate the brake light switch at the top of the brake pedal **(see illustration)**.

4   Unplug the switch connector.

5   Check for continuity across switch terminals B and C with an ohmmeter **(see illustration)**. When the brake pedal is depressed, there should be continuity; when it's released, there should be no continuity.

6   On models with cruise control, check for continuity across switch terminals A and D with an ohmmeter. When the brake pedal is depressed, there should be no continuity; when it's released, there should be continuity. If the switch doesn't operate as described, replace it.

Replacement

7   Disconnect the electrical connector from the switch, if you haven't already done so.

8   Remove the locknut on the pedal side of the switch and unscrew the switch from the bracket.

9   Installation of the brake light switch is the reverse of the removal procedure.

Adjustment

10   Loosen the brake light switch locknut and back off the brake light switch until it's not touching the brake pedal.

11   Loosen the master cylinder pushrod locknut and screw the pushrod in or out with pliers until the pedal height from the floor is correct (as listed in this Chapter's Specifications). **Note:** *Measure from the top face of the pedal pad to the floor (not the carpet).*

12   Tighten the locknut securely.

14.2 Use an ohmmeter to check the brake fluid level switch with the float in the UP position (there should be no continuity)

13   Screw in the brake light switch until its plunger is fully depressed (threaded end touching the pad on the pedal arm), then back off the switch 1/2-turn and tighten the locknut securely.

14   Depress the pedal with your hand and measure the pedal freeplay. It should be within the dimensions listed in this Chapter's Specifications. Make sure the brake lights operate when the pedal is depressed and go off when the pedal is released.

14 Brake fluid level switch - check and replacement

Check

Refer to illustration 14.2 and 14.3

1   To check the brake fluid level switch, disconnect the electrical connector and remove the cap from the brake fluid reservoir on top of the master cylinder.

2   Check the switch continuity with the float in the UP position **(see illustration)**. There should be no continuity.

3   Check the switch continuity with the float in the DOWN position **(see illustration)**. There should be continuity.

4   If the switch doesn't operate as described, replace it.

Replacement

5   Disconnect the electrical connector from

14.3 The ohmmeter will indicate continuity when the float is at the bottom of its travel

the switch, if you haven't already done so.

6   Remove the cap from the brake fluid reservoir. Replace the cap as a complete unit.

7   Installation of the brake fluid level switch and cap is the reverse of the removal procedure.

15 Traction Control System (Legend models) - general information

The Traction Control System (TCS) limits wheel slip during acceleration by cutting fuel to certain cylinders, by retarding the ignition, by upshifting the transmission, or by some combination of the three. The TCS control unit monitors vehicle speed, direction and wheel speed through the ABS wheel sensors, steering angle sensor and lateral acceleration sensor. When one or more wheels begins to spin faster than the others, the TCS control unit calculates the reduction in torque needed to stop wheelspin and restore traction. Depending on the torque reduction necessary, the calculated torque reduction is some combination of fuel cutoff, spark retard, and/or upshifting the transmission. This recommendation is relayed from the TCS control unit to the Engine Control Module (ECM), which manipulates fuel cutoff and spark retard to produce the requisite torque. If the wheel strip spins, the ECM requests an upshift to the next higher gear.

Chapter 10
Suspension and steering systems

Contents

Specifications

General

Power steering fluid type	See Chapter 1

Torque specifications

Ft-lbs (unless otherwise indicated)

Front suspension

Shock absorber	
Shock absorber-to-body mounting nuts	
Integra	
1990 and 1991	29
1992 and 1993	36
Legend	28
Shock absorber damper rod upper nut	22
Damper fork	
Pinch bolt	
Integra	32
Legend	37
Fork-to-lower arm through-bolt nut	
Integra	47
Legend	51
Upper control arm	
Anchor bolt nuts	47
Pivot bolt nuts	22
Lower control arm	
Integra (pivot bolt)	43
Legend	
Front pivot nut	76
Rear pivot flange nut	90
Radius rod (Integra)	
Nut	32
Bolts	76
Stabilizer bar	
Link nuts	
Integra (upper and lower)	16
Legend	
Upper	40
Lower	28
Bushing clamp nuts/bolts	16
Upper balljoint nut	29 to 35
Lower balljoint nut	
Integra	36 to 43
Legend	51 to 58

10

Torque specifications

Ft-lbs (unless otherwise indicated)

Rear suspension

Integra

Compensator arm	
Compensator arm-to-body pivot bolt	29
Compensator arm-to-trailing arm bolt	29
Hub-to-spindle nut	134
Lower arm	
Lower arm-to-body pivot bolt	40
Lower arm-to-trailing arm bolt	40
Shock absorber	
Damper rod nut	22
Shock-to-lower arm bolt	40
Shock upper mounting nuts	
1990 and 1991	29
1992 and 1993	36
Trailing arm bushing bracket-to-body bolts	47
Upper arm	
Bushing bracket-to-body bolts	29
Upper arm-to-trailing arm bolt	40
Stabilizer bar	
Upper link bolt	16
Lower link nut	29
Bushing clamp nuts	16

Legend

Hub-to-spindle nut	206
Lower arm	
Front lower arm-to-body pivot bolt	76
Front lower arm-to-radius rod nut	61
Front lower arm to knuckle nut	36 to 43
Rear lower arm-to-body bolt	40
Rear lower arm-to-knuckle nut	47
Shock absorber	
Damper rod nut	22
Shock-to-lower arm bolt	76
Shock upper mounting nuts	28
Radius rod-to-body bolts	76
Upper arm-to-body bolts	36
Upper arm-to-knuckle nut	36 to 43
Stabilizer bar	
Link bolts	
Upper	22
Lower	16
Bushing clamp nuts	16

Steering system

Integra

Steering wheel nut	36
Steering gear mounting bolts	
Left (driver's side)	32
Right (passenger's) side	29
Gearbox guard	72 in-lbs
Tie-rod end-to-steering knuckle nut	32
Intermediate shaft pinch-bolt	16
Center beam bolts	33

Legend

Steering wheel nut	36
Airbag module Torx bolts	84 in-lbs
Steering gear mounting bolts	
Clamp bolts	28
Mounting bolts	43
Splash guard bolts	28
Tie-rod end-to-steering knuckle nut	36 to 43
Intermediate shaft pinch-bolt	16

1.1a Front suspension and steering components (Integra models)

1	Steering gear	4	Shock absorber/coil spring assembly	6	Tie-rod end
2	Lower control arm	5	Steering knuckle	7	Stabilizer bar
3	Damper fork				

1 General information

Refer to illustrations 1.1a, 1.1b, 1.2a and 1.2b

The front suspension **(see illustrations)** is a fully independent design with upper and lower control arms, shock absorber/coil spring assemblies and a stabilizer bar.

The rear suspension on Integra models is composed of trailing arms, upper and lower control arms, shock absorber/coil spring units and a stabilizer bar. The rear sus-pension on Legend models uses radius rods, two lower control arms per side, one upper control arm per side, knuckle/hub assem-blies, shock absorber/coil spring units and a stabilizer bar **(see illustrations)**.

All models use power-assisted rack-

1.1b Front suspension and steering components (Legend models)

1 Shock absorber/coil spring assembly
2 Upper control arm
3 Steering knuckle
4 Tie-rod end
5 Damper fork
6 Lower control arm
7 Steering gear
8 Splash guard

10

1.2a Rear suspension components (Integra models)

1 Trailing arm	*3 Stabilizer bar*	*5 Shock absorber/coil spring assembly*
2 Compensator arm	*4 Lower arm*	

1.2b Rear suspension components (Legend models)

1 Radius rod	*3 Shock absorber/coil*	*4 Stabilizer bar*	*6 Knuckle*
2 Front lower arm	*spring assembly*	*5 Rear lower arm*	*7 Upper arm*

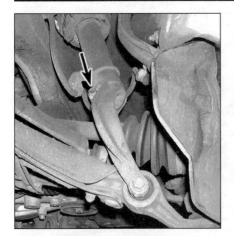

2.4 Remove the damper fork pinch bolt (arrow)

2.5a Remove the through-bolt that connects the damper fork to the lower control arm

2.5b Detach the damper fork from the shock absorber

and-pinion steering. The power steering system employs an engine-driven pump connected by hoses to the steering gear.

Frequently, when working on the suspension or steering system components, you may come across fasteners which seem impossible to loosen. These fasteners on the underside of the vehicle are continually subjected to water, road grime, mud, etc., and can become rusted or "seized," making them extremely difficult to remove. In order to unscrew these stubborn fasteners without damaging them (or other components), be sure to use lots of penetrating oil and allow it to soak in for a while. Using a wire brush to clean exposed threads will also ease removal of the nut or bolt and prevent damage to the threads. Sometimes a sharp blow with a hammer and punch is effective in breaking the bond between a nut and bolt threads, but care must be taken to prevent the punch from slipping off the fastener and ruining the threads. Heating the stuck fastener and surrounding area with a torch sometimes helps too, but isn't recommended because of the obvious dangers associated with fire. Long breaker bars and extension, or "cheater," pipes will increase leverage, but never use an extension pipe on a ratchet - the ratcheting mechanism could be damaged. Sometimes, turning the nut or bolt in the tightening (clockwise) direction first will help to break it loose. Fasteners that require drastic measures to loosen should always be replaced with new ones.

Since most of the procedures that are dealt with in this chapter involve jacking up the vehicle and working underneath it, a good pair of jackstands will be needed. A hydraulic floor jack is the preferred type of jack to lift the vehicle, and it can also be used to support certain components during various operations. **Warning:** *Never, under any circumstances, rely on a jack to support the vehicle while working on it. Whenever any of the suspension or steering fasteners are loosened or removed they must be inspected and, if necessary, be replaced with new ones of the same part number or of original equipment quality and design. Torque specifications*

must be followed for proper reassembly and component retention. Never attempt to heat or straighten any suspension or steering component. Instead, replace any bent or damaged part with a new one.

---

2 Shock absorber/coil spring assembly (front) - removal and installation

Note: *The manufacturer recommends replacing all self-locking fasteners with new ones during reassembly.*

Removal

Refer to illustrations 2.4, 2.5a, 2.5b and 2.6

1   Loosen the wheel lug nuts, raise the vehicle and support it securely on jackstands. Remove the wheel.
2   Unbolt the brake hose from the shock absorber assembly.
3   Place a floor jack under the lower control arm to support it when the damper fork is detached.
4   Remove the damper fork pinch bolt **(see illustration)**.
5   Remove the damper fork-to-lower control arm bolt and remove the fork **(see illustrations)**. It may be necessary to tap the fork from the shock absorber.
6   Support the shock absorber and coil spring assembly and remove the upper mounting nuts **(see illustration)**. Remove the unit from the fenderwell.

Installation

7   Guide the shock absorber assembly up into the fenderwell and insert the upper mounting studs through the holes in the body. Once the studs protrude from the holes, install the nuts so the assembly won't fall back through, but don't tighten the nuts completely yet. The shock absorber is heavy and awkward, so get an assistant to help you, if possible.
8   Insert the lower end of the shock

absorber into the damper fork. Make sure the aligning tab on the back of the shock body enters the slot in the damper fork.
9   Connect the damper fork to the lower control arm, tightening the self-locking nut to the torque listed in this Chapter's Specifications. Now tighten the damper fork pinch bolt to the torque listed in this Chapter's Specifications.
10   Attach the brake hose to its bracket and tighten the bolt securely.
11   Install the wheel and lug nuts, lower the vehicle and tighten the lug nuts to the torque listed in the Chapter 1 Specifications.
12   Tighten the upper mounting nuts to the torque listed in this Chapter's Specifications.

---

3 Shock absorber or coil spring - replacement

Refer to illustrations 3.5, 3.6a and 3.6b
Note: *The manufacturer recommends replacing all self-locking fasteners with new ones during reassembly.*

1   Remove the shock absorber/coil spring assembly (see Section 2 or 10).

2.6 Remove the nuts (arrows) from the shock absorber mounting studs (Legend shown; Integra models have only two nuts)

10

3.5 Install the spring compressor according to the tool manufacturer's instructions and compress the spring until all pressure is relieved from the mounting base

3.6a Exploded view of an Integra front shock absorber/coil spring assembly

1   Self-locking nut
2   Damper mounting washer
3   Damper mounting rubber
4   Damper mounting collar
5   Damper mounting base
6   Damper mounting rubber
7   Spring mounting rubber
8   Spring
9   Dust cover plate
10 Dust cover
11 Bump stop plate
12 Bump stop
13 Damper unit

3.6b Exploded view of a Legend front shock absorber/coil spring assembly

1   Self-locking nut
2   Damper mounting base
3   Damper mounting washer
4   Dust cover plate
5   Spring
6   Dust cover
7   Spring mounting rubber
8   Bump stop plate
9   Bump stop
10 Damper unit

4.2a Unscrew the nuts (arrows) and remove the stabilizer bar link bushings, washers and spacer (Integra)

4.2b Remove the stabilizer bar link nuts (arrows) (Legend)

2   Check the shock absorber for leaking fluid, dents, cracks or other obvious damage. Check the coil spring for chips or cracks which could cause premature failure and inspect the spring seats for hardness or general deterioration. The shock absorber assemblies, complete with the coil springs, are available on an exchange basis which eliminates much time and work. So, before disassembling your shock to replace individual components, check on the availability of parts and the price of a complete rebuilt unit. **Warning:** *Disassembling a shock absorber/coil spring assembly is potentially dangerous and utmost attention must be directed to the job, or serious injury may result. Use only a high-quality spring compressor and carefully follow the manufacturer's instructions furnished with the tool. After removing the coil spring from the shock absorber, set it aside in a safe, isolated area.*

3   Mount the shock absorber assembly in a vise. Line the vise jaws with wood or rags to prevent damage to the unit and don't tighten the vise excessively.

4   Mark the relationship of the damper mounting base to the spring (or if the spring is being replaced, put the mark on the

damper unit). This will ensure correct positioning of the mounting base when the unit is reassembled.

5   Following the tool manufacturer's instructions, install the spring compressor (which can be obtained at most auto parts stores or equipment yards on a daily rental basis) on the spring and compress it sufficiently to relieve all pressure from the damper mounting base **(see illustration)**.

6   Remove the damper cap **(see illustrations)**. Unscrew the self-locking nut while holding the damper shaft with an Allen wrench to prevent it from turning. Remove the parts from the upper part of the shock and lay them out in the exact order in which they're removed.

7   Carefully lift the compressed spring from the assembly and set it in a safe place, such as inside a steel cabinet. **Warning:** *Keep the ends of the spring facing away from your body!*

8   Slide the rest of the parts off of the damper shaft and lay them out in the exact order in which they're removed.

9   Install the bump stop, bump stop plate (if equipped), dust cover and dust cover plate onto the new damper unit. Extend the damper shaft as far as it will go and slide the

components down to the damper body.

10   Carefully place the coil spring onto the shock absorber body, with the end of the spring resting in the lowest part of the seat.

11   Install the spring mounting rubber, lower mounting rubber, damper mounting collar, damper mounting base, seal, upper mounting rubber, damper mounting washer and a new self-locking nut. Before tightening the nut, align the previously applied marks on the mounting base and the spring (or damper body).

12   Tighten the self-locking nut to the torque listed in this Chapter's Specifications, again using the Allen wrench to prevent the shaft from turning. Remove the spring compressor. Install the damper cap.

13   Install the shock absorber/coil spring assembly (see Section 2 or 10).

4   Stabilizer bar and bushings (front) - removal and installation

Refer to illustrations 4.2a, 4.2b, 4.3a and 4.3b
Note: *The manufacturer recommends replacing all self-locking fasteners with new ones during reassembly.*

1   Apply the parking brake. Loosen the front wheel lug nuts, raise the front of the vehicle and support it securely on jackstands. Remove the wheels.

2   If you're working on an Integra model, remove the nuts from the stabilizer bar link bolts **(see illustration)**. Note the order in which the spacers, washers and bushings are arranged on the link bolt. If you're working on a Legend, remove the nuts from the stabilizer bar links.

3   Remove the bolts which attach the stabilizer bar brackets to the underside of the vehicle **(see illustrations)**.

4   Remove the bar from under the vehicle.

5   Pull the brackets off the stabilizer bar and inspect the bushings for cracks, hardness and other signs of deterioration. If the bushings are damaged, replace them.

6   Installation is the reverse of removal.

10

4.3a Remove the bolts (arrows) attaching the stabilizer bar bracket to the chassis (Integra)

4.3b Stabilizer bar bracket-to-chassis nuts (arrows) (Legend)

5.2a Loosen - but don't remove - the
upper balljoint castle nut (arrow)

5.2b On Legend models you'll have to
remove this bolt and cover for
access to the castle nut

5.3 Install a puller and separate the upper
control arm balljoint stud from the
steering knuckle

5   Upper control arm (front) - removal and installation

Refer to illustrations 5.2a, 5.2b, 5.3 and 5.4
Note: *The manufacturer recommends replacing all self-locking fasteners with new ones during reassembly.*

1   Loosen the front wheel lug nuts, raise the vehicle, place it securely on jackstands and remove the wheel. Support the lower control arm with a floor jack. On Legend models, unbolt the ABS wheel speed sensor bracket from the upper control arm.

2   Remove the cotter pin and loosen, but do not remove, the castle nut **(see illustration)** from the upper balljoint stud. The nut will prevent the upper control arm and the steering knuckle from separating violently in the next step.

3   Separate the upper control arm from the steering knuckle with a puller **(see illustration)**, then remove the balljoint nut. Don't let the top of the steering knuckle fall out. If necessary, secure it to the shock absorber with a piece of wire.

4   Remove the upper control arm-to-shock tower nuts, then guide the arm out around the coil spring **(see illustration)**. If the bushings in the upper control arm mounting studs

are worn out, remove the nuts and pivot bolts and remove the mounting studs. When reassembling, make sure the heads of the pivot bolts face each other (inwards). Tighten the pivot bolt nuts to the torque listed in this Chapter's Specifications.

5   Installation is the reverse of removal. Be sure to tighten all of the fasteners to the torque values listed in this Chapter's Specifications. **Note:** *Tighten the balljoint nut to the lower torque value given in the Specifications, then try inserting the cotter pin. If necessary, tighten the nut a little more to line up the slots in the nut with the hole in the balljoint stud. Never loosen the nut to allow cotter pin insertion.*

6   Lower control arm (front) - removal and installation

Refer to illustrations 6.4, 6.6a and 6.6b
Note: *The manufacturer recommends replacing all self-locking fasteners with new ones during reassembly.*

1   Loosen the front wheel lug nuts, raise the vehicle, place it securely on jackstands and remove the wheel.

2   Detach the stabilizer bar link from the lower control arm (see Section 4).

3   Detach the damper fork from the lower control arm (see Section 2).

4   Remove the cotter pin from the castle nut on the lower balljoint stud. Loosen the nut, but don't remove it yet. Using a puller, separate the lower control arm from the balljoint in the steering knuckle **(see illustration)**. Remove the nut.

5   On Integra models, remove the bolts and separate the radius rod from the lower control arm.

6   Remove the pivot bolt(s)/nut(s) from the inner end of the lower control arm **(see illustrations)** and separate the arm from the chassis.

7   Installation is the reverse of removal. Be sure to tighten all fasteners to the torque listed in this Chapter's Specifications. **Note:** *Tighten the balljoint nut to the lower torque value given in the Specifications, then try inserting the cotter pin. If necessary, tighten the nut a little more to line up the slots in the nut with the hole in the balljoint stud. Never loosen the nut to allow cotter pin insertion.* **Note:** *The manufacturer recommends replacing the inner pivot bolt with a new one during reassembly.*

7   Steering knuckle and hub assembly - removal and installation

Removal

Refer to illustrations 7.1a and 7.1b

1   Remove the wheel cover. Unstake the driveaxle/hub nut, then loosen it **(see illustrations)**. Loosen the wheel lug nuts, raise the front of the vehicle and support it securely on jackstands. Remove the wheel and the driveaxle/hub nut.

2   Unbolt the brake hose bracket from the steering knuckle. Unbolt the brake caliper and hang it out of the way with a piece of wire. Remove the caliper mounting bracket and remove the brake disc (see Chapter 9).

5.4 To detach the upper control arm
from the shock tower, remove
these two nuts (arrows)

6.4 Separate the lower control arm from
the steering knuckle balljoint with a puller

6.6a On Legend models, remove the self-locking nut (arrow) from the forward end of the lower control arm . . .

6.6b . . . and the nut and bolt (arrow) from the rear end of the arm

On models equipped with an Anti-lock Brake System (ABS), unbolt the wheel speed sensor and its bracket from the steering knuckle.

3   Disconnect the tie-rod end from the steering knuckle (see Section 16).

4   Separate the lower control arm from the balljoint in the bottom of the steering knuckle (see Section 6).

5   Separate the upper end of the knuckle from the upper control arm balljoint.

6   Carefully pull the knuckle and hub assembly off of the driveaxle. Tap the end of the driveaxle with a soft-faced hammer to break the driveaxle loose from the hub. Support the driveaxle with a piece of wire to prevent damage to the inner CV joint.

Installation

7   Apply a light coat of wheel bearing grease to the driveaxle splines. Insert the driveaxle through the splined bore of the hub while guiding the steering knuckle into position.

8   Connect the upper end of the knuckle to the upper control arm balljoint (see Section 5). Tighten the balljoint stud nut to the torque listed in this Chapter's Specifications, then install a new cotter pin. **Note:** *Tighten*

the nut to the lower torque value given in the Specifications, then try inserting the cotter pin. If necessary, tighten the nut a little more to line up the slots in the nut with the hole in the balljoint stud. Never loosen the nut to allow cotter pin insertion.

9   Connect the lower control arm to the balljoint on the bottom of the knuckle (see Section 6). **Note:** *Tighten the nut to the lower torque value given in the Specifications, then try inserting the cotter pin. If necessary, tighten the nut a little more to line up the slots in the nut with the hole in the balljoint stud. Never loosen the nut to allow cotter pin insertion.*

10   Install a new driveaxle/hub nut and tighten it securely.

11   Install the brake disc, caliper mount and caliper (see Chapter 9). Attach the brake hose bracket. Connect the brake hose bracket and, if equipped, the wheel speed sensor and bracket to the knuckle.

12   Install the wheel and lug nuts, lower the vehicle and tighten the lug nuts to the torque listed in the Chapter 1 Specifications.

13   Tighten the new driveaxle/hub nut to the torque listed in the Chapter 8 Specifications, then stake it in place.

14   Install the wheel cover.

8   Hub and bearing assembly (front) - removal and installation

1   Remove the steering knuckle and hub assembly (see Section 7).

2   Due to the special tools and expertise required to press the hub from the steering knuckle, the assembly should be taken to an automotive machine shop or other qualified repair facility to have the bearing replaced if it is worn.

9   Balljoints - replacement

1   The front suspension uses two balljoints. The upper balljoint, located in the upper control arm, can't be removed. If it's worn or damaged, replace the upper control arm (see Section 5). The balljoint boot, however, can be replaced separately.

2   The lower balljoint, located in the steering knuckle, can be replaced individually, but special tools are needed. If it's worn or damaged, remove the steering knuckle (see Section 7) and take it to an automotive machine shop or other qualified repair facility to have it replaced.

3   The rear suspension on Legend models also uses two balljoints; one on the outer end of the upper arm and one on the outer end of the forward lower arm. If either of these balljoints require replacing, the entire arm must be replaced. The balljoint boots are replaceable individually.

10

10   Shock absorber/coil spring assembly (rear) - removal and installation

Refer to illustrations 10.2a, 10.2b, 10.2c, 10.3 and 10.4

Note: *The manufacturer recommends replacing all self-locking fasteners with new ones during reassembly.*

7.1a Use a hammer and a small punch to unstake the driveaxle/hub nut . . .

7.1b . . . then loosen the nut with a socket and breaker bar

10.2a On Integra models, detach the cover for access to the upper shock absorber mounting nuts

10.2b On Legend models remove the rear speaker (arrow) . . .

10.2c . . . then detach the rubber cover (arrow) for access to the shock absorber upper mounting nuts

1   Loosen the rear wheel lug nuts, raise the rear of the vehicle and support it securely on jackstands. Remove the rear wheels.
2   Remove the damper upper cover (Integra) or the speaker and cover (Legend) **(see illustrations)**.
3   Remove the shock absorber upper

mounting nuts **(see illustration)**.
4   Remove the shock absorber lower mounting bolt **(see illustration)**.
5   Remove the shock absorber/coil spring assembly. If you're working on an Integra, pull down on the lower arm to gain some working clearance.

6   To inspect or replace the shock absorber or coil spring, see Section 3.
7   Installation is the reverse of removal. Be sure to tighten all fasteners to the torque values listed in this Chapter's Specifications.

11   Stabilizer bar and bushings (rear) - removal and installation

Refer to illustrations 11.2a and 11.2b
Note: *The manufacturer recommends replacing all self-locking fasteners with new ones during reassembly.*
1   Loosen the rear wheel lug nuts, raise the rear of the vehicle and support it securely on jackstands. Remove the rear wheels.
2   Remove the stabilizer bar-to-link bolts and the stabilizer bar bracket bolts and remove the stabilizer bar **(see illustrations)**.
3   Pull the brackets off the stabilizer bar and inspect the bushings for cracks, hardness and other signs of deterioration. If the bushings are damaged, replace them.
4   Installation is the reverse of removal.

10.3 Remove the upper mounting nuts (arrows)

10.4 Remove the shock absorber lower mounting bolt (arrow) (Legend shown)

11.2a Remove the stabilizer bar-to-link bolts (arrow) . . .

11.2b . . . then remove the clamp bolts (arrows)

12 Hub and bearing assembly (rear) - removal and installation

Refer to illustrations 12.3, 12.4a, 12.4b and 12.5

Note 1: *The rear hub and bearing are combined into a single assembly. The bearing is sealed for life and requires no lubrication or attention. If the bearing is worn or damaged, replace the entire hub and bearing assembly.*

Note 2: *The manufacturer recommends replacing all self-locking fasteners with new one s during reassembly.*

1   Loosen the rear wheel lug nuts, raise the rear of the vehicle and support it securely on jackstands. Remove the rear wheels.

2   Remove the brake caliper, caliper mounting bracket and brake disc (see Chapter 9). Hang the caliper out of the way with a piece of wire (it isn't necessary to disconnect the brake hose).

3   Remove the dust cover **(see illustration)**.

4   Unstake the hub retaining nut **(see illustration),** unscrew the nut, then remove the thrust washer and the hub assembly **(see illustration)**.

5   Install the new hub assembly and thrust washer, install and tighten a new nut to the torque listed in this Chapter's Specifications, then stake its edge into the groove in the spindle **(see illustration)**.

6   Install the dust cover by tapping lightly around the edge until it is seated.

7   The remainder of installation is the reverse of removal. Tighten the brake caliper mounting bracket bolts and the caliper mounting bolts to the torque listed in the Chapter 9 Specifications.

13 Rear suspension arms (Integra models) - removal and installation

Note: *The manufacturer recommends replacing all self-locking fasteners with new ones during reassembly.*

1   Loosen the rear wheel lug nuts, raise the rear of the vehicle and support it securely on jackstands. Remove the rear wheels.

Upper arm

Refer to illustration 13.2

2   Remove the upper arm-to-trailing arm bolt and nut **(see illustration)**.

3   Remove the mounting bolts from the

12.3 Using a hammer and chisel, remove the dust cover

upper arm inner bushing bracket and remove the upper arm.

4   Inspect the bushing for cracking or deterioration. If it's worn, have it pressed out, and a new one installed, by an automotive machine shop or other qualified repair facility.

5   Installation is the reverse of removal. Be sure to tighten all fasteners to the torque values listed in this Chapter's Specifications.

12.4a Unstake the hub nut

12.4b The hub assembly should come off easily, but to remove it if it's stuck, pull it from the rear knuckle with a slide hammer

12.5 Stake the hub nut into place

13.2 To remove the upper arm, remove the bolt and nut (right arrows) that attach it to the trailing arm, then remove the two bolts (left arrows) that attach the inner bushing bracket to the body

10

13.7 To disconnect the inner end of the lower arm from the chassis, remove the pivot bolt (arrow)

13.10 To remove the compensator arm, remove the bolt (right arrow) that attaches the arm to the body, then remove the bolt that attaches the compensator arm to the trailing arm (left arrow)

Lower arm

Refer to illustration 13.7

6   Detach the lower end of the shock absorber from the lower arm. Remove the lower arm-to-trailing arm bolt.

7   Remove the inner pivot bolt and nut from the lower arm **(see illustration)**, then remove the lower arm.

8   Inspect the lower arm bushings for cracks and deterioration. If any of them are worn, have them pressed out, and new ones installed, by an automotive machine shop or other qualified repair facility.

9   Installation is the reverse of removal. Be sure to tighten all fasteners to the torque values listed in this Chapter's Specifications.

Compensator arm

Refer to illustration 13.10

10   Remove the compensator arm-to-trailing arm bolt **(see illustration)**.

11   Mark the relationship of the compensator arm-to-body bolt nut and bolt. Detach the compensator arm.

12   Inspect the compensator arm bushings for wear and deterioration. If either of them need to be replaced, have them pressed out, and new ones installed, by an automotive machine shop or other qualified repair facility.

13   Installation is the reverse of removal. Align the compensator arm-to-body bolt with the mark you made in Step 11, then tighten the fasteners to the torque values listed in this Chapter's Specifications. It would be a good idea to have the wheel alignment checked and, if necessary, adjusted.

Trailing arm

Refer to illustrations 13.18a and 13.18b

14   Disconnect the brake hose from the rear caliper and plug the hose to prevent leakage or contamination. Remove the rear caliper and disc. Disconnect the parking brake cable (see Chapter 9).

15   Remove the rear hub and bearing assembly (see Section 12).

16   Remove the brake backing plate.

17   Detach the upper, lower and compensator arms from the trailing arm.

18   Disconnect the parking brake cable bracket from the trailing arm, then remove the bolts from the trailing arm bushing bracket **(see illustrations)** and remove the trailing arm.

19   Inspect the trailing arm bushing for cracks and deterioration. If it needs to be replaced, have it pressed out, and a new one installed, by an automotive machine shop or other qualified repair facility.

20   Installation is the reverse of removal. Be sure to tighten all fasteners to the torque values listed in this Chapter's Specifications and bleed the brake hydraulic system (see Chapter 9). It would be a good idea to have the wheel alignment checked and, if necessary, adjusted.

14   Rear suspension arms and knuckle (Legend models) - removal and installation

Note: *The manufacturer recommends replacing all self-locking fasteners with new ones during reassembly.*

1   Loosen the rear wheel lug nuts, raise the rear of the vehicle and support it securely on jackstands. Remove the rear wheels.

Knuckle

Refer to illustrations 14.8a and 14.8b

2   Remove the hub and bearing assembly (see Section 12).

3   Remove the bolts and detach the parking brake cable and ABS wheel sensor (don't disconnect the harness).

4   Remove the nuts and detach the backing plate and parking brake assembly from the knuckle.

5   Remove the lower shock absorber bolt (see Section 10).

6   Detach the rear lower arm from the knuckle **(see illustration 14.21)**.

7   Remove the radius rod nut from the

13.18a To disconnect the trailing arm from the body, remove the left bushing bracket bolt (arrow) . . .

13.18b . . . and the right bolt (right arrow); don't forget to detach the bracket for the parking brake cable by removing the bolt indicated by the left arrow

14.8a Separate the upper and lower balljoints from the knuckle with a puller or a balljoint separator . . .

14.8b . . . then detach the knuckle from the arms

14.11 Remove the nut from the upper radius rod, remove the two upper arm-to-chassis bolts, then detach the balljoint from the knuckle

14.16 Remove the nut from the lower radius rod, detach the lower balljoint from the knuckle, then remove the inner pivot bolt

upper arm, then unbolt the upper arm from the chassis **(see illustration 14.11)**.

8   Remove the cotter pins and nuts and use a balljoint remover to separate the upper

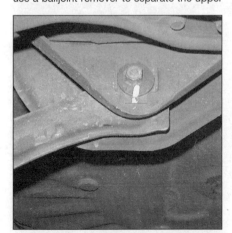

14.20 Make a match mark on the adjuster cam at the inner end of the rear lower arm . . .

and lower balljoints. Remove the knuckle **(see illustrations)**.

9   Installation is the reverse of removal. Tighten the suspension fasteners to the torque listed in this Chapter's Specifications, and tighten the brake fasteners to the torque listed in the Chapter 9 Specifications.

Upper arm

Refer to illustration 14.11

10   Unbolt the shock absorber from the knuckle **(see illustration 10.4)**.

11   Remove the radius rod nut from the upper arm **(see illustration)**.

12   Unbolt the upper arm from the chassis **(see illustration 14.11)**.

13   Separate the upper arm from the knuckle **(see illustration 14.8a)**, pivot the arm on the radius rod and slide it off. It may be necessary to push the shock absorber out of the way for clearance.

14   Installation is the reverse of removal. Tighten all fasteners to the torque values listed in this Chapter's Specifications.

Lower arms

Front

Refer to illustration 14.16

15   Detach the wheel speed sensor brackets from the arm.

16   Remove the radius rod nut from the lower arm **(see illustration)**.

17   Separate the arm from the knuckle as described in Step 8.

18   Remove the inner pivot bolt, separate the arm from the chassis bracket and slide it off the radius rod.

19   Installation is the reverse of removal. Tighten all fasteners to the torque values listed in this Chapter's Specifications.

Rear

Refer to illustrations 14.20 and 14.21

Note: *The right and left rear lower arms are not interchangeable.*

20   Mark the relationship of the toe adjuster cam to the chassis bracket at the inner end of the arm **(see illustration)**.

10

14.21 . . . then remove the adjuster bolt and nut at the inner end of the arm, and the nut and washer at the outer end of the arm

14.22 Remove the nuts attaching the radius rods to the upper and lower arms

21   Remove the nut and washer from the outer end of the arm, and the nut, bolt and adjuster cam from the inner end of the arm **(see illustration)**. Detach the arm from the chassis bracket and the knuckle. Installation is the reverse of removal. Be sure to align the mark on the toe adjuster cam with the mark on the chassis bracket, then tighten all fasteners to the torque values listed in this Chapter's Specifications.

Radius rods

Refer to illustrations 14.22 and 14.26

22   Remove the nuts from the rear ends of both radius rods **(see illustration)**.
23   Detach the parking brake cable brackets from the radius rod.
24   Remove the shock absorber lower mounting bolt.
25   Unbolt the upper arm from the chassis **(see illustration 14.11)**.
26   Remove the bolts from the radius rod bracket at the forward end of the rods **(see illustration)**.
27   Pull down on the front of the radius rods and slide the rods out of the upper and lower

arms. It may be helpful to have an assistant push down on the rear knuckle to gain working clearance at the forward end of the rods. **Caution:** *Be careful not to damage the brake hose.*
28   Installation is the reverse of removal. Tighten all fasteners to the torque values listed in this Chapter's Specifications.

15   Steering wheel - removal and installation

Warning: *All Legend models covered by this manual are equipped with a Supplemental Restraint System (SRS), more commonly known as an airbag(s). Always disable the airbag system before working in the vicinity of the SRS unit, steering column or instrument panel to avoid the possibility of accidental deployment of the airbag, which could cause personal injury (see Chapter 12).*
1   Disconnect the cable from the negative battery terminal, and if you're working on a Legend model, disconnect the positive battery cable. **Caution:** *If the radio in your vehi-*

cle is equipped with an anti-theft system, make sure you have the correct activation code before disconnecting the battery.

Integra

Refer to illustrations 15.2, 15.3 and 15.4

Removal

2   Pry out the steering wheel center cover **(see illustration)**.
3   Remove the steering wheel retaining nut. Paint or scribe a mark indicating the relationship of the steering wheel hub to the steering shaft **(see illustration)**.
4   Remove the steering wheel by rocking it back and forth while pulling it straight off the shaft **(see illustration)**. **Caution:** *Do not hammer on the wheel or the shaft.*

Installation

5   Install the steering wheel on the steering shaft, aligning the mark on the wheel with the mark on the shaft. Install the nut and tighten it to the torque listed in this Chapter's Specifications.
6   Install the center cover.

14.26 Remove the bolts attaching the radius rod bracket to the chassis

15.2 Use a flat-bladed screwdriver to pry out the center cover of the steering wheel

15.3 Mark the relationship of the wheel to the shaft

15.4 Grasp the steering wheel and rock it back and forth while pulling straight out to remove it

15.7a Remove this screw and detach the access plate from the underside of the steering wheel

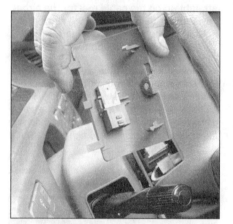

15.7b The shorting connector is stowed on the inside of the access plate

15.7c Unplug the yellow connector (arrow) for the airbag module

15.7d Plug the shorting connector into the airbag module connector to disable the airbag module

Legend

Removal

Refer to illustrations 15.7a, 15.7b, 15.7c, 15.7d, 15.8a, 15.8b, 15.9 and 15.11

7 Remove the access plate from the steering wheel. Remove the shorting connector from the access plate **(see illustrations)**.

Unplug the airbag module-to-cable reel connector and plug the shorting connector into the airbag module side of this connector to safely isolate the airbag module **(see illustrations)**.

8 Remove the access panels from each side of the steering wheel. Remove the Torx screws that secure the airbag module from

the steering wheel **(see illustrations)**.
9 Remove the airbag module from the steering wheel **(see illustration)**. **Warning:** *Carry the airbag module with the trim side facing away from your body and set it in an isolated area with the trim side facing up.*
10 Unplug the electrical connectors for the

15.8a Remove the left Torx screw (arrow) that attaches the airbag module to the steering wheel . . .

15.8b . . . then remove the right Torx screw (arrow)

15.9 Remove the airbag module from the steering wheel and set it aside (always store the airbag module with the trim side facing UP)

10

horn and the cruise control system.

11   Remove the steering wheel retaining nut. Paint or scribe a mark indicating the relationship of the steering wheel hub to the steering shaft **(see illustration)**.

12   Remove the steering wheel by pulling it straight off the shaft. **Warning:** *While the steering wheel is removed, DO NOT turn the steering shaft. If you do so, the airbag cable reel could be damaged.*

Installation

Refer to illustration 15.14

13   Make sure that the wheels are pointed straight ahead.

14   Make absolutely sure that the cable reel is centered with the arrow on the cable reel pointing up **(see illustration)**. This shouldn't be a problem as long as you have not turned the steering shaft while the wheel was removed. If for some reason the shaft was turned, center the cable reel as follows:

a) *Rotate the cable reel clockwise until it stops.*

b) *Rotate the cable reel counterclockwise about two turns until the yellow gear tooth lines up with the mark on the cover and the arrow on the cable reel points straight up.*

15   Be sure to align the index mark on the steering wheel hub with the mark on the shaft when you slip the wheel onto the shaft. And make sure the locating pins on the steering column engage the holes in the backside of the steering wheel. Install the mounting nut and tighten it to the torque listed in this Chapter's Specifications.

16   Plug in the horn connector and, if equipped, the cruise control connector.

17   Reattach the airbag module with NEW Torx bolts and tighten the bolts to the torque listed in this Chapter's Specifications. Install the Torx bolt access panels.

18   Unplug the shorting connector from the airbag connector.

19   Plug the airbag and cable reel connector halves together.

20   Secure the shorting connector to the access plate and install the access plate.

15.11 After removing the steering wheel nut, mark the relationship of the wheel to the shaft

15.14 Before installing the steering wheel, make sure that the wheels are pointed straight ahead and the "Top" mark points straight up on the cable reel for the airbag system; also, make sure the yellow gear tooth at the 7 o'clock position is lined up with its mark on the cover

16   Tie-rod ends - removal and installation

Removal

Refer to illustrations 16.2a, 16.2b and 16.4

1   Loosen the wheel lug nuts. Raise the front of the vehicle, support it securely on jackstands and remove the wheel.

2   Hold the tie-rod end with an open-end wrench and loosen the jam nut enough to mark the position of the tie-rod end in relation to the threads **(see illustrations)**.

3   Remove the cotter pin and loosen the nut on the tie-rod end stud. Don't completely remove the nut.

4   Separate the tie-rod end from the steering knuckle arm with a puller **(see illustration)**. Remove the nut and detach the tie-rod end from the knuckle.

5   Unscrew the tie-rod end from the tie-rod.

Installation

6   Thread the tie-rod end on to the marked position and insert the tie-rod stud into the steering knuckle arm. Don't tighten the jam nut yet.

7   Install the nut on the stud and tighten it to the torque listed in this Chapter's Specifications. Install a new cotter pin. **Note:** *Tighten the nut to the lower torque value given in the Specifications, then try inserting the cotter pin. If necessary, tighten the nut a*

16.2a Loosen the tie-rod end jam nut

16.2b Make an alignment mark on the exposed threads, along the edge of the tie-rod end, so the new tie-rod end will be installed in the exact same position

16.4 Use a puller to separate the tie-rod end from the steering knuckle arm

17.3 Cut off the steering gear boot clamps (arrows)

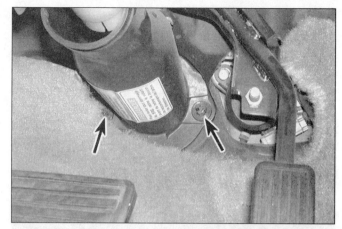

18.1 Pop off the upper and lower clamps, pry out the plastic retainers and slide off the cover

little more to line up the slots in the nut with the hole in the balljoint stud. Never loosen the nut to allow cotter pin insertion.

8   Tighten the jam nut securely.
9   Install the wheel and lug nuts. Lower the vehicle and tighten the lug nuts to the torque listed in the Chapter 1 Specifications.
10   Have the alignment checked by a dealer service department or an alignment shop.

17 Steering gear boots - replacement

Refer to illustration 17.3

1   Loosen the lug nuts, raise the front of the vehicle and support it securely on jackstands. Remove the wheel.
2   Remove the tie-rod end and jam nut (see Section 16).
3   Remove the steering gear boot clamps and slide off the boot **(see illustration)**.
4   Before installing the new boot, wrap the threads and serrations on the end of the tie-rod with a layer of tape so the small end of the new boot isn't damaged.
5   Slide the new boot into position on the steering gear until it seats in the groove in the steering rod and install new clamps.
6   Remove the tape and install the tie-rod end (see Section 16).
7   Install the wheel and lug nuts. Lower the vehicle and tighten the lug nuts to the torque listed in the Chapter 1 Specifications.

18 Steering gear - removal and installation

Note: *The manufacturer recommends replacing all self-locking fasteners with new ones during reassembly.*

Integra

Removal

Refer to illustrations 18.1, 18.8 and 18.9

1   Working under the dash, remove the steering joint cover **(see illustration)**.
2   Mark the relationship of the intermediate shaft universal joint to the steering gear input shaft and remove the pinch bolt.
3   Raise the front of the vehicle and support it securely on jackstands. Apply the parking brake. Lock the steering wheel with the ignition key.

4   Remove the shift and extension rods (manual transaxle) or shift control cable (automatic transaxle) from the transaxle (see Chapter 7A or B).
5   Remove the catalytic converter (see Chapter 4).
6   Place a drain pan under the steering gear. Disconnect the power steering fluid lines and cap them to prevent contamination and loss of fluid.
7   Separate the tie-rod ends from the steering knuckle arms (see Section 16). Remove the left tie-rod end.
8   Remove center beam to provide clearance so the steering gear can be removed **(see illustration)**.
9   Remove the steering gear shield for access, support the steering gear and remove the mounting bolts **(see illustration)**. Lower the unit, separating the intermediate shaft from the steering gear input shaft. Move the steering gear as far as possible to the right. Rotate the steering gear so that the input shaft is facing forward. Lower the left end past the frame and remove the steering gear from the vehicle as you move it to the left side.

18.8 Remove the bolts (arrows) and detach the center beam

18.9 Remove the bolts (arrows) and lower the shield for access to the steering gear

10

18.18 Remove the bolts (arrow) and lower the splash guard

18.19a Disconnect the pressure line fittings (arrows) . . .

Installation

9   Maneuver the steering gear into position by reversing the removal method and connect the intermediate shaft, aligning the marks. An assistant would be helpful here.

10   Install the steering gear mounting bolts and washers and tighten them to the torque listed in this Chapter's Specifications.

11   Install the left tie-rod end and connect

18.19b . . . and the return hoses (arrow)

the tie-rod ends to the steering knuckle arms (see Section 16).

12   Connect the power steering hoses/lines to the steering gear.

13   Install the transaxle control rods or cable, center beam, steering gear shield and the catalytic converter.

14   Lower the vehicle, install the intermediate shaft pinch bolt and tighten it to the torque listed in this Chapter's Specifications. Install the steering joint cover. Proceed to Step 30.

Legend

Removal

Refer to illustrations 18.18, 18.19a, 18.19b, 18.20 and 18.22

Warning: *Make sure the steering shaft is not turned while the steering gear is removed or you could damage the airbag cable reel. To prevent the shaft from turning, place the ignition key in the LOCK position or thread the seat belt through the steering wheel and clip it into place.*

15   Mark the relationship of the intermediate shaft universal joint to the steering gear input shaft.

16   Loosen, but do not remove, the lower pinch bolt.

17   Raise the front of the vehicle and support it securely on jackstands. Apply the parking brake. Lock the steering wheel with the ignition key.

18   Remove the bolts and detach the splash guard **(see illustration)**.

19   Place a drain pan under the steering gear. Disconnect the power steering lines and plug them to prevent contamination and loss of fluid **(see illustrations)**.

20   Remove the bolts and detach the fluid line assembly from the steering gear **(see illustration)**.

21   Separate the tie-rod ends from the steering knuckle arms (see Section 16).

22   Support the steering gear and remove the mounting clamp bolts **(see illustration)**.

23   Remove the intermediate shaft pinch bolt, then lower the unit, separating the intermediate shaft from the steering gear input shaft.

Installation

24   Raise the steering gear into position and connect the intermediate shaft, aligning the marks.

18.20 Remove the bolts and separate the fluid line assembly from the steering gear

18.22 Remove the mounting clamp bolts

19.2a To remove the power steering pump on Integra models, disconnect the pressure line bolts and the return line clamp (A), then remove the adjuster and mounting bolts (B) (lower mounting bolt not visible)

19.2b On Legend models, disconnect the pressure line bolts and the return line clamp (A), then remove the mounting bolt and nut (B) and the adjuster bolt (C)

25   Install the fluid line assembly and clamps loosely. Align the return lines with the steering gear fittings and connect them. Connect the suction lines. Tighten the fluid line clamp assembly bolts securely.

26   Place the steering gear mounting clamp in position and tighten the bolts to the torque listed in this Chapter's Specifications.

27   Install the splash guard and tighten the bolts to the torque listed in this Chapter's Specifications.

28   Install the intermediate shaft pinch bolt and tighten it to the torque listed in this Chapter's Specifications.

29   Connect the tie-rod ends to the steering knuckle arms (see Section 16).

All models

30   Fill the power steering pump reservoir with the recommended fluid (see Chapter 1) and bleed the steering system (see Section 21).

19   Power steering pump - removal and installation

Refer to illustrations 19.2a and 19.2b

1   Disconnect the cable from the negative battery terminal. **Caution:** *If the radio in your vehicle is equipped with an anti-theft system, make sure you have the correct activation code before disconnecting the battery.*

2   Disconnect the fluid lines at the pump **(see illustrations)**. Note the difference between the pressure and the return hoses; the return hose is held to the pump with a spring type clamp, and the pressure line has two bolts holding it to the pump body. Cap or plug both hoses to prevent leakage or contamination. Install a new O-ring on the end of the pressure line.

3   Remove the pump adjusting bolt.

4   Remove the pump mounting bolts and remove the pump from the engine.

5   Installation is the reverse of removal. Be

sure to bleed the power steering system (see Section 21) and adjust the drivebelt tension (see Chapter 1).

20   Power steering speed sensor - check and replacement

Check

Refer to illustration 20.3

1   Check the power steering fluid level and drivebelt tension (see Chapter 1).

2   With the engine idling at normal operating temperature, pull on the steering wheel with a spring scale until the front tires begin to turn and record the reading on the scale. On Integra models the reading should be 7-lbs and on Legend models it should be 6.6-lbs.

3   If the readings are higher or lower, turn the engine off, disconnect the hose from the speed sensor and plug the hose **(see illustration)**.

4   Restart the engine and allow it to idle and repeat the check in Step 2. If the spring scale reading is now 7 lbs (Integra) or 6.6 lbs (Legend) or less, replace the speed sensor with a new one. If reading is higher, there is a

20.3 Disconnect the speed sensor hose from the fitting (arrow) and plug the hose

problem with the power steering pump or the steering gear.

Replacement

5   Disconnect the hoses from the speed sensor.

6   On Integra models, pull the speedometer cable up, remove the retaining clip and detach the cable from the sensor. On Legend models, unplug the speed sensor connector.

6   Remove the retaining bolt and lift the speed sensor out of the transmission/transaxle.

7   Installation is the reverse of removal.

21   Power steering system - bleeding

1   Following any operation in which the power steering fluid lines have been disconnected, the power steering system must be bled to remove all air and obtain proper steering performance.

2   With the front wheels in the straight ahead position, check the power steering fluid level (see Chapter 1). If it's low, add fluid until it reaches the lower mark on the reservoir.

3   Start the engine and allow it to run at fast idle. Recheck the fluid level and add more if necessary to reach the Cold mark on the dipstick.

4   Bleed the system by turning the wheels from side-to-side, without hitting the stops. This will work the air out of the system. Keep the reservoir full of fluid as this is done.

5   When the air is worked out of the system, return the wheels to the straight ahead position and leave the vehicle running for several more minutes before shutting it off.

6   Road test the vehicle to be sure the steering system is functioning normally and noise free.

7   Recheck the fluid level to be sure it is up to the Hot mark on the reservoir while the engine is at normal operating temperature. Add fluid if necessary (see Chapter 1).

10

METRIC TIRE SIZES

P 185 / 80 R 13

TIRE TYPE
P-PASSENGER
T-TEMPORARY
C-COMMERCIAL

ASPECT RATIO
(SECTION HEIGHT)
――――――――――
(SECTION WIDTH)
70
75
80

RIM DIAMETER
(INCHES)
13
14
15

SECTION WIDTH
(MILLIMETERS)
185
195
205
ETC

CONSTRUCTION TYPE
R-RADIAL
B-BIAS - BELTED
D-DIAGONAL (BIAS)

SECTION WIDTH

SECTION HEIGHT

22.1 Metric tire size code

CAMBER ANGLE (FRONT VIEW)

FRONT

CASTER ANGLE (SIDE VIEW)

FRONT

TOE-IN (TOP VIEW)

23.1 Wheel alignment details

A minus B = C (degrees camber)
D = caster (expressed in degrees)
E minus F = toe-in (measured in inches)
G = toe-in (expressed in degrees)

22 Wheels and tires - general information

Refer to illustration 22.1

All vehicles covered by this manual are equipped with metric-sized steel belted radial tires **(see illustration)**. Use of other size or type of tires may affect the ride and handling of the vehicle. Don't mix different types of tires, such as radials and bias belted, on the same vehicle as handling may be seriously affected. It's recommended that tires be replaced in pairs on the same axle, but if only one tire is being replaced, be sure it's the same size, structure and tread design as the other.

Because tire pressure has a substantial effect on handling and wear, the pressure on all tires should be checked at least once a month or before any extended trips (see Chapter 1).

Wheels must be replaced if they are bent, dented, leak air, have elongated bolt holes, are heavily rusted, out of vertical symmetry or if the lug nuts won't stay tight. Wheel repairs that use welding or peening are not recommended.

Tire and wheel balance is important to the overall handling, braking and performance of the vehicle. Unbalanced wheels can adversely affect handling and ride characteristics as well as tire life. Whenever a tire is installed on a wheel, a shop with the proper equipment should balance the tire and wheel.

23 Wheel alignment - general information

Refer to illustration 23.1

A wheel alignment refers to the adjustments made to the wheels so they are in proper angular relationship to the suspension and the ground. Wheels that are out of proper alignment not only affect steering control, but also increase tire wear. Toe-in can be adjusted on the front and rear wheels. The front and rear camber and caster angles should be checked to determine if any of the suspension components are worn out or bent **(see illustration)**.

Getting the proper wheel alignment is a very exacting process, one in which complicated and expensive machines are necessary to perform the job properly. Because of this, you should have a technician with the proper equipment perform these tasks. We will, however, use this space to give you a basic idea of what is involved with wheel alignment so you can better understand the process and deal intelligently with the shop that does the work.

Toe-in is the turning in of the wheels. The purpose of a toe specification is to ensure parallel rolling of the wheels. In a vehicle with zero toe-in, the distance between the front edges of the wheels will be the same as the distance between the rear edges of the wheels. The actual amount of toe-in is normally only a fraction of an inch. At the front end, toe-in is controlled by the tie-rod end position on the tie-rod. At the rear on Legend models it is adjusted by turning an adjuster

cam bolt on the inner end of the rear lower arm. On Integra models it is adjusted by moving the compensator arm in-or-out within its bracket on the body. Incorrect toe-in will cause the tires to wear improperly by making them scrub against the road surface.

Camber is the tilting of the wheels from the vertical when viewed from the front or rear of the vehicle. When the wheels tilt out at the top, the camber is said to be positive (+). When the wheels tilt in at the top the camber is negative (-). The amount of tilt is measured in degrees from the vertical and this measurement is called the camber angle. This angle affects the amount of tire tread which contacts the road and compensates for changes in the suspension geometry when the vehicle is cornering or traveling over an undulating surface. Camber isn't adjustable on these vehicles.

Caster is the tilting of the top of the steering axis from the vertical. A tilt toward the rear is positive caster and a tilt toward the front is negative caster. Caster isn't adjustable on these vehicles.

Chapter 11 Body

Contents

Specifications

Torque specifications

	Ft-lbs (unless otherwise indicated)
Passenger's airbag retaining nuts	86 in-lbs
Steering column mounting bolts	
Integra	
Flange nuts	144 in-lbs
Bracket bolts	16
Legend	
Flange nuts/bolts	108 in lbs
Bracket nuts	16

1 General information

These models feature a "unibody" layout, using a floor pan with front and rear frame side rails which support the body components, front and rear suspension systems and other mechanical components.

Certain components are particularly vulnerable to accident damage and can be unbolted and repaired or replaced. Among these parts are the body moldings, bumpers, the hood and trunk lid (or liftgate) and all glass.

Only general body maintenance practices and body panel repair procedures within the scope of the do-it-yourselfer are included in this Chapter.

2 Body - maintenance

1 The condition of your vehicle's body is very important, because the resale value depends a great deal on it. It's much more difficult to repair a neglected or damaged body than it is to repair mechanical components. The hidden areas of the body, such as the wheel wells, the frame and the engine compartment, are equally important, although they don't require as frequent attention as the rest of the body.
2 Once a year, or every 12,000 miles, it's a good idea to have the underside of the body steam cleaned. All traces of dirt and oil will be removed and the area can then be inspected carefully for rust, damaged brake lines, frayed electrical wires, damaged cables and other problems.
3 At the same time, clean the engine and the engine compartment with a steam cleaner or water soluble degreaser.
4 The wheel wells should be given close attention, since undercoating can peel away and stones and dirt thrown up by the tires can cause the paint to chip and flake, allowing rust to set in. If rust is found, clean down to the bare metal and apply an anti-rust paint.
5 The body should be washed about once a week. Wet the vehicle thoroughly to soften the dirt, then wash it down with a soft sponge and plenty of clean soapy water. If the surplus dirt is not washed off very carefully, it can wear down the paint.
6 Spots of tar or asphalt thrown up from

11

the road should be removed with a cloth soaked in solvent.

7   Once every six months, wax the body and chrome trim. If a chrome cleaner is used to remove rust from any of the vehicle's plated parts, remember that the cleaner also removes part of the chrome, so use it sparingly.

3   Vinyl trim - maintenance

Don't clean vinyl trim with detergents, caustic soap or petroleum based cleaners. Plain soap and water works just fine, with a soft brush to clean dirt that may be ingrained. Wash the vinyl as frequently as the rest of the vehicle.

After cleaning, application of a high quality rubber and vinyl protectant will help prevent oxidation and cracks. The protectant can also be applied to weatherstripping, vacuum lines and rubber hoses, which often fail as a result of chemical degradation, and to the tires.

4   Upholstery and carpets - maintenance

1   Every three months remove the carpets or mats and clean the interior of the vehicle (more frequently if necessary). Vacuum the upholstery and carpets to remove loose dirt and dust.

2   Leather upholstery requires special care. Stains should be removed with warm water and a very mild soap solution. Use a clean, damp cloth to remove the soap, then wipe again with a dry cloth. Never use alcohol, gasoline, nail polish remover or thinner to clean leather upholstery.

3   After cleaning, regularly treat leather upholstery with a leather wax. Never use car wax on leather upholstery.

4   In areas where the interior of the vehicle is subject to bright sunlight, cover leather seats with a sheet if the vehicle is to be left out for any length of time.

5   Body repair - minor damage

Plastic body panels

The following repair procedures are for minor scratches and gouges. Repair of more serious damage should be left to a dealer service department or qualified auto body shop. Below is a list of the equipment and materials necessary to perform the following repair procedures on plastic body panels. Although a specific brand of material may be mentioned, it should be noted that equivalent products from other manufacturers may be used instead.

Wax, grease and silicone removing solvent
Cloth-backed body tape
Sanding discs
Drill motor with three-inch disc holder
Hand sanding block
Rubber squeegees
Sandpaper
Non-porous mixing palette
Wood paddle or putty knife
Curved tooth body file
Flexible parts repair material

Flexible panels (front and rear bumper fascia)

1   Remove the damaged panel, if necessary or desirable. In most cases, repairs can be carried out with the panel installed.

2   Clean the area(s) to be repaired with a wax, grease and silicone removing solvent applied with a water-dampened cloth.

3   If the damage is structural, that is, if it extends through the panel, clean the backside of the panel area to be repaired as well. Wipe dry.

4   Sand the rear surface about 1-1/2 inches beyond the break.

5   Cut two pieces of fiberglass cloth large enough to overlap the break by about 1-1/2 inches. Cut only to the required length.

6   Mix the adhesive from the repair kit according to the instructions included with the kit, and apply a layer of the mixture approximately 1/8-inch thick on the backside of the panel. Overlap the break by at least 1-1/2 inches.

7   Apply one piece of fiberglass cloth to the adhesive and cover the cloth with additional adhesive. Apply a second piece of fiberglass cloth to the adhesive and immediately cover the cloth with additional adhesive insufficient quantity to fill the weave.

8   Allow the repair to cure for 20 to 30 minutes at 60-degrees to 80-degrees F.

9   If necessary, trim the excess repair material at the edge.

10   Remove all of the paint film over and around the area(s) to be repaired. The repair material should not overlap the painted surface.

11   With a drill motor and a sanding disc (or a rotary file), cut a "V" along the break line approximately 1/2-inch wide. Remove all dust and loose particles from the repair area.

12   Mix and apply the repair material. Apply a light coat first over the damaged area; then continue applying material until it reaches a level slightly higher than the surrounding finish.

13   Cure the mixture for 20 to 30 minutes at 60-degrees to 80-degrees F.

14   Roughly establish the contour of the area being repaired with a body file. If low areas or pits remain, mix and apply additional adhesive.

15   Block sand the damaged area with sandpaper to establish the actual contour of the surrounding surface.

16   If desired, the repaired area can be temporarily protected with several light coats of primer. Because of the special paints and techniques required for flexible body panels, it is recommended that the vehicle be taken to a paint shop for completion of the body repair.

Steel body panels

See photo sequence

Repair of minor scratches

17   If the scratch is superficial and does not penetrate to the metal of the body, repair is very simple. Lightly rub the scratched area with a fine rubbing compound to remove loose paint and built-up wax. Rinse the area with clean water.

18   Apply touch-up paint to the scratch, using a small brush. Continue to apply thin layers of paint until the surface of the paint in the scratch is level with the surrounding paint. Allow the new paint at least two weeks to harden, then blend it into the surrounding paint by rubbing with a very fine rubbing compound. Finally, apply a coat of wax to the scratch area.

19   If the scratch has penetrated the paint and exposed the metal of the body, causing the metal to rust, a different repair technique is required. Remove all loose rust from the bottom of the scratch with a pocket knife, then apply rust inhibiting paint to prevent the formation of rust in the future. Using a rubber or nylon applicator, coat the scratched area with glaze-type filler. If required, the filler can be mixed with thinner to provide a very thin paste, which is ideal for filling narrow scratches. Before the glaze filler in the scratch hardens, wrap a piece of smooth cotton cloth around the tip of a finger. Dip the cloth in thinner and then quickly wipe it along the surface of the scratch. This will ensure that the surface of the filler is slightly hollow. The scratch can now be painted over as described earlier in this section.

Repair of dents

20   When repairing dents, the first job is to pull the dent out until the affected area is as close as possible to its original shape. There is no point in trying to restore the original shape completely as the metal in the damaged area will have stretched on impact and cannot be restored to its original contours. It is better to bring the level of the dent up to a point, which is about 1/8-inch below the level of the surrounding metal. In cases where the dent is very shallow, it is not worth trying to pull it out at all.

21   If the back side of the dent is accessible, it can be hammered out gently from behind using a soft-face hammer. While doing this, hold a block of wood firmly against the opposite side of the metal to absorb the hammer blows and prevent the metal from being stretched.

22   If the dent is in a section of the body which has double layers, or some other factor makes it inaccessible from behind, a different technique is required. Drill several small holes through the metal inside the damaged area, particularly in the deeper sections. Screw long, self-tapping screws into the holes just enough for them to get a good grip in the metal. Now the dent can be pulled out by pulling on the protruding heads of the screws

with locking pliers.

23   The next stage of repair is the removal of paint from the damaged area and from an inch or so of the surrounding metal. This is done with a wire brush or sanding disk in a drill motor, although it can be done just as effectively by hand with sandpaper. To complete the preparation for filling, score the surface of the bare metal with a screwdriver or the tang of a file, or drill small holes in the affected area. This will provide a good grip for the filler material. To complete the repair, see the subsection on filling and painting later in this Section.

Repair of rust holes or gashes

24   Remove all paint from the affected area and from an inch or so of the surrounding metal using a sanding disk or wire brush mounted in a drill motor. If these are not available, a few sheets of sandpaper will do the job just as effectively.

25   With the paint removed, you will be able to determine the severity of the corrosion and decide whether to replace the whole panel, if possible, or repair the affected area. New body panels are not as expensive as most people think and it is often quicker to install a new panel than to repair large areas of rust.

26   Remove all trim pieces from the affected area except those which will act as a guide to the original shape of the damaged body, such as headlight shells, etc. Using metal snips or a hacksaw blade, remove all loose metal and any other metal that is badly affected by rust. Hammer the edges of the hole in to create a slight depression for the filler material.

27   Wire brush the affected area to remove the powdery rust from the surface of the metal. If the back of the rusted area is accessible, treat it with rust inhibiting paint.

28   Before filling is done, block the hole in some way. This can be done with sheet metal riveted or screwed into place, or by stuffing the hole with wire mesh.

29   Once the hole is blocked off, the affected area can be filled and painted. See the following subsection on filling and painting.

Filling and painting

30   Many types of body fillers are available, but generally speaking, body repair kits which contain filler paste and a tube of resin hardener are best for this type of repair work. A wide, flexible plastic or nylon applicator will be necessary for imparting a smooth and contoured finish to the surface of the filler material. Mix up a small amount of filler on a clean piece of wood or cardboard (use the hardener sparingly). Follow the manufacturer's instructions on the package, otherwise the filler will set incorrectly.

31   Using the applicator, apply the filler paste to the prepared area. Draw the applicator across the surface of the filler to achieve the desired contour and to level the filler surface. As soon as a contour that approximates the original one is achieved, stop working the paste. If you continue, the paste will begin to stick to the applicator. Continue to add thin layers of paste at 20-minute intervals until the level of the filler is just above the surrounding metal.

32   Once the filler has hardened, the excess can be removed with a body file. From then on, progressively finer grades of sandpaper should be used, starting with a 180-grit paper and finishing with 600-grit wet-or-dry paper. Always wrap the sandpaper around a flat rubber or wooden block, otherwise the surface of the filler will not be completely flat. During the sanding of the filler surface, the wet-or-dry paper should be periodically rinsed in water. This will ensure that a very smooth finish is produced in the final stage.

33   At this point, the repair area should be surrounded by a ring of bare metal, which in turn should be encircled by the finely feathered edge of good paint. Rinse the repair area with clean water until all of the dust produced by the sanding operation is gone.

34   Spray the entire area with a light coat of primer. This will reveal any imperfections in the surface of the filler. Repair the imperfections with fresh filler paste or glaze filler and once more smooth the surface with sandpaper. Repeat this spray-and-repair procedure until you are satisfied that the surface of the filler and the feathered edge of the paint are perfect. Rinse the area with clean water and allow it to dry completely.

35   The repair area is now ready for painting. Spray painting must be carried out in a warm, dry, windless and dust free atmosphere. These conditions can be created if you have access to a large indoor work area, but if you are forced to work in the open, you will have to pick the day very carefully. If you are working indoors, dousing the floor in the work area with water will help settle the dust, which would otherwise be in the air. If the repair area is confined to one body panel, mask off the surrounding panels. This will help minimize the effects of a slight mismatch in paint color. Trim pieces such as chrome strips, door handles, etc., will also need to be masked off or removed. Use masking tape and several thickness of newspaper for the masking operations.

36   Before spraying, shake the paint can thoroughly, then spray a test area until the spray painting technique is mastered. Cover the repair area with a thick coat of primer. The thickness should be built up using several thin layers of primer rather than one thick one. Using 600-grit wet-or-dry sandpaper, rub down the surface of the primer until it is very smooth. While doing this, the work area should be thoroughly rinsed with water and the wet-or-dry sandpaper periodically rinsed as well. Allow the primer to dry before spraying additional coats.

37   Spray on the top coat, again building up the thickness by using several thin layers of paint. Begin spraying in the center of the repair area and then, using a circular motion, work out until the whole repair area and about two inches of the surrounding original

paint is covered. Remove all masking material 10 to 15 minutes after spraying on the final coat of paint. Allow the new paint at least two weeks to harden, then use a very fine rubbing compound to blend the edges of the new paint into the existing paint. Finally, apply a coat of wax.

6   Body repair - major damage

1   Major damage must be repaired by an auto body shop specifically equipped to perform unibody repairs. These shops have the specialized equipment required to do the job properly.

2   If the damage is extensive, the body must be checked for proper alignment or the vehicle's handling characteristics may be adversely affected and other components may wear at an accelerated rate.

3   Due to the fact that all of the major body components (hood, fenders, etc.) are separate and replaceable units, any seriously damaged components should be replaced rather than repaired. Sometimes the components can be found in a wrecking yard that specializes in used vehicle components, often at considerable savings over the cost of new parts.

7   Hinges and locks - maintenance

Once every 3000 miles, or every three months, the hinges and latch assemblies on the doors, hood and trunk (or liftgate) should be given a few drops of light oil or lock lubricant. The door latch strikers should also be lubricated with a thin coat of grease to reduce wear and ensure free movement. Lubricate the door and trunk (or liftgate) locks with spray-on graphite lubricant.

8   Windshield and fixed glass - replacement

Replacement of the windshield and fixed glass requires the use of special fast-setting adhesive/caulk materials and some specialized tools and techniques. These operations should be left to a dealer service department or a shop specializing in glass work.

9   Hood and trunk lid support struts - removal and installation

Warning: *The support strut is filled with pressurized gas - do not disassemble this component, if it is faulty replace it with a new one.* **Note:** *The hood and rear trunk lid are heavy and somewhat awkward to hold securely while replacing struts - at least two people should perform this procedure.*

11

These photos illustrate a method of repairing simple dents. They are intended to supplement *Body repair - minor damage* in this Chapter and should not be used as the sole instructions for body repair on these vehicles.

1   If you can't access the backside of the body panel to hammer out the dent, pull it out with a slide-hammer-type dent puller. In the deepest portion of the dent or along the crease line, drill or punch hole(s) at least one inch apart . . .

2   . . . then screw the slide-hammer into the hole and operate it. Tap with a hammer near the edge of the dent to help 'pop' the metal back to its original shape. When you're finished, the dent area should be close to its original contour and about 1/8-inch below the surface of the surrounding metal

3   Using coarse-grit sandpaper, remove the paint down to the bare metal. Hand sanding works fine, but the disc sander shown here makes the job faster. Use finer (about 320-grit) sandpaper to feather-edge the paint at least one inch around the dent area

4   When the paint is removed, touch will probably be more helpful than sight for telling if the metal is straight. Hammer down the high spots or raise the low spots as necessary. Clean the repair area with wax/silicone remover

5   Following label instructions, mix up a batch of plastic filler and hardener. The ratio of filler to hardener is critical, and, if you mix it incorrectly, it will either not cure properly or cure too quickly (you won't have time to file and sand it into shape)

6   Working quickly so the filler doesn't harden, use a plastic applicator to press the body filler firmly into the metal, assuring it bonds completely. Work the filler until it matches the original contour and is slightly above the surrounding metal

7   Let the filler harden until you can just dent it with your fingernail. Use a body file or Surform tool (shown here) to rough-shape the filler

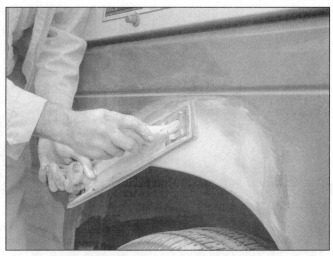

8   Use coarse-grit sandpaper and a sanding board or block to work the filler down until it's smooth and even. Work down to finer grits of sandpaper - always using a board or block - ending up with 360 or 400 grit

9   You shouldn't be able to feel any ridge at the transition from the filler to the bare metal or from the bare metal to the old paint. As soon as the repair is flat and uniform, remove the dust and mask off the adjacent panels or trim pieces

10   Apply several layers of primer to the area. Don't spray the primer on too heavy, so it sags or runs, and make sure each coat is dry before you spray on the next one. A professional-type spray gun is being used here, but aerosol spray primer is available inexpensively from auto parts stores

11   The primer will help reveal imperfections or scratches. Fill these with glazing compound. Follow the label instructions and sand it with 360 or 400-grit sandpaper until it's smooth. Repeat the glazing, sanding and respraying until the primer reveals a perfectly smooth surface

12   Finish sand the primer with very fine sandpaper (400 or 600-grit) to remove the primer overspray. Clean the area with water and allow it to dry. Use a tack rag to remove any dust, then apply the finish coat. Don't attempt to rub out or wax the repair area until the paint has dried completely (at least two weeks)

9.1 On Legend models, remove the two bolts securing the strut to the hood

9.2 Remove the nut securing the lower end of the strut

9.3a On Integra models, a nut (arrow) secures both ends of the strut

Hood

Refer to illustrations 9.1 and 9.2

1   Support the hood and remove the bolts securing the upper end of the strut **(see illustration)**.
2   Remove the nut from the lower end and remove the strut **(see illustration)**.

9.3b On Legend models, the struts are held in place by a bolt at each end - the lower end has a plastic cover

Trunk lid

Refer to illustrations 9.3a and 9.3b

3   Remove the nuts/bolts from both ends of the strut and detach it from the vehicle **(see illustrations)**.
4   Installation is the reverse of removal.

---

10   Hood - removal, installation and adjustment

Removal and installation

Refer to illustration 10.2

Note: *The hood is heavy and somewhat awkward to remove and install - at least two people should perform this procedure.*

1   Use blankets or pads to cover the fenders and cowl areas. This will protect the body and paint as the hood is lifted off.
2   Scribe or draw alignment marks around the bolt heads to ensure proper alignment during installation **(see illustration)**.
3   Disconnect any cables or wire harnesses, which will interfere with removal.
4   Have an assistant support the weight of the hood and remove the support struts (see Section 9). Remove the hinge-to-hood bolts and any shims, if already installed. If there are

any shims, make sure you keep the shims for each side with their respective bolts. Don't mix them up.
5   Lift off the hood.
6   Installation is the reverse of removal. If you fit the hood so that the hinges fit within the scribe marks you made before loosening the bolts and if you install the shims, if any, in the same number and location they were in prior to removal, then the hood should still be aligned. Of course, if you're installing a new hood, or forgot to scribe the hinge positions, or mixed up the shims, etc. then you'll need to readjust the hood position.

Adjustment

Refer to illustrations 10.10 and 10.11

7   You can adjust the hood fore-and-aft and right-and-left by means of the elongated holes in the hinges.
8   Scribe a line around the entire hinge plate so you can judge the amount of movement.
9   Loosen the bolts and move the hood into correct alignment. Move it only a little at a time. Tighten the hinge bolts or nuts and carefully lower the hood to check the alignment.
10   If necessary after installation, the entire hood latch assembly can be adjusted up-

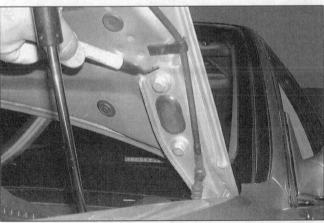

10.2 Scribe or draw alignment marks around the hood hinges to ensure proper alignment of the hood when it's reinstalled

10.10 Scribe a line around the hood latch so you can judge the movement, then loosen the bolts (arrows) and adjust the latch position

10.11 To adjust the vertical height of the leading edge of the hood so it's flush with the fenders, turn each edge cushion clockwise (to lower the hood) or counterclockwise (to raise the hood)

and-down as well as from side-to-side on the upper radiator support so the hood closes securely and is flush with the fenders **(see illustration)**. To do this, scribe a line around the hood latch mounting bolts to provide a reference point. Then loosen the bolts and reposition the latch assembly as necessary. Following adjustment, retighten the mounting bolts.

11   Adjust the vertical height of the leading edge of the hood by screwing the edge cushions in or out so that the hood, when closed, is flush with the fenders **(see illustration)**. Finally, adjust the rear edge of the hood until it's flush with the fenders by using shims (available at a dealer parts department) between the hood and the hinge plates.

12   The hood latch assembly, as well as the hinges, should be periodically lubricated with white lithium-base grease to prevent sticking and wear.

11   Hood latch and release cable - removal and installation

Latch

Refer to illustration 11.2

1   Remove the radiator grille opening cover, then scribe a line around the latch to aid alignment when installing, detach the latch retaining bolts from the radiator support **(see illustration 10.10)** and remove the latch.

2   Disconnect the hood release cable by disengaging the cable from the latch assembly **(see illustration)**.

3   Installation is reverse of the removal.

Note: *Adjust the latch so the hood engages securely when closed and the hood bumpers are slightly compressed.*

Cable

Refer to illustrations 11.5a and 11.5b

4   Disconnect the hood release cable from the latch assembly as described above.

11.2   Detach the cable and unhook the end from the latch

5   Working in the passenger's compartment, remove the driver side kick panel (Integra) or lift up the release lever for access. Remove the release lever mounting bolts and detach the hood release lever **(see illustrations)**. Detach the cable from the lever.

6   Attach a piece of stiff wire to the latch end of the cable, then detach all the cable retaining clips.

7   Push the grommet through the firewall and pull the cable into the engine compartment. Ensure that the new cable has a grommet attached, then remove the old cable from the wire and replace it with the new cable.

8   Pull the wire back through the firewall.

9   Installation is the reverse of the removal

Note: *Push on the grommet to seat it in the firewall completely.*

12   Bumper cover - removal and installation

Warning: *Models covered by this manual are equipped with a Supplemental Restraint System (SRS), more commonly known as airbags. Always disable the airbag system before working in the vicinity of the SRS unit, steering column or instrument panel to avoid the possibility of accidental deployment of the airbag, which could cause personal injury (see Chapter 12).*

Caution: *If the radio in your vehicle is equipped with an anti-theft system, make*

11.5a   On Integra models, remove the kick panel for access, then remove the latch assembly bolts (arrows) and detach the cable

11.5b   On Legend models, lift up the lever for access to the retaining bolt (arrow)

sure you have the correct activation code before disconnecting the battery.

Integra

Front bumper

Refer to illustrations 12.3, 12.4, 12.5 and 12.6

1   Apply the parking brake, raise the vehicle and support it securely on jackstands.

2   Disconnect the negative battery cable.

3   Working under the vehicle, detach the screws securing the lower edges of the front spoiler **(see illustration)**.

4   Working in the front wheel opening,

12.3   Remove the Integra spoiler retaining bolts (arrows)

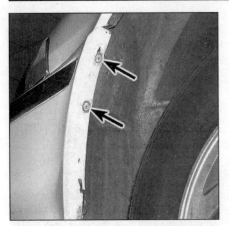

12.4 Remove the screws (arrows) at the front edge of the wheel wells

12.5 Remove the bolts (arrows) located in the turn signal openings

12.6 The bumper cover is retained to the body on each side by a nut (arrow)

12.10 Screws (arrows) retain the ends of the rear bumper cover

12.11 The bumper cover is retained by two nuts (arrows) on each side under the vehicle

12.12 Remove the nut (arrow) on each side in the trunk

detach the plastic retaining screws securing the bumper cover to inner fenderwell splash shields **(see illustration)**.

5   Remove the front turn signal assembly and remove the bumper cover retaining bolts **(see illustration)**.

6   Remove the two nuts retaining the bumper cover to the body brackets and pull assembly out and away from the vehicle **(see illustration)**.

7   Disconnect any electrical connections, which would interfere with removal and detach the bumper cover from the vehicle.

8   Installation is the reverse of removal.

Rear bumper

Refer to illustrations 12.10, 12.11 and 12.12

9   Apply the parking brake, raise the vehicle and support it securely on jackstands.

10   Remove the screws securing the each side of bumper cover in the rear wheel openings **(see illustration)**.

11   Working under the vehicle, remove the nuts securing the each side of the bumper cover **(see illustration)**.

12   Open the trunk or rear liftgate and remove the nuts securing the bumper cover **(see illustration)**. Pull the bumper cover assembly out and away from the vehicle.

13   Installation is the reverse of removal.

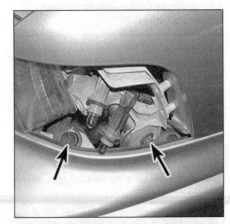

12.16 Remove the two bolts (arrows) in each parking light opening

Legend

Front bumper

Refer to illustrations 12.16, 12.17, 12.18 and 12.19

14   Apply the parking brake, raise the vehicle and support it securely on jackstands.

15   Disconnect the negative battery cable.

16   Remove the turn signal lights and park-

12.17 Remove the bolts (arrows) retaining the bumper cover to the chassis

ing lights (see Chapter 12) and remove the bumper cover retaining bolts in the openings **(see illustration)**.

17   Working through the openings in the bumper, remove the bumper cover-to-chassis bolts **(see illustration)**.

18   Remove the grille for access to the retaining screw securing the top of the bumper cover **(see illustration)**.

12.18 Remove the screw (arrow) retaining the top edge of the bumper cover

12.19 Pull the bumper cover out sharply to detach it from the clip (arrow) at each rear corner

12.24 Remove the three screws (arrows) along the top edge of the bumper cover

12.25 Remove the two screws (arrows) at the lower edge of the rear bumper cover

19 Grasp the bumper cover assembly securely and pull it forward sharply to detach it from the retaining clips at both sides (see illustration).
20 Disconnect any electrical connections, which would interfere with removal and remove the cover.
21 Installation is the reverse of removal.

Rear bumper

Refer to illustrations 12.24 and 12.25
22 Apply the parking brake, raise the vehi-cle and support it securely on jackstands.
23 Detach the wheel well cover and remove the two nuts securing the each side of bumper cover in the rear wheel openings.
24 Open the trunk, detach the weather stripping and remove the plastic screws securing the bumper cover (see illustration).
25 Working under the vehicle, remove the screws securing the each side of the bumper cover (see illustration). Pull the bumper cover assembly out and away from the vehicle.
26 Installation is the reverse of removal.

13 Front fender - removal and installation

Refer to illustrations 13.3, 13.4a, 13.4b, 13.4c and 13.4d
1 Raise the vehicle, support it securely on jackstands and remove the front wheel.
2 Remove the front bumper cover (see Section 12).
3 Remove the plastic retaining screws securing the inner fender housing panel and detach the panel (see illustration).
4 Remove the remaining fender mounting

13.3 Remove the plastic retaining screws (arrows) retaining the inner panel to the fender

13.4a Remove the bolts (arrows) at the front end of the fender

13.4b The upper rear corner of the fender is retained to the A-pillar with a bolt (arrow)

13.4c Remove the bolts (arrows) along the top of the fender

13.4d Two bolts (arrows) retain the lower rear corner of the fender

14.2a Integra trunk lid latch screw locations (arrows)

a line around the trunk lid latch assembly for a reference point to aid the installation procedure.

2   Remove the bolts/nuts retaining the trunk lid latch **(see illustrations)**.

3   Remove the latch and disconnect the cable and electrical connections **(see illustrations**.

4   Installation is the reverse of removal.

Lock cylinder

Refer to illustration 14.5

5   Open the trunk. Disconnect the latch rod and remove the lock cylinder retaining bolt **(see illustration)**.

6   Grasp the lock cylinder twist it counterclockwise 90-degrees to align the tabs on the lock cylinder with the slots in the body and lower it from the trunk lid.

7   Installation is the reverse of removal.

bolts **(see illustrations)**.

5   Detach the fender. It's a good idea to have an assistant support the fender while it's being moved away from the vehicle to prevent damage to the surrounding body panels.

6   Installation is the reverse of removal.

14 Trunk lid latch and lock cylinder - removal and installation

Trunk lid latch

Refer to illustrations 14.2a and 14.2b

1   Open the trunk or hatchback and scribe

15 Trunk lid - removal, installation and adjustment

Note: *The trunk lid is heavy and somewhat awkward to remove and install - at least two people should perform this procedure.*

14.2b Legend trunk lid latch screw locations (arrows)

14.5 Disconnect the latch rod (A) and remove the lock cylinder bolt (B)

15.1 Use a small pry tool to remove the trunk release trim cover retainers (arrows)

15.3 Draw around the hinge end with a marking pen so the trunk can be installed in the same position

15.4 With an assistant holding the trunk lid, remove the four trunk lid retaining bolts

15.9 Mark the trunk lid striker position before loosening the bolts

Removal and installation

Refer to illustrations 15.1, 15.3 and 15.4

1   Open the trunk lid and cover the edges of the trunk compartment with pads or cloths to protect the painted surfaces when the lid is removed. Remove the trunk lid finish panel **(see illustration)**.

2   Disconnect any cables or wire harness connectors attached to the trunk lid that would interfere with removal.

3   Make alignment marks around the hinge mounting bolts with paint or a marking pen **(see illustration)**.

4   While an assistant supports the trunk lid, remove the lid-to-hinge bolts on both sides and lift it off **(see illustration)**.

5   Installation is the reverse of removal. **Note:** *When reinstalling the trunk lid, align the lid-to-hinge bolts with the marks made during removal.*

Adjustment

Refer to illustration 15.9

6   Fore-and-aft and side-to-side adjust-ment of the trunk lid is accomplished by mov-ing the lid in relation to the hinge after loosen-ing the bolts or nuts.

7   Scribe a line around the entire hinge

plate as described earlier in this Section so you can determine the amount of movement.

8   Loosen the bolts or nuts and move the trunk lid into correct alignment. Move it only a little at a time. Tighten the hinge bolts or nuts and carefully lower the trunk lid to check the alignment.

9   If necessary after installation, the entire trunk lid striker assembly can be adjusted up and down as well as from side to side on the trunk lid so the lid closes securely and is flush

with the rear quarter panels. To do this, scribe a line around the trunk lid striker assembly to provide a reference point. Then loosen the bolts and reposition the striker as necessary **(see illustration)**. Following adjustment, retighten the mounting bolts.

10   The trunk lid latch assembly, as well as the hinges, should be periodically lubricated with white lithium-base grease to prevent sticking and wear.

11   Finally, adjust the height of the trunk lid in relation to the body by screwing the rubber bumpers in-or-out.

16 Trunk release and fuel door cables - removal and installation

Refer to illustrations 16.2a, 16.2b, 162c and 16.5

1   Remove the left door sill plate(s) (both front and rear doors on sedan models). Remove the rear seat and the left rear quarter trim panel. Remove the left-side trunk trim panel. On Integra hatchback models, remove the rear trim panel. Pull the carpet back on the left side to access the cable retainers.

2   Remove the screw and detach the trim cover for access the release lever retaining bolts **(see illustration)**. Remove the release

16.2a Remove the cover from the release lever assembly

16.2b Remove the retaining bolts . . .

11

16.2c . . . and detach the cable from the release lever assembly

16.5 From inside the trunk or hatch area, rotate the fuel door release latch (arrow) 90-degrees so the tabs line up with the slots in the body, then withdraw the cable

17.1 Remove the window crank by pulling the clip off with a wire hook or special tool (handle removed for clarity)

17.2 Remove the screw and the inside door handle cover

17.3 Remove the screw and detach the armrest pocket

17.4a Remove the screws from the pull handle (arrows)

lever assembly retaining bolts, pull the assembly out and detach the cable(s) **(see illustrations)**.

3   Detach the cable(s) from the retainers and clips along the entire length of the cable(s).

4   On Integra models, remove the trunk lid or hatchback latch and disconnect the cable from the latch.

5   To detach the fuel door latch and cable, twist the latch 90-degrees to align the tabs on the striker assembly with the slots in the body and withdraw the latch and cable **(see illustration)**.

6   Working in the trunk compartment, pull the cable assembly towards the rear of the vehicle. Be careful not to bend the cable(s).

7   Installation is the reverse of removal.

17   Door trim panel - removal and installation

Warning: *Models covered by this manual are equipped with a Supplemental Restraint System (SRS), more commonly known as* airbags. Always disable the airbag system before working in the vicinity of the SRS unit, steering column or instrument panel to avoid the possibility of accidental deployment of the airbag, which could cause personal injury (see Chapter 12).

Caution: *If the radio in your vehicle is equipped with an anti-theft system, make sure you have the correct activation code before disconnecting the battery.*

Integra

Refer to illustrations 17.1, 17.2, 17.3, 17.4a, 17.4b, and 17.5

1   On manual window regulator equipped models, remove the window crank **(see illustration)**.

2   Remove the screw and the inside door handle cover **(see illustration)**.

3   Remove the screw and detach the armrest pocket **(see illustration)**.

4   Remove the door trim panel retaining screws from the pull handle and remove the plastic retainer in the front upper corner of the panel **(see illustrations)**.

5   Remove the screw from the rear edge of the panel **(see illustration)**.

Legend

Refer to illustrations 17.6a, 17.6b and 17.7

6   Carefully pry off the door handle trim plate and remove the two screws **(see illustrations)**. **Note:** *Do not remove the handle from the trim panel, but disconnect the cable*

17.4b Remove the retainer from the front upper corner

17.5 Remove the screw from the rear edge of the door panel

17.6a On Legend models, pry off the door handle cover . . .

17.6b . . . and remove the screws from the door handle

17.7 Remove the two screws from below the armrest (arrows)

17.8 Carefully pry the clips free so the door trim panel can be removed

17.9 On Legend models, pull the trim panel away from the door and disconnect the cable from the inside door handle

from the handle when the panel is removed.
7   Remove the two screws from below the armrest **(see illustration)**.

All models

Refer to illustrations 17.8 and 17.9
8   Carefully pry loose the retaining clips with a trim pad remover or a putty knife between the trim panel and the door. Work slowly and carefully around the outer edge of the trim panel until it's free **(see illustration)**.
9   After all of the clips are disengaged, pull the trim panel up, unplug any wire harness connectors and remove the panel. On legend models, disconnect the door handle cable from the door handle **(see illustration)**.
10   For access to the door inner panel, carefully pry out the retainers and detach the plastic shield.
11   Prior to installation of the door trim panel, be sure to reinstall any clips in the panel which may have come out when you removed the panel.
12   Plug in the wire harness connectors for the power door lock switch and the power window switch, if equipped, and place the panel in position in the door. Press the door panel into place until the clips are seated.

Install the trim panel retaining screws. If equipped, install the manual regulator crank handle.

18   Door - removal, installation and adjustment

Note: *The door is heavy and somewhat awkward to remove and install - at least two people should perform this procedure.*

Removal and installation

Refer to illustrations 18.6, 18.8a and 18.8b
1   Lower the window completely in the door and then disconnect the negative cable from the battery.
2   Open the door all the way and support it on jacks or blocks covered with rags to prevent damaging the paint.
3   Remove the door trim panel and water deflector as described in Section 17.
4   Disconnect all electrical connections, ground wires and harness retaining clips from the door. **Note:** *It is a good idea to label all connections to aid the reassembly process.*
5   From the door side, detach the rubber

conduit between the body and the door. Then pull the wiring harness through conduit hole and remove from the door.
6   Remove the door stop strut center pin **(see illustration)**.
7   Mark around the door hinges with a pen

18.6 Use a small hammer to tap out the door strut stop retaining pin (arrow)

11

18.8a Remove the door hinge bolts (arrows)

18.8b Open the rear doors for easier access to the bolts (arrows)

18.11 Loosen the hinge-to-body bolts to adjust the doors

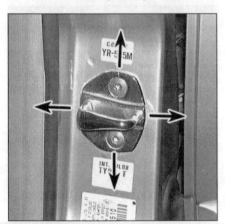

18.13 Adjust the door lock striker by loosening the mounting screws and gently tapping the striker in the desired direction

19.2 Detach the actuating rod link (arrow) from the latch

19.4 Remove the latch screws and nut (Legend models) (arrows) from the end of the door and pull the latch assembly through the access hole

or a scribe to facilitate realignment during reassembly.

8　With an assistant holding the door, remove the hinge to door bolts **(see illustrations)** and lift the door off.

9　Installation is the reverse of removal.

Adjustment

Refer to illustrations 18.11 and 18.13

10　Having proper door to body alignment is a critical part of a well functioning door assembly. First check the door hinge pins for excessive play. Fully open the door and lift up and down on the door without lifting the body. If a door has 1/16-inch or more excessive play, the hinges should be replaced.

11　Door-to-body alignment adjustments are made by loosening the hinge-to-body bolts **(see illustration)** or hinge-to-door bolts and moving the door. Proper body alignment is achieved when the top of the doors are parallel with the roof section, the front door is flush with the fender, the rear door is flush with the rear quarter panel and the bottom of the doors are aligned with the lower rocker panel. If these goals can't be reached by adjusting the hinge-to-body or hinge-to-door

bolts, body alignment shims may have to be purchased and inserted behind the hinges to achieve correct alignment.

12　To adjust the door closed position, scribe a line or mark around the striker plate to provide a reference point, then check that the door latch is contacting the center of the latch striker. If not adjust the up and down position first.

13　Finally adjust the latch striker sideways position, so that the door panel is flush with the center pillar or rear quarter panel and provides positive engagement with the latch mechanism **(see illustration)**.

19　Door latch, lock cylinder and handles - removal and installation

---

Door latch

Refer to illustrations 19.2 and 19.4

1　Raise the window then remove the door trim panel and watershield as described in Section 17.

2　Working through the large access hole, disengage the outside door handle-to-latch rod, outside door lock-to-latch rod, the inside

lock-to-latch rod, the inside handle-to-latch rod and the lock solenoid-to-latch rod (if equipped) **(see illustration)**.

3　All door locking rods are attached by plastic clips. The plastic clips can be removed by unsnapping the portion engaging the connecting rod and then pulling the rod out of its locating hole.

4　Remove the screws securing the latch to the door **(see illustration)**. Remove the latch assembly from the door.

5　Installation is the reverse of removal.

Outside handle and lock cylinder

6　Raise the window and remove the door trim panel and watershield as described in Section 17.

Integra

Refer to illustration 19.8

7　Working through the access hole, remove the clip retaining the lock cylinder to the outside handle assembly and remove the lock cylinder.

8　Carefully pry the latch rod swivel out of the handle **(see illustration)**.

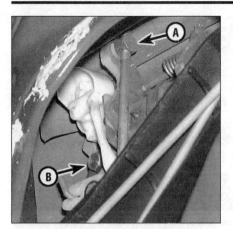

19.8 Pry the latch rod swivel (A) out of the handle and remove the mounting bolts (B) (only one bolt visible)

19.12 Pry the latch rod swivel (A) from the handle assembly and remove the bolt (B) and the handle holder - to remove the lock cylinder pull off the retaining clip (C)

19.15 Remove the handle base bolts (arrows) from the outside of the door and slide the handle base toward the front of the vehicle

19.19 Remove the inside handle retaining screws (arrows), pull the handle out and detach the actuating rod from the backside

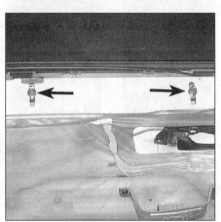

20.4 Remove the nuts (arrows) and detach the stopper plates at the top of the door

20.10 On Legend models, remove the nut (arrow) and detach the stopper plate

9   Remove the outside handle retaining bolts and remove the handle assembly from the door.

10   Installation is the reverse of removal.

Legend

Refer to illustrations 19.12 and 19.15

11   Disconnect the security system electrical connector and detach the harness from the retaining clips.

12   Remove the bolt and the holder from the handle base and pry the latch rod swivel from the handle assembly **(see illustration)**.

13   Remove the outer door handle by sliding it back and rotating the front out of the handle base and door.

14   Remove the screw covers and remove the mounting base bolts.

15   Slide the mounting base toward the front of the vehicle and remove it from the door **(see illustration)**.

16   To remove the lock cylinder, pull the retaining clip off the lock cylinder **(see illustration19.12)** and withdraw the lock cylinder from the outside of the door.

17   Installation is the reverse of removal.

Inside handle

Refer to illustration 19.19

Integra

18   Remove the door trim panel as described in Section 17 and peel away the watershield.

19   Remove the door handle retaining screws **(see illustration)**.

20   Pull the handle out, disconnect the actuating rod from the backside and remove the handle from the door.

21   Installation is the reverse of removal.

Legend

22   Remove the door trim panel (see Section 17).

23   Remove the screw and detach the inside handle from the trim panel.

24   Installation is the reverse of removal.

20   Door window glass - removal and installation

1   Remove the door trim panel and the plastic watershield (see Section 17).

Integra

Refer to illustration 20.4

2   Lower the window glass all the way down into the door.

3   Carefully pry the weatherstrip out of the door window opening.

4   Remove the nuts and detach the stopper plates from the door **(see illustration)**.

5   Raise the window just enough to access the window retaining bolts through the hole in the door frame.

6   Place a rag over the glass to help prevent scratching the glass and remove the two glass mounting nuts and remove the glass by pulling it up and out.

7   Installation is the reverse of removal.

Legend

Refer to illustrations 20.10, 20.11 and 20.12

8   Lower the window glass all the way down into the door.

9   Carefully pry the weatherstrip out of the door window opening.

10   Remove the nut and detach the stopper plate at the top of the door **(see illustration)**.

11

20.11 Remove the window run channel bolts (arrows) from the end of the door

20.12 Raise the window just enough to access the glass retaining bolts (arrows) through the holes in the door frame - loosen the bolts securing the glass to the regulator arm

21.4 Detach the window roller guide retaining nuts (A) and remove the window regulator bolts (B)

21.9 Remove the window roller guide and regulator bolts (arrows)

11   Remove the screw(s) and detach the front glass run channel from the window **(see illustration)**.

12   Raise the window just enough to access the window retaining bolts through the hole in the door frame and loosen the bolts **(see illustration)**.

13   Place a rag over the glass to help prevent scratching the glass and remove the two glass mounting bolts.

14   Remove the glass by pulling it to the rear, then lifting it up and out.

15   Installation is the reverse of removal.

21   Door window glass regulator - removal and installation

1   Remove the door trim panel and the plastic watershield (see Section 17).

Integra

Refer to illustration 21.4

2   Remove the window glass assembly (see Section 20).

3   On power operated windows, disconnect the electrical connector from the window regulator motor.

4   On all models, mark the location of the roller guide and regulator nuts and bolts. On power operated windows, remove the roller guide and the regulator mounting bolts **(see illustration)**. On manually operated windows remove the regulator mounting bolts, then slide the regulator assembly out of the lower channel guide.

5   Pull the roller guide and regulator assemblies through the service hole in the door frame to remove it.

6   Installation is the reverse of removal.

Legend

Refer to illustration 21.9

7   Remove the window glass assembly (see Section 20).

8   On power operated windows, disconnect the electrical connector from the window regulator motor.

9   On all models, mark the location of the roller guide and regulator nuts and bolts. On power operated windows, remove the roller guide and the regulator mounting bolts **(see illustration)**. On manually operated windows remove the regulator mounting bolts, then slide the regulator assembly out of the lower channel guide.

10 Pull the roller guide and regulator assemblies through the service hole in the door frame to remove it.

11 Installation is the reverse of removal.

22.2 Use a small screwdriver to pry off the mirror cover

22   Rearview mirrors - removal and installation

Outside mirrors

Refer to illustration 22.2 and 22.4

1   Remove the door trim panel and the plastic watershield (see Section 18).

2   Pry off the mirror trim cover **(see illustration)**.

**22.4 To remove the mirror, remove these three screws (arrows) -
if the vehicle has power mirrors, unplug the electrical connector**

22.8 Remove the screw (arrow) and lower the mirror

**23.4 Remove the front console retaining screws (arrows) (not all
screws visible)**

**23.6 Detach the cover and remove the screws (arrows) from the
front edge of the rear console**

3   Disconnect the electrical connector from the mirror (if equipped).

4   Remove the three mirror retaining nuts and detach the mirror from the vehicle **(see illustration)**.

5   Installation is the reverse of removal.

Inside mirror

Refer to illustration 22.8

6   Disconnect the electrical connector from the mirror (if equipped).

7   Detach the cover from the retaining bracket.

8   Remove the screws and lower the mirror **(see illustration)**.

9   Installation is the reverse of removal.

23   Center console - removal and installation

Warning: *Models covered by this manual are equipped with a Supplemental Restraint System (SRS), more commonly known as airbags. Always disable the airbag system before working in the vicinity of the SRS unit, steering column or instrument panel to avoid the possibility of accidental deployment of*

the airbag, which could cause personal injury (see Chapter 12).

1   Disconnect the negative battery cable. **Caution:** *If the radio in your vehicle is equipped with an anti-theft system, make sure you have the correct activation code before disconnecting the battery.*

2   Apply the parking brake and block the wheels, On automatic transaxle models, place the shift lever in Drive, On manual transaxle models, remove the shift lever knob.

Integra

Refer to illustrations 23.4 and 23.6

3   Remove the lower dashboard trim panels from both sides (see Section 24).

4   Pry off the rear cover and remove the front console retaining screws **(see illustration)**.

5   Lift the front console up and over the shift lever. Disconnect any electrical connections and remove the console from the vehicle.

6   Pry up the cover and remove the two rear console screws **(see illustration).**

7   Pull up on the parking brake handle. Slide the console to the rear of the vehicle to disengage the hooks and lift it over the park-

ing brake handle.

8   Installation is the reverse of removal.

Legend

Refer to illustration 23.9, 23.10, 23.11a, 23.11b, 23.11c, 23.13a and 23.13b

9   Remove the lower dashboard trim panels and the glove box (see Section 24). On automatic transmission models, carefully pry

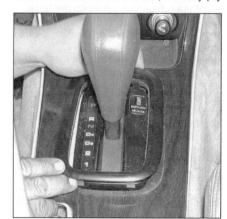

**23.9 On automatic transmission models,
pry off the shift lever trim plate**

11

23.10 Remove the two screws (arrows) and carefully remove the trim panel from the console

23.11a Remove the two screws at the front edge of the center armrest/storage compartment (arrows)

23.11b Open the lid and remove the screws from inside the storage compartment

23.11c After prying off the cover, remove the screws from each side of the center armrest/storage compartment

23.13a Remove the screws (arrows) and the glove box side cover from the right side of the center console

off the shift lever trim plate (see illustration).

10   Remove the two screws retaining the console trim panel, pry the console trim panel off and disconnect the electrical connector for the cigar lighter (see illustration).

11   Carefully pry the cover off the backside of the center armrest/storage compartment. Remove the screws at the front, rear and inside the compartment (see illustrations).

12   Remove the center armrest/storage compartment by lifting it up over the parking brake lever.

13   Remove the cover from the right side of the console (see illustration). Remove the three screws from each side, the two screws at the top and the two screws at the rear of the console (see illustration).

14   Lift the console up and over the shift lever. Disconnect any electrical connections and remove the console from the vehicle.

15   Installation is the reverse of removal.

24 Dashboard trim panels - removal and installation

Warning: *Models covered by this manual are*

23.13b Remove the retaining screws on each side at the rear of the console

equipped with a Supplemental Restraint System (SRS), more commonly known as airbags. Always disable the airbag system before working in the vicinity of the SRS unit, steering column or instrument panel to avoid the possibility of accidental deployment of the airbag, which could cause personal injury (see Chapter 12).

Caution: *If the radio in your vehicle is equipped with an anti-theft system, make*

sure you have the correct activation code before disconnecting the battery.

Instrument cluster bezel

Refer to illustrations 24.2a, 24.2b and 24.3

1   Tilt the steering wheel down to the lowest position.

2   On Integra models, remove the screws at the top of the bezel (see illustration). Remove the screws at the lower edge of the

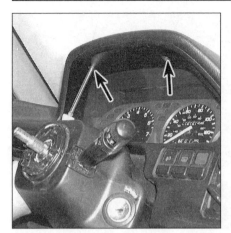

24.2a Remove the screws along the top of the bezel

24.2b Remove the blower fan switch cover and remove the screws

24.3 Remove the screws on each side of the lower edge of the bezel (Legend)

24.8a Driver's side instrument panel lower cover screw locations (arrows) - Integra

24.8b Driver's side instrument panel lower cover screw locations (arrows) - Legend

bezel (one on each side of the steering column). Remove the blower fan and air conditioning switch knobs and pry off the cover. Remove the screws behind the cover **(see illustration)**. Remove the screw at the right end of the bezel (to the right of the heater/air conditioning control panel).

3   On Legend models, remove the instrument panel lower cover and remove the two screws (one on each side of the steering column) **(see illustration)**.

4   Grasp the bezel securely and pull back sharply to detach the clips from the instrument panel.

5   Unplug any electrical connectors that interfere with removal.

6   Installation is the reverse of removal.

Instrument panel lower cover (driver side)

Refer to illustrations 24.8a and 24.8b

7   On Integra models, remove the lower pocket. On Legend models, carefully pry out the interior lights dimmer panel and disconnect the electrical connector

8   Detach the retaining screws and remove

24.11 Remove the knee bolster reinforcement panel bolts (arrows) (Integra model shown)

the cover **(see illustrations)**.

9   Installation is the reverse of removal.

Knee bolster reinforcement panel

Refer to illustration 24.11

10   Remove the driver side instrument panel lower cover (see above).

11   Remove the bolts and detach the knee

bolster reinforcement panel **(see illustration)**.

12   Installation is the reverse of removal.

Instrument panel lower cover (passenger side)

Refer to illustration 24.13a and 24.13b

13   Remove the screws or clips along the lower edge, then detach the lower cover from

11

24.13a On Integra models, remove the screws (arrows) from the lower edge of the passenger side lower cover and pull the cover straight back

24.13b On Legend models, pry out the three clips (arrows) to remove the passenger side lower cover

24.15a Integra model glove box retaining screws (arrows)

24.15b On Legend models, remove the four hinge screws (arrows) and detach the glove box

the dashboard **(see illustrations)**.
14   Installation is the reverse of the removal.

Glove box

Refer to illustration 24.15a and 24.15b
15   To remove the glove box, remove the screws and lower the glove box from the instrument panel **(see illustrations)**.
16   Installation is the reverse of the removal.

Clock (Integra models)

Refer to illustration 24.17
17   Use a screwdriver to detach the clock **(see illustration)**.
18   Unplug the clock electrical connector and remove the clock from the instrument panel.
19   Installation is the reverse of the removal.

Glove box side cover (Legend models)

Refer to illustration 24.21
20   Remove the passenger side lower cover and glove box (see above).
21   Remove the screws and detach the cover from the instrument panel **(see illustration)**.
22   Installation is the reverse of the removal.

24.17 Using a flat-blade screwdriver, carefully pry the clock from the instrument panel

25   Steering column cover - removal and installation

Refer to illustrations 25.3a and 25.3b
Warning: *Models covered by this manual are equipped with a Supplemental Restraint Sys-*

24.21 Remove the glove box side cover retaining screws (arrows)

tem (SRS), more commonly known as airbags. Always disable the airbag system before working in the vicinity of the SRS unit, steering column or instrument panel to avoid the possibility of accidental deployment of the airbag, which could cause personal injury (see Chapter 12).
Caution: *If the radio in your vehicle is equipped with an anti-theft system, make*

25.3a Remove the screws (arrows) from the lower steering column cover (Integra)

25.3b Legend model steering column cover screws (arrows)

26.8 Remove the steering column retaining nuts (arrows) and lower the steering column

26.9 Remove the side covers on Integra models for access to the instrument panel retaining bolts

26.13 Remove the screws (arrows) securing the lower center of the instrument panel

26.14a Remove the screws securing the left and . . .

sure you have the correct activation code before disconnecting the battery.

1   Remove the driver's side instrument panel lower cover (see Section 26).

2   On tilt steering columns, move the column to the lowest position.

3   Remove the retaining screws, then separate the halves and remove the covers (see illustrations).

4   Installation is the reverse of the removal procedure.

26 Instrument panel - removal and installation

Refer to illustrations 26.8, 26.9, 26.13, 26.14a and 26.14b

Warning: *Models covered by this manual are equipped with a Supplemental Restraint System (SRS), more commonly known as airbags. Always disable the airbag system before working in the vicinity of the SRS unit, steering column or instrument panel to avoid the possibility of accidental deployment of the airbag, which could cause personal injury* (see Chapter 12).

Caution: *If the radio in your vehicle is*

equipped with an anti-theft system, make sure you have the correct activation code before disconnecting the battery.

1   Disconnect the negative battery cable. Disable the airbags (see Chapter 12).

2   Remove the driver's side airbag (if equipped) and the steering wheel (see Chapter 10).

3   Remove the center floor console (see Section 23).

4   Remove the instrument cluster bezel (see Section 24).

5   Remove the instrument cluster (see Chapter 12).

6   Remove all of the dashboard trim panels described in Section 24.

7   Detach the nuts and bolts securing the fuse box and the hood release handle (see Chapter 12 and Section 11).

8   Remove the nuts and lower the steering column (see illustration). Place protective padding on the front seat to protect the upholstery.

9   Remove the instrument panel side covers (see illustration).

10   Detach the air vent grilles.

11   Remove the radio (see Chapter 12) and the heater/air conditioning control assembly

26.14b . . . right side of the instrument panel

(see Chapter 3).

12   Remove the bolts securing each end of the instrument panel.

13   Remove the screws securing the lower center part of the instrument panel (see illustration).

14   Remove the bolts securing the lower half of the instrument panel (see illustrations).

11

27.2a Remove the screws (arrows) and detach the cowl (Integra)

27.2b Remove the windshield base molding for access and remove the screws (arrows) on each side of the cowl (Legend)

15   Remove the bolts retaining the front edge of instrument panel to the firewall.

16   Pull the instrument panel towards the rear of the vehicle and detach any electrical connectors interfering with removal.

17   Lift the instrument panel over the steering column and remove it from the vehicle.

18   Installation is the reverse of removal.

27   Cowl cover - removal and installation

Refer to illustrations 27.2a and 27.2b

1   Remove the windshield wiper arm retaining nuts and remove the wiper arms.

2   Remove the retaining screws and plastic clips securing the rear of the cowl cover and remove the cowl cover from the vehicle (**see illustrations**).

3   Installation is the reverse of removal.

28   Seats - removal and installation

Front seat

Refer to illustrations 28.2, 28.5, 28.6a and 28.6b

1   Position the seat all the way back and remove the front retaining bolts.

2   Position the seat all the way forward and remove the rear retaining bolts (**see illustration**).

28.2 Remove the cover for access to the front seat retaining bolts (arrow)

3   Tilt the seat upward to access the underneath, then disconnect any electrical connectors and lift the seat from the vehicle.

4   Installation is the reverse of removal.

Rear seat

Integra

5   Remove the rear seat back hinge bolts and remove the rear seat backs.

6   Remove the seat cushion rear retaining bolts and pull the back of the seat up to detach the hooks at the front.

28.7 Detach the rear seat cushion retaining clip (arrow) on each side

Legend

Refer to illustrations 28.7, 28.8a and 28.8b

7   Pull the rear seat cushion up and detach the seat cushion retaining clips (**see illustration**). Pull the front of the seat up to detach the hooks at the back and remove the cushion.

8   Pull the bolt covers back and remove the seat back mounting bolts (four at the bottom, two at the top) (**see illustration**). Pull the seat back up and out to detach the hooks and remove the seat back.

9   Installation is the reverse of removal.

28.8a Remove the bolts at the bottom (arrows) . . .

28.8b . . . and top (arrow) of the seat back

Chapter 12
Chassis electrical system

Contents

1 General information

The electrical system is a 12-volt, negative ground type. A lead/acid-type battery charged by the alternator supplies power for the lights and all electrical accessories.

This Chapter covers repair and service procedures for the various electrical components not associated with the engine. Information on the battery, alternator, distributor and starter motor can be found in Chapter 5. It should be noted that when portions of the electrical system are serviced, the negative battery cable should be disconnected from the battery to prevent electrical shorts and/or fires. **Caution:** *If the radio in your vehicle is equipped with an anti-theft system, make sure you have the correct activation code before disconnecting the battery.*

2 Electrical troubleshooting

Refer to illustration 2.15

A typical electrical circuit consists of an electrical component, any switches, relays, motors, fuses, fusible links or circuit breakers related to that component and the wiring and connectors that link the component to both the battery and the chassis. To help you pinpoint an electrical circuit problem, wiring diagrams are included at the end of this Chapter.

Before tackling any troublesome electrical circuit, first study the appropriate wiring diagrams to get a complete understanding of what makes up that individual circuit. Trouble spots, for instance, can often be narrowed down by noting if other components related to the circuit are operating properly. If several components or circuits fail at one time, chances are the problem is in a fuse or ground connection, because several circuits are often routed through the same fuse and ground connections.

Electrical problems usually stem from simple causes, such as loose or corroded connections, a blown fuse, a melted fusible link or a failed relay. Visually inspect the condition of all fuses, wires and connections in a problem circuit before troubleshooting the circuit.

If test equipment and instruments are going to be utilized, use the diagrams to plan ahead of time where you will make the necessary connections in order to accurately pinpoint the trouble spot.

The basic tools needed for electrical troubleshooting include a circuit tester or voltmeter (a 12-volt bulb with a set of test leads can also be used), a continuity tester, which includes a bulb, battery and set of test leads, and a jumper wire, preferably with a circuit breaker incorporated, which can be used to bypass electrical components. Before attempting to locate a problem with test instruments, use the wiring diagram(s) to decide where to make the connections.

Voltage checks

Voltage checks should be performed if a circuit is not functioning properly. Connect one lead of a circuit tester to either the negative battery terminal or a known good ground. Connect the other lead to a connector in the circuit being tested, preferably nearest to the battery or fuse. If the bulb of the tester lights, voltage is present, which means that the part of the circuit between the connector and the battery is problem free. Continue checking the rest of the circuit in the same fashion. When you reach a point at which no voltage is present, the problem lies between that point and the last test point with voltage. Most of the time the problem can be traced to a loose connection. **Note:** *Keep in mind that some circuits receive voltage only when the ignition key is in the Accessory or Run position.*

Finding a short

One method of finding shorts in a circuit is to remove the fuse and connect a test light or voltmeter in place of the fuse terminals. There should be no voltage present in the circuit. Move the wiring harness from side-to-side while watching the test light. If the bulb goes on, there is a short to ground somewhere in that area, probably where the insulation has rubbed through. The same test can be performed on each component in the circuit, even a switch.

Ground check

Perform a ground test to check whether a component is properly grounded. Disconnect the battery and connect one lead of a self-powered test light, known as a continuity tester, to a known good ground. Connect the other lead to the wire or ground connection being tested. If the bulb goes on, the ground is good. If the bulb does not go on, the ground is not good.

Continuity check

A continuity check is done to determine if there are any breaks in a circuit - if it is passing electricity properly. With the circuit off (no power in the circuit), a self-powered continuity tester can be used to check the circuit. Connect the test leads to both ends of the circuit (or to the "power" end and a good ground), and if the test light comes on the circuit is passing current properly. If the light doesn't come on, there is a break somewhere in the circuit. The same procedure can be used to test a switch, by connecting the continuity tester to the switch terminals. With the switch turned On, the test light should come on.

2.15 To backprobe a connector, insert a small diameter probe with a sharp point (such as a straight pin) into the back of the connector along side the desired wire until the probe contacts the metal terminal; connect your meter leads to the probes - this allows you to test a functioning circuit

Finding an open circuit

When diagnosing for possible open circuits, it is often difficult to locate them by sight because oxidation or terminal misalignment are hidden by the connectors. Merely wiggling a connector on a sensor or in the wiring harness may correct the open circuit condition. Remember this when an open circuit is indicated when troubleshooting a circuit. Intermittent problems may also be caused by oxidized or loose connections.

Electrical troubleshooting is simple if you keep in mind that all electrical circuits are basically electricity running from the battery, through the wires, switches, relays, fuses and fusible links to each electrical component (light bulb, motor, etc.) and to ground, from which it is passed back to the battery. Any electrical problem is an interruption in the flow of electricity to and from the battery.

Connectors

Most electrical connections on these vehicles are made with multiwire plastic connectors. The mating halves of many connectors are secured with locking clips molded into the plastic connector shells. The mating halves of large connectors, such as some of those under the instrument panel, are held together by a bolt through the center of the connector.

To separate a connector with locking clips, use a small screwdriver to pry the clips apart carefully, then separate the connector halves. Pull only on the shell, never pull on the wiring harness as you may damage the individual wires and terminals inside the connectors. Look at the connector closely before trying to separate the halves. Often the locking clips are engaged in a way that is not immediately clear. Additionally, many connectors have more than one set of clips.

Each pair of connector terminals has a

3.1a On Integra models, the interior fuse box (arrow) is located under the left (driver's side) of the instrument panel, under a cover

male half and a female half. When you look at the end view of a connector in a diagram, be sure to understand whether the view shows the harness side or the component side of the connector. Connector halves are mirror images of each other, and a terminal shown on the right side end view of one half will be on the left side end view of the other half.

It is often necessary to take circuit voltage measurements with a connector connected. Whenever possible, carefully insert the test probes of your meter into the rear of the connector shell to contact the terminal inside. This kind of connection is called "backprobing" **(see illustration).** When inserting a test probe into a male terminal, be careful not to distort the terminal opening. Doing so can lead to a poor connection and corrosion at that terminal later. If the connector openings are too small for your meter's probes, insert small straight pins into the openings and attach the meter probes to them.

3   Fuses - general information

Refer to illustrations 3.1a, 3.1b, 3.1c and 3.3

1   The electrical circuits of the vehicle are protected by a combination of fuses and circuit breakers. The two fuse blocks (three fuse blocks on models equipped with ABS) are located under the instrument panel and on the side of the engine compartment **(see illustrations).**

2   Each of the fuses is designed to protect a specific circuit (or circuits), and the various circuits are identified on the fuse panel itself.

3   Miniaturized fuses are employed in the fuse blocks. These compact fuses, with blade terminal design, allow fingertip removal and replacement. If an electrical component fails, always check the fuse first. To check the fuses, turn the ignition key to the On position and, using a test light, probe each exposed terminal of each fuse. If the test light glows on both terminals of a fuse, the fuse is

3.1b On Integra models, the engine compartment fuse box (arrow) is located in the right rear corner of the engine compartment

3.1c On Legend models, the engine compartment fuse box (arrow) is located next to the battery

good. If power is available on one side of the fuse but not the other, the fuse is blown. When removed, a blown fuse is easily identified through the clear plastic body **(see illustration)**. Visually inspect the element for evidence of damage.

4   Be sure to replace blown fuses with the correct type. Fuses of different ratings are physically interchangeable, but only fuses of the proper rating should be used. Replacing a fuse with one of a higher or lower value than

3.3 The fuses can easily be inspected visually to see if they are blown

specified is not recommended. Each electrical circuit needs a specific amount of protection. The amperage value of each fuse is molded into the fuse body.

5   If the replacement fuse immediately fails, don't replace it again until the cause of the problem is isolated and corrected. In most cases, the cause will be a short circuit in the wiring caused by a broken or deteriorated wire.

6   All models are equipped with a main fuse (either an 80A or 100A) which protects all the circuits coming from the battery. If these circuits are overloaded, the main fuse blows, preventing damage to the main wiring harness. The main fuse consists of a metal strip, which will be visibly melted when overloaded. Always disconnect the battery before replacing a main fuse (available from your dealer). **Caution:** *If the stereo in your vehicle is equipped with an anti-theft system, make sure you have the correct activation code before disconnecting the battery.* The main fuse is located in the engine compartment fuse block. It's very similar in appearance to standard fuses and is replaced in the same way. If you have to replace a main fuse, make sure you install a replacement unit that's

equivalent to the old fuse. In other words, if the old main fuse is an 80A unit, replace it with an 80A fuse; if it's a 100A unit, replace it with a 100A fuse. Don't switch amperage ratings on the main fuse!

4   Circuit breakers - general information

Circuit breakers protect components such as sunroof motors, power window motors and airbag inflator resistors.

On some models the circuit breaker resets itself automatically, so an electrical overload in a circuit breaker protected system will cause the circuit to fail momentarily, then come back on. If the circuit does not come back on, check it immediately. Once the condition is corrected, the circuit breaker will resume its normal function. Some circuit breakers must be reset manually.

5   Relays - general information

General information

Refer to illustrations 5.1a, 5.1b and 5.1c

1   Several electrical accessories in the vehicle, such as the fuel injection system, horns, starter, and cooling fans use relays to transmit the electrical power to the component. Relays use a low-current circuit (the control circuit) to open and close a high-current circuit (the power circuit). If the relay is defective, that component will not operate properly. The various relays are mounted in engine compartment fuse box and several locations throughout the vehicle **(see illustrations)**. If a faulty relay is suspected, it can be removed and tested using the procedure below. Defective relays must be replaced as a unit.

Testing

Refer to illustration 5.5

2   It's best to refer to the wiring diagram for the circuit to determine the proper hook-ups for the relay you're testing. However, if

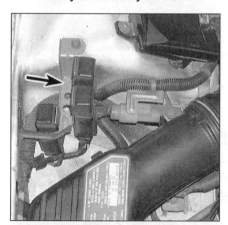

5.1a On Integra models, the ABS relays (arrow) are located on the right side of the engine compartment

5.1b On Legend models, several relays are located in the right rear corner of the engine compartment

5.1c On Legend models, the main relay center is located next to the battery (arrow)

12

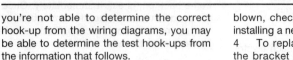

5.5 To test a typical four-terminal normally open relay, connect an ohmmeter to the two terminals of the power circuit - the meter will indicate no continuity until battery power and ground are connected to the two terminals of the control circuit, then the relay will click and continuity will be indicated

42025-12-5.5 HAYNES

6.1a On Integra models, the turn signal/hazard flasher (arrow) is located next to the steering column

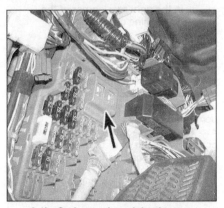

6.1b On Legend models, the turn signal/hazard flasher is located on the interior fuse box (arrow)

7.2 On Legend models, disconnect the electrical connector for the lighting switch or wiper switch at the base of the steering column

you're not able to determine the correct hook-up from the wiring diagrams, you may be able to determine the test hook-ups from the information that follows.

3   On most relays, two of the terminals are the relay's control circuit (they connect to the relay coil which, when energized, closes the large contacts to complete the circuit). The other terminals are the power circuit (they are connected together within the relay when the control-circuit coil is energized).

4   Most relays are marked as an aid to help you determine which terminals are the control circuit and which are the power circuit.

5   Connect an ohmmeter to the two terminals of the power circuit. Connect a fused jumper wire between one of the two control circuit terminals and the positive battery terminal. Connect another jumper wire between the other control circuit terminal and ground. When the connections are made, the relay should click and continuity will be indicated on the meter **(see illustration)**. On some relays, polarity may be critical, so, if the relay doesn't click, try swapping the jumper wires on the control circuit terminals.

6   If the relay fails the above test, replace it.

6   Hazard/turn signal flashers - check and replacement

Refer to illustrations 6.1a and 6.1b

1   The hazard/turn signal flasher is located next to the steering column (Integra) or in the interior fuse block under the left side of the instrument panel (Legend) **(see illustrations)**

2   If the flasher unit is functioning properly, you can hear an audible clicking sound when it's operating. If the turn signals fail on one side or the other and the flasher unit doesn't make its characteristic clicking sound, look for a faulty turn signal bulb.

3   If both turn signals fail to blink, the problem may be due to a blown fuse (in the engine compartment fuse box), a faulty flasher unit, a broken switch or a loose or open connection. If a quick check of the fuse box indicates that the turn signal fuse has

blown, check the wiring for a short before installing a new fuse.

4   To replace the flasher, remove it from the bracket and disconnect the connector (Integra) or pull it out of the fuse block (Legend).

5   Make sure that the replacement unit is identical to the original. Compare the old one to the new one before installing it.

6   Installation is the reverse of removal.

7   Steering column switches - check and replacement

Warning: *Legend models are equipped with a Supplemental Restraint system (SRS), more commonly known as airbags. Always disable the airbag system before working in the vicinity of the impact sensors, steering column or instrument panel to avoid the possibility of accidental deployment of the airbag, which could cause personal injury (see Section 26). Do not use electrical test equipment on any of the airbag system wiring or tamper with them in any way.*

Combination light switch and windshield wiper/washer switch

Check

Refer to illustrations 7.2, 7.3a, 7.3b, 7.3c, 7.3d and 7.3e

1   The exterior lighting and wiper switches

SWITCH POSITION	CONTINUITY BETWEEN
Headlight switch	
Low beam	D and E; F and I
High beam	D and E; I and J
Flash-to-pass	I and J
Turn signal switch	
Right	A and C
Left	A and B

7.3a Combination light switch terminal guide and continuity table - Integra

SWITCH POSITION	CONTINUITY BETWEEN
Windshield wiper switch	
Off	A and F
Int	A and F; C and D
Low	A and G
High	B and G
Mist	B and G
Washer	D and E
Rear wiper switch	
Off	J and K
On	J and L
Washer	H and I

7.3b Wiper/washer switch terminal guide and continuity table - Integra

1	2	3			4	5	6
7	8	9	10	11	12	13	14

SWITCH POSITION	CONTINUITY BETWEEN
Headlight switch	
Low beam	2, 3 and 12
High beam	2 and 11
Flash-to-pass	2, 11 and 12
Turn signal switch	
Right	6 and 4 (diode)
Left	5 and 6 (diode)

Note: *The turn signal switch contains a diode; if continuity is not indicated, reverse the meter leads and retest.*

7.3c Combination light switch terminal guide and continuity table - Legend

1	2	3			4	5	6
7	8	9	10	11	12	13	14

SWITCH POSITION	CONTINUITY BETWEEN
Int	3 and 11
Low	4 and 10
High	5 and 10
Mist	5 and 10
Washer	3 and 13
Intermittent time controller	8 and 2 (0 to 30 K-ohms)

**7.3d Windshield wiper/washer switch terminal guide and continuity table - Legend
(with Traction Control System)**

1	2			3	4
5	6	7	8	9	10

SWITCH POSITION	CONTINUITY BETWEEN
Int	2 and 8
Low	3 and 7
High	4 and 7
Mist	4 and 7
Washer	2 and 10
Intermittent time controller	1 and 5 (0 to 30 K-ohms)

**7.3e Windshield wiper/washer switch terminal guide and continuity table - Legend
(without Traction Control System)**

are located on the steering column. The combination light switch incorporates the turn signal, headlight, dimmer and parking light switches into one switch on the left side of the column. The windshield wiper/washer functions are incorporated into another switch on the right side of the column. The cruise control and radio remote switch (some models) are located on the steering wheel.

2   On Integra models, because of difficulty in accessing the terminals for testing, remove the switch (see Step 4). On Legend models, remove the lower instrument panel cover and disconnect the appropriate switch electrical connector at the base of the steering column **(see illustration)**.

3   Using an ohmmeter or self-powered test light and the accompanying diagrams, check for continuity between the indicated switch terminals with the switch in each of the indicated positions **(see illustrations)**. If the continuity isn't as specified, replace the switch.

Replacement

Refer to illustrations 7.5a and 7.5b

4   On Integra models, remove the steering wheel and the steering column covers. Use a small screwdriver to carefully detach the electrical connectors from the switch. Remove the two retaining screws and detach the switch from the steering column. Installation is the reverse of removal.

5   On Legend models, remove the lower instrument panel cover and the steering column covers. Disconnect the electrical connector at the base of the steering column. Remove the switch retaining screws by positioning the steering wheel spokes vertically to one side or the other **(see illustrations)**. Remove the switch. Installation is the reverse of removal.

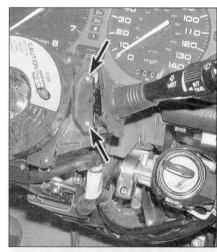

7.5a On Legend models, to remove either of the steering column switches, remove the two retaining screws (arrows) (steering wheel removed for clarity only, position the spokes vertically to access the screws) . . .

12

7.5b . . . and carefully pry the switch out of the steering column bracket

Cruise control switch

Check

Refer to illustrations 7.7a and 7.7b

6   On Integra models, remove the steering wheel for access to the switch connector. On Legend models, remove the switch from the steering wheel (see Step 10).

7   Using an ohmmeter and the accompanying diagram, check for continuity between the indicated terminals with the switch in each of the indicated positions **(see illustrations)**. If the continuity isn't as specified, replace the switch.

Replacement

Refer to illustration 7.10

8   Disconnect the negative battery cable (see **Warning** above). **Caution:** *If the radio in your vehicle is equipped with an anti-theft system, make sure you have the correct activation code before disconnecting the battery.*

9   On Integra models, remove the steering wheel, remove the two screws and detach the switch.

10   On Legend models, remove the cover over the cruise control switch. Detach the switch retaining screws **(see illustration)**. Then disconnect the electrical connections and remove the switch from the steering wheel.

11   Installation is the reverse of removal.

7.10 On Legend models, remove the two mounting screws (arrows) and remove the cruise control switch

SWITCH POSITION	CONTINUITY BETWEEN
Off	
Set (On)	A and C
Resume (On)	B and C

7.7a Cruise control switch terminal guide and continuity table - Integra

SWITCH POSITION	CONTINUITY BETWEEN
Set (On)	C and B
Resume (On)	C and A
Cancel (On)	C and B; C and A (diode)

Note: *The cancel switch contains a diode, if continuity is not indicated, reverse the meter leads and retest.*

7.7b Cruise control switch terminal guide and continuity table - Legend

Radio remote switch (Legend models)

Check

Refer to illustration 7.13

12   Remove the switch from the steering wheel (see below).

13   Using an ohmmeter or self-powered test light and the accompanying diagram, measure the resistance between the two terminals with the switch in each position **(see**

illustration). If the resistance isn't as specified, replace the switch.

Replacement

Refer to illustration 7.14

14   Remove the cover over the radio remote switch. Detach the switch retaining screws, disconnect the electrical connections and remove the switch from the steering wheel **(see illustration)**

15   Installation is the reverse of removal.

SWITCH POSITION	RESISTANCE
Off	3,600 ohms
Seek	800 ohms
Volume up	350 ohms
Volume down	100 ohms

7.13 Radio remote control terminal guide and resistance table - Legend

7.14 Remove the two mounting screws (arrows) and remove the radio remote switch

8.3 Disconnect the ignition switch connectors from the fuse box and wiring harness (arrow)

8   Ignition switch and key lock cylinder - check and replacement

Warning: *Legend models are equipped with a Supplemental Restraint system (SRS), more commonly known as airbags. Always disable the airbag system before working in the vicinity of the impact sensors, steering column or instrument panel to avoid the possibility of accidental deployment of the airbag, which could cause personal injury (see Section 26). Do not use electrical test equipment on any of the airbag system wiring or tamper with them in any way.*

Ignition switch

Refer to illustrations 8.3, 8.4a, 8.4b, 8.7a and 8.7b

1   Disconnect the negative battery cable (see **Warning** above). **Caution:** *If the radio in your vehicle is equipped with an anti-theft system, make sure you have the correct activation code before disconnecting the battery.*

2   Remove the lower instrument panel cover and the steering column covers (see Chapter 11).

3   Follow the wire harness for the ignition switch down the steering column and discon-

nect the connectors from the fuse box and wiring harness **(see illustration)**.

4   Check the ignition switch for continuity between the indicated connector terminals with the ignition switch in each position **(see illustrations)**.

5   If the continuity is not as specified, replace the switch.

6   Insert the key and turn it to the Lock position.

7   Remove the two retaining screws and detach the switch **(see illustrations)**.

8   Installation is the reverse of removal.

Lock cylinder and steering column lock assembly

Note: *On Integra models with a manual transaxle, the lock cylinder can be replaced separately. On all other models, the lock cylinder and steering column lock must be replaced as an assembly.*

9   Check the lock cylinder in each position to make sure it isn't worn or loose and that the key position corresponds to the markings on the housing.

10   Disconnect the negative battery cable (see **Warning** above). **Caution:** *If the radio in your vehicle is equipped with an anti-theft system, make sure you have the correct activation code before disconnecting the battery.*

SWITCH POSITION	CONTINUITY BETWEEN
I	2 and 4
II	2, 4 and 6; 7, 1 and 3
III	7,1 and 5

8.4a Ignition switch terminal guide (as viewed from backside of connector) and continuity table - Integra

SWITCH POSITION	CONTINUITY BETWEEN
I	1 and 4
II	1, 2, 3 and 4
III	1, 2 and 5

8.4b Ignition switch terminal guide (as viewed from backside of connector) and continuity table - Legend

8.7a Ignition switch screw locations (arrows) - Integra

8.7b Ignition switch screw locations (arrows) - Legend

12

8.12　On Integra models with a manual transaxle, remove the lock cylinder set screw (arrow)

8.13　With the key in the Acc (I) position, push in on the release pin with a punch or screwdriver and pull the cylinder straight out

8.24　On Legend models, use a chisel and hammer to make a notch in the head of the shear-bolt, then unscrew the bolt and detach the bracket

Integra

Refer to illustrations 8.12 and 8.13

Manual transaxle

11　Remove the steering wheel (see Chapter 10) and the steering column covers (see Chapter 11). Remove the ignition switch.

12　Insert the key and place the ignition switch in the Acc (I) position. Remove the set screw from the lock cylinder housing **(see illustration)**.

13　Using a small screwdriver or sharp awl, depress the pin and withdraw the lock cylinder from the housing **(see illustration)**.

14　To install the new lock cylinder, turn the key to the Lock (0) position and align the lock cylinder with the housing. Holding the lock cylinder, turn the key to the Acc (I) position, depress the pin and guide the pin into the slot in the housing. Press the lock cylinder in until the pin locks in place and install the set screw.

15　Check the lock operation and install the ignition switch, steering column covers and steering wheel.

Automatic transaxle

16　Remove the steering wheel (see Chapter 10). Remove the steering column covers, lower instrument panel cover and knee bolster (see Chapter 11).

17　Remove the steering column mounting nuts/bolts. Lower and support the steering column. Remove the ignition switch from the lock assembly.

18　Center-punch the two shear-head bolts and drill the bolt heads off with a 3/16-inch drill bit. **Caution:** *Be careful not to damage the lock housing if you intend to reuse it.* Separate the clamp and remove the lock assembly from the steering column.

19　Install the lock assembly and loosely install new shear-head bolts. Install the ignition switch and make sure the lock operates properly and the ignition key does not bind.

20　Tighten the shear head bolts until the heads break off.

21　Raise the steering column into position and tighten the mounting bolts to 114 in-lbs.

22　The remainder of installation is the reverse of removal.

Legend

Refer to illustrations 8.24, 8.25 and 8.26

23　Remove the steering column covers and lower instrument panel cover and knee bolster (see Chapter 11). Remove the ignition switch and disconnect the wiring harness from the lock assembly.

24　Use a chisel and hammer or a file to cut a notch in the head of the shear-head bolt. Tap the bolt head counterclockwise and remove the bolt **(see illustration)**. Remove the knee bolster bracket.

25　Remove the steering column mounting flange nuts and the lower bracket. Carefully lower and support the steering column **(see illustration)**.

26　Insert the key and place the ignition switch cylinder to the Acc (I) position. Using a small screwdriver or sharp awl, depress the pin and withdraw the lock assembly from the steering column **(see illustration)**.

27　To install the new lock assembly, insert the key and place the lock in the Acc (I) position. Depress the retaining pin and insert the lock assembly into the steering column until

8.25　Lower the steering column for access to the lock cylinder

8.26　To remove the ignition lock assembly on a Legend, place the key in the Acc (I) position, depress the release pin with a tool and pull the assembly straight out of the steering column

9.1a Instrument panel switch location - Integra

1   Hazard switch
2   Rear window defogger switch
3   Fog light switch

9.1b Instrument panel switch location - Integra

4   Instrument panel light dimmer
5   Cruise control main switch
6   Moon roof control switch
7   Power mirror control switch

the pin locks in place. Loosely install a new shear-head bolt and the knee bolster bracket.
28   Raise the steering column into position. Tighten the flange nuts to 144 in-lbs and the lower clamp bolts to 16 ft-lbs.
30   Temporarily install the lower instrument panel cover and make sure the lock fits through the hole provided. Turn the lock assembly slightly to make it fit, if necessary. Insert the key and make sure the lock operates properly and the ignition key does not bind. When satisfied all is correct, tighten the shear-head bolt until the head breaks off.
31   Install the ignition switch, knee bolster, instrument panel lower cover and steering column covers.
32   The remainder of installation is the reverse of removal.

9   Instrument panel switches - check and replacement

Warning: *Legend models are equipped with a Supplemental Restraint system (SRS), more commonly known as airbags. Always disable the airbag system before working in the vicinity of the impact sensors, steering column or instrument panel to avoid the possibility of accidental deployment of the airbag, which could cause personal injury (see Section 26). Do not use electrical test equipment on any of the airbag system wiring or tamper with them in any way.*

Integra

Refer to illustrations 9.1a, 9.1b, 9.2, 9.3a, 9.3b, 9.3c, 9.3d and 9.3e

1   The Hazard switch, defogger switch, fog light switch, instrument panel lights dimmer switch, cruise control main switch, moon roof switch and power mirror control switch are attached to the instrument cluster bezel **(see illustration).**

2   To remove a switch for testing or replacement, remove the cluster bezel (see Chapter 11). Depress the locking tabs and remove the switch from the bezel **(see illustration).**
3   To check the hazard switch, defogger switch, fog light switch, cruise control switch or moon roof switch, use an ohmmeter or self-powered test lamp and the accompanying diagrams to check for continuity between each of the indicated switch terminals with the switch in each of the indicated positions **(see illustrations).** If the continuity isn't as specified, replace the individual switch.
4   Refer to Section 26 to check the power mirror control switch.

9.2 To remove a switch from the bezel, press on the locking tabs at the base and push the switch through the front of the bezel

SWITCH POSITION	CONTINUITY BETWEEN
ON	1, 2 and 3; 6 and 7
(bulb check)	4 and 5
OFF	7 and 8
(bulb check)	4 and 5

9.3a Hazard switch terminal guide and continuity table - Integra (if continuity is not indicated during a bulb check replace only the defective bulb)

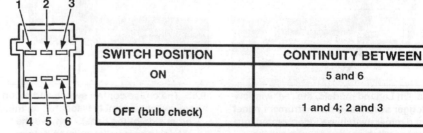

SWITCH POSITION	CONTINUITY BETWEEN
ON	5 and 6
OFF (bulb check)	1 and 4; 2 and 3

9.3b Rear window defogger switch terminal guide and continuity table - Integra (if continuity is not indicated during a bulb check replace only the defective bulb)

12

5   The instrument panel lights dimmer switch control circuitry is contained within the switch, so the instrument panel lights dimmer switch cannot be checked using conventional methods. The following procedure tests each individual circuit. If there is a problem with the system and the circuits are good, the switch is assumed defective. Inspect the switch terminals, if they're corroded or bent, repair them if possible or replace the switch. Working on the wiring harness connector:

a) *Connect an ohmmeter between the black wire terminal of the connector and a good chassis ground. There should be continuity. If not, check the circuit for an open or bad connection.*

b) *With the headlight switch ON, connect a voltmeter between the red/black wire terminal of the connector and ground. There should be battery voltage. If not, check the circuit back to the under-dash fuse box and combination switch.*

c) *With the headlight switch ON, connect a jumper wire between the red wire terminal of the connector and a good chassis ground. The instrument panel lights should come on at full brightness.*

d) *If the wiring test results were correct and the switch doesn't work properly, replace the switch.*

Legend

Refer to illustrations 9.6a, 9.6b, 9.6c, 9.8a, 9.8b, 9.8c and 9.8d

6   On Legend models, the rear window defogger switch, instrument panel lights dimmer, cruise control main switch and moon roof switch are attached to the instrument cluster bezel **(see illustrations)**. The hazard switch is attached to the heater/air conditioning control unit below the center air distribution duct **(see illustration)**.

7   To remove a switch for testing or replacement, remove the instrument cluster bezel, remove the screws and detach the switch from the bezel. To remove the hazard switch, remove the heater/air conditioning

SWITCH POSITION	CONTINUITY BETWEEN
ON	3 and 5
OFF (bulb check)	1 and 2; 3 and 4

12021-12-9.3c HAYNES

9.3c Fog light switch terminal guide and continuity table - Integra (if continuity is not indicated during a bulb check replace only the defective bulb)

SWITCH POSITION	CONTINUITY BETWEEN
ON	1 and 2
ON (bulb check)	1, 2 and 3; 4 and 5
OFF (bulb check)	2 and 3; 4 and 5

12021-12-9.3D HAYNES

9.3d Cruise control main switch terminal guide and continuity table - Integra (if continuity is not indicated during a bulb check replace only the defective bulb)

SWITCH POSITION	CONTINUITY BETWEEN
ON	2 and 3
(bulb check)	2 and 4
OFF (bulb check)	3 and 4

12021-12-9.3E HAYNES

9.3e Moon roof switch terminal guide and continuity table - Integra

control panel, remove the screws and separate the air distribution duct from the control panel, remove the clock assembly from the control panel and separate the hazard switch from the clock assembly.

8   Use an ohmmeter or self-powered test lamp and the accompanying diagrams to check for continuity between the indicated switch terminals with the switch in the indicated positions **(see illustrations)**. If the continuity isn't as specified, replace the individual switch. To check the instrument panel lights dimmer, check the resistance at the indicated terminals as you turn the adjusting knob. the meter should indicate approximately 0 to 20 K-ohms as the knob is turned. If the resistance is not as specified, replace the dimmer switch.

10   Instrument panel gauges - check

Warning: *Legend models are equipped with a Supplemental Restraint System (SRS), more commonly known as an airbag(s). Always disable the airbag system before working in the vicinity of the SRS unit, steering column or instrument panel to avoid the possibility of accidental deployment of the airbag, which could cause personal injury (see Section 26).*

Fuel and temperature gauges

1   All tests below require the ignition switch to be turned to ON position when testing.

2   If the gauge pointer does not move from the empty or cold positions, check the fuse. If

9.6a On Legend models, the rear window defogger switch and the instrument panel light dimmer switch are incorporated into one switch assembly - remove the retaining screws (arrows) to detach the switch from the bezel

9.6b The cruise control switch and moon roof switch assembly is located on the other side of the bezel - remove the retaining screws (arrows) to detach the switch from the bezel

9.6c On Legend models, the hazard switch (arrow) is attached to the heater/air conditioning control panel

SWITCH POSITION	CONTINUITY BETWEEN
ON	4 and 5
OFF (bulb check)	1 and 6; 2 and 3

12021-12-9.8A HAYNES

9.8a Defogger switch terminal guide and continuity table - Legend (if continuity is not indicated during a bulb check replace only the defective bulb)

12021-12-9.8B HAYNES

9.8b Instrument panel lights dimmer switch terminal guide - Legend (there should be approximately zero to 20 K-ohms resistance indicated on terminals 1 and 2 as the knob is turned)

SWITCH POSITION	CONTINUITY BETWEEN
CRUISE CONTROL	
ON	2 and 3
OFF (bulb check)	1 and 2; 4 and 5
MOON ROOF	
OFF (bulb check)	4 and 5
OPEN	6 and 8 (diode)
CLOSE	7 and 8 (diode)

12021-12-9.8c HAYNES

NOTE: *The switch contains a diode, if continuity is not indicated, reverse the meter leads and retest.*

9.8c Cruise control main switch and moon roof switch terminal guide and continuity table - Legend (if continuity is not indicated during a bulb check replace only the defective bulb)

SWITCH POSITION	CONTINUITY BETWEEN
ON	3 and 2; 3 and 4 (diode)
OFF (bulb check)	1 and 5

12021-12-9.8d HAYNES

NOTE: *The switch contains a diode, if continuity is not indicated, reverse the meter leads and retest.*

9.8d Hazard switch terminal guide and continuity table - Legend (if continuity is not indicated during a bulb check replace only the defective bulb)

the fuse is OK, locate the particular sending unit for the circuit you're working on (see Chapter 4 for fuel sending unit location or Chapter 3 for the temperature sending unit location). Connect the sending unit connector to ground momentarily. If the pointer goes to the full or hot position replace the sending unit. If the pointer stays in the same position, use a jumper wire to ground the sending unit terminal on the back of the gauge. If necessary, refer to the wiring diagrams at the end of this Chapter. If the pointer moves, the problem lies in the wiring between the gauge and the sending unit. If the pointer does not move with the sending unit terminal on the back of the gauge grounded, check for volt-age at the other terminal of the gauge. If voltage is present, replace the gauge.

11 Instrument cluster - removal and installation

Refer to illustrations 11.4a, 11.4b and 11.4c
Warning: *Legend models are equipped with a Supplemental Restraint system (SRS), more commonly known as airbags. Always disable the airbag system before working in the vicinity of the impact sensors, steering column or instrument panel to avoid the possibility of accidental deployment of the airbag, which could cause personal injury (see Section 26). Do not use electrical test equipment on any of the airbag system wiring or tamper with them in any way.*

1   Disconnect the negative battery cable (see **Warning** above). **Caution:** *If the radio in your vehicle is equipped with an anti-theft system, make sure you have the correct activation code before disconnecting the battery.*
2   Tilt the steering wheel to its lowest position and remove the instrument cluster bezel (see Chapter 11).
3   Pad the steering column to protect it.
4   Remove the cluster mounting screws, carefully pull it straight out of the instrument panel and disconnect the electrical connectors **(see illustrations).** On Integra models, disconnect the speedometer cable.
5   Installation is the reverse of removal.

11.4a Instrument cluster screw locations (arrows) - Integra

11.4a Instrument cluster screw locations (arrows) - Legend

12

11.4c Pull the cluster out of the dash, turn it over and disconnect the electrical connectors from the backside

12.3a On Integra models, reach under the radio and remove the retaining screws (arrows)

12 Radio and speakers - removal and installation

Warning: *Legend models are equipped with a Supplemental Restraint system (SRS), more commonly known as airbags. Always disable the airbag system before working in the vicinity of the impact sensors, steering column or instrument panel to avoid the possibility of accidental deployment of the airbag, which could cause personal injury (see Section 26). Do not use electrical test equipment on any of the airbag system wiring or tamper with them in any way.*

Radio

Refer to illustrations 12.3a and 12.3b

1   Detach the cable from the negative terminal of the battery (see **Warning** above). **Caution:** *If the radio in your vehicle is equipped with an anti-theft system, make sure you have the correct activation code before disconnecting the battery.*
2   On Integra models, remove the center console (see Chapter 11). On Legend models remove the console trim panel (see Chapter 11).

3   Remove the two retaining screws **(see illustrations)**. Pull out the radio and unplug the electrical connector and antenna lead.
4   Installation is the reverse of removal.

Speakers

Front main speakers

Refer to illustration 12.6

5   On Integra models, remove the speaker trim cover. On legend models, remove the door trim panel.
6   Remove the speaker mounting screws, pull out the speaker and unplug the electrical connector **(see illustration)**.
7   Installation is the reverse of removal.

Front tweeters (Legend)

8   Remove the door trim panel.
9   Disconnect the tweeter electrical connector.
10   Remove the tweeter mounting screws and take it out.
11   Installation is the reverse of removal.

Rear speakers

Refer to illustration 12.12

12   On Integra hatchback models, remove the screws and detach the speaker trim

cover. Remove the speaker mounting screws, pull the speaker up and disconnect the speaker wires **(see illustration)**.
13   On Integra sedan models, from inside the trunk, remove the nuts retaining the speaker box assembly to the package tray and disconnect the speaker wires. From inside the passenger compartment, remove the speaker assembly. Remove the screws and the speaker grille, then remove the screws and the speaker from the speaker box.
14   On legend models, pry off the speaker grille, remove the speaker mounting screws, lift the speaker up and disconnect the speaker wires.
15   Installation is the reverse of removal.

13 Antenna - removal and installation

Antenna mast

Refer to illustrations 13.1, 13.2 and 13.3

1   Tape the fender to protect it from scratches. Remove the nut and spacer **(see illustration)**.

12.3b Legend model radio mounting bolts (arrows)

12.6 Remove the screws (arrows) and detach the speaker from the door

12.12 Remove the screws (arrows), pull the speaker out and unplug it (Integra hatchback)

13.1 Tape the fender to protect it and remove the antenna nut with snap-ring pliers

13.2 With the ignition key and the radio in the ON position, guide the antenna mast out of the motor assembly

13.3 Insert the new antenna so that the antenna cable teeth face the rear of the vehicle

2   Have an assistant switch the radio ON to extend the antenna. Guide the mast as it extends, then remove it from the vehicle **(see illustration)**.

3   Install the antenna with teeth facing the rear of the vehicle and engage the antenna teeth with the drive cable. Switch the radio ON and let the antenna motor pull the mast into the fender **(see illustration)**.

4   Install the spacer and antenna nut. **Note:** *If the spacer has a flat seal, it goes inside the collar, below the spacer. If the spacer has an O-ring, it goes on top of the spacer.*

Power antenna motor

Refer to illustration 13.6

5   If you're working on a sedan, remove the side trim panel from inside the trunk. If you're working on a hatchback, remove the quarter trim panel from the vehicle interior.

6   Remove the antenna nut and washer **(see illustration 13.1)**. Remove the antenna motor mounting nuts/bolts **(see illustration)**. Disconnect the electrical connector and antenna lead and withdraw the assembly.

7   Installation is the reverse of removal.

14 Headlight - replacement

Warning: *Halogen gas-filled bulbs are under pressure and may shatter if the surface is scratched or the bulb is dropped. Wear eye protection and handle the bulbs carefully, grasping only the base whenever possible. Do not touch the surface of the bulb with your fingers because the oil from your skin could cause it to overheat and fail prematurely. If you do touch the bulb surface, clean it with rubbing alcohol.*

Integra

1   Remove the air cleaner housing if you are removing the right side headlight bulb.

2   Reach behind the headlight, unplug the electrical connector rotate the plastic retaining collar counterclockwise and remove it. Grasp the bulb assembly securely and pull straight out to remove it.

3   Installation is the reverse of removal (see **Warning** above).

Legend

Refer to illustrations 14.4 and 14.5

4   Reach behind the headlight assembly

and remove the bulb cover **(see illustration)**.

5   Release the retaining clip, then pull the bulb assembly out. Disconnect the electrical connector and remove the bulb **(see illustration)**.

6   Installation is the reverse of removal (see **Warning** above).

15 Headlights - adjustment

Refer to illustrations 15.1a, 15.1b and 15.3

Note: *The headlights must be aimed correctly. If adjusted incorrectly they could blind the driver of an oncoming vehicle and cause a serious accident or seriously reduce your ability to see the road. The headlights should be checked for proper aim every 12 months and any time a new headlight is installed or front end body work is performed. It should be emphasized that the following procedure is only an interim step, which will provide temporary adjustment until the headlights can be adjusted by a properly equipped shop.*

1   Headlights have spring-loaded adjusting screws for controlling up-and-down (inner) and left-and-right movement (outer - nearest the parking light) **(see illustrations)**.

13.6 Remove the mounting nuts and unplug the electrical connector (arrows) to detach the antenna motor

14.4 On Legend models, grasp the bulb cover securely and detach it

14.5 Pull the bulb out and unplug the connector

15.1a On Integra models, use a screwdriver to make vertical (1) and horizontal (2) adjustments to the headlight and vertical adjustments to the fog light (3)

15.1b Legend model vertical (1) and horizontal (2) headlight adjuster locations - after adjustment the bubbles should be centered in the horizontal (3) and vertical (4) indicators

2   There are several methods of adjusting the headlights. The simplest method requires a blank wall and a level floor.

3   Position masking tape vertically on the wall in reference to the vehicle centerline and the centerlines of both headlights **(see illustration)**.

4   Position a horizontal tape line in reference to the centerline of all the headlights. **Note:** *It may be easier to position the tape on the wall with the vehicle parked only a few inches away.*

5   Adjustment should be made with the vehicle parked 25 feet from the wall, sitting level, the gas tank half-full and no unusually heavy load in the vehicle.

6   Starting with the low beam adjustment, position the high intensity zone so it is two inches below the horizontal line and two inches to the right of the headlight vertical line. Adjustment is made by turning the vertical adjusting screw. The horizontal adjusting screw should be used to move the beam left or right.

7   With the high beams on, the high intensity zone should be vertically centered with the exact center just below the horizontal line. **Note:** *It may not be possible to position the headlight aim exactly for both high and low beams. If a compromise must be made, keep in mind that the low beams are the most used and have the greatest effect on safety.*

8   Have the headlights adjusted by a dealer service department or service station at the earliest opportunity.

16   Headlight housing - replacement

Refer to illustrations 16.3a and 16.3b

1   Unplug the electrical connectors, and remove the halogen bulbs (see Section 14).

2   Remove the front bumper cover (see Chapter 11). On Legend models, remove the parking light assembly.

3   Remove the headlight housing mounting bolts/nuts and remove the housing **(see illustrations)**.

4   Installation is the reverse of removal. After you're done, adjust the headlights (see Section 15).

15.3 Headlight adjustment details

16.3a On Integra models, remove the four headlight housing mounting bolts (arrows)

16.3b On Legend models, remove the five headlight housing bolts (arrows)

17.4a Remove the retaining screw (arrow) from the panel below the turn signal lamp housing . . .

17.4b . . . then pry the panel out

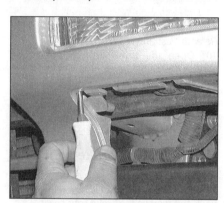

17.5a Remove the lamp housing screw (arrow) . . .

17 Bulb replacement

Front turn signal lights

Integra

1   Remove the lens securing screws and pull the turn signal light assembly out of the bumper. Unplug the electrical connector and remove the light assembly.

2   Turn the bulb holder counterclockwise and remove the bulb from the holder.

3   Installation is the reverse of removal.

Legend

Refer to illustrations 17.4a, 17.4b, 17.5a and 17.5b

4   Working below the spoiler, remove the screw from the panel below the turn signal light, then detach the panel with a screwdriver **(see illustrations)**.

5   Remove the housing securing screw and rotate the turn signal light assembly out of the bumper **(see illustrations)**. Rotate the bulb holder counterclockwise to remove it. Push in on the bulb and rotate it to replace it.

6   Installation is the reverse of removal.

Front parking and side marker lights

Refer to illustrations 17.7a and 17.7b

7   Remove the screw and pull the lamp assembly out of the fender **(see illustrations)**.

8   Detach the parking light bulb holder and pull the parking light bulb straight out to remove it. Turn the turn signal bulb holder 1/8-turn counterclockwise and pull it out of the housing. Remove the bulb from the bulb holder.

9   Installation is the reverse of removal.

17.5b . . . and rotate the housing out for access to the bulb holder

17.7a Remove the side marker and parking light housing screw . . .

17.7b . . . and pull out the housing for access to the bulb holders

12

17.10 Remove nuts and detach the cover from the inner panel to access the bulbs

17.11 Detach the housing and push in on the bulb, then rotate it counterclockwise for removal

17.23 On Legend models, the high mount brake light (arrow) is accessible from inside the trunk

Tail light and brake light

Refer to illustrations 17.10 and 17.11

10   Open the trunk or rear hatch and remove the access cover (**see illustration**).
11   Remove the bulb holders for access to the bulbs (**see illustration**).
12   Push in on the bulb and turn it counterclockwise, then pull it out of the bulb holder.
13   Installation is the reverse of removal.

High-mounted brake light

Integra

14   On hatchback models, open the hatchback and remove the brake light cover.
15   Twist the bulb holder 1/4-turn counterclockwise and pull it out of the housing.
16   Pull the bulb straight out of the bulb holder.
17   On sedan models, open the trunk lid to access the high-mounted brake light housing.
18   Press in on the centers of the retainers with a small screwdriver or punch, then pry the retainers out.
19   Unplug the electrical connector and twist the holder 1/4-turn counterclockwise, then pull it out of the housing.

20   Pull the bulb straight out of the bulb holder.
21   Installation is the reverse of removal.

Legend

Refer to illustration 17.23

22   Working in the trunk, rotate the bulb holder counterclockwise and detach it for access to the bulb (**see illustration**).
23   Twist the bulb holder counterclockwise, remove it from the housing and remove the bulb.
24   Installation is the reverse of removal.

Instrument panel lights

25   To gain access to the instrument panel lights, the instrument cluster will have to be removed first (see Section 11).
26   Rotate the bulb holder counterclockwise and remove it from the instrument cluster.
27   Pull the bulb straight out of the holder.
28   Installation is the reverse of removal.

License plate lights

Refer to illustration 17.29

29   Remove the two screws and pull out the

lens (**see illustration**).
30   Rotate the bulb holder 1/8-turn counterclockwise and detach it from the lens housing.
31   Pull the bulb straight out of the holder.
32   Installation is the reverse of removal.

Dome/cargo/trunk lights

Refer to illustration 17.33

33   Carefully pry the lens off for access to the bulb (**see illustration**).
34   Remove the bulb(s) from the terminals. It may be necessary to pry the bulb out - if this is the case, pry only on the ends of the bulb (otherwise the glass may shatter).
35   Installation is the reverse of removal.

18 Daytime Running Lights (DRL) - general information

The Daytime Running Lights (DRL) system used on Canadian models illuminates the headlights whenever the engine is running. The only exception is with the engine running and the parking brake engaged. Once the parking brake is released, the lights will

17.29 Remove the screws (arrows) and detach the license plate light lens

17.33 Carefully pry the interior light lens out for access to the bulb(s)

19.2 Windshield wiper motor terminal identification - to check the motor for operation connect a fused jumper wire to the positive terminal of a 12 volt battery and terminal no. 4; the motor will operate on low speed when terminal no. 2 is grounded and high speed when terminal no. 1 is grounded

Integra   **Legend**

12021-12-19.2 HAYNES

19.7 To remove a wiper arm, remove the nut and pull the arm off the shaft

remain on as long as the ignition switch is on, even if the parking brake is later applied.

The DRL system supplies reduced power to the headlights so they won't be too bright for daytime use, while prolonging headlight life.

19 Wiper motor - check and replacement

Wiper motor and circuit check

Refer to illustration 19.2

Note: *Refer to the wiring diagrams for wire colors and locations in the following checks. When checking for voltage, probe a grounded 12-volt test light to each terminal at the connector until it lights; this verifies voltage (power) at the terminal. If the following checks fail to locate the problem, have the system diagnosed by a dealer service department or other properly equipped repair facility.*

1   If the wipers work slowly, make sure the battery is in good condition and has a strong charge (see Chapter 1). Check for binding linkage and pivots. Lubricate or repair the linkage or pivots as necessary. Check for loose or corroded connections, especially the ground connection.

2   If the wipers fail to operate when activated, check the fuse. If the fuse is OK, disconnect the electrical connector to the motor, turn the wiper switch to the HI position and check for voltage at the green/black wire terminal of the connector. Check for

continuity between the black wire terminal of the connector a good chassis ground. If there's voltage supplied to the motor, check the motor with fused jumper wires from the battery **(see illustration)**. If the motor fails to operate, replace it. If there's voltage at the motor connector, and the wiper motor tested good, check the wiper switch for continuity (see Section 7). On Legend models, also check the wiper relays (see Section 5).

3   If the interval (delay) function is inoperative, check the continuity of all the wiring between the switch and integrated control unit. If the wiring is OK, have the integrated control unit checked by a dealership or properly equipped repair facility.

4   If the wipers stop at the position they're in when the switch is turned off (fail to park), check for voltage at the park feed wire of the wiper motor connector when the wiper switch is OFF but the ignition is ON. If no voltage is present, check for an open circuit between the wiper motor and the fuse panel.

5   If the wipers won't shut off unless the ignition is OFF, disconnect the wiring from the wiper control switch. If the wipers stop, replace the switch. If the wipers keep running, there's a defective limit switch in the motor; replace the motor.

6   If the wipers won't retract below the hood line, check for mechanical obstructions in the wiper linkage or on the vehicle's body, which would prevent the wipers from parking. If there are no obstructions, check the wiring between the switch and motor for continuity. If the wiring is OK, replace the wiper motor.

Wiper motor replacement

Front

Refer to illustration 19.7

7   Remove the windshield wiper arms **(see illustration)**.

8   On legend models, remove the windshield base molding. Remove the cowl cover and hood seal (see Chapter 11).

9   Disconnect the electrical connector from the wiper motor.

Integra

10   Carefully pry the wiper linkage off the motor arm. Remove the four retaining bolts, detach the wiper motor from the firewall and lift it out of the engine compartment.

11   Installation is the reverse of removal.

Legend

Refer to illustrations 19.12 and 19.13

12   Remove the bolts and remove the complete wiper motor and linkage assembly **(see illustration)**.

13   Remove the nut and detach the linkage arm, then remove wiper motor retaining bolts **(see illustration)**.

14   Remove the wiper motor from the frame.

15   Installation is the reverse of removal.

19.12 Remove the wiper assembly mounting bolts (arrows) and remove the complete assembly from the vehicle

19.13 Remove the wiper motor arm nut and the three mounting bolts (arrows) and remove the motor from the frame

12

19.16 To remove a rear wiper arm, flip up the cover and remove the nut

19.19 Rear wiper motor mounting bolts (arrows)

20.3 Check for voltage at the horn terminal

Rear (Integra hatchback)

Refer to illustrations 19.16 and 19.19

16   Pull the rear wiper arm cover back to access the wiper arm retaining nut. Detach the nut and pull the wiper arm straight off the shaft to remove it **(see illustration)**.

17   Open the rear hatch and remove the trim panel (see Chapter 11).

18   Disconnect the electrical connector from the wiper motor.

19   Remove the wiper motor mounting bracket bolts and remove the motor **(see illustration)**.

20   Installation is the reverse of removal.

---

20   Horn - check and replacement

Check

Refer to illustration 20.3

Note: *Check the fuses before beginning electrical diagnosis.*

1   Disconnect the electrical connector from the horn.

2   To test the horn(s), connect battery voltage and ground to the horn terminals with a pair of jumper wires. If the horn doesn't sound, replace it.

3   On Integra models, if the horn is good, check for battery voltage at the horn connector **(see illustration)**. Battery voltage should be present at the white/green wire terminal with the ignition key On. When the blue/red wire is grounded by the horn switch the horn should sound. If voltage is present, check the horn switch and related wiring for continuity to ground.

4   On Legend models, check for battery voltage at the blue wire terminal of the horn connector when the horn switch is depressed. If there's no voltage at the horn, check the relay (see Section 5).

5   If the relay is OK, check for voltage to the relay power and control circuits. If either of the circuits is not receiving voltage, inspect the wiring between the relay and the fuse panel.

6   If the relay circuits are receiving voltage, depress the horn switch and check the circuit

from the relay to the horn switch for continuity to ground. If there's no continuity, check the circuit for an open. If there's no open circuit, replace the horn switch.

7   If there's continuity to ground through the horn switch, check for an open or short in the circuit from the relay to the switch.

Replacement

Refer to illustration 20.9

8   To access the horns, the front bumper must first be removed on Integra models and the right side horn on Legend models (see Chapter 11). The left side horn on Legend models is located next to the battery.

9   Disconnect the electrical connectors and remove the bracket bolt **(see illustration)**.

10   Installation is the reverse of removal.

---

21   Rear window defogger - check and repair

---

1   The rear window defogger consists of a number of horizontal heating elements baked onto the inside surface of the glass. Power is supplied to the heater grid by a defogger relay and fuse located in the interior fuse box on Integra models, or in the underhood fuse and relay box on Legend models. The defogger relay is controlled by the instrument panel switch. The timer is controlled by the integrated control unit.

2   Small breaks in the element can be repaired without removing the rear window.

Check

Refer to illustrations 21.5, 21.6 and 21.8

3   Turn the ignition switch and defogger system switches to the ON position.

4   Using a voltmeter, place the positive probe against the defogger grid positive terminal and the negative probe against the ground terminal. If battery voltage is not indicated, check the fuse, relay, defogger switch and related wiring. If voltage is indicated, but all or part of the defogger doesn't heat, proceed with the following tests.

20.9 Horn mounting bolt (arrow)

5   When measuring voltage during the next two tests, wrap a piece of aluminum foil around the tip of the voltmeter positive probe and press the foil against the heating element with your finger **(see illustration)**. Place the negative probe on the defogger grid ground terminal.

6   Check the voltage at the center of each heating element **(see illustration)**. If the voltage is 5 to 6 volts, the element is okay (there

21.5 When measuring the voltage at the rear window defogger grid, wrap a piece of aluminum foil around the positive probe of the voltmeter and press the foil against the wire with your finger

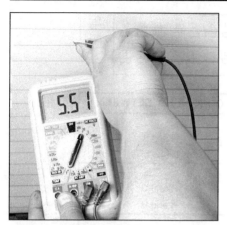

21.6 To determine if a wire has broken, check the voltage at the center of each wire. If the voltage is 5 to 6 volts, the wire is unbroken; if the voltage is 10 to 12 volts, the wire is broken between the center of the wire and the ground side; if the voltage is 0 volts, the wire is broken between the center of the wire and the power side

is no break). If the voltage is 0 volts, the element is broken between the center of the element and the positive end. If the voltage is 10 to 12 volts the element is broken between the center of the element and the ground side. Check each heating element.

7   If none of the elements are broken, connect the negative probe to a good chassis ground. The voltage reading should stay the same, if it doesn't the ground connection is bad.

8   To find the break, place the voltmeter negative probe against the defogger ground terminal. Place the voltmeter positive probe with the foil strip against the heating element at the positive side and slide it toward the negative side. The point at which the voltmeter deflects from several volts to zero is the point where the heating element is broken **(see illustration)**.

Repair

Refer to illustration 21.14

9   Repair the break in the element using a repair kit specifically for this purpose, such as Dupont paste No. 4817 (or equivalent). The kit includes plastic conductive epoxy.

10   Before repairing a break, turn off the system and allow it to cool for a few minutes.

11   Lightly buff the element area with fine steel wool; then clean it thoroughly with rubbing alcohol.

12   Use masking tape to mask off the area being repaired.

13   Thoroughly mix the epoxy, following the kit instructions.

14   Apply the epoxy material to the slit in the masking tape, overlapping the undamaged area about 3/4-inch on either end **(see illustration)**.

15   Allow the repair to cure for 24 hours before removing the tape and using the system.

21.8 To find the break, place the voltmeter negative lead against the defogger ground terminal, place the voltmeter positive lead with the foil strip against the heat wire at the positive terminal end and slide it toward the negative terminal end - the point at which the voltmeter deflects from several volts to zero volts is the point at which the wire is broken

22 Cruise control system - description and check

1   The cruise control system maintains vehicle speed with a servo motor located in the engine compartment on the driver's side fenderwell, which is connected to the throttle linkage by a cable. The system consists of the servo motor, brake switch, control switches, speed sensors and relays. Some features of the system require special testers and diagnostic procedures, which are beyond the scope of this manual. Listed below are some general procedures that may be used to locate common problems.

2   Locate and check the fuse (see Section 3).

3   The brake pedal switch (or stop lamp switch) deactivates the cruise control system. Have an assistant press the brake pedal

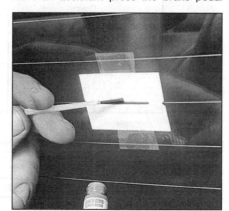

21.14 To use a defogger repair kit, apply masking tape to the inside of the window at the damaged area, then brush on the special conductive coating

while you check the stop lamp operation.

4   If the brake lights do not operate properly, correct the problem and retest the cruise control.

5   Check the control cable between the cruise control actuator and the throttle linkage and replace as necessary.

6   The cruise control system uses a speed sensing device. The speed sensor is located in the transaxle on Integra models and in the differential housing on Legend models. To test the speed sensor, see Chapter 6.

7   Test drive the vehicle to determine if the cruise control is now working. If it isn't, take it to a dealer service department or an automotive electrical specialist for further diagnosis.

23 Power window system - description and check

Refer to illustrations 23.12a, 23.12b, 23.12c and 23.12d

1   The power window system operates electric motors, mounted in the doors, which lower and raise the windows. The system consists of a relay, the control switches, the motors, regulators, glass mechanisms and associated wiring.

2   The power windows can be lowered and raised from the master control switch by the driver or by remote switches located at the individual windows. Each window has a separate motor, which is reversible. The position of the control switch determines the polarity and therefore the direction of operation.

3   The circuits are protected by fuses. Each motor is also equipped with an internal circuit breaker, which prevents one stuck window from disabling the whole system.

4   The power window system will only operate when the ignition switch is ON. In addition, many models have a window lockout switch at the master control switch which, when activated, disables the switches at the rear windows and, sometimes, the switch at the passenger's window also. Always check these items before troubleshooting a window problem.

5   These procedures are general in nature, so if you can't find the problem using them, take the vehicle to a dealer service department or other properly equipped repair facility.

6   If the power windows won't operate, always check the fuse and the relay first.

7   If only the rear windows are inoperative, or if the windows only operate from the master control switch, check the rear window lockout switch for continuity in the unlocked position. Replace it if it doesn't have continuity.

8   Check the wiring between the switches and fuse panel for continuity. Repair the wiring, if necessary.

9   If only one window is inoperative from the master control switch, try the other control switch at the window. **Note:** *This doesn't apply to the driver's door window.*

10   If the same window works from one switch, but not the other, check the switch

12

for continuity.

11   If the switch tests OK, check for a short or open in the circuit between the affected switch and the window motor.

12   If one window is inoperative from both switches, remove the trim panel from the affected door and check for voltage at the switch and at the motor while the switch is operated. If a defective switch is suspected, remove the switch and check it for continuity as indicated **(see illustrations)**.

13   If voltage is reaching the motor, disconnect the glass from the regulator (see Chapter 11). Move the window up and down by hand while checking for binding and damage. Also check for binding and damage to the regulator. If the regulator is not damaged and the window moves up and down smoothly, replace the motor. If there's binding or damage, lubricate, repair or replace parts, as necessary. **Note:** *The window motor is an integral part of the window regulator assembly. See Chapter 11 for the removal procedures.*

14   If voltage isn't reaching the motor, check the wiring in the circuit for continuity between the switches and motors. You'll need to consult the wiring diagram for the vehicle. If the circuit is equipped with a relay, check that the relay is grounded properly and receiving voltage.

15   Test the windows after you are done to confirm proper repairs.

24   Power door lock system - description and check

Refer to illustrations 24.3 and 24.6

The power door lock system operates the door lock actuators mounted in each door. The system consists of the switches, actuators, a control unit and associated wiring. Diagnosis can usually be limited to simple checks of the wiring connections and actuators for minor faults, which can be easily repaired. Since this system uses an electronic control unit, in-depth diagnosis should be left to a dealership service department. The door lock control unit is located behind the instrument panel, to the right of the fuse box on Integra models or to the right of the steering column on Legend models.

Power door lock systems are operated by bi-directional solenoids located in the doors. The lock switches have two operating positions: Lock and Unlock. When activated, the switch sends a ground signal to the door lock control unit to lock or unlock the doors. Depending on which way the switch is activated, the control unit reverses polarity to the solenoids, allowing the two sides of the circuit to be used alternately as the feed (positive) and ground side.

Some vehicles may have an anti-theft systems incorporated into the power locks. If you are unable to locate the trouble using the following general Steps, consult your a dealer service department or other qualified repair shop.

Hatchback   Sedan

SWITCH POSITION	CONTINUITY BETWEEN
LEFT FRONT	
Up	N and K
Down	N and M
RIGHT FRONT	
Up	H and C
Down	H and D
LEFT REAR	
Up	G and A
Down	G and B
RIGHT REAF	
Up	J and E
Down	J and F

`12021-12-23.12a HAYNES`

23.12a Master window switch terminal guide and continuity table - Integra (test with master lockout switch on)

SWITCH POSITION	CONTINUITY BETWEEN
UP	A and B; D and E
DOWN	B and D; C and E

`12021-12-23.12b HAYNES`

23.12b Passenger window switch terminal guide and continuity table - Integra

SWITCH POSITION	CONTINUITY BETWEEN
LEFT FRONT	The driver's switch cannot be tested for continuity
RIGHT FRONT	
Up	C and P; G and Q
Down	C and G; P and Q
LEFT REAR	
Up	F and D; E and Q
Down	F and E; D and Q
RIGHT REAR	
Up	O and M; N and Q
Down	O and N; M and Q

`12021-12-23.12c HAYNES`

23.12c Master window switch terminal guide and continuity table - Legend (test with master lockout switch on)

SWITCH POSITION	CONTINUITY BETWEEN
UP	D and E; C and G
DOWN	C and D; G and H

`12021-12-23.12d HAYNES`

23.12d Passenger window switch terminal guide and continuity table - Legend

SWITCH POSITION	CONTINUITY BETWEEN
LOCK	1 and 2
UNLOCK	2 and 3

42025-12-24.3 HAYNES

24.3 Power door lock switch terminal guide and continuity table

1   Always check the circuit protection first. Some vehicles use a combination of circuit breakers and fuses.

2   Operate the door lock switches in both directions (Lock and Unlock) with the engine off. Listen for the click of the solenoids operating.

3   Test the switches for continuity **(see illustration)**. Replace the switch if there's not continuity in both switch positions.

4   Check the wiring between the switches, control unit and solenoids for continuity. Repair the wiring if there's no continuity.

24.6 Remove the door trim panel and check for power to the door lock while the appropriate switch is depressed

5   Check for a bad ground at the switches or the control unit.

6   If all but one lock solenoids operate, remove the trim panel from the affected door (see Chapter 11) and check for voltage at the solenoid while the lock switch is operated One of the wires should have voltage in the Lock position; the other should have voltage in the Unlock position **(see illustration)**.

7   If the inoperative solenoid is receiving voltage, replace the solenoid.

8   If the inoperative solenoid isn't receiving voltage, check for an open or short in the wire between the lock solenoid and the control unit. **Note:** *It's common for wires to break in the portion of the harness between the body and door (opening and closing the door fatigues and eventually breaks the wires).*

25   Electric rear view mirrors - description and check

Refer to illustrations 25.7a and 25.7b

1   Electric rear view mirrors use two motors to move the glass; one for up-and-down adjustments and one for left-to-right adjustments.

2   The control switch has a selector portion, which sends voltage to the left or right side, mirror. With the ignition ON, engine OFF, roll down the windows and operate the mirror control switch through all functions

(left-right and up-down) for both the left and right side mirrors.

3   Listen carefully for the sound of the electric motors running in the mirrors.

4   If the motors can be heard but the mirror glass doesn't move, there's probably a problem with the drive mechanism inside the mirror. Remove and disassemble the mirror to locate the problem.

5   If the mirrors don't operate and no sound comes from the mirrors, check the fuse (see Section 3).

6   If the fuse is OK, remove the mirror control switch from its mounting without disconnecting the wires attached to it. Turn the ignition ON and check for voltage at the switch. There should be voltage at the black/yellow wire terminal. If there's no voltage at the switch, check for an opening or short in the wiring between the fuse panel and the switch.

7   If there's voltage at the switch, disconnect it. Check the switch for continuity in all its operating positions **(see illustrations)**. If the switch does not have continuity, replace it.

8   Re-connect the switch. Locate the wire going from the switch to ground. Leaving the switch connected, connect a jumper wire between this wire and ground. If the mirror works normally with this wire in place, repair the faulty ground connection.

9   If the mirror still doesn't work, remove the cover and check the wires at the mirror for voltage with a test light. Check with ignition ON and the mirror selector switch on the appropriate side. Operate the mirror switch in all its positions. There should be voltage at one of the switch-to-mirror wires in each switch position (except the neutral position).

10   If there's not voltage in each switch position, check the wiring between the mirror and control switch for opens and shorts.

11   If there's voltage, remove the mirror and test it off the vehicle with jumper wires. Replace the mirror if it fails this test (see Chapter 11).

Not used

1 2 3 4 5 6 7 8 9 10

SWITCH POSITION	CONTINUITY BETWEEN
RIGHT MIRROR	
Up	5 and 9
Down	3 and 9; 6 and 9
Left	5 and 9; 6 and 9
Right	3 and 9
LEFT MIRROR	
Up	5 and 9
Down	4 and 9; 7 and 9
Left	5 and 9; 7 and 9
Right	4 and 9

12021-12-25.7a HAYNES

25.7a Rear view mirror control switch terminal guide and continuity table - Integra

1	2	3		4	5
6	7	8	9		

SWITCH POSITION	CONTINUITY BETWEEN
RIGHT MIRROR	
Up	3 and 7
Down	4 and 7; 5 and 7
Left	3 and 7; 5 and 7
Right	4 and 7
LEFT MIRROR	
Up	3 and 7
Down	2 and 7; 1 and 7
Left	3 and 7; 1 and 7
Right	2 and 7

25.7b Rear view mirror control switch terminal guide and continuity table - Legend

12

26.8 Remove the access panel, then remove the short connector (arrow) and the two-pin connector between the airbag and the cable reel

26.12 When disabling the passenger's side airbag, unplug the two-pin connector from the SRS main harness and install the short connector (arrow)

26.18 Passenger side airbag mounting nuts (arrows)

26 Airbag system - general information

Description

1   Legend models are equipped with a Supplemental Restraint System (SRS), more commonly known as an airbag. All models have two airbags, one for the driver and one for the front seat passenger. The SRS system is designed to protect the driver and passenger) from serious injury in the event of a head-on or frontal collision.

2   The SRS system consists of an SRS unit - which contains an impact sensor, safing sensor, self-diagnosis circuit and a back-up power circuit - located under the dash, right in front of the floor console, an airbag assembly in the center of the steering wheel and a second airbag assembly for the front seat passenger, located in the top of the dashboard right above the glove box.

Operation

3   For the airbag(s) to deploy, the impact and safing sensors must be activated. When this condition occurs, the circuit to the airbag inflator is closed and the airbag inflates. If the battery is destroyed by the impact, or is too low to power the inflator, a back-up power unit inside the SRS unit provides power.

Self-diagnosis system

4   A self-diagnosis circuit in the SRS unit displays a light when the ignition switch is turned to the On position. If the system is operating normally, the light should go out after about six seconds. If the light doesn't come on, or doesn't go out after six seconds, or if it comes on while you're driving the vehicle, there's a malfunction in the SRS system. Have it inspected and repaired as soon as possible. Do not attempt to troubleshoot or service the SRS system yourself. Even a small mistake could cause the SRS system to malfunction when you need it.

Servicing components near the SRS system

5   Nevertheless, there are times when you need to remove the steering wheel, radio or service other components on or near the dashboard. At these times, you'll be working around components and wire harnesses for the SRS system. Do not unplug the connectors for these wires. And do not use electrical test equipment on SRS wires. *ALWAYS DISABLE THE SRS SYSTEM BEFORE WORKING NEAR THE SRS SYSTEM COMPONENTS OR RELATED WIRING.*

Disabling the SRS system

Refer to illustrations 26.8 and 26.12
Warning: *Anytime you are working in the vicinity of airbag wiring or components, DISABLE THE SRS SYSTEM.*

6   Disconnect the battery negative cable, then disconnect the positive cable and wait three minutes. **Caution:** *The radio in your vehicle may be equipped with an anti-theft system. Make sure you have the correct activation code before disconnecting the battery.*

7   Connect the short (red) connectors to the airbag side of the connectors as described in the following steps.

Driver's side airbag

8   Remove the access panel below the airbag and remove the short (red) connector **(see illustration)**.

9   Unplug the two-pin connector between the airbag and the cable reel.

10   Plug the short (red) connector into the airbag side of the three-pin connector.

Passenger's side airbag

11   Remove the glove box (see Chapter 11).

12   Unplug the electrical connector between the passenger side airbag and the SRS main wiring harness. Install the red short connector on the airbag side of the connector **(see illustration)**.

Enabling the SRS system

13   After you've disabled the airbag and performed the necessary service, unplug the short connector from the airbag connector and plug in the two-pin airbag connector into the two-pin cable reel connector (driver's side) or the SRS main harness (passenger's side). Attach the short connector to its holder and reinstall the lid to the underside of the steering wheel or reinstall the glove box.

14   Turn the ignition switch to the Off position.

15   Reattach the positive (first) and negative (last) battery cables (see Chapter 5).

Airbag removal and installation

Refer to illustration 26.18

16   Disable the system (see above).

17   To remove the driver's side airbag, see Chapter 10.

18   To remove the passenger's side airbag, remove its mounting nuts **(see illustration)**.

19   Installation is the reverse of removal. Enable the SRS system as described above.

27 Wiring diagrams - general information

Since it isn't possible to include all wiring diagrams for every year and model covered by this manual, the following diagrams are those that are typical and most commonly needed.

Prior to troubleshooting any circuits, check the fuse and circuit breakers (if equipped) to make sure they're in good condition. Make sure the battery is properly charged and check the cable connections (see Chapter 1).

When checking a circuit, make sure that all connectors are clean, with no broken or loose terminals. When unplugging a connector, do not pull on the wires. Pull only on the connector housing.

Starting and charging systems - Integra

Engine control system - 1990 and 1991 Integra (1 of 2)

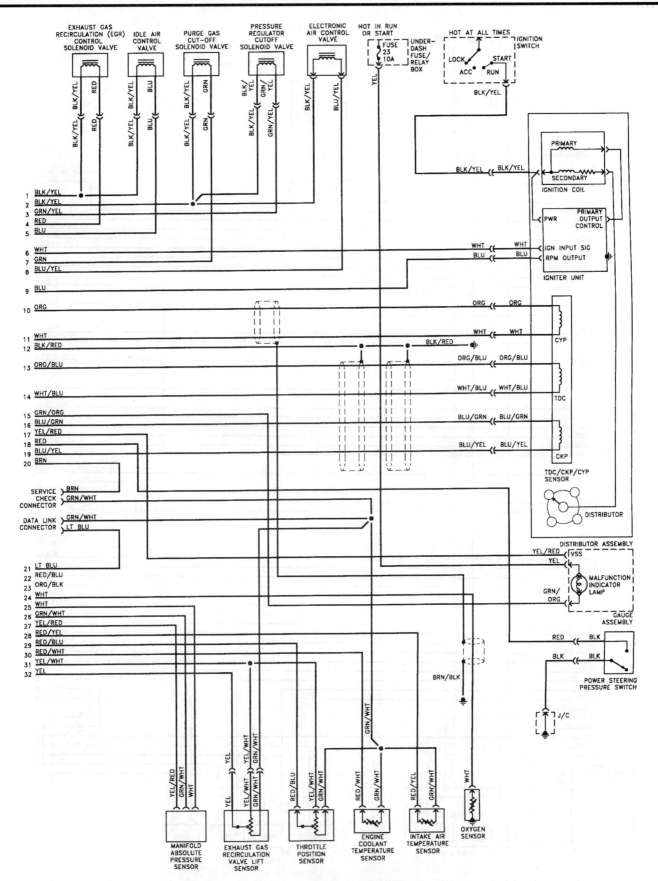

Engine control system - 1990 and 1991 Integra (2 of 2)

Engine control system - 1992 and 1993 Integra (1 of 2)

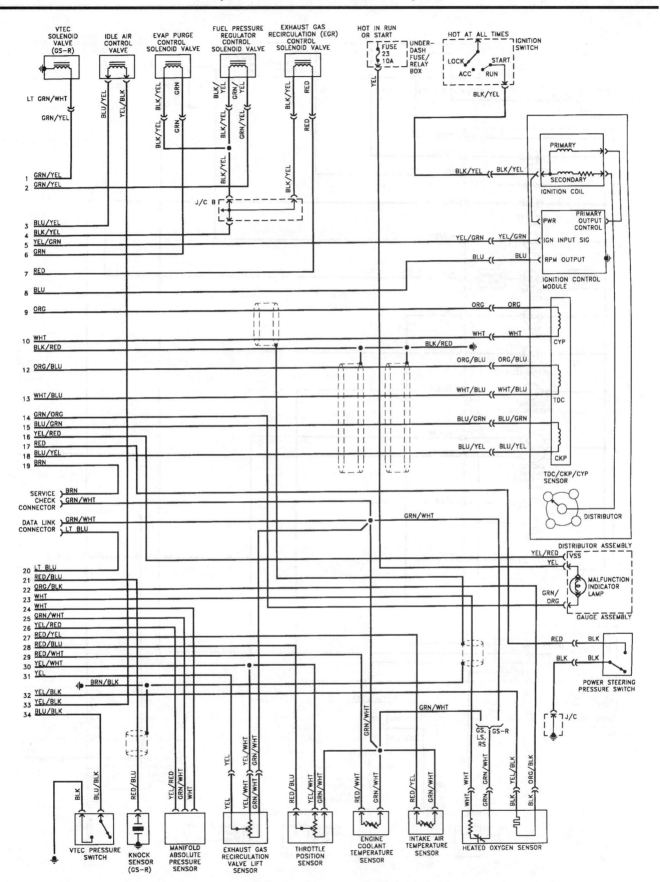

Engine control system - 1992 and 1993 Integra (2 of 2)

Instrument panel warning lights and gauges system - Integra

Exterior lighting system (except headlights) - Integra (1 of 2)

Exterior lighting system (except headlights) - Integra (2 of 2)

Headlight system - Integra USA models

Headlight system - 1990 Integra Canada models

Headlight system - 1991 thru 1993 Integra Canada models

Courtesy lighting system - Integra

Instrument panel lighting system - Integra

Power window system - Integra

Power door lock system - Integra hatchback

Power door lock system - Integra sedan

12

Rear window wiper and washer system - Integra

Windshield wiper and washer system - Integra

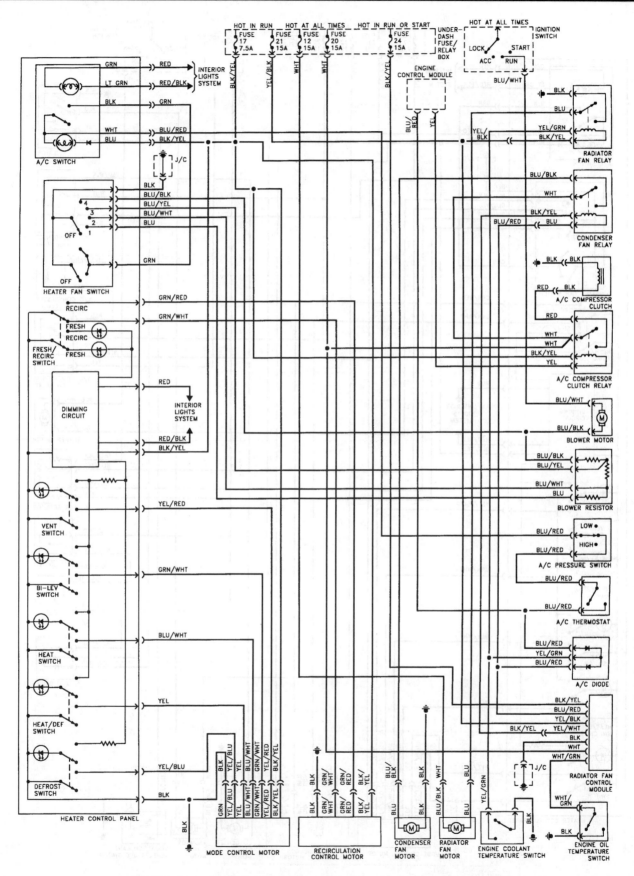

Heater, air conditioning and engine cooling fan system - Integra USA models

Heater, air conditioning and engine cooling fan system - Integra Canada models

Typical stereo system - Integra

Engine cooling fan system (without air conditioning) - Integra

12

Cruise control system - Integra

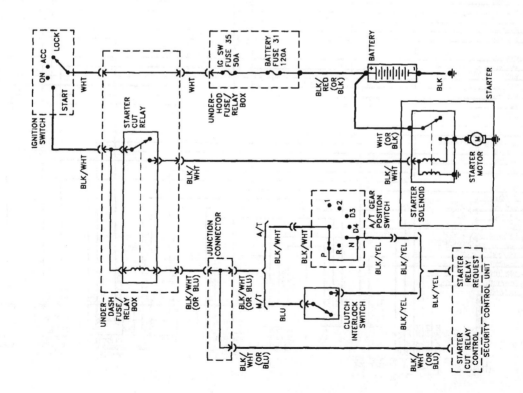

Starting and charging systems - Legend

12

Engine control system - Legend (1 of 3)

Engine control system - Legend (2 of 3)

Engine control system - Legend (3 of 3)

Instrument panel warning lights and gauges system - Legend (1 of 2)

Instrument panel warning lights and gauges system - Legend (2 of 2)

Exterior lighting system (except headlights) - Legend (1 of 3)

12

Exterior lighting system (except headlights) - Legend (2 of 3)

Exterior lighting system (except headlights) - Legend (3 of 3)

Headlight system (without daytime running lights) - Legend

Headlight system (with daytime running lights) - Legend

Interior lighting system - Legend (1 of 3)

Interior lighting system - Legend (2 of 3)

Interior lighting system - Legend (3 of 3)

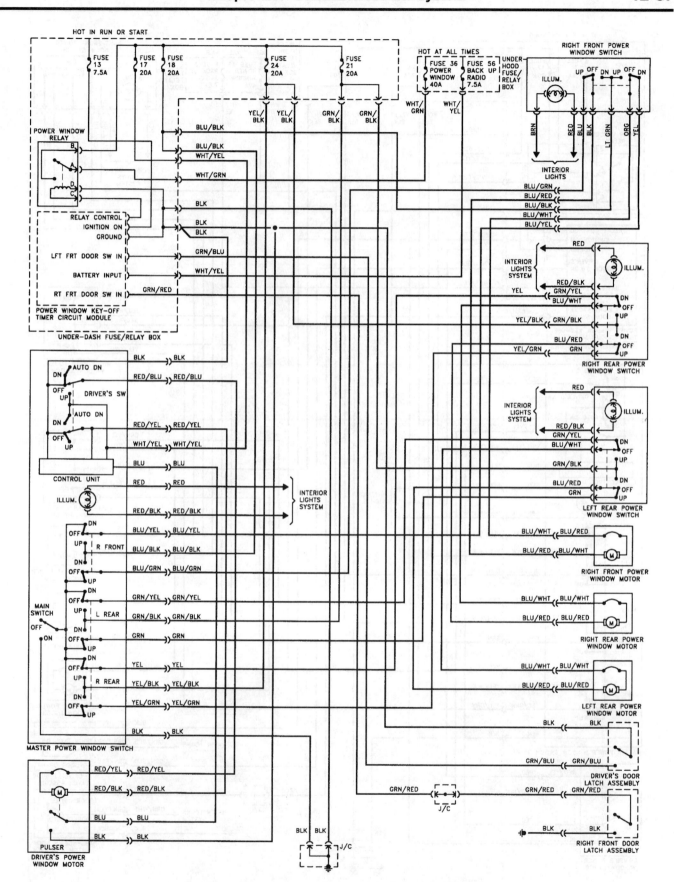

Power window system - 1991 thru 1993 Legend sedan

Power window system - 1991 thru 1993 Legend coupe

Power window system - 1994 and 1995 Legend (1 of 2)

Power window system - 1994 and 1995 Legend (2 of 2)

Power door lock system - 1991 and 1992 Legend sedan

12

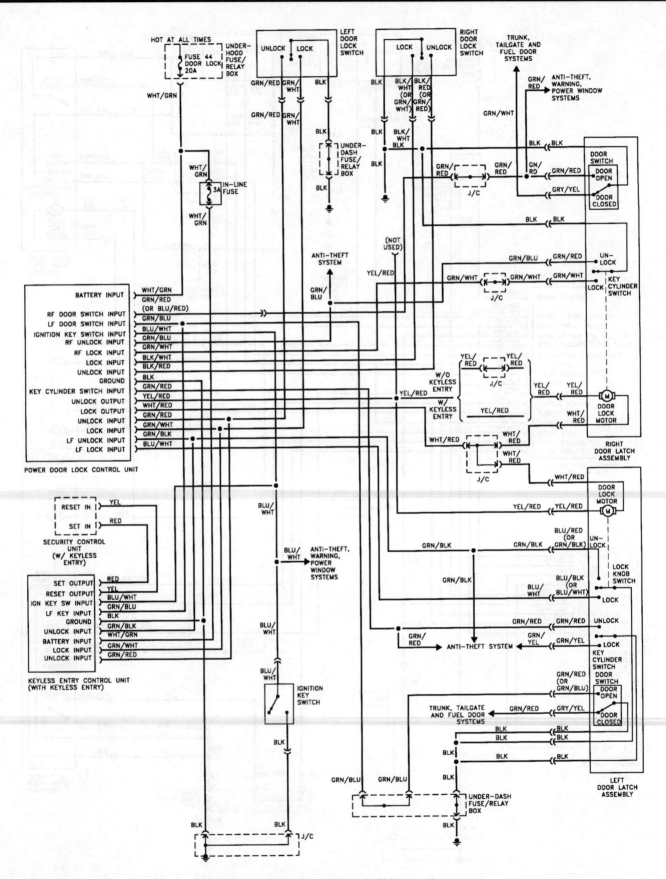

Power door lock system - 1991 and 1992 Legend coupe

Power door lock system - 1993 Legend sedan

Power door lock system - 1993 Legend coupe

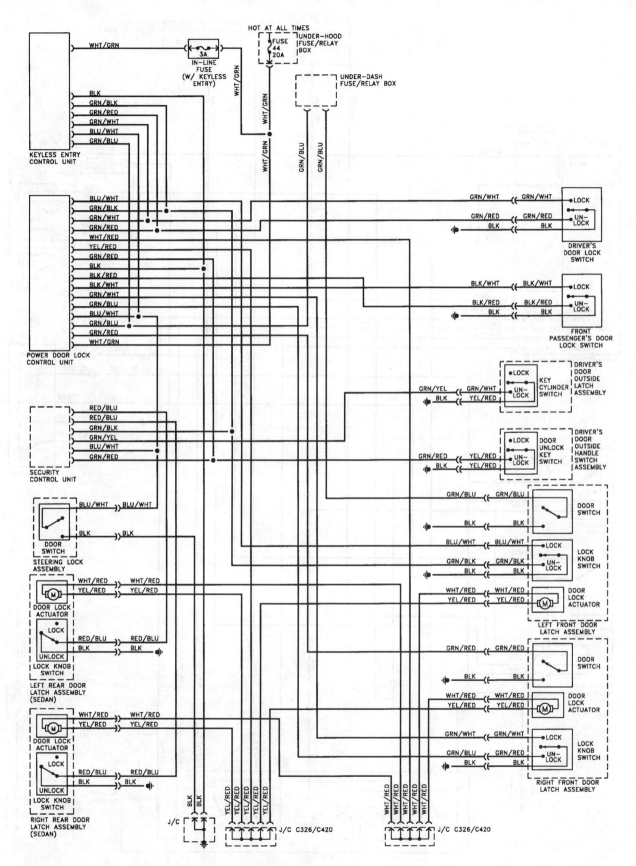

Power door lock system - 1994 and 1995 Legend

Windshield wiper and washer system - 1991 thru 1993 Legend

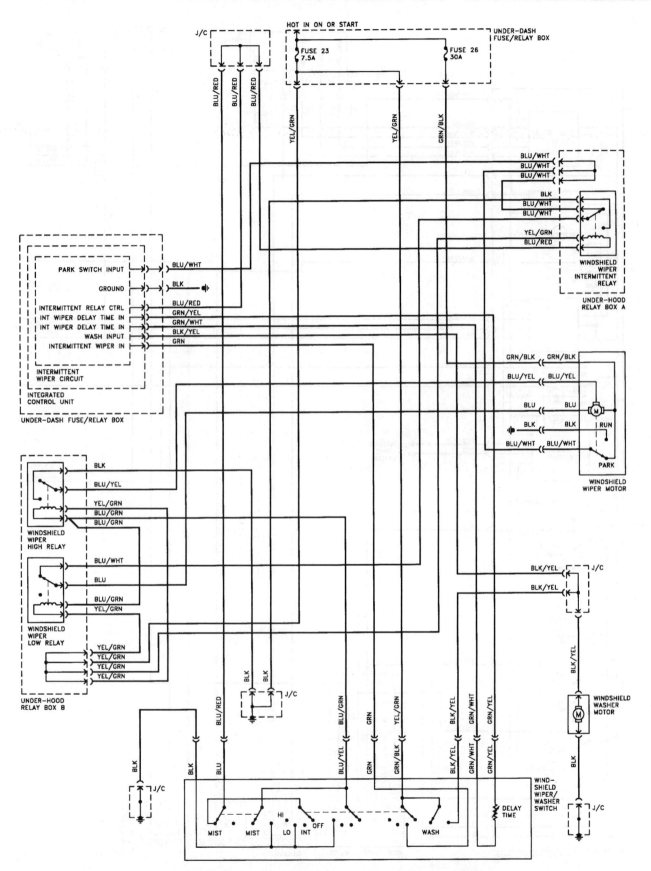

Windshield wiper and washer system - 1994 and 1995 Legend

Heater, manual air conditioning and engine cooling fan systems - Legend (1 of 2)

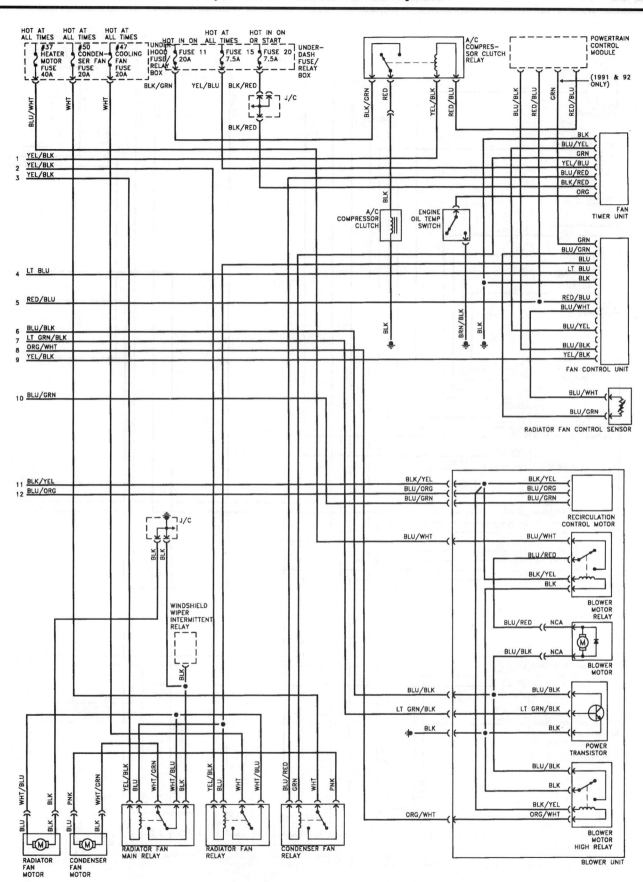

Heater, manual air conditioning and engine cooling fan systems - Legend (2 of 2)

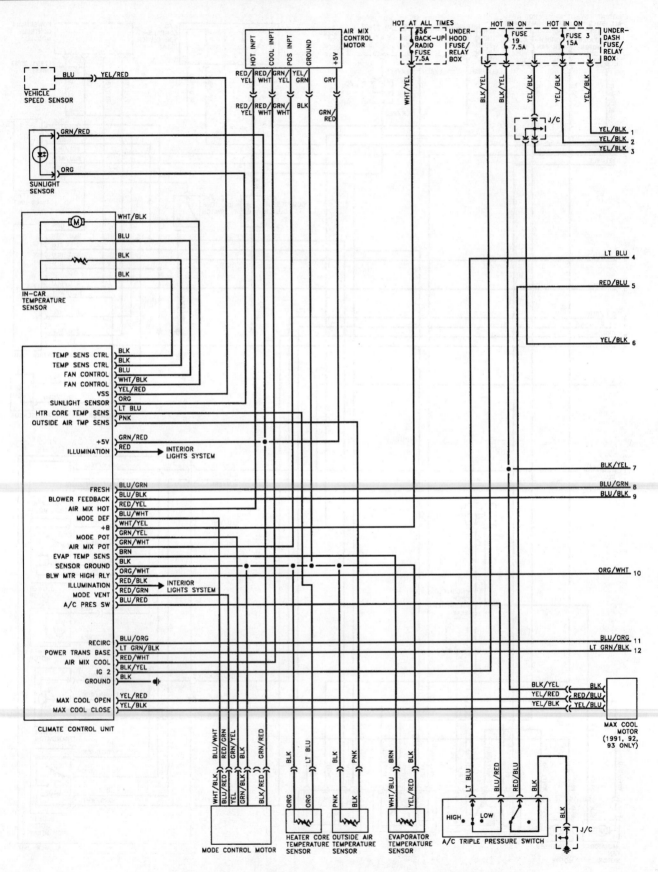

Heater, automatic air conditioning and engine cooling fan systems - Legend (1 of 2)

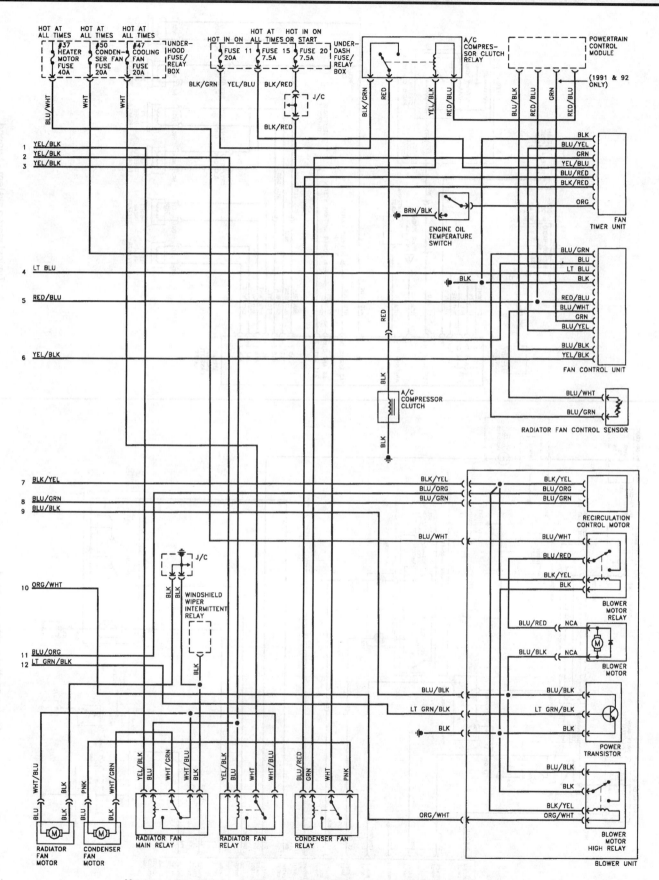

Heater, automatic air conditioning and engine cooling fan systems - Legend (2 of 2)

12

Typical stereo system - Legend

Cruise control system - Legend

Index

Haynes Automotive Manuals

NOTE: New manuals are added to this list on a periodic basis. If you do not see a listing for your vehicle, consult your local Haynes dealer for the latest product information.

ACURA
*12020 Integra '86 thru '89 & Legend '86 thru '90

AMC
Jeep CJ - see JEEP (50020)
14020 Concord/Hornet/Gremlin/Spirit '70 thru '83
14025 (Renault) Alliance & Encore '83 thru '87

AUDI
15020 4000 all models '80 thru '87
15025 5000 all models '77 thru '83
15026 5000 all models '84 thru '88

AUSTIN
Healey Sprite - see MG Midget (66015)

BMW
*18020 3/5 Series '82 thru '92
*18021 3 Series except 325iX models '92 thru '97
18025 320i all 4 cyl models '75 thru '83
18035 528i & 530i all models '75 thru '80
18050 1500 thru 2002 except Turbo '59 thru '77

BUICK
Century (FWD) - see GM (38005)
*19020 Buick, Oldsmobile & Pontiac Full-size
(Front wheel drive) '85 thru '98
Buick Electra, LeSabre and Park Avenue;
Oldsmobile Delta 88 Royale, Ninety Eight
and Regency; Pontiac Bonneville
19025 Buick Oldsmobile & Pontiac Full-size
(Rear wheel drive)
Buick Estate '70 thru '90, Electra '70 thru '84,
LeSabre '70 thru '85, Limited '74 thru '79
Oldsmobile Custom Cruiser '70 thru '90,
Delta 88 '70 thru '85,Ninety-eight '70 thru '84
Pontiac Bonneville '70 thru '81,
Catalina '70 thru '81, Grandville '70 thru '75,
Parisienne '83 thru '86
19030 Mid-size Regal & Century '74 thru '87
Regal - see GM (38010)
Skyhawk - see GM (38020)
Skylark - see GM (38020, 38025)
Somerset - see GENERAL MOTORS (38025)

CADILLAC
*21030 Cadillac Rear Wheel Drive '70 thru '93
Cimarron, Eldorado & Seville - see
GM (38015, 38030)

CHEVROLET
10305 Chevrolet Engine Overhaul Manual
*24010 Astro & GMC Safari Mini-vans '85 thru '93
24015 Camaro V8 all models '70 thru '81
24016 Camaro all models '82 thru '92
Cavalier - see GM (38015)
Celebrity - see GM (38005)
24017 Camaro & Firebird '93 thru '97
24020 Chevelle, Malibu, El Camino '69 thru '87
24024 Chevette & Pontiac T1000 '76 thru '87
Citation - see GENERAL MOTORS (38020)
*24032 Corsica/Beretta all models '87 thru '96
24040 Corvette all V8 models '68 thru '82
*24041 Corvette all models '84 thru '96
24045 Full-size Sedans Caprice, Impala,
Biscayne, Bel Air & Wagons '69 thru '90
24046 Impala SS & Caprice and
Buick Roadmaster '91 thru '96
Lumina '90 thru '94 - see GM (38010)
24048 Lumina & Monte Carlo '95 thru '98
Lumina APV - see GM (38035)
24050 Luv Pick-up all 2WD & 4WD '72 thru '82
24055 Monte Carlo all models '70 thru '88
Monte Carlo '95 thru '98 - see LUMINA
24059 Nova all V8 models '69 thru '79
*24060 Nova/Geo Prizm '85 thru '92
24064 Pick-ups '67 thru '87 - Chevrolet & GMC,
all V8 & in-line 6 cyl, 2WD & 4WD '67 thru '87;
Suburbans, Blazers & Jimmys '67 thru '91
*24065 Pick-ups '88 thru '98 - Chevrolet & GMC,
all full-size pick-ups '88 thru '98; Blazer &
Jimmy '92 thru '94; Suburban '92 thru '98;
Tahoe & Yukon '95 thru '98
*24070 S-10 & GMC S-15 Pick-ups '82 thru '93
24071 S-10, Gmc S-15 & Jimmy '94 thru '96
*24075 Sprint & Geo Metro '85 thru '94
*24080 Vans - Chevrolet & GMC '68 thru '96

CHRYSLER
10310 Chrysler Engine Overhaul Manual
*25015 Chrysler Cirrus, Dodge Stratus,
Plymouth Breeze, '95 thru '98
*25020 Full-size Front-Wheel Drive '88 thru '93
K-Cars - see DODGE Aries (30008)
Laser - see DODGE Daytona (30030)
25025 Chrysler LHS, Concorde & New Yorker,
Dodge Intrepid, Eagle Vision, '93 thru '97
*25030 Chrysler/Plym. Mid-size '82 thru '95
Rear-wheel Drive - see DODGE (30050)

DATSUN
28005 200SX all models '80 thru '83
28007 B-210 all models '73 thru '78
28009 210 all models '78 thru '82
28012 240Z, 260Z & 280Z Coupe '70 thru '78
28014 280ZX Coupe & 2+2 '79 thru '83
300ZX - see NISSAN (72010)
28016 310 all models '78 thru '82
28018 510 & PL521 Pick-up '68 thru '73
28020 510 all models '78 thru '81
28022 620 Series Pick-up '73 thru '79
720 Series Pick-up - see NISSAN (72030)
28025 810/Maxima all gas models, '77 thru '84

DODGE
400 & 600 - see CHRYSLER (25030)
*30008 Aries & Plymouth Reliant '81 thru '89
30010 Caravan & Ply. Voyager '84 thru '95
*30011 Caravan & Ply. Voyager '96 thru '98
*30012 Challenger/Plymouth Saporro '78 thru '83
Challenger '67-'76 - see DART (30025)
30016 Colt/Plymouth Champ '78 thru '87
*30020 Dakota Pick-ups all models '87 thru '96
30025 Dart, Challenger/Plymouth Barracuda
& Valiant 6 cyl models '67 thru '76
*30030 Daytona & Chrysler Laser '84 thru '89
Intrepid - see Chrysler (25025)
30034 Dodge & Plymouth Neon '95 thru '97
*30035 Omni & Plymouth Horizon '78 thru '90
30040 Pick-ups all full-size models '74 thru '93
30041 Pick-ups all models '94 thru '96
*30045 Ram 50/D50 Pick-ups & Raider and
Plymouth Arrow Pick-ups '79 thru '93
30050 Dodge/Ply./Chrysler RWD '71 thru '89
*30055 Shadow/Plymouth Sundance '87 thru '94
*30060 Spirit & Plymouth Acclaim '89 thru '95
*30065 Vans - Dodge & Plymouth '71 thru '96

EAGLE
Talon - see MITSUBISHI Eclipse (68030)
Vision - see CHRYSLER (25025)

FIAT
34010 124 Sport Coupe & Spider '68 thru '78
34025 X1/9 all models '74 thru '80

FORD
10355 Ford Automatic Transmission Overhaul
10320 Ford Engine Overhaul Manual
*36004 Aerostar Mini-vans '86 thru '96
Aspire - see FORD Festiva (36030)
*36006 Contour/Mercury Mystique '95 thru '98
36008 Courier Pick-up all models '72 thru '82
36012 Crown Victoria & Mercury
Grand Marquis '88 thru '96
36016 Escort/Mercury Lynx '81 thru '90
36020 Escort/Mercury Tracer '91 thru '96
Expedition - see FORD Pick-up (36059)
*36024 Explorer & Mazda Navajo '91 thru '95
36028 Fairmont & Mercury Zephyr '78 thru '83
36030 Festiva & Aspire '88 thru '97
36032 Fiesta all models '77 thru '80
36036 Ford & Mercury Full-size,
Ford LTD & Mercury Marquis ('75 thru '82);
Ford Custom 500,Country Squire, Crown
Victoria & Mercury Colony Park ('75 thru '87);
Ford LTD Crown Victoria &
Mercury Gran Marquis ('83 thru '87)
36040 Granada & Mercury Monarch '75 thru '80
36044 Ford & Mercury Mid-size,
Ford Thunderbird & Mercury
Cougar ('75 thru '82);
Ford LTD & Mercury Marquis ('83 thru '86);
Ford Torino,Gran Torino, Elite, Ranchero
pick-up, LTD II, Mercury Montego, Comet,
XR-7 & Lincoln Versailles ('75 thru '86)
36048 Mustang V8 all models '64-1/2 thru '73
36049 Mustang II 4 cyl, V6 & V8 '74 thru '78
36050 Mustang & Mercury Capri incl. Turbo
Mustang, '79 thru '93; Capri, '79 thru '86
*36051 Mustang all models '94 thru '97
*36054 Pick-ups and Bronco '73 thru '79
*36058 Pick-ups and Bronco '80 thru '96
*36059 Pick-ups, Expedition &
Lincoln Navigator '97 thru '98
36062 Pinto & Mercury Bobcat '75 thru '80
36066 Probe all models '89 thru '92
*36070 Ranger/Bronco II all models '83 thru '92
*36071 Ford Ranger '93 thru '97 &
Mazda Pick-ups '94 thru '97
*36074 Taurus & Mercury Sable '86 thru '95
*36075 Taurus & Mercury Sable '96 thru '98
*36078 Tempo & Mercury Topaz '84 thru '94
36082 Thunderbird/Mercury Cougar '83 thru '88
36086 Thunderbird/Mercury Cougar '89 and '97
36090 Vans all V8 Econoline models '69 thru '91
*36094 Vans full size '92 thru '95
*36097 Windstar Mini-van '95 thru '98

GENERAL MOTORS
*10360 GM Automatic Transmission Overhaul
*38005 Buick Century, Chevrolet Celebrity,
Olds Cutlass Ciera & Pontiac 6000
all models '82 thru '96
*38010 Buick Regal, Chevrolet Lumina,
Oldsmobile Cutlass Supreme & Pontiac
Grand Prix front wheel drive '88 thru '95
*38015 Buick Skyhawk, Cadillac Cimarron,
Chevrolet Cavalier, Oldsmobile Firenza
Pontiac J-2000 & Sunbird '82 thru '94
*38016 Chevrolet Cavalier &
Pontiac Sunfire '95 thru '98
38020 Buick Skylark, Chevrolet Citation,
Olds Omega, Pontiac Phoenix '80 thru '85
38025 Buick Skylark & Somerset, Olds Achieva,
Calais & Pontiac Grand Am '85 thru '95
38030 Cadillac Eldorado & Oldsmobile
Toronado '71 thru '85, Seville '80 thru '85,
Buick Riviera '79 thru '85
*38035 Chevrolet Lumina APV, Oldsmobile
Silhouette & Pontiac Trans Sport '90 thru '95
General Motors Full-size
Rear-wheel Drive - see BUICK (19025)

GEO
Metro - see CHEVROLET Sprint (24075)
Prizm - see CHEVROLET (24060) or
TOYOTA (92036)
*40030 Storm all models '90 thru '93
Tracker - see SUZUKI Samurai (90010)

GMC
Safari - see CHEVROLET ASTRO (24010)
Vans & Pick-ups - see CHEVROLET

HONDA
42010 Accord CVCC all models '76 thru '83
42011 Accord all models '84 thru '89
42012 Accord all models '90 thru '93
*42013 Accord all models '94 thru '95
42020 Civic 1200 all models '73 thru '79
42021 Civic 1300 & 1500 CVCC '80 thru '83
42022 Civic 1500 CVCC all models '75 thru '79
42023 Civic all models '84 thru '91
42024 Civic & del Sol '92 thru '95
Passport - see ISUZU Rodeo (47017)
*42040 Prelude CVCC all models '79 thru '89

HYUNDAI
*43015 Excel all models '86 thru '94

ISUZU
Hombre - see CHEVROLET S-10 (24071)
*47017 Rodeo '91 thru '97, Amigo '89 thru '94,
Honda Passport '95 thru '97
*47020 Trooper '84 thru '91, Pick-up '81 thru '93

JAGUAR
*49010 XJ6 all 6 cyl models '68 thru '86
*49011 XJ6 all models '88 thru '94
*49015 XJ12 & XJS all 12 cyl models '72 thru '85

JEEP
*50010 Cherokee, Comanche & Wagoneer
Limited all models '84 thru '96
50020 CJ all models '49 thru '86
*50025 Grand Cherokee all models '93 thru '98
*50029 Grand Wagoneer & Pick-up '72 thru '91
*50030 Wrangler all models '87 thru '95

LINCOLN
Navigator - see FORD Pick-up (36059)
59010 Rear Wheel Drive all models '70 thru '96

MAZDA
61010 GLC (rear wheel drive) '77 thru '83
61011 GLC (front wheel drive) '81 thru '85
61015 323 & Protegé '90 thru '97
*61016 MX-5 Miata '90 thru '97
*61020 MPV all models '89 thru '94
Navajo - see FORD Explorer (36024)
61030 Pick-ups '72 thru '93
Pick-ups '94 on - see Ford (36071)
61035 RX-7 all models '79 thru '85
*61036 RX-7 all models '86 thru '91
61040 626 (rear wheel drive) '79 thru '82
*61041 626 & MX-6 (front wheel drive) '83 thru '91

MERCEDES-BENZ
63012 123 Series Diesel '76 thru '85
*63015 190 Series 4-cyl gas models, '84 thru '88
63020 230, 250 & 280 6 cyl sohc '68 thru '72
63025 280 123 Series gas models '77 thru '81
63030 350 & 450 all models '71 thru '80

MERCURY
See FORD Listing

MG
66010 MGB Roadster & GT Coupe '62 thru '80
66015 MG Midget & Austin Healey Sprite
Roadster '58 thru '80

MITSUBISHI
*68020 Cordia, Tredia, Galant, Precis &
Mirage '83 thru '93
*68030 Eclipse, Eagle Talon &
Plymouth Laser '90 thru '94
*68040 Pick-up '83 thru '96, Montero '83 thru '93

NISSAN
72010 300ZX all models incl. Turbo '84 thru '89
*72015 Altima all models '93 thru '97
*72020 Maxima all models '85 thru '91
*72030 Pick-ups '80 thru '96, Pathfinder '87 thru '95
72040 Pulsar all models '83 thru '86
72050 Sentra all models '82 thru '94
*72051 Sentra & 200SX all models '95 thru '98
*72060 Stanza all models '82 thru '90

OLDSMOBILE
*73015 Cutlass '74 thru '88
For other OLDSMOBILE titles, see
BUICK, CHEVROLET or
GENERAL MOTORS listing.

PLYMOUTH
For PLYMOUTH titles, see DODGE.

PONTIAC
79008 Fiero all models '84 thru '88
79018 Firebird V8 models except Turbo '70 thru '81
79019 Firebird all models '82 thru '92
For other PONTIAC titles, see
BUICK, CHEVROLET or
GENERAL MOTORS listing.

PORSCHE
*80020 911 Coupe & Targa models '65 thru '89
80025 914 all 4 cyl models '69 thru '76
80030 924 all models incl. Turbo '76 thru '82
*80035 944 all models incl. Turbo '83 thru '89

RENAULT
Alliance, Encore - see AMC (14020)

SAAB
*84010 900 including Turbo '79 thru '88

SATURN
*87010 Saturn all models '91 thru '96

SUBARU
89002 1100, 1300, 1400 & 1600 '71 thru '79
*89003 1600 & 1800 2WD & 4WD '80 thru '94

SUZUKI
*90010 Samurai/Sidekick/Geo Tracker '86 thru '96

TOYOTA
92005 Camry all models '83 thru '91
*92006 Camry all models '92 thru '96
92015 Celica Rear Wheel Drive '71 thru '85
*92020 Celica Front Wheel Drive '86 thru '93
92025 Celica Supra all models '79 thru '92
92030 Corolla all models '75 thru '79
92032 Corolla rear wheel drive models '80 thru '87
*92035 Corolla front wheel drive models '84 thru '92
*92036 Corolla & Geo Prizm '93 thru '97
92040 Corolla Tercel all models '80 thru '82
92045 Corona all models '74 thru '82
92050 Cressida all models '78 thru '82
92055 Land Cruiser Series FJ40, 43, 45 & 55
'68 thru '82
*92056 Land Cruiser Series FJ60, 62, 80 &
FZJ80 '68 thru '82
*92065 MR2 all models '85 thru '87
92070 Pick-up all models '69 thru '78
92075 Pick-up all models '79 thru '95
*92076 Tacoma '95 thru '98,
4Runner '96 thru '98, T100 '93 thru '98
*92080 Previa all models '91 thru '95
92085 Tercel all models '87 thru '94

TRIUMPH
94007 Spitfire all models '62 thru '81
94010 TR7 all models '75 thru '81

VW
96008 Beetle & Karmann Ghia '54 thru '79
96012 Dasher all gasoline models '74 thru '81
*96016 Rabbit, Jetta, Scirocco, & Pick-up gas
models '74 thru '91 & Convertible '80 thru '92
*96017 Golf & Jetta '93 thru '97
96020 Rabbit, Jetta, Pick-up diesel '77 thru '84
96030 Transporter 1600 all models '68 thru '79
96035 Transporter 1700, 1800, 2000 '72 thru '79
96040 Type 3 1500 & 1600 '63 thru '73
96045 Vanagon air-cooled models '80 thru '83

VOLVO
97010 120, 130 Series & 1800 Sports '61 thru '73
97015 140 Series all models '66 thru '74
*97020 240 Series all models '76 thru '93
97025 260 Series all models '75 thru '82
*97040 740 & 760 Series all models '82 thru '88

TECHBOOK MANUALS
10205 Automotive Computer Codes
10210 Automotive Emissions Control Manual
10215 Fuel Injection Manual, 1978 thru 1985
10220 Fuel Injection Manual, 1986 thru 1996
10225 Holley Carburetor Manual
10230 Rochester Carburetor Manual
10240 Weber/Zenith/Stromberg/SU Carburetor
10305 Chevrolet Engine Overhaul Manual
10310 Chrysler Engine Overhaul Manual
10320 Ford Engine Overhaul Manual
10330 GM and Ford Diesel Engine Repair
10340 Small Engine Repair Manual
10345 Suspension, Steering & Driveline
10355 Ford Automatic Transmission Overhaul
10360 GM Automatic Transmission Overhaul
10405 Automotive Body Repair & Painting
10410 Automotive Brake Manual
10415 Automotive Detailing Manual
10420 Automotive Eelectrical Manual
10425 Automotive Heating & Air Conditioning
10430 Automotive Reference Dictionary
10435 Automotive Tools Manual
10440 Used Car Buying Guide
10445 Welding Manual
10450 ATV Basics

SPANISH MANUALS
98903 Reparación de Carrocería & Pintura
98905 Códigos Automotrices de la Computadora
98910 Frenos Automotriz
98915 Inyección de Combustible 1986 al 1994
99040 Chevrolet & GMC Camionetas '67 al '87
99041 Chevrolet & GMC Camionetas '88 al '95
99042 Chevrolet Camionetas Cerradas '68 al '95
99055 Dodge Caravan/Ply. Voyager '84 al '95
99075 Ford Camionetas y Bronco '80 al '94
99077 Ford Camionetas Cerradas '69 al '91
99083 Ford Modelos de Tamaño Grande '75 al '87
99088 Ford Modelos de Tamaño Mediano '75 al '86
99091 Ford Taurus & Mercury Sable '75 al '86
99095 GM Modelos de Tamaño Grande '70 al '88
99100 GM Modelos de Tamaño Mediano '70 al '88
99110 Nissan Camionetas '80 al '96,
Pathfinder '87 al '95
99118 Nissan Sentra '82 al '94
99125 Toyota Camionetas y 4-Runner '79 al '95

---

* Listings shown with an asterisk (*) indicate model coverage as of this printing. These titles will be periodically updated to include later model years - consult your Haynes dealer for more information.

Nearly 100 Haynes motorcycle manuals also available

5-98

Haynes North America, Inc., 861 Lawrence Drive, Newbury Park, CA 91320 • (805) 498-6703